The BUSINESS ONE IRWIN Guide to Using The Wall Street Journal

About the author . . .

MICHAEL B. LEHMANN is Professor of Economics at the University of San Francisco. He is a graduate of Grinnell College and received his Ph.D. from Cornell University.

Professor Lehmann lectures extensively on business and investment conditions and has developed a popular seminar based on this book, which he offers to investors, the business community, and corporations as an in-house training program.

The BUSINESS ONE IRWIN Guide to Using The Wall Street Journal

Third Edition

Michael B. Lehmann

BUSINESS ONE IRWIN
Homewood, Illinois 60430

This publication is designed to provide accurate and authoritative information in regard to the subject matter covered. It is sold with the understanding that the publisher is not engaged in rendering legal, accounting, or other professional service. If legal advice or other expert assistance is required, the services of a competent professional person should be sought.

From a Declaration of Principles jointly adopted by a Committee of the American Bar Association and a Committee of Publishers.

Project editor: Rita McMullen
Production manager: Bette K. Ittersagen
Jacket designer: Tim Kaage
Compositor: Publication Services, Inc.
Typeface: 11/13 Times Roman
Printer: R.R. Donnelley & Sons Company

Library of Congress Cataloging-in-Publication Data

Lehmann, Michael B.
The BUSINESS ONE IRWIN guide to using the Wall Street journal / Michael B. Lehmann.—3d ed.
p. cm.
ISBN 1-55623-242-X
1. Wall Street journal. 2. Business cycles—United States. 3. Economic indicators—United States. I. BUSINESS ONE IRWIN II. Wall Street journal. III. Title.
HB3743.L44 1990
332.6—dc20
89–17232
CIP

Printed in the United States of America
4 5 6 7 DO 9 9 8 7 6 5 4 3 2 1

To My Father
Dr. Frederick Lehmann

CONTENTS

PREFACE

When I first proposed this book to BUSINESS ONE IRWIN, they asked me if its purpose was to show the reader "how to be your own economist." Not exactly, I said. The objective was to show the reader "how to use *The Wall Street Journal* to be your own economist."

After all, the *Journal* is the authoritative source for business news in America; it is published coast to coast; and it has the largest daily circulation of any newspaper in the country. By focusing on a handful of key statistical reports in the *Journal*, you can acquire a surprisingly quick and firm comprehension of the ups and downs of the American business economy. This book will facilitate that comprehension, clearly and accurately—but, I hope, in a pleasing and nontechnical manner.

The BUSINESS ONE IRWIN Guide to Using the Wall Street Journal is designed to help you develop a sound overview of our economy so that your grasp of economic events as well as your business and investment decisions will be more informed and more confident. But it is not a get-rich-quick manual. You should always seek competent professional counsel before placing business or personal capital at risk.

Michael B. Lehmann

ACKNOWLEDGMENTS

This edition of *The BUSINESS ONE IRWIN Guide to Using the Wall Street Journal* is a substantial revision of the first two and, I hope, a substantial improvement as well. The chapters on commodities, stocks, bonds, and the money markets present new and thoroughly revised material, researched and developed by my student and teaching assistant, Jane O'Neil. She helped prepare the rough draft of these chapters while compiling an up-to-date listing of the recently added statistical series presented in the *Journal's* new third section, on money and investing. Jane also maintained a file of all *The Wall Street Journal* articles used to illustrate the other chapters, revised and updated the appendixes, and compiled the bibliographies of additional sources accompanying the chapters on investing as well as the list of on-line data sources. And as if that were not enough, she put in a heroic stint at her personal computer in the mad rush to meet the publication deadline. It is no overstatement to say that without her efforts, this edition would not have been possible.

Authors always owe and often express a word of thanks to their secretaries and typists. But Lindy Chris of the University of San Francisco's Economics Department was far more than secretary and typist. Not only did she have the tedious duty of preparing draft after draft while keeping an eye on the deadline, she also served as coordinator and critic, taking the reader's point of view and advising me what ought and ought not to be included. Her services were critical to the project's success.

Once again, as with the earlier editions, I owe a great debt to my wife, Millianne, and to Alan Heineman, my principal editor. Both criticized, amended, rewrote, and suggested deletions from and additions to the early drafts. Their editorial efforts spurred me to labor over revisions that otherwise would not have been undertaken, forcing me to clarify my ideas and manner of expression.

Cindy Forman, of the College for Financial Planning, made numerous suggestions for strategic revisions designed to increase the usefulness of this edition for financial professionals.

Bob Meier reviewed the second edition for BUSINESS ONE IRWIN and recommended many changes designed to increase the new edition's appeal to investors. Among those changes are the lists of suggested further reading that he helped me assemble.

Josh Feinman at the Fed was very patient with me as he explained why banks no longer avail themselves of the discount window when the Fed tightens.

Dow Jones and *The Wall Street Journal* were generous in contributing the resources of their staffs. Dan Hinson and John Prestbo of the New York office spent hours of their time enhancing my understanding of the statistical format and presentation in the *Journal's* third section, on money and investing. Gilbert Sherman and Phyllis Pierce of the Massachusetts office were generous with their help in obtaining historical figures for the Dow Jones Commodity Index.

Elaine Zuckerman at the Conference Board in New York provided back data for the Board's Consumer Confidence Index.

For this edition as for previous editions, Fr. Richard Mulcahy, S.J., of the University of San Francisco's Economics Department, and Tom Soden, a former student and now a vice president with Shearson Lehman Hutton in Larkspur, California, provided valuable assistance on the stock market.

Prof. Barry Doyle, at the University of San Francisco's McLaren College of Business, helped with the chapters on stocks, bonds, and commodities.

Martin Pring and Stan Weinstein contributed background for the discussion of technical analysis.

Bob Ferraro reminded me not to delete what little I said concerning social justice and those who really suffer because of the vagaries of the business cycle.

Robert O'Donnell and Jeff Currie of Smith Barney and Joseph Schlater of Dean Witter also gave much-needed advice on stocks, bonds, and commodities.

Patrick McGovern provided invaluable computer assistance.

Finally, Susan Russell at Precision Graphics did a great job on the charts, and Annette Kulmaczewski of Publication Services patiently shepherded the manuscript through the production process.

House rules and regulations prohibit me from recognizing individuals on the staff at BUSINESS ONE IRWIN, so I thank them all collectively now.

M.B.L.

PART I

THE BIG PICTURE: THE ECONOMIC CLIMATE AND THE INVESTMENT OUTLOOK

CHAPTER 1

INTRODUCTION

GOLD VS. STOCKS

Some say that we learn best by doing . . . that we should plunge right in.

Give it a try. Examine Chart 1–1 on page 4 with an investor's eye. The vertical axis provides values for the Dow Jones Industrial Average and the price of gold. Years are on the horizontal axis. Where would you have placed your assets—into gold or stocks—at two critical junctures or turning points: 1970 and 1980? And where will you place them at the third critical juncture, 1990?

Before you answer, you should be aware that the U.S. Treasury had set the price of gold at $35 an ounce from 1934 to 1971. Since the Treasury stood ready to buy or sell gold at $35 an ounce, and since the United States had most of the world's gold, there was no reason for any seller of gold to take one penny less than $35 or any buyer to pay one penny more than $35. So the price just sat at $35, year after year.

Just in case the stagnant price was not disincentive enough, Americans were prohibited by law from owning gold as an investment. Gold was to be used exclusively by the Treasury to settle international accounts. All that changed dramatically in the early 1970s, when the United States stopped selling gold for international settlement purposes and Americans were granted permission to own gold as an investment.

Although Americans were not permitted to own gold until December 31, 1974, place yourself in the hypothetical position of an investor who *could* have chosen between gold and stocks in 1970. With the wisdom of hindsight, can there be any doubt about your choice?

Look at Chart 1–1 again. You already know that gold was $35 in 1970. The Dow Jones Industrial Average, which most people view as

CHART 1–1

Gold vs. Stocks: Gold—Engelhard High Price through 1987, Average Thereafter; Dow Jones Industrial Average

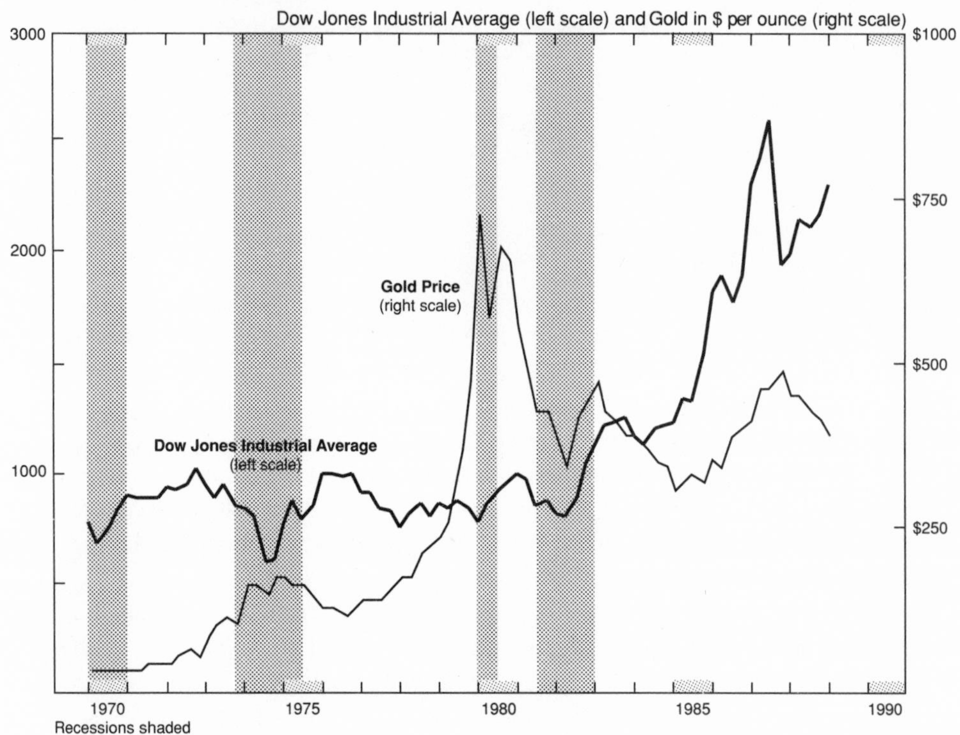

Source: U.S. Bureau of Mines, *Minerals Yearbook*; Standard & Poor's *Statistical Service*; Phyliis S. Pierce, ed., *The Dow Jones Investor's Handbook* (Homewood, IL: Dow Jones-Irwin, 1989); *Barron's*.

a proxy for the stock market, began and ended the 1970s at about 800. It fluctuated in a limited range for these 10 years, going nowhere. Had you bought stock in 1970, you would have enjoyed no investment appreciation. Gold, on the other hand, exploded in value, climbing to over $800 by early 1980. The smart money was in gold, not stocks.

Your choice was equally clear in 1980. Gold stood at over $800 an ounce; the Dow was under 1000. Then gold began to plunge. By mid-decade it had fallen to around $300. The price rose briefly to $500 in late 87 but by the end of the decade was down around the $400 mark. Stock prices, on the other hand, broke free in 1982, climbing intermittently, until in a burst of activity the Dow topped 2700 in August of 1987. Then came the crash and the recovery that followed, so that the Dow had made up most of its loss and was on the way to regaining its 1987 high by the end of the decade.

Looking back over the 1980s, there's no doubt that you should have taken all your money out of gold and put it all in stocks at the beginning of the decade. Stocks more than doubled (from under 1000 to over 2000), while gold was cut in half (from over $800 to $400). You would have done very well in stocks, *despite the crash*. And even though the gain was not as great as the spectacular appreciation of gold during the 1970s, remember you could not have bought gold until December 31, 1974, when the price was $186.

But what do you do now? Are you trying to decide between stocks and gold once more? You can see from the chart that there is little evidence that stocks and gold move in the same direction for long. As a matter of fact, the chart indicates they are more likely to move in opposite directions over the long run. What should your investments be for the 1990s—gold or stocks?

Your response at this point might well be, "Now wait a minute, there are other investment avenues. I don't have to restrict my choice to gold or stocks." True, not every investment need be in the stock market or in gold, but most investments will be either "goldlike" or "stocklike" in their behavior. Conditions favorable to the stock market will also favor other paper investments such as bonds, while tangible investments such as commodities will move with gold. So, to simplify the discussion at this point, continue as if stocks and gold were the only investment opportunities. (Short-term money market investments will also be discussed later.) The principles illustrated will be easy to apply later to the full spectrum of investment possibilities.

Diversification is one time-honored method for protecting investment income from the vagaries of the economic climate. Yet, putting half your money in stocks and half in gold in 1970 would have gained you much less over these decades. Diversification by itself is not an optimal strategy. Your store of investments must be minded. Investments must be shifted from gold (i.e., tangibles) to stocks (i.e., paper investments) and back again as conditions change. Investment timing is the key.

In order to call these moves, you will have to know why gold and stocks behaved as they did. What force propelled gold upward in the 1970s and held stocks back? And was it the same force or a different one that boosted stocks and depressed gold in the 1980s? Could the same force have generated such remarkably different turns of events?

Yes. Could and did. In a word, *inflation* was responsible for both sets of events. But you need to modify that word in order to describe the 70s and 80s accurately. *High* inflation drove gold upward and held stocks down in the 70s, and *low* inflation had the opposite effect in the 1980s—raising stocks and depressing gold.

That means you will need to forecast the investment climate of the 1990s from the perspective of inflation. In order to do that, you will not only have to make an educated guess with respect to inflation, you will also need to know how to forecast inflation based on the readily available economic data. And that forecast must be completed reasonably far in advance, so that your actions can anticipate investment trends (long-run movements in gold and stocks) before they occur. You don't want to react to events after the profitable opportunities have passed. You want to beat the market to the punch . . . and that's not easy.

Investor's Tip

- Diversification by itself is not an optimal strategy.
- Timing is the key
- Buy gold, commodities, and other tangibles when high (more than 8 percent) inflation threatens; sell if you expect low (less than 7 percent) inflation.
- Buy stocks, bonds, and other paper investments if you anticipate low inflation; get out when high inflation looms.

ON YOUR OWN

This means you will have to use the investment data on your own, without an interpreter. You will have to decipher the Dow Jones Industrial Average, GNP, capacity utilization, price/earnings ratio, housing starts, advance/decline linc, auto sales, and other statistical series and reports. *You* must use them to gain an understanding of developing business and investment trends so that your judgments and opinions are not merely based on (and therefore biased by) popular analyses and secondary sources.

It's worth some time and effort to learn how to deal with the data on your own, because until you come to grips with the data you can't honestly say that you have formed your own opinion about current economic and business events, let alone about what the future holds. The news media now serve as intermediaries between you and the data. Furthermore, no matter how many experts are quoted, you still aren't dealing with the facts, only with someone else's interpretation of them. And these interpretations are often contradictory—and therefore confusing. At some point you have to wonder, do the "experts" know what they're talking about? And while you are waiting for them to sort things out, your investment opportunities may have passed.

On the other hand, your desire to master the data may also stem from your own business needs. Will demand for your product be weak or strong two quarters from now or two years from now? Is this the time to lay in additional inventory, hire key personnel, and build more plant? Or, despite the current level of orders, would it be more prudent to cancel those plans? Can you beat the competition to the punch, one way or another? Are interest rates likely to rise or to fall? Is disinflation (as deflation is sometimes called) merely a buzzword, or has inflation really been licked? That's just a hint of the issues you can begin to analyze on your own; all it takes is learning to come to grips with a small number of regularly released statistical reports.

You may also wish to conduct your own analysis of current economic events because they form the foundation for so many other social and political developments. Were President Reagan's tax cut and supply-side economics responsible for the early 1980s decline in inflation and today's healthy economic environment, or should the Federal Reserve System take the credit? And how serious are the problems of the federal government's budget deficit and the balance-of-trade deficit? Do your answers to these questions reflect your analysis of the data, your political point of view, or the opinions of your favorite commentator? Maybe they should reflect all three, but they can reflect only the last two until you learn to deal with the numbers on your own. Once you do that, your own judgment will be of greater importance to you and others.

Don't misunderstand: dispensing with expert advice is not the objective. Even the world's leading authority on a subject must consult other experts as a continual check on his or her understanding. This challenges the authority and helps prevent sloppy thinking. The point is: become the expert by handling the data on your own, and you will know whether or not the other experts make sense. Otherwise, you'll never be certain whether you're receiving sound or flimsy advice.

If you want to be your own economist and investment advisor, if you wish to master the daily data, you need two things: (1) a readily available, reliable, and comprehensive statistical source and (2) a guide to organizing and interpreting the information you receive.

As to the first requirement, *The Wall Street Journal* is your best source of investment, business, and economic information; you really don't need anything else. It contains all the reports necessary to conduct your own analysis.

With respect to the second requirement, this book can be your guide. In it, the nature of the statistics will be explained so that what they measure and how they are computed will be clear. GNP, capacity utilization, the price/earnings ratio, and the Dow Jones Industrial Average cannot remain vague and indefinite terms if you are going to be in control of the information.

For example, when the *Journal* reports that the money supply has increased, it is important to know that this fact has virtually nothing to do with the availability of paper money. The money supply is composed largely of checking accounts; currency is the petty cash of the economy.

Understanding the nature of the various statistical series is, of course, not enough. You must be able to place them in both historical and contemporary context. For instance, the price/earnings (P/E) ratio for the Dow stocks hit a 25-year high of 22 in August 1987, just as the Dow peaked immediately prior to the October crash. A year later the P/E ratio was only 12, and the outlook for stocks was bright. The savvy investor understood these developments and was prepared to act on them.

These essential skills will develop and gain strength with each chapter. Your historical perspective will deepen, providing the background or benchmark for evaluating contemporary events. When a *Journal* article states that the trade deficit or the budget deficit is the largest ever, or that the Dow Jones Industrial Average has hit a new high, the comparison can provide perspective only if you grasp the frame of reference: knowledge of the past aids evaluation of the present by providing a standard against which recent developments are measured. For instance, auto sales and housing starts may be slightly higher or lower than they were a year ago, but if you know that current levels of activity are substantially lower than the peaks reached in the 1970s, your perspective provides evidence that today's economy has not yet approached boom conditions.

As you read on, you will become aware that none of the statistical reports stands alone. Understanding the relationships among them provides insight into the economy's operation and the investment scene, for each is a piece of the puzzle, and together they compose the picture. For instance, mortgage interest rates and home construction have been featured in the *Journal* lately, and there is a simple, vital link between them: as mortgage interest rates fall, home construction increases.

Consider another example. In 1985 we asked our major trading partners to intervene in the foreign exchange markets in order to depress the value of the dollar. The hope was that cheaper dollars—and hence cheaper prices for American goods in world markets—would boost our exports and reduce our balance-of-trade deficit. Thus, the statistical reports on the value of the dollar and on our ability to export are inextricably linked, as you will see in more detail in Chapter 16.

All of the statistics analyzed in this book can be interrelated in this fashion, so they need not be a series of isolated events, released piecemeal on a day-to-day basis. Instead, they will form an unfolding pattern that clearly reveals the direction of economic and business activity.

Finally, you need a framework, a device to give a coherent shape to these historical insights and contemporary interrelationships. The business cycle, that wavelike rise and fall of economic activity, provides that necessary framework. You are already familiar with the cycle in your own investing , business, or personal situation, and the news media have provided increased coverage of the ups and downs of the economy in recent years. Economic expansion and contraction, easy or tight credit conditions, inflation, and unemployment are recurring facts of life. Who escapes them?

The business cycle is the best vehicle for illuminating the *Journal*'s regularly appearing statistical series. Its phases bring life and meaning to the statistical reports. They establish the perspective through which the illustrations and examples in the book are interwoven into a unified exposition.

Each chapter will introduce one or more statistical series, and each will be devoted to a theme (such as the money and credit markets) that is used to describe and explain the statistical series introduced in the chapter, beginning with the simplest and most basic elements of the business cycle and proceeding to additional topics that will complete your understanding. This step-by-step progression of topics will not, however, prevent you from breaking into any chapter, out of order, if you wish to examine a particular statistical series or group of series. Indeed, you may already have a firm grasp of some of these topics and need only to fill in the missing elements to round out your comprehension of the essential workings of American business. A complete listing of all the statistical series discussed in this guide can be found in the appendixes following Chapter 17.

Each chapter will describe its statistical series in the context of the business cycle and explain the relationship of the new series to the overall picture. Analysis will be based on charts drawn from official publications so that you can visualize the data and put the current information in perspective. Recent articles in *The Wall Street Journal* containing the statistical series will be reproduced and discussed so that you can interpret the data in light of the visual presentation made by the charts. Finally, you will be alerted to what future developments can be expected.

You will enjoy putting the puzzle together yourself. Anyone can do it, with a little help. The ebb and flow of the business cycle will channel the stream of data that now floods you in seemingly random fashion, and you will experience a genuine sense of accomplishment in creating order out of something that may previously have appeared chaotic.

A word of caution before you begin. This will not be an economics or business cycle course or text, nor will it be a precise forecasting device. There will be no formula or model. The business cycle is used strictly as a vehicle to make the statistical information usable in as easy a manner as possible. The objective is not to make a professional economist out of you but to enable you to conduct your own analysis of the data just as soon as you are able. You will dive into the data and "get your hands dirty" by taking apart the cycle, analyzing it, and reassembling it. When you have finished this book, you will feel confident that you can deal with the data on your own.

Returning to the chart and example at the beginning of this chapter, you will be able to forecast the outlook for inflation and decide whether stocks (paper investments) or gold (tangible investments) are best for you. But a full discussion of that choice must wait till Chapter 8.

Now, before exploring the business cycle in detail, take time for a leisurely overview.

CHAPTER 2

THE BUSINESS CYCLE

A BIT OF HISTORY

The business cycle is nothing new. It's been a characteristic of every capitalist economy in the modern era. Nations have endured boom followed by bust, prosperity and then depression—periods of growth and confidence trailing off into a decade of despair.

It is all so familiar to us that images of its human effects are scattered among our popular stereotypes. Men in top hats peer at ticker tape emerging from a little glass dome. They wheel and deal, corner wheat markets, play with railroads, and organize steel companies. Fortunes are quickly won and just as quickly lost. Former tycoons are seen selling apples on street corners. Factory gates shut and signs go up saying, "No help wanted." Soup kitchens appear, and desperate families flee the dust bowl in Model A pickup trucks.

These caricatures—based on real history, actual power, blows of ill fortune, human suffering—persist in our collective consciousness, permanently etched by the Great Depression. Although the stock market collapse of 1929 is the most notorious such event in our history, it is by no means unique. Cycles in the American economy can be traced and analyzed going back to the beginning of the 19th century.

The settlement of the West is an example. The frontier assumes such importance in our history and folklore that we tend to think of the westward migration as a smooth, if hazardous, inevitable flow, driven by the doctrine of Manifest Destiny. It didn't happen that way. The settlement of the West proceeded in a cyclical pattern.

Farmers and ranchers were (and are) businesspeople. The sod house and subsistence farming of the 1800s were temporary inconveniences, converted as quickly as possible to growing cash crops and raising livestock for the market. The settlers wanted to know the bottom line, the difference between revenue and expense. They wanted the best price for their cotton, corn, cattle, wheat, and hogs. They wanted to maximize production and minimize cost by using modern cultivation techniques and the latest equipment. Railroads and banks concerned them because transportation and interest rates affected the cost of doing business and thus their profit margin. Finally, and most important, farmers wanted their capital to grow. They expected their net worth to increase as their farms appreciated in value and their mortgages were paid.

This experience was not confined to the United States; European settlers in Canada, Australia, and Argentina produced the same commodities under similar conditions. All were part of the growing world economy. Every farmer and rancher counted on industrialization and urbanization at home and in Europe to build demand for his or her commodities.

And worldwide demand for food and fiber did increase rapidly. Farmers responded by boosting production as best they could on existing holdings. Eventually, however, their output reached its limit, even though demand continued to grow. As a result, prices began to creep, and then race, upward. The venturesome dreamed of moving west and doubling or tripling their acreage. Record crop and livestock prices made the costs of moving and financing a new spread seem manageable, and existing farms could always be sold to the less intrepid. Thousands upon thousands of families streamed across the frontier, claiming millions of acres offered by generous government policies or buying from speculators who held raw land.

Nobody planned the westward migration; nobody coordinated it; nobody governed it. Each individual involved made his or her own calculation of the market. Farmers borrowed in order to purchase land and building materials and to buy livestock, seed, and equipment. Newly opened banks faced an insatiable demand for credit. Towns sprang up at railroad sidings where grain elevators and livestock yards were constructed. Merchants and Main Street followed. High prices brought a land boom, and the land boom brought settlement and opened the West.

It took a while for the newly converted prairie to produce a cash crop. But when it did, thousands of new farms began dumping their output on the market. The supply of agricultural commodities increased dramatically. Shortage changed to surplus, and prices dropped. Time after time during the 19th century, commodity prices fell to record lows after a period of inflation and the subsequent land rush.

Many farmers were wiped out. They could not pay their debts while commodity prices scraped bottom, and banks foreclosed on farm property. If a bank made too many loans that went bad, then it was dragged down too. Merchants saw their customers disappear and had to close up shop. Settlers abandoned their land, and boomtowns became ghost towns.

Prices inevitably remained low for years, and most farmers, living on returns far below expectations, barely made it. In every instance, it took a while before the steady growth in world demand absorbed the excess agricultural commodities.

But as time passed, the cycle would repeat itself. After the inflation that accompanied the Civil War, western settlement continued to occur in waves until the end of the century, despite 30 years of deflation. The process happened at least half a dozen times until the frontier closed in the last years of the 19th century.

By the turn of this century, progress had been spectacular. Many thousands of acres of prairie had been transformed into productive field and pasture. Commodities worth billions of dollars were produced annually for the domestic and world markets. Billions of dollars of wealth had been created in the form of improved farmland. But the discipline of the business cycle governed the advance. For every two steps forward, there had been one step backward, as those who borrowed or lent the least wisely, settled the poorest land, or had the worst luck went broke.

Things haven't changed. Agriculture's fortunes are still guided by the cycle. Remember the boom of the early 70s? Consumption of beef was up; President Nixon negotiated the wheat deal with Russia; the Peruvian anchovy harvest had failed, and soy beans were used to fill the gap (as a protein extender). Agricultural commodity prices doubled, even tripled, and therefore, of course, farm income shot up. As a result, farmers spent the rest of the decade investing heavily in land and equipment. Ultimately, supply outstripped demand, and farm prices deteriorated throughout the early 80s.

We've seen the result. It's nothing that hasn't happened before: foreclosures, bankruptcies, falling land values, broken families, and ruined lives. Eventually, of course, prices will stabilize—until the next cycle comes along to start the process all over again.

Oil presents a similar picture. Billions were spent on exploration, recovery, and production projects in Texas, Louisiana, Oklahoma, Wyoming, Colorado, and Alaska when prices were high. Houston, Dallas, Denver, and Anchorage were boomtowns in the early 1980s. Then, when prices fell (and they always do), the money dried up. Soon you could get a condominium in Anchorage or Denver for $15,000 because whole city blocks of new housing developments were abandoned—left by their owners for bank foreclosure.

What was true for farming and oil was equally true for the nation's railroads: they developed in the same cyclical pattern. On the eve of World War I, America's railway system was complete, representing a total capital investment second only to that of agriculture. It was a remarkable feat of creative engineering and equally creative financing.

We marvel at the colorful exploits of the Goulds, Fisks, Drews, Vanderbilts, Stanfords, Hills, and others. History refers to some of them as "robber barons"; they seemed to skim off one dollar for every two invested, and it's a wonder that the railway system was ever completed or operated safely. Yet there it was, the largest in the world, a quarter of a million miles of track moving the nation's freight and passenger traffic with unparalleled efficiency.

Promoters speculatively pushed the railroads westward in anticipation of the freight and passenger traffic that settlement would bring. Federal, state, and local governments, vying for the routes that would generate progress and development, gave the railroad companies 10 percent of the nation's land. Improving rights-of-way, laying track, building trestles, stations, and marshaling yards, and purchasing locomotives and rolling stock required the railway company to raise more capital than had ever been mobilized for any other single business venture. The companies floated billions of dollars in stocks and bonds, and investors eagerly ventured their capital to take advantage of prospective success. Flush with funds, the railroads raced toward the Pacific Coast, hoping that revenue would grow quickly enough to justify their huge investment. Periodically, however, the generous rate of expansion exceeded the growth in traffic. Prospects for profits, which had seemed so bright, grew dim. Investors stopped providing funds, and railroad track construction came to a halt. Since operating revenues could not recover costs, many railroads were forced into receivership and were reorganized. Stock and bond prices plunged, wiping out investors long after the promoters had made off with their killings.

Eventually, traffic grew sufficiently to justify existing lines and raise hopes that construction could profitably resume. Investors were once again lured into advancing their funds, and a new cycle of railway expansion began. It, too, was followed by a bust, and then by another wave of construction, until the nation's railway system was complete.

The tracks spanned a continent, from New York, Philadelphia, and Baltimore to Chicago, and from there to New Orleans, Los Angeles, San Francisco, Portland, and Seattle. Profit had motivated the enterprise, and enormous tangible wealth had been created. Losses had periodically and temporarily halted the undertaking and impoverished those who had speculated unwisely or who had been duped. Construction had proceeded in waves. It was an unplanned and often disorganized adventure but, given the institutions of the time, no other method could have built the system as rapidly.

In this century, we have seen the business cycle not only in the heroic proportions of the Roaring Twenties and the Great Depression but also during every succeeding business expansion or recession. We're in the cycle now, and we will be tomorrow and next year.

Business activity always expands and then contracts. There are periods when production, employment, and profits surge ahead, each followed by a period when profits and output fall, and unemployment increases. Then the entire cycle repeats itself once again. During the expansion, demand and production, income and wealth grow. Homes and factories are constructed, and machinery and equipment are put in place. The value of these assets grows too, as home prices and common stock prices increase. But then comes the inevitable contraction, and all the forces that mark the expansion shift into reverse. Demand, production, and income fall. The level of construction and the production of machinery and equipment are drastically curtailed. Assets lose their value as home prices and common stock prices fall.

No doubt you already realize that business cycles occur and repeat themselves in this way. But why? No completely satisfactory theory has yet been created. No one can accurately predict the length and course of each cycle. Economics, unlike physics, cannot be reduced to experiments and repeated over and over again under ideal conditions. There is no economic equivalent to Galileo on the Tower of Pisa, proving that objects of unequal weight fall with equal speed, because the economic "tower" is never quite the same height; the "objects" keep changing in number, size, and even nature; and the "laws of gravity" apply unequally to each object. Yet one thing is certain: the business cycle is generated by forces within the economic system, not by outside forces. These internal forces create the alternating periods of economic expansion and contraction. And you should recognize that certain crucial features of the cycle endure.

A THUMBNAIL SKETCH

First, the forces of supply and demand condition every cycle. Our ability to enjoy increasing income depends on our ability to supply or create increased production or output; we must produce more to earn more. But the level of demand, and the expenditures made in purchasing this output, must justify the level of production. That is, we must sell what we produce in order to earn. With sufficient demand, the level of production will be sustained and will grow, and income will increase; if demand is insufficient, the reverse will occur. During the expansionary phase of the cycle, demand and supply forces are in a relationship that permits the growth of production and income; during the contractionary phase, their relationship compels a decrease in production and income.

Second, neither consumers nor businesses are constrained to rely solely on the income they have generated in the process of production. They have recourse to the credit market; they can borrow money and spend more than they earn. Spending borrowed funds permits demand to take on a life of its own and bid up a constantly and rapidly growing level of production. This gives rise to the expansionary phase of the cycle. Eventually, the growth in production becomes dependent on the continued availability of credit, which sustains the growth in demand. But once buyers can no longer rely on borrowed funds (because of market saturation, the exhaustion of profitable investment opportunities, or tight credit), demand falls and, with it, the bloated level of production and income. The contractionary phase has begun.

Third, every expansion carries with it the inevitability of "overexpansion" and the subsequent contraction. Overexpansion may be impelled by businesses that invest too heavily in new plant and equipment in order to take advantage of a seemingly profitable opportunity, or by consumers who borrow too heavily in order to buy homes, autos, or other goods. But when businesses realize that the expected level of sales will not support additional plant and equipment, and when consumers realize that they will have difficulty paying for that new home or car, then businesses and consumers will curtail their borrowing and expenditure. Since production and income have spurted ahead to meet the growth in demand, they fall when the inevitable contraction in demand takes place.

Fourth, during contractions, production and income recede to a sustainable level, that is, to a level not reliant on a continuous growth in credit. The contraction returns the economy to a more efficient level of operation.

Fifth, every contraction sows the seeds of the subsequent recovery. Income earned in the productive process, rather than bloated levels of borrowing, maintains the level of demand. Consumers and businesses repay their debts. Eventually, lower debt burdens and interest rates encourage consumer and business borrowing and demand. The economy begins expanding once more.

And there is progress over the course of the cycle. Overall growth takes place because some, or even most, of the increase in output remains intact. Nor is all the created wealth subsequently destroyed. The abandoned steel mills of the "rust belt" will be scrapped, but the plant and equipment used to make personal computers will remain on-stream. Subdivisions developed in 1986, when interest rates were low, turned a profit for their developers, while those completed in 1980, when interest rates rose, were liquidated at a loss after standing empty for a year. And so on. The tree grows, but the rings in its trunk mark the cycles of seasons that were often lush but on occasion were beset by drought.

Yet the American economy grew steadily throughout the 1980s after the recession of 1981–82. Had the business cycle been repealed? Some seemed to think so, just as others had thought so before them, only to be disappointed by the next recession.

Why did the economy just keep growing? Why didn't it stop? Did President Reagan and his supply-side policies deserve the credit? Was the Federal Reserve responsible?

And will the economy keep on growing, without recession, through the 1990s? At the end of the 1980s there were signs that it might.

Therefore, the chapters that follow will not only discuss the cycle's dynamic, they will also describe the forces that have "stretched out" the cycle and postponed recession's expected return. And they will also discuss the likelihood that inflation will be reignited, signaling a turn for investors from stocks to gold.

But as you may already suspect, the business cycle does not operate in a vacuum. It is conditioned, shortened and stretched, and initiated and forestalled by the institutions of our economy. So before embarking on an investigation of the cycle, take a quick look at Chapter 3, which discusses the attempts to influence the economy since World War II.

CHAPTER 3

THE TRANSFORMATION OF THE POSTWAR ECONOMY

To this point we have discussed the business cycle as if it were independent and autonomous. But in fact, in modern history, the American business cycle has been influenced by a variety of attempts to guide and direct it. The economic events of the 15 years from 1965 to 1980 provide a vivid example of well-intentioned economic meddling gone awry.

During these years the federal government and the Federal Reserve System attempted to stimulate demand for goods and services with liberal spending, tax, and credit policies. Their objective was to boost the economy higher and faster, thereby generating increased employment opportunities. They thought that as supply rose to meet demand, increased production would accomplish their objectives. Unfortunately, as demand grew more rapidly than supply, prices spiraled upward. As inflation became more severe, the only solution appeared to be a periodic reversal of those policies of liberal spending, tax, and credit—which invariably plunged the economy into recession. These policy reversals exacerbated the cycle so that inflation *escalated* during boom and unemployment *rose* during bust.

The actions of the Federal Reserve and federal government had their origin in the 30s, when economists were attempting to cope with the ravages of the Great Depression. At that time it was obvious that the economy was stagnating due to insufficient demand for the goods and services business could produce. The factories were there; the machines were there; the labor was there; only the customers were missing. The great question of the day was, "How can we generate effective demand for goods and services?"

Traditional economists had no solution to the problem. They viewed the Depression as a trough in a particularly severe cycle that would correct itself with time. Therefore, they prescribed laissez-faire (leave it alone) as the best possible course of action. Why not? It had always worked in the past.

A new generation of economists surveyed the scene and came up with a different diagnosis. They saw the Great Depression as inaugurating an era in which demand was (and might remain) chronically depressed. To deal with the problem they recommended a two-pronged solution.

First, stimulate demand directly. Clearly consumers were not going to spend more, for many were unemployed, and those who were working were afraid to spend because they might lose their jobs. Business was not going to buy new factories and machinery since even existing facilities were underutilized. Only the government was in a position to spend more. Such government spending would involve deficit financing as the level of expenditures exceeded tax revenues, but the New Dealers were prepared to run the risk. If the government had to borrow now, it could pay back later. In this way the government would be the employer of last resort, hiring people to build dams, bridges, roads, and parks.

Second, the Federal Reserve System (the nation's central bank, known as the Fed) could push interest rates down and thereby depress the cost of borrowing money. This would motivate businesses (to the extent that they could be motivated) to borrow funds in order to buy equipment and machinery and to build additional factories and other establishments. Making credit easy was a way of stimulating economic activity.

These policies, applied in the late 30s, were interrupted by World War II, at which point there was no need to stimulate the economy. But when the war came to an end, it was feared that the economy would again slip back into a chronic state of depression. That anxiety was unfounded, but was so strongly felt that the ideological revolution of the 1930s survived. The new school of economists believed it was the government's duty to stimulate demand until the economy reached its maximum potential of full employment. This attitude meshed with other liberal and progressive views regarding government's responsibility for the social welfare of all.

Conservatives, on the other hand, continued to feel that laissez-faire was the best policy. Thus, throughout the Eisenhower years, the conservative administration drew fire from progressive economists for not implementing the lessons that had been learned in the 30s. They wanted additional federal spending and easy money in order to spur the economy.

When John F. Kennedy ran for office in 1960, he charged that the

Eisenhower administration's conservative policies had reduced the rate of economic growth, and he promised to get the economy moving again. After he took office in 1961, he made good on that pledge by inviting the new school of economists into his administration, urging them to apply the progressive policies that had been developed under Roosevelt.

They did prescribe those policies, but with a new wrinkle. Rather than stimulate demand directly with increased government spending, they proposed putting more purchasing power in the pockets of consumers by cutting taxes. The government would still have to borrow to meet the deficit, except that this time it would do so to pay for a shortfall of revenue rather than a growth in expenditure. One way or the other, demand would grow. Increased consumer spending was just as good as government spending—and, as a rule, politically more advantageous. The extra spending would stimulate economic growth and create jobs as production expanded to meet the surge in consumer demand. At the same time, President Kennedy's economists urged the Federal Reserve to maintain an easy policy so that liberal credit would be available at low rates of interest for consumer and business needs.

These views remained in fashion for two decades. A generation of students was trained to believe that an inadequate level of demand was the paramount problem facing the economy and that they should study economics in order to determine how the federal government and the Federal Reserve could best stimulate the level of economic activity to provide full employment. They all recognized that excessive stimulation of demand could lead to inflation, but they felt that inflation would not be a severe problem until the economy attained full employment.

In each recession the Federal Reserve depressed interest rates, and the government stimulated spending directly with tax cuts for consumers and business. Demand roared ahead in short order, and when it exceeded supply at current prices, prices surged upward. At this point the federal government and the Federal Reserve reversed course and employed policies designed to dampen inflation. They slammed on the brakes, raising taxes and interest rates, depressing demand temporarily, and causing recession. But as soon as the inflation rate dropped, they reversed course and helped bring on the next round of expanding demand and inflation.

No one—not the economists, not the government, not the Federal Reserve—realized that World War II had profoundly changed the underlying circumstances and that policies appropriate for the 30s were not suited for the 60s and 70s. The Great Depression, which preceded the war, was a time of inadequate demand. But government borrowing from banks during the war, and the expenditures of those funds, had placed a wealth of liquid assets at the consumer's disposal. When the war ended, consumers were prepared to spend those funds, and were also increasingly prepared to borrow in order to supplement their expenditures. In the postwar world, demand, buttressed by borrowing, would chronically exceed supply, thus bidding prices upward. Excessive demand, not inadequate demand, would be the problem.

Thus began the first American peacetime period with significant and continuing inflation. In all other eras inflation had been the product of wartime government spending financed by borrowing, while peacetime had been a period of stable prices or even deflation. Consequently, government spending financed by borrowing, whether in time of war or peace, was viewed by almost everyone as the single source of inflation, and this mindset spilled over into the postwar world. No one comprehended that a new economic dynamic was at work in which inflation would be generated by private (consumer and business) borrowing and spending. Ever greater waves of borrowing by the private sector (not government) would drive the inflationary cycle.

The new generation of economists and their students, whose intellectual mold had been cast during the New Deal, were like generals who conduct a war by fighting the previous campaign. But the real issue facing the postwar world was how to keep demand under control, how to restrain it and prevent it from generating inflation. The Eisenhower years, when demand did seem to stall, confused economists, making them believe that the chronically depressed conditions of the 1930s were a real possibility in the postwar world.

A major miscalculation. In fact, the escalating inflation of the 70s showed us that the potential runaway horse of the economy was champing at the bit—and all the while economists and policy makers were wondering how to apply the spurs more vigorously.

By 1980, after two decades of inappropriate policies, the Federal Reserve determined to come to grips with the problem. New Deal economics had to be discarded. The spurs had to be removed, the reins taken in hand, the runaway horse restrained. So the Fed tightened up, interest rates reached the stratosphere, borrowing and spending dried up, and the economy came closer to collapsing in 1981–82 than at any time since the war. After the recession of 1981–82 contained demand and eliminated inflation, the Fed slowly began to ease up. But the Fed was determined not to return to the errors of the past; it would not let credit become easy, or demand grow too rapidly, or inflation get out of control again.

In the 1980s, even though the "new" generation of economists had aged and their policy prescriptions had been largely discredited, the contrasting wisdom of the Federal Reserve's restraint came under increasing attack from another quarter. A still newer generation of supply-side economists demanded that the Fed open the gate and permit a flood of credit at low rates of interest to irrigate the economy's productive forces. They weren't afraid of inflation—or mindful of past errors. If the Fed had relented, and those who wished to abandon restraint had won the day, inflation would have gripped the economy once again.

But the Fed did not relent; it maintained interest rates at levels high enough to keep borrowing and thus demand in check. And, as long as it continues to do so, the Fed can prevent the economy from roaring forward and escalating into the inflationary spiral that brings inevitable recession.

Thus, the Fed acted single-handedly to stretch out the business cycle and forestall recession. By squashing the cycle flat in the early 1980s, and then restraining inflation in the mid and late 80s, the Fed interrupted the cycle's regular and periodic oscillations. This created a period of steady expansion during which the economy did not overheat. By the end of the 80s it was impossible to forecast whether that brief period would stretch indefinitely into a long era, postponing the recession that is the cycle's concluding phase. But there were some clear signs that inflation had been brought under control, giving the edge to stocks and other paper investments over gold and similar tangible investments.

So before you consider *The Wall Street Journal*'s reports on business cycle developments, read Chapters 4 and 5 to review the role of the Federal Reserve System and the federal government in today's business and investment scene.

CHAPTER 4

THE FEDERAL RESERVE SYSTEM: MONETARY POLICY AND INTEREST RATES

THE FED AND INFLATION

Inflation and the business cycle have the greatest imaginable impact on economic conditions and the value of your investments. Because the Federal Reserve System (the Fed) is the only modern American institution that has been able to constructively control and shape these forces, you should begin by learning how to use *The Wall Street Journal* to decipher the Fed's operations.

The Fed is your first order of business because the power of the Fed squashed the business cycle flat in the early 1980's, bringing an end to excessive inflation for the foreseeable future. Before that, during the high-inflation 70s, business cycle fluctuations had grown more severe and inflation's pace had accelerated. *Thus, the Fed's stand against inflation in 1981–82 was the most important turning point in our post–World War II economic history.* And, as you already know, the Fed's anti-inflation policies of the late 80s were crucial in postponing recession and stretching out the cycle.

The business cycle and inflation had spun out of control in the late 1960s and 70s because consumers and businesses had borrowed ever more heavily to finance ever larger expenditures on homes, cars, and other durable goods, as well as plant, equipment, and inventory. As oceans of borrowing supported tidal waves of spending (i.e., demand for goods and services), supply could not keep pace, and prices rose.

To understand this phenomenon, consider a hypothetical example in which people had just as much to spend at the end of a given year as at the beginning, but had increased their output of goods and services by 5 percent during that year. Prices would have to fall by 5 percent before the same amount of spending (demand) could absorb an additional 5 percent of goods and services (supply). And if folks continued each year to produce 5 percent more while their spending did not grow, then prices would fall by 5 percent year after year. We would have chronic deflation.

Similarly, if people's ability to spend (demand) grew by 20 percent while output (supply) grew by 5 percent, you can imagine prices being bid up by 15 percent in that year. And if their spending continued to grow by 20 percent a year while their output grew by only 5 percent, you can imagine chronic inflation of 15 percent. Now you understand how changing supply and demand generate deflation and inflation.

But you may ask, "How is it possible for spending (demand) to grow more rapidly than the output (supply) of society? You can spend only what you have, after all." No, not if people have access to credit provided by banks. For instance, suppose you earn $50,000 a year and your income is a measure of the value of the goods and services that you produce or supply for the market. Also suppose that your spending (demand) is limited by your income. Demand and supply ($50,000) are equal, so prices don't change. Now suppose that you have access to bank credit, so that you can borrow $200,000 to have a house built. Your demand (spending) rises to $200,000 even though your income (supply) remains at $50,000. Demand exceeds supply in this case, and if your situation is repeated often enough in others, prices rise. Whenever demand exceeds supply at current prices, made possible by borrowing (credit), inflation (rising prices) occurs.

The $200,000 provided by the banks was *not* produced and saved by someone else, thereby equating earlier supply with new demand. It was created out of thin air by the banking system, and that is why your bank-financed spending is inflationary. It also serves to illustrate the point that you have to understand the banking and credit system to comprehend the reasons for the ever-escalating business cycle and inflation of 1965–80.

Private borrowing by consumers and businesses has always been a feature of our economy, but it did not begin to reach heroic proportions and grow at an explosive pace until the late 1960s. From that point on, credit *doubled* every five years. There was no way production could keep pace with these surges in demand, so rising inflation filled the gap.

But borrowing and spending did not grow smoothly. They surged forward periodically, generating the wavelike action of the business cycle. The rise of borrowing and spending carried inflation with it, and interest rates, too, as spiraling borrowing drove up the cost of credit. Steep increases in prices and interest rates eventually choked off the boom, discouraging consumers and businesses from continued borrowing and spending. The wave crashed and the cycle completed itself as the economy contracted into recession.

The Fed exacerbated the worst aspects of the cycle in the late 60s and throughout the 70s by attempting to alleviate them. Reining in credit expansion at the peak of the cycle, in order to curb inflation, merely contributed to the severity of the inevitable downturn and made recession worse. Easing up during recession, in order to encourage borrowing and spending and thus pull the economy out of a slump, contributed to the excesses of the next boom. And with each wave of the cycle, inflation and interest rates ratcheted higher and higher.

The Fed reversed course in 1981–82 and brought an end to 15 years of escalating inflation and cyclical instability by applying a chokehold of high interest rates. The economy was brought to the brink of collapse. But when the Fed relaxed its grip and interest rates declined from exorbitant to merely high, the manic rounds of boom and bust had ceased. The economy set out on a healthy expansion without inflation that lasted through the late 80s and could postpone recession until well into the 90s.

Tight money had done the trick and continues to do so. Borrowing no longer doubles every five years. It is now discouraged by interest rates too high to be ignored. Inflation had been contained. The Fed had won.

Bankrolling Inflation

- Bank lending finances spending; spending generates inflation.
- The Fed controls bank lending and can thereby control inflation.

But what is the Fed? How does it work? What, exactly, did it (and does it) do? Start your investigation with a bit of background.

THE FED'S HISTORY

The United States was the last major industrial nation to establish a central bank. The modern German state commissioned a central bank in 1875; the Bank of France was founded in 1800; and the Bank of England had entered its third century of operation when the Federal Reserve System was created in 1913.

America's tardiness was due to our traditional suspicion of centralized financial power and authority. Historically, we have felt more comfortable with small banks serving a single community. In fact, some states limit branch banking to this day, requiring that most of a bank's business be conducted under one roof. Ironically, the Continental Illinois Bank in Chicago is one of the nation's biggest, even though Illinois law severely constrains its branch facilities. California's liberal branch banking laws once helped Bank of America build its position as the nation's largest bank, whereas the big New York City banks (until recently) were hampered by legislation that confined them to the city and its suburbs and kept their branches out of upstate New York.

Alexander Hamilton proposed a central bank shortly after the country's founding. The two early attempts to create one failed when confronted with the nation's suspicion of the Eastern financial community. Consequently, our economy grew until the eve of World War I without benefit of coordination or control of its banking activity. Banking, like the sale of alcohol following the repeal of Prohibition, was largely subject to local option.

Under these circumstances, the banks had to fend for themselves, and the business cycle created perils for them as well as opportunities for profit. During recessions, when business income was down (usually following periods of speculative excess), banks found it difficult to collect on loans.

At the same time, nervous businesspersons and investors made large withdrawals, sometimes demanding payment in gold or silver specie. These precious metal coins composed the ultimate reserve for deposits; however, no bank possessed enough of them to secure every depositor, and the banking system functioned on the assumption that only a minority of depositors would demand their funds on any one day. When panic set in and a queue formed out the door and around the block, a bank could be wiped out in a matter of hours. As rumor spread, one bank after another failed, until only the most substantial institutions, with the greatest specie reserve, were left standing. The chain reaction damaged many people, not the least of whom were innocent depositors who could not reach their funds in time.

Congress took up the issue after the panic of 1907. In that crisis—as the story goes—J.P. Morgan kept New York's most important bankers locked up in his home overnight until they agreed to contribute a pool of specie to be lent to the weakest banks until the run subsided. It worked—but the near-disaster had made it clear that the time had come to establish an American central bank that could lend to all banks in time of panic; the nation's financial system could no longer rely on the private arrangements of J.P. Morgan. Thus, the Federal Reserve System was established by Congress in 1913. All member banks were required to make deposits to the system, creating a pool of reserves from which financially strapped banks could borrow during a crisis.

The system was originally conceived as a lender of last resort. In times of severe economic stress, it would use the pooled reserves of the banking system to make loans to banks under stress. When conditions improved, the loans were to be repaid. As time went by, however, the Fed discovered two things: first, that the reserve requirement could be used to control banking activity; and second, that control over the banking system provided a means of influencing the business cycle.

The reasoning was straightforward. Bank lending is a key ingredient in the business cycle, driving the cyclic expansion of demand. It cannot, however, grow beyond the limits set by bank reserves; so when the Fed wants to give the economy a boost by encouraging banks to lend more, it increases reserves. On the other hand, by decreasing reserves and thereby shrinking available credit, the Fed exerts a restraining effect on the economy.

OPEN-MARKET OPERATIONS

The mechanism used by the Fed to manipulate the banking system's reserves is astonishingly simple: it buys or sells securities on the open market. Briefly put, when the Fed buys securities, the sellers deposit the proceeds of the sale in their banks, and the banking system's reserves grow. On the other hand, when the Fed sells securities, buyers withdraw funds from their banks in order to make the purchases, and bank reserves fall.

This illustration may help you understand the process. Imagine that the Fed, a government securities dealer, and all banks (not an individual bank) are the only players in this example. (At the end of the 1980s, there were approximately 40 major U.S. Treasury securities dealers with which the Fed conducted business.)

Keep in mind that there are trillions of dollars of U.S. Treasury securities outstanding and that anyone (domestic and foreign corporations, individuals, state, local and foreign governments, private banks, and central banks) can buy them. Billions of dollars are traded each day in New York City.

The Fed increases and reduces bank reserves by its actions in this market. It trades in U.S. Treasury securities rather than some other instrument because the government securities market is so broad and Federal Reserve activities have a relatively small impact on that market.

When the Fed purchases a security from one of the 40-odd dealers, it pays the dealer by instructing the dealer's bank to credit the checking account of the dealer by the amount of the transaction. At the same time, the Fed pays the bank by crediting the bank's reserve account at the Fed.

Returning to the example, Treasury bills are denominated in amounts of $10,000. Thus, when the Fed buys a Treasury bill from a securities dealer, it instructs the dealer's bank to credit the dealer's account by $10,000 to pay for the Treasury bill. At the same time the Fed credits the dealer's bank's reserve account by $10,000. As a result of the transaction, the dealer has exchanged one asset (Treasury bills ↓ $10,000) for another (checking account ↑ $10,000), the bank's assets (reserves at the Fed ↑ $10,000) and liabilities (dealer's checking account ↑ $10,000) have both increased, and the Fed's assets (Treasury bills ↑ $10,000) and liabilities (bank reserves ↑ $10,000) have both increased.

You may ask, "What gives the Fed the authority to execute these transactions: to pay for a Treasury bill by instructing the dealer's bank to credit the dealer's checking account and then to compensate the bank by crediting its reserve account at the Fed? It's as if the Fed has the right to fund the purchase of an asset by creating its own liability." That's how it works. The Fed has the right under the authority vested in it by the Federal Reserve Act of 1913.

In other words, the Fed can increase the nation's bank reserves by purchasing U.S. Treasury securities from securities dealers, and all it need do to pay for those securities is inform the banks that it has provided them with more reserves. And that's not all: be aware that unless the

Fed continues to buy those securities and pay for them by crediting the banks' reserve accounts, bank reserves won't grow. The Fed can halt the economy's expansion by no longer purchasing Treasury bills. Once the Fed stops buying, bank reserves stop growing and so must bank lending. If the Fed wishes to keep a growing economy supplied with bank reserves, it must increase its holdings of Treasury securities over the long haul.

But suppose the Fed wishes to slow the economy's growth temporarily by curtailing banks' ability to lend. Easy—it just stops *buying* securities and starts *selling* them. The securities dealer pays for the Treasury bill it acquires (dealer's assets ↑) when the Fed instructs the dealer's bank to debit the dealer's bank account (dealer's assets ↓). The Fed collects from the dealer's bank by debiting the bank's reserve account at the Fed (bank's assets ↓) and the bank is compensated when it debits the dealer's checking account (bank's liabilities ↓). Consequently, bank lending must cease because the banks are deprived of reserves. Meanwhile, the Fed has merely reduced its assets (Treasury securities ↓) as well as its liabilities (bank reserves ↓).

Consider a few additional points. Don't worry whether or not the securities dealer is willing to buy or sell Treasury securities. There are dozens of dealers competing for the Fed's (and everyone else's) business. There's as much likelihood of the Fed not being able to find a buyer or seller for its Treasury securities as there is of someone not being able to buy or sell a share of stock at the market price. If one stockbroker won't do it, another will.

Also, don't be confused because these open-market operations involve the buying and selling of Treasury securities. Remember that the Fed is not an agency of the U.S. government. The Fed could just as easily deal in common stock or automobiles, but it wouldn't do that because it doesn't want its actions to upset the stock market or the car market. Nonetheless, keep in mind that the Fed could pay for shares of stock or autos by instructing banks to credit stockbrokers' or auto dealers' accounts (and then credit those banks' reserve accounts) in the same fashion that it instructs banks to credit U.S. Treasury securities dealers' accounts. Then the Fed would credit the reserve accounts of the banks that held the stockbrokers' and car dealers' accounts. If the Fed sold common stock or used cars, it would drain away bank reserves just as surely as when it sold Treasury bills in the open market.

To resume the historical account, the Fed has exercised increasing power over the economy since 1913. Periodically, this has led to conflict with the president and Congress. On occasion, politicians took the Fed to task for being too restrictive, for not permitting the economy to grow rapidly enough. At other times, the Fed was criticized for being too lenient and permitting demand to grow so rapidly that inflation threatened.

Why the conflict? Shouldn't the Fed's policy reflect the wishes of Congress and the president? Maybe, but it need not, for—as many do not realize—the Fed is *not* an agency of the U.S. government, but a corporation owned by banks that have purchased shares of stock. Federally chartered banks are required to purchase this stock and be members of the Federal Reserve System; state-chartered banks may be members if they wish. All banks, however, are subject to the Fed's control.

True, the Fed does have a quasi-public character because its affairs are managed by a Board of Governors appointed by the president of the United States with the approval of Congress. Nonetheless, once appointed, the Board of Governors is independent of the federal government and is free to pursue policies of its own choosing. New laws could, of course, change its status. That's why the chairman of the board is so frequently called upon to defend the policies of the Fed before Congress, and why Congress often reminds the Fed that it is a creature of Congress, which can enact legislation to reduce, alter, or eliminate the Fed's powers. Indeed, legislators and others do suggest from time to time that the Fed be made an agency of the U.S. government in order to remove its autonomy. So far, however, Congress has kept it independent, and it is likely to remain so, exercising its best judgment in guiding the nation's banking activity.

In some ways, the Fed's control over the banking system's reserves is the most important relationship between any two institutions in the American economy. The Fed can increase or reduce bank reserves at will, making it easier or more difficult for the banks to lend, and thus stimulating or restricting business and economic activity.

THE FED AND THE MONEY SUPPLY

But how is it that bank lending increases the supply of money? Where does the money come from? There is an astonishingly simple answer to these questions: the banks create it by crediting the checking account deposits of their borrowers. Thus, bank lending creates money (deposits).

And the only limits to the money supply are

1. The Fed's willingness to provide the banks with reserves.
2. The banks' ability to find borrowers.

It may sound strange that banks create money, but nonetheless it's true.

The reason so much controversy surrounds the money supply is that many people misunderstand its nature. Checking accounts (or demand deposits, as they are formally called) constitute three quarters of the money supply, and currency and coins in circulation together make up the remaining quarter. The one quarter of the money supply that exists as cash comes from a two-tiered source: the U.S. Treasury mints coins and prints paper money for the Fed, and the Fed distributes them.

These arrangements have an interesting and important history. Before the Civil War, with the exception of the two short-lived attempts at a central bank that were mentioned earlier, all paper money was issued by private banks and was called bank notes. These bank notes resembled modern paper currency and entered circulation when banks lent them to customers.

The banks' incentive to issue bank notes to borrowers, instead of gold and silver coins, came from the limited supply of gold and silver coins (specie). Each bank kept a specie reserve that was no more than a fraction of its outstanding bank notes. This reserve was used to satisfy those who demanded that a bank redeem its notes with specie; as long as the bank could do so, its notes were accepted at face value and were "good as gold." Bank notes and minted coins circulated together.

After the Civil War, checking accounts replaced bank notes. They were safer and more convenient because the customer (borrower) had to sign them and could write in their exact amount. In modern times, all customers, whether depositors or borrowers, began to make use of checking accounts. The private bank note passed into history.

The U.S. Treasury first issued paper money during the Civil War, and it continued to do so until some time after World War II. During the 20th century, however, most of our paper money has been issued by the Federal Reserve System, and today the Fed has that exclusive responsibility; if you examine a piece of currency, you will see that it is a "Federal Reserve Note." Thus, ironically, bank notes constitute all of our currency today, just as they did before the Civil War. But today the notes are issued by the central bank rather than by a host of private banks.

Since the Treasury prints currency at the Fed's request to meet the public's needs, the common notion that the federal government cranks out more paper money to finance its deficits has no factual basis. The amount of paper money in circulation has nothing to do with the deficits of the federal government. When the federal government runs a deficit (expenditures exceed revenue), the Treasury borrows by issuing bonds that are bought by investors: the government gets the money, and the investors get the bonds. If a bond is sold to a bank (and banks are major purchasers of U.S. Treasury securities), the bank pays for it by crediting the checking account of the U.S. Treasury, thus increasing the total volume of all checking accounts. This is called *monetizing the debt*; it enlarges the money supply but does not affect currency in circulation. (If the bond is purchased by the Fed, the transaction is also characterized as monetizing the debt, and the effect is similar to an expansionary monetary policy in which the Fed buys U.S. Treasury securities through open-market operations.)

By contrast, the Fed issues paper money in response not to the budget deficits of the *federal government* but to the *public's* requirements for cash. It supplies banks with cash, and the banks pay for it with a check written on their reserve account. Checks written to "cash" by bank customers then determine the amount of currency circulating outside banks. This demand for cash has no impact on the money supply because checking accounts decrease by the amount currency increases when the check is "cashed."

How then does the money supply grow? In the same fashion that bank notes outstanding grew in the 19th century. When banks lend, they create demand deposits (checking accounts) or credit an existing demand deposit. The more that banks lend, the more that the money supply (which is mostly demand deposits) increases. Today, as 100 years ago, bank reserves set the only limit on bank lending and, therefore, on the money supply. The difference is that instead of keeping specie as reserves, the banks must maintain reserves with the Fed.

Remember: bank loans create deposits (checking accounts), not the other way around. As long as the banking system has sufficient reserves, it can make loans in the form of demand deposits (money). You must abandon the notion that depositors' funds provide the wherewithal for bank lending. That may be true for the traditional mortgage-lending activity of a savings and loan association, but it is not true for commercial banks. After all, where would depositors get the funds if not by withdrawing them from another checking account? But this actually does not increase deposits for the entire system; it only reshuffles deposits among banks. The total is unchanged.

Thus, demand deposits (checking accounts), and with them the money supply, grow when banks lend, and it makes no difference who the borrower is. When a business borrows from its bank in order to stock goods for the Christmas season, the bank creates a deposit (money) on which the business writes checks to pay for merchandise. If you borrow from your bank to buy a car, the loan creates a demand deposit that increases the money supply. Therefore, as you can see, it is not just the federal government that "monetizes debt" when it borrows from the banking system; businesses and consumers "monetize" their debt too.

One last point must be made about the nature of bank reserves. A hundred years ago, they consisted of gold and silver specie; today, they are deposits that banks maintain with the Federal Reserve System. Of what do these reserves consist, if not specie? They are merely checking accounts that the banks have on deposit with the Fed, very much like the checking account you have at your own bank. Recall that the banks' checking accounts (reserves) increase when the Fed buys securities from a government securities dealer.

If it sounds like a house of cards, or like bookkeeping entries in a computer's memory, that's because it is. Nothing "backs up" the money supply except our faith in it, expressed every time we accept or write a check. And those checking accounts, and hence the money supply, built on borrowing, *must keep growing* if the economy is to grow over the business cycle. The forward surge of the cycle, when demand grows rapidly and pulls the economy's output with it, is founded on spenders' ability and willingness to borrow, to go into debt.

This, then, is the critical significance of the money supply: it measures the increase in demand made possible by bank lending. With that in mind, it is now time to discuss the price borrowers are willing to pay for those funds.

THE FED AND INTEREST RATES

Every commodity has a price; the *interest rate* is the price of money. As with any commodity, that price fluctuates according to the laws of supply and demand.

The demand for money increases and interest rates rise during economic expansion as consumers and businesses finance increased spending. They do so by drawing on three sources of funds: current savings, liquidation of financial assets, and borrowing from banks and other financial intermediaries.

During recessions, as the economy moves from trough to recovery, cash becomes plentiful again. Savings are ample, financial assets accumulate, and debt is repaid. Interest rates fall as the supply of funds exceeds the demand for funds at current rates.

The cyclical rise and fall of interest rates would occur with or without the Federal Reserve System. Yet the Fed's influence on interest rates is so pervasive that it is now time to study the Fed's actions in detail. Begin with *The Wall Street Journal*'s weekly report on the Fed's operations. The basic information you need to follow the Fed's impact on the banks, the money supply, and interest rates will be found in this article.

FEDERAL RESERVE DATA

"Federal Reserve Data" contains Wednesday figures that are released on Thursday for publication the following day, and in revised form a week later. Thus, statistics for Wednesday, May 3, 1989 appeared on Friday, May 12, 1989 (see pages 36 and 37).

Look at **Free Reserves**, the next-to-last line under the heading **Reserve Aggregates**. It reveals the impact of the Fed's actions on the banking system. This section will explain its derivation and how to use it.

In examining free reserves, keep in mind that the discussion refers to all banks collectively, not to individual banks. This distinction is important. Banks can competitively drain one another of reserves to augment their ability to lend, but this activity does not increase the entire system's reserves even though it explains the fierce rivalry among banks for deposits. When deposits are moved from one bank to another, the reserves of the first bank fall and those of the second bank increase. The first bank must restrain its lending, while the second bank can lend more. This competitive reshuffling of reserves, however, has not altered the overall level of reserves, and so the lending ability of the banking system remains the same.

Consequently, the reserves of the entire banking system depend on the Fed's open-market operations (buying and selling U.S. Treasury

FEDERAL RESERVE DATA

MONETARY AGGREGATES
(daily average in billions)

	One week ended: May 1	Apr. 24
Money supply (M1) sa	781.7	786.9
Money supply (M1) nsa	778.0	790.7
Money supply (M2) sa	3071.3	3082.1
Money supply (M2) nsa	3063.0	3084.8
Money supply (M3) sa	3953.2	3965.5
Money supply (M3) nsa	3939.1	3958.9
	Four weeks ended: May 1	**Apr. 3**
Money supply (M1) sa	783.0	784.8
Money supply (M1) nsa	791.2	774.6
Money supply (M2) sa	3080.6	3079.6
Money supply (M2) nsa	3091.3	3075.2
Money supply (M3) sa	3961.6	3954.5
Money supply (M3) nsa	3965.4	3951.3
	Month: Apr.	**Mar.**
Money supply (M1) sa	782.9	786.3
Money supply (M2) sa	3081.1	3079.5
Money supply (M3) sa	3961.3	3952.2

nsa-Not seasonally adjusted. sa-Seasonally adjusted.

KEY ASSETS AND LIABILITIES OF THE 10 LEADING NEW YORK BANKS
(in millions of dollars)

ASSETS:	May 3, 1989	Change from April 26, 1989
Total loans, leases and investments, adjusted	208,378	– 486
Commercial and industrial loans	58,983	+ 732
Loans to depository and financial institutions	17,593	+ 221
Loans to individuals	19,368	– 495
Real estate loans	51,679	+ 47
U.S. government securities	14,962	– 152
Other securities including municipal issues	17,436	– 18
Municipal securities	12,018	– 34
LIABILITIES:		
Demand deposits	50,785	+ 1,190
Other transaction deposits including NOW accounts	8,544	– 375
Savings and other nontransaction deposits	102,910	+ 9
Includes large time deposits of $100,000 or more	42,680	– 274

COMMERCIAL PAPER OUTSTANDING
(in millions of dollars)

All issuers	501,842	+ 3,940
Financial companies	380,310	+ 1,385
Nonfinancial companies	121,532	+ 2,555

MEMBER BANK RESERVE CHANGES

Changes in weekly averages of reserves and related items during the week and year ended May 10, 1989 were as follows (in millions of dollars)

Reserve bank credit:	May 10 1989	Chg fm May 2 1989	wk end May 11 1988
U.S. Gov't securities:			
Bought outright	234,123	+ 726	+ 10,657
Held under repurch agreemt	10,189	+ 601	+ 7,401
Federal agency issues:			
Bought outright	6,654	....	– 625
Held under repurch agreemt	3,736	– 407	+ 2,702
Acceptances—bought outright			
Held under repurch agreemt	....	....	....
Borrowings from Fed	1,743	– 175	– 337
Seasonal borrowings	314	+ 21	+ 75
Extended credit	1,221	– 10	– 510
Float	797	+ 159	– 26
Other Federal Reserve Assets	22,622	+ 1,177	+ 6,428
Total Reserve Bank Credit	279,863	+ 2,030	+ 2,199
Gold Stock	11,061	....	– 2
SDR certificates	5,611	+ 93	+ 593
Treasury currency outstanding	19,031	+ 14	+ 62
Total	315,566	+ 2,187	+ 27,410
Currency in circulation	345,206	+ 1449	+ 15,134
Treasury cash holdings	490	+ 13	+ 9
Treasury dpts with F.R. Bnks	23,141	+ 1,156	+ 9,989
Foreign dpts with F.R. Bnks	206	– 61	– 73
Other dpts with F.R. Bnks	281	– 157	– 27
Service related balances, adj	1,785	– 163	– 161
Other F.R. liabilities & capital	8,826	– 56	+ 1,593
Total	279,936	+ 2,201	+ 26,465

RESERVE AGGREGATES ← Reserve Aggregates
(daily average in millions)

	Two weeks ended: May 3	Apr. 19
Total Reserves (sa)	60,409	58,610
Nonborrowed Reserves (sa)	58,441	56,028
Required Reserves (sa)	59,159	58,375
Excess Reserves (nsa)	1,251	235
Borrowings from Fed (nsa)-a	581	612
Free Reserves (nsa)	670	–377
Monetary Base (sa)	280,051	277,448

a-Excluding extended credit. nsa-Not seasonally adjusted. sa-Seasonally adjusted.

Free Reserves Positive (+) $670 million for two weeks ending May 3,1989

Source: *The Wall Street Journal*, May 12, 1989.

securities), which were described earlier. The banks cannot augment their reserves independently through their own actions. The Fed *supplies* the banking system with reserves by *buying* securities, and it *deprives* the system of reserves by *selling* securities. When the Fed buys securities, the seller deposits the proceeds of the sale in his or her bank, thus increasing bank reserves. When it sells them, the buyer pays with funds withdrawn from his or her bank, thus decreasing bank reserves. More reserves make it easier for the banks to lend, stimulating economic activity; fewer reserves make it more difficult for the banks to lend, restraining economic activity.

That sounds very hard on the banks. Suppose the Fed's policy becomes restrictive in the midst of an economic expansion; it sells securities, and so deprives the banks of reserves. If the banks are making loans while the Fed is reducing the level of bank reserves, the banking system will be short of reserves. Do the banks have a cushion to protect them in such an event?

Yes, they may borrow reserves from the Fed at a rate of interest called *the discount rate*. And to avoid a penalty for falling short, banks initiate such borrowing before their reserves are completely exhausted, thus maintaining a margin of *excess reserves*.

Now you can calculate the *free reserve* figure for the entire banking system, which appears in the **Reserve Aggregates** section of "Federal Reserve Data."

When bank lending grows rapidly and the Fed is not supplying the banks with sufficient reserves, the banks will be obliged to borrow heavily from the Fed. If borrowing exceeds excess reserves, free reserves is a negative (–) figure. This is a signal that bank lending is expanding at a rapid pace and that the Fed is trying to restrain the banks and the expansion of economic activity.

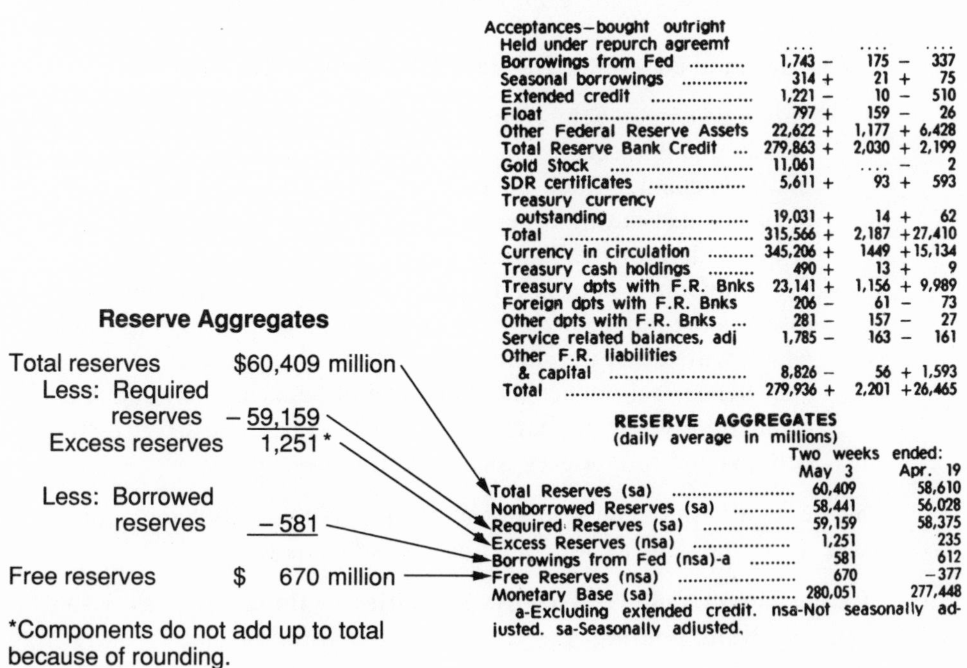

Acceptances–bought outright			
Held under repurch agreemt	....	....	....
Borrowings from Fed	1,743	– 175	– 337
Seasonal borrowings	314	+ 21	+ 75
Extended credit	1,221	– 10	– 510
Float	797	+ 159	– 26
Other Federal Reserve Assets	22,622	+ 1,177	+ 6,428
Total Reserve Bank Credit ...	279,863	+ 2,030	+ 2,199
Gold Stock	11,061	....	– 2
SDR certificates	5,611	+ 93	+ 593
Treasury currency outstanding	19,031	+ 14	+ 62
Total	315,566	+ 2,187	+27,410
Currency in circulation	345,206	+ 1449	+15,134
Treasury cash holdings	490	+ 13	+ 9
Treasury dpts with F.R. Bnks	23,141	+ 1,156	+ 9,989
Foreign dpts with F.R. Bnks	206	– 61	– 73
Other dpts with F.R. Bnks ...	281	– 157	– 27
Service related balances, adj	1,785	– 163	– 161
Other F.R. liabilities & capital	8,826	– 56	+ 1,593
Total	279,936	+ 2,201	+26,465

RESERVE AGGREGATES
(daily average in millions)

	Two weeks ended: May 3	Apr. 19
Total Reserves (sa)	60,409	58,610
Nonborrowed Reserves (sa)	58,441	56,028
Required Reserves (sa)	59,159	58,375
Excess Reserves (nsa)	1,251	235
Borrowings from Fed (nsa)-a	581	612
Free Reserves (nsa)	670	–377
Monetary Base (sa)	280,051	277,448

a-Excluding extended credit. nsa-Not seasonally adjusted. sa-Seasonally adjusted.

Source: *The Wall Street Journal*, May 12, 1989.

On the other hand, during a period of slack economic activity, bank lending (and hence required reserves) will decline. Banks will not have to borrow reserves from the Fed. When excess reserves are large and bank borrowing is negligible, free reserves will be positive (+). A high level of free reserves shows that the Fed is not restraining the banks.

Returning to the May 12, 1989 "Federal Reserve Data," you can see that free reserves averaged $670 million in the two weeks ending May 3, 1989. The Fed had provided banks with sufficient reserves. Excess reserves exceeded the banks' borrowing from the Fed, so free reserves were positive (+).

In summary, free reserves will be positive (+) when the Fed is supplying the banks with enough reserves through its open-market operations that the banks need not borrow. Free reserves are negative (–) when the Fed is restricting bank reserves. When, in the course of the business cycle, the former is true, the Fed's actions are referred to as an *easy money* policy or an *expansionary* monetary policy. When the latter is true, and free reserves are negative by a large amount, the Fed's actions are referred to as a *tight money* policy or a *contractionary* monetary policy.

What are the Fed's objectives in implementing these policies?

- *Expansionary policy:* If the Fed buys securities, thus increasing member bank reserves, the banks will be able to lend more, stimulating demand. Such an expansionary policy has traditionally been pursued during a period of recession when the economy is at the bottom of the business cycle.
- *Contractionary policy:* If the Fed sells securities, and bank reserves are reduced, the banks will not be able to lend as much, which will curtail the share of demand that depends on borrowing and, hence, will reduce the total level of demand. This policy has been followed at the peak of the cycle to restrain the growth of demand and inflationary increases in prices.

These relationships can be easily summarized in the following manner: (Read ↑ as "up," ↓ as "down," and → as "leads to.")

Expansionary policy: Fed buys securities → Bank reserves ↑ → Bank lending ↑ → Demand ↑ → Inflation ↑ .

Contractionary policy: Fed sells securities → Bank reserves ↓ → Bank lending ↓ → Demand ↓ → Inflation ↓ .

Thus, free reserves are positive (+) when the Fed pursues an expansionary policy, because open-market operations (Fed buys securities) have provided banks with such a large volume of reserves that excess reserves exceed bank borrowing from the Fed. Free reserves are negative (–) when Fed policy turns contractionary and open-market sales of securities deprive banks of reserves, obliging them to borrow more than their excess reserves from the Fed.

The Fed was traditionally activist, alternately pursuing easy (supplying banks with reserves) or tight (depriving banks of reserves) money policies, depending on the state of the business cycle. During periods of recession and through the recovery stage and the early period of expansion, the Fed's easy money policy contributed to rapid growth in the money supply (demand deposits or checking accounts) as banks lent money (demand deposits or checking accounts) freely in response to plentiful reserves. As the expansionary phase of the cycle reached its peak, the Fed switched to a tight money policy, restricting the growth of bank reserves and, hence, the money supply.

The Fed's actions with respect to the *money supply* may be added to the earlier set of directed arrows and summarized as shown:

Expansionary policy: Fed buys securities → Bank reserves ↑ → Bank lending ↑ → Money supply ↑ → Demand ↑ .

Contractionary policy: Fed sells securities → Bank reserves ↓ → Bank lending ↓ → Money supply ↓ → Demand ↓ .

You can track the money supply, sometimes referred to as M1, in each Friday's Federal Reserve Data under **Monetary Aggregates. M1** is demand deposits (checking accounts) and currency in circulation. In the report that appeared on Friday, May 12, 1989, M1 averaged $781.7 billion for the week ending May 1, 1989, $783.0 billion for the four weeks ending May 1, and $782.9 billion in April of 1989 (see page 40).

The annotation "sa" means *seasonally adjusted*. All seasonal fluctuations, such as the large increase and subsequent decline in the money supply associated with the Christmas shopping season, have been removed from the data.

You'll see references now and then to a variety of "M's," and the *Journal* tracks them on Fridays together with the Fed's targets for their growth. See the excerpt from the February 17, 1989 issue on page 40. **M2** is M1 plus savings accounts and money market fund shares, and

One-Week Money Supply Figure
M1 averaged $781.7 billion
during week ending May 1, 1989

Four-Week Money Supply Figure
M1 averaged $783.0 billion
during four weeks ending May 1, 1989

Monthly Money Supply Figure
M1 averaged $782.9 billion
in April 1989

FEDERAL RESERVE DATA

MONETARY AGGREGATES
(daily average in billions)

	One week ended: May 1	Apr. 24
Money supply (M1) sa	781.7	786.9
Money supply (M1) nsa	778.0	790.7
Money supply (M2) sa	3071.3	3082.1
Money supply (M2) nsa	3063.0	3084.8
Money supply (M3) sa	3953.2	3965.5
Money supply (M3) nsa	3939.1	3958.9
	Four weeks ended: May 1	**Apr. 3**
Money supply (M1) sa	783.0	784.8
Money supply (M1) nsa	791.2	774.6
Money supply (M2) sa	3080.6	3079.6
Money supply (M2) nsa	3091.3	3075.2
Money supply (M3) sa	3961.6	3954.5
Money supply (M3) nsa	3965.4	3951.3
	Month: Apr.	**Mar.**
Money supply (M1) sa	782.9	786.3
Money supply (M2) sa	3081.1	3079.5
Money supply (M3) sa	3961.3	3952.2

nsa-Not seasonally adjusted. sa-Seasonally adjusted.

KEY ASSETS AND LIABILITIES OF THE 10 LEADING NEW YORK BANKS
(in millions of dollars)

	May 3, 1989	Change from April 26, 1989
ASSETS:		
Total loans, leases and investments, adjusted	208,378	− 486
Commercial and industrial loans	58,983	+ 732
Loans to depository and financial institutions	17,593	+ 221
Loans to individuals	19,368	− 495
Real estate loans	51,679	+ 47
U.S. government securities	14,962	− 152
Other securities including municipal issues	17,436	− 18
Municipal securities	12,018	− 34
LIABILITIES:		
Demand deposits	50,785	+ 1,190
Other transaction deposits including NOW accounts	8,544	− 375
Savings and other nontransaction deposits	102,910	+ 9
Includes large time deposits of $100,000 or more	42,680	− 274

COMMERCIAL PAPER OUTSTANDING
(in millions of dollars)

All issuers	501,842	+ 3,940
Financial companies	380,310	+ 1,385
Nonfinancial companies	121,532	+ 2,555

MEMBER BANK RESERVE CHANGES

Changes in weekly averages of reserves and related items during the week and year ended May 10, 1989 were as follows (in millions of dollars)

	May 10 1989	Chg fm May 2 1989	wk end May 11 1988
Reserve bank credit:			
U.S. Gov't securities:			
Bought outright	234,123	+ 726	+ 10,657
Held under repurch agreemt	10,189	+ 601	+ 7,401
Federal agency issues:			
Bought outright	6,654	....	− 625
Held under repurch agreemt	3,736	− 407	+ 2,702
Acceptances—bought outright			
Held under repurch agreemt	....	....	....
Borrowings from Fed	1,743	− 175	− 337
Seasonal borrowings	314	+ 21	+ 75
Extended credit	1,221	− 10	− 510
Float	797	+ 159	− 26
Other Federal Reserve Assets	22,622	+ 1,177	+ 6,428
Total Reserve Bank Credit	279,863	+ 2,030	+ 2,199
Gold Stock	11,061	....	− 2
SDR certificates	5,611	+ 93	+ 593
Treasury currency outstanding	19,031	+ 14	+ 62
Total	315,566	+ 2,187	+ 27,410
Currency in circulation	345,206	+ 1449	+ 15,134
Treasury cash holdings	490	+ 13	+ 9
Treasury dpts with F.R. Bnks	23,141	+ 1,156	+ 9,989
Foreign dpts with F.R. Bnks	206	− 61	− 73
Other dpts with F.R. Bnks	281	− 157	− 27
Service related balances, adj	1,785	− 163	− 161
Other F.R. liabilities & capital	8,826	− 56	+ 1,593
Total	279,936	+ 2,201	+ 26,465

RESERVE AGGREGATES
(daily average in millions)

	Two weeks ended: May 3	Apr. 19
Total Reserves (sa)	60,409	58,610
Nonborrowed Reserves (sa)	58,441	56,028
Required Reserves (sa)	59,159	58,375
Excess Reserves (nsa)	1,251	235
Borrowings from Fed (nsa)-a	581	612
Free Reserves (nsa)	670	−377
Monetary Base (sa)	280,051	277,448

a-Excluding extended credit. nsa-Not seasonally adjusted. sa-Seasonally adjusted.

Source: *The Wall Street Journal*, May 12, 1989.

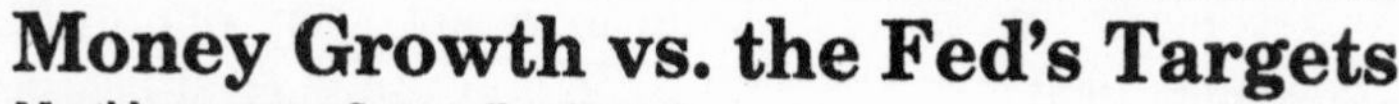

Monthly averages, Seasonally adjusted

M1 Checking deposits plus cash held by the public. The Fed didn't set a target for M1 growth this year or last year. The inset shows the latest period.

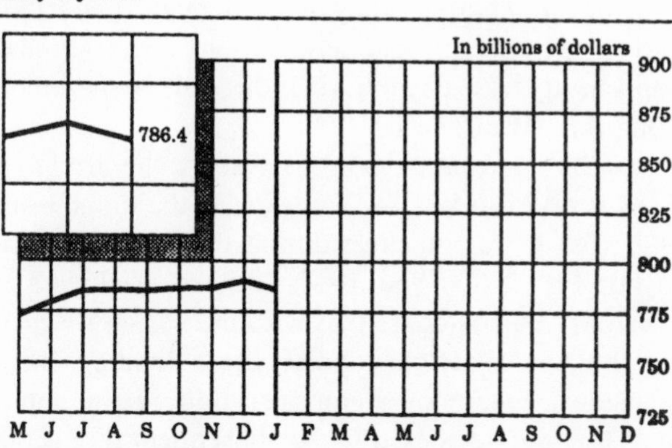

M2 Includes everything in M1 plus most types of savings, including money market deposit accounts. The Fed's tentative growth target for this year, as shown by the large cone as well as the dotted lines, is 3%-to-7% growth, compared with 4%-to-8% last year.

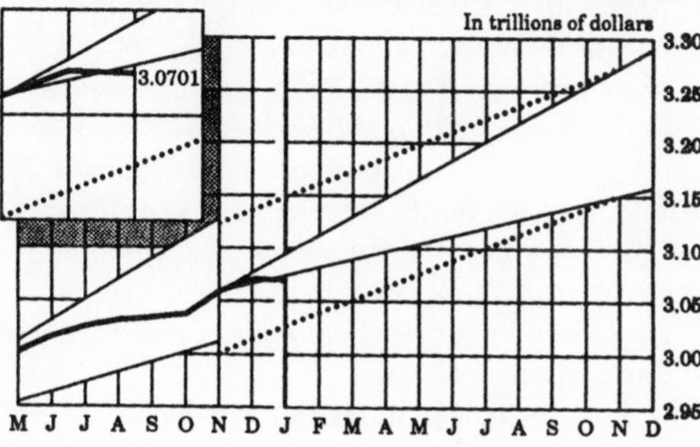

M3 Includes M2 plus some investments such as large certificates of deposit and money market funds sold to institutions. The Fed's tentative target this year is 3.5%-to-7.5% growth, down from 4%-to-8% last year.

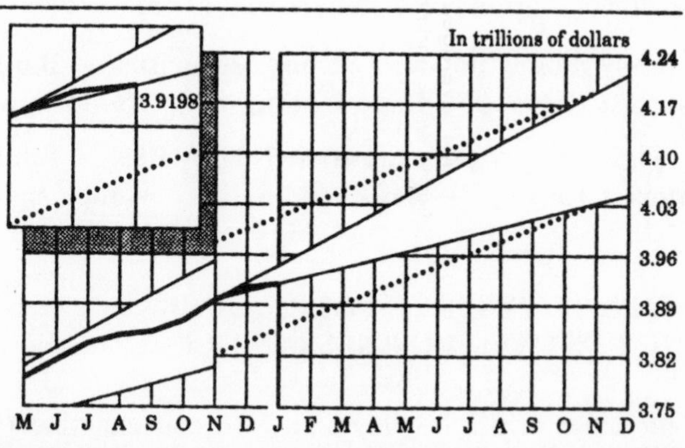

Source: *The Wall Street Journal*, February 17, 1989.

M3 is M2 plus certain other large accounts at financial institutions. All of these have become increasingly volatile in recent years due to the revolution in consumer banking. The public can now use interest-bearing savings accounts as if they were demand deposits, and the distinction between savings and loan associations and commercial banks is rapidly disappearing. As a result, it's difficult to maintain the dividing lines among the "M's."

Use Chart 4–1 on page 43 to observe the growth in the money supply (M1) since World War II. You can see the money supply's rapid increase in the 70s. It was quickest during the business cycle expansions of the late 60s, 1972–73, and 1977–78, and it slowed with the subsequent recessions. This is consistent with the earlier discussion of bank lending over the course of the cycle. Bank lending increased with cyclical expansions, generating a commensurate rise in demand deposits (money supply), and it decreased in the subsequent recessions, restricting money supply growth. As you will see shortly, some observers bitterly criticized the Fed for these oscillations in money supply's growth.

As you can imagine, the Fed's actions also had an impact on interest rates. The Fed traditionally pursued an "easy money" policy to hold interest rates down and promote relaxed credit conditions in order to boost demand during the recovery phase of the cycle. Eventually, when the expansion was fully under way, the peak of the cycle was not far off, and credit availability was constricting on its own, the Fed switched to a "tight money" policy, which reduced the supply of credit even further and drove up interest rates.

The Fed's actions with respect to *interest rates* may be included with the directed arrows and summarized as follows:

Easy money policy: Fed buys securities → Bank reserves ↑ → Interest Rates ↓ → Bank lending ↑ → Money supply ↑ → Demand ↑ .

Tight money policy: Fed sells securities → Bank reserves ↓ → Interest Rates ↑ → Bank lending ↓ → Money supply ↓ → Demand ↓ .

FEDERAL RESERVE POLICY AND THE POSTWAR BUSINESS CYCLE

With these principles in mind, you can examine the Fed's record of expansionary (free reserves positive and low interest rates) and contractionary (free reserves negative and high interest rates) monetary policies

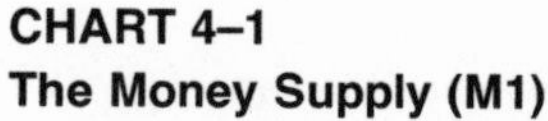

CHART 4–1
The Money Supply (M1)

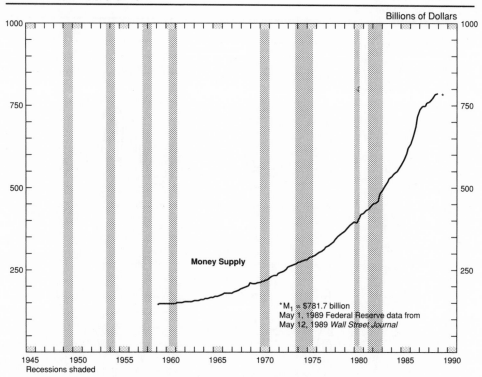

Source: U.S. Department of Commerce, *Business Statistics* and *Survey of Current Business*, various issues, and Federal Reserve Board.

since World War II. (See Charts 4–2, 4–3, and 4–4 on pages 44, 45, and 46.) Negative free reserves are called *net borrowed reserves*.

Remember that the Fed's objective had always been to counteract the natural swing of the cycle, stimulating demand at the trough with low interest rates, making it easy for the banks to lend, and curbing inflation at the peak with high interest, making it difficult for the banks to lend. The peaks and valleys of the cycle are reflected in the bank borrowings of reserves. Recessions are shaded in gray, and data quoted from *The Wall Street Journal* is indicated with an asterisk.

The economic events that began in the early 70s clearly illustrate these ideas. Do you recall the feverish inflationary boom of 1973, when demand for autos and housing was so insistent that the United Auto

CHART 4–2
Bank Borrowings of Reserves from Fed, Excess Reserves, and Free and Net Borrowed Reserves

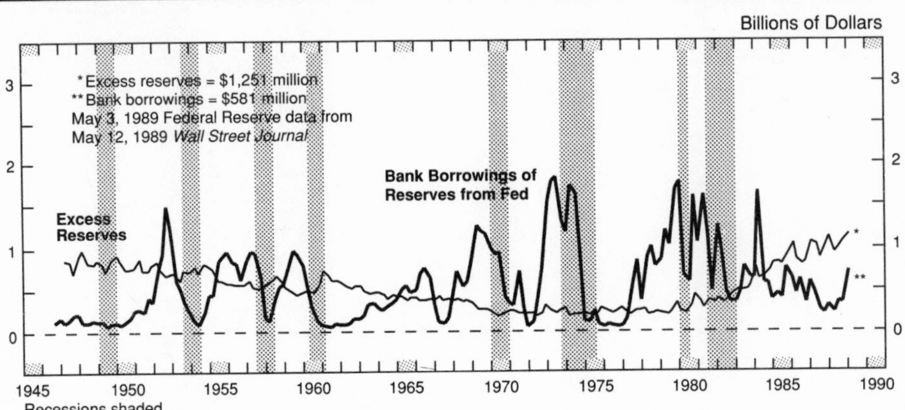

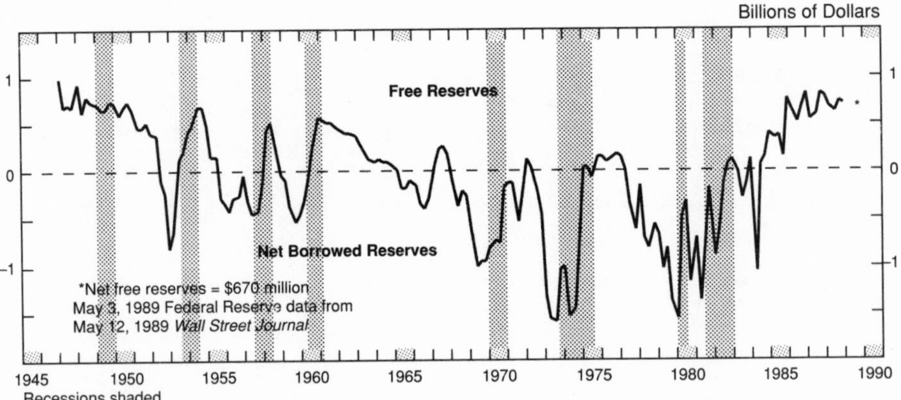

Source: *Federal Reserve Bulletin.*

Workers Union was complaining of compulsory overtime and there were shortages of lumber? The demand for borrowed funds was very strong; bank lending was heavy; and required reserves grew apace. Accordingly, the Fed instituted a tight money policy, compelling banks to borrow heavily from the Fed (see top of Chart 4–2 and Charts 4–3 and 4–4 for years 1973 to 74) in order to maintain adequate reserves and forcing interest rates upward. You can see the consequences in the (mirror image) bottom of Chart 4–2: net borrowed reserves reached $2 billion in 1974.

CHART 4–3
Short-Term Interest Rates: The Prime Rate, the Federal Funds Rate, and the Treasury Bill Rate

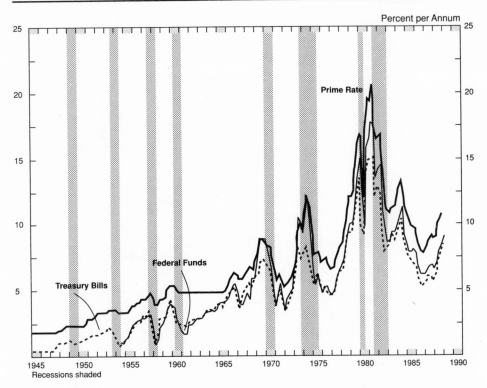

Source: U.S. Department of Commerce, *Business Conditions Digest* and *Handbook of Cyclical Indicators*, series 109, 114, and 119.

As the Fed applied the brakes and raised interest rates, the boom came to a halt.

More than 2 million people were thrown out of work when the full force of recession hit in late 1974 and early 1975. The Fed switched to an easy money policy to stimulate the economy. As a result, bank borrowings of reserves from the Fed dropped sharply, so that for most of the period from 1975 through 1977 the banks had free reserves (excess reserves exceeding borrowing from the Fed) and interest rates were low.

By 1977 economic expansion was in progress. In response, the Fed reversed itself again, adopting a tight money policy, and the banks'

CHART 4–4

Long-Term Interest Rates: Secondary Market Yields on FHA Mortages, Yield on New Issues of High-Grade Corporate Bonds, and Yield on Long-Term Treasury Bonds

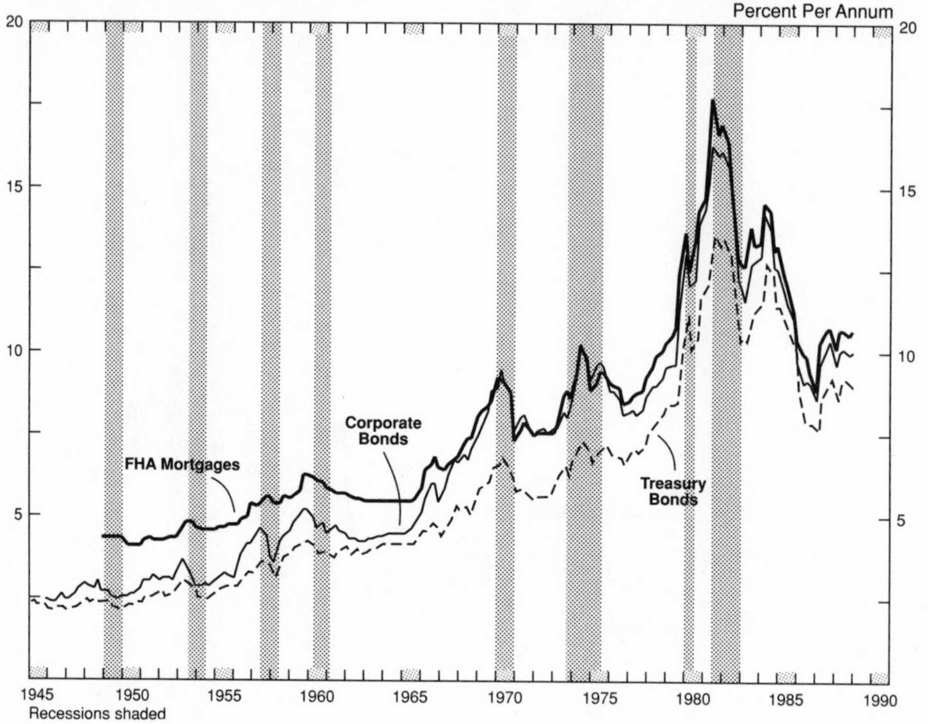

Source: U.S. Department of Commerce, *Business Conditions Digest* and *Handbook of Cyclical Indicators*, series 115, 116, and 118.

position swung back into net borrowed reserves. First, bank lending to business increased steadily, and with it the level of required reserves. Second, the Fed began to exercise a policy of restraint in order to prevent too rapid an expansion of the economy. As the Fed pursued a restrictive policy, bank reserves became less adequate, which forced the banks to borrow reserves from the Fed and drove interest rates up once again.

Net borrowed reserves grew from 1977 onward, averaging almost $2 billion monthly by early 1980; it was 1974 all over again, except that inflation was even more severe. While the Fed pursued its traditional tight money policy, President Carter instituted voluntary wage and price controls.

President Carter reshuffled his cabinet in 1979, appointing Fed Chairman G. William Miller to the position of Secretary of the Treasury, and asking Paul Volcker, President of the Federal Reserve Bank of New York, to replace Mr. Miller. Paul Volcker accepted the appointment and immediately rallied the members of the Board to maintain the fight against inflation, obtaining a commitment from them to pursue the struggle beyond the cycle's present phase.

By the week of March 12, 1980, net borrowed reserves exceeded $3 billion, and interest rates were at a postwar high. The cyclical peak had arrived, and a downturn was inevitable. When the recession struck, net borrowed reserves plummeted as the Fed's stance eased, until free reserves appeared briefly on July 9, 1980.

The downturn had been so sharp that the Board of Governors had set aside its inflation–fighting stance temporarily, providing banks with sufficient reserves and lowering interest rates to prevent undue hardship. Paul Volcker's battle plan, which will be described more fully in a moment, had been postponed by the exigencies of the moment.

In summary, then, the overall aim of the Fed since World War II had been to curb and ultimately reverse the extremes of the cycle: to dampen inflation and to stimulate a depressed economy.

THE MONETARIST CRITIQUE

However, another look at the charts of net borrowed and free reserves and interest rates on pages 44, 45 and 46 reveals that the Fed's policies contributed to the cycle's severity. Like an inexperienced driver with one foot on the gas and the other on the brake, attempting to achieve a steady speed but only able to surge forward after screeching to a halt, the Fed alternately stimulated and restrained the economy. Record levels of net borrowed reserves and interest rates at the cyclical peaks of the late 60s and the middle and late 70s provide evidence of the Fed's desperate attempts to bring inflationary expansion under control. Yet these sudden stops were partly the result of previous attempts, such as those made in 1972 and 1976, to stimulate rapid expansion by providing banks with plentiful free reserves and borrowers with low interest rates. As the economy accelerated and inflation began to go out of control, the Fed hit the brakes.

Meanwhile, the business cycle of the 70s rose higher and higher, with inflation becoming more severe with each boom and unemployment becoming more severe with each bust. The Fed's policies had failed.

In the 70s, a growing group of economists began to criticize the Fed's policy, accusing the Fed of contributing to the severity of the business cycle instead of reducing cyclical fluctuations. In their view, the Fed's contractionary policy, applied at the peak of the cycle, only added to the severity of the impending recession, while its expansionary policy, during the early stages of recovery, only set the stage for the subsequent inflations.

These economists, known as the *monetarist* school, believe that the rate of increase in the money supply is the single most important determinant of business cycle conditions. If the money supply grows rapidly, the economy expands; if the money supply does not grow rapidly, or even contracts, economic activity also contracts. The monetarists also believe that because other forces intrinsic to the economy will lead to normal cyclical activity and fluctuation in the rate of growth in the money supply, the Fed's best course of action is to attempt to keep the money supply's growth on an even keel, preferably at a low rate, reflecting the economy's long-range ability to increase output. According to the monetarists' view, anything beyond that rate will lead to inflation, and attempts to reduce the swings of the cycle will instead only exacerbate them.

It's as if the monetarists were saying, "If you want a comfortable temperature, set the thermostat and leave it. Don't fiddle with it by alternately raising and lowering it every time you feel a little chilly or a bit too warm, because this will just cause wide swings in temperature, which only heighten discomfort rather than reduce it."

The Road to Hell Is Paved with Good Intentions

- The effect of the Fed's policies in the 70s was the opposite of its intentions.
- The Fed's policies increased the amplitude of the cycle's swings.

DEBT AND THE CYCLE

Now, although the Fed was unable to control the cycle or inflation in the 70s, it was not solely responsible for the course of events. You can see tidal waves of consumer and business borrowing (referred to earlier) in Chart 4–5 on page 52, doubling every five years: $100 billion in 1969, $200 billion in 1974, and $400 billion in 1979. This borrowing drove demand forward during the expansionary phase of the cycle, creating the inflationary conditions that provoked the Fed's tight money policy and the subsequent crash into recession. The downturn would have occurred in the Fed's absence; the Fed's policies just made it more severe. Unfortunately, after recession took hold, the quick shift to an easy money policy fostered the next giant wave of borrowing, spending, and inflation, and this inevitably produced (once the wave's internal energy was spent and the Fed tightened up) a major collapse.

Be sure to notice as well that interest rates rose over time due to the ever-escalating demand for funds. You saw this in Chart 4–3 on page 45, when consumer and business borrowing doubled every five years in the 1970s. Since the demand for funds continuously exceeded the supply of funds at current prices, interest rates (the price of borrowed money) climbed in the long run.

Inflation's Engine: the 1970s

- Explosive borrowing → explosive spending → explosive inflation.

THE FED'S REVOLUTION

Although the Fed may not have been entirely responsible for the debacle of the late 70s, the monetarists' criticism of its "stop-go" policies had hit home. In October 1979, shortly after Paul Volcker began his term of office, the Fed announced an accommodation with the monetarist position. Henceforth, Mr. Volcker said, the Fed would set targets for monetary growth that it believed were consistent with an acceptable (low) rate of inflation.

In the summer of 1980, Mr. Volcker persuaded the Fed that it would have to renew immediately its commitment to halting inflation, a commitment that it had suspended briefly during the recession of the previous spring. In earlier recessions, the Fed had always permitted a substantial period (see Charts 4–2, 4–3, and 4–4 on pages 44, 45 and 46) during which the banks could maintain free reserves or benefit from a decline in net borrowed reserves. Following the 1980 slump, however, the Fed decided to prevent rapid recovery and expansion by maintaining a very tight money policy during the early phases of recovery. Mr. Volcker persuaded the Board of Governors that inflation had become so severe that the economy could not tolerate the usual easy–money-aided recovery. The rate of inflation had risen over each successive cycle and had barely declined during the 1980 recession. Rapid stimulation and recovery of demand would quickly bid prices up once again. This time, tight money was the only appropriate remedy, even if it stunted the recovery.

In consequence, the Fed's 1980, 1981, and 1982 tight money policies drove the prime rate to 21½ percent and first mortgage rates to 18 percent, unleashing the worst recession since World War II. For the first time, the Fed had stopped a recovery in its tracks and watched the economy slide off into back-to-back recessions. The Fed had made up its mind that restraining demand in order to control inflation was worth the price of economic contraction.

But the Fed relaxed its grip in the summer of 1982, first, because inflation had been wrung out of the economy and unemployment had reached an intolerable level; and second, because there were strong signs that Congress was losing patience with the Fed's restrictive policies. The Fed had accomplished its objective, so there was no need to antagonize further those who had the power to terminate the Fed's independent status. Yet, despite the eventual relaxation, you should realize that the Fed's 1981 policies marked a major shift in strategy that had significant and far-reaching consequences for our economy. *If severe inflation has been eliminated for the foreseeable future, it is no exaggeration to say that the Fed beat it back single-handedly.*

The Fed Beats Back Inflation: Early 80s

- **Restrictive policy → Bank reserves ↓ → Interest rates ↑ → Borrowing ↓ → Spending ↓ → Inflation ↓ .**

Events since 1982 have nonetheless required the Fed's constant vigilance. When the Fed permitted easier conditions in late 1982, the economy roared ahead, as you can see from Chart 4–5 on page 52. Business and consumer borrowing grew rapidly in 1983, reaching $500 billion (a record high at the time) by early 1984. Was this to be a repeat of earlier inflationary cycles, where demand, financed by easy credit, would be permitted to leap upward, bidding the rate of inflation to a new record? Would the bitter and wrenching experience of 1981–82, which had brought inflation under control, have been suffered in vain?

Immediate action was required if just such a painful reaction was to be avoided. So the Fed fine-tuned a minislowdown, restricting bank reserves sufficiently through open-market operations to compel banks to borrow reserves from the Fed. Chart 4–2 on page 44 shows net borrowed reserves growing quickly in spring 1984 (followed by rising interest rates in Charts 4–3 and 4–4, on pages 45, and 46), as banks were obliged to dip into the Fed in order to maintain their required reserves. That solved the problem: the growth in demand was stymied, and the economy cooled off.

The Fed's policies in the early 80s were a radical departure from those of the 60s and 70s. The 1981–82 recession and the minislowdown of 1984 signaled a new era, a major turning point in postwar economic history. The Fed had abandoned its old game plan: spurring the economy onward during slack conditions only to apply a chokehold when boom and inflation got out of hand, and then dealing with a repeat performance in the next cycle but on a new, ratcheted, higher plateau. General restraint over the course of the cycle was the new master strategy.

Paul Volcker knew that easy conditions and a pro-growth attitude had contributed to the disaster of the 70s. He also knew that he was on a tightrope, and that the cautious attitude described above could not lapse into complacency. But by the mid-80s, new appointees to the Board of Governors who favored an easy money policy had begun to undermine Mr. Volcker's go-slow approach. You will notice (pages 44, 45 and 46) that free reserves became positive once again and interest rates fell, signaling dramatically easier conditions.

Why did these new appointees to the Board of Governors pursue a policy which appeared to be such a reckless reversal of the Fed's successful approach? And why were they appointed? Because President Reagan and his advisers, who called themselves "supply-side" economists, wanted supply-siders on the Board. And supply-siders favor

CHART 4–5
Total Private Borrowing

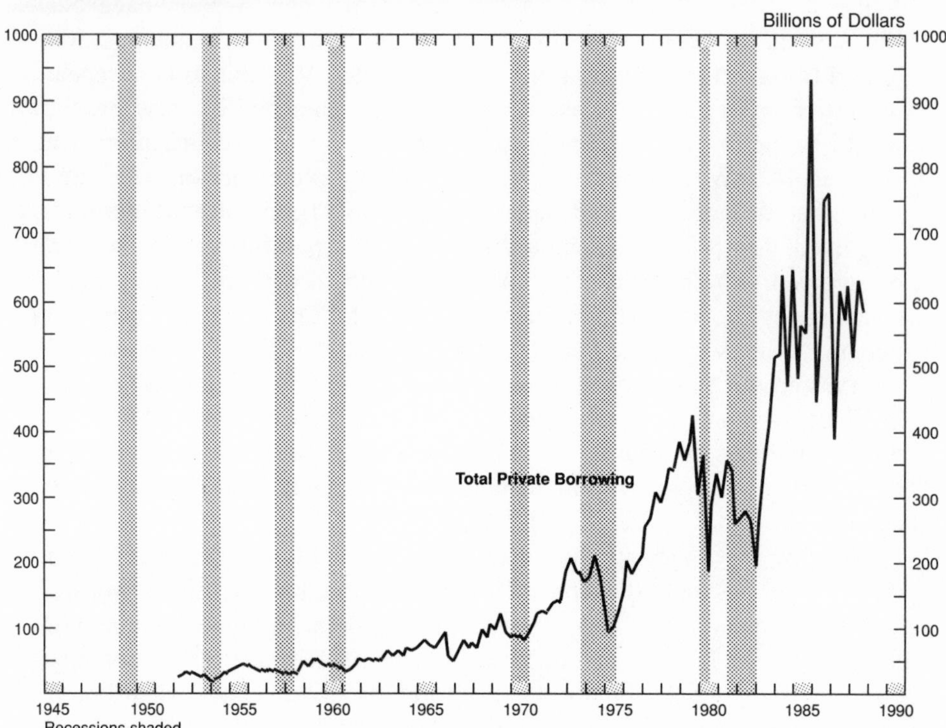

Source: U.S. Department of Commerce, *Business Conditions Digest* and *Handbook of Cyclical Indicators*, series 110.

easy credit and low interest rates. By 1987, at the end of Paul Volcker's second four-year term as the Board's chair, he was the only veteran of the tight money campaign of the early 80s. As the supply-siders pushed easier and easier conditions, and free reserves remained positive, Mr. Volcker informed President Reagan that he did not wish to be appointed to another term as chair—a term in which the Board's policy of restraint could be undone by a new majority that favored easy money, and a term in which easy money could once again unleash the forces of inflation upon the economy.

So President Reagan appointed Alan Greenspan to succeed Paul Volcker. Many observers were pessimistic and did not believe that Mr.

Greenspan would be any more successful in controlling the supply-siders. But these fears were unfounded because under Mr. Greenspan the Board continued to be responsible, refusing to permit a rekindling of the inflation of the 1970s. Although free reserves have remained positive, you can see in Chart 4–5 on page 52 that the trend of private borrowing has not increased in the late 1980s, fluctuating around $500 billion to $600 billion annually since 1984. Thus the Board has maintained sufficient restraint to prevent the headlong expansion of private borrowing, and with it the explosion in demand that precedes a new round of inflation.

(The big jump in borrowing in the last quarter of 1985 was due to state and local government borrowing in anticipation of tax law changes that never came about. State and local borrowing is included with these private borrowing figures but is usually quite small.)

The Fed Controls Inflation: Late 80s

- **Moderate restraint → Moderately high interest rates → Moderate borrowing → Moderate spending → Moderate inflation.**

Any student of the economy must be concerned with the composition of the Board of Governors and any tendency to appoint new members to the board who are predisposed to easier conditions. Mr. Greenspan (or any subsequent chair) needs a Board that understands the errors of the past and will maintain restraint. If this policy is frustrated, the economy will once again grow too quickly, and a new round of damaging inflation will inevitably result.

FINE-TUNING AND DEREGULATION

That carries the Fed's story to the present date and raises the issue of economic "fine-tuning." How did the Fed manage to bring about an effective minislowdown in 1984, when it seemed incapable of such sensitive fine-tuning in the 70s? And why should we be optimistic that the Fed can fine-tune in the future? The answer is partly that the Fed had a relatively small and easy task before it in 1984. But that's not all. In the 70s and earlier, interest rate regulations restricted the Fed to operating a switch that was either "off" or "on." But deregulation in the late 70s and early 80s permitted a metamorphosis; the switch became a valve, and the flow of credit could be more finely calibrated.

The history of this transition deserves some explanation. Until the end of the 70s, banks and savings and loan companies were not permitted to pay more than a statutory maximum of slightly over 5 percent on consumer savings accounts. During the rapid expansions of 1968–69 and 1973–74, Treasury bill interest rates climbed to well above 5 percent, providing an incentive for large depositors to withdraw their funds from these financial intermediaries and invest them in Treasury bills in order to earn the higher market return.

This process was called *disintermediation* (a coinage only an economist could love) because savers bypassed the financial intermediaries to invest their funds directly in Treasury bills; S&Ls suffered severely because of their dependence on consumer savings accounts.

The upshot was that as soon as boom conditions developed and the Fed began exercising a tight money policy, driving interest rates up, an ocean of deposits drained out of the banks and especially out of the S&Ls. The savings and loans literally ran out of money. They couldn't make mortgage loans, even if borrowers were willing to pay exorbitant rates of interest.

You can understand, then, why the Fed's tight money policies during these earlier periods did not cause credit to constrict gradually as interest rates climbed; instead, the availability of credit suddenly dried up for certain key areas of the economy (e.g., residential construction almost shut down).

Then, when the boom peaked and the economy slipped off into recession, the Fed switched to an easy money policy. As soon as Treasury bill interest rates fell below the statutory maximum that banks and S&Ls were able to pay, depositors sold their Treasury bills and redeposited the funds, propelling a tidal wave of deposits back into the financial intermediaries. As a result, S&Ls practically gave money away to finance home building.

These fund flows out of and then back into the banks and S&Ls exacerbated the business cycle. In 1969 and 1974, analysts didn't talk about tight conditions; they talked about the "credit crunch" and how it had stopped the economy in its tracks. Then, as deposits came flooding back into the system in 1970–72 and 1975–77, demand fueled by cheap credit took off like a rocket.

By 1980, deregulation had begun to remove interest rate ceilings from consumer savings accounts. The new, flexible-rate accounts were even called "T-bill accounts" because they were pegged to the Treasury bill rate and were designed to prevent consumers from defecting to the savings account's chief competitor, the Treasury bill, as interest rates rose.

When the Fed made its desperate stand against inflation in 1981–82, deregulation had been partially accomplished: the T-bill accounts prevented a run on the savings and loan companies' deposits. However, these accounts required a minimum deposit of $10,000, so many savers were attracted by recently created money market mutual funds that had much smaller minimum deposit requirements and invested in commercial paper and other short-term instruments, thus providing yields slightly higher than those of Treasury bills. Consequently, banks and S&Ls still faced a partial drain on their deposits.

But deregulation had begun to work. The S&Ls did not run out of money in 1981–82, although they were obliged to raise mortgage rates to prohibitive levels as T-bill account interest rates went up with the yield on Treasury bills. Residential construction was at last constrained by the *price* borrowers had to pay for funds rather than by the *availability* of those funds.

After the Fed eased up in mid-1982, and as the economy rebounded strongly in 1983, banks and S&Ls received permission to offer "money market accounts," which competed directly with the money market funds. Although deregulation was not 100 percent complete, depositors now had little reason to keep their funds elsewhere, and so a large volume of funds returned to the banks and S&Ls from the money market mutual funds.

Now that the Fed had a finely honed scalpel, it could maintain interest rates at sufficiently low levels to encourage demand but could easily nudge them upward whenever inflationary conditions threatened. And it would not have to fear the destructive flows of funds out of and into banks and S&Ls.

Early 1984 provided the first test; to confirm the results, review the interest rate record in Charts 4–3 and 4–4 on pages 45 and 46 once again. Interest rates collapsed in late 1982, but the Fed didn't wait long before it began to tighten up again. Demand had roared ahead throughout 1983; and, by the end of the year, there were many alarming signs that inflation was about to be rekindled. Although the Fed had allowed interest rates to drift upward throughout 1983, by early 1984 more decisive, positive action was required.

Recall from Chart 4–2 on page 44 that the Fed's tight money policy in the spring of 1984 had forced the banks to borrow reserves from the Fed. You can see in Charts 4–3 and 4–4 that interest rates quickly shot upward in response, inducing the minislowdown of 1984. There was talk of recession, but the Fed had carefully tuned the slowdown and did not let it develop into recession. Once the danger was past, the Fed permitted interest rates to drop sharply (remember the decline in net borrowed reserves), and demand began to grow once again.

Although deregulation became suspect in the late 80s because of the excesses and consequent failures associated with unregulated lending practices by the savings and loan industry, the deregulation of interest rates helped the Fed alter the course of America's economic history.

The Fed continues to fine-tune credit conditions carefully today, keeping interest rates low enough to permit demand's steady growth but high enough to prevent its reckless advance. Look once again at the record in Charts 4–2, 4–3, and 4–4 on pages 44, 45, and 46. Although the Fed announced a restrictive policy in late 1988 and conducted open–market operations designed to deprive the banks of reserves, you can see that the banks were not obliged to borrow from the Fed. Yet interest rates rose, seemingly breaking their connection with banks' borrowing from the Fed. In all earlier instances, the Fed's restrictive policies had obliged the banks to borrow. Now they didn't, yet interest rates rose.

The Fed could not explain this development—nor, at this point has anyone else satisfactorily done so. It was as if the Fed had reached its intended destination by traveling a route it did not recognize.

In any event, and to repeat an earlier admonition, the Fed cannot let interest rates fall to their 1971–72 or 1976–77 levels because demand and inflation will explode. That's why the Fed permitted cyclical forces to bid interest rates upward after mid-1986. *Credit restraint is the Fed's challenge for the 1990s.*

THE NEW CREDIT RATIONING

Recall once again the credit craziness of the late 70s, when rampant recourse to borrowed funds pumped up the inflationary balloon. Many observers suggested credit rationing as a solution. That was the only way, they argued, to provide funds for productive business investment in new technology and capital goods, while curtailing unproductive consumer expenditures financed by installment plans, credit cards, and so forth. Otherwise, industry had to compete with consumers in the capital markets for scarce funds. Consumers, the argument continued, were notoriously insensitive to interest rates; all they cared about was the size of the monthly payment, and this could be held down by stretching out the length of payment.

Consequently, as consumers borrowed more and more for second homes, boats, the latest electronic gadget, or whatever, business was forced to pay ever higher interest rates as it competed for scarce funds. This not only limited industry's ability to modernize and improve our nation's capital stock, it also added *business* debt-financed demand on top of *consumer* debt-financed demand. Too many dollars chased too few goods (i.e., supply could not keep pace with demand at current prices) and therefore prices inevitably rose too quickly. So the advocates of credit rationing recommended their solution.

They suggested that legal minimums be set for auto and home loan down payments and legal maximums established for the term of the loan. For instance, 50 percent minimum down payments with a 10–year maximum loan term for housing and 2 years for autos. There was no way Congress would enact, or the President sign, such legislation. The auto and construction industries would not permit it.

You don't hear many suggestions for credit rationing today. Deregulation and the Fed's determination to bring inflation under control have kept interest rates at the point where consumer expenditures are sensitive to the cost of borrowing. Now the Fed can fine-tune the level of residential building and auto manufacturing, permitting sufficient ease to maintain a healthy level of activity, yet sufficient restraint to prevent runaway expansion and inflation. The same is true for business borrowing.

The Fed has a unique opportunity in the 1990s to keep interest rates at just the right level to maintain an adequate, but not too rapid, growth in demand without inflation. But that means that interest rates in the 1990s cannot return to the low levels of yesteryear. *High interest rates (which is not to say chronically rising rates) are the new credit rationing, and they will be with us for many years.*

Investors should keep that in mind. And they should be aware that the Fed's anti-inflation posture will bode ill for gold and other tangibles but well for stocks and other paper investments. All of which Chapter 8 will discuss in greater detail.

Take another look at Chart 4–5 on page 52. Except for the stalagmite of borrowing in late 1985, private borrowing fluctuated around $500 or $600 billion annually for half a decade. Despite all the discussion of debt in the media, by the late 80s it appeared that debt had stopped growing at an increasing rate. This was more than just a signal of the effectiveness of the Fed's high interest rate policies. It lies at the root of the minimal inflation of the 80s and the stretching of the cycle into the 90s.

Growing oscillations in borrowing, as well as ever higher amounts of borrowing, caused the increasingly severe inflation and cyclical activity of the late 60s and the 70s. If an ever higher rate of borrowing is a thing of the past, and the Fed seems to have found a way of ensuring that, then the 1990s may be part of a new trend of noninflationary and noncyclical activity.

SUMMARY

To summarize this experience, think of the economy as a frisky horse where the rider (the Fed) must continually pull back on the reins (tight money) in order to prevent a runaway, breakneck gallop (inflation). The rider has learned a lesson the hard way, by periodically letting the reins go slack and permitting the horse to break into a gallop, only to be thrown from the horse as it reared when the rider desperately yanked on the reins (pre–1981/82 stop-go policy).

The stop-go policy is over; the Fed has a firm grip on the reins. Its present governors know it must restrain borrowing with high interest rates into the foreseeable future in order to dampen both the business cycle and inflation.

CHAPTER 5

FEDERAL FISCAL POLICY

THE CONVENTIONAL WISDOM

The federal deficit needs no introduction. It was an issue for debate in every presidential election campaign in the 1980s. The federal government borrowed $200 billion in some years of that decade and over a trillion dollars throughout the decade. This chapter will deal principally with one aspect of that issue: the deficit's impact on the rate of inflation.

Chapter 4 asserted that the Fed had "single-handedly" overcome inflation in the 1980s by the exercise of monetary policy. This runs contrary to the conventional wisdom that it is federal deficits that generate inflation. How do we reconcile the conventional wisdom that deficits generate inflation with the earlier analysis of the Fed's role? Let's look at the evidence.

The facts portrayed in Chart 5–1 on page 60 show that the deficit grew dramatically in 1975 and 1981–82, and shrank to an insignificant number in 1979. If the conventional wisdom made sense, inflation should have jumped in 1975 and 1981–82 with the increase in the federal deficit and subsided in 1979 when the budget balanced.

But that didn't happen. As a matter of fact, the opposite occurred. Inflation narrowed in 1975 and 1981–82 and peaked in 1979. In other words, not only do the facts not support the conventional wisdom, they seem to indicate the opposite. Inflation fell with the increases in the federal deficit (1975 and 1981–82) and rose when the deficit declined (1979). Does this mean that balanced budgets *generate* inflation while deficits *reduce* inflation? Now that *would* be a scoop.

To resolve the problem, you must put the federal deficit in perspective. Chart 4–5 on page 52, reproduced as Chart 5–2 on page 61, depicts private borrowing. Compare it with the federal deficit in Chart 5–1 on

CHART 5–1
Federal Government Expenditures, Receipts, and Deficit

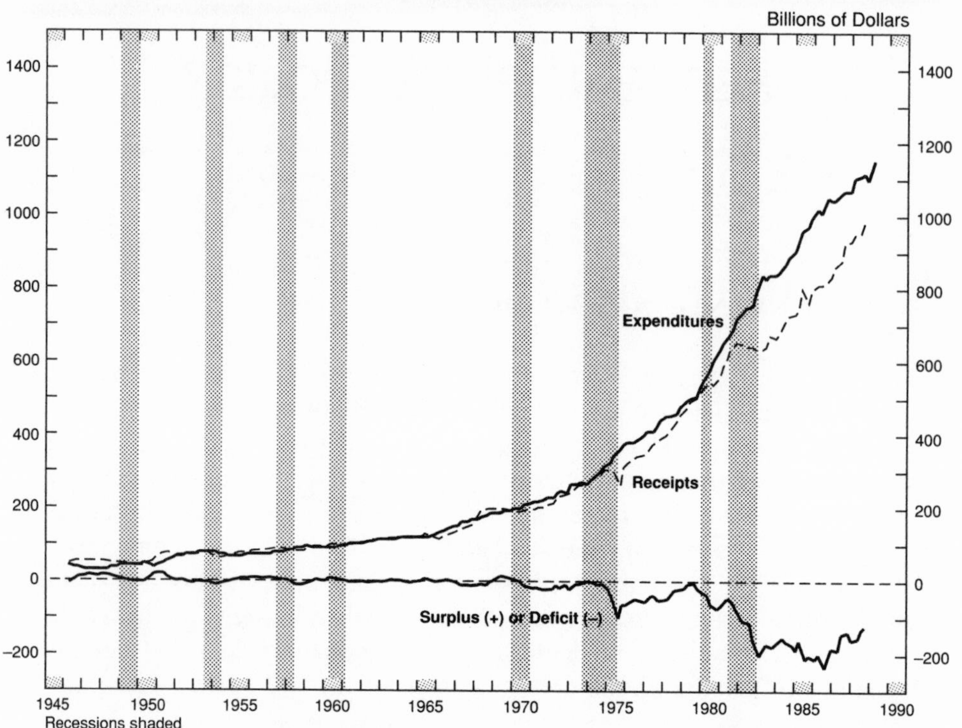

Source: U.S. Department of Commerce, *Business Conditions Digest* and *Handbook of Cyclical Indicators*, series 500, 501, and 502.

page 60. Recall that private borrowing includes mortgage borrowing to support residential construction, installment credit to finance the purchase of autos and other consumer durables, and business indebtedness to pay for expenditures on plant, equipment, and inventory. But it also includes (unfortunately, because it is confusing) borrowing by state and local governments, for reasons that need not be developed here.

Keep in mind that both charts portray annual borrowing, not outstanding debt. By the end of the 80s, outstanding federal debt was over $2 trillion and outstanding private debt was over $9 trillion. Each year's borrowing adds to the outstanding figure, so that an annual federal deficit of $100 billion would boost the outstanding federal figure from $2 trillion

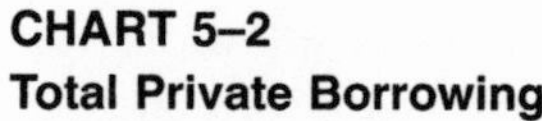

CHART 5–2
Total Private Borrowing

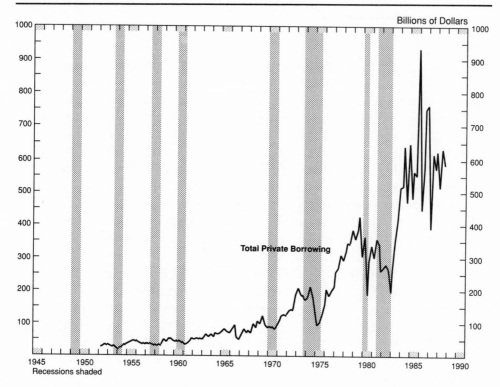

Source: U.S. Department of Commerce, *Business Conditions Digest* and *Handbook of Cyclical Indicators*, series 110.

to $2.1 trillion and annual private borrowing of $500 billion might lift the private total to $9.5 trillion. (Don't confuse either of these with the balance of trade deficit, to be examined in Chapter 16.)

Now compare private borrowing with the federal deficit in 1975, and note that both were approximately $100 billion. Then they move in opposite directions: the federal deficit shrinks to nothing in 1979 and private borrowing balloons to $400 billion. So total borrowing grew from $200 billion in 1975 ($100 billion of private plus $100 billion of federal) to $400 billion in 1979 (all private).

This explains the burst of inflation in the late 70s. Total borrowing doubled, financing the huge increase in demand (greater than the economy's increase in production at current prices) that drove up inflation. Thus, the growth in private borrowing in the late 70s overwhelmed the decline in federal borrowing, generating rapid price increases.

On the other hand, if you continue to look at the record in Charts 5–1 and 5–2 on pages 60 and 61, you'll notice that private borrowing slumped in 1981 and 1982, dropping to almost $200 billion annually from its $400 billion peak in 1979. The federal deficit, however, popped back up from next to nothing in 1979 to about $200 billion in 1982. Once again, when you add private and federal borrowing, you see an offset: the total is $400 billion in both years ($400 billion private in 1979 with no federal deficit and $200 billion for each in 1982). When total borrowing stopped growing from 1979 through 1982, the rate of inflation subsided as demand came into line with supply.

This illustrates the fallacy in the conventional wisdom and explains why inflation seemed to behave so perversely when compared to the federal deficit. You can't ignore private borrowing when analyzing inflation. As a matter of fact, the explosion of private borrowing from 1970 to 1973 ($100 billion to $200 billion) and from 1975 to 1979 ($100 billion to $400 billion) explains that decade's two great rounds of inflation. Inflation did not grow in the 1980s because private borrowing fluctuated in a narrow range (except for 1985) and demonstrated no upward trend after 1984. By the end of the decade, private borrowing was still fluctuating around $600 billion annually, the level it had reached more than five years earlier.

The burst of borrowing in late 1985 needs an explanation. It was due to state and local governments' trying to beat an anticipated change in tax laws that never came to pass. Some Congressmen had suggested that interest paid on state and local bonds no longer be tax–exempt. Enactment of this legislation would have increased state and local interest payments because their bonds had paid below–market rates for years due to the tax–exempt benefit to investors (i.e., bond holders were willing to receive below market yields, provided they were tax–exempt). State and local governments moved up their borrowing in anticipation of the 1986 change that never came to pass.

But the main point to bear in mind is that the large federal deficits of the 1980s have not generated inflation, despite the attention paid them. They shrank from the $200 billion range in the middle of the decade to about $100 billion at the end, and should shrink further in the early 1990s. Private borrowing continued to overshadow federal borrowing at the end of the 1980s by a ratio of 4:1 ($600 billion : $150 billion). Any future change in the federal deficit is likely to be small when compared to private borrowing.

Investor's Tip

- Forget about the federal deficit; it won't influence our rate of inflation for the foreseeable future and therefore *won't* influence the value of your investments.

ALONG CAME KEYNES

Nonetheless, you ought to consider the federal government's deficits in some detail for no other reason than that they drew so much attention in the 1980s. In order to sort out the continuing debate surrounding the federal government's taxing and spending programs and their impact on the economy, you must go back to the 19th and early 20th centuries. Economics then was governed by an axiom known as *Say's Law*: "Supply creates its own demand." This meant that economic recession and depression and their accompanying unemployment were temporary and self-correcting phenomena. After all, capitalists produce goods for market, and workers offer their labor for hire *so that they in turn can demand goods in the marketplace*. If the goods cannot be sold or the labor is not hired, then a lower price or wage will be asked, until price and wage cutting permit all of the goods or labor to be sold. No goods will remain chronically unsold and no labor will remain chronically unemployed as long as prices and wages remain flexible.

Using this line of reasoning, 19th-century economists argued that recession and its concomitant unemployment were transitory phenomena and should generate neither a great deal of concern nor any corrective policy prescription by the government. Society and government ought to let well enough alone (i.e., follow the policy of laissez-faire) and let market forces prevail. The operation of the market would eventually restore full employment.

With Say's Law as their guide, no wonder economists could not understand the Great Depression, which began in 1929 and hit bottom in 1933. Nor could they understand why the economy's performance remained anemic for so long after 1933. After all, they reasoned, the economy should naturally return to conditions of full production and full employment as business cut prices in order to sell its products and workers took wage cuts in order to find employment. If the economy continued in a slump, that was the fault, not of the economists and their theories, but of employers and employees who refused to cut prices and wages.

The economists' logic did not help the businesses that were failing or the workers who were out of jobs. Prices and wages had fallen, yet conditions remained dismal; something was dreadfully wrong, and somebody had to do something about it.

In America, President Roosevelt was elected. He responded with massive public-works programs, which, by the way, were funded by federal deficits. The economic community was horrified and they insisted that the federal government's efforts would merely deny resources to the private sector, and thus provide no net benefit. F.D.R. ignored economic theory. He was a practical man with a practical solution: if people were out of work, then the government would be the employer of last resort and put them to work building roads, parks, bridges, dams, and other public projects.

In 1936 an Englishman named John Maynard Keynes (rhymes with *brains*) gave intellectual credentials to F.D.R.'s practical policies by proposing that the problem was the economists' theories, not the economy. Keynes tackled Say's Law (and the economics establishment) at the knees by declaring that demand *could* be chronically insufficient and the economy *could* be chronically plagued with substantial excess capacity and unemployment. Keynes scolded his fellow economists for arguing that their theories were right and that the problem lay with the practical world of business and work that was not living up to theoretical expectations. Science—even "the dismal science" of economics—dictates that a theory that does not conform to the facts must be discarded.

Keynes declared that it was ridiculous to expect price and wage cuts to solve the economy's problem. A totally new approach had to be devised. He believed the only answer was to boost demand by the use of some exogenous (outside) force. Workers could not be expected to buy more under conditions of actual and threatened unemployment nor business to spend more on plant and equipment when excess capacity and weak profits were the rule. But if consumers and business would not spend, how could the economy pull out of its slump? Through government spending, Keynes argued, even if the government had to borrow funds. Once government began to spend on public works, the people who were employed on these projects would spend their earnings on privately produced goods and services. In a multiplier effect, the total level of demand would be lifted and full employment restored. When the pump-priming operation was over and the private economy was back on its feet, the government could gradually withdraw from the economic scene. Pump-priming by government intervention became known as *Keynesian* economics.

Keynesian (rhymes with "brainsian") theory came to dominate economics, rendering Say's Law archaic. The next generation of economists pushed Keynesian theory a bit further, reasoning that a tax cut could be as effective in priming the pump as an increase in government expenditures. Reducing taxes would increase consumers' disposable income and their consumption expenditures. The new generation believed this would be as effective as an increase in government expenditures for restoring demand to a level sufficient to ensure full employment.

Economists now argued that it didn't matter how the pump was primed, whether through expenditure increases or tax cuts. Putting more into the expenditure stream than was removed from the income stream (in the form of taxes) would always create a net boost in total demand. If government expenditures increased while tax revenues remained the same, the increase in public expenditures would boost demand. If government expenditures remained the same while taxes were cut, the increase in private consumption expenditures would boost demand. In either case, or in both together, a net addition to total demand was made possible by the increased government deficit and the borrowing needed to fund that deficit.

The federal government borrows from the public by selling bonds. Now, it might seem that borrowing from the public would have the same effect as taxing the public since it removes funds from the private sector and would thus neutralize the spending increase. After all, if the public refrains from spending to buy government bonds, isn't the public's expenditure reduced? The answer is yes, if the bonds are purchased by private citizens; however, this is generally not the case. The largest share of bonds is sold to the banking system, which purchases them by creating a demand deposit (checking account) for the government. This is known as "monetizing" the debt, as described in Chapter 4. The fact that the government borrows from the banks permits an increase in government spending without a decrease in private spending.

The federal government's attempts to influence economic activity through its power to tax and spend is known as *fiscal policy*. Although this chapter discusses fiscal policy in the context of the need to stimulate demand in order to deal with recession, it should be clear that fiscal policy could also be employed to deal with inflation. For example, increasing taxes or reducing government expenditures, which would create a surplus, drains spending from the economy, reducing total demand and, consequently, cooling inflation.

As the discussion of fiscal policy continues, remember that it is not the same thing as *monetary policy*, which was discussed in Chapter 4. Monetary policy refers to the actions of the Federal Reserve System; *fiscal policy* refers to the actions of the federal government. Monetary policy works through its influence on the banking system, the money supply, bank lending, and interest rates, whereas fiscal policy works through its direct impact on aggregate demand.

Also keep in mind that fiscal policy is the province solely of the federal government, not of state or local government. Only the federal government has the flexibility to run the necessary budget deficits or surpluses large enough to influence total demand. Most state and local governments are limited, either de facto or de jure, to operating with a balanced budget.

THE KENNEDY TAX CUT

Keynesian economics, with its emphasis on fiscal policy, had won the hearts and minds of academic economists by the early 1960s. Not everyone, however, was convinced. When President Kennedy assumed office in 1961 and proposed a tax cut to stimulate the level of economic activity, Republicans and conservative Democrats in Congress attacked it as fiscally irresponsible. They demanded a balanced budget and argued that tax cuts would generate unacceptable deficits. President Kennedy's Keynesian reply was that the deficits would disappear as soon as the tax cut stimulated the level of demand, output, and income, providing even greater tax revenues despite the decline in the tax rate. These arguments did not immediately persuade Congress, and the tax cut did not pass until the spring of 1964, following President Kennedy's assassination.

The nation enjoyed full employment and a balanced budget in 1965, and Keynesian fiscal policy became an accepted method of "fine-tuning" the economy. Indeed, this technique became so legitimate that it was employed by the next two Republican presidents. President Nixon cut taxes to deal with the 1970 recession, and President Ford cut taxes to deal with the 1974–75 recession. In each case, the Federal Reserve also pursued an easy money policy in order to stimulate demand. Conservatives joined liberals and Republicans agreed with Democrats that tax cuts were necessary to get the economy moving.

By the late 1970s, however, severe inflation prompted a new and growing group of economists to conclude that attempts to stimulate demand with easy money and easy fiscal policies had gone awry. Escalating inflation, which reduced real income, had drawn more and more people into the labor force. The new entrants to the labor force, usually the secondary or tertiary wage earners in the family, had fewer skills and thus were more difficult to employ. Unemployment grew as inflation escalated. The economy had the worst of both worlds. Thus, this new group of economists and politicians argued that what was known as "full-employment policy," actually the Keynesian prescription of stimulating demand through easy monetary and easy fiscal policies, had been a failure.

Moreover, they continued, increased inflation had discouraged savings and investment. Rising prices penalized savers for their thrift, because the value of real savings fell. This encouraged personal indebtedness rather than saving, and inasmuch as saving is the ultimate source of all funds for investment, the level of investment was bound to shrink over time. These critics charged that the lack of savings and the resulting lack of investment were reflected by the low levels of business investment in new machinery and technology and by the resulting decline in productivity.

Finally, they attacked the progressive income tax, which propelled people into higher tax brackets despite a drop in real income. Higher marginal tax rates, they said, removed the incentive to work more and to work harder. Why should businesses invest in new ideas, new products, and more efficient ways of doing things if higher taxes confiscated the profits? Why should workers put in more hours on the job if higher taxes reduced the additional pay to a meaningless figure?

SUPPLY-SIDE ECONOMICS

The views of these economists and politicians came to be called *supply-side* economics, which they developed in contrast to *demand-side*, or Keynesian, economics. The supply-siders argued that it was more important to support policies that bolstered the economy's ability to supply or produce more goods than to enhance demand. Therefore, the supply-side economists advocated drastic federal income tax reductions over a three-year period, with deficits to be avoided by a parallel reduction in federal spending. Federal expenditure programs, in their view, tended to over-regulate private activity and to waste tax dollars in a variety of boondoggles and unnecessary transfer payments.

Supply-side theory claimed that a massive, across-the-board tax cut would accomplish two major objectives. First, it would provide incentives for increased work, thus boosting output. A greater supply, or output, of goods and services would dampen inflation. Second, increased disposable income would lead to increased savings, providing a pool of funds to finance investment. Once again, the supply of goods and services would be stimulated, and increased output would reduce inflation.

Supply-side economics was a total contradiction of Keynesian fiscal policy, which had prevailed for almost half a century. It was widely and correctly viewed as a device to restrict and contract the federal government and so was admired and promoted by conservatives and viewed with suspicion by liberals. The supply-siders began to make their voices heard during President Carter's administration, placing him in a potential quandary. He had pledged to balance the federal budget by the end of his first term in office. Rapid economic expansion and inflation had pushed revenues upward more rapidly than expenditures; consequently, his goal was in sight by late 1979. The tax cut proposed by the supply-siders would have postponed that goal, unless, of course, it was accompanied by large reductions in federal expenditures, which, as a Democrat, President Carter could not endorse.

The 1980 recession created an even sharper dilemma for him. He might have advocated a tax cut (the traditional Keynesian prescription for recession), but this would have played into the hands of the supply-siders, who would have demanded compensating spending cuts. By now the supply-siders had a presidential candidate, Ronald Reagan, as their principal spokesman. The situation was further complicated for President Carter by the fact that the supply-side tax cut favored upper-income groups, rather than the lower-income groups traditionally targeted for tax cuts by the Democrats. Thus, political circumstances precluded President Carter from trying to deal with the 1980 recession by means of tax reductions.

After his inauguration in 1981, as the economy slid into the 1981–82 recession, President Reagan pushed for and obtained the supply-side tax cuts. What a strange historical reversal: 20 years after President Kennedy battled Republicans and conservatives for his tax cut, President Reagan now had to battle Democrats and liberals for his. Whereas Democrats had once advocated tax cuts to stimulate the economy and the Republicans had opposed those cuts, it was now the Republicans who were advocating tax cuts over the opposition of the Democrats. The parties had done a complete about-face.

The shift of the mantle of fiscal conservatism from Republicans to Democrats is one of the most important political changes since World War II. President Reagan's supply-side tax cut of 1981–83 accompanied the recession of 1981–82. It generated a chaotic reduction in federal revenue, because a smaller proportion of a declining level of income was collected in taxes. Meanwhile, total expenditures continued to grow despite reductions in the budget left by President Carter. Democrats criticized the resulting deficit and demanded that the tax cuts be rescinded. Republicans insisted that there be no tax increase, despite the deficits.

The debate occurred in the midst of recession and recovery. The Republicans contended that any tax increase would jeopardize the supply-side expansion. The Democrats countered that continued deficits and the accompanying government borrowing drove up interest rates and jeopardized the expansion. Beneath the economic details of the debate, both sides had ideological positions to defend. The Democrats realized that continued deficits put relentless pressures on domestic expenditures. Only a tax increase could generate the revenue that made these expenditure programs affordable. The Republicans too were aware that the only way to deliver a knockout punch to the domestic programs, while increasing military expenditures, was to hold taxes down and let the clamor to end the deficits force legislators to curtail domestic spending. So the real battle was over domestic programs, not taxes, the deficit, or even supply-side economics. Indeed, there are some political analysts who believe that the whole supply-side argument was only a cynical "Trojan Horse" whose sole purpose was to decimate federal assistance programs and repeal the New Deal.

In the end, no compromise of these issues was attained. The Democrats held on to the social programs, the Republicans held on to the military programs, and President Reagan made it clear that he would veto any tax increase. The deficit remained. Finally, in a desperate attempt to at least seem to be doing something about the problem, Congress passed the Gramm-Rudman Balanced Budget Act in late 1985, mandating gradual elimination of deficits over a five-year period. The political fight was pushed into the future. The Democrats hoped that military expenditures would be cut and taxes raised, the Republicans and the president hoped that domestic expenditures would be cut, and they all hoped that this procrustean bed would dismember someone else.

CROWDING OUT

Meanwhile, the argument over supply-side economics (never the real issue) was lost in the shuffle as the political wrangling over the impact of the deficit continued. The Democrats insisted that the increased federal borrowing due to the tax cut would crowd out private borrowing (and hence capital expenditures). Ironically, Republicans had criticized President Carter's (shrinking) deficits in the late 1970s on precisely the same grounds. Yet you have seen that private borrowing exploded in those years. The inconsistencies in the political debate provide further evidence that the real issues were not (and are not) economic.

Indeed, any fear about "crowding out" was misplaced, for it was the actions of the Federal Reserve that largely determined whether private borrowing at reasonable rates was possible. Whenever the Fed pursues a tight money policy, private borrowers must compete with the government for funds; whenever the Fed pursues a sufficiently easy policy, there is room for both private and public borrowing. The point is that difficulty or ease of credit conditions is determined largely by the Fed and not by any crowding out dynamic.

Keep in mind that the Fed's objective throughout the 80s was to restrain the expansion rather than stimulate it, so perhaps a little crowding out, if it helped prevent credit conditions from becoming too easy, was not so unhealthy. Tight money restricted consumer borrowing more than business borrowing, allocating funds (and resources) away from consumption expenditures toward investment expenditures in new plant and equipment. And as the economy and tax revenues grew in the late

80s, private borrowing held its own while federal borrowing shrank (see Chart 5–1 on page 60 and Chart 5–2 on page 61).

Forget about Crowding Out

- The Fed's influence on interest rates is far more important than the federal government's borrowing.

In order to relate this discussion of fiscal policy to the business cycle, you need to know how *not* to relate it. Please realize that the huge federal deficits were responsible for neither the 1981–82 recession nor the subsequent recovery and expansion. The Federal Reserve's tight money policy generated the recession; the recession choked off inflation; and the stifling of inflation, along with the release of the Fed's grip, is what produced recovery and expansion in the mid and late 80s.

Thus, President Reagan's administration should be neither blamed for the recession nor lauded for the recovery and expansion or inflation's demise. Those phenomena were created by monetary policy, not fiscal policy.

BALANCING THE BUDGET

You can see from Chart 5–1 on page 60 that the federal deficit has grown enormously with each recession—for two chief reasons. First, recession reduced receipts because of lower personal income tax revenues, unemployment (the unemployed paid no income tax), and lower profits tax revenues. Second, tax cuts accompanied the recessions of 1970, 1974–75, and 1981–82. In addition, note that federal expenditures continued to grow during each recession despite revenue's setback, generating the budget gap. Since the deficit grew with each successive recession, closing this deficit gap became more difficult and took longer every time.

In order for President Bush to close the continuing deficit gap without a tax increase in the early 90s, receipts must grow more rapidly than expenditures. It took four years after the 1970 recession and five years after the 1974–75 recession to balance the federal budget. How long will it take this time? That's hard to say. The gap began to shrink in the late 80s and it will continue to shrink as long as a growing economy generates additional tax revenues. A recession, if and when one occurs, will bring about renewed deficits by reducing tax revenues. If future deficits are to be avoided, a substantial budgetary surplus must be built to provide a cushion for the inevitable decline in revenue that accompanies recession.

But wait a minute. Perhaps we should stop worrying about the deficit altogether since its impact on the business cycle and on crowding out is so negligible. Not quite. There are still two good reasons for concern. First, as the federal government's debt mounts, interest payments become an increasing share of federal expenditures. There are historical examples of nations borrowing to the point that debt service composed the majority of their budget, compelling increased borrowing to meet the interest payments on old debt and thereby severely restricting the nation's ability to cope with any social or military issue. Second, if the financial markets begin to question whether the federal government can meet its debts, it could become increasingly difficult for the government to obtain credit, subjecting its day-to-day operations to cash-flow irregularities.

Therefore, the soundness of both government finance and the economy would be strengthened by deficit reduction and a balanced budget. But, to repeat, that does not mean that continued federal deficits should be your primary concern with respect to inflation's outlook. Your attention should focus on the private sector and whether or not the Fed can continue to rein in private borrowing and spending.

CHAPTER 6

THE POSTWAR BUSINESS CYCLE: THE ROLE OF CONSUMER DEMAND

CONSUMER DEMAND AND INFLATION

Chapter 4 developed three concepts:

1. The Fed brought inflation under control in the 1980s by restraining borrowing and thus demand.
2. The Fed "fine-tuned" gradual expansion in the 1980s, abandoning the "stop-go" policies of the 1970s and thereby postponing recession.
3. High interest rates will be the credit-rationing mechanism of the 1990s, restraining demand and inflation.

This chapter will build on these concepts by analyzing the role of the consumer in the post–World War II business cycle, showing how consumer demand led the business cycle by generating ever higher waves of inflation until that inflation broke on the rocks of the Fed's 1981–82 tight money policy. It will also illustrate how the Fed's fine-tuning smoothed out consumer demand, thereby not only limiting inflation but also postponing the next recession.

To begin the analysis of inflation, start with a definition and consider that definition in its historical context. *Inflation* is an increase in prices due to excessive spending financed by borrowing from banks. "Too many dollars chasing too few goods" is a standard way of putting it. Economists are more formal: "Inflation occurs when demand exceeds supply at current prices, and prices are bid up."

Both explanations conjure up the image of a gigantic auction at which customers bid for both goods and services. The more money the customers have to spend, the higher prices go. Where do they get the money? From banks that create it.

Now look at inflation's record in Chart 6–1.

Although we wait and hope for it to subside, we tend to assume that inflation, like death and taxes, is inevitable. In fact, however, chronic inflation is a recent problem. Before the late 1940s, severe inflation was a temporary phenomenon, usually associated with war. When the federal government's wartime expenditures overshot tax revenues and the government covered the difference by selling bonds to the banking system or by printing paper money (which the federal government has not done recently), prices increased swiftly. That's how the conventional wisdom arose that government deficits cause inflation.

CHART 6–1
Wholesale Prices

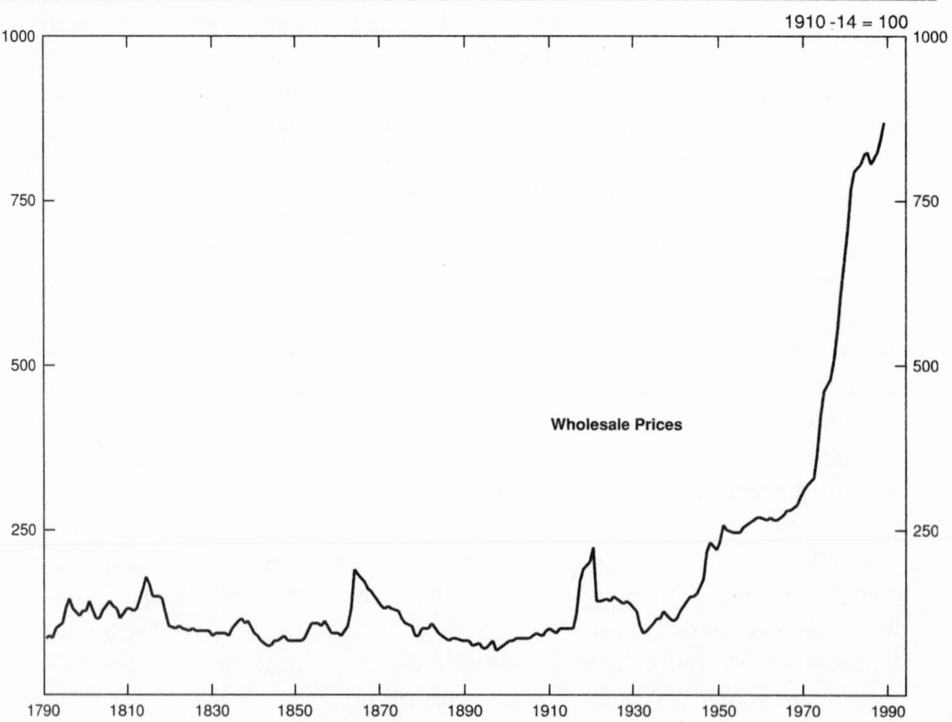

Source: U.S. Bureau of the Census, *Historical Statistics of the U.S.* (Washington, D.C., 1975), series E52 and 23; U.S. Department of Commerce, *Business Conditions Digest* and *Handbook of Cyclical Indicators*, series 334.

From 1789 until after World War II, except for war-related inflations, prices in America always fell more often than they rose. As a matter of fact, prices were actually lower in 1914, on the eve of World War I, than they were in 1815, at the end of the Napoleonic Wars and the War of 1812!

Prices dropped during the 19th century because supply grew more rapidly than demand. Business mobilized the technological advances of the Industrial Revolution to produce standard items of consumption in large quantities at considerably lower cost. Occasionally, prices rose during the upswing of the business cycle, because investment expenditures were financed by bank borrowing or because there were temporary shortages of agricultural commodities. But these increases were more than offset in recession years when prices tumbled as huge additions to supply were brought to market.

The institutions that, in our day, enable and encourage headlong private borrowing and spending had not yet evolved. A hundred years ago it wasn't easy to obtain a home mortgage. Typically, the purchase of a new home required a 50–percent down payment with interest-only mortgage payments on a seven-year loan, followed by a balloon payment of the entire principal at the end. The stretch-out of automobile financing, reducing the size of the monthly payment to put a new car within a broader reach, is a post–World War II development. Fifty years ago, most of the major consumer durables that we now buy on credit were available exclusively to a small portion of the population on a cash-only basis, if they existed at all.

It was not until after World War II that vast amounts of consumer borrowing came into common use, financing residential construction, autos, and other goods. At the same time, new institutions evolved to facilitate business borrowing.

Only the Civil War and World Wars I and II had provided great inflationary experiences; even the period between World War I and World War II was a time of deflation (falling prices). War brought inflation, and peace brought deflation, because government borrowed and spent more massively in wartime than business borrowed and spent in peacetime. The difference was more a matter of degree than a matter of kind; peacetime investment expenditures and borrowing by farmers, railroads, and manufacturers, though substantial, were usually not large enough to boost the growth in demand beyond the increase in supply. Thus prices fell in most years because supply exceeded demand at current prices.

To summarize, prices fell unless there was a rapid increase in demand (spending) financed by bank borrowing or the printing press (greenbacks during the Civil War). Only when outside financing provided a boost did demand take on a life of its own and grow more rapidly than supply. It made little difference whether it was government spending for war or business spending for investment, as long as banks printed bank notes or created demand deposits, or the government printed paper money. Once demand grew more rapidly than supply, and too many dollars chased too few goods, prices rose.

History does not note or dwell upon the pre–World War II examples of private borrowing and spending that generated inflation because there were so few of them; they were insignificant when compared to wartime episodes.

But what was responsible for the post–World War II inflationary experience? Why have prices risen so steadily? The answer lies in consumer spending. This period marked the first time that consumers borrowed continually and prodigiously to finance purchases of luxury goods. The level of activity grew decade after decade, and with each cycle, so that in the 1970s tidal waves of credit roared through the system, rapidly swelling demand to record levels.

It started in the 1920s, a kind of brief test run for the full-scale activity that followed World War II. At first, following World War I, consumer purchases financed by credit were limited to homes and automobiles, but by modern times credit-backed demand expanded to include kitchen and laundry appliances, furniture and furnishings, and electronic equipment such as television sets, VCRs, stereos, and personal computers. All were financed by credit, and the terms became more liberal over time, even as interest rates rose. The American consumer was encouraged—indeed, came to feel obligated—to mortgage the future so that present expenditures could exceed present income, with borrowing covering the difference.

The economy's health thus developed a dependence on the chronic fix of greater consumer expenditures, financed by borrowing. These circumstances were entirely different from the circumstances of the 19th century; during that era, consumers were largely confined to standard items of consumption purchased with current income (not debt), and economic growth was propelled by increased supply, which pushed prices downward. Now the situation became quite different. Full production and employment became the hostages of ever larger waves of consumer expenditure on discretionary purchases financed by borrowing.

CONSUMER DEMAND AND THE BUSINESS CYCLE

Unfortunately, these surges in consumer demand always led to their own demise, because expansion brought inflation, which depleted real incomes and generated the downturn of the cycle. Only then did inflation abate, real income recover, and expansion begin anew. Thus every boom inevitably went bust and each recession was also self-correcting and carried with it the seeds of economic recovery.

But *why* does the business cycle always rebound from recession, never falling into permanent depression, and why can't there be continuous expansion?

Well, to begin with, every expansion ends inevitably in recession because every expansion is fueled by credit. Consumers and businesses can borrow to buy new homes, cars, factories, and machinery. The more they borrow and spend, the faster demand grows, and production is pushed into high gear in order to keep pace with demand. But sooner or later, the upward spiral of borrowing and spending comes to an end. The strain on productive facilities forces costs higher, pushing prices up, too. Inflation depresses consumer sentiment and consumers respond by curtailing their expenditures. Consumers also find that their incomes cannot support the burden of additional debt repayment. Businesses, having accomplished their targeted growth in plant and equipment, see that demand will not greatly increase in the near future and cut back or cease their expenditures in this area. Once business and consumer borrowing and spending start to decline, the slump begins and production and income fall. Inflation subsides with the drop in demand.

The recession hits bottom just before consumers recover their confidence, due to inflation's decline, and begin spending again. Components of demand that were financed by credit stop shrinking. Remember that these components are a limited, though highly volatile, share of total demand. (The demand for many items that are not financed by credit, such as food and medical care, will hardly decline at all during recession.) As consumers and businesses cease borrowing and turn their attention to liquidating their expansion-generated debts, the price of credit, namely interest rates, falls until finally the debt burden and interest rates are low enough that consumers can borrow and spend again. At this juncture, auto production, home construction, and business investment in new plant and equipment stop falling, the slide ends, and economic recovery is in sight.

Generally speaking, expansion ceases when consumers are no longer willing to borrow and spend; contraction ends when their confidence returns. In the 1970s, these cyclical changes in consumer confidence were closely tied to the rate of inflation. Rapid economic expansion brought swiftly rising prices with an attendant and sobering drop in real income and consumer confidence. Recession cooled the pace of inflation, encouraging a resurgence of confidence.

In the 1980s, the normal course of the cycle was interrupted by the Fed's tight money policy of 1981–82 and was also strongly influenced by the Fed's new posture toward inflation. The Fed squashed the cycle flat and squeezed high inflation out of the system. The economy expanded gradually and steadily in the mid and late 80s. Yet, it would be foolish to say that the Fed had repealed the business cycle. Although future cycles may not have the same sort of extreme peaks and troughs as in the 1970s, they will still recognizably recur.

Chapter 4, which examined the Federal Reserve System and the money and credit markets, described the 70's cycle, and the new climate of the 80s, in financial terms. Look at the cycle now from a different perspective, weaving in the elements of production, income, and consumer demand.

Consumers borrowed heavily in 1972 and 1973 to make record purchases of new homes and automobiles. Business responded by adding plant and equipment to meet the demand and by stockpiling inventory to satisfy customer orders. The sharp growth in consumer and business demand boosted prices rapidly, and the rate of inflation increased from 4 percent in 1972 to 12 percent in 1974. Interest rates moved in parallel fashion. Soon consumers became discouraged because their incomes failed to keep pace, so their expenditures on homes, autos, and other goods plunged.

This led to a general decline in production, and by early 1975 unemployment was at a postwar record high. The cycle was complete. The drop in demand reduced both inflation and interest rates, thereby restoring consumer confidence and spending. Recovery and expansion brought boom conditions. Rising inflation and interest rates returned in 1978, eroding consumer confidence once again. Consumer demand fell, and the 1980 recession began; another cycle had come full circle.

Recovery from the 1980 recession had barely begun when the Fed strangled the credit markets in 1981–82. The ensuing recession, designed to curb inflation, had the typical impact on consumer confidence (dramatic improvement due to reduced inflation), and as soon as the Fed relaxed its grip, consumer expenditures surged forward in 1983.

But why didn't the 80s repeat the experience of the 70s? Why didn't burgeoning consumer demand, backed by exploding credit, drive inflation upward once again? Because the Fed fine-tuned a reduction in demand. And if the Fed maintains its vigilant attitude toward inflation, the current expansion could last well into the 90s. Thus you should now learn which signposts to observe in order to follow the dynamic of inflation and consumer demand.

So far, the business cycle has been painted with fairly broad strokes. The time has come to take up a finer brush so that essential details and connections can be clearly drawn. This chapter shows you how to use *The Wall Street Journal* to understand each step in the growth of consumer demand.

The first statistical series to be examined in this chapter is the *consumer price index* (CPI), whose fluctuations chart the course of inflation. Lower inflation leads to improved consumer sentiment and demand, which drives economic expansion forward. You can gauge the latter through data on auto sales, consumer credit, and housing starts, which will serve as the leading indicators of consumer demand.

CONSUMER PRICE INDEX (CPI)

The Bureau of Labor Statistics' CPI release usually appears in *The Wall Street Journal* in the fourth week of the month. In the Wednesday, March 22, 1989 article, the first paragraph informs you of the CPI's monthly increase. Multiply by 12 to approximate the annual rate. (See pages 80, 81, and 82.)

The CPI compares relative price changes over time. An index must be constructed because consumers purchase such a wide variety of goods and services that no single item could accurately reflect the situation. (See Chart 6–2 on page 83.)

After a base period (1982–84) is selected and assigned an index number of 100.0, prices for other periods are then reported as percentage changes from this base. For instance, if prices rose 5 percent, the index would be 105.0. If prices fell by 10 percent, the index would be 90.0.

The Bureau of Labor Statistics (BLS) calculates the CPI by compiling a list of the goods and services purchased by the typical consumer, including such items as food, clothing, shelter, public utilities, and medical care. These make up the "market basket." The base-period price of each item is recorded and assigned a weight according to its

Consumer Prices Rose 0.4% Last Month And Fears of Rampant Inflation Let Up

Modest Rise Is Below January's, Far Below Producer-Price Jump

By Hilary Stout
Staff Reporter of The Wall Street Journal

Consumer Price Index

WASHINGTON—Consumer prices rose 0.4% in February, slower than their January pace and far below the February jump in producer prices, the Labor Department said.

The report brought cautious relief to the financial markets, which were alarmed by the department's report Friday that prices producers charged for finished goods soared 1.0% in February for the second month in a row. That was the largest two-month increase since early 1981.

"I think the inflation statistics have returned to sanity," said Michael Evans, president of Evans Economics, an economic forecasting firm here.

President Bush said he was "encouraged" by the figures. "They're better than we expected," he continued, saying he was "concerned" when he saw the producer price figures. But he added, "We'll be vigilant" about inflation.

Many economists remain wary that the low unemployment, high demand and tight productive capacity in the economy will continue to generate pressure on prices.

"The financial markets were pleased because it was not similar to the horrific producer price index, but I think it suggests that while inflation is not galloping upward it is still creeping," said William Dudley, senior economist at Goldman, Sachs & Co.

Consumer Prices

In percent (1982-84=100).

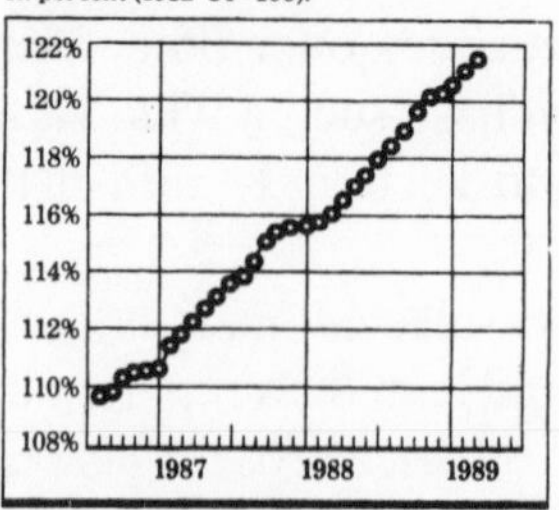

CONSUMER PRICES rose in February to 121.6% of the 1982-84 average from 121.1% in January, the Labor Department reports. (See story on page A2)

February's climb in the prices consumers paid for a variety of goods and services follows an increase of 0.6% in January, the largest monthly rise in two years. So far in 1989, consumer prices have risen at an annual rate of 6.1%, well above the 4.4% increases posted for 1988 and 1987.

No Worst-Case Scenario Seen

Many economists said there is no doubt inflation will continue at a quicker clip than during the past few years, though they said the latest consumer price numbers suggest the country isn't in danger of tumbling into an inflationary spiral.

"Certainly 1989 will deliver a noticeably higher inflation rate than 1988," said William Dunkelberg, dean of the Temple University School of Business and Management and chief economist of the National Federation of Independent Business.

But Jerry Jasinowski, chief economist of the National Association of Manufacturers, said the latest consumer price numbers show, "in essence, fears of inflation getting out of control look premature."

"After the temporary spike in the first quarter," he added, "inflation should settle into the 5% (annual) range by midyear."

Except for medical care and housing, inflation slowed in every category of the consumer price report. Medical costs rose 0.8% for the second month in a row. Energy and transportation costs both rose 0.6%, smaller than the January increases in both those categories.

Even excluding food and energy, where wide price swings can distort the overall index, consumer prices rose 0.4% during the month.

CONSUMER PRICES

Here are the seasonally adjusted changes in the components of the Labor Department's consumer price index for February:

	% change from Jan. 1989	Feb. 1988
All items	0.4	4.8
Minus food & energy	0.4	4.8
Food and beverage	0.5	6.0
Housing	0.3	3.9
Apparel	−0.2	4.6
Transportation	0.6	4.5
Medical care	0.8	7.2
Entertainment	0.4	5.1
Other	0.6	7.4

consumer price indexes (1982-1984 equals 100), unadjusted for seasonal variation, together with the percentage increases from 1988 were:

All urban consumers	121.6	4.8
Urban wage earners & clerical	120.2	4.8
Chicago	122.2	4.8
Detroit	120.1	5.6
Los Angeles	125.5	4.8
New York	127.6	5.4
Philadelphia	125.4	5.1
San Francisco	124.0	5.2
Dallas-Fort Worth	117.5	3.1
Detroit	120.1	5.6
Houston	112.7	4.4
Pittsburgh	117.9	4.1

Source: *The Wall Street Journal*, March 22, 1989.

CPI–First Paragraph

WASHINGTON—Consumer prices rose 0.4% in February, slower than their January pace and far below the February jump in producer prices, the Labor Department said.

Source: *The Wall Street Journal*, March 22, 1989.

relative importance in the basket. Changes in the price of each item are noted, and the percentage change in the total price is reflected in the change of the index number.

The ways consumers spend are continuously shifting because tastes change, as do incomes and the relative prices of goods. New goods and services are frequently introduced. It would be impossible, however, to generate a consistent index of consumer prices if the components of the market basket were constantly changed; a balance must be struck between the need for consistency and the need for an accurate reflection of consumer buying patterns. Therefore, the BLS revises the contents of the market basket only occasionally, after conducting a survey of consumer expenditure patterns.

Contrary to the popular image, the CPI is not really a "cost-of-living" index. The BLS's market basket is fixed; the individual consumer's is not. Substitutions are made with changes in prices and with changes in income. Your cost of living can vary (or can be made to vary) independently of any change in the CPI.

A final point should be made. In the early 80s, the BLS replaced the cost of homeownership with an imputation (or estimate) of the rental value of owner-occupied homes. The cost of home ownership, which includes mortgage interest rates and home purchase prices, had swiftly escalated in the late 1970s, so that this component of the CPI was pulling the entire index upward. Many found this an unjustified upward bias. Accordingly, the BLS adjusted the shelter component to estimate the increase in rental value of an owner-occupied home, which more closely approximates its usage value than does actual appreciation in price. Ironically, interest rates and home prices fell soon afterward, so that the

Consumer Prices

In percent (1982-84=100).

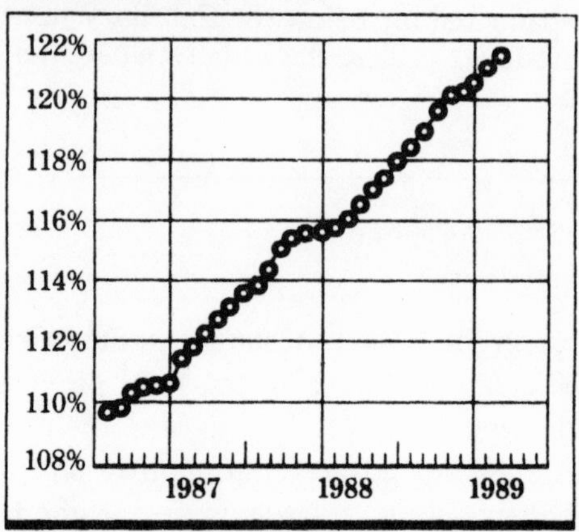

CONSUMER PRICES rose in February to 121.6% of the 1982-84 average from 121.1% in January, the Labor Department reports. (See story on page A2)

CONSUMER PRICES

Here are the seasonally adjusted changes in the components of the Labor Department's consumer price index for February:.

	% change from Jan. 1989	% change from Feb. 1988
All items	0.4	4.8
Minus food & energy	0.4	4.8
Food and beverage	0.5	6.0
Housing	0.3	3.9
Apparel	−0.2	4.6
Transportation	0.6	4.5
Medical care	0.8	7.2
Entertainment	0.4	5.1
Other	0.6	7.4

consumer price indexes (1982-1984 equals 100), unadjusted for seasonal variation, together with the percentage increases from 1988 were:

All urban consumers	121.6	4.8
Urban wage earners & clerical	120.2	4.8
Chicago	122.2	4.8
Detroit	120.1	5.6
Los Angeles	125.5	4.8
New York	127.6	5.4
Philadelphia	125.4	5.1
San Francisco	124.0	5.2
Dallas-Fort Worth	117.5	3.1
Detroit	120.1	5.6
Houston	112.7	4.4
Pittsburgh	117.9	4.1

Source: *The Wall Street Journal*, March 22, 1989.

CHART 6–2
Consumer Price Index (CPI) (1982–84 = 100); **Change in Index at Annual Rates** (smoothed)

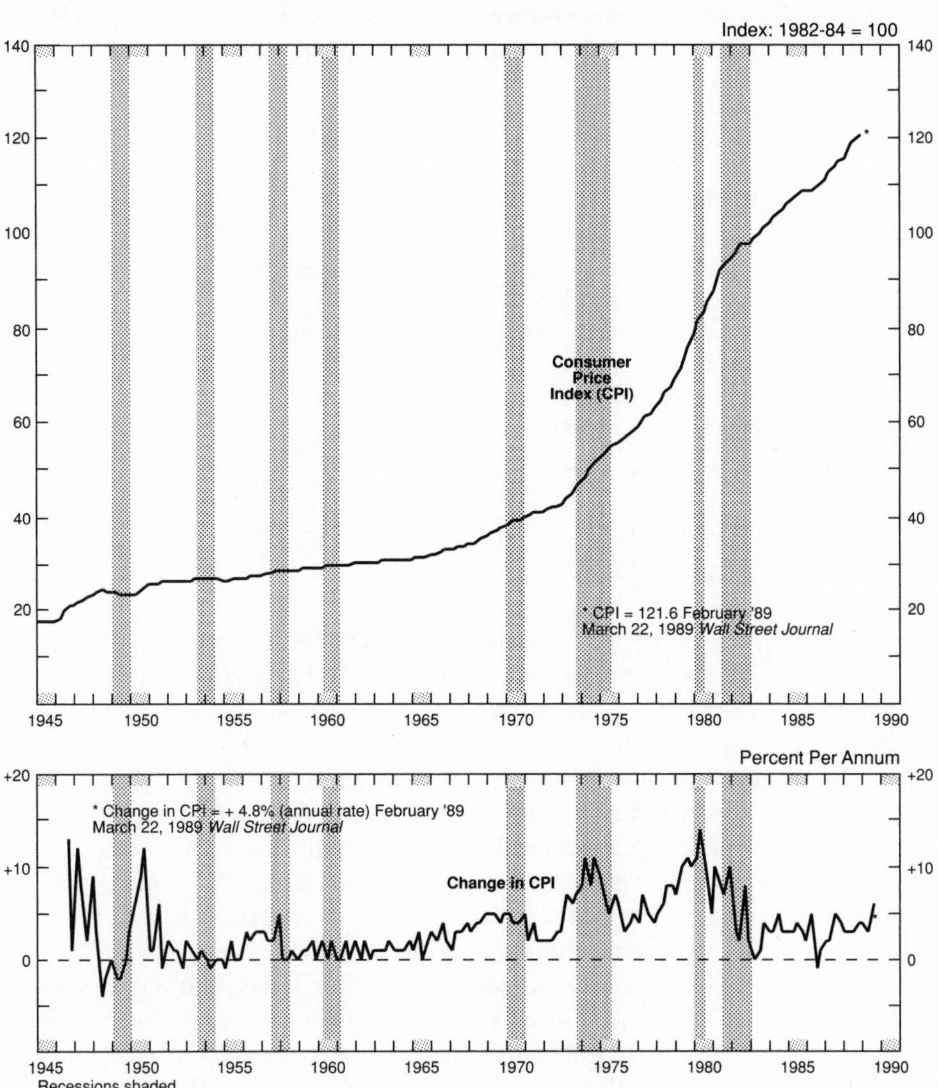

Source: U.S. Department of Commerce, *Business Conditions Digest* and *Handbook of Cyclical Indicators*, series 320 and 320c.

old index, had it remained in use, would have displayed a downward bias and risen less rapidly than the new index.

Make a mental note that the *Journal's* March 22, 1989 report updates Chart 6–2 on page 83 and confirms inflation's continued abatement; the CPI increased by about 5 percent annually in the late 80s. The Fed's fine-tuning worked.

Investor's Tip

- If the CPI increases by 8 percent or more (at an annual rate) for three months running, watch out!
- If that performance is repeated over the next three months, the Fed has failed.
- Bail out of paper investments like stocks and bonds; get into gold and other tangible assets.

CONSUMER SENTIMENT

The Fed's tight money policies and the ensuing recession forced the rate of inflation down to a moderate level in 1982. Let's now consider the impact of that on economic recovery in general and on the consumer's leading role in particular.

The Institute for Social Research at the University of Michigan compiles the *Index of Consumer Sentiment.* Consumers are asked a variety of questions regarding their personal financial circumstances and their outlook for the future. Responses are tabulated according to whether conditions are perceived as better or worse than a year earlier, and an index is constructed comparing the outcome to that for a base year (1966). *The Wall Street Journal* occasionally reports this index, but more often publishes the Conference Board's index of consumer confidence. (See the Thursday, March 2, 1989 article on page 86.) A glance at Chart 6–3 on page 87 shows you that the Michigan and Conference Board indexes have similar records.

Compare the CPI with the Michigan index (see Chart 6–4 on page 87), and you will find that inflation and consumer sentiment move in opposite directions as consumers respond to the rate of inflation.

But consumers are influenced by more than inflation. Employment opportunities, interest rates, and current events (like the stock market crash of October 1987) all play a role. Consumer psychology is complicated. Yet you can see that the singular impact of inflation has been too strong to overlook since the early 1970s; inflation and consumer sentiment have demonstrated a clear and predictable inverse relationship.

Note the dramatic improvement in consumer sentiment after 1980 as inflation slackened due to the recession forced on the economy by the Fed's 1981–82 tight money policy. Then, when the Fed relaxed its grip and the economy began to recover, consumer sentiment exploded in the most dramatic gain since the construction of the index. You can see (Chart 6–4 on page 87) that by 1983–84 it was in the 90–100 range and remained above 90 until the stock market crash of 1987.

Feelings Are Facts

- Inflation causes recession by depressing consumer sentiment.

Before moving on, however, reflect on the robust condition of consumer sentiment today and the spectacular improvement in consumer sentiment between its 1979–80 low and the mid-80s. This turnaround can be explained by comparing the 1955–65 period with 1965–80. The principal difference between these periods is the moderate rate of inflation in the first decade and the cyclical increase of inflation after that. With each boom (1969, 1974, 1979), the rate of inflation hit a new high and consumer sentiment reached a new low. Although the mid-70s recession was worse than the 1970 recession, the rate of inflation did not drop to as low a number. No wonder consumer sentiment deteriorated for 15 years: inflation and the attendant swings of the business cycle were becoming more severe. Once inflation's grip was broken in the early 80s, however, consumers began feeling positively upbeat again for the first time in 20 years. The key had been the interruption of the inflationary boom/bust cycle.

But what about the stock market crash of October 1987? You can see (Chart 6–4) that consumer sentiment plunged to the low 80s in late 1987 and then snapped back to the mid-90s by early 1988, demonstrating that

Despite Greater Confidence, Rising January Income, Spending Was Up Little

By HILARY STOUT
And JAMES T. AREDDY
Staff Reporters of THE WALL STREET JOURNAL

Signs are emerging that the gradual rise in interest rates over the past year may be starting to have an effect on consumers.

The Commerce Department reported yesterday that Americans' personal income spurted in January but their spending stayed nearly flat. At the same time the Conference Board in New York released a survey that showed confidence in the economy in February at its highest level since December 1969 but suggested rising interest rates are crimping people's plans to purchase costly items such as cars and houses.

Personal income in the U.S. increased 1.8% in January, to an annual rate of $4.282 trillion, according to the government report, prodded in part by special factors such as farm subsidies, a federal pay raise and annual cost-of-living adjustments for Social Security recipients.

January's jump in personal income followed a rise of 0.9% in December. And even discounting the special factors, income grew 1.6% in the month, Commerce Department officials said.

But despite the extra money, personal spending edged up only 0.1%, to an annual rate of $3.353 trillion, after jumping 0.8% in December. Consequently, the personal savings rate leaped to 5.8% of disposable income from 4.3%.

The Conference Board's Consumer Confidence Index escalated to 122 in February from a revised 115.8 in January and 114.9 a year earlier. But a scant 2.7% of the re-

Source: *The Wall Street Journal,* March 2, 1989.

CHART 6–3
Consumer Sentiment: Michigan and Conference Board Surveys

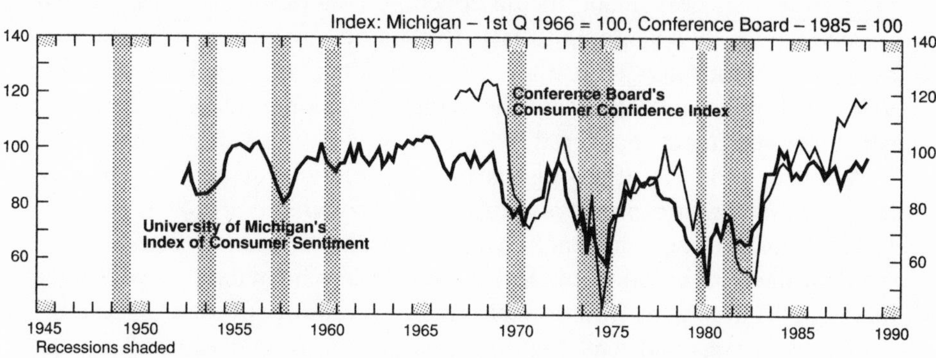

Source: *Public Opinion*, August/September 1985, pp. 22–23; The Conference Board.

CHART 6–4
Index of Consumer Sentiment and Change in CPI at Annual Rate

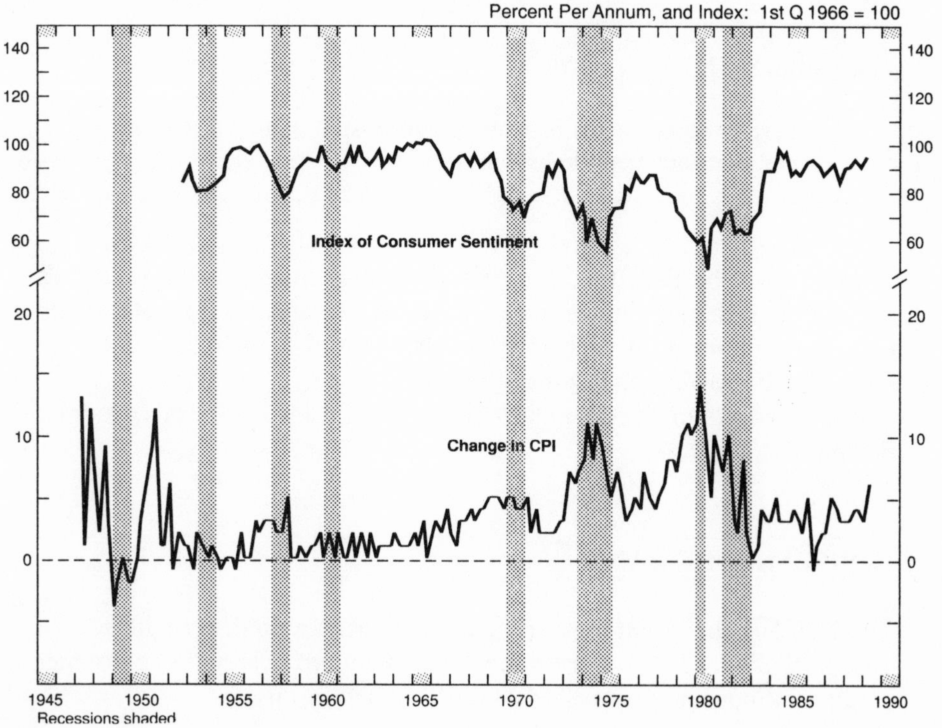

Percent Per Annum, and Index: 1st Q 1966 = 100

Index of Consumer Sentiment

Change in CPI

Recessions shaded

Source: U.S. Department of Commerce, *Business Conditions Digest* and *Handbook of Cyclical Indicators*, series 58 and 320c.

consumer sentiment responds to more than consumer prices. Although only 20 percent of the American public owns stock directly (other than in pension plans), pessimistic media coverage convinced most people that the economic sky was going to fall. Bombarded by bad news, consumer sentiment plummeted. But after a few months, when it became clear that the sky had not fallen and the economy was not going to collapse, consumer sentiment recovered.

And here's the nub of this discussion: *the relationship between the CPI and consumer sentiment drives consumer borrowing and spending*. Low inflation and strong consumer sentiment propel consumer demand forward, while high inflation and low consumer sentiment depress consumer demand. That's why inflation brings on recession (it depresses consumer sentiment) and why low inflation generates recovery and expansion (it boosts consumer sentiment). Low inflation in the 1980s has maintained consumer sentiment and postponed the cycle's peak and the next recession. Credit the Fed's fine-tuning for that.

Investor's Tip

- There'll be no recession until inflation surges past 8 percent and consumer sentiment drops below 80.

And credit the Fed, too, for restraining consumer demand (and thus preventing inflation) in the face of robust consumer sentiment. With consumer sentiment at such lofty levels, only high interest could keep consumer borrowing and demand in check.

It's now time to consider the most important indicators of consumer demand.

CONSUMER DEMAND

The Wall Street Journal regularly publishes articles on three indicators of consumer demand that merit your close attention: auto sales, consumer credit, and housing starts. Let's examine each in turn.

Auto Sales

Around the 5th, 15th, and 25th of the month *The Journal* reports automobile sales data compiled by the manufacturers. Look at the Friday, March 24, 1989 report on page 90.

The 4.3 percent increase for mid-March reported in the first paragraph compares all auto sales with auto sales in the same month one year ago. But you need *seasonally adjusted data at an annual rate* to make a comparison with recent months as well as years past. Thus, the third paragraph and the accompanying chart report the mid-March rate of 6.8 million domestically-produced automobiles as slightly lower than the 7.2 million figure of a year ago, as indicated on Chart 6–5 (page 92).

The well-equipped auto has symbolized the American consumer economy since the 1920s. The automobile industry pioneered such now-familiar techniques as planned obsolescence, mass production, and mass marketing and advertising campaigns in the 1920s and 30s. Henry Ford's Model T was the first mass-produced automobile. His assembly line production methods were state-of-the-art; his marketing concept, however, was vintage 19th century. He emphasized the cheapest possible serviceable car at the lowest price. Henry Ford reduced the price of a Model T to $300 in the early 1920s, and provided customers with any color they wanted, as long as it was black. Ford dominated the market until the late 1920s, when General Motors saw the profit potential in continually inflating the product by offering colors, options, and model changes and increased size, weight, and speed. This strategy enabled GM to take the sales lead from Ford; and, from then on, competition in autos meant more (and different) car for more money, not the same car for a lower price. The option of less car for less money was eliminated until the German and Japanese imports arrived.

Ford had grafted 20th-century technology onto 19th-century marketing techniques, driven the price down as far as it could go, and seen sales go flat in the mid-1920s as the market was saturated. GM pioneered the 20th-century marketing technique of product inflation on a mass scale and gambled that the consumer would borrow ever more in order to buy next year's model.

Product inflation boosts sales by cajoling the consumer into buying something new at a higher price. The customer isn't swindled, just convinced by marketing and advertising techniques that he or she needs an

Vehicle Sales Increased 4.3% In Mid-March

Outlook Is Said to Be Mixed At Best as a Softening In Car Buying Continues

By JOSEPH B. WHITE

Staff Reporter of THE WALL STREET JOURNAL

Auto Sales–
year ago comparison

DETROIT – Sales of cars and light trucks in the U.S. rose 4.3% during mid-March compared with a mediocre year-ago performance. But dealers and analysts said the outlook is mixed at best, with car sales continuing to look soft.

Auto makers are watching carefully for signs that rising interest rates or recession fears are scaring customers out of showrooms. Most analysts said it's too soon to tell for sure. But some dealers said there's no question consumers are skittish.

Auto Sales–
seasonally adjusted
annual rate

Car sales are clearly soft, with deliveries of domestic models in the latest period running at a 6.8 million seasonally adjusted annual pace compared with last year's 7.2 million. The results "are weaker than I expected and continue the gradual softening trend," said Drexel Burnham Lambert Inc. analyst David Healy.

However, truck sales were up 7.8% over last year, belying theories that financing costs are causing a broad reluctance to buy vehicles now. "The signals on the industry are mixed," said **Chrysler** Corp. sales analyst Steven Torok.

Dealers are sending mixed signals too. "Anyone who tells you it's great is full of" it, said Tim Crowley, sales manager at Hollywood Chrysler-Plymouth, a high volume dealer near Miami. At Winner Ford in Cherry Hill, N.J., showroom traffic is down 20% from both last month and a year ago, said general manager Hank Berry. At Wellesley Toyota in affluent suburban Boston, sales manager Mike Christopher said sales are down 30%.

But at Prospect Motors, which carries several **General Motors** Corp. lines, general manager Frank Halvorson said he's having a good month. Sales to fleet buyers have been "tremendous. We did 3,500 [vehicles] this month." Fleet business at the Jackson, Calif., dealership has been buoyed by "big incentives" from GM, Mr. Halvorson added.

Overall, the eight major U.S. auto makers sold 194,597 domestically built cars in the latest ten days, up 2.8% from 189,245 a year earlier. (Because of the effects of the Commerce Department seasonal adjustment formulas, the increased unit volume translates into a lower seasonally adjusted annual sales pace this year.)

Sales of trucks, minivans and sport utility vehicles from the eight major domestic producers totaled 119,868, compared with 111,194 a year earlier.

Of the Big Three U.S. makers, Chrysler suffered a sharp drop. The No. 3 auto maker's domestic car sales skidded 16.2%, while total car and light truck sales for the mid-March period fell 6.3% from a year ago. However, Mr. Torok said the company had expected a weak first quarter and is optimistic sales will turn around in April to June.

At GM, domestic car sales nudged up 0.2%, while truck sales rose 5% over last year. The No. 1 auto maker's total vehicle sales for the latest ten days were up 0.7%.

Ford Motor Co.'s total vehicle sales for mid-March rose 8.2% compared with a year earlier. The No. 2 auto maker's domestic car sales rose 6.1%, while truck sales jumped 10.6%.

The five Japanese auto makers who build vehicles in the U.S. sold 23,229 domestic-made cars and trucks in the latest ten days, up 70% from a year ago.

RETAIL U.S. CAR AND LIGHT TRUCK SALES-a

	1989 Mar 11-20	1988 Mar 11-20	x-% Chg.
GM total vehicles	**143,429**	**142,387**	+ **0.7**
Domestic car	92,362	92,173	+ 0.2
Imported car	3,443	4,838	– 28.8
Total car	95,805	97,011	– 1.2
Domestic truck	47,376	45,376	+ 4.4
Imported truck	248	0	d
Total truck	47,624	45,376	+ 5.0
FORD total vehicles	**100,460**	**92,835**	+ **8.2**
Domestic car	57,479	54,186	+ 6.1
Imported car	2,257	1,837	+ 22.9
Total car	59,736	56,023	+ 6.6
Domestic truck	40,724	36,812	+ 10.6
CHRYSLER tot. veh.	**56,514**	**60,317**	– **6.3**
Domestic car	25,824	30,801	– 16.2
Imported car	3,467	3,140	+ 10.4
Total car	29,291	33,941	– 13.7
Domestic truck	26,333	24,691	+ 6.7
Imported truck	890	1,685	– 47.2
Total truck	27,223	26,376	+ 3.2
NISSAN total vehicles	**7,209**	**4,499**	+ **60.2**
Domestic car	2,912	1,869	+ 55.8
Domestic truck	4,297	2,630	+ 63.4
HONDA domestic car	**9,052**	**7,270**	+ **24.5**
VW domestic car-b	**0**	**1,034**	
TOYOTA domestic car	**5,027**	**1,169**	**d**
MAZDA domestic car	**1,384**	**743**	+ **86.3**
MITSUBISHI-c	**557**	**0**	**d**
Total cars	**203,764**	**199,060**	+ **2.4**
Domestic	194,597	189,245	+ 2.8
Imported	9,167	9,815	– 6.6
Total trucks	**119,868**	**111,194**	+ **7.8**
Domestic	118,730	109,509	+ 8.4
Imported	1,138	1,685	– 32.5
Total dom. veh.	**313,327**	**298,754**	+ **4.9**
Total vehicles	**323,632**	**310,254**	+ **4.3**

a-Totals include only vehicle sales reported in the period.
b-Volkswagen ceased U.S. car production in July 1988.
c-Domestic car
d-Percentage change is over 99%.
x-There were 8 selling days in the most recent period and 8 a year earlier. Percentage differences based on daily sales rate rather than sales volume.

U.S. Auto Sales

Seasonally adjusted annual rate of domestic cars sold, in 10-day selling periods, in millions

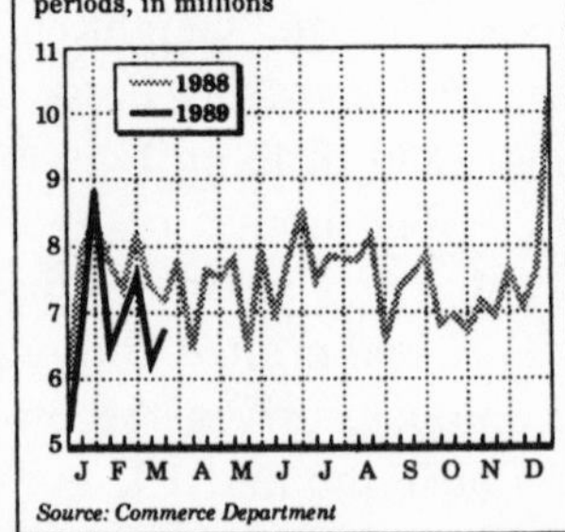

Source: Commerce Department

Source: *The Wall Street Journal*, March 24, 1989.

Seasonally Adjusted Annual Data–Third Paragraph

Car sales are clearly soft, with deliveries of domestic models in the latest period running at a 6.8 million seasonally adjusted annual pace compared with last year's 7.2 million. The results "are weaker than I expected and continue the gradual softening trend," said Drexel Burnham Lambert Inc. analyst David Healy.

Source: *The Wall Street Journal*, March 24, 1989

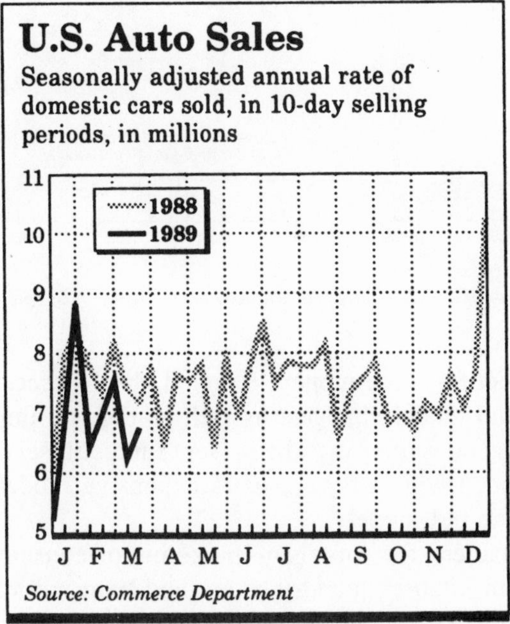

Source: *The Wall Street Journal*, March 24, 1989.

CHART 6–5
New Auto Sales, Domestic Type (excluding imports)

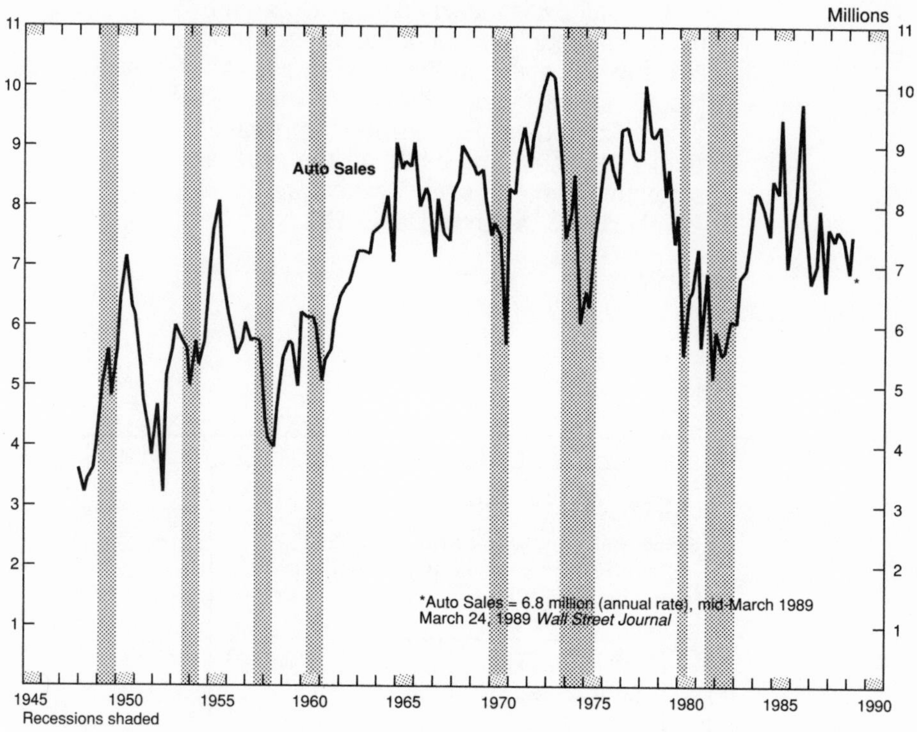

Source: Federal Reserve Board; U.S Department of Commerce, *Survey of Current Business*.

improved product for more money. Planned obsolescence is a corollary, because style and model changes, as well as product improvement, aid in persuading the consumer that the present (and still serviceable) model should be replaced with a better, more expensive model, not a lower-cost repeat of the old model.

That set the pattern for American marketing of consumer goods. You can see it in your kitchen, laundry room, and living room, not just your driveway. TV replaced radio, color TV replaced black-and-white TV, and VCRs are now perceived as near-compulsory accessories. With each innovation, the price goes up and so does debt.

The 1970s and 80s, however, brought a rude shock to the domestic automobile manufacturers. The American public was no longer willing to buy whatever the manufacturers wished to sell. Consumers balked at continued product inflation, especially if it meant buying features, such as increased size and weight, that were no longer attractive. In addition, consumers were willing to accept less car for less money, especially if it meant a better made and more fuel efficient vehicle. So the domestic manufacturers lost market share to the imports, and are still struggling to stem the tide.

Yet domestic auto sales remained a leading indicator of economic activity, turning down as soon as escalating inflation eroded consumer sentiment (see Charts 6–4 and 6–5 on pages 87 and 92) and recovering quickly when inflation subsided and consumer sentiment improved. Domestic auto sales have led the cycle into both expansion and contraction.

This will help you understand domestic auto sales' role in the economy and why you should regularly track them. It's not just that the auto industry, along with the bloc of industries that depends upon it (e.g., rubber tire, steel, glass, upholstery), represents a significant share of total economic activity. It's also that the fortunes of the auto industry lead the cycle, foretelling recession and prosperity. What's good for GM may not necessarily be good for America, but GM's sales are a reliable leading indicator of overall economic activity.

The Fed's high interest rate policies in the 80s helped restrain auto sales, keeping them in the 7 to 8 million annual range (see Chart 6–5) and thus holding down costs and inflation. Will the domestic manufacturers soon reach the 10-million-a-year sales volume they occasionally enjoyed in the 70s? Not unless the Fed dramatically reverses course and deliberately depresses interest rates.

Investor's Tip

- Auto sales above 8 million threaten inflation; 10 million assure inflation.

Consumer Credit

The Wall Street Journal publishes the Commerce Department's release on *consumer installment debt* in the second week of the month. The second paragraph of the Friday, March 10, 1989 *Journal* article provides the figure you need. Changes in consumer credit are an important barometer of

Consumer Credit Rose in January At a 7.9% Rate

By Hilary Stout
Staff Reporter of The Wall Street Journal

WASHINGTON—The pace of consumer borrowing, from credit-card spending to car loans, picked up slightly in January, the Federal Reserve reported.

Consumer credit expanded at a 7.9% annual rate to $4.36 billion during the month after climbing at a 7.8% annual rate to $4.30 billion in December, according to the Fed. December's rate of increase was revised yesterday from an initial calculation of 9.9%.

Consumer credit

All the numbers are adjusted for seasonal variations.

The solid growth seemed to suggest that rising interest rates haven't had a strong impact on consumer borrowing. The Fed's policy makers have been pushing up interest rates in an effort to curb borrowing by making credit more costly. They hope the lower demand will slow price increases.

Car loans, a type of consumer borrowing closely affected by interest rates, led the credit increase in January, growing by $2.22 billion, an annual rate of 9.2%. While that is slightly slower than the 9.8% rate of December, it is well above November's 5.7% rate of increase.

"So far it looks like interest rates are not biting into consumer credit," said Michael Penzer, senior economist at Bank of America in San Francisco.

But Irwin Kellner, chief economist for Manufacturers Hanover, said the January rise in consumer credit was far below rises of a few years ago. "I think what we're seeing here is a gradual slowing in the rate of growth in consumer credit, in part because of the bite of higher interest rates and in part because this is the seventh year of economic expansion, and consumer needs for the big-ticket items, where credit is often needed, have been satisfied," Mr. Kellner said.

The growth of revolving credit, which includes credit card borrowing, continued to slow, climbing $823 million in January, or an annual rate of 5.3%, after growing at an 8.4% annual rate in December and 21.1% in November.

Mobil-home credit grew $82 million, or at an annual rate of 3.8%, in January after declining at a 12.9% annual rate in December.

Source: *The Wall Street Journal*, March 10, 1989.

consumer activity because of the phenomenon just described: borrowing to finance purchases of autos and other expensive and postponable items.

Now multiply the $4.36 billion reported in the second paragraph of the *Journal* article by 12 (slightly more than $52 billion) to determine the annual rate, and update Chart 6–6 with that figure.

Consumer credit rose gradually and cyclically until the 1970s. Then it exploded. You can see the cyclical maximum of $10 billion in the late 60s, $20 billion in the early 70s, and $50 billion in the late 70s. In the latest expansion, before and after 1984's minislowdown (the Fed's policies hit installment rates, too), installment borrowing reached $80 billion at an annual rate (Chart 6–6). No wonder the Fed is concerned; indeed, it's amazing that inflation has not been even more severe in the face of this stimulus to demand.

CHART 6–6
Change in Consumer Installment Credit

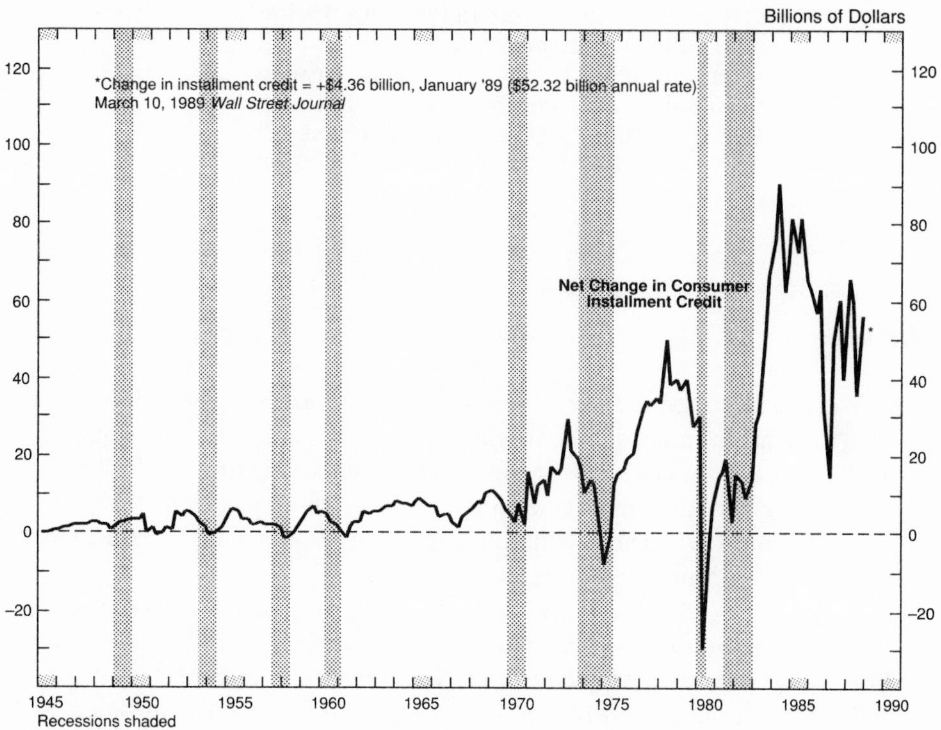

Source: U.S. Department of Commerce, *Business Conditions Digest* and *handbook of Cyclical Indicators*, series 113.

You should also notice that the increases in consumer installment debt have eased since the initial surge of the early and mid-80s. Figures in the late 80s have been closer to $60 billion than $100 billion (Chart 6–6). The Fed's tighter policies have been partly responsible for this by restraining growth in that part of consumer demand financed by debt, and thereby helping keep output, costs, and inflation under control.

Investor's Tip

- Consumer credit growth of $80 billion threatens inflation; $100 billion assures inflation.

Consumer Credit–Second Paragraph

Consumer credit expanded at a 7.9% annual rate to $4.36 billion during the month after climbing at a 7.8% annual rate to $4.30 billion in December, according to the Fed. December's rate of increase was revised yesterday from an initial calculation of 9.9%.

Source: *The Wall Street Journal*, March 10, 1989.

You can also see the cyclical sensitivity of consumer credit and its reaction to changes in consumer sentiment (compare Chart 6–6 on page 95 with Chart 6–4 on page 87). Increases in consumer credit trailed off with the surge of inflation and the drop in consumer sentiment in the late 60s, 1973–74, and 1979. Then, with each recession and the return of consumer confidence, consumer credit rebounded.

Following World War II and until recently, consumer credit was notoriously impervious to the long-run rise in interest rates since World War II. Consumers were primarily concerned with the size of monthly payments, and stretching out the term of the loan was usually regarded as sufficient to mitigate the steady rise in the interest rate. But the Fed's 1981 tight money policy crushed this piece of conventional wisdom. Monthly payments became so large that many consumers were forced to forsake consumer credit and postpone purchases of autos and other expensive items. The Fed's tight money policies proved effective once again in 1984, although borrowing bounced back up as soon as the Fed eased off. Despite present installment credit figures being lower than earlier in the decade, consumers' continued willingness to take on ever larger amounts of debt is one reason the Fed should maintain fairly tight credit conditions in the foreseeable future.

Housing Starts

The Commerce Department's monthly release on *housing starts* is usually published in *The Wall Street Journal* between the 17th and the 20th of the month. Always direct your attention to the seasonally adjusted monthly figure, presented at an annual rate. The second paragraph and the chart accompanying the Friday, February 17, 1989 story on page 98 tell you that there were 1.69 million home and apartment unit construction starts in January of 1989.

The cyclical sensitivity of housing starts to consumer sentiment and the availability of mortgage credit is striking. (See Chart 6–7 on page 100.) Housing starts turned down well before the onset of recession, as soon as rising inflation reduced consumer confidence and the Fed slammed on the brakes, drying up mortgage credit. But you can see that they turned back up even before the recession ended as consumer confidence returned with the decline of inflation and the Fed's switch to an easy money policy.

You have already reviewed the dramatic impact of the Fed's 1981–82 tight money policy on residential construction. The Fed's policy put a new home beyond the reach of most consumers, and mortgage borrowing and housing starts plunged. Although housing starts and mortgage borrowing have since recovered, housing starts will not surpass the record levels of the early 70s (2.5 million at an annual rate in 1972) unless the Fed once again tolerates the low interest rates that prevailed back then. That would be dangerous, because the flat performance of housing starts, in the 1.5–1.7 million range in the mid and late 80s, is the most reassuring feature of the charts on pages 99 and 100.

Investor's Tip

- As housing starts approach 2 million, inflation looms.

What was said earlier about industries related to auto sales can be repeated for residential construction. Lumber, cement, glass, roofing materials, heating, plumbing and electrical supplies, kitchen and laundry appliances, and furniture and furnishings are all part of the bloc of industries that fluctuate with housing starts. The Fed's policy of restraint held all of these activities in check and thereby maintained moderate levels of inflation in those industries as well.

Housing Starts Jumped 8% in January, But Warm-Spell Rise Is Called a Fluke

By HILARY STOUT
Staff Reporter of THE WALL STREET JOURNAL

WASHINGTON—Unusually mild winter weather sent new housing construction soaring 8.0% in January, the Commerce Department reported.

Housing Starts — Work began on homes and apartments at an annual rate of 1.69 million units in January, a sharp rise from December's annual rate of 1.57 million units and well beyond the rate housing analysts expect for 1989.

Most housing economists dismissed the jump as a fluke, propelled by a warm streak that swept much of the country last month, including the Northeast and Midwest.

"I would call it an aberration," said Willard Gourley, president of the Mortgage Bankers Association and vice chairman of Barclays American/Mortgage Corp. in Charlotte, N.C.

"We are by no means expecting this 1.69 (million) starts rate to hold," said David Seiders, chief economist for the National Association of Home Builders.

In fact, most analysts predict rising mortgage rates in 1989 will crimp demand in the housing market. And changing demographics—with a smaller generation of young adults entering the home market—will probably hold construction down for the next few years, some add.

A mammoth 52% leap in new housing construction in the Northeast catapulted the overall figure. But the Northeast market has been softening for the past year, and analysts attributed the huge growth in January almost entirely to the weather.

"Builders always have a stock or backlog of permits to use, and when they have surprise weather there is a tendency to go ahead and put something into the ground," Mr. Seiders said.

Work began on single-family homes at an annual rate of 1.2 million in January, a 7.1% increase over December. On multi-unit complexes, work began at an annual rate of 490,000 units, 10.1% higher than the December rate.

Monthly figures are adjusted for seasonal variation. The housing start figures often are thought to be imprecise and, generally, the Commerce Department revises them heavily after their initial release. Yesterday, for example, the department changed its calculation of December's housing starts to a 0.1% rise. Originally, it tallied a 2.2% rise.

Building permits were issued at an annual rate of 1.52 million in January, a 2.7% decline from the month before.

Housing Starts

Annual rate, in millions of dwelling units.

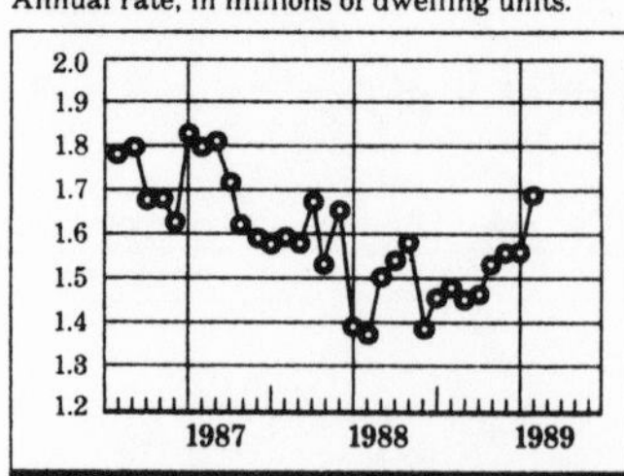

HOUSING STARTS in January rose to a seasonally adjusted rate of 1,693,000 units from a revised 1,568,000 units in December, the Commerce Department reports. (See story on page A2.)

Source: *The Wall Street Journal*, February 17, 1989.

Housing Starts–Second Paragraph

Work began on homes and apartments at an annual rate of 1.69 million units in January, a sharp rise from December's annual rate of 1.57 million units and well beyond the rate housing analysts expect for 1989.

Source: *The Wall Street Journal*, February 17, 1989.

Housing Starts

Annual rate, in millions of dwelling units.

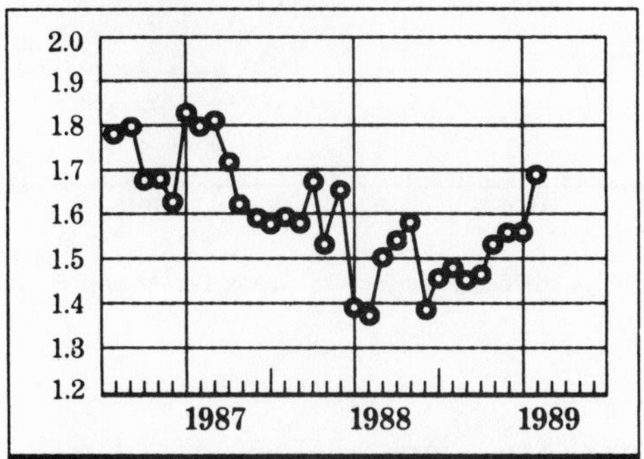

HOUSING STARTS in January rose to a seasonally adjusted rate of 1,693,000 units from a revised 1,568,000 units in December, the Commerce Department reports. (See story on page A2.)

Source: *The Wall Street Journal*, February 17, 1989.

CHART 6–7
Housing Starts

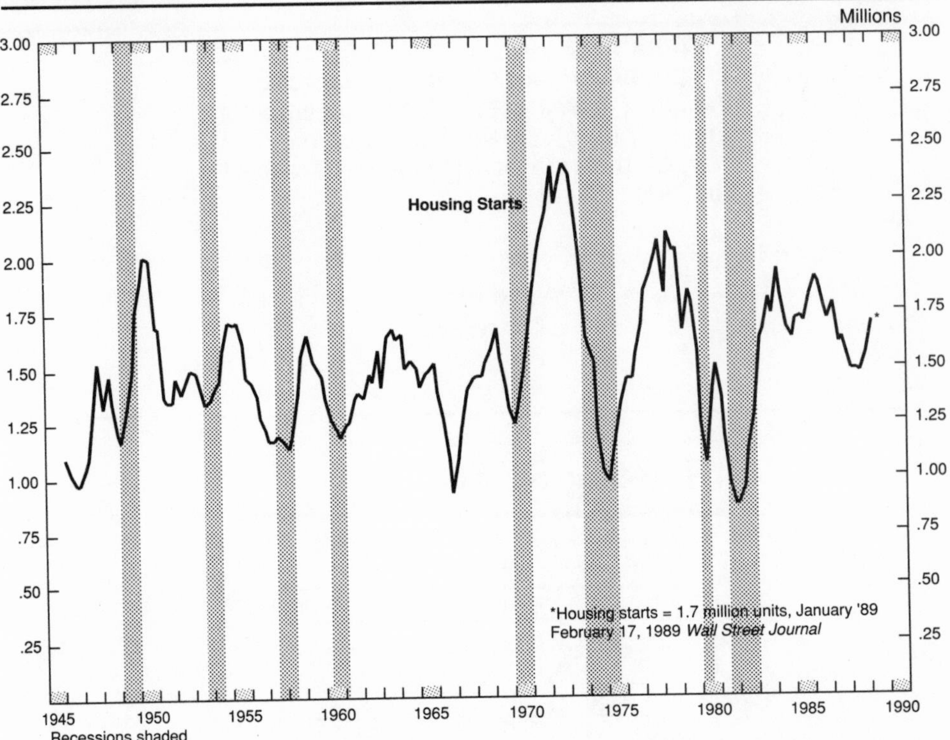

Source: U.S. Department of Commerce, *Business Conditions Digest* and *Handbook of Cyclical Indicators*, series 28.

CONSUMER DEMAND AND THE RECESSION OF 1980

So now you can see how much the modern American economy has come to depend on product inflation and ever larger volumes of debt. These sustain the growth in demand required to maintain production and income at adequate levels. Moreover, consumer debt and consumer demand have been the leading edge of the post–World War II business cycle. Paradoxically, their strong growth led to cyclical problems with inflation, which periodically tended to choke off credit, demand, and economic expansion, generating recession.

The 1980 recession is a good example. By late 1979, rapid increases in the producer price index had pushed the rate of inflation, as measured by the CPI, to 15 percent at an annual rate (see Chart 6–4, page 87). Employee compensation grew at 10 percent a year, but that was hardly enough to offset the effect of inflation.

The Index of Consumer Sentiment had sunk steadily through 1978 and 1979 as inflation surged upward. In late 1979, it matched 1974's dismal performance. Consumers were discouraged. Their take-home pay was losing the race with inflation, interest rates were high and rising, relief was nowhere in sight, and so they had no cause for anything but pessimism.

Slumping auto sales and housing starts were the first omens of recession. Both declined throughout 1979. Housing starts fell from a 1.8 million annual rate to 1.4 million, and auto sales declined from 9 million to 7 million (see Chart 6–7, page 100, and Chart 6–5, page 92).

Thus, 1980 began with most of the important leading indicators of consumer activity heading downward or showing weakness. They were beginning to drag the rest of the economy with them.

Nonetheless, interest rates and inflation hit postwar highs (at the time) in the first quarter of 1980. The Federal Reserve System clamped down hard on consumer credit, restricting its availability and raising interest rates even higher. This was the proverbial last straw, and in the second quarter consumer credit fell more steeply than at any other time in the postwar period. All consumer activities that had come to depend on consumer credit were affected; auto sales and housing starts plunged. The Fed's action had brought the entire process to a head and hastened the recession that had been inevitable for over a year.

SUMMING UP: THE CYCLE AND ITS CONSEQUENCES

In summary, as the cycle moves from *expansion to peak,* rapidly rising inflation depresses consumer real income and consumer sentiment, bringing on a collapse in consumer demand and inevitable recession.

CPI ↑ → Consumer sentiment ↓ → Consumer demand ↓
(Auto sales ↓ + Consumer credit ↓ + Housing starts ↓).

Recession let the steam out of the economy and that cooled inflation.

The temporary reduction in the rate of inflation permitted the business cycle to resume its course after each recession. Reduced inflation encouraged consumers to indulge in a new wave of borrowing and spending, moving the cycle from *recovery to expansion* and launching another round of inflation.

CPI ↓ → Consumer sentiment ↑ → Consumer demand ↑ (Auto sales ↑ + Consumer credit ↑ + Housing starts ↑).

There was no human villain in this drama. Blame the inanimate forces of credit and inflation, which periodically swept over the economy to leave recession's wreckage behind. The Fed finally came to grips with the problem in 1981 when, in its attempt to bring inflation under control, it tightened credit sufficiently to turn recovery into recession. That is why the 1980 recession, rather than the 1981–82 experience, was used as an illustration: the most recent recession was engineered by the Fed to reduce inflation, while the recession of 1980 was a more natural outcome of cyclical developments.

There are no villains, but there are victims. There is no doubt who bore the burden of recession: the unemployed. Their loss of income is not shared by the rest of us as the economy contracts. Moreover, unemployment hits hardest those industries that depend heavily on big-ticket consumer expenditures financed by borrowing. It is worst in construction, autos, and other durable goods industries and in the steel and nonferrous metal industries. Workers in communications, services, finance, and government are largely spared.

Through no fault of their own, therefore, workers (and their families) in a narrow band of industries must bear most of the cycle's burden. They are not responsible for the economy's fluctuations, but they are the chief victims in every downturn. Someone must build the homes and cars and mill the lumber and steel. Yet, as if caught in a perverse game of musical chairs, those who do are always left without a seat when the music stops.

WHAT NEXT?

Is the next recession inevitable? Yes, because all economic expansions end in recession. But whether it will be mild or severe depends on the current expansion. A strong and rapid expansion, driven by large increases in consumer and business borrowing and ending in virulent inflation, will produce a sharp and severe recession. A mild and gradual expansion, lacking excessive borrowing and ending with only slight inflation, will produce a mild recession. We are in that kind of prolonged and moderate expansion now and have been spared recession because of the expansion's relaxed pace.

Data on auto sales, consumer credit, and housing starts in the late 80s provided evidence that the excesses of the 70s can be avoided if the Fed has the resolve to keep interest rates at restrictive levels. It is better to avoid the rapid growth of demand and the resurrection of inflation, the lethal twins that have killed all previous booms. If demand grows slowly because credit is restrained, the expansion will last longer and not be set back so severely by the next recession.

Investor's Tip

- If housing starts exceed 1.8 million, consumer credit $80 billion, and auto sales 8 million, inflation is around the corner.

All of this illustrates the effectiveness of the Fed's fine-tuning in the late 80s. The Fed maintained interest rates at sufficiently high levels to restrain consumer borrowing and demand. Despite robust consumer sentiment, the Fed did not permit consumers to borrow and spend their way into the next inflationary boom and recession.

Investor's Tip
Statistical Indicators and Danger Signals

- Follow these indicators in *The Wall Street Journal* and watch for the following danger signals:

Indicator	*When Published*	*End of 80s Level*	*Danger Level*	*Potential Problem*
Auto Sales	Every ten days	7–8 million	8 million	Sales urge leads to inflation
Consumer Credit	2nd week	$40–60 billion	$80 billion	Borrowing binge leads to inflation
Housing Starts	17th to 20th of month	1.5–1.7 million	1.8 million	Construction boom leads to inflation
CPI	4th Week	5%	8%	High inflation threatens consumer sentiment
Consumer Sentiment	1st week	100–120	80	Low consumer sentiment will lead to drop in consumer demand and recession

- If these indicators flash a warning, move out of paper assets and into tangible assets before inflation surges.

CHAPTER 7

THE POSTWAR BUSINESS CYCLE: THE ROLE OF COSTS AND INFLATION

INTRODUCTION

There must be a recession in the future, and there must be a recovery after that. The statistical series you have examined so far are your surveyor's tools. By using them you know that inflation and recession have been postponed because the Fed's restraint has prolonged the current expansion. But suppose demand *does* swell out of control. What is the dynamic that rekindles inflation?

You can find inflation's bellwether in the statistical series that chart output and efficiency. Gross national product, industrial production, and capacity utilization measure the economy's output; productivity measures its efficiency. As output increases, efficiency decreases, and inflation (as reported by the producer price index) inevitably becomes a problem.

At the peak of the cycle, when output is at its maximum, production facilities are strained to the point where production costs rise sharply. Overburdened equipment fails, accelerating the expense of maintenance and repair. The quantities of labor added to the production process are relatively greater than the increase in output. Inevitable inefficiencies force up costs and consequently prices, even though the product itself has not changed. As the obvious result, inflation increases rapidly.

With the recession's drop in production, the strain on facilities and labor eases. Costs fall, inflation declines, and the stage is set for a new round of expansion and growth.

The connections between output, efficiency, and inflation form this chapter's central theme. Turn now to an examination of the statistical releases that will be of particular importance in charting the course of production and the interaction of efficiency and inflation as the economy moves from trough to recovery.

GROSS NATIONAL PRODUCT (GNP)

GNP is a good place to start. As the broadest available measure of economic activity, it provides the official scale with which fluctuations in the economy are measured.

The Wall Street Journal publishes the U.S. Department of Commerce's quarterly release on the GNP about three weeks after the close of each quarter. Then, around the 20th of the two subsequent months of the next quarter, it reports revisions of the data. The first quarter of 1989 figures appeared in the Thursday, April 27, 1989 *Journal*.

Look for the following features: *constant-dollar (real) GNP, current-dollar (nominal) GNP,* the *rate of inflation,* and the *statistical summary.*

Constant-Dollar (Real) GNP

The first paragraph tells you of ". . . a vigorous expansion in the first quarter at a 5.5% annual rate . . . ." What does this mean?

Constant-dollar (real) GNP measures the final output of goods and services produced in the American economy in one year, without including the impact of changed prices on the value of those goods. Thus, this

---

Constant Dollar (Real) GNP–First Paragraph

WASHINGTON – A return to normal farm production following last year's devastating drought propelled the U.S. economy to a vigorous expansion in the first quarter at a 5.5% annual rate, the Commerce Department reported.

Source: *The Wall Street Journal*, April 27, 1989.

Economy, Propelled by Farm Recovery, Grew at Vigorous 5.5% Rate in 1st Period

Some Economists View Pace As Snappy, but Others See Clear Slowing Trend

ECONOMY

By HILARY STOUT
Staff Reporter of THE WALL STREET JOURNAL

Constant Dollar (real) GNP

WASHINGTON – A return to normal farm production following last year's devastating drought propelled the U.S. economy to a vigorous expansion in the first quarter at a 5.5% annual rate, the Commerce Department reported.

Outside of the farm sector, the economy slowed from its fourth-quarter clip, but the pace was still faster than some inflation-conscious Federal Reserve officials have said they would like to see.

Discounting the statistical catch-up from the drought, the gross national product–the value of the nation's output of goods and services–grew at a 3% annual rate in the first three months of 1989, the Commerce Department said. In the fourth quarter, GNP expanded at an annual rate of 2.4%, but the pace would have been 3.5% had it not been for the drought's effects.

All the numbers are adjusted for inflation and for seasonal changes.

GNP Changes
(Seasonally adjusted annual rate after inflation)
■ Advance ▩ Preliminary □ Final 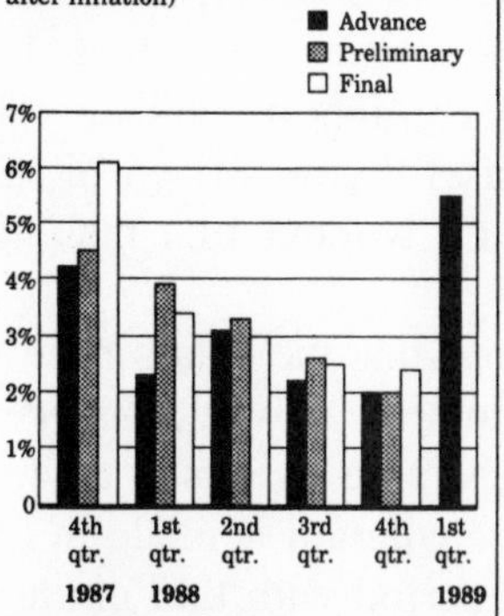
7% 6% 5% 4% 3% 2% 1% 0
4th qtr. 1987 | 1st qtr. 1988 | 2nd qtr. | 3rd qtr. | 4th qtr. | 1st qtr. 1989
Source: Commerce Department

Mild Surprise

Some economists expressed mild surprise that the underlying economic growth continued at so snappy a pace, given the Fed's efforts to curb economic activity by pushing up interest rates. But many others said the GNP numbers show the economy is following a clear slowing trend.

"I think this slowdown is precisely what the doctor ordered," said Lyle Gramley, chief economist of the Mortgage Bankers Association and a former Fed governor. "We were in great danger of the pot boiling over."

Many analysts have feared that the economy's pace was generating inflationary pressures by absorbing too much of the country's industrial capacity and using nearly all of the available work force. Some policy makers at the Fed have made it known they would like to see the economy expand no more than 2.5% this year.

"A pattern of growth that favors exports and investment in plant and equipment is a desirable one for the sustainability of the economic expansion," Commerce Secretary Robert Mosbacher said in a statement issued shortly after the report was released.

Laying Groundwork

Expansion of business investment and sales of products overseas don't generate the worrisome pressures on prices that come from voracious consumer demand. Indeed, investment in new facilities and equipment can ease inflation by laying the groundwork for gains in productivity and efficiency.

Consequently, the GNP report "was basically good news," said James F. Smith, a professor of finance at the University of North Carolina Business School in Chapel Hill. "You've got consumers backing off and businesses continuing to modernize and serve or regain foreign customers."

Current Dollar (nominal) GNP

Yesterday's GNP report contained a historic footnote as the economy, before adjustment for inflation, passed the $5 trillion mark for the first time, hitting a $5.117 trillion annual rate in the quarter. On that unadjusted basis, the economy grew at a 9.7% annual rate in the first quarter.

Rate of Inflation

The report did include evidence that inflation is rising. A price index that measures the change in costs of a fixed basket of goods and services increased to a 5% annual rate in the first quarter from 4.2% in the fourth. Another price measure–known as the implicit price deflator–dropped to 3.9% from 5.3%. Commerce Department economists say the first measure is a more meaningful gauge of inflation because it isn't influenced by changes in the mix of goods and services produced in any one quarter.

Statistical Summary

GROSS NATIONAL PRODUCT

Here are some of the major components of the gross national product expressed in seasonally adjusted annual rates in billions of constant (1982) dollars:

	1st Qtr. 1989	4th Qtr. 1988
GNP	4,088.2	4,033.4
less: inventory chng	53.8	29.1
equals: final sales	4,034.5	4,004.4
Components of Final Sales		
Personal Consumption	2,634.8	2,626.2
Nonresidential Invest.	502.8	491.4
Residential Invest.	194.8	196.6
Net Exports	−95.6	−105.4
Gov't Purchases	797.7	795.5

In the first quarter, the implicit price deflator fell to 3.9% of the 1982 average, from 5.3% in the previous quarter.

Source: *The Wall Street Journal*, April 27, 1989.

year's output (as well as last year's output, next year's, or any year we wish to measure) is calculated in the prices of the base year (1982).

GNP includes only *final* goods and services. This eliminates measuring the same thing more than once at various stages of its production. For instance, bread purchased by the consumer appears in GNP, but both the flour from which the bread is baked and the wheat from which the flour is milled are omitted because the value of the bread comprises the value of all its ingredients. Thus, the economy's output of *all* goods and services is far greater than its output of *final* (GNP) goods and services. We use very little steel, chemicals, or advertising agency services directly. Their value is subsumed in our purchases of well-promoted Chevrolets and Saran Wrap.

Paragraph 1 refers to a 5.5 percent increase in final output. This measurement was made at a *seasonally adjusted annual rate* in the first quarter. Adjusting for seasonal factors merely means correcting the distortion in the data arising from the measurement being taken during this rather than any other quarter. Obviously, no seasonal adjustment is required when a whole year's data is measured, but when the year is divided up and data extracted for a run of months, the risk of distortion attributable to the season is great. For instance, retail trade is particularly heavy around Christmas and particularly light immediately after the first of the year; you could not make a useful comparison of the first quarter's retail sales with the last quarter's without first making a seasonal adjustment.

The reference to "annual rate" shows that the data for the first quarter, which of course covers only three months' activity, has been multiplied by four to increase it to a level comparable to annual data.

The constant-dollar or real GNP calculation is made in order to compare the level of output in one time period with that in another without inflation's distorting impact. If the inflation factor were not removed, you would not know whether differences in dollar value were due to output changes or price changes. Real GNP gives you a dollar value that measures output changes only.

One last point should be made before moving on. The first paragraph referred to the 5.5 percent growth rate as "vigorous." Three percent or better is good, and more than 5 percent is unusual and unsustainable for any length of time. The economy just can't supply (turn out) more than that without an increase in prices because of the limits on our productive capacity at any moment. On the other hand, 5.5 percent is well above the rate of population growth and therefore provides a substantial per capita gain.

Current-Dollar (Nominal) GNP

Nominal (current-dollar) GNP includes inflation and is therefore higher than real (constant-dollar) GNP, which does not. Distinguishing clearly between these expressions will help you avoid a good deal of confusion.

The second paragraph from the end of the article informs you that before adjustment for inflation (i.e., including current, inflated prices) GNP was $5.117 trillion, considerably more than the real figure (at 1982 prices) of $4.0882 trillion, reported in the statistical summary at the end of the article. You can see how rising prices inflate the nominal value of GNP. Both measurements calibrate the same level of output, but the greatly increased value of the current-dollar GNP figure is a direct consequence of the higher level of prices prevailing now.

Rate of Inflation

The last paragraph reports that the *implicit price deflator* "dropped to 3.9% from 5.3%." This index yields the broadest measure of inflation, since GNP is the most broadly based measure of economic activity. It is derived by dividing current-dollar (nominal) GNP, which includes inflation, by constant-dollar (real) GNP, which does not include inflation. Dividing the figure that includes inflation by the figure that does not provides a measurement of price increase.

The more familiar consumer price index includes consumption expenditures only, while the implicit price deflator includes production for business and government use as well. The producer price index, which

Current Dollar (Nominal) GNP–Second Paragraph from end of article

...lion mark for the first time, hitting a $5.117 trillion annual rate in the quarter. On that unadjusted basis, the economy grew at a 9.7% annual rate in the first quarter.

Source: *The Wall Street Journal*, April 27, 1989.

Rate of Inflation–Last Paragraph

The report did include evidence that inflation is rising. A price index that measures the change in costs of a fixed basket of goods and services increased to a 5% annual rate in the first quarter from 4.2% in the fourth. Another price measure—known as the implicit price deflator—dropped to 3.9% from 5.3%. Commerce Department economists say the first measure is a more meaningful gauge of inflation because it isn't influenced by changes in the mix of goods and services produced in any one quarter.

Source: *The Wall Street Journal*, April 27, 1989.

is explained later in this chapter, covers wholesale prices of goods but not services.

Statistical Summary

The statistical summary at the end of the article provides a convenient breakdown of the major GNP components.

Now you are ready to put GNP's current performance in historical perspective. Compare it with Chart 7–1.

Statistical Summary–End of Article

GROSS NATIONAL PRODUCT

Here are some of the major components of the gross national product expressed in seasonally adjusted annual rates in billions of constant (1982) dollars:

	1st Qtr. 1989	4th Qtr. 1988
GNP	**4,088.2**	**4,033.4**
less: inventory chng	53.8	29.1
equals: final sales	4,034.5	4,004.4
Components of Final Sales		
Personal Consumption	2,634.8	2,626.2
Nonresidential Invest.	502.8	491.4
Residential Invest.	194.8	196.6
Net Exports	–95.6	–105.4
Gov't Purchases	797.7	795.5

In the first quarter, the implicit price deflator fell to 3.9% of the 1982 average, from 5.3% in the previous quarter.

Source: *The Wall Street Journal*, April 27, 1989.

CHART 7–1
Gross National Product (GNP) In Constant (1982) Dollars; Quarterly Change in GNP at Annual Rates

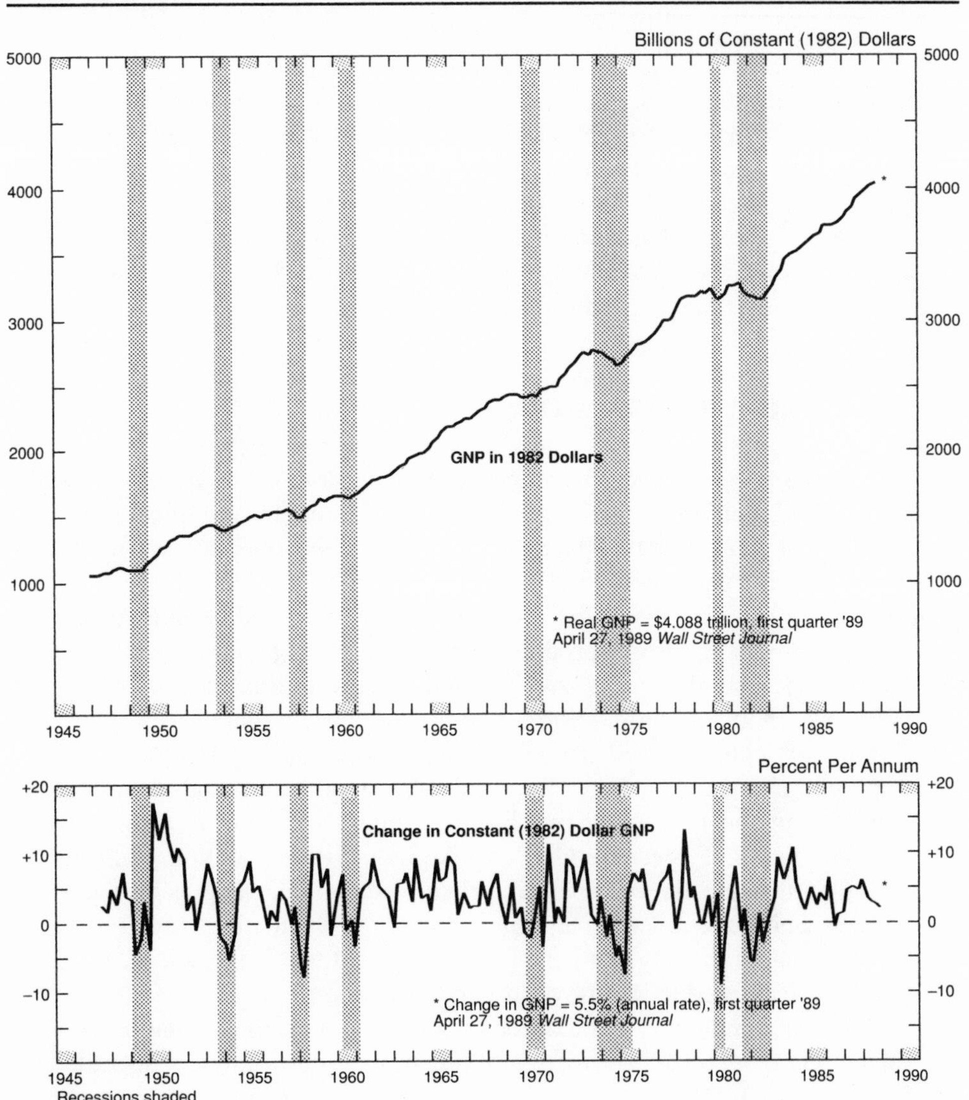

Source: U.S. Department of Commerce, *Business Conditions Digest* and *Handbook of Cyclical Indicators*, series 50 and 50c.

The top graph portrays the actual level of GNP, while the bottom graph depicts quarterly percentage changes at annual rates. When the bottom series is above the zero line, GNP has increased; a drop in GNP is indicated by points below the zero line.

As you look at these graphs, pay special attention to the setback to GNP growth during the back-to-back recessions of 1980 and 1981–82. You can also see that GNP shot out of that ditch in 1983, although it was dented again during the minislowdown of 1984. Since then GNP has grown moderately.

Industrial production and capacity utilization will mirror GNP's performance and also provide important additional detail, so you should now become acquainted with these series.

INDUSTRIAL PRODUCTION

The Wall Street Journal reports the Federal Reserve's data on *industrial production* in an article that usually appears midmonth. A typical report was published on Friday, March 17, 1989. The headline, accompanying chart, second paragraph, and statistical table at the end of the story summarize matters, while the article provides detail and commentary.

The index of industrial production measures changes in the output of the mining, manufacturing, and gas and electric utilities sectors of our economy. Industrial production is a narrower concept than GNP because it omits agriculture, construction, wholesale and retail trade, transportation, communications, services, finance, government, and American activities in the rest of the world. Industrial production is also more volatile than GNP, because GNP, unlike industrial production, includes activities that are largely spared cyclical fluctuation, such as services, finance, and government. The brunt of cyclical fluctuations falls on the mining, manufacturing, and public utilities sectors. Nonetheless, GNP and industrial production move in parallel fashion.

Industrial production is measured by an *index*, a technique that focuses on the relative size and fluctuation of physical output without concern for its dollar value. To construct the index, a base year (1977) was selected to serve as a benchmark and assigned a value of 100.0. (Think of it as 100 percent.) Data for all other months and years is then expressed in relative proportion (numerical ratio) to the data for the base year. For example, according to the statistical summary at the end of the article,

Industrial Output Was Flat in February; Operating Rate, Housing Starts Dropped

By Hilary Stout
Staff Reporter of The Wall Street Journal

WASHINGTON—Three new government reports show further signs of slowing in major sectors of the economy.

Industrial Production

U.S. industry in February failed to increase its production for the first time in a year, the Federal Reserve reported. At the same time, the Fed said, the nation's factories, utilities and mines used a slightly smaller portion of their capacity than in January. And new housing construction plunged 11.4% in February, the Commerce Department reported.

Many economists have been hoping for slower economic growth, contending that the economy has expanded to the point where rapid advancement is breeding inflation. The Fed has been actively trying to rein in the economy by coaxing up interest rates. But until recently, report after report had signaled persistent vigor in the economy.

Capacity Utilization

The leveling-off of industrial production in February followed a 0.4% rise in December, according to the Fed's report. Meanwhile, industry's operating rate fell to 84.3% of capacity from 84.5% in January, the first decline since September, the Fed said.

But Edward Yardeni, chief economist at Prudential-Bache Securities Inc., said that although the numbers show the economy "isn't booming," it's "expanding in the right places."

The industrial production figures, for example, reflected declines in production of automobiles and construction supplies but a rising level of output of business equipment.

The growth in business equipment "confirms the view that capacity is expanding . . .and the fact that the capacity utilization rate is down in the face of flat production shows that capacity is expanding," Mr. Yardeni said.

Tight capacity is worrisome because it can lead to production bottlenecks and shortages, which can drive prices up.

In the area of production, Mr. Yardeni said, "A lot of weakness was in car sales. I have no problem with an economy where we have consumer spending growing at a slower pace and capital spending at a faster pace."

He added: "If we keep this up, we'll start looking like Japan."

Industrial Production

In percent (1977=100), seasonally adjusted.

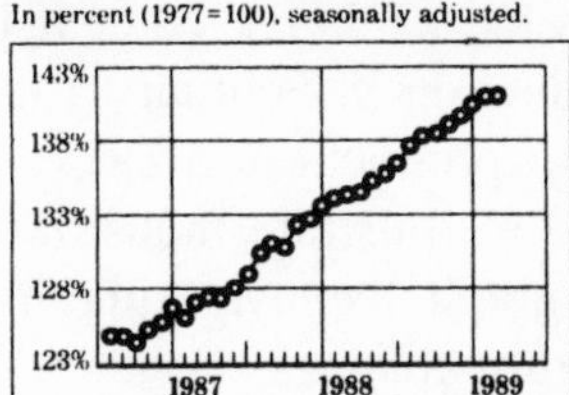

Statistical Summary

INDUSTRIAL PRODUCTION

Here is a summary of the Federal Reserve Board's report on industrial production in February. The figures are seasonally adjusted.

	% change from Jan. 1989	Feb. 1988
Total	0.0	5.0
Consumer goods	0.1	5.8
Business equipment	0.8	8.5
Defense and space	−0.2	−5.4
Manufacturing only	0.0	5.7
Durable goods	0.1	6.1
Nondurable goods	−0.1	5.0
Mining	−1.8	0.0
Utilities	1.9	1.2

The industrial production index for February stood at 141.1% of the 1977 average.

Source: *The Wall Street Journal*, March 17, 1989.

Industrial Production

In percent (1977=100), seasonally adjusted.

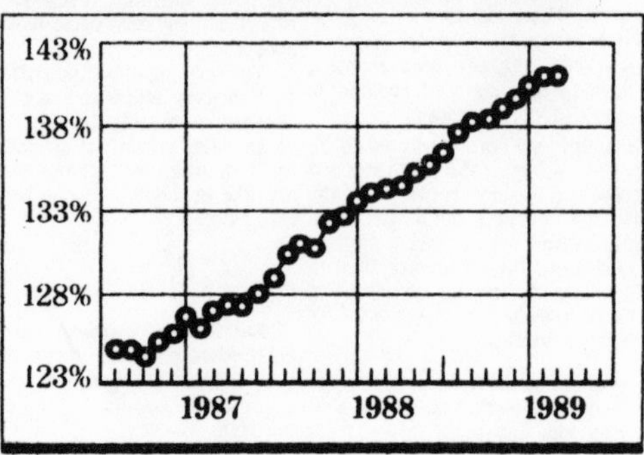

Source: *The Wall Street Journal*, March 17, 1989.

industrial production had an index value of 141.1 percent in February 1989. This means that industrial production in February 1989 was 41.1 percent higher than the average rate of production in 1977.

As with GNP, two graphs are used to illustrate industrial production (see Chart 7–2 on page 115). The top graph displays actual index values, and the bottom graph illustrates monthly changes.

Statistical Summary–End of Article

INDUSTRIAL PRODUCTION

Here is a summary of the Federal Reserve Board's report on industrial production in February. The figures are seasonally adjusted.

	% change from	
	Jan. 1989	Feb. 1988
Total	0.0	5.0
Consumer goods	0.1	5.8
Business equipment	0.8	8.5
Defense and space	−0.2	−5.4
Manufacturing only	0.0	5.7
Durable goods	0.1	6.1
Nondurable goods	−0.1	5.0
Mining	−1.8	0.0
Utilities	1.9	1.2

The industrial production index for February stood at 141.1% of the 1977 average.

Source: *The Wall Street Journal*, March 17, 1989.

CHART 7–2
Industrial Production Index (1977 = 100); **Quarterly Change in Index at Annual Rates**

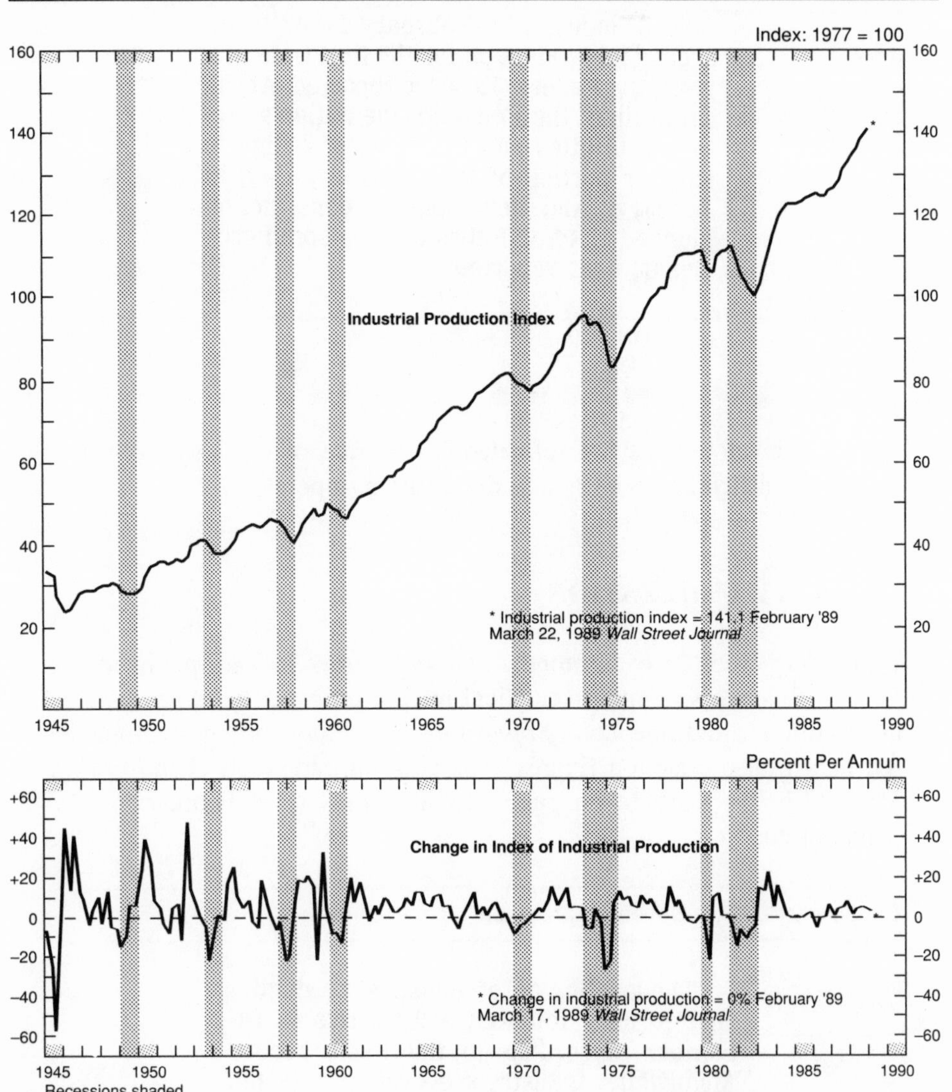

Source: U.S. Department of Commerce, *Business Conditions Digest* and *Handbook of Cyclical Indicators*, series 47 and 47c.

Industrial Production–Second Paragraph

U.S. industry in February failed to increase its production for the first time in a year, the Federal Reserve reported. At the same time, the Fed said, the nation's factories, utilities and mines used a slightly smaller portion of their capacity than in January. And new housing construction plunged 11.4% in February, the Commerce Department reported.

Source: *The Wall Street Journal*, March 17, 1989.

These developments are reflected in the rate of capacity utilization and in the efficiency with which the economy operates.

CAPACITY UTILIZATION

In the third week of each month, *The Wall Street Journal* publishes the Federal Reserve's monthly statistical release on *capacity utilization*, or, as it is often called, the *factory operating rate*. Frequently it accompanies the industrial production figures. The seventh paragraph of the Friday, March 17, 1989 article on page 113 informs you of February's 84.3 percent rate.

Capacity Utilization–Seventh Paragraph

The leveling-off of industrial production in February followed a 0.4% rise in December, according to the Fed's report. Meanwhile, industry's operating rate fell to 84.3% of capacity from 84.5% in January, the first decline since September, the Fed said.

Source: *The Wall Street Journal*, March 17, 1989.

Capacity utilization is the rate at which mining, manufacturing, and public utilities industries operate, expressed as a percentage of the maximum rate at which they could operate under existing conditions. Putting the matter differently, think of capacity utilization as measuring what these industries are currently producing compared (in percentage terms) to the most they could produce using all of their present resources. Thus, if an industry produces 80 tons of product in a year, while having plant and equipment at its disposal capable of producing 100 tons a year, that industry is operating at 80 percent of capacity; its capacity utilization is 80 percent.

Capacity utilization is a short-run concept determined by a company's current physical limits; at any moment in which capacity utilization is reported, it is assumed that the company's plant and equipment cannot be increased, although labor and other inputs can. This defines the short run. Although manufacturing industry continually adds new plant and equipment, it is useful to snap a photograph at a particular moment to enable measurement and comparison.

What bearing does capacity utilization have on the efficiency or productivity of industry? Consider a hypothetical analogy. Your car operates more efficiently at 50 miles per hour than at 70 miles per hour if its maximum speed is 80, for you will obtain better gas mileage at the lower speed. Efficiency is expressed as a relationship between inputs (gas gallons) and outputs (miles driven). Your car's engine operates more efficiently at lower speeds, or at lower levels of capacity utilization.

You are therefore confronted with the problem of diminishing returns: as your speed increases, you obtain fewer miles for each additional gallon of gas. At 50 miles per hour, you can go 30 miles on an additional gallon of gas; at 52 miles per hour, 29 miles on an additional gallon; at 54 miles per hour, 28 miles; and so on. Your output (miles) per unit of input (gallon) falls as you push toward full capacity utilization (maximum speed).

Likewise, as capacity utilization increases, an industry also passes the point of diminishing returns. This may be at 70 percent, 80 percent, or 90 percent of capacity utilization, depending on the industry, but the point will ultimately be reached where the percentage increases in output will become smaller than the percentage increases in input. For instance, a 15 percent increase in labor input, once we have passed the point of diminishing returns, may provide only a 10 percent increase in output. This phenomenon does not occur because of some mystical mathematical relationship nor because people are just like automobile engines. There are common-sense reasons for it, and you probably know many of them already.

First, at low levels of capacity utilization, there is ample time to inspect, maintain, and repair equipment; accidental damage can be held to a minimum; and production increases can be achieved easily in a smoothly efficient plant. Above a certain level of capacity utilization, however, management finds it more difficult to inspect, maintain, and repair equipment because of the plant's heavier operating schedule. Perhaps a second shift of workers has been added or additional overtime scheduled. There is less time for equipment maintenance, and accidental damage becomes inevitable. The labor force is in place and on the payroll, and production does increase, but not as rapidly as does labor input, because equipment frequently breaks down.

Second, as production increases and more labor is hired, the last people hired are less experienced and usually less efficient than the older workers; furthermore, crowding and fatigue can become a problem if more overtime is scheduled. Poor work quality and accidental damage result. All of this ensures that output will not increase as rapidly as labor input.

Third, low levels of capacity utilization occur at the trough of a recession. Business firms typically suffer a sharp drop in profit, if not actual losses, and under these circumstances, the employer reduces the work force as much as possible. In fact, he or she usually reduces it more than the drop in output, once the decision to cut back has been made. Why more than the drop in output? Because by the trough of recession, the seriousness of the situation is recognized, and industry has embarked on a thorough restructuring. The alarm has sounded and costs (work force) are slashed. That's why recession often generates the sharpest increases in efficiency.

Even after output has begun to recover, an extended period of labor reduction may continue as part of a general cost-cutting program. As recovery boosts capacity utilization, however, hiring additional workers becomes inevitable. When a factory reaches full capacity utilization near the peak of a boom, the cost-cutting program will be long forgotten as management scrambles for additional labor in order to meet the barrage of orders. At this point, additions to labor are greater than increments in output, even though (to repeat) output will be rising somewhat.

You can summarize business's decisions regarding labor as follows. During rapid expansion and into economic boom, when orders are heavy and capacity utilization is strained, business will sacrifice efficiency and short-run profits to maintain customer loyalty. Management adds labor more rapidly than output increases in order to get the job done. But when the recession hits in earnest, and it becomes apparent that orders will not recover for some time, management cuts labor costs to the bone with layoffs and a freeze on hiring. This is especially true during a prolonged recession, such as that of 1981–82, which followed on the heels of an earlier recession (in 1980) and an incomplete recovery. Even after recovery and expansion begin, however, business will still attempt to operate with a reduced labor force in order to reap the benefits of cost cutting in the form of higher profits. Operating efficiency (productivity) improves rapidly, and it will not be threatened until the expansion heats up and boom conditions develop.

Remember the motor in your car? Efficiency is expressed as the relationship between inputs (fuel) and outputs (distance traveled). It is useful to think of the economy as if it were a machine, like the engine. Since your engine is fixed in size (at any moment in time), you can only push a finite amount of fuel through it. Depressing the accelerator rapidly increases your speed and the distance traveled, but the increment in fuel used is greater than the increment in speed and distance. Hence the efficiency of your engine falls despite your greater speed and distance. You are getting fewer miles per gallon and it's taking more fuel to go a mile because you are driving faster.

Just as a bigger engine would help you accelerate more quickly, more industrial capacity would permit the economy to operate more efficiently. But for the moment it is limited to the amount at hand, making it useful to speak about the rate of capacity utilization now. And it is important to realize that, like your car engine, the economy becomes less efficient if it is pushed too hard.

Now compare capacity utilization's historical record with that of GNP and industrial production, noting once again the figure reported in the March 17, 1989 *Journal* article (see Chart 7–3 on page 120). Each of the series examined thus far (GNP, industrial production, capacity utilization) tells the same story. The economy has moved well past the trough of the cycle since 1981–82, although the impact of the 1984 minislowdown is clear in all three series. Note especially the plateau in capacity utilization that lingered long after 1984.

Now you can discern the Fed's reasons for that 1984 slowdown. Too rapid an increase in output and capacity utilization would have

CHART 7–3
GNP, Industrial Production, and Capacity Utilization

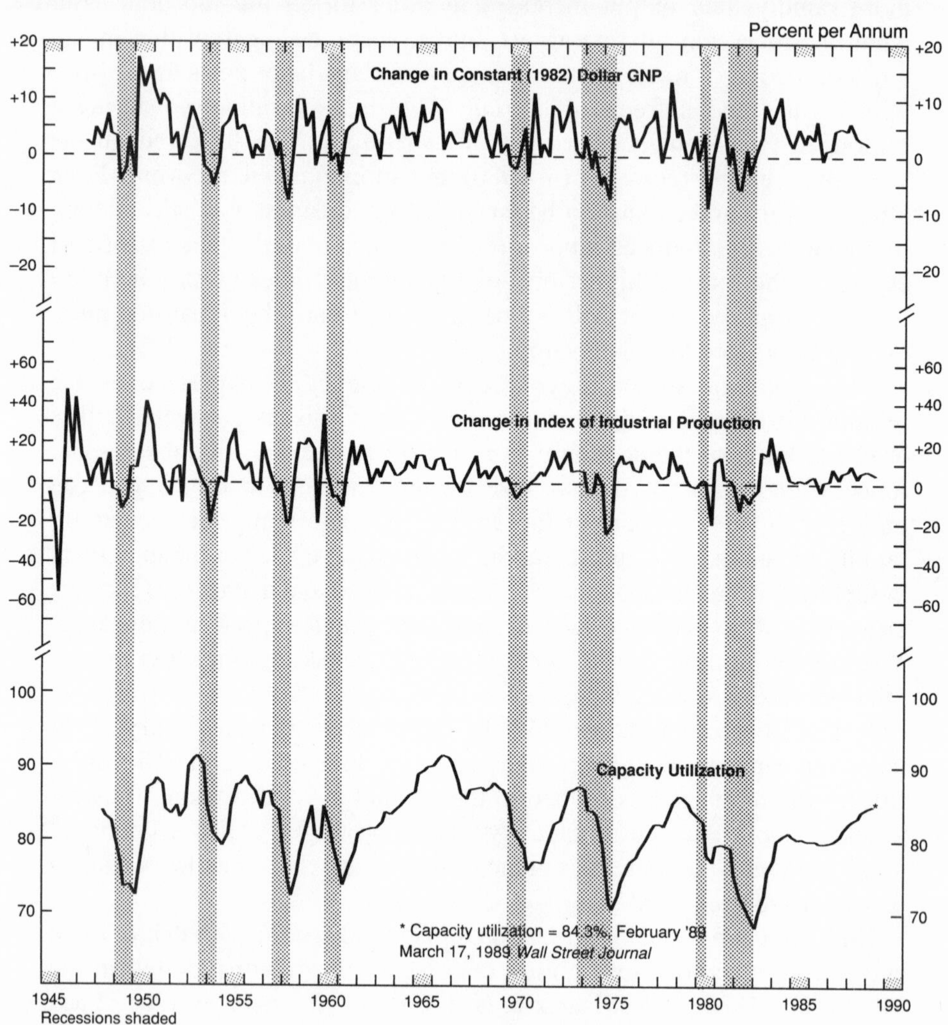

Source: U.S. Department of Commerce, *Business Conditions Digest* and *Handbook of Cyclical Indicators*, series 47c, 50c and 82.

eliminated any gain in efficiency created by the slack conditions during and immediately following the 1981–82 recession. The Fed wanted slow, steady growth, not a rush to full capacity utilization, so it held back the economy in 1984 because capacity utilization had improved too quickly (from a 70 percent to an 80 percent rate in about one year).

The mid-80s capacity utilization plateau (hovering around 80 percent for almost five years) explains the low inflation rates we have had throughout the 1980s. The economy had not been pushed to a sufficiently high level of capacity utilization to produce inefficiencies by the late 1980s, although it had approached the 85 percent range.

Capacity utilization approached 85% in the late 80s because of our surging exports and strong markets for producers durable goods (see Chapter 15). But these sectors were not large enough to overwhelm the consumer sectors which still had considerable slack.

When you examine the 1970s, on the other hand, you can see that the rate of capacity utilization periodically rose to the 90 percent level, generating the inefficiency that brings on inflation. That's why the severe cyclical fluctuations of the 70s were bad for the economy and the slow, steady growth of the 80s was good.

Capacity Utilization and Inflation

- Robust consumer demand for housing and autos and other durables leads to surging capacity utilization and inflation.
- Capacity utilization over 85% generates inflation.

The next series in this chapter, labor productivity and unit labor costs, will provide the statistical measurements needed to calibrate these fluctuations in efficiency.

LABOR PRODUCTIVITY AND UNIT LABOR COSTS

The Wall Street Journal reports the U.S. Department of Labor's preliminary release on *labor productivity* about a month after the end of the quarter, and publishes a revision about a month later. The Wednesday,

March 8, 1989 article presents revisions for the fourth quarter of 1988, which appeared earlier in preliminary form.

The first and sixth paragraphs inform you that a 3.7 percent improvement in output, combined with a 3.6 percent increase in labor input,

---

Nonfarm Worker Output Rose at 0.1% Annual Rate

By a WALL STREET JOURNAL *Staff Reporter*

Labor Productivity — WASHINGTON—Worker productivity in nonfarm businesses edged up at a 0.1% annual rate in the fourth quarter, the Labor Department said in revisions of an earlier report that said the figure was unchanged.

Productivity, or output for each hour of work, climbed at an annual rate of 2% in the third quarter and dropped at a 2.4% rate in the second.

The department estimated that productivity for all businesses, including farms, declined at a 2% annual rate in the fourth quarter, the same as originally reported. A drop in farm output stemming from last summer's drought was largely responsible.

Growth in productivity is critical to the economy if it is to continue expanding without inflation.

Unit labor costs increased at an annual rate of 5.6% in the fourth quarter, as the department initially calculated, after increasing at a 3.7% annual rate in the third quarter and a 6.8% annual rate in the second.

Output and Hours — The department changed its estimate of the rise in fourth-quarter nonfarm output to an annual rate of 3.7% from a rate of 3.6%. It altered its calculation of the increase in hours laborers worked to an annual rate of 3.6% from 3.5%.

For all of 1988, nonfarm productivity grew 1.4%, a significant improvement from the 1987 rise of 0.8%.

Source: *The Wall Street Journal*, March 8, 1989.

Labor Productivity–First Paragraph

WASHINGTON–Worker productivity in nonfarm businesses edged up at a 0.1% annual rate in the fourth quarter, the Labor Department said in revisions of an earlier report that said the figure was unchanged.

Output and Hours–Sixth Paragraph

The department changed its estimate of the rise in fourth-quarter nonfarm output to an annual rate of 3.7% from a rate of 3.6%. It altered its calculation of the increase in hours laborers worked to an annual rate of 3.6% from 3.5%.

Source: *The Wall Street Journal*, March 8, 1989.

drove up output per worker by 0.1 percent for all *nonfarm business*. It's simple subtraction: 3.7 minus 3.6 equals (roughly) 0.1.

Chart 7–4 on page 124 presents the record for all business (including farms). The series are similar.

Labor productivity measures output or production per unit of labor input (e.g., output per hour) and is *the most important gauge* of our nation's efficiency. Its significance cannot be overemphasized, for *per capita real income cannot improve*—and thus the country's standard of living cannot rise—*without an increase in per capita production.*

Unit labor cost measures the cost of labor per unit of output. Thus, unit labor cost is the *inverse* of labor productivity, since unit labor costs fall as labor productivity rises, and vice versa. Unit labor cost tells you how much added labor is required to produce an additional unit of output. Because labor is hired for a wage, requiring more labor time to produce each unit of output will raise labor costs per unit of output, and vice versa.

CHART 7–4
Productivity: Output per Hour, All Persons, Private Business Sector (1977 = 100); **Change in Output per Hour** (smoothed)

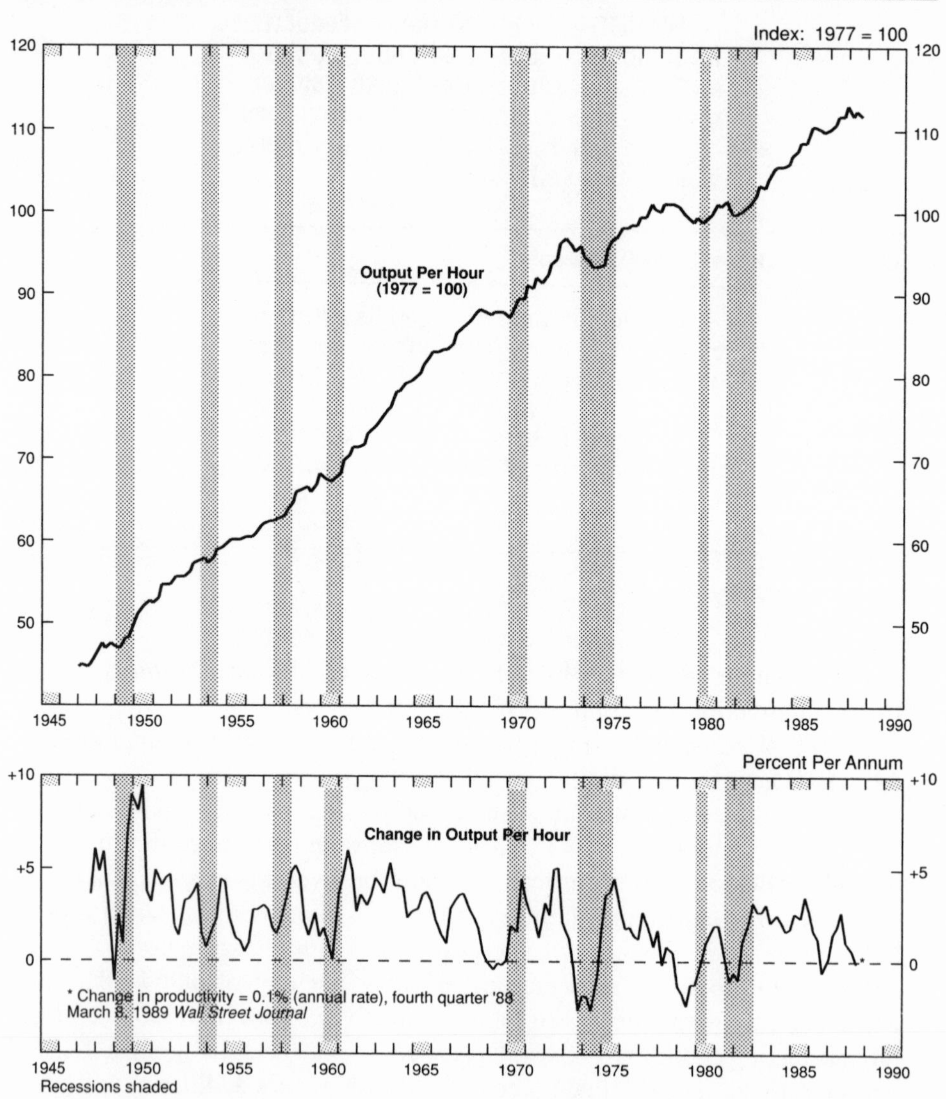

Source: U.S. Department of Commerce, *Business Conditions Digest* and *Handbook of Cyclical Indicators*, series 370 and 370c.

Consider, for instance, a factory that assembles hand-held calculators. If the production of a calculator has required an hour of labor and a technological innovation permits the production of two calculators per hour, labor productivity has doubled, from one to two calculators per hour. The output per hour of work is twice what it was.

If the wage rate is $10 per hour, and before the innovation an hour of work was required to produce a calculator, the labor cost per unit of output was then $10. After the innovation, however, two calculators can be produced in an hour, or one calculator in half an hour, so unit labor cost has fallen to $5. Note that as labor productivity doubled, from one to two calculators per hour, unit labor costs were halved, from $10 to $5 per unit of output. The gain in labor productivity drove down unit labor costs without any change in the wage rate.

Now compare the record of labor productivity and unit labor costs with the other indicators examined so far (see Chart 7–5 on page 126).

GNP, industrial production, and capacity utilization together define the business cycle in the 1970s. Since 1970 their fluctuations have indicated prosperity and recession. You can also see that labor productivity plunged and unit labor costs soared with the peak of each cycle in the 1970s. Then labor productivity improved and unit labor costs declined with each recession and into the next recovery. But as soon as expansion got under way, labor productivity's growth began to weaken and unit labor costs began to rise, until productivity slumped and costs peaked at the end of the boom.

And this brings you full circle to the discussion of efficiency included in the earlier investigation of capacity utilization: the economy's efficiency deteriorated in the 70s with each boom and improved in each recession and into recovery. All that this section has done is to provide the labels and devices (labor productivity and unit labor costs) necessary to measure that efficiency. During boom conditions, efficiency (labor productivity) declines and expenses (unit labor costs) mount. During recession the opposite is true.

At first you might ask yourself, "Why would management ever place itself in the position of risking a drop in the efficiency of its operations in order to push output and capacity utilization too far? Why not limit production to an efficient level of operations, at say 80 percent capacity utilization, rather than risk declining productivity at 90 percent of capacity utilization?"

The answer is easy, if you put yourself in management's shoes. Suppose you're the boss at Bethlehem Steel, and Ford Motor Co. is

CHART 7–5
GNP, Industrial Production, Capacity Utilization, Labor Productivity, and Unit Labor Costs

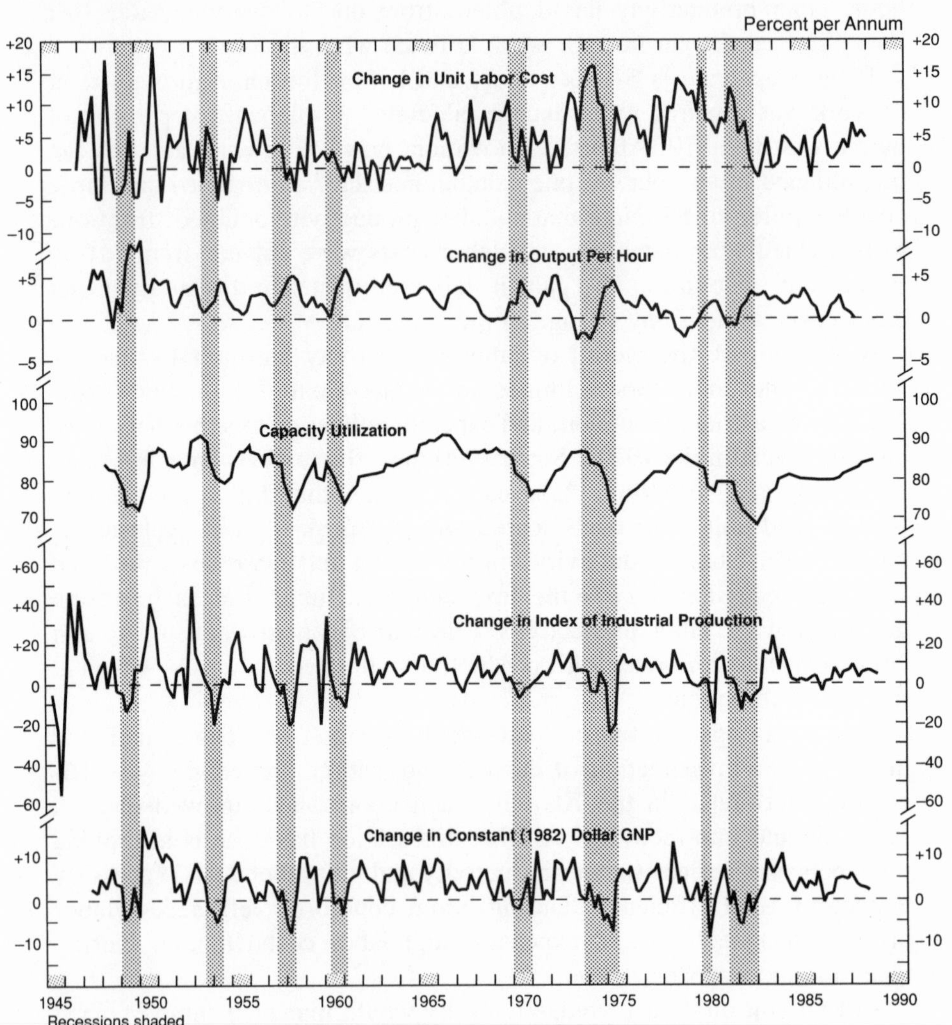

Source: U.S. Department of Commerce, *Business Conditions Digest* and *Handbook of Cyclical Indicators*, series 47c, 50c, 82, and 370c; Bureau of Labor Statistics.

your best customer. Suppose also that you're running two production shifts at your mill, sixteen hours a day, and a small maintenance crew is employed during the remaining eight-hour shift. The maintenance crew inspects, maintains, and repairs the equipment so that everything is up and running during the daily sixteen hours of production.

Now Ford calls and says their Taurus model has been a big success and they need more steel in a hurry. Do you tell Ford that you're sorry, that you're running flat out, that you have no idle capacity, and that they should come back during the next recession when you have plenty of idle capacity and would be happy to take their order? Only if you want to lose your best customer. No, you tell them you will move heaven and earth to fill their order, and you cancel the maintenance shift and put on another production shift.

Putting on another shift of workers increases the size of your production crew (and labor costs) by 50 percent (from sixteen to twenty-four hours a day). Yet your output increases by only 30 percent because of periodic breakdowns in equipment that cannot be properly maintained. But if you only require a 30 percent increase in output in order to fill the order, you may very well be willing to put up with a 50 percent increase in labor hours and costs. Sure, output per worker (productivity) falls on this order and maybe you won't turn a profit either. That's okay as long as you keep your best customer. You're interested in maximizing your profit in the long run, not the short run.

As a result, you've met your deadline by pushing your mill's output to the maximum. Productivity has declined and costs have increased. But that's acceptable, especially if you can pass those higher costs on in the form of higher prices (the subject of the next section of this chapter).

The charts inform you that productivity growth was moderate during the 80s as output grew more rapidly than labor input. The economy was far better off than in the 70s, when periodic declines in productivity were associated with excessive rates of capacity utilization.

Productivity and the Cycle

- The economy is like your car's engine—far more efficient at a steady, moderate pace than in stop-and-go traffic.
- If you push the accelerator to the floor and rev the engine (high capacity utilization), efficiency (productivity) drops.

Turn now to the object of all the effort to contain costs: producer prices.

PRODUCER PRICES

The *producer price index*, until recently referred to as the wholesale price index, is compiled by the U.S. Department of Labor and shows the changes in prices charged by producers of finished goods—changes that are, of course, reflected in the prices consumers must pay. The Labor Department's new release on producer prices is usually published by *The Wall Street Journal* on the third Monday of the month.

The Monday, March 20, 1989 article is an example, and the headline and second paragraph tell you that the producer price index rose 1.0 percent in February 1989. The chart accompanying the article (see page 130) shows the index at 112.1 (1982 = 100).

Despite the article's alarm at February's increase, Chart 7–6 (see page 131) confirms that inflation for most of the 80s, as measured by the producer price index, was still well below the double-digit levels of the 1970s. The drop since the 1979–80 peak has been dramatic.

You can also see from Chart 7–7 on page 132 that in the 70s the cyclical trends in producer prices mirrored those of unit labor costs. With each boom in output and capacity utilization, productivity dropped and unit labor costs rose, driving producer prices up. Then, when recession hit and output and capacity utilization fell, improved labor productivity and lower unit labor costs were reflected in reduced inflation. The 1981–82 recession illustrates the principle: inflation's trend followed unit labor costs downward. As the economy's efficiency improved, stable prices followed on the heels of stable costs. Inflation remained low throughout the 1980s because unit labor costs increased at a moderate pace.

"But isn't it true," you may ask "that moderate wage increases restrained unit labor costs in the 1980s? Perhaps the emphasis on productivity is misplaced and we should instead focus attention on wages as the driving force propelling prices upward."

True, wage increases subsided in the low-inflation 80s, contributing to the meager growth in unit labor costs. But generally speaking, *wage rates follow the cycle, they do not lead it*. Wages lagged behind prices during inflation's surge in the late 70s and fell less rapidly than prices in the early 80s. If boom conditions return and sharp cost increases due to

Producer-Price Jump of 1% in February Fuels Inflation Fears and Rocks Markets

Spurt, After January Surge, Costs Stocks 48.57 Points And Sets Bonds Reeling

By David Wessel
And Hilary Stout
Staff Reporters of The Wall Street Journal

WASHINGTON—Inflation is busting out all over.

Producer Prices

In February, for the second month in a row, producer prices rose 1%, the equivalent of a 12.7% annual rate, the Labor Department said. Not only were there sharp rises in food and energy prices, which sometimes show wide swings from month to month, but prices of other finished goods from flatware to pharmaceuticals also shot up.

Although the Bush administration continued to predict that inflation will abate, private economists expressed alarm, and prices on financial markets plunged. The Dow Jones Industrial Average fell 48.57 points Friday. Bond prices plummeted, pushing up long-term yields on government bonds to their highest level in more than six months.

Price increases of this magnitude, if they continue, "cannot be absorbed by the economy without tremendous negative consequences," said Dirk Van Dongen, president of the National Association of Wholesalers-Distributors.

But Michael Boskin, the chief White House economist, said he expects the inflation figures "to subside to more-reasonable levels in the coming months." He emphasized the need to "remain vigilant" against inflation, but said, "We had expected a couple of bad months of inflation numbers."

Inflation specialist Donald Ratajczak, a Georgia State University economist, didn't react so calmly. "Back-to-back double digits! If that's not inflation, I'm going to send them a pair of glasses."

'Me-Too Pricing'

He warned, "We're starting to get what I call me-too pricing." Producers in some industries where cost pressures aren't substantial are raising prices anyhow—simply because everyone else is, he explained. "That's a sign that inflationary expectations are greater than we thought," he said.

Signs that inflation is accelerating—and the strong reaction from financial markets to Friday's report—increase the chances that the Federal Reserve will raise interest rates further in order to slow the economy and relieve pressure on prices.

The producer-price report capped a week of confusing economic data for February. A week earlier, the government said unemployment fell to 5.1%, a 15-year low, and employers added 289,000 jobs. A few days later, however, other reports showed retail sales falling in February, industrial production unchanged for the first time in a year and factories' use of capacity declining, all hints of an economic slowdown that would lessen the chances of an inflationary outbreak.

The government's index of consumer prices rose 0.6% in January, the fastest clip in two years. The report for February comes out tomorrow.

Fastest Rising Prices

Increase in producer price of selected consumer goods

	FEBRUARY*	PAST 12 MONTHS
Vegetables	35.3%	38.1%
Processed turkeys	5.3	28.8
Household flatware	4.1	12.4
Gasoline	4.1	5.6
Consumer paper goods	2.9	8.0
Prescription drugs	1.5	10.0
Books	1.2	6.6
Natural gas	1.9	9.3
All consumer goods	1.2	5.9
All finished goods	1.0	5.3

*Seasonally adjusted, except books and natural gas

Source: Bureau of Labor Statistics

The February increase in producer prices was more widespread than in January. Excluding volatile food and energy prices, producer prices climbed 0.6% in February, compared with 0.4% in January and 0.7% in December.

Prices of household flatware, for instance, climbed 4.1% in February, and stand 12.4% higher than a year earlier. Producers blame higher prices for nickel and chrome. These increases have forced up stainless-steel prices by 50% over the past year, said Peter Fobare, vice president, sales, at Oneida Ltd. Silversmiths. Oneida absorbed the higher costs through the end of 1988 and had planned on doing the same through this spring. "The increases became too large to not pass along," he said.

Prescription-drug prices rose 1.5% in February after rising 1% in January. Drug companies, which have been raising prices 8% or 9% a year, now are charging fully 10% more than they did a year earlier, the Labor Department said. "It's an early sign that something may be changing," said Thomas Simone, vice president and controller at McKesson Corp., a major drug distributor based in San Francisco.

Some industry executives see signs of buying in anticipation of further price increases, the kind of market behavior that makes economists worry. Mr. Simone noted that recent data may be distorted because some companies put off until February price increases that customarily would have been made in January. That would tend to overstate the Labor Department's seasonally adjusted figure for February.

Green Squash

Food prices in February rose 1.2%, led by a 35.3% increase in fresh and dried vegetables. And those increases apparently are continuing in March. "Two weeks ago, the price of 25 pounds of green beans from Florida went up within three days from $12 to $24, and 20 pounds of green squash went up from $8.60 to $20," said Rob Bildner,

Please Turn to Page A6, Column 1

Source: *The Wall Street Journal*, March 20, 1989.

Producer Prices–Second Paragraph

In February, for the second month in a row, producer prices rose 1%, the equivalent of a 12.7% annual rate, the Labor Department said. Not only were there sharp rises in food and energy prices, which sometimes show wide swings from month to month, but prices of other finished goods from flatware to pharmaceuticals also shot up.

Source: *The Wall Street Journal*, March 20, 1989.

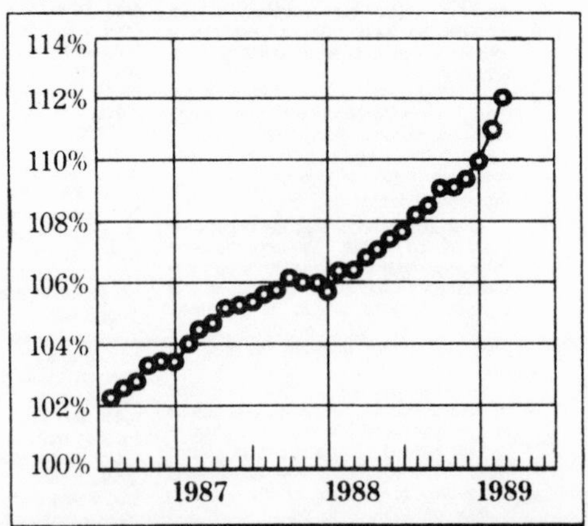

PRODUCER PRICES on finished goods in February rose at a seasonally adjusted rate of 112.1% of the 1982 average, vs. 111% in January, the Labor Department reports. (See story on page A2.)

Source: *The Wall Street Journal*, March 20, 1989.

CHART 7–6
Producer Price Index (1982 = 100); **Quarterly Change in Index at Annual Rates** (smoothed)

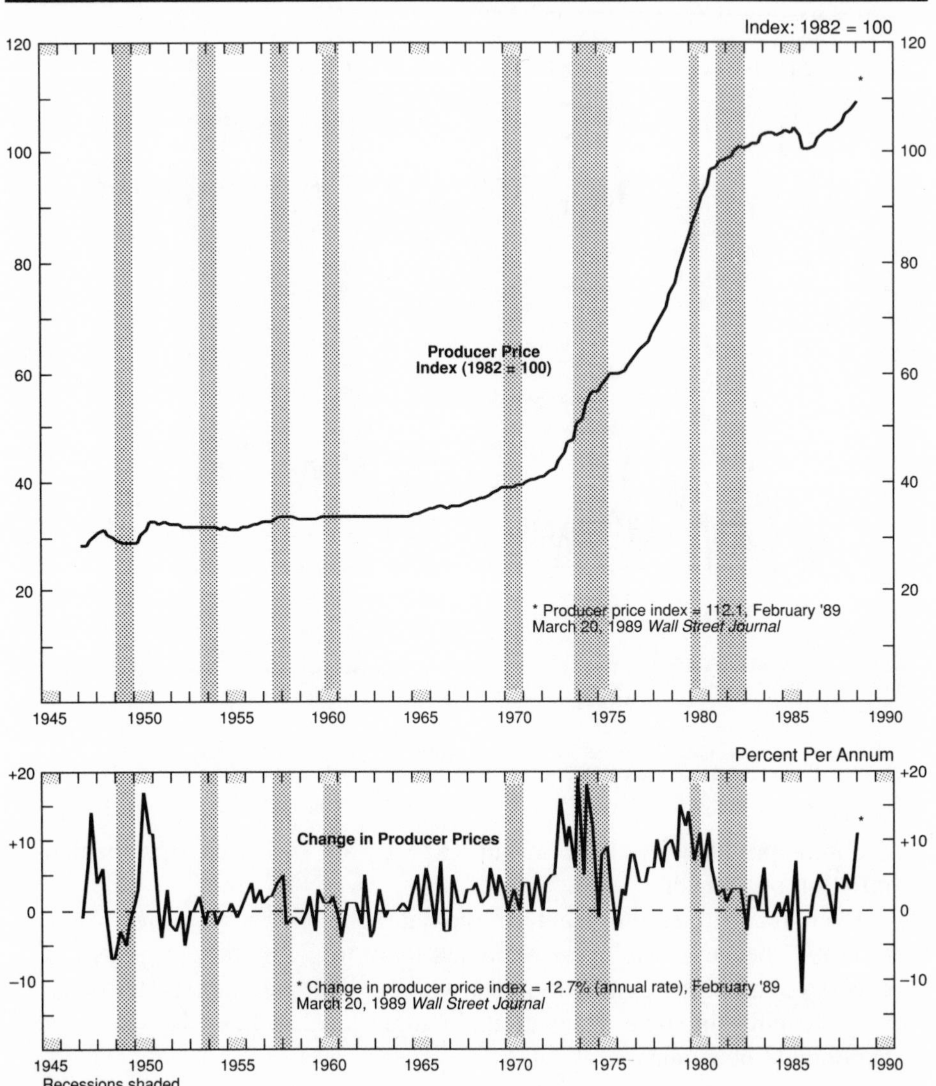

Source: U.S. Department of Commerce, *Business Conditions Digest* and *Handbook of Cyclical Indicators*, series 334 and 334c.

CHART 7–7
Changes in Unit Labor Costs and Producer Prices

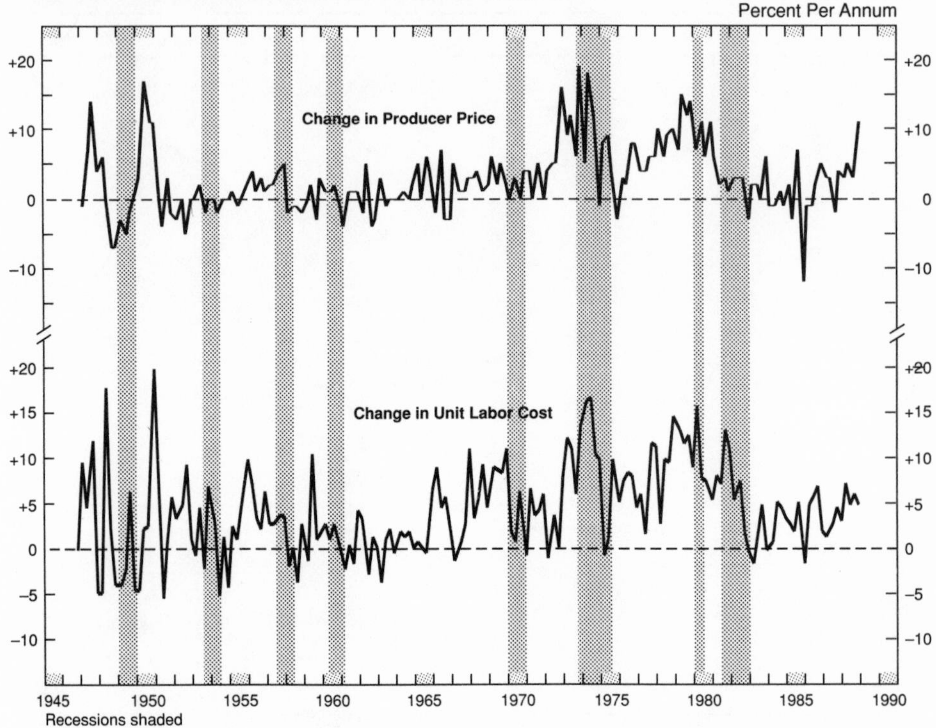

Source: U.S. Department of Commerce, *Business Conditions Digest* and *Handbook of Cyclical Indicators*, series 334c; Bureau of Labor Statistics.

declining productivity are the result, expect wage increases to lag behind inflation once again.

Even the full employment of the late 80s didn't generate "wage inflation" because employers remained loath to grant wage increases in excess of inflation. Competition for workers in some markets did boost wages rapidly in some occupations in some locales, but this was not a nationwide phenomenon.

THE COST/PRICE DYNAMIC

To conclude, summarize the cycle's progress from *trough to recovery* as follows:

GNP $\downarrow \rightarrow$ Industrial production $\downarrow \rightarrow$ Capacity utilization $\downarrow \rightarrow$ Labor productivity $\uparrow \rightarrow$ Unit labor costs $\downarrow \rightarrow$ Producer prices $\downarrow$.

When GNP and industrial production fall, capacity utilization declines. This leads to an increase in labor productivity and a drop in unit labor costs, driving down the rate of inflation as measured by producer prices.

Like the reveler's hangover, recession grips the economy following the bender of boom and inflation. Rest is the only cure, and recovery is marked not by a renewed round of expansion and growth but by a slack period in which steadiness is restored.

But it would surely be naive to assume that low inflation will be forever with us. What forces can propel it upward once again? Why may we have a renewed round of price increases?

If you ask a businessperson why prices rise, he or she will answer, "Rising costs," probably referring to personal experience. When you ask an economist the same question, the response will be, "Demand exceeds supply at current prices, and therefore prices rise," probably referring to the textbook case. These points of view seem to have nothing in common. Yet an analysis of economic expansion shows that they meld into a single explanation. Consider an idealized (and hypothetical) situation.

Suppose all the indicators of economic expansion (demand)—auto sales, consumer credit, housing starts—are strong. This will initiate broad-based growth as incomes increase in the construction, auto, and other durable goods industries, spilling over and boosting demand for other consumer goods. Boom conditions will intensify as business invests in additional factories and machinery to meet the rush in orders.

As the expansion unfolds, capacity utilization increases with the growth in demand and production. Soon factories move from, say, 70 percent to 90 percent of their rated maximum. Productive facilities strain to meet the demands and retain the loyalty of customers.

Next, high levels of capacity utilization drive labor productivity down and unit labor costs up; efficiency is sacrificed for increased output. Machinery that is always in use cannot be adequately maintained, and so it breaks down. Inexperienced workers often do not make the same contribution as old hands. The amount of labor employed increases more rapidly than output, and as output per worker falls, the labor cost per unit of output rises. This generates a surge in production costs.

Finally, rapidly increasing costs are translated into rapidly increasing prices, and a renewed round of inflation begins.

All the forces that led to a reduction in the rate of inflation are now reversed as the cycle moves from *expansion to peak.*

GNP ↑ → Industrial production ↑ → Capacity utilization ↑ → Labor productivity ↓ → Unit labor costs ↑ → Producer prices ↑ .

So the practical (businessperson's) and the theoretical (economist's) explanations of inflation are not at odds. During expansion, demand bids production to a level that is inefficient and costly. The businessperson experiences the increased cost and attributes inflation directly to that experience. The economist sees increased demand as the ultimate cause of the production gain that drives costs up. Each explanation covers different aspects of the single phenomenon, economic expansion.

THE 1970s AS AN ILLUSTRATION

The late 1970s illuminate the process graphically. You will need the same statistical series employed earlier to illustrate expansion's impact on inflation: *GNP, industrial production, capacity utilization, labor productivity* and *unit labor costs*, and the *producer price index*. Each of these statistical series has already been introduced, so excerpts from *The Wall Street Journal* will not be presented again.

Although subsequently eclipsed by the 1981–82 recession, the 1974 recession established a postwar record at the time. GNP declined for four quarters, and industrial production tumbled 15 percent. By the spring of 1975, the unemployment rate was over 9 percent.

Like all recessions, however, this one prepared the way for the subsequent recovery. Capacity utilization fell to a postwar low, and labor productivity began to rise immediately. The resulting decline in unit labor costs cut the rate of inflation.

At the same time, the Federal Reserve System switched from a tight to an easy money policy, reducing interest rates and providing ample credit. A sharp recovery and strong expansion began as the decline in the rate of inflation dramatically improved consumer real income and boosted consumer sentiment. At long last, consumers were pulling ahead of inflation; their pleasure was reflected in demand's rapid increase.

By 1977–78, new housing starts were 2 million annually and domestic automobile sales peaked at approximately 10 million, while consumer installment borrowing hit annual rates of $50 billion.

The evidence of a robust economic expansion was all around as GNP and industrial production surged ahead. Rapid growth in demand, production, and capacity utilization had its inevitable result: the nation's factories and other productive facilities were strained, and increases in the labor force no longer made a proportional contribution to output (see Chart 7–5 on page 126).

In 1979 labor productivity stopped improving and began to fall. As a result, unit labor costs increased steadily, and by early 1980 the rate of inflation, as measured by the producer price index, had reached 15 percent (see Chart 7–7 on page 132).

Declining labor productivity is the focal point of this analysis. Once output is pushed past the point of diminishing returns, unit labor costs become an inevitable problem. Most people believe that rising wages are chiefly responsible for this condition; wages do play a minor role, naturally, but unit labor costs will increase swiftly even if wage gains run well below the rate of inflation (i.e., even if real wages are falling).

Falling real wages, coupled with the forward surge in labor costs, creates one of the cruelest features of inflation. Because labor productivity has declined, there is less per capita output and therefore less real income per person. Declining real income pits one segment of American society against another, fighting over a shrinking pie. Labor-management relations become especially bitter in these periods of boom without prosperity. Employers blame workers' wages for rising labor costs and shrinking profits, while workers blame employers' profits for shrinking real wages; in reality, neither one is responsible for the other's misfortune.

In such times, the public's support for wage and price controls becomes insistent (although, of course, management has a greater interest in controlling wages and labor has a greater interest in controlling prices). Yet you can see from this chapter's analysis that rising costs due to reduced efficiency (falling labor productivity) are responsible for the increase in prices that captures everyone's attention. No one's greed is to blame. And therefore controls designed to limit greed are bound to be ineffective.

There have been two recent attempts at wage and price controls: the first under President Nixon in 1971–72 and the second under President Carter in 1979–80. President Nixon's controls were certain to "succeed" because they were implemented during the transition from recovery to expansion, while capacity utilization was low and labor productivity was high. As a result, the rate of inflation was still falling from its 1970 cyclical peak. It would have continued to decline in any event and remain low until the expansion gained strength. The controls did slightly dampen inflation, but their impact was marginal.

President Carter's controls were destined to "fail," just as President Nixon's were destined to succeed, because President Carter's were implemented during the virulent expansion of 1977–79. As labor productivity fell and unit costs climbed, business merely passed its increased costs on to the consumer. Rising prices reflected rising costs, not greed, and business did not earn excessive profits.

Keep in mind also that more stringent wage controls could not have restrained business costs. Some of the increase in unit labor costs was due to the increase in wage rates, but most of it was due to declining productivity caused by high capacity utilization. Workers were no more culpable than their employers.

This is an important point. We really can't blame the declines in labor productivity in the 1970s on the American worker, as some are prone to do. Productivity lapses in that decade occurred cyclically, when the economy overheated, and thus they really reflected the limitations of plant and equipment under extreme conditions rather than failures of diligence in the labor force.

And harking back to World War II for an example of successful wage and price controls is not the answer, either. Wage and price (and profit) controls worked then because the economy was on a war footing. About half of the economy's output was devoted to the war effort, much of it under a system of planning and direct resource allocation that operated outside ordinary market relationships. You couldn't bid up the price of a car (none were produced because the auto plants were converted to war production) or buy all the gasoline and steak you wanted (these were rationed). And despite the patriotism aroused by the war effort, black markets arose to subvert the controls. Therefore, it's doubtful whether such a system could work to contain peacetime inflation, for which, unlike war-induced inflation, there is no end in sight.

Imposing wage and price controls during the expansionary phase of the business cycle (as was attempted in the late 70s) is a little like trying to stop the rattle of a boiling kettle by taping down the lid. Demand heats the expansion, and inflation is the natural result. Turning down the heat is the only practical solution.

Finally, there's the question of "supply-side shocks." These are sudden increases in the price of important commodities (imposed by the sellers) or reductions in supply due to forces beyond our control. Some believe that the late 70s' inflation was due to these sorts of shocks, but this argument should be taken with a grain of salt. First, any explanation that places the blame on others should be suspect; if you wish to find fault, it is always best to look in the mirror. Second, neither OPEC nor the Russian wheat deal nor the failure of the Peruvian anchovy harvest can explain the price explosions of the 70s. They may have contributed to the inflation, but they did not cause it. If demand had been weak, prices would have remained stable. After all, prices stopped climbing as soon as recession hit in 1981–82, well before the oil price collapse of early 1986.

And whether you are dealing with free-market farm prices or OPEC, repealing the laws of supply and demand is not easy. Farm prices eased down in the commodity deflation of the 80s, while oil prices collapsed in a matter of months in early 1986. In both cases, high prices and profits in the 70s had attracted investment in new productive facilities and therefore created excess capacity (supply). Once supply exceeded demand at current prices, the price collapse was inevitable.

CONCLUSION

The expansion of the late 80s did not generate inflation as virulent as that of 1977–79 because the Fed restrained the growth in demand by restraining the growth in credit. The minislowdown of 1984 demonstrated the Fed's determination to act at the first sign of danger, and the Fed's actions throughout the 1980s confirm its resolve to keep demand under control by restraining credit and keeping interest rates high. The Fed's actions stretched out the cycle and thereby postponed the onset of recession.

Investor's Tip

- Moderate levels of consumer demand (auto, housing, consumer credit) → Moderate capacity utilization → Moderate inflation.
- Booming auto sales (8 million +) + Housing starts (1.8 million +) + Consumer credit ($80 billion +) → High capacity utilization (85 + percent) → rapid (8 + percent) producer price inflation.
- A booming economy is your first hint that you should anticipate inflation by disposing of paper investments and buying tangible investments.

Investor's Tip
Statistical Indicators and Danger Signals

- Follow these indicators in *The Wall Street Journal* and watch for the following danger signals:

Indicator	*When Published*	*End of 80s Level*	*Danger Level*	*Potential Problem*
GNP	20th of the month	3%	5%	High rate leads to inflation
Industrial Production	Mid-month	5%	10%	High rate leads to inflation
Capacity Utilization	Mid-month	80–85%	85%	High rate leads to inflation
Labor Productivity	End of month	2%	0	Low rate leads to inefficiency, rising costs, & inflation
Producer Prices	Mid-month	5%	8%	High inflation will reduce consumer demand & lead to recession

- If these indicators reach the danger level, move out of paper assets and into tangible assets before inflation becomes a problem.

CHAPTER 8

STOCKS VS. GOLD

If you return to the comparison of stocks' and gold's performance (see Chart 8–1 on page 140) first mentioned in Chapter 1, you will note, to repeat, that stocks did poorly in the high-inflation 70s and well in the low-inflation 80s, and that gold performed in the opposite fashion. Recall the promise in Chapter 1 that you would be able to forecast stocks' and gold's future performance once you had mastered (1) an understanding of the forces that shaped inflation, and (2) an ability to use *The Wall Street Journal* to analyze those forces. Now is the time to put your knowledge to work.

GOLD

Compare gold's performance to an index of a dozen commodity prices (including gold) presented on page 141 in Chart 8–2, and recall the suggestion in Chapter 1 that you view gold as a proxy for all tangible investments. When you mention commodities as an investment, most people think of gold.

The similarity in movement between gold prices and the commodity index is easily explained. All commodity prices (and gold is a commodity) measure inflation, which is after all nothing more than rising prices. Copper, cattle, hogs, lumber, wheat, and gold will move along the same path in the long run because the price of each is subject to the same supply and demand forces. When demand exceeds supply at current prices because spenders have access to credit, all prices rise. Sure, there are occasions when a commodity will defy the price trend for a while because of circumstances peculiar to its production and market. But these are exceptional cases.

Gold is a good investment (as are most tangibles) in times of high and rising inflation because its price climbs more rapidly than standard

CHART 8–1
Gold vs. Stocks: Gold—Engelhard High Price through 1987, Average Thereafter; Dow Jones Industrial Average

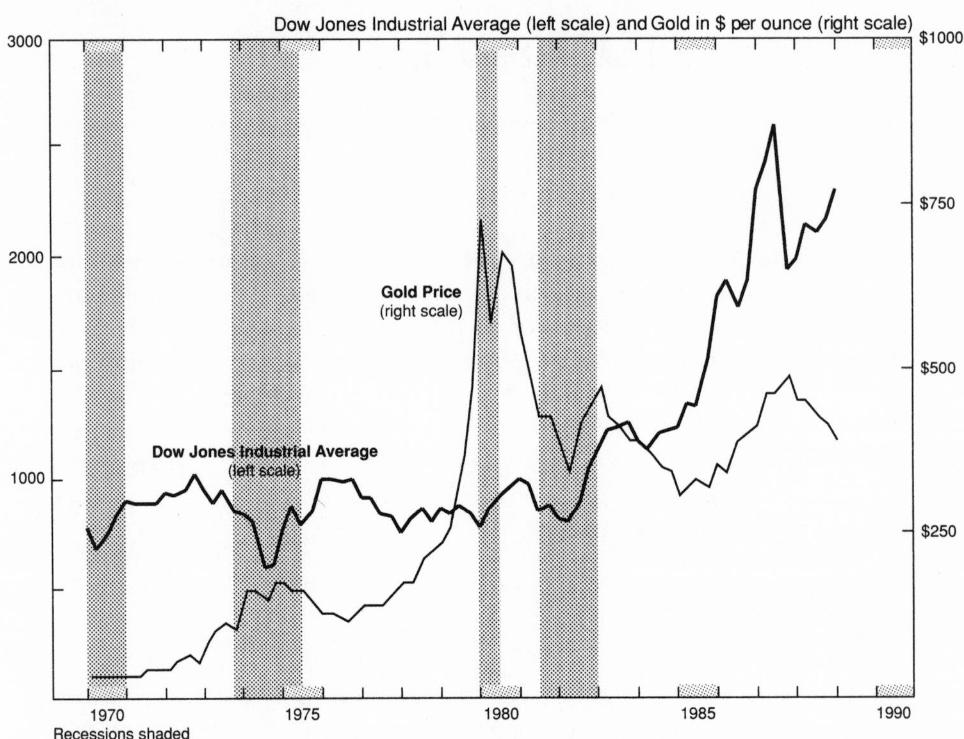

Source: U.S. Bureau of Mines, *Minerals Yearbook*; Standard & Poor's *Statistical Service*; Phyllis S. Pierce, ed., *The Dow Jones Investor's Handbook* (Homewood, IL: Dow Jones-Irwin, 1989); *Barron's*.

measures of inflation such as the CPI. In times of low inflation, gold prices will be weak or actually fall. Why does gold beat the averages during a period of severe inflation and then fall when inflation subsides (although prices generally are still rising)?

What is true for gold is true for commodities generally. All occupy a position early in the production chain, before a great deal of value has been added in the productive process. Value added, which is the labor and technology applied to raw materials that turn them into useful products, acts as a cushion between the prices we pay for the finished product and the volatile prices paid for the commodities from which the product was fashioned.

CHART 8–2
Gold and Dow Jones Commodity Futures Index

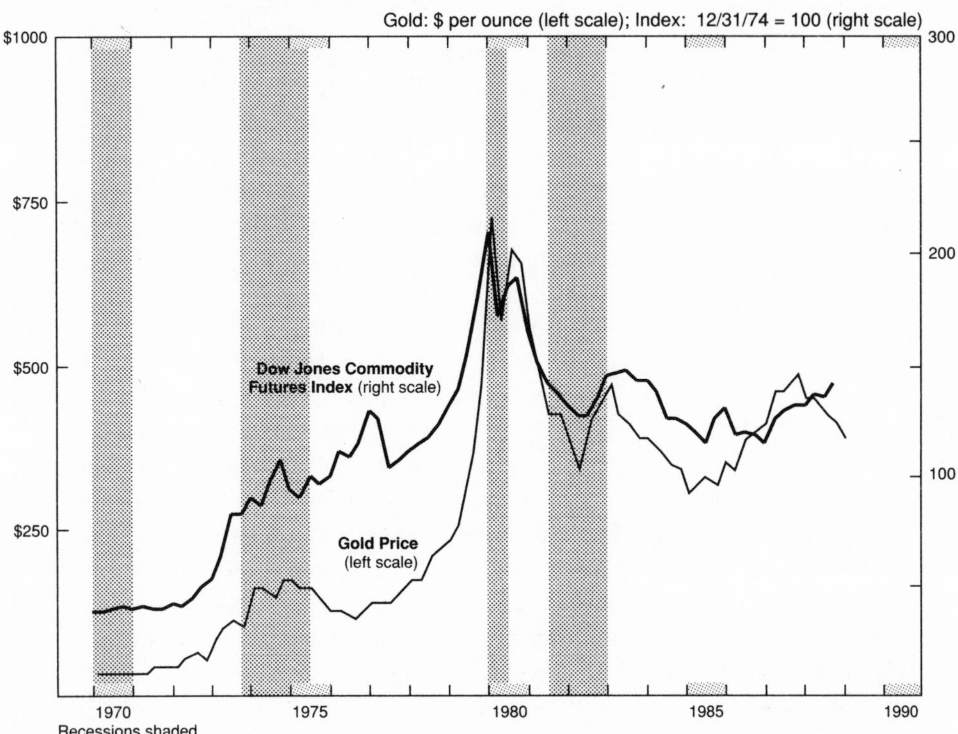

Source: U.S. Bureau of Mines, *Minerals Yearbook*; Standard & Poor's *Statistical Service*; Phyllis S. Pierce, ed., *The Dow Jones Investor's Handbook* (Homewood, IL: Dow Jones-Irwin, 1989); *Barron's*.

Consider an example. If air travel increases, airlines order more planes from the aircraft manufacturers. Airplane prices may rise 10 percent with the costs of designing, developing, manufacturing, and assembling. Most of these costs are payments to people. Yet the price of aluminum, the aircrafts' principal ingredient, may rise 50 percent in the face of rapidly growing demand. And bauxite, the raw material from which aluminum is produced, may jump 100 percent, even as the cost of electricity (aluminum's other principal ingredient) hardly grows at all. Thus, a 10 percent increase in airplane prices may be consistent with a 100 percent increase in the price of bauxite, a mineral taken from the ground.

Conversely, a drop in the demand for aircraft will not generate a decline in aircraft prices as labor costs continue to grow. Yet bauxite prices may fall.

Other examples are more commonplace. The price of a loaf of bread or a hamburger may increase slightly while wheat and cattle prices double, only to keep rising as wheat and cattle prices fall. Ketchup prices may rise slightly while tomato prices fluctuate. And so on.

It's as if fluctuations in the demand for finished goods had a whipsaw effect on the price of commodities, with slight variations at one end magnified in the fluctuations at the other end. It's a kind of reverse ripple effect, with the waves escalating in size and intensity as you move away from the splash.

Chart 8–3 provides an illustration by presenting a number of price indexes, from raw commodity prices to semifinished goods to the CPI.

The sharp break presented by the early 1980s is never lost, but is clearly muted as you go up the productive process from raw to finished goods. Commodity prices rise most steeply among all the indexes and actually fall in the 80s. The CPI rises least rapidly of all the indexes in the 1970s, yet continues to rise most rapidly in the 1980s, a period in which many commodity prices fell.

As a general rule, commodity prices rise more rapidly than consumer prices in high inflation, but rise less rapidly than consumer prices when inflation is low (and can actually fall).

Once again, the farther back you go in the chain of production, the more volatile the price index. Gold is no exception to this rule. Glance back to Chart 8–2 and you can see gold's explosion in the 70s and its weak performance in the 80s. It will stay weak in the 90s if inflation remains in check. Yet it could climb beyond its 1980 high of about $800 an ounce if inflation is rekindled.

Investor's Tip

- Stay away from gold, commodities, and other tangibles unless inflation exceeds 8 percent for a quarter.

CHART 8–3
Price Index Comparisons: Dow Jones Commodity Futures Index, Raw Industrial Materials (spot), Producer Price Index, Consumer Price Index

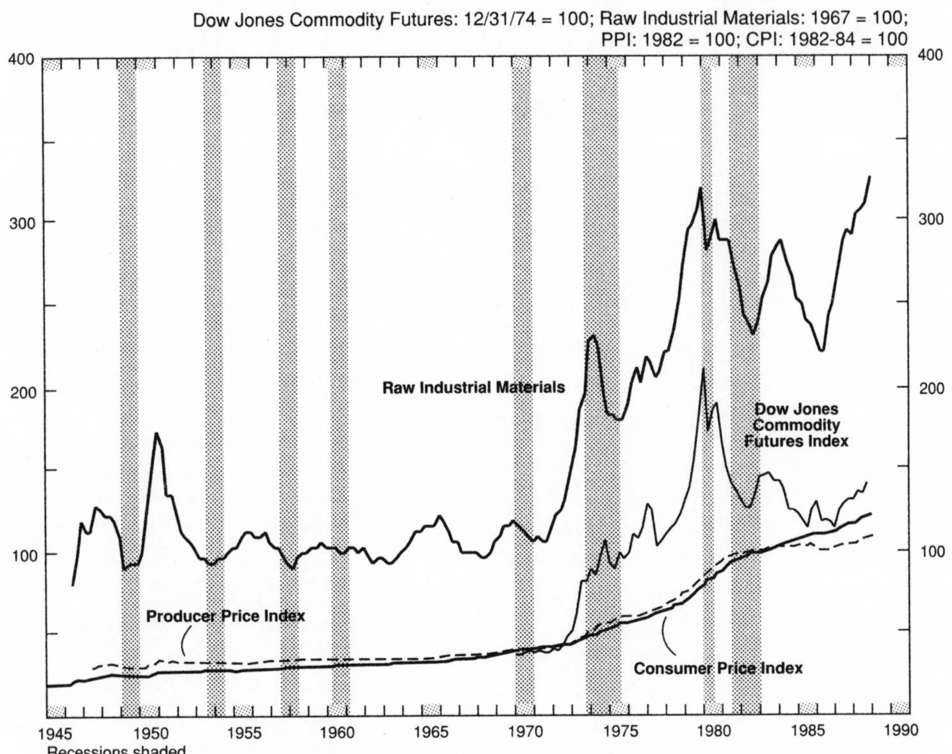

Source: U.S. Department of Commerce, *Business Conditions Digest* and *Handbook of Cyclical Indicators*, series 23, 320, 334; Phyllis S. Pierce, ed. *The Dow Jones Investor's Handbook* (Homewood, IL: Dow Jones-Irwin, 1989); *Barron's*; Knight-Ridder, Commodity Research Bureau.

PROFITS AND STOCKS

Stocks are more complex than commodities because you must analyze profits first. You can't measure a company's value until you know how much it can earn. *The Wall Street Journal survey of corporate profits* for over 500 corporations appears about two months after the close of the quarter. The second paragraph of the Tuesday, February 21, 1989 report for the fourth quarter of 1988 states that profits rose 22 percent from the same period a year earlier (see page 144).

Companies' Net Income Rose 20% In the Fourth Period of Last Year

Corporate profits wound up a strong year in the fourth quarter of 1988, aided in part by foreign-based earnings bolstered by further declines in the dollar. By mid-1989, however, analysts expect earnings to begin posting year-to-year declines. And the quality of profits is already slipping as a result of tax-law changes.

Corporate Profits

In the quarter ended Dec. 31, after-tax earnings on continuing operations of 645 major corporations rose 22% from the 1987 fourth quarter, a period of strong profits. Net income climbed 20%.

The substantial gain compares with an 11% rise in net income in this year's third quarter, when many economists thought they saw signs of a slowing economy. The third-quarter rise followed a string of four larger year-to-year gains.

Canadian Profits Rise

Another strong performance by Canada's mining sector pushed the nation's corporate profits higher in the fourth quarter. Story on page B10.

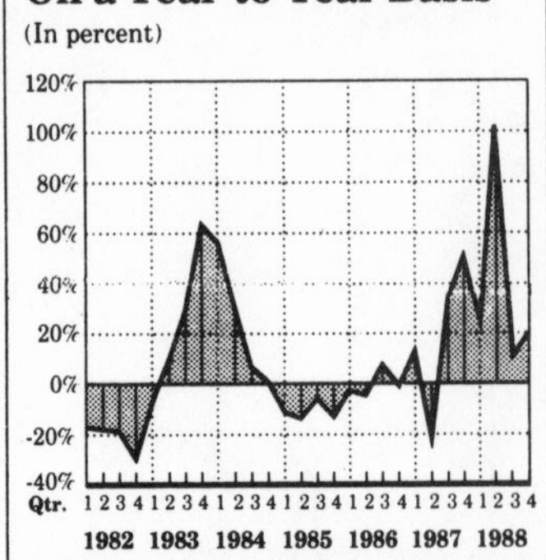

"The main story in the fourth quarter," according to analysts at Drexel Burnham Lambert, "was the continuation of favorable operating conditions in domestic and international markets."

Looking ahead, Christopher Caton of DRI/McGraw Hill, an economic consulting firm, says the 1986 tax law will hold the growth of corporate depreciation allowances down to 2% between 1988 and 1991, although over that period "actual economic depreciation will grow by 20%." With this business cost kept lower, reported profits will look better than they actually are, and a larger share of income will be subject to tax. Even so, Mr. Caton expects conventionally measured profits this year to fall 2% from 1988.

Jerry L. Jordan, the chief economist of First Interstate Bancorp in Los Angeles, sees a profits time bomb lurking in the savings and loan mess. "There is a great deal of real estate that will have to be sold off to clear up all of this," he warns. "If the holders wait until the economy slips into a recession to sell the properties, prices will be down, and profits will have a very heavy hit." Mr. Jordan, incidentally, expects a recession to start in mid-1989.

Among the nine major industry sectors, the best showings were in energy, which swung to a big profit from a loss in the 1987 fourth quarter; financial services, up 77%, and basic materials, up 51%. The technology group was the big loser, sustaining a 73% drop from a year earlier.

The automobile industry, which started the 1980s in a near-depression, is ending the decade on a high note. Thanks to the second-best sales year in history, combined profits of Detroit's Big Three hit a record $11.25 billion, easily topping the 1984 record. Only Chrysler's net fell, mainly because of heavy investments to modernize an aging lineup of cars. All three had higher fourth-quarter earnings. Analysts expect strong first-quarter earnings, although the outlook for all 1989 is less cer-

Profit Survey Is Revised To Match Stock Groups

Beginning with this quarterly profits roundup, The Wall Street Journal is revising its compilation of corporate earnings to conform with the Dow Jones Industry Groups published in the newspaper every day.

This change will facilitate comparisons of profit figures with the stock movements of the various industrial groups. It also will increase the companies involved to about 700 from some 530, although not all of them report in time to be listed in a given roundup.

The companies are selected mainly on the basis of market capitalization, although some smaller ones are included to give a representative sampling of the industry. A few additional companies are included because of their broad interest to investors even though their capitalizations may have dwindled.

Source: *The Wall Street Journal*, February 21, 1989.

Fourth-Quarter Profits–Second Paragraph

In the quarter ended Dec. 31, after-tax earnings on continuing operations of 645 major corporations rose 22% from the 1987 fourth quarter, a period of strong profits. Net income climbed 20%.

Source: *The Wall Street Journal*, February 21, 1989.

The Commerce Department's quarterly survey of profits, usually included in the GNP article, appears about 20 days later and covers a much larger sample. Examine the Friday, March 24, 1989 report, especially the second paragraph (see page 146).

Don't be confused by different comparisons. Profits were 2.8 percent higher in the *fourth quarter* of 1988 than in the *third quarter* according to the Commerce Department survey, but 22 percent higher in the fourth quarter than in the *same quarter one year earlier* according to *The Wall Street Journal* survey. Be sure you understand which time periods are being compared.

Compare *fourth-quarter* 1988 profits of $173.9 billion, as reported in paragraph nine, with the postwar record of profits in Chart 8–4 on page 147. You can see that profits deteriorated in the 1981–82 recession, following a meager recovery from the 1980 recession, and were finally approaching the levels of the late 70s after a ten-year hiatus. How will profits perform in the 1990s? Will they continue to grow to record highs? The answers to these questions are found in an examination of profits over the business cycle.

Profits measure efficiency by comparing revenues to costs. Recall that the economy's efficiency improves during the early phases of the cycle and deteriorates during the latter phases. Thus, profits grow during recovery and expansion and deteriorate during peak and contraction.

A bit of logic reveals the relationship between general changes in economic efficiency over the cycle and the specific measurement of profit. Efficiency rises early in the cycle because factories are operating with excess capacity and producing less than maximum output. The general reduction in costs due to enhanced productivity increases the spread between prices and costs, known as the *profit rate* or profit per

Economy Grew At 2.4% Rate In 4th-Period

Pace Topped Prior Estimate Of 2%, But It Declined From the 3rd Quarter

By Alan Murray
Staff Reporter of The Wall Street Journal

WASHINGTON—The economy grew at a 2.4% annual rate in the fourth quarter of last year, more rapidly than previously reported although still less than the third quarter's 2.5% pace, the Commerce Department said.

Corporate Profits

The department also reported that after-tax profits of U.S. corporations rose 2.8% in the fourth quarter, after increasing 3.9% in the third quarter, while corporate cash flow expanded a hefty 3.2%, following a 0.8% rise in the previous period.

The agency's previous estimates of real gross national product—the total output of goods and services, adjusted for inflation—put the fourth-quarter increase at a 2% annual rate. But new statistics showed that government spending and business investment had both been stronger than previously estimated.

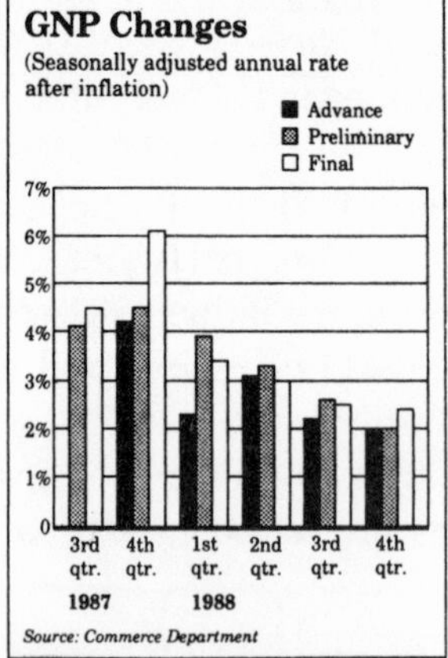

Excluding the effects of last year's drought, the Commerce Department estimated the fourth-quarter growth rate at a hefty 3.5%.

Analysts said growth in the economy and in profits is already slowing from their year-end paces. Kathleen Cooper, chief economist at Security Pacific National Bank in Los Angeles, said consumer spending "has slackened off in the first quarter" and is likely to hold down growth.

Donald Straszheim, president of Merrill Lynch Economics Inc., said profits are likely to be flat this year. "Profits are not going to advance at all in 1989," he said. "We are clearly in a period when profitability is being squeezed, and will be squeezed more as the year progresses."

Even if the economy's underlying growth rate is slowing, however, the growth rate for the first quarter is likely to prove exceptionally strong because of a rebound following the drought. Commerce Department economists say recovery from the drought will add more than two percentage points to growth in the first quarter.

The new report continued to show signs of price increases. A GNP-based price measure known as the "deflator," which is adjusted for changes in the composition of the nation's output, rose to a 5.3% annual rate in the fourth quarter, the same as in the previous report, exceeding the 4.7% rate of the third period. A separate price measure based on a fixed basket of goods rose to a 4.2% pace, also the same as previously reported but less than the third quarter's 5.3%.

Fourth-quarter corporate profits rose to an annual rate of $173.9 billion after taxes, while corporate cash flow rose to an annual rate of $409.2 billion.

Corporate Profits

Before taxes, corporate profits rose 1.8% to $319.5 billion, after rising 2.6% in the third quarter.

Adjusting for depreciation of capital and changes in the value of inventory, profits from current production rose 3% in the fourth quarter to $339.9 billion, after rising 1.1% in the prior period.

All the figures are adjusted for seasonal variations.

GROSS NATIONAL PRODUCT

Here are some of the major components of the gross national product expressed in seasonally adjusted annual rates in billions of constant (1982) dollars:

	4th Qtr. 1988	3rd Qtr. 1988
GNP	4,033.4	4,009.4
less: inventory chng	29.1	39.5
equals: final sales	4,004.4	3,969.9
Components of Final Sales		
Personal Consumption	2,626.2	2,603.8
Nonresidential Invest.	491.4	495.0
Residential Invest.	196.6	191.6
Net Exports	−105.4	−93.9
Gov't Purchases	795.5	773.5

In the fourth quarter, the implicit price deflator rose to 5.3% of the 1982 average, from in the previous quarter.

Source: *The Wall Street Journal*, March 24, 1989.

Corporate Profits–Second and Ninth Paragraphs

The department also reported that after-tax profits of U.S. corporations rose 2.8% in the fourth quarter, after increasing 3.9% in the third quarter, while corporate cash flow expanded a hefty 3.2%, following a 0.8% rise in the previous period.

Fourth-quarter corporate profits rose to an annual rate of $173.9 billion after taxes, while corporate cash flow rose to an annual rate of $409.2 billion.

Source: *The Wall Street Journal*, March 24, 1989.

CHART 8–4
Corporate Profits after Taxes

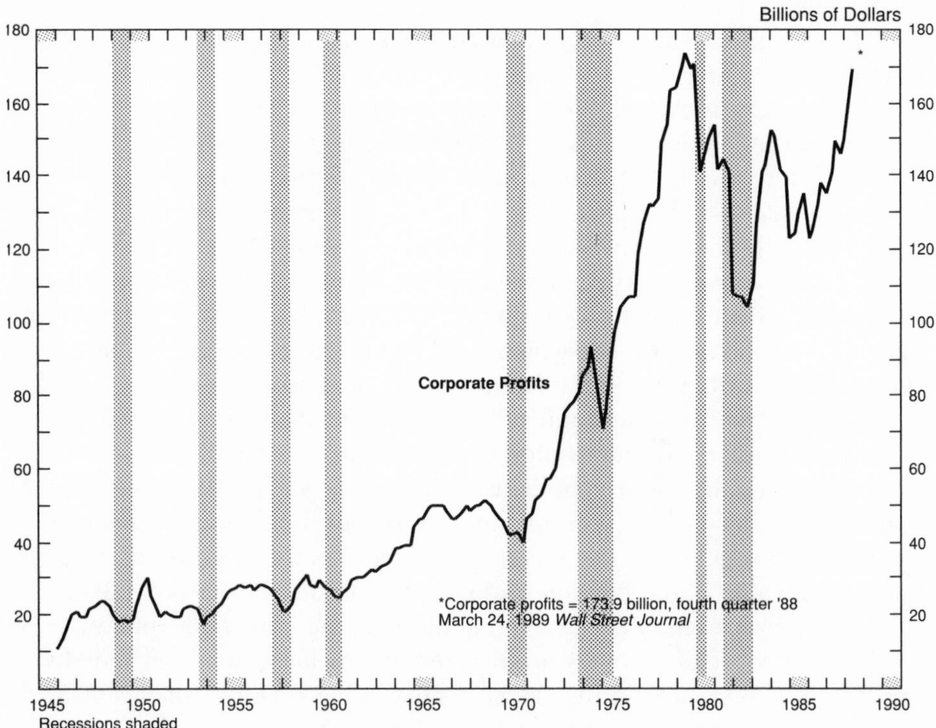

Source: U.S. Department of Commerce, *Business Conditions Digest* and *Handbook of Cyclical Indicators*, series 16.

unit of output. As sales increase, total profit grows because of both higher output and higher profits per unit of output.

Efficiency deteriorates late in the cycle as factories strain to produce maximum output. Costs rise as productivity falls, and industry is forced into a "profit squeeze," meaning that costs push up against prices. Total profits fall as sales volume stops growing, or actually contracts, and profit per unit of output (the profit rate) falls.

It may help to think of it in these terms: costs rise as output increases and industry reaches full capacity utilization. As costs come up from below, they bump prices upward. But competition prevents management from raising prices as rapidly as it would like. If costs rise more rapidly than prices, the margin between price and cost is squeezed. Profit margins decline.

On the other hand, management has the opportunity to rebuild its profit margins in the slack period following recession. Costs are no longer rising as rapidly because capacity utilization is low. This provides management the opportunity to recover profit margins by raising prices more rapidly than costs.

Thus, paradoxically, profit margins shrink when prices rise most rapidly.

The top graph in Chart 8–5 gives a bedrock picture of real profits, stripped of inflationary gains. It portrays the quality of profits by removing inventory profits swollen by inflation and by taking into account the replacement cost of depreciating plant and equipment (rather than the unrealistically low original cost). The bottom graph depicts the ratio of price to unit labor cost (i.e., the relative strength of prices and unit labor cost) and is therefore a proxy for profit margins. This informs you of the extent of labor cost's encroachment on prices and of business's ability to hold down labor costs in relation to the prices received.

Keep in mind that the ratio of price to unit labor cost is a fraction in which price is the numerator (top half) and cost the denominator (bottom half). In boom conditions, when costs are rising rapidly and pushing prices upward, profit margins are squeezed because competition prevents management from raising prices as rapidly as costs increase. Thus, the value of the fraction (ratio of price to unit labor cost) falls as the denominator (cost) rises more rapidly than the numerator (price).

In recession and recovery from recession, management can rebuild profit margins because costs are no longer rising rapidly. Management raises prices somewhat more quickly than costs increase, and profit margins are rebuilt. As a result, the ratio of price to unit labor cost

CHART 8–5
Corporate Profits in 1982 Dollars with Inventory Valuation and Capital Consumption Adjustment; and Ratio, Price to Unit Labor Cost, Nonfarm Business

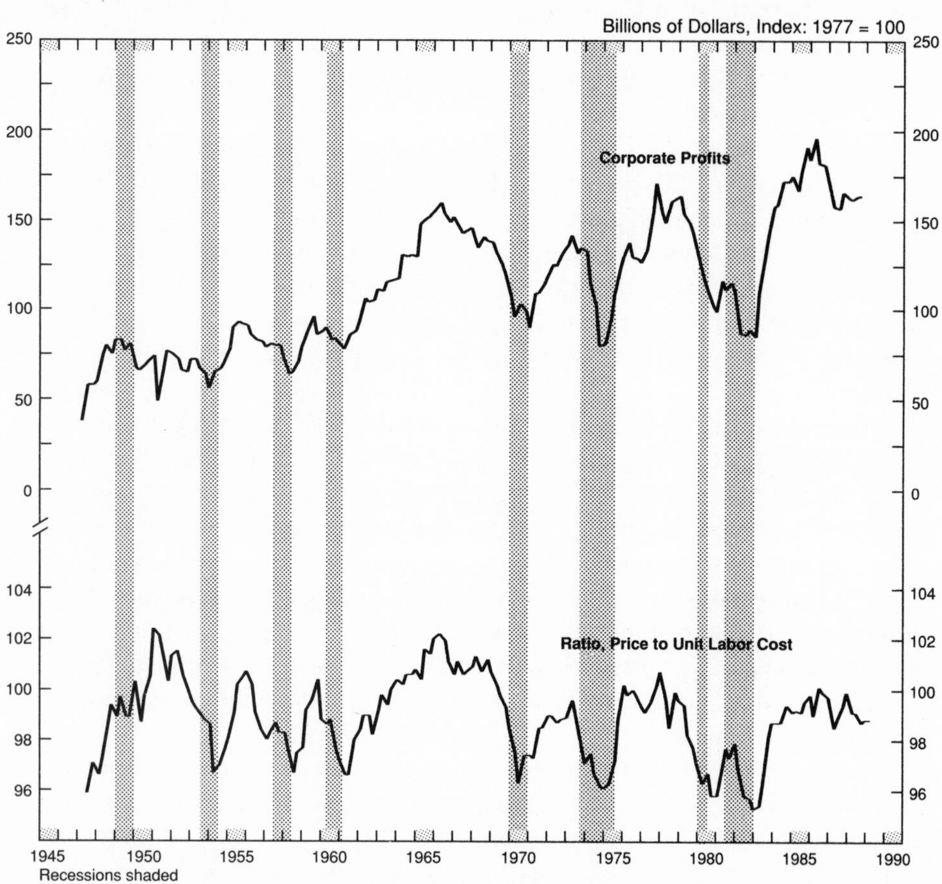

Source: U.S. Department of Commerce, *Business Conditions Digest* and *Handbook of Cyclical Indicators*, series 26 and 80.

rises as the numerator of the fraction now gains more rapidly than the denominator.

Each of the cycles in the 1970s demonstrates the same sequence of events. Start with a typical recovery and expansion, such as the recovery and expansion of 1971–72 or 1975–77. Unit labor cost was kept down by good gains in labor productivity due to modest levels of capacity utilization. As a result, the ratio of price to unit labor cost (our proxy for the term *profit margins*) improved and held up well. Since sales volume and output were growing, total real profits grew sharply.

Then, in 1973 and 1978–79, as production and capacity utilization peaked, labor productivity declined and unit labor cost increased. As a result, the ratio of price to unit labor cost fell as profit margins were pinched. Since, at the peak of the cycle, sales and output had also stalled, real profits tumbled and continued to fall throughout the ensuing recessions of 1974–75 and 1980.

Chapter 7 discussed wage and price controls, and Chart 8–5 illustrates the foolishness of this adventure. The rate of inflation declined in 1971–72, during President Nixon's controls, despite rising profit margins (ratio of price to unit labor cost) and rising real profits. Since real profits were rising, what use were the wage and price controls? Inflation subsided, not because of the controls, but because the rate of cost increase subsided due to *improved productivity brought about by the recovery phase of the business cycle*.

The rate of inflation increased in 1979–80, during President Carter's controls, despite falling profit margins (ratio of price to unit labor cost) and falling real profits. Since real profits were falling, why weren't controls effective in limiting greed? Because the inflation was not due to greed, it was due to *the increasingly rapid rise in costs brought on by cyclical expansion's negative impact on productivity*. Controls could not stem the rising spiral of prices.

To summarize, profits, when calculated for the entire economy, measure efficiency, not greed. Prices simply can't be controlled by limiting profits.

You can see in Chart 8–5 on page 149 that real profits improved substantially in the mid-80s, as low rates of capacity utilization boosted labor productivity and held down unit labor costs, providing an increased spread between prices and costs (improved profit margins).

Profits and margins stumbled in the late 80s because the economy grew too languidly. Keep in mind, however, that neither fell as severely as they had in the 70s during the cyclical course of boom conditions.

The important point (see Chart 8–6) is that inflation's cyclical squeeze on profit margins and real earnings in the 1970s regularly depressed the stock market so that it could not advance out of the trading range in which it was trapped. *Inflation is murder on profit margins and therefore is the death of the stock market*. On the other hand, once inflation subsided, continued strong margins provided a boost to the stock market in the 1980s.

CHART 8–6

Dow Jones Industrial Average and Real Earnings (corporate profits in 1982 dollars with inventory valuation and capital consumption adjustment)

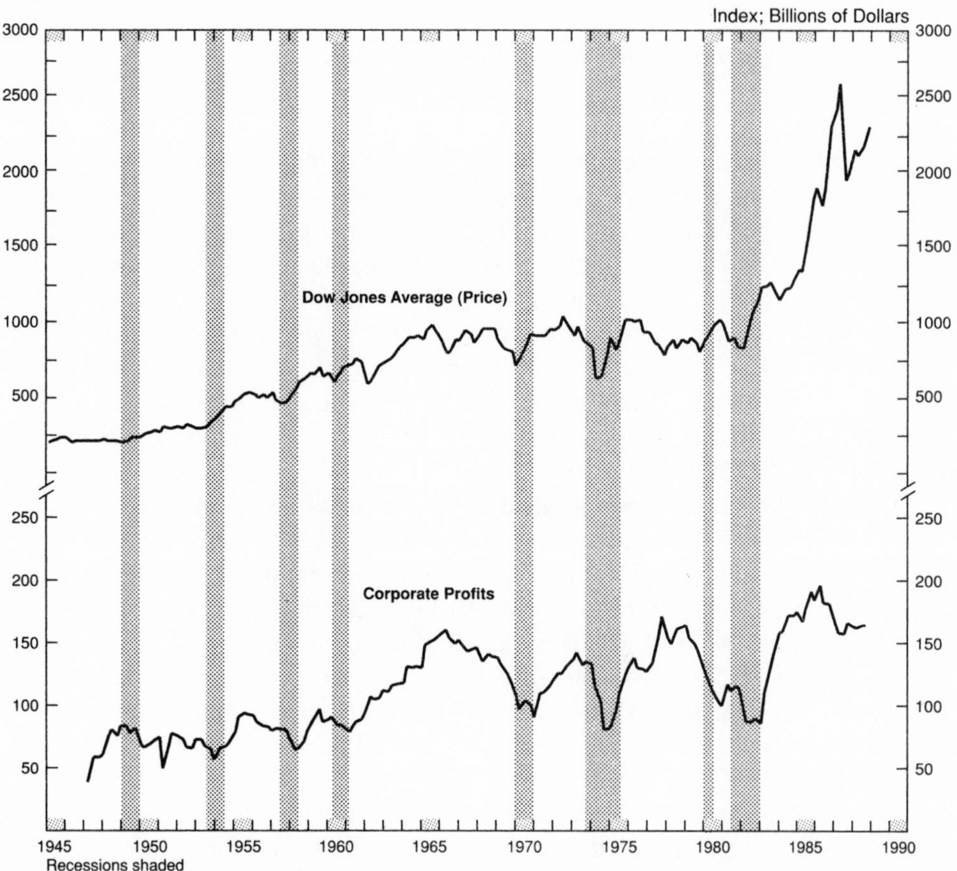

Source: Phyllis S. Pierce, ed., *The Dow Jones Investor's Handbook* (Homewood, IL: Dow Jones-Irwin, 1989); *Barron's*; and U.S. Department of Commerce, *Business Conditions Digest* and *Handbook of Cyclical Indicators*, series 80.

Investor's Tip

- Stay away from stocks if the annual rate of inflation exceeds 8 percent for a quarter.

The stock market loves low inflation because profit margins and real earnings can grow. If the Fed does what it should, the 90s ought to be good for stocks.

STOCKS AND THE PRICE/EARNINGS RATIO

Let's return to the Dow Jones Industrial Average. You know that the price of a share of stock reflects the ability of the corporation to earn profits. This relationship is expressed as the *price/earnings* (P/E, or price divided by per share earnings) *ratio* between the price of the stock and the profits per share of stock earned by the corporation (profits divided by number of shares outstanding). The price/earnings ratio answers this question: "What is the price an investor must pay to capture a dollar of earnings?" For instance, a P/E ratio of 10 might mean that a company earned $10 per share per annum and that a share sold for $100, or it might mean that a company earned $7 per share per annum and that a share sold for $70, and so on.

The investor, of course, seeks the highest yield consistent with safety. The earnings yield is annual profit expressed as a percentage of market price. If you earn $100 a year on an investment of $1,000 the yield is 10 percent. A P/E ratio of 10 (10/1) represents a 10 percent yield because earnings are 1/10 (10 percent) of the price per share. Similarly, a P/E ratio of 5 (5/1) is the equivalent of a 20 percent yield because earnings per share are one fifth (20 percent) of invested capital. A P/E ratio of 20 (20/1) represents a 5 percent earnings yield. And so on.

Chart 8–7 shows the Dow's P/E ratio fell from the end of World War II until the beginning of the Korean War, because earnings grew while share prices languished. Following the uncertainties of the 1930s and World War II, investors were still tentative about the market.

Then the great *bull market* (stock prices fall in a *bear market*) of the 1950s began, and the P/E ratio rose as investors bid up share prices more rapidly than earnings increased. Investors were at last convinced of a "return to normalcy" and were willing to stake their future in shares of stock. The market was clearly "undervalued" (a P/E ratio of seven was roughly a 15 percent earnings yield), so it is not surprising that stock prices climbed rapidly. Stocks were a good buy because their price was very low compared to their earnings per share and their potential for even higher earnings. As investors rushed into the market, stock prices

CHART 8–7
Dow Jones Industrial Average (price), **Earnings per Share, and Price/Earnings Ratio**

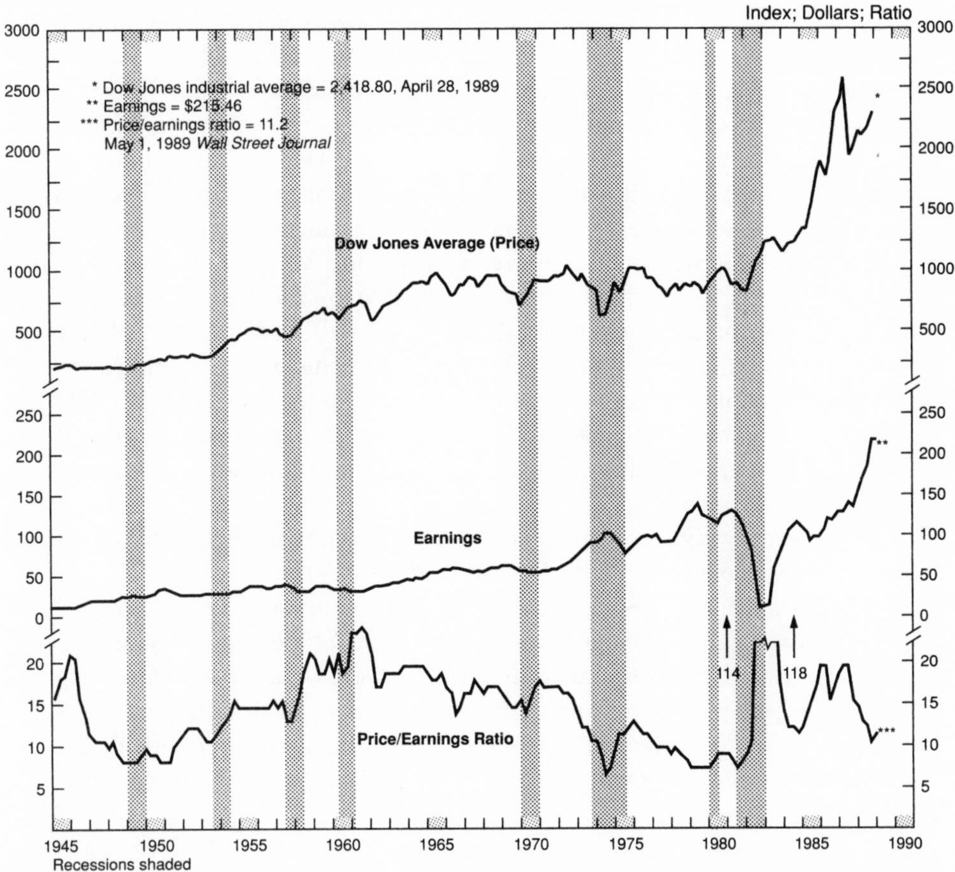

Source: Phyllis S. Pierce, ed., *The Dow Jones Investor's Handbook* (Homewood, IL: Dow Jones-Irwin, 1989), and *Barrons'*.

soared. Enthusiasm was so great and share prices advanced so rapidly that the P/E ratio rose despite stronger earnings per share.

The P/E ratio had climbed to more than 20 (a 5 percent yield) by the early 60s, so the market was no longer undervalued. The ratio plateaued or fell slightly to the end of the 60s because share prices were no longer increasing faster than corporate earnings. The great bull market had ended.

During the 70s, investors became frightened of the impact of inflation and severe cyclical fluctuation on profit margins, since margins fell sharply with each burst of inflation. At the first hint of declining margins, investors unloaded their shares and stock prices plunged. As a result, the Dow remained mired within a range for a decade, fluctuating between the high 500s and just over 1,000. Investors had been so badly burned by the market's decline in 1969 and 1974 that they refused to be swayed by the strong recovery of profits after each recession.

Yet nominal (not adjusted for inflation) profits rose over the decade, and thus the P/E ratio fell, so that by the early 1980s it was almost as low as it had been at the outset of the Korean War. The market had not kept pace with nominal earnings, and stocks were undervalued once again.

To some, this indicated that we were on the verge of another bull market. The situation seemed similar to that of the late 1940s, with investors hesitant after years of bad news, yet willing to take the plunge when it became clear that the fundamentals had changed. One indication of this sentiment was that stock prices fell little in the recessions of 1980 and 1981–82 when compared with those of 1970 and 1974. It was as if investors were positioning themselves for the bull market that was just around the corner.

There were two very auspicious signs. First, the breaking of the boom-and-bust inflationary spiral with the back-to-back recessions of 1980 and 1981–82 was a key signal that henceforth corporations could produce growing and stable real earnings in a climate of high profit margins. Second, the low P/E ratio meant that stocks were undervalued. Growing earnings would generate rising share prices, and when sufficient numbers of investors realized that the earnings improvement was permanent, the P/E ratio would rise to higher levels as buying pressure drove stock prices up.

The bull market of the 80s began in the summer of 1982, when it became clear that the Fed had loosened its monetary vise. The decline in interest rates mattered to investors because interest-earning assets are an alternative to stocks. As interest rates fell, investors moved out of interest-earning instruments and into stocks.

The shift into stocks continued because investors now recognized the growing potential for both increased nominal and real corporate profits. The sharp and sustained improvement in profit margins and real earnings shown in Chart 8–5 on page 149 and Chart 8–6 on page 151 was the source of this optimism. Once real earnings cracked the plateau of the 1965–80 period, nominal earnings could not be far behind, and investors correctly predicted that the Dow would respond by breaking out of its 1965–80 range.

TABLE 8–1

Year	*Quarter Ended*	*Dow*	*Earnings per share*	*P/E Ratio*
1983	March 31	1,130.03	9.52	118.4
	June 30	1,211.96	11.59	105.4
	Sept. 30	1,233.13	56.12	30.0
	Dec. 30	1,258.64	72.45	17.4
1984	March 30	1,164.89	87.38	13.3
	June 29	1,132.40	102.07	11.1
	Sept. 28	1,206.71	108.11	11.2
	Dec. 31	1,211.57	113.58	10.7
1985	March 29	1,226.78	107.87	11.7
	June 28	1,335.46	102.26	13.1
	Sept. 30	1,328.63	90.78	14.6
	Dec. 31	1,546.67	96.11	16.1
1986	March 31	1,818.61	94.63	18.9
	June 30	1,892.72	103.39	18.9
	Sept. 30	1,767.58	118.80	14.9
	Dec. 31	1,895.95	115.59	16.4
1987	March 31	2,304.69	126.49	18.2
	June 30	2,418.53	126.23	19.2
	Aug 25	2,722.42	126.23	21.6
	Sept. 30	2,596.28	137.99	18.8
	Dec. 31	1,938.83	133.05	14.6
1988	March 31	1,988.06	144.45	13.8
	June 30	2,141.70	168.54	12.7
	Sept. 30	2,112.91	181.04	11.7
	Dec. 30	2,168.57	215.46	10.1
1989	April 28	2,418.80	215.46	11.2

Source: *Barrons'* and *The Wall Street Journal.*

But Chart 8–7 on page 153 and Table 8–1 demonstrate that investors responded too enthusiastically to the improved profit potential. Speculation bid share prices up much faster than either real or nominal earnings. By August 1987 the Dow had doubled its 1983 level and stood at more than 2700, while earnings per share at $125 were not much greater than they had been four years earlier. The P/E ratio climbed to 22:1, higher than it had been since the early 60s.

Clearly the market was overvalued, ripe for a correction. It began to fold after its peak of 2722.42 on August 25, 1987, and declined 500 points by October 16. Then on October 19 it crashed another 500 points.

Yet earnings per share continued to grow in a climate of low inflation. They reached $215 in early 1989, sending the P/E back down to 12. Now the Dow was undervalued once again and investors began to recover

P/E RATIOS & YIELDS ON INDEXES

	--P/E Ratios--		Dividend Yields	
	4/28/89	Yr. Ago	4/28/89	Yr. Ago
DJ Industrials	11.2	15.3	3.45%	3.45%
DJ Tranportations	10.8	13.6	1.53%	6.23%
DJ Utilities	15.8	9.2	7.78%	9.19%
S&P 500	13.04	14.93	3.53%	3.65%

Price earnings ratios for the Dow Jones Averages are based on per share earnings for the 12 months ended December 31, 1988 of $215.46 for the 30 Industrials; $105.82 for the 20 transportation issues; $12.17 for the 15 utilities.

P/E Ratio and Earnings per Share

Source: *The Wall Street Journal*, May 1, 1989.

from their postcrash jitters. By early 89 they had bid the Dow up over 2246.74, its close on October 16, 1987, the trading day just prior to the October 19 crash.

What was the source of their bullish attitude? Strong margins, low inflation, and a low P/E. What did investors have to fear? Either inflation's return or speculation; the first because of its depressing impact on profit margins, the second because excessive stock market appreciation would create overvaluation (a high P/E) of the kind that existed before the 1987 crash.

Investor's Tip

- If the P/E exceeds 15, be cautious: stocks may be overvalued; if the P/E reaches 20, get out.

Follow the earnings and P/E for the Dow stocks each Monday on the third page (C3) of the *Journal*'s third section, called *Money and Investing*. An example from the May 1, 1989 *Journal* appears above.

STOCKS VS. GOLD

Smart investors picked stocks and stayed away from gold in the late 80s. The Fed had inflation under control, which was a good omen for stocks (and bonds and other paper investments) and a bad omen for gold (and commodities and other tangible investments).

As for the crash of 87, that had proved to be a correction for the excessive speculation in stocks that occurred despite a lofty P/E ratio. Now that the P/E ratio was in a low to normal range, the danger of speculative excess had passed.

WHAT ABOUT REAL ESTATE?

In the 1980s some real estate markets were definitely an exception to the rule that paper assets were a better buy than tangible assets in a decade of slack economic conditions. Housing prices rose rapidly in the Northeast and in the San Francisco and Los Angeles areas as well as selected markets in between. But rural America and the oil-dependent areas saw their real estate values collapse.

Real estate was a regional play in the 80s, unlike the 70s when prices rose everywhere. It would be tempting to generalize about the 1980s, but it can't be done. Selected real estate markets were an exception to the rule that tangible investments were a bad bet in the 1980s.

Investor's Tip
Statistical Indicators and Danger Signals

- Follow these indicators in the *The Wall Street Journal* and watch for the following danger signals:

Indicator	*When Published*	*End of 80s Level*	*Danger Level*	*Potential Problem*
P/E for Dow Stocks	Every Monday	12	15	High P/E means overvalued stocks
Gold Price	Daily	$375–$400	$450	Smart money betting on inflation

- When the P/E for the Dow stocks exceeds 15, get ready to get out of the market. When it reaches 20, you should be gone.
- If there's a run-up in gold's price, ask yourself, "What do they know about the inflation outlook that I don't?" It probably is time to dump your stocks.

APPENDIX TO PART I

DANGER SIGNALS, CYCLE DIAGRAMS, AND SUGGESTIONS FOR FURTHER READING

STATISTICAL INDICATORS AND DANGER SIGNALS

Follow these indicators in *The Wall Street Journal* and watch for the following danger signals.

Indicator	*When Published*	*End of 80s Level*	*Danger Level*	*Potential Problem*
Auto sales	Every 10 days (5th, 15th, 25th)	7–8 million	8 million	Sales surge leads to inflation
Consumer credit	2nd week of month	$40–60 billion	$80 billion	Borrowing binge leads to inflation
Housing starts	17th to 20th of month	1.5–1.7 million	1.8 million	Construction boom leads to inflation
GNP	20th of the month	3%	5%	High rate leads to inflation
Industrial production	Mid-month	5%	10%	High rate leads to inflation
Capacity utilization	Mid-month	80–85%	85%	High rate leads to inflation
Labor productivity	End of month	2%	0	Low rate leads to inefficiency, rising costs, and inflation

Indicator	*When Published*	*End of 80s Level*	*Danger Level*	*Potential Problem*
Producer prices	Mid-month	5%	8%	High inflation will reduce consumer demand and lead to recession
Consumer prices (CPI)	4th week	5%	8%	High inflation threatens consumer sentiment
Consumer sentiment (Conference Board)	1st week	100–120	80	Low consumer sentiment will lead to drop in consumer demand and recession
Dow Jones P/E ratio	Monday	12/1	15/1	High P/E indicates stocks overvalued and Dow ripe for correction

Stylized Summary of Generic Cycle

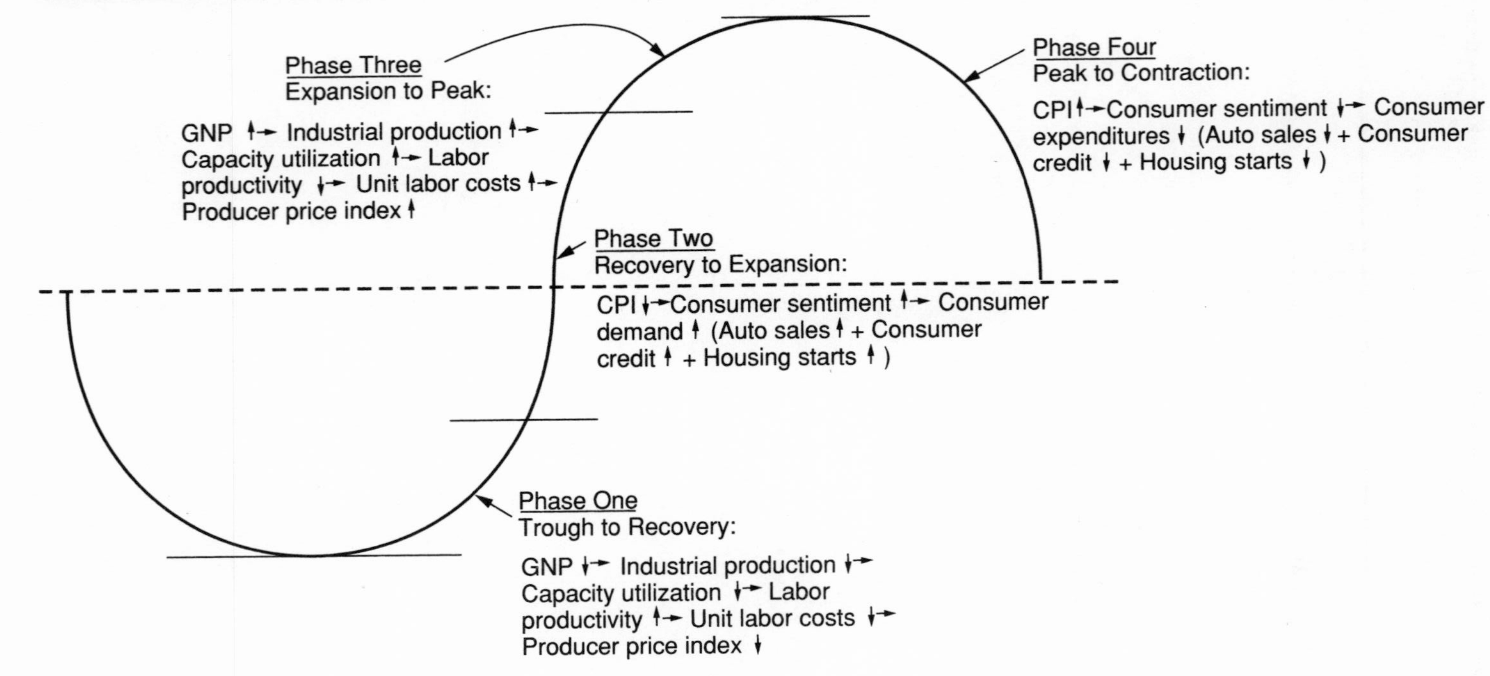
Phase Three
Expansion to Peak:
GNP ↑→ Industrial production ↑→
Capacity utilization ↑→ Labor
productivity ↓→ Unit labor costs ↑→
Producer price index ↑
Phase Four
Peak to Contraction:
CPI ↑→Consumer sentiment ↓→ Consumer
expenditures ↓ (Auto sales ↓ + Consumer
credit ↓ + Housing starts ↓)
Phase Two
Recovery to Expansion:
CPI ↓→Consumer sentiment ↑→ Consumer
demand ↑ (Auto sales ↑ + Consumer
credit ↑ + Housing starts ↑)
Phase One
Trough to Recovery:
GNP ↓→ Industrial production ↓→
Capacity utilization ↓→ Labor
productivity ↑→ Unit labor costs ↓→
Producer price index ↓

Stylized Summary of 1980s Cycle; Hypothetical Alternative Scenarios for the 1990s

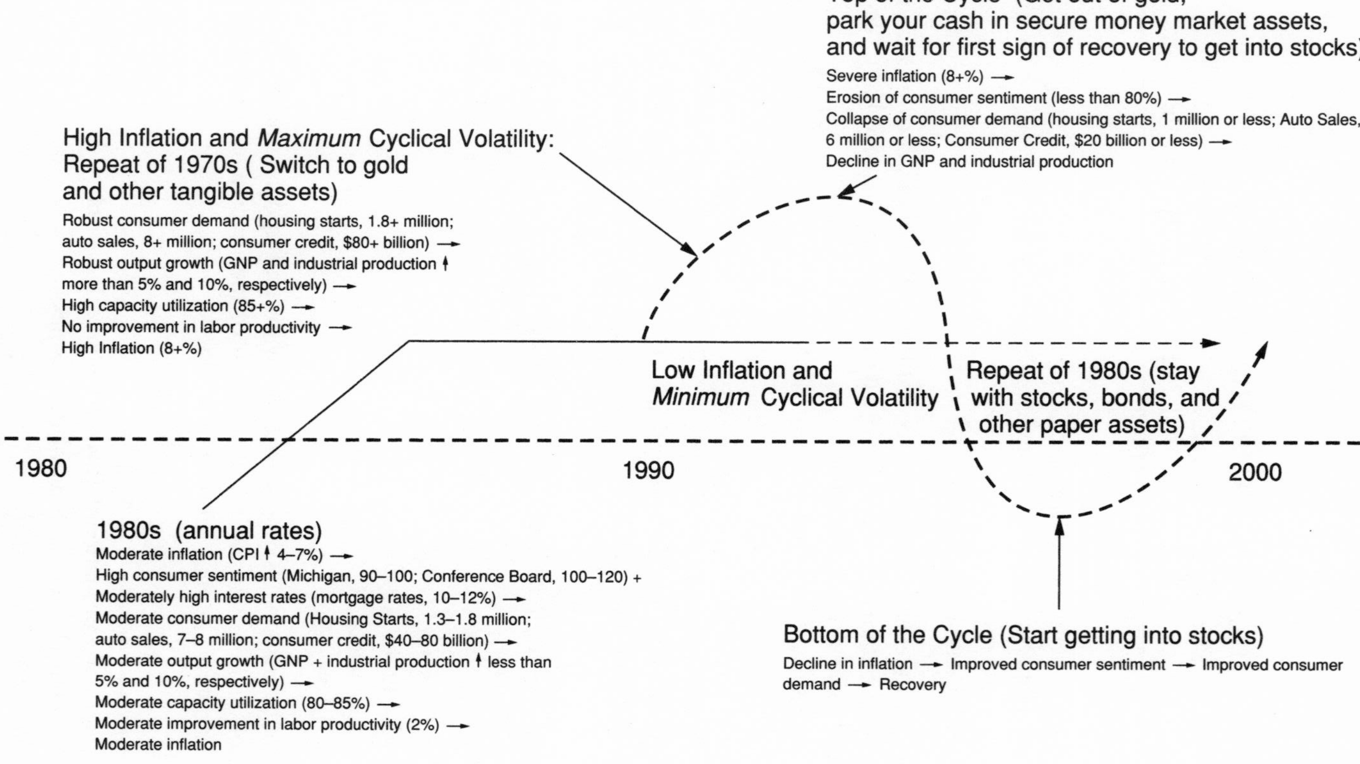
Top of the Cycle (Get out of gold,
park your cash in secure money market assets,
and wait for first sign of recovery to get into stocks)
Severe inflation (8+%) →
Erosion of consumer sentiment (less than 80%) →
Collapse of consumer demand (housing starts, 1 million or less; Auto Sales, 6 million or less; Consumer Credit, $20 billion or less) →
Decline in GNP and industrial production
High Inflation and *Maximum* Cyclical Volatility:
Repeat of 1970s (Switch to gold
and other tangible assets)
Robust consumer demand (housing starts, 1.8+ million; auto sales, 8+ million; consumer credit, $80+ billion) →
Robust output growth (GNP and industrial production ↑ more than 5% and 10%, respectively) →
High capacity utilization (85+%) →
No improvement in labor productivity →
High Inflation (8+%)
Low Inflation and
Minimum Cyclical Volatility
Repeat of 1980s (stay
with stocks, bonds, and
other paper assets)
1980
1990
2000
1980s (annual rates)
Moderate inflation (CPI ↑ 4–7%) →
High consumer sentiment (Michigan, 90–100; Conference Board, 100–120) +
Moderately high interest rates (mortgage rates, 10–12%) →
Moderate consumer demand (Housing Starts, 1.3–1.8 million; auto sales, 7–8 million; consumer credit, $40–80 billion) →
Moderate output growth (GNP + industrial production ↑ less than 5% and 10%, respectively) →
Moderate capacity utilization (80–85%) →
Moderate improvement in labor productivity (2%) →
Moderate inflation
Bottom of the Cycle (Start getting into stocks)
Decline in inflation → Improved consumer sentiment → Improved consumer demand → Recovery

SUGGESTIONS FOR FURTHER READING

These selected publications will assist your analysis of the business cycle and general economic conditions.

Business Conditions Digest
U.S. Department of Commerce
U.S. Government Printing Office
Washington, D.C. 20402

As you can see from the source listings in this book, *Business Conditions Digest* contains chart and table data on a comprehensive list of economic and business cycle indicators.
Monthly; annual subscription $44.

Handbook of Cyclical Indicators
U.S. Department of Commerce
U.S. Government Printing Office
Washington D.C. 20402

The companion reference to *Business Conditions Digest*, this source describes in detail each of the statistical series in the *Digest*.
Purchase price $5.50.

The Lehmann Letter
1855 Eighth Avenue
San Francisco, CA 94122-4708
(415) 564-4252

The author's newsletter carries forward and updates the analysis in this book and employs it in a discussion of the investment outlook.
Monthly, annual subscription $45.

Recession-Recovery Watch
Center for International Business Cycle Research
Columbia University School of Business
New York, NY 10027

A more advanced and technical analysis.
Quarterly; annual subscription $95.

PART II

YOUR CHOICE OF INVESTMENTS

CHAPTER 9

THE STOCK MARKET

A FIRST GLANCE: MARKETS DIARY

Chapter 8 compared the fortunes of stocks and gold in condition of high and low inflation. Now it's time to study these competing investments in depth.

Start with stocks, not only because they are a more common investment, but also because you have seen that our economy's health and the stock market's health are inextricably intertwined.

You probably want to plunge right in and find out how you can make money in the market and use *The Wall Street Journal* to see how much you've made, but slow down a little instead and take the time for a step-by-step approach.

The stock market is a good barometer of economic activity because it reflects the value of owning the businesses responsible for most of our economy's output. *The Dow Jones Industrial Average* is the most popular indicator of stock market performance, and that's why Chapters 1 and 8 employed it to portray the entire market.

The Dow represents share prices of 30 blue-chip industrial corporations, chosen because their operations cover the broad spectrum of industrial America, although you can see from the list presented below that not all of these firms are literally "industrials" (e.g., American Express, AT&T, McDonalds, and Woolworth are in financial services, communications, and retailing). (Dow Jones publishes separate indexes for public utilities and transportation companies.)

There are broader stock market barometers that include more corporations. For example, Standard & Poor's index of 500 stocks, known as the S & P 500, depicts the combined fortunes of 500 companies. The Wilshire Index follows 5000. They all move in more or less parallel fashion. But the Dow Industrials remains the most closely watched average because it was first and, more significant, because its handful of blue-chip companies do reflect stock market activity with surprising precision.

You probably already know a fair bit of the information in the next several pages, but it will provide a good basis for some more complex ideas presented later in this chapter.

Every day, on the first page (C1) of the third section, *The Wall Street Journal* publishes a summary account of the activity of the stock market as measured by several major indexes. It is always the lead item under the heading **Markets Diary** (see the excerpt from the Thursday, March 30, 1989 *Journal*). The Dow Jones Industrial Average is featured in the two charts under the **Stocks** caption. The chart on the left pictures the fluctuations in the Dow since September 1987, while the one on the right shows the Dow's weekly movement. The table just below the charts features four major domestic indexes and two international indexes: the Dow Jones Industrial Average, the Dow Jones Equity Index, the S & P 500, the NASDAQ Composite Index, the London Financial Times, and the Tokyo Nikkei Index. The Dow Jones Equity Index is a very

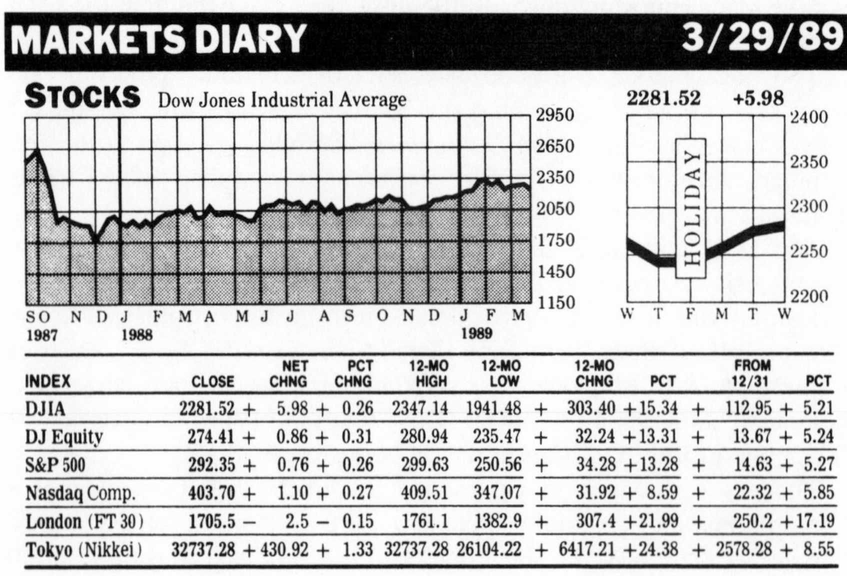

MARKETS DIARY 3/29/89

STOCKS Dow Jones Industrial Average

INDEX	CLOSE	NET CHNG	PCT CHNG	12-MO HIGH	12-MO LOW	12-MO CHNG	PCT	FROM 12/31	PCT
DJIA	2281.52	+ 5.98	+ 0.26	2347.14	1941.48	+ 303.40	+15.34	+ 112.95	+ 5.21
DJ Equity	274.41	+ 0.86	+ 0.31	280.94	235.47	+ 32.24	+13.31	+ 13.67	+ 5.24
S&P 500	292.35	+ 0.76	+ 0.26	299.63	250.56	+ 34.28	+13.28	+ 14.63	+ 5.27
Nasdaq Comp.	403.70	+ 1.10	+ 0.27	409.51	347.07	+ 31.92	+ 8.59	+ 22.32	+ 5.85
London (FT 30)	1705.5	– 2.5	– 0.15	1761.1	1382.9	+ 307.4	+21.99	+ 250.2	+17.19
Tokyo (Nikkei)	32737.28	+430.92	+ 1.33	32737.28	26104.22	+ 6417.21	+24.38	+ 2578.28	+ 8.55

Source: *The Wall Street Journal*, March 30, 1989.

broad-based index (June 30, 1982 = 100) of about 700 stocks, to be discussed more fully below. You can find a listing of these companies on pages 211 and 212. The NASDAQ (National Association of Securities Dealers Automated Quotations) Composite Index covers the over-the-counter (OTC) market, which is also discussed below. This market typically trades shares of smaller companies not listed on any exchange.

You should use this chart and table for your first quick assessment of the previous day's stock market activity. Notice that while all American indexes improved by about the same (percentage) amount on Wednesday, March 29, 1989, the major markets did better than the OTC market in the 12 months ending March 29, although the OTC improved more since the first of the year.

But take a moment to consider the Dow Industrials in more detail.

CALCULATING THE DOW

Each day, on the third page (C3) of the last section, the *Journal* publishes in chart form a detailed summary of the **Dow Jones Averages** over the past six months (see pages 168 and 169). It records the progress of the 30 industrials, the 20 stocks in the transportation average, and the 15 stocks in the utility average, as well as trading volume.

After glancing at the top chart of the **Dow Jones Averages**, your first question—once you know what this index signifies—probably is, "How

The 30 Stocks in the Dow Jones Industrial Average

Alcoa	International Paper
Allied-Signal	McDonald's
American Express	Merck
AT&T	Minnesota Mining & Manufacturing
Bethlehem Steel	Navistar
Boeing	Phillip Morris
Chevron	Primerica
Coca-Cola	Procter & Gamble
DuPont	Sears Roebuck
Eastman Kodak	Texaco
Exxon	Union Carbide
General Electric	United Technologies
General Motors	USX
Goodyear	Westinghouse
IBM	Woolworth

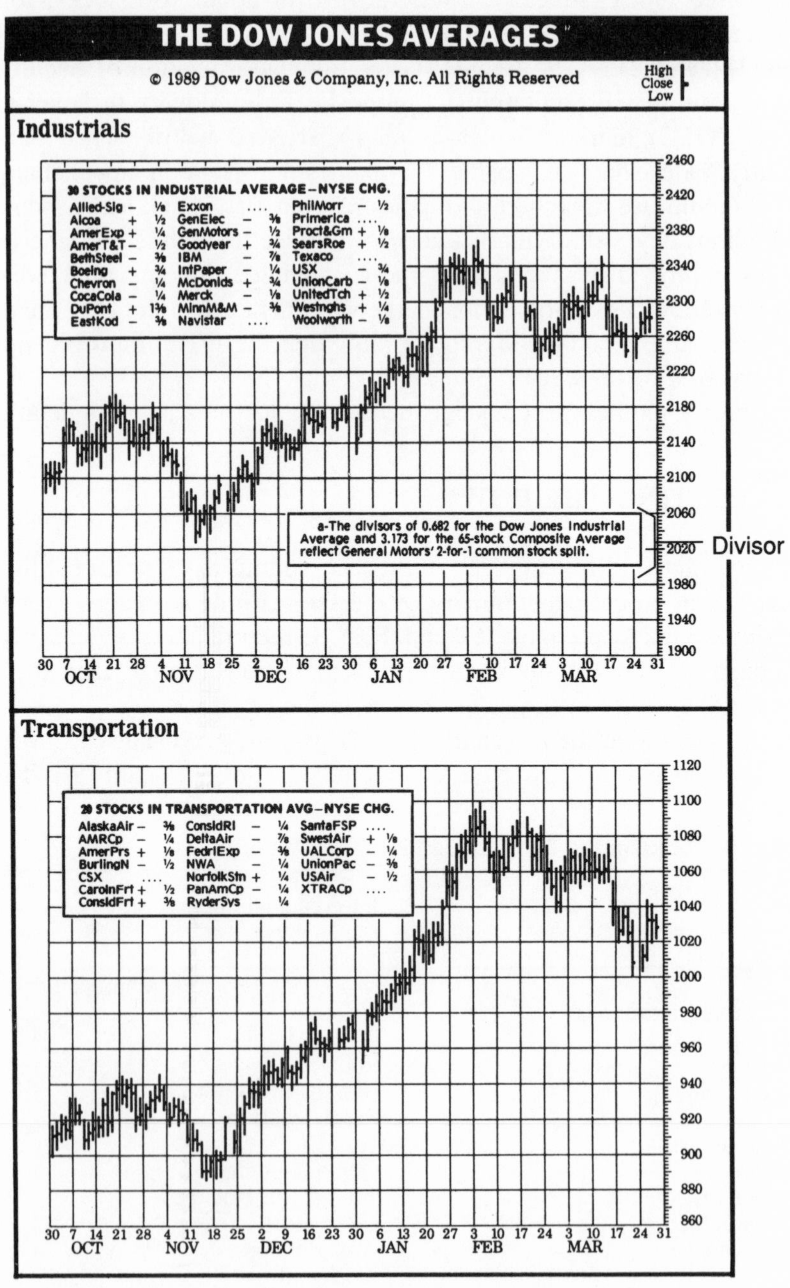
THE DOW JONES AVERAGES
© 1989 Dow Jones & Company, Inc. All Rights Reserved
High
Close
Low
Industrials
30 STOCKS IN INDUSTRIAL AVERAGE—NYSE CHG.
Allied-Sig – ⅛ Exxon .... PhilMorr – ½
Alcoa + ½ GenElec – ⅜ Primerica ....
AmerExp + ¼ GenMotors – ½ Proct&Gm + ⅛
AmerT&T – ½ Goodyear + ¾ SearsRoe + ½
BethSteel – ⅜ IBM – ⅞ Texaco ....
Boeing + ¾ IntPaper – ¼ USX – ¾
Chevron – ¼ McDonlds + ¾ UnionCarb – ⅛
CocaCola – ¼ Merck – ⅛ UnitedTch + ½
DuPont + 1⅜ MinnM&M – ⅜ Westnghs + ¼
EastKod – ⅜ Navistar .... Woolworth – ⅛
a-The divisors of 0.682 for the Dow Jones Industrial Average and 3.173 for the 65-stock Composite Average reflect General Motors' 2-for-1 common stock split.
Divisor
2460
2420
2380
2340
2300
2260
2220
2180
2140
2100
2060
2020
1980
1940
1900
30 7 14 21 28 4 11 18 25 2 9 16 23 30 6 13 20 27 3 10 17 24 3 10 17 24 31
OCT NOV DEC JAN FEB MAR
Transportation
20 STOCKS IN TRANSPORTATION AVG—NYSE CHG.
AlaskaAir – ⅜ ConsldRl – ¼ SantaFSP ....
AMRCp – ¼ DeltaAir – ⅞ SwestAir + ⅛
AmerPrs + ⅛ FedrlExp – ⅜ UALCorp – ¼
BurlingN – ½ NWA – ¼ UnionPac – ⅜
CSX .... NorfolkStn + ¼ USAir – ½
CaroinFrt + ½ PanAmCp – ¼ XTRACp ....
ConsldFrt + ⅜ RyderSys – ¼
1120
1100
1080
1060
1040
1020
1000
980
960
940
920
900
880
860
30 7 14 21 28 4 11 18 25 2 9 16 23 30 6 13 20 27 3 10 17 24 3 10 17 24 31
OCT NOV DEC JAN FEB MAR

Source: *The Wall Street Journal*, March 31, 1989

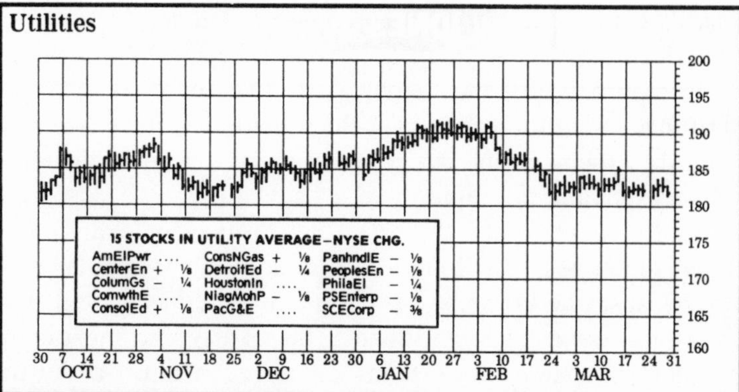

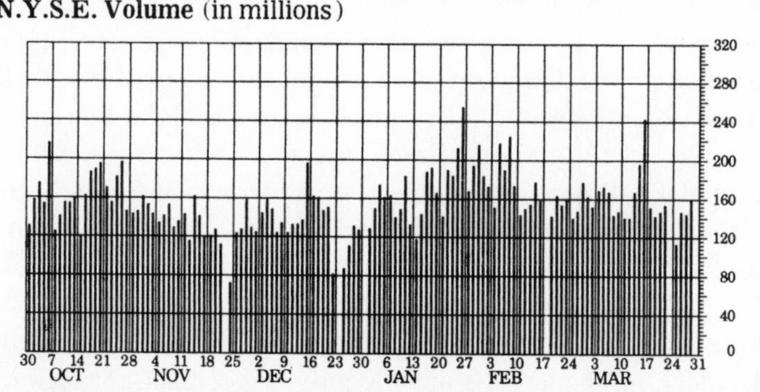

Following are the Dow Jones averages of INDUSTRIAL, TRANSPORTATION and UTILITY stocks with the total sales of each group for the period indicated.

DATE	OPEN	10 AM	11 AM	12 NOON	1 PM	2 PM	3 PM	CLOSE	CH	%	HIGH*	LOW*	VOLUME
30 INDUSTRIALS													
Mar 30	2281.34	2277.68	2275.11	2277.13	2279.51	2278.96	2284.09	2281.34	– 0.18	– 0.01	2296.92	2264.30	17,801,200
Mar 29	2274.01	2280.24	2276.39	2278.41	2273.64	2274.19	2274.19	a2281.52	+ 5.98	+ 0.26	2293.62	2262.65	14,516,900
Mar 28	2269.46	2268.21	2278.04	2274.11	2274.64	2268.04	2273.39	2275.54	+ 17.68	+ 0.78	2287.86	2258.93	17,322,800
Mar 27	2240.54	2245.71	2250.89	2248.93	2254.46	2254.64	2253.57	2257.86	+ 14.82	+ 0.66	2264.29	2234.46	12,491,300
Mar 23	2265.71	2268.21	2264.46	2264.11	2253.75	2248.57	2241.79	2243.04	– 20.17	– 0.89	2274.82	2235.89	20,521,800
20 TRANSPORTATION COS.													
Mar 30	1031.86	1028.78	1025.55	1026.52	1027.49	1027.98	1030.40	1027.98	– 4.04	– 0.39	1035.74	1021.35	3,439,600
Mar 29	1033.15	1034.61	1028.30	1027.17	1025.71	1025.71	1025.39	1032.02	– 0.16	– 0.02	1041.56	1018.92	4,764,300
Mar 28	1016.17	1015.20	1024.90	1034.77	1035.41	1032.83	1031.86	1032.18	+ 20.38	+ 2.01	1043.98	1009.06	8,460,500
Mar 27	1007.92	1008.25	1013.42	1010.03	1012.29	1011.97	1011.80	1011.80	+ 3.71	+ 0.37	1018.60	1002.91	3,426,200
Mar 23	1026.03	1027.33	1022.48	1015.04	1011.00	1004.85	1005.01	1008.09	– 16.65	– 1.62	1032.50	1000.16	5,850,200
15 UTILITIES													
Mar 30	182.31	182.08	182.02	182.14	182.14	182.08	182.43	181.84	– 0.89	– 0.49	182.97	181.31	4,468,300
Mar 29	182.85	183.62	183.26	182.97	182.61	182.73	182.67	182.73	– 0.18	– 0.10	184.09	182.02	2,636,200
Mar 28	182.61	182.43	182.61	182.61	182.55	182.49	182.49	182.91	+ 0.48	+ 0.26	183.85	181.42	4,777,200
Mar 27	181.84	181.78	182.08	181.90	182.43	182.08	182.14	182.43	+ 0.29	+ 0.16	183.03	181.01	2,293,700
Mar 23	182.49	182.49	182.37	182.25	181.84	181.84	181.84	182.14	– 0.23	– 0.13	183.26	181.42	3,560,900
65 STOCKS COMPOSITE AVERAGE													
Mar 30	862.91	861.21	859.83	860.58	861.33	861.29	863.22	861.65	– 1.61	– 0.19	867.63	856.01	25,709,100
Mar 29	862.00	864.21	861.61	861.57	859.95	860.15	860.03	a863.26	+ 1.26	+ 0.15	869.09	855.54	21,917,400
Mar 28	856.64	856.02	860.60	862.12	862.35	860.25	861.18	862.00	+ 9.04	+ 1.06	868.13	851.87	30,560,500
Mar 27	847.87	849.04	851.60	850.24	852.34	852.06	851.83	852.96	+ 4.31	+ 0.51	856.37	844.81	18,211,200
Mar 23	858.12	858.97	856.92	854.98	851.48	848.88	847.45	848.65	– 8.54	– 1.00	862.15	844.73	29,932,900

Averages are compiled daily by using the following divisors: Industrials, 0.682; Transportation, 0.773; Utilities, 2.109; Composite, 3.173.

*Averages of the highs and lows reached at any time during the day on the New York Stock Exchange by the individual stocks.

Source: *The Wall Street Journal*, March 31, 1989

can an average of stock market prices be over $2,000? I don't know of *one* stock that trades that high, much less *30* of them."

The answer involves the manner in which the Dow deals with "stock splits." Companies split their stock (say, two for one) to prevent the stock from becoming too expensive. Shareholders receive two shares for each share they own and the stock's price is halved; thus, the total value of the shares remains the same.

This usually occurs when the price of a "round-lot" transaction (100 shares) gets too expensive. Round-lot transactions are popular with large investors because the commission per share is reduced, and it's much easier to buy a round lot at $50 than $100 a share. So most companies would rather split their stock than see it become too expensive and discourage investors' purchases.

Here's how this applies to the Dow Jones Industrial Average.

Suppose you are calculating the average of a group of 30 stocks (such as the Dow) by adding the share prices of all of them and dividing by 30. If (to make the arithmetic simple and the point clear) each of the 30 were selling at $100, obviously the average would be $100 ($3,000/30). However, if each of the 30 happened to split two for one, then each would be worth $50, per share; that is, the average price per share of these 30 stocks would suddenly be $50 not $100. Clearly it makes no sense to reduce the average because of such splits, since someone who owns the stock has exactly as much equity (percentage ownership) value after a split as before it.

Lowering the divisor from 30 to 15 is one solution: 30 shares at $50 each ($1,500) divided by 15 (not 30) keeps the average at 100. Future stock splits can be handled in a similar fashion with an appropriate adjustment in the divisor.

Another, though less important, reason for changing the divisor is that occasionally Dow Jones replaces one of the 30 industrial stocks with another. Here, too, it wouldn't make sense to change the average; just because one stock is substituted for another doesn't mean the market, itself, has changed. Therefore, the divisor is adjusted at the same time, to keep the average constant.

Now consider a real-life example (see page 172) using the Dow on Monday, May 15, 1989. Add the share prices of all 30 companies in the Dow. The total comes to $1,680.38, and, when you divide that by the divisor of 0.682, you get $2,463.89—the Dow average for May 15, 1989. There had been so many stock splits that the divisor had fallen to 0.682.

Divisors

a-The divisors of 0.682 for the Dow Jones Industrial Average and 3.173 for the 65-stock Composite Average reflect General Motors' 2-for-1 common stock split.

Averages are compiled daily by using the following divisors: Industrials, 0.682; Transportation, 0.773; Utilities, 2.109; Composite, 3.173.

Source: *The Wall Street Journal*, March 31, 1989.

The figures used on page 172 to compute the Dow are the closing May 15, 1989 prices for the New York Stock Exchange (NYSE). NYSE *Composite Transactions* prices (to be discussed below) vary slightly from the prices used here. For example, Alcoa closed in New York at 67, while the Composite for May 15, 1989 listed its price at 67¼. Why the discrepancy? Because the composite includes the closing prices of the Pacific Stock Exchange, which continues its operations for half an hour after the New York Exchange closes. On May 15, 1989 that half-hour was enough time for the price of Alcoa to be bid up an additional quarter of a point.

So much for the Dow; you are now ready to move on to a more detailed analysis of stock market performance.

STOCK MARKET DATA BANK

The Stock Market Data Bank appears daily on the second page (C2) of the third section. See pages 173 through 174 for an example from the Friday, March 31, 1989 *Wall Street Journal*. It presents a comprehensive summary of stock market activity in five sections: **Major Indexes, Most Active Issues, Diaries, Price Percentage Gainers and Losers, Volume Percentage Gainers and Losers, Volume Percentage Leaders,** and **Breakdown of Trading in NYSE Stocks**. Look at it after you have examined the **Markets Diary** in order to get a more detailed view of the previous day's trading activity.

Major Indexes lists the Dow averages as well as a variety of other indexes in greater detail than provided in the **Markets Diary** on the first page (C1) of the third section. These statistics permit you to compare the performance of your own investments with the broadest gauges of stock market activity.

May 15, 1989 Closing Stock Prices

Company	*Price*
Alcoa	$ 67
Allied-Signal	33
American Express	33.625
AT&T	34.50
Bethlehem Steel	23.25
Boeing	81.625
Chevron	52.875
Coca-Cola	56.375
DuPont	110.625
Eastman Kodak	42.75
Exxon	43
General Electric	52.125
General Motors	40.75
Goodyear	54.25
IBM	112.75
International Paper	49.25
McDonald's	58.75
Merck	70.625
Minnesota Mining & Manufacturing	74
Navistar	5.25
Phillip Morris	133.625
Primerica	21.25
Procter & Gamble	99
Sears Roebuck	46
Texaco	54.125
Union Carbide	29
United Technologies	52.50
USX	34.375
Westinghouse	61
Woolworth	53.125
Total	$1,680.375

$$\frac{1{,}680.375}{0.682} = \$2{,}463.89 \text{ (The Dow average on May 15, 1989)}$$

$$\frac{\text{Sum of stock prices}}{\text{Divisor}} = \text{The Dow Jones Industrial Average}$$

STOCK MARKET DATA BANK 3/30/89

MAJOR INDEXES

HIGH	LOW	(12 MOS)	CLOSE	NET CHG	% CHG	12 MO CHG	% CHG	FROM 12/31	% CHG
DOW JONES AVERAGES									
2347.14	1941.48	30 Industrials	2281.34	− 0.18	− 0.01	+ 293.28	+14.75	+ 112.77	+ 5.20
1087.97	784.05	20 Transportation	1027.98	− 4.04	− 0.39	+ 164.93	+19.11	+ 58.14	+ 5.99
191.15	167.08	15 Utilities	x181.84	− 0.89	− 0.49	+ 10.37	+ 6.05	− 4.44	− 2.38
896.15	719.30	65 Composite	x861.65	− 1.61	− 0.19	+ 110.78	+14.75	+ 35.71	+ 4.32
280.94	235.47	Equity Mkt. Index	274.60	+ 0.19	+ 0.07	+ 31.71	+13.06	+ 13.86	+ 5.32
NEW YORK STOCK EXCHANGE									
168.10	142.21	Composite	164.38	+ 0.13	+ 0.08	+ 17.78	+12.13	+ 8.12	+ 5.20
203.84	172.22	Industrials	198.65	+ 0.06	+ 0.03	+ 20.83	+11.71	+ 9.23	+ 4.87
78.93	67.79	Utilities	77.56	− 0.01	− 0.01	+ 8.17	+11.77	+ 2.87	+ 3.84
165.27	122.27	Transportation	157.17	− 0.78	− 0.49	+ 23.09	+17.22	+ 10.57	+ 7.21
140.43	118.43	Finance	139.34	+ 0.81	+ 0.58	+ 17.82	+14.66	+ 11.15	+ 8.70
STANDARD & POOR'S INDEXES									
299.63	250.83	500 Index	292.52	+ 0.17	+ 0.06	+ 33.63	+12.99	+ 14.8U_	
346.41	290.74	Industrials	336.86	− 0.06	− 0.02	+ 36.47	+12.14	+ 15.60	+ 4.86
255.19	187.76	Transportation	239.47	− 1.19	− 0.49	+ 28.67	+13.60	+ 11.30	+ 4.95
118.56	101.21	Utilities	116.72	+ 0.12	+ 0.10	+ 12.51	+12.00	+ 4.08	+ 3.62
27.57	21.83	Financials	27.57	+ 0.23	+ 0.84	+ 5.25	+23.52	+ 3.08	+ 12.58
NASDAQ									
409.51	363.26	Composite	404.56	+ 0.86	+ 0.21	+ 29.92	+ 7.99	+ 23.18	+ 6.08
413.09	356.15	Industrials	396.22	+ 1.18	+ 0.30	+ 12.55	+ 3.27	+ 17.27	+ 4.56
476.70	384.52	Insurance	469.33	+ 0.89	+ 0.19	+ 71.68	+18.03	+ 40.19	+ 9.37
464.97	433.41	Banks	457.37	+ 1.68	+ 0.37	+ 8.60	+ 1.92	+ 22.06	+ 5.07
178.11	156.88	Nat. Mkt. Comp.	176.00	+ 0.40	+ 0.23	+ 14.07	+ 8.69	+ 10.35	+ 6.25
160.10	138.03	Nat. Mkt. Indus.	154.36	+ 0.48	+ 0.31	+ 5.93	+ 4.00	+ 6.94	+ 4.71
OTHERS									
332.52	285.37	Amex	325.47	− 0.11	− 0.03	+ 29.04	+ 9.80	+ 19.46	+ 6.36
248.67	220.76	Value-Line (geom.)	244.11	+ 0.19	+ 0.08	+ 15.97	+ 7.00	+ 11.43	+ 4.91
159.27	139.20	Russell 2000	156.76	− 0.04	− 0.03	+ 14.61	+10.28	+ 9.40	+ 6.38
2953.14	2506.94	Wilshire 5000	2892.62	+ 3.49	+ 0.12	+ 308.67	+11.95	+ 154.20	+ 5.63

MOST ACTIVE ISSUES

NYSE	VOLUME	CLOSE	CHANGE
Illinois Power	4,311,400	14	− 1¾
BankAmerica	3,551,200	24½	+ ⅝
Citicorp	2,569,500	29½	+ 1
SCEcorp	2,528,700	x31	− ⅜
Freeport McMo	2,432,600	34	+ ⅝
Brunswick	1,946,400	20⅜	+ 1
Western No Am	1,934,000	3/32	− 3/128
Black & Decker	1,818,800	18¾	− ½
Sears Roebuck	1,738,200	43½	+ ½
IBM	1,652,400	108¾	− ⅞
Smithkln Beck	1,608,600	55⅝	+ ⅞
AT&T	1,570,200	30¾	− ½
Amer Express	1,518,400	31⅜	+ ¼
Exxon Corp	1,491,600	43½	− ⅛
Chase Manhat	1,347,600	37	+ 1⅜
NASDAQ NMS			
M C I Comm	2,523,800	28⅞	.....
MiniScribe	1,578,600	3¼	− 7/16
Corp Cap Res	1,573,400	9/16	− 11/16
Oceaneering	1,537,000	4⅛	+ 7/16
Intel Corp	1,355,100	25¼	+ ¾
Seagate Tech	1,223,500	11¾	+ ⅜
Sun State S&L	1,085,500	2⅛	− 2¾
Tele-Comm A	1,060,200	29¼	+ ½
K L A Instr	1,014,100	11	+ ¾
Mobile cl A	970,700	34⅝	− 1⅛
Apple Cmptr	933,600	34¾	+ ½
US Healthcare	848,100	10	+ ⅜
Equitex Inc	725,800	3/16	+ 1/32
AMEX			
Texas Air Corp	956,300	13⅝	+ ¾
Energy Svc	683,700	3	.....
D W G Corp	358,200	12¾	− ⅝
Houston Oil Tr	355,600	1¼	+ ⅛
Amdahl Corp	322,100	16⅝	− ⅜

DIARIES

NYSE	THUR	WED	WK AGO
Issues traded	1,940	1,960	1,965
Advances	726	741	584
Declines	716	658	814
Unchanged	498	561	567
New highs	43	37	24
New lows	40	29	33
zAdv vol (000)	74,838	69,880	46,427
zDecl vol (000)	61,214	48,323	86,026
zTotal vol (000)	159,950	144,240	153,750
Closing tick[1]	+41	+24	−155
Closing trin[2]	.83	.78	1.35
zBlock trades	3,337	3,026	3,011
NASDAQ			
Issues traded	4,468	4,470	4,469
Advances	952	1,016	952
Declines	977	895	983
Unchanged	2,539	2,559	2,534
New highs	77	84	61
New lows	37	41	35
Adv vol (000)	44,590	46,837	55,030
Decl vol (000)	34,905	34,464	30,379
Total vol (000)	115,613	122,960	149,178
Block trades	1,893	2,030	2,018
AMEX			
Issues traded	875	864	849
Advances	262	288	272
Declines	326	261	276
Unchanged	287	315	301
New highs	20	30	21
New lows	12	14	18
zAdv vol (000)	4,119	4,903	3,125
zDecl vol (000)	3,690	2,970	3,834
zTotal vol (000)	9,780	10,180	9,660
Comp vol (000)	12,399	12,577	11,612
zBlock trades	151	154	172

Illinois Power,
Volume Leader
Advancing Issues
Led Declining issues
Now Highs Exceeded
New lows
Advance Volume
Led Decline Volume

Positive(+)
closing tick means
more stocks advanced
than declined
in last trade.

Trin of less than
one indicates
buying pressure.

The Wall Street Journal, March 31, 1989

Source: *The Wall Street Journal*, March 31, 1989.

Soo Line down 18.8%

PRICE PERCENTAGE GAINERS . . .

NYSE	CLOSE		CHANGE		% CHG
Cmprhnsv Care	11½	+	1⅞	+	19.5
Todd Shipyrd	2¼	+	¼	+	12.5
Ensource Inc	9⅞	+	1	+	11.3
Ensearch Explr	10¼	+	1	+	10.8
Tyler Corp	7¾	+	¾	+	10.7
Varco Intl	4½	+	⅜	+	9.1
House Fabrics	23¾	+	1⅞	+	8.6
Mesabi Trust	3½	+	¼	+	7.7
Service Resou	3½	+	¼	+	7.7
Daniel Indus	15	+	1	+	7.1
Recognitn Eq	9⅜	+	⅝	+	7.1
WMS Indus	7⅝	+	½	+	7.0
Chyron Corp	3⅞	+	¼	+	6.9
Service Merch	15⅝	+	⅞	+	5.9
Avon Products	22½	+	1¼	+	5.9
Thortec Intl	2¼	+	⅛	+	5.9
Bankers Tr NY	x41⅞	+	2¼	+	5.7
Rockwell Intl	22	+	1⅛	+	5.4
Crossland Savs	14¾	+	¾	+	5.4
Mitel Corp	2½	+	⅛	+	5.3
NASDAQ NMS					
Prof Invtrs	4	+	¾	+	23.1
City Holding Co	18	+	3	+	20.0
Synercom Tech	4¼	+	11/16	+	19.3
Atl Fncl Fed	2⅜	+	⅜	+	18.8
Old Fash Food	4¾	+	¾	+	18.8
Possis Corp	4⅛	+	⅝	+	17.9
Miller Bldg	5 3/16	+	¾	+	16.9
Quadra Logic	4⅛	+	½	+	13.8
Sierra RE 1984	7⅜	+	⅞	+	13.5
Nova Pharm	4⅝	+	½	+	12.1
Oceaneering	4⅛	+	7/16	+	11.9
Vitronics Corp	2⅜	+	¼	+	11.8
Tekelec	14¾	+	1½	+	11.3
Circon Corp	5	+	½	+	11.1
AMEX					
Concord Fab	3¾	+	½	+	15.4
Sierra Cap VI	5¾	+	¾	+	15.0
Decorator Ind	5	+	½	+	11.1
Spartech	4⅝	+	⅜	+	8.8
Inco Oppty Rlty	4⅝	+	⅜	+	8.8

AND LOSERS

NYSE	CLOSE		CHANGE		% CHG
SooLineCorp	19½	–	4½	–	18.8
IllinoisPower	14	–	1¾	–	11.1
WickesCos	7	–	¾	–	9.7
WedgestnFn	2⅜	–	¼	–	9.5
GreenTree	6⅜	–	⅝	–	8.9
GenentechInc	17¾	–	1⅝	–	8.4
TISMtgInv	5½	–	½	–	8.3
EkcoGrp	3⅛	–	¼	–	7.4
BondIntlGold	8⅛	–	⅝	–	7.1
EMCCorp	3½	–	¼	–	6.7
USHomeCorp	1⅞	–	⅛	–	6.3
Winchells	1⅞	–	⅛	–	6.3
ZenithLabs	2	–	⅛	–	5.9
LTVCorp	2⅛	–	⅛	–	5.6
IdealBasicInd	2⅛	–	⅛	–	5.6
PanAmCorp	4⅜	–	¼	–	5.4
RepubGypsm	4½	–	¼	–	5.3
BordenChem	20⅞	–	1⅛	–	5.1
BordenChemPl	20⅞	–	1⅛	–	5.1
KanebServices	2⅜	–	⅛	–	5.0
NASDAQ NMS					
SunStateS&L	2⅛	–	2¾	–	56.4
NobelInsur	2	–	½	–	20.0
AmerContl	3⅜	–	⅝	–	15.6
JRMHldg	2¾	–	½	–	15.4
ElectronicTele	4½	–	¾	–	14.3
HuffmanKoos	3¼	–	½	–	13.3
AltronInc	2⅝	–	⅜	–	12.5
PacNuclearSys	11⅝	–	1⅝	–	12.3
MiniScribe	3¼	–	7/16	–	11.9
Microsemi	4⅝	–	⅝	–	11.9
ComstockGrp	1⅞	–	¼	–	11.8
AmerRice	1⅞	–	¼	–	11.8
HarvardKnit	2⅞	–	⅜	–	11.5
Plasti-LineInc	10	–	1¼	–	11.1
AMEX					
YankeeCos	1¾	–	¼	–	12.5
Nichols(SE)	2⅞	–	⅜	–	11.5
PrincetnDiag	2⅜	–	¼	–	9.5
Jewelmasters	4⅛	–	⅜	–	8.3
GiantYellow	10	–	⅞	–	8.0

BREAKDOWN OF TRADING IN NYSE STOCKS

BY MARKET	Thur	Wed	WK AGO
New York	159,950,000	144,240,000	153,750,000
Midwest	10,389,800	10,175,900	10,661,700
Pacific	6,640,100	5,134,100	5,122,200
NASD	4,611,110	4,714,180	5,385,880
Phila	2,541,300	2,566,400	2,558,800
Boston	3,123,300	3,042,800	2,884,100
Cincinnati	851,500	771,200	499,100
Instinet	303,000	290,600	391,700
Composite	188,410,110	170,935,180	181,253,480

Composite Volume of All NYSE Stocks Traded in All Exchanges

[1]The net difference of the number of stocks closing higher than their previous trade from those closing lower; NYSE trading only.

x-Ex-dividend of SCECorp. 62 cents lowered the Utility average 0.30. This lowered the Composite average 0.20.

z-NYSE or Amex only.

½-HOURLY	Thur	Wed	WK AGO
9:30-10	20,200,000	24,510,000	22,420,000
10-10:30	16,300,000	13,860,000	13,820,000
10:30-11	10,990,000	11,760,000	15,700,000
11-11:30	11,030,000	10,220,000	10,560,000
11:30-12	11,960,000	10,800,000	10,140,000
12-12:30	12,810,000	8,820,000	8,760,000
12:30-1	7,450,000	11,680,000	13,250,000
1-1:30	7,660,000	5,830,000	13,850,000
1:30-2	9,100,000	5,790,000	7,330,000
2-2:30	9,240,000	8,180,000	10,690,000
2:30-3	14,650,000	7,610,000	7,890,000
3-3:30	12,830,000	9,900,000	8,050,000
3:30-4	15,730,000	15,280,000	11,290,000

Source: *The Wall Street Journal*, March 31, 1989.

Dow Industrials Down 0.01%

NYSE Composite Up 0.08%

S&P 500 Up 0.06%

STOCK MARKET DATA BANK **3/30/89**

MAJOR INDEXES

HIGH	LOW	(12 MOS)	CLOSE	NET CHG	% CHG	12 MO CHG	% CHG	FROM 12/31	% CHG
DOW JONES AVERAGES									
2347.14	1941.48	30 Industrials	2281.34	− 0.18	− 0.01	+ 293.28	+14.75	+ 112.77	+ 5.20
1087.97	784.05	20 Transportation	1027.98	− 4.04	− 0.39	+ 164.93	+19.11	+ 58.14	+ 5.99
191.15	167.08	15 Utilities	x181.84	− 0.89	− 0.49	+ 10.37	+ 6.05	− 4.44	− 2.38
896.15	719.30	65 Composite	x861.65	− 1.61	− 0.19	+ 110.78	+14.75	+ 35.71	+ 4.32
280.94	235.47	Equity Mkt. Index	274.60	+ 0.19	+ 0.07	+ 31.71	+13.06	+ 13.86	+ 5.32
NEW YORK STOCK EXCHANGE									
168.10	142.21	Composite	164.38	+ 0.13	+ 0.08	+ 17.78	+12.13	+ 8.12	+ 5.20
203.84	172.22	Industrials	198.65	+ 0.06	+ 0.03	+ 20.83	+11.71	+ 9.23	+ 4.87
78.93	67.79	Utilities	77.56	− 0.01	− 0.01	+ 8.17	+11.77	+ 2.87	+ 3.84
165.27	122.27	Transportation	157.17	− 0.78	− 0.49	+ 23.09	+17.22	+ 10.57	+ 7.21
140.43	118.43	Finance	139.34	+ 0.81	+ 0.58	+ 17.82	+14.66	+ 11.15	+ 8.70
STANDARD & POOR'S INDEXES									
299.63	250.83	500 Index	292.52	+ 0.17	+ 0.06	+ 33.63	+12.99	+ 14.8U_	
346.41	290.74	Industrials	336.86	− 0.06	− 0.02	+ 36.47	+12.14	+ 15.60	+ 4.86
255.19	187.76	Transportation	239.47	− 1.19	− 0.49	+ 28.67	+13.60	+ 11.30	+ 4.95
118.56	101.21	Utilities	116.72	+ 0.12	+ 0.10	+ 12.51	+12.00	+ 4.08	+ 3.62
27.57	21.83	Financials	27.57	+ 0.23	+ 0.84	+ 5.25	+23.52	+ 3.08	+ 12.58

Source: *The Wall Street Journal*, March 31, 1989.

Most Active Issues lists the day's most heavily traded stocks on the three major markets: New York Stock Exchange (NYSE), the National Association of Security Dealers Automated Quotation (NASDAQ) system in the over-the-counter (OTC) market, and the American Stock Exchange (AMEX). For instance, under NYSE you can see that over 4 million shares of Illinois Power changed hands on Wednesday, March 30, 1989. This stock fell sharply under heavy selling pressure.

The **Diaries** provide another important measure of the day's trading activity: *advances versus declines, new highs versus new lows*, and the

Illinois Power – Volume Leader

MOST ACTIVE ISSUES

NYSE	VOLUME	CLOSE	CHANGE
Illinois Power	4,311,400	14	− 1¾
BankAmerica	3,551,200	24½	+ ⅝
Citicorp	2,569,500	29½	+ 1
SCEcorp	2,528,700	x31	− ⅜

Source: *The Wall Street Journal*, March 31, 1989.

DIARIES

NYSE	THUR	WED	WK AGO
Issues traded	1,940	1,960	1,965
Advances	726	741	584
Declines	716	658	814
Unchanged	498	561	567
New highs	43	37	24
New lows	40	29	33
zAdv vol (000)	74,838	69,880	46,427
zDecl vol (000)	61,214	48,323	86,026
zTotal vol (000)	159,950	144,240	153,750
Closing tick[1]	+41	+24	−155
Closing trin[2]	.83	.78	1.35
zBlock trades	3,337	3,026	3,011

Advancing Issues led Declining Issues
New Highs exceeded New Lows
Advance Volume led Decline Volume
(+) Positive closing tick means more stocks advanced than declined in last trade
Trin of less than one indicates buying pressure

Source: *The Wall Street Journal*, March 31, 1989.

volume of the stocks advancing and declining. On Thursday, March 30, 1989, 726 issues advanced and 716 declined on the New York exchange. The advancers were comparatively a bit more actively traded: 74,838,000 to 61,214,000. These figures are not inconsistent with the slight incline in the Dow that day, but the margin of stocks that hit new highs (43) over those that hit new lows (40) is a sign of a market with only marginal upward strength. These figures can signal strength or weakness in the market if there is a sharp disproportion between issues advancing (and their volume) as well as stocks that reach new highs on the one hand versus issues declining and stocks that reach new lows on the other.

Closing tick and *closing trin* are even finer measures of stock market strength or weakness.

A *tick* in a measure of movement in closing stock prices: a positive (+) tick means prices were rising at the end of the day, and the negative (–) tick indicates falling prices. The closing tick nets all stocks whose last trade was higher than the previous trade (+) on the NYSE against all stocks whose last trade was lower (–); a "+" closing tick means that more stocks were rising than falling and a "–" closing tick means that more stocks were falling than rising. On March 30, 41 more stocks were rising than falling at their last trade, and so the closing tick for the day was +41.

A *trin* also measures market strength. A trin less than one (0.83 on Thursday, March 30, 1989) indicates money flowing into stocks (bullish sign), while a trin greater than one indicates money flowing out of stocks (bearish sign). The trin is computed by dividing two ratios:

$$\frac{\frac{\text{Advances}}{\text{Declines}}}{\frac{\text{Advance Volume}}{\text{Decline Volume}}} = \frac{\frac{726}{716}}{\frac{74,838}{61,214}} = 0.83$$

As an investor, you want to know the percentage performance of your stocks. A $1 rise in the price of a stock that you purchased at $100 a share is an event to note, but if you had paid $2 a share for the stock, the same $1 rise is a cause for celebration. In the first case your investment increased by 1 percent, in the second by 50 percent. In **Price Percentage Gainers and Losers** you can track this daily. On March 30, 1989, SooLine Corporation fell 18.8 percent in a single day (ouch!) on a drop of $4.50 to a price of $19.50.

Volume Percentage Leaders represent the stocks that traded the largest volume of shares on March 30. The percentage gain refers to the increase in volume over the average for the previous 65 trading days.

The **Breakdown of Trading in NYSE Stocks** provides trading volume on all stock exchanges of securities listed on the New York Stock Exchange, as well as trading volume by half-hours. Trading of all NYSE stocks on all exchanges was a composite volume of 188,410,110 shares for Thursday, March 30.

AND LOSERS

NYSE	CLOSE		CHANGE		% CHG
SooLineCorp	19½	–	4½	–	18.8
IllinoisPower	14	–	1¾	–	11.1
WickesCos	7	–	¾	–	9.7
WedgestnFn	2⅜	–	¼	–	9.5

Soo Line down 18.8% → SooLineCorp

Source: *The Wall Street Journal*, March 31, 1989.

BREAKDOWN OF TRADING IN NYSE STOCKS

BY MARKET	Thur	Wed	WK AGO
New York	159,950,000	144,240,000	153,750,000
Midwest	10,389,800	10,175,900	10,661,700
Pacific	6,640,100	5,134,100	5,122,200
NASD	4,611,110	4,714,180	5,385,880
Phila	2,541,300	2,566,400	2,558,800
Boston	3,123,300	3,042,800	2,884,100
Cincinnati	851,500	771,200	499,100
Instinet	303,000	290,600	391,700
Composite	188,410,110	170,935,180	181,253,480

Composite Volume of all NYSE stocks traded on all exchanges → Composite

Source: *The Wall Street Journal*, March 31, 1989.

Finally, the **Diaries** component of the **Stock Market Data Bank** listed the number of stocks that hit new highs and lows (i.e., the number that closed higher or lower than at any time in the past 52 weeks). You saw that on March 30, 1989, 43 reached new highs and 40 reached new lows. **NYSE Highs/Lows** (in the front-page indexes of the first and last sections) lists these stocks. Consider this example from the Friday, March 31, 1989 *Journal*.

NYSE HIGHS/LOWS

Thursday, March 30, 1989

NEW HIGHS – 43

AmBldgMnt	Craig Corp	KubotaLtd	StoneWeb
AmIntGrp	DanielInd	LandsEnd	SunElec
Anthony s	Ensource	MarshMcl	TrnCdaPipe g
Aon cp	FstChicago pf	Mesabi Tr	Tribune
BankAmer	FreeptMcM pf	Mestek	UGI Corp
BauschLmb	GenMills	Newell s	UNUM
BeckmanInst n	Hanna pf	PS Group	UniTel
ChaseManh	HelmrPayne	PepsiCo	UnvHltRIT
ChemBank	HiltonHtl s	PhilVanH	Warn Lamb
ClubMed	HouseFab	PlainsPtr	WasteMgt
ContBank n	HouseIntl	Polaroid wd	

NEW LOWS – 40

ARX Inc	GreenTree	OHM Cp	SavanEP pfA
Adams Exp	INA InvSec	PanhECp	Svcmstr
ArizPS adj pf	Ill Power	PortG 2.60pf	SooLine
BancoBilV n	IllPw 4.08pf	PrimeMotr	Soumrk adj pf
Bunker Hill	IllPw 4.70pf	PrimMtrLt	Soumrk pfH
CIllLt 4.50pf	IllPw 7.56pf	PrudIntInc n	TIS Mtg n
ConEd 5pfA	IllPw 11.75pf	PrudStrat	TemplGlGv n
DataGenl	LVI Grp pf	PSEG 4.30pf	VnKmpMerIn n
EMC Cp	NatSemi	Quantum	vjWstCoNA
Fairchld pf	NewAmerHi	RegalIntl	Xerox 3.68pf

s-Split or stock dividend of 25 per cent or more in the past 52 weeks. High-low range is adjusted from old stock. n-New issue in past 52 weeks and does not cover the entire 52 week period.

Source: *The Wall Street Journal*, March 31, 1989.

THE ODD-LOT TRADER

So far this discussion has proceeded without regard to the magnitude of individual investments, except for the observation that companies split their stock chiefly in order to keep its price within the small investor's reach. Remember that round lots are trades of 100 shares whose commission per share is lower than that on *odd-lot* (less than 100 shares) transactions. Yet many small investors still trade in odd lots because they cannot afford to deal in round lots. For instance, IBM closed at $112.50 on Friday, March 17, 1989, putting the cost of a round-lot purchase at $11,250 ($112.50 × 100) and out of the reach of many small investors.

Many market analysts used to believe that odd-lot transactions were a contrary (negative) indicator, because they saw the small investor as a market follower who buys more as the market peaks and sells more as it bottoms out (the opposite of the savvy, bigtime trader who gets in at the bottom and out at the top). Therefore, according to this wisdom, a high ratio of odd-lot buying to selling is a sign of a market peak (time to sell), while the opposite indicates a market trough (time to buy). However, since a great many small investors in recent years have abandoned odd-lots in favor of mutual funds, this omen has become less significant to analysts.

The *Journal* provides a daily record of **Odd-Lot Trading** for the day preceding the previous trading day. You'll find it beneath NYSE Highs/Lows. See the example on page 180 from the Friday, June 16, 1989 issue that indicated sales of 569,020 and purchases of 274,158 on June 14, 1989.

A more detailed report appears on Mondays (also beneath NYSE Highs/Lows). See for yourself when examining the **Odd-Lot Trading** report from the Monday, March 20, 1989 *Wall Street Journal*. Odd-lot sales (547,889 shares) exceeded odd-lot purchases (252,982) on Thursday, March 16, 1989 in NYSE trading by odd-lot specialists and shares sold (3,750,543) exceeded shares purchased (1,812,874) by all NYSE member firms for the week ended Friday, March 3, 1989.

Perhaps the conventional wisdom *was* true since small (odd-lot) investors were busy selling into the rising market in the spring of 89. Maybe they had purchased these shares just prior to the 87 crash and were happy to unload them now at no loss. Too bad they didn't know that low inflation and low PEs (see Chapter 8) made stocks a good bet.

NYSE HIGHS/LOWS

Thursday, June 15, 1989

NEW HIGHS – 69

AmGvTrmTr n	DuqLt 2pf	Munsingwr	SanDie Gas
AHlthPr	Eastn Util	NSPw 4.11pf	ScottysInc
AmerHotel	Eldon	NSPw 8.80pf	SIGNET
Aon cp	FtBkSv pf	Norwest	SourceCap
ApPw 7.40pf	FstUnionCp	NovoNord	SouUnCo
ArchDnM	Hershey	OhEd 7.36pf	StdFdBk
CML Gp	HiltonHtl	OhEd 8.64pf	StoneridgeRs
ChasMn pfG	IdahoPwr	OrionCap	viTodShp pf
CinG 7.44pf	IntPub wi	OrionCa pf	Torchmark
CinG 9.52pf	JerCe 8.12pf	OrionCa pf	Transco pf
Circus	JerCe 7.88pf	OverShip s	Tri-Cont pf
ClubMed	KansCtyPL	PacifiCorp	UnEl 6.40pf
CwE 1.42pf	LIL Co pfI	PhEl 3.80pf	UnEl 7.44pf
Crane	LongsDrug	PhEl 7.75pf	UnTel 1.50pf
Curtiss Wrt	Marriott	PortGenCp	ValerNGs
DaytPL pfF	MetEd pfI	PSInd 8.52pf	VaEP 7.45pf
Duqsne Lt	MorgGrnfl	PSEG 7.52pf	WarnrComm
		RepubNY	

NEW LOWS – 24

Alleen Inc	BlueArrow n	IntegRsc	Quantum
AlaPw adj pf	CtytrstBcp	IntgRs adj pf	Repsol n
AmRlEst	CollnvGrd n	IntgRs 4.25pf	Soumrk pfH
ArizPS adj pf	EquitecFn	IntgRs 8.1pf	StoneCont s
Bairnco	GlblGovt	Matsush El	Wabaninc n
BenetonGp n	Idex cp n	NIM adj pf	WeirtonStl n

s-Split or stock dividend of 25 per cent or more in the past 52 weeks. High-low range is adjusted from old stock. n-New issue in past 52 weeks and does not cover the entire 52 week period.

ODD-LOT TRADING

NEW YORK – The New York Stock Exchange specialists reported the following odd-lot transactions (in shares):

	Customer Purchases	Short Sales	Other Sales	Total Sales
June 14, 1989	274,158	46,161	522,859	569,020

Odd-lot sales exceed odd-lot purchases on June 14,1989 ⟶

Source: *The Wall Street Journal*, June 16, 1989.

ODD-LOT TRADING

NEW YORK – The New York Stock Exchange specialists reported the following odd-lot transactions (in shares):

	Customer Purchases	Short Sales	Other Sales	Total Sales
March 16, 1989	252,982	15,068	532,821	547,889

⟵ Odd-lot sales exceed purchases on March 16, 1989

New York Stock Exchange odd-lot trading for all member firms dealing in odd-lots, for the week ended March 3, 1989 are:

	Shares	Values
Customers' Orders to Buy ..	1,812,874	$67,035,246
Customers' Orders to Sell ...	3,750,543	$142,673,456
Customers' Short Sales	75,124	$3,083,337

⟵ Odd-lot sales exceed odd-lot purchases in week ending March 3,1989

Round-Lot transactions (in shares) for the week ended March 3, 1989:

	Purchases	Sales (incl. Short Sales)	Short Sales
Total	780,873,450	780,873,450	53,271,880
For Member Accounts:			
As Specialists-a,b	68,145,460	71,970,090	19,996,570
As Floor Traders	....	2,700	....
Others-a	104,460,195	118,635,145	15,398,950

a-Including offsetting round-lot transactions arising from odd-lot dealer activity by specialists and other members.

b-Includes transactions effected by members acting as Registered Competitive Market Makers.

American Stock Exchange round-lot and odd-lot trading statistics for the week ended March 3, 1989, are:

	Purchases	Sales (incl. Short Sales)	Short Sales
Total	46,914,145	46,914,145	1,222,000
For Member Accounts:			
As Specialists	5,009,595	5,456,380	75,700
As Floor Traders	96,600	40,600	3,100
Others	3,184,394	3,019,082	341,700
Customer odd-lots	78,749	169,173	....

Source: *The Wall Street Journal*, March 20, 1989.

FOLLOW YOUR STOCK

Suppose now that you have studied the various stock market indicators and indexes, decided that the time was right to get into the market, and did so. You will want to follow the progress of your investment. Here's how you do it.

If you own shares of Anheuser-Busch, you can follow their daily performance in *The Wall Street Journal* by turning to **New York Stock Exchange Composite Transactions**. Recall that this composite report includes a small amount of trading activity on regional exchanges. You'll find a reference to all exchanges in the index on the front pages of the first (A1) and third (C1) sections.

In the accompanying Tuesday, May 16, 1989 excerpts (page 182 and below), the first and second columns tell you the highest and lowest value of one share of the stock in the past 52 weeks, expressed in dollars and fractions of a dollar. Thus, Anheuser-Busch stock was as low as 29 dollars ($29) and as high as 40½ dollars ($40.50) in the year preceding May 15, 1989.

Footnotes and symbols, including arrows and underlining, are fully explained in the box on the lower left of the first page of the Composite listings.

The third and fourth columns give the company name and stock ticker symbol (BUD).

The fifth column of data reports the latest annual cash dividend of 72 cents per share. The dividend is expressed as a percentage of the closing price in the next column ($0.72 / $41.25 = 1.74 percent, rounded to 1.7 percent).

The seventh column shows the price-earnings (P-E) ratio, which is obtained by dividing the price of the stock by its earnings per share. (This important statistic is discussed in detail in Chapter 8.) On May

---

	52 Weeks Hi	Lo	Stock	Sym	Div	Yld %	PE	Vol 100s	Hi	Lo	Close	Net Chg	
	16⅛	9⅞	AnalogDevcs	ADI		...	13	529	11¼	10⅞	11	− ¼	
	18⅞	7⅛	AnchorGlass	ANC	.08	.8	...	671	10⅜	9⅞	10¼	+ ⅛	
	27¼	19⅝	Angelica	AGL	.76	3.3	13	82	23⅝	23⅜	23⅜	− ⅛	
	11⅜	8	AngellRE	ACR	1.52	14.0	...	35	10⅞	10⅝	10⅞	+ ¼	
↑	40½	29	AnheuserB	BUD	.72	1.7	16	8183	41¼	40½	41¼	+ ¾	← Anheuser Busch
	14⅜	7⅞	AnthemElec	ATM		...	10	250	11	10¾	10¾	...	
s	19⅜	8½	Anthonyind	ANT	.44	2.4	12	100	18½	18¼	18¼	− ⅛	

Source: *The Wall Street Journal*, May 16, 1989.

NEW YORK STOCK EXCHANGE COMPOSITE TRANSACTIONS

Quotations as of 4:30 p.m. Eastern Time
Monday, May 15, 1989

	52 Weeks Hi	52 Weeks Lo	Stock	Sym	Div	Yld %	PE	Vol 100s	Hi	Lo	Close	Net Chg
	15¼	11⅛	Amcastind	AIZ	.48	3.7	10	126	13⅛	13	13	...
	15⅝	8⅜	Amdura	ADU		...	3	131	15⅜	15	15⅛	– ⅛
	27¼	19½	Amdura pf		1.95	7.5	...	9	26⅛	26	26	– ⅜
	40½	25¾	AmerHess	AHC	.60	1.5	12	1990	39¾	39¼	39⅝	+ ⅝
	23⅛	14¾	AmBarrick	ABX	.13e	...	...	283	20⅜	20¼	20¼	– ½
	71¾	43½	AmBrand	AMB	2.44	3.5	11	2791	70⅜	68⅝	69¾	+ ⅜
	30⅝	26⅝	AmBrand pf		2.75	10.0	...	76	27½	27¼	27½	+ ¼
↑	137½	89	AmBrand pf		2.67	1.9	...	1	141	141	141	+3¾
	39¾	24⅛	AmBldgMaint	ABM	.92	2.6	19	71	36	36	36	...
	29¾	23¼	AmBusnPdts	ABP	.96	3.4	12	2	28⅝	28⅝	28⅝	+ ⅛
	22⅛	19⅛	AmCapBdFd	ACB	2.20e	11.2	...	85	19⅞	19⅝	19⅝	– ⅛
	24	19¼	AmCapCvSec	ACS	2.93e	13.2	...	19	22⅛	21½	22⅛	+ ⅝
x	10⅛	8⅜	AmCapIncTr	ACD	1.10a	12.2	...	x169	9⅛	8⅞	9	+ ⅛
	12⅜	8¼	AmCapMgt	ACA	.60	6.4	10	4	9⅜	9⅜	9⅜	...
	13/16	⅛	**AmCentury**	**ACT**		...	...	16	¼	¼	¼	+1/32
	55⅞	44	AmCyanmd	ACY	1.35	2.5	16	3472	55⅜	54⅝	54¾	– ⅛
	29¼	25¾	AmElecPwr	AEP	2.32a	8.6	9	3054	27⅛	26⅞	27	...
↑	34	22⅞	AmExpress	AXP	.84	2.5	14	13155	34¼	33¼	33⅝	– ⅜
x	19⅛	11½	AmFamily	AFL	.28	1.6	13	x642	17⅝	17⅜	17½	– ¼
	36½	27⅜	AmGenerl	AGC	1.50	4.2	11	1705	36⅛	35¼	36⅛	+ ¾
	8½	7⅜	AmGvIncFd	AGF	.84a	10.8	...	331	8	7¾	7¾	– ¼
n	10⅛	8⅞	AmGvIncoP	AAF	1.06a	11.3	...	123	9½	9⅜	9⅜	...
n	10⅛	9¼	AmGvTermTr	AGT	.26e	2.7	...	116	9⅝	9½	9½	+ ⅛
	20½	17	AmHlthProp	AHE	2.20	11.0	13	388	20⅛	19⅞	20	+ ⅛
	94	70¾	AmHomePdts	AHP	3.90	4.1	14	2032	94	93	94	+ ⅞
s	57¾	42¾	Ameritech	AIT	2.92	5.1	12	2168	57⅛	56½	56⅞	– ⅛
	84¼	50	AmIntGroup	AIG	.40	.5	11	3663	83⅜	81¼	83⅜	+2
	22⅛	14¼	AMI	AMI	.72	3.3	23	2549	21¾	21⅝	21⅝	...
↑	38¾	27	AmPresidnt	APS	.60	1.7	13	316	40⅞	35¼	35⅜	– ⅛
	65	53½	AmPresidnt pf		3.50	5.8	...	91	60⅝	60⅛	60⅛	...
	16⅞	13⅞	AmRE Ptnrs	ACP	2.00	13.9	8	78	14⅝	14⅜	14⅜	– ¼
	4⅞	3⅞	AmRltyTr	ARB	.72	16.9	3	72	4¼	4	4¼	...
	18¾	11¾	AmSvgBk	ASB	.80	5.2	3	106	15⅜	15⅛	15⅜	– ⅛
	19½	15⅞	AmSvgBk pf		1.81	10.5	...	18	17½	17¼	17¼	– ⅜
	5⅞	3	AmShipBldg	ABG		...	...	29	3½	3⅜	3½	+ ⅛
	65	47⅝	AmStores	ASC	1.00	1.7	24	686	60⅞	60¼	60⅜	– ¼
	70¾	56	AmStores pf		4.38	6.7	...	112	65⅝	65⅜	65⅝	+ ⅛
	35⅛	24⅛	AmT&T	T	1.20	3.5	17	20065	34½	34⅛	34½	+ ½
	21½	14⅞	AmWaterWks	AWK	.74	4.2	10	96	18	17⅝	17¾	– ¼
	15¼	13¼	AmWaterWks pf		1.25	9.3	...	z1350	14	13½	13½	+ ¼
↑	15¾	13¼	AmWater pf		1.25	7.8	...	z240	16	15¾	16	+ ⅝
	14¼	12⅜	AmHotel	AHR		...	77	14	14	13⅞	13⅞	– ⅛
	40¼	29¾	Ameron	AMN	1.28	3.5	13	34	37	36¾	36¾	– ½
	18¾	**12⅞**	**AmesDeptStr**	**ADD**	.10	.6	14	1443	17	16	17	+ ⅞
	16½	12¼	Ametek	AME	.60	4.5	21	692	13½	13¼	13¼	...
	11⅜	9¾	AMEV Sec	AMV	1.08a	10.5	...	79	10⅜	10⅛	10¼	...
s	45⅛	34	Amoco	AN	1.90	4.4	11	7938	43½	43	43¼	– ⅛
	52	40½	AMP	AMP	1.20	2.8	14	3588	42¾	42¼	42¾	+ ⅝
	15⅝	11⅞	AmpcoPgh	AP	.30	2.0	...	219	14¾	14⅝	14¾	+ ⅛
s	16⅛	6¾	AMRE	AMM	.08	1.0	16	158	7⅝	7⅜	7⅝	+ ¼
	9¾	7⅛	AMREP	AXR		...	46	11	8¼	8¼	8¼	– ⅛
	26⅞	22⅜	AmSouthBcp	ASO	1.32	5.0	8	123	26¼	26	26¼	+ ¼
	11½	4⅝	Anacomp	AAC		...	12	2669	6¼	5¾	6¼	– ¼
	29¼	22	AnadrkPete	APC	.30	1.1	28	285	28⅜	28	28⅜	+ ⅛
	16⅛	9⅞	AnalogDevcs	ADI		...	13	529	11¼	10⅞	11	– ¼
	18⅞	7⅛	AnchorGlass	ANC	.08	.8	...	671	10⅜	9⅞	10¼	+ ⅛
	27¼	19⅝	Angelica	AGL	.76	3.3	13	82	23⅝	23⅜	23⅜	– ⅛
	11⅜	8	AngellRE	ACR	1.52	14.0	...	35	10⅞	10⅝	10⅞	+ ¼
Anheuser Busch → ↑	40½	29	AnheuserB	BUD	.72	1.7	16	8183	41¼	40½	41¼	+ ¾
	14⅜	7⅞	AnthemElec	ATM		...	10	250	11	10¾	10¾	...
s	19⅜	8½	AnthonyInd	ANT	.44	2.4	12	100	18½	18¼	18¼	– ⅛
↑	33⅜	23	AonCp	AOC	1.40	4.1	12	791	33¾	32¾	33¾	+1
	10⅞	6	ApacheCp	APA	.28	2.7	24	866	10⅝	10⅜	10½	+ ⅛
	86	80¼	AppalchPwr pf		8.12	10.0	...	z100	81	81	81	+ ¼
	78	73	AppalchPwr pf		7.40	9.8	...	z1200	75¼	75	75¼	+ ¾
	37½	27½	AppleBk	APK		...	7	42	36⅛	35⅞	36	+ ⅛
	17½	11½	AppliedMagn	APM		...	10	152	12¾	12½	12⅝	– ⅛
	28	17¾	ArcherDan	ADM	.10b	.4	13	4525	27⅝	27⅛	27¼	– ⅛
	38⅛	26¼	ARCO Chm	RCM	2.50	6.8	7	410	37	36⅛	36½	+ ¼
s	27⅝	16¼	AristChm	ARS	1.00	4.9	5	2079	20½	20	20⅜	...
↓	39⅝	37¾	BankNY adA		1.76e	4.7	...	50	37½	37½	37½	– ½
	26¼	9¾	BankAmer	BAC	.30e	1.2	8	6302	25¾	25½	25¾	+ ⅛
	37⅛	32½	BankAmer pf		3.66e	10.5	...	71	35¼	34¼	34¾	– ⅛
	61½	53½	BankAmer pf		6.00e	10.1	...	8	59½	59⅜	59½	...
	7⅝	5¼	BankAmer pf		2.25	...	...	264	6¼	6⅛	6¼	+ ⅛
	45⅞	30	BankTrst	BT	2.08	4.6	5	2970	45⅝	44	45⅝	+1⅝
s	25⅞	11¾	BannerInd	BNR		...	15	32	23⅛	22⅞	23	+ ⅜
	33⅜	21	Barclays	BCS	1.78e	5.7	5	10	31½	31½	31½	...
s	24⅝	18⅜	Bard CR	BCR	.32	1.3	17	1280	24⅛	23¾	24	– ⅛
	36⅜	32⅛	BarnesGp	B	1.40	4.0	12	21	35⅛	34⅞	35⅛	+ ⅛
↑	37⅜	29⅜	BarnettBks	BBI	1.20	3.2	10	1688	37¾	36⅞	37¾	+ ¾
n	8⅞	4⅜	BaroidCp	BRC	.20	2.3	52	945	8⅞	8⅝	8⅞	...
	8⅞	4¼	BarryWrgt	BAR		...	90	55	5⅜	5⅜	5⅜	– ⅛
	13/16	⅛	vjBasix	BAS		...	...	34	11/32	5/16	11/32	...
	19⅛	13	BattleMtn	BMG	.10	.7	15	955	13⅜	13⅛	13⅜	+ ⅛
↑	56½	39⅞	BauschLomb	BOL	1.16	2.1	17	997	56¾	55⅛	56⅜	+1½
	22½	16¼	BaxterInt	BAX	.56	2.7	15	10223	20¾	20	20⅝	+ ⅜
	47¾	37⅛	BaxterInt pf		3.65e	9.6	...	281	38¼	38	38	– ⅛
	73	56¾	BaxterInt pf		3.50	5.3	...	279	66⅜	65⅝	66	+ ⅞
	19¾	9⅜	BayFnl	BAY		...	...	16	9⅞	9⅝	9⅞	+ ¼
	27⅛	21¼	BayStGas	BGC	1.80	6.8	10	31	26⅜	26⅛	26⅜	...
	16⅛	11⅛	BearStearns	BSC	.56b	3.8	10	2127	14⅞	14⅜	14⅝	+ ¼
	45¼	31¼	BearingsInc	BER	.80a	1.8	13	92	44⅜	44⅛	44⅜	+ ⅝
n	22¾	17⅛	BeckmanInstr	BEC	.07e	.4	13	212	19⅞	19⅝	19⅝	– ¼
	57⅞	46½	BectonDksn	BDX	1.00	1.8	13	1208	55¾	55⅜	55⅝	– ⅛
	40	26¾	BeldenHem	BHY	.52	1.4	12	9	36¾	36½	36½	+ ¼
↑	84	65	BellAtlantic	BEL	4.40	5.3	12	2161	84½	83½	83⅝	– ⅜
	16⅞	13½	BellIndus	BI	.28	1.8	19	94	15¾	15⅝	15¾	+ ⅛
↑	47½	38½	BellSouth	BLS	2.52	5.3	14	5290	47¾	47¼	47⅝	+ ¼
x	34⅝	22⅜	Belo AH	BLC	.44	1.3	59	x42	34	33¾	33⅞	...
	29⅝	18⅝	Bemis	BMS	.60	2.2	18	114	27⅞	27½	27¾	...
	53¾	41⅝	Beneficial	BNL	2.20	4.3	12	327	51½	51⅛	51⅜	...
	46¼	39½	Beneficial pf		4.30	10.1	...	12	42½	42½	42½	+ ¾
	4⅞	3⅜	Benguet B	BE	.19r	4.2	7	168	4⅝	4½	4½	– ⅛
	2⅛	⅛	vjBerkey	BKY		...	...	10	3/16	3/16	3/16	...
	6475	3625	BerkHathwy	BRK		...	...	z130	6075	5950	6075	+175
	15⅜	6⅞	BestBuy	BBY		...	16	99	7⅝	7⅜	7⅜	– ⅛
	28½	18¼	BethSteel	BS		...	5	3487	23¼	22⅝	23¼	+ ¾
	56¼	46¼	BethSteel pf		5.00	9.8	...	111	51¼	50⅞	51⅛	+ ⅛
	27⅝	22½	BethSteel pf		2.50	10.0	...	79	25¼	24⅞	25⅛	+ ⅛
	9⅜	3¾	BeverlyEnt	BEV		...	...	1077	8⅝	8⅜	8⅝	...
	16¼	7½	BiocraftLabs	BCL		...	25	808	14	13	13⅜	– ⅝
s	29⅞	18	BirmghamStl	BIR	.50	2.3	7	4881	26¼	20¾	22	–1
	25¼	18⅛	BlackDeck	BDK	.40	2.0	11	5372	20⅝	20	20⅛	– ⅜
	28¼	24½	BlackHills	BKH	1.52	5.8	11	92	26⅜	25¾	26	– ½
n	10⅛	8¼	BlackstnIncTr	BKT	1.10	12.1	...	672	9¼	9⅛	9⅛	– ⅛
n	10⅛	8¾	BlackstnTgt	BTT	1.00	10.7	...	1624	9½	9⅜	9⅜	...
	30¼	22¾	BlockHR	HRB	1.04	3.8	16	1864	27¾	27¼	27⅝	+ ⅝
s	36½	11	BlockbstrE	BV		...	41	13014	28¼	25	28⅛	+1
n	22¾	14⅝	BlueArrow	BAW	.34e	2.0	...	2908	16¾	16⅝	16¾	– ¼
	6¾	5½	BlueChipFd	BLU	.48e	7.2	...	149	6⅝	6½	6⅝	...
↑	80⅛	48⅜	Boeing	BA	1.80	2.2	20	8048	81⅝	80	81⅝	+1⅝
	47½	39¼	BoiseCasc	BCC	1.40	3.1	7	544	45½	45	45⅛	– ⅜
	18⅝	7	BoltBerNew	BBN	.06	.8	...	340	7⅝	7⅜	7⅝	– ⅛
n	11¾	6¾	BondIntGold	BIG		...	...	33	7¼	7⅛	7⅛	– ⅛
	24	14⅜	BordChm un	BCP	3.40e	17.0	6	914	20¼	19¾	20	+ ⅛
n	24	17	BordChm	BCU	3.40e	17.2	6	213	20⅛	19¾	19¾	– ⅛
	64½	48⅜	BordenInc	BN	1.80	2.8	15	1739	64½	64	64½	...
	15¾	12¼	BostCelts	BOS	1.60e	11.5	7	29	13⅞	13⅝	13⅞	...
	17¼	13¼	BostEdsn	BSE	1.82	11.1	9	453	16⅜	16	16⅜	+ ¼
	88½	82	BostEdsn pf		8.88	10.6	...	z200	84	84	84	...
	14⅞	13¾	BostEdsn pf		1.46	10.2	...	13	14¼	14⅛	14¼	+ ⅛
	35⅞	25¼	Bowater	BOW	1.12	3.4	7	6450	33½	32	33	+1¼
	12⅞	7⅛	BrazilFd	BZF	.80e	7.0	...	236	11⅜	11⅛	11⅜	+ ⅛
	36	24¾	BriggsStrat	BGG	1.60	5.9	37	782	27½	27	27⅛	– ⅜
↑	50⅜	38⅛	BristMyrs	BMY	2.00	3.9	17	8229	50¾	50	50¾	+ ⅜
	36½	24¾	BritAir	BAB	1.41e	4.1	8	906	34¾	34⅛	34¼	– ½
	34½	27⅞	BritGas	BRG	1.72e	5.7	12	275	30½	30¼	30¼	– ¼
	61⅝	48¼	BritPetrol	BP	3.27e	5.8	15	2395	56½	56⅛	56⅜	– ¼
	9⅜	6⅛	BritPetrol wt			...	...	33	7½	7½	7½	...
	15⅛	11	BritSteel pp	BST		...	...	3332	14⅝	14½	14⅝	– ⅛
	52	37¾	BritTelcom	BTY	1.95e	4.3	10	366	45¾	45½	45½	– ¾
	10	6¾	BroadInc	BRO	.10	1.3	...	2045	7⅞	7¾	7⅞	...

Source: *The Wall Street Journal*, May 16, 1989.

15, Anheuser-Busch's stock was worth 16 times the profits per share of stock.

The eighth column informs you of the number of shares traded that day, expressed in hundreds of shares. Thus, 818,300 shares of Anheuser-Busch stock were traded. If a **z** appears before the number in this column, the figure represents the actual number (not hundreds) of shares traded.

The ninth, tenth, and eleventh columns reveal the stock's highest, lowest, and closing (last) price for the trading day. (Note in the caption under the date in the illustration that these quotes are a composite of transactions on the NYSE and the other exchanges listed. So the closing price listed may be that on the Pacific Stock Exchange in San Francisco rather than the closing price on the NYSE.) Thus, on Thursday, March 30, 1989, Anheuser-Busch stock traded as high as 41¼ and as low as 40½ before closing at 41¼.

The last column provides the change in the closing price of the stock from the price at the close of the previous day. You can see that this stock closed at a price 75 cents higher than the previous closing price.

Shares of other companies, usually smaller than those listed on the NYSE, trade on the **American Stock Exchange (AMEX)**. *The Wall Street Journal*'s AMEX report, called **American Stock Exchange Composite Transactions**, is identical in form to NYSE Composite Transactions.

Over-the-counter (OTC) stocks, generally issued by even smaller or newer companies, are not traded on an exchange. (There are exceptions: Apple Computer is not small, yet continues to trade on the OTC market.) Instead, dealers have established a market for them using a computer network referred to as *NASDAQ* (National Association of Securities Dealers Automated Quotations). You can follow this market in **NASDAQ National Market Issues**, which is similar to the New York and American Exchange listings. Take a look at the reprint from the Friday, March 31, 1989 *Journal* (on page 184), using **Microsoft** as an example.

The first two columns give the high and low prices for the past year. The column after the price-earning ratio lists sales in hundreds, informing you that 324,600 shares of Microsoft traded on Thursday, March 30, 1989.

The next three columns provide the high (50), low (49⅛) and closing (49⅞) prices of the day, and the final column tells you that Microsoft's stock closed at a price 37.5 cents higher than its price at the previous close.

NASDAQ NATIONAL MARKET ISSUES

	52 Weeks Hi	52 Weeks Lo	Stock	Sym	Div	Yld %	PE	Vol 100s	Hi	Lo	Close	Net Chg
	18⅜	13¼	Jerrico	JERR	.16	.9	14	1173	17⅝	17⅜	17⅝	+ ⅛
s	23¾	6¼	JesupGp	JGRPD		...	...	5	6½	6½	6½	...
	6⅜	2⅛	JetbornInt	JETS		...	28	287	2⅞	2 11/16	2 13/16	+ 1/16
	12⅝	**4¾**	**JiffyLub**	**JLUB**		**...**	**...**	**2200**	**5⅞**	**5½**	**5½**	**− ⅜**
	4⅝	2¾	JHansnSvg	JHSL		...	5	25	3⅛	2¾	2¾	...
	2⅛	**1½**	**JohnsnElec**	**JHSN**		**...**	**...**	**26**	**2 1/16**	**2 1/16**	**2 1/16**	**+ ⅛**
	25	15½	JohnsnWld	JWAIA		...	12	108	23	22¼	22½	− ½
	7½	**5½**	**JohnstnSvg**	**JSBK**		**...**	**10**	**34**	**6½**	**6**	**6**	**− ½**
	16¾	11	JonesIntcbl	JOIN		...	...	44	16¼	16¼	16¼	− ¼
	16¾	10⅜	JonesIntcbl A	JOINA		...	...	47	15¾	15⅜	15⅝	+ ⅛
	7	4⅛	JonesMed	JMED	.04e	.6	16	20	6¼	6	6¼	+ ⅛
	3¼	1¾	JonesSpclk	SPLKA		...	...	183	2 9/16	2 7/16	2½	+ 1/16
	31¼	27	Joslyn	JOSL	1.60	5.9	10	3	27¼	27¼	27¼	−1
	25¾	13	JunoLight	JUNO	.16	1.1	12	11	14⅝	14⅜	14⅜	...
	16¾	13¾	JustinInd	JSTN	.40	2.5	12	20	15⅞	15⅞	15⅞	− ⅛
			−K−K−K−									
	4¾	**2¾**	**KCS Grp**	**KCSG**		**...**	**...**	**20**	**4⅝**	**4⅜**	**4⅝**	**+ ¼**
	21	**9½**	**KLA Instrm**	**KLAC**		**...**	**18**	**10141**	**11**	**10¼**	**11**	**+ ¾**
	14¾	11¼	KLLM Trnspt	KLLM		...	10	1	11¾	11¾	11¾	...
	5⅝	2½	KMS Ind	KMSI	.12	2.4	16	62	5	4¾	5	...
	14½	10	KTronInt	KTII		...	7	3	11¾	11¼	11¾	+ ¼
	21	14	Kahler	KHLR		...	81	2	19½	19½	19½	+ ½
	18½	12	KamanCp	KAMNA	.44	3.2	10	1339	13⅞	13¾	13⅞	+ ⅛
	4½	1⅞	MKamnstn	MKCO		...	8	42	4¼	4¼	4¼	...
	26½	14½	CarlKarchr	CARL	.16	.6	15	170	25½	25	25⅜	+ ⅜
	11¼	7⅝	Kasler	KASL	.05e	.5	24	16	10¾	10⅝	10⅝	...
	31½	24¼	Kaydon	KDON	.30	1.0	12	142	29¼	28¾	28¾	− ½
	⅞	¼	Kaypro	KPRO		...	...	910	9/32	¼	¼	...
	32½	8½	KeaneInc	KEAN		...	14	129	32½	30½	30½	− ½
	45½	32½	KellySvc A	KELYA	.64	1.8	14	61	35	33½	35	+1½
	44½	**32½**	**KellySvc B**	**KELYB**	**.64**	**1.8**	**14**	**35**	**35**	**34¾**	**35**	**+1¾**
	32½	20¾	KemperCp	KEMC	.84	2.6	9	719	32½	32¼	32½	+ ⅛
	15½	12½	KenanTrnspt	KTCO	.18	1.3	7	46	13⅝	13½	13½	− ¼
	11/16	**¼**	**KenlwthSys**	**KENS**		**...**	**...**	**430**	**9/32**	**¼**	**9/32**	**+ 1/32**
	14⅜	10⅞	KyCtlLf	KENCA	.40	3.0	6	813	13⅜	13	13⅜	+ ¼
	7¼	4¼	Keptel	KPTL		...	30	24	6⅞	6⅝	6⅞	...
	4⅜	2½	KevlinMcrw	KVLM		...	24	7	2 11/16	2 11/16	2 11/16	...
	9½	8	KewneeSci	KEQU	.04e	.5	30	6	8⅛	8	8	− ⅛
s	18⅞	12	KeyCenturn	KEYC	.52b	3.9	12	582	13½	13	13½	+ ½
	2¾	1¾	KeyProdctn wi	KPCI	.12e	4.8	...	56	2½	2½	2½	− 1/16
s↓	204	145	MerchBkNY	MBNY	1.00a	.7	24	9	150	138	150	−3
	7	**3¼**	**MerchCap A**	**MCBKA**	**.40**	**9.4**	**...**	**259**	**4⅞**	**4¼**	**4¼**	**− ⅜**
	28	21¾	MerchNtl	MCHN	1.00	3.8	9	19	26¼	26	26	...
	15⅞	10⅝	MercuryGen	MRCY	.40	2.9	6	11	14	14	14	− ⅛
	2¼	**¼**	**MeretInc**	**MRET**		**...**	**...**	**30**	**13/16**	**¾**	**¾**	**− 1/16**
	21⅞	18⅛	MeridnBcp	MRDN	1.10	5.5	9	294	20⅜	20⅛	20⅛	− ⅛
	5¼	**2**	**MeridnDiagn**	**KITS**		**...**	**89**	**22**	**3⅝**	**3 9/16**	**3 9/16**	**− 3/16**
	6⅜	3⅛	MeritorSvg	MTOR		...	...	769	3¾	3½	3¾	...
	9½	6¼	MerrillCp	MRLL		...	18	100	8¾	8½	8¾	+ ⅛
	15¾	8¼	MerryGoRd	MGRE		...	13	374	15⅛	14⅞	15⅛	+ ⅛
	8½	**5**	**MerryLdInv**	**MERY**	**.80**	**14.5**	**6**	**26**	**5½**	**5⅛**	**5½**	**+ ⅜**
	4½	3¼	MesaAirl	MESL		...	16	20	4⅛	3⅞	3⅞	− ⅛
	7⅞	4⅞	MetCoilSys	METS	.12	1.7	11	4	7⅛	6⅞	7⅛	+ ¼
	18¾	15⅛	Metcalf	METC		...	19	15	17¾	17¾	17¾	− ¼
	6⅝	4	MethodEl A	METHA	.07	1.6	11	21	4⅜	4¼	4¼	...
	6½	4	MethodEl B	METHB	.06	1.5	15	7	4	4	4	− ⅛
	9½	3	MetroAirl	MAIR		...	47	342	8½	8⅜	8⅜	...
	31	10⅞	MetroSvTN	MFTN		...	...	104	11⅜	11	11	+ ⅛
	2⅛	**¾**	**MetroTel**	**MTRO**		**...**	**...**	**152**	**1⅜**	**1¼**	**1⅜**	**+ ⅛**
	8	**¼**	**MetroFnlS&L**	**MSLA**		**...**	**...**	**20**	**7/16**	**7/16**	**7/16**	**+ ⅛**
	17½	12⅞	MeyerFred	MEYR		...	11	108	16⅞	16¾	16¾	...
	5¼	2¼	MicAnthJwl	MAJL		...	...	6	2⅞	2½	2½	...
s↑	19⅝	13⅜	MichlFood	MIKL	.20	1.0	16	944	19¾	18⅞	19½	+ ⅜
	52¼	41¾	MichNtl	MNCO	2.00	4.6	7	400	44¼	43½	43¾	− ¼
	9¼	4⅞	MicroAge	MICA		...	7	52	6¾	6½	6½	− ⅛
↓	9¼	3⅜	MicoMask	MCRO		...	5	173	3⅝	3¼	3½	+ ⅛
	7⅝	5½	MicroAm	MRAC		...	11	440	6⅞	6¾	6⅞	+ ⅛
s	14	8¾	MicroBilt	BILT	.10	.8	17	8	13½	13	13	− ⅝
	26	14½	MicronTech	MCRN		...	5	1990	18⅞	18½	18⅞	+ ⅛
	26	5⅞	Micropolis	MLIS		...	...	142	6¼	6⅛	6⅛	− ⅛
	3½	**1¾**	**MicroPro**	**MPRO**		**...**	**...**	**800**	**2 1/16**	**1 13/16**	**2 1/16**	**+ ¼**
↓	**7⅝**	**4⅞**	**Microsemi**	**MSCC**		**...**	**17**	**251**	**5¼**	**4⅝**	**4⅝**	**− ⅝**
	36¼	18	Microcom	MNPI		...	18	74	30	29¼	29¼	...
	70½	45¼	Microsoft	MSFT		...	18	3246	50	49⅛	49⅞	+ ⅜ ← Microsoft
	19	15	MidAmBcp	MABC	.60b	3.2	10	33	19	19	19	...
	20	17	MidAmInc	MIAM	1.00	5.6	10	1	18	18	18	+ ¼
	15	9½	MidConnBk	MIDC	.56	4.2	...	33	13⅜	13¼	13¼	− ¼
	10¾	5¼	MidSouthIns	MIDS	.24	4.2	5	26	5⅞	5¾	5¾	+ ¼
↓	22¼	14	MidStS&L	MSSL	.40	2.9	26	210	14⅛	13½	13¾	− ¼
	28¾	25½	MidsexWtr	MSEX	1.78	6.8	12	1	26¼	26¼	26¼	− ½

Source: *The Wall Street Journal*, March 31, 1989.

	52 Weeks Hi	52 Weeks Lo	Stock	Sym	Div	Yld %	PE	Vol 100s	Hi	Lo	Close	Net Chg
	3½	**1¾**	**MicroPro**	**MPRO**		**...**	**...**	**800**	**2 1/16**	**1 13/16**	**2 1/16**	**+ ¼**
↓	**7⅝**	**4⅞**	**Microsemi**	**MSCC**		**...**	**17**	**251**	**5¼**	**4⅝**	**4⅝**	**− ⅝**
	36¼	18	Microcom	MNPI		...	18	74	30	29¼	29¼	...
Microsoft →	70½	45¼	Microsoft	MSFT		...	18	3246	50	49⅛	49⅞	+ ⅜
	19	15	MidAmBcp	MABC	.60b	3.2	10	33	19	19	19	...
	20	17	MidAmInc	MIAM	1.00	5.6	10	1	18	18	18	+ ¼
	15	9½	MidConnBk	MIDC	.56	4.2	...	33	13⅜	13¼	13¼	− ¼
	10¾	5¼	MidSouthIns	MIDS	.24	4.2	5	26	5⅞	5¾	5¾	+ ¼
↓	22¼	14	MidStS&L	MSSL	.40	2.9	26	210	14⅛	13½	13¾	− ¼
	28¾	25½	MidsexWtr	MSEX	1.78	6.8	12	1	26¼	26¼	26¼	− ½

Source: *The Wall Street Journal*, March 31, 1989.

The remainder of the OTC stocks are quoted currently with bid (what buyers are willing to pay) and ask (what sellers are willing to offer) prices, although all OTC stocks will eventually be quoted with closing prices. Look at the daily report, **NASDAQ Bid & Asked Quotations**, from the Thursday, March 30, 1989 edition of the *Journal* (page 186).

With this information, you can track the performance of any share of stock traded on the New York or American exchanges or the OTC market.

MUTUAL FUNDS

But at this point you may feel that the discussion has strayed from the goals established in Chapters 1 and 8. If you've decided to pick stocks instead of gold, can the wisdom of that decision be offset by the selection of the wrong stock? If so, is there a way to get into the stock market without purchasing a particular stock?

Yes, and yes. Mutual funds provide a way to invest in the stock market indirectly. Investment companies establish mutual funds to pool the resources of many investors and thus create a large, shared portfolio of investments. Individuals invest in mutual funds by purchasing shares in the fund from the investment company. The return on the portfolio is passed through to the individual investors according to the number of shares held. Mutual funds are popular because they permit diversification in a wide variety of securities with very small capital outlay. In addition, a mutual fund lets you take advantage of the professional management skills of the investment company.

When you purchase a mutual fund share, you own a fraction of the total assets in the portfolio. The price of that share is equal to its *net asset value* (net value of assets held by the fund divided by the number of mutual fund shares outstanding plus any sales commission.). As with any pooled investment in common stock, price appreciation and dividends earned will determine the gain in net asset value.

Mutual funds are classified according to whether or not they charge a sales commission called a *load*. Every day, **Mutual Fund Quotations** lists the major funds available to investors. See the indexes on the front pages of the first (A1) and third (C1) sections. See page 187 for an excerpt from the Thursday, March 30, 1989 edition of the *Journal*.

No-Load (NL) Funds don't require a commission to purchase or sell the shares of the fund. There is, however, a "management fee" on the

NASDAQ BID & ASKED QUOTATIONS

Stock & Div		Sales 100s	Bid	Asked	Net Chg.
-A-A-A-					
AA Imp		3	1 3/4	2 1/4	...
AFN h		954	7/8	15/16	− 1/16
AFP		110	1 1/8	1 3/16	...
AMR wt		20	153	157	...
APAOp		39	10 3/4	12 1/4	...
ASK Cp		1403	1 1/16	1 3/32	+ 1/32
ATC		103	3 1/8	3 1/4	...
ATC wt		10	1 1/4	1 11/16	...
Acclaim		340	3 13/16	3 7/8	+ 1/8
Aclm wtA		61	2 1/8	2 3/16	+ 3/16
Acl wtB		230	1 3/8	1 7/16	+ 1/8
ActnStf		794	2 1/8	2 1/4	+ 1/16
Adelph h		100	26 1/2	27	...
AdNMR		119	4	4 3/8	...
A NMR wt		94	4	4 1/4	...
AdvPr		21	1 7/8	2	...
AdPd wtC		50	23/32	7/8	...
AdvCo un		100	2 1/4	3 1/8	+ 1/4
Advatex		45	3 1/16	3 3/16	...
AdvCa s		15	1/8	5/32	...
Aeroson		12	1 11/16	1 13/16	...
AirSen		45	1 5/16	1 3/8	...
Alcide		264	3 1/16	3 1/4	+ 1/16
Alden	.10e	14	4 1/8	4 1/2	...
Alfaint		123	7/8	15/16	+ 1/16
Amribc	.10e	14	20 7/8	21 1/2	− 3/8
AAcft		453	13/16	27/32	...
AmBcp s	.43e	2	26	29	...
ABionet		631	7/16	15/32	...
AmBio		22	1 1/8	1 3/8	...
AmBdy		383	5 5/8	5 3/4	...
ABsCpt		335	1 5/16	1 7/16	− 1/8
ACty pf	1.50	120	14	14 3/4	...
ACont pf	3.44	52	8 3/8	8 3/4	+ 1/8
AmFB		2	4 3/4	5 1/4	...
AmInPt		312	1 1/4	1 5/16	+ 1/32
ANtPt		10	1 13/16	2	...
ARecr	.13	62	7 3/8	7 5/8	...
AmTelc		35	7/8	15/16	...
AmVacn		30	7 5/8	7 7/8	...
AmVisn		15	1 5/8	1 11/16	...
Amnws		8	2 1/2	2 7/8	...
An-Con		150	13/16	7/8	− 1/8
AnlySur		50	4 1/8	4 1/4	...
AndwGp		144	5 1/2	[illegible]	[illegible]
Angecn		[illegible]	[illegible]	[illegible]	[illegible]
[illegible]		[illegible]	[illegible]	[illegible]	[illegible]
[illegible]		[illegible]	[illegible]	[illegible]/16	...
[illegible]		4	3 1/8	3 3/4	...
[illegible]		3	5 1/2	5 7/8	...
CredoPt		31	1 7/8	2	...
CrwnBd		25	1 1/4	1 1/2	...
CrwnR s		56	3 1/8	3 3/8	...
CrwnA	.40	48	11 1/4	12	+ 1/2
CybrOpt		36	5 1/4	5 5/8	...
CytrxBi		108	17/32	3/4	− 1/32
CytrxB un		62	2 5/8	3	− 1/4
-D-D-D-					
DMI		82	2 1/2	2 3/4	+ 1/8
DSP un		20	1 1/4	1 5/8	...
DVIFn		35	3 1/4	3 3/8	...
Daltex		40	5/8	23/32	...
DartDg		691	1 1/4	1 3/8	+ 1/8
DtTrNw		6	14 1/4	14 1/2	...
Dtamg		792	3 3/16	3 1/4	− 3/16
Datvnd		404	1 1/2	1 5/8	− 1/8
Datvd un		60	6 1/4	7	− 3/8
DefltPr		65	1 13/16	1 15/16	− 1/16
DefltP wt		64	3/4	13/16	− 1/16
DefltP un		20	2 1/2	2 3/4	− 1/4
Denning		106	1 3/32	1 5/32	− 1/32
DnsPc s		178	1 1/2	1 9/16	− 1/16
DiagDt		15	3	3 1/2	...
DigtlSol		158	2 1/4	2 3/8	...
DimV un		129	18 3/4	19 1/4	− 1/2
DivTch		61	1 3/4	1 7/8	...
DrgScr		169	7	7 3/8	...
Dyncp pf	†	30	14	14 1/2	...
-E-E-E-					
EFIEle		20	1 7/16	1 1/2	...
Estmaq		29	2 13/16	2 15/16	...
Egghead		830	10 3/4	11	...
Elctmd		210	1 15/16	2	+ 1/32
ElcMis		1	1 1/2	1 3/4	...
Elctsrc		66	4	4 1/4	...
Endtrn		15	15/16	1	...
EngCn h		478	7	7 1/8	− 1/4
ECnv wt91		116	1/4	1/2	...
Enscor		10	2 1/8	2 1/4	− 1/16
Entorge		50	1 1/4	1 5/16	...
EnvDia		2916	1 3/8	1 7/16	− 1/16
Epitope		244	7 1/2	7 3/4	− 1/4
EqtG pf		12	3 1/8	3 1/2	...
ExecBc		58	8 1/4	8 5/8	− 1/4
-F-F-F-					
FA Cptr		212	1 1/4	1 5/16	...
FNB Cp	.24b	5	15	16 1/2	...
FalcLt g	5.75e	1823	24 1/8	24 1/4	+ 3/8
Falstaff		17	11 1/2	11 3/4	...
FamShp		49	1 9/16	1 11/16	...
FamSh un		5	4 3/8	4 3/4	− 1/4
FamSh pf	.20	20	2 3/8	2 3/4	− 1/4
FarmCB	1.00	10	28 1/2	29	...
FarmT un		55	3/4	7/8	...
Fayette	.15e	20	13	13 3/4	...
FAM unA		1	23 1/2	25 1/2	...
Filmstr		634	4 1/8	4 3/16	...
FnBenA	†	10	3	3 1/2	...
Finlind		1	7	9	...
Fd SVP s		77	1 7/8	2 3/16	...
FtCarin	.50	1	29 1/2	31	...
FstLI	.47r	2	25 1/2	27	...
FtMed		2	1 5/8	1 3/4	...
FUtdSv	.30	1	10 3/4	11	...
FishBu		61	3	3 1/4	...
Fisons	.78e	1	19 1/8	19 1/4	...
Flexwat		130	1	1 1/4	− 1/8
Florfx		270	1 1/4	1 5/16	...
Foreind		197	2 1/4	2 7/16	...
FrmRe	.01e	148	9/16	3/4	+ 1/16
Franch		797	1 1/2	1 9/16	+ 3/16
FrJuce s		25	29/32	1 1/16	...
FrntSvg		10	1 5/8	2	...
Furnsh		8	1 5/8	1 7/8	...
FutMed		135	25/32	13/16	+ 1/32
-G-G-G-					
GTEC 5pf	1.00	4	10 1/8	10 1/2	...
Galgph		86	1 1/4	1 1/2	...
Galgr un		3	3 1/2	4	...
GlxyCh		12	4 1/8	4 3/8	...
Gamogn		4	7/16	17/32	− 1/8
Gamo un		160	3/4	27/32	− 1/16
Garnet		14	5 1/8	5 7/8	...
GnMicro		129	4 1/8	4 1/4	− 1/8
GnSci		2	6 1/2	8	...
GenesCp	1.20a	2	42 1/2	45 1/2	...
Geotek		49	2 3/8	2 3/4	...
GliMed		780	3 3/4	3 7/8	...
GoVide		523	10	10 1/4	...
GoldCo		28	4	4 1/4	...
GoldRs		190	1 7/16	1 15/32	...
GldStd		67	2 15/16	3 1/16	...
GldKngt		4	7 7/8	8 1/8	− [illegible]
GldNth		51	[illegible]	[illegible]	[illegible]
GravEl		[illegible]	[illegible]	[illegible]	[illegible]
[illegible]		[illegible]	[illegible]	[illegible]	...
[illegible]		[illegible]	5	5 1/8	...
[illegible]an pf		200	4	5	...
MotnCtl		447	4 5/8	4 11/16	− 1/16
MultnA	.45e	14	8 1/4	9 1/4	− 1/4
Muscoch		109	3	3 1/16	− 1/16
vjMustR		23	13/32	1/2	...
Mylex		855	2 7/16	2 1/2	+ 3/16
MyoT un		60	1 1/2	1 3/4	− 1/16
-N-N-N-					
NMR		261	3 1/2	3 3/4	− 1/8
NY COM		1005	1 9/16	1 19/32	− 1/32
NtlAset		890	1 3/16	1 5/16	...
Ntl FSI		309	5 5/8	5 7/8	+ 1/8
NtlInBc		110	1 7/16	1 11/16	+ 1/8
NLamp		50	4 5/8	4 3/4	...
NtTeam		95	4 3/16	4 5/16	...
Neolens		206	1 7/32	1 1/4	+ 1/16
Neoln un		20	1 3/8	1 7/16	+ 1/8
NetAir		80	3/32	1/8	+ 1/32
NwfldMn		60	1/8	3/16	− 1/32
NobiltyH	.08	13	3 1/8	3 3/4	...
NAMtl		75	1 5/8	1 13/16	− 1/4
NAmSv		12	5 1/4	6	+ 1/4
NE Ins		138	1 9/16	1 11/16	− 1/16
NthLily		145	2 5/16	2 1/2	− 1/16
Novfrn		255	1 3/4	1 7/8	...
Noven		147	2 3/4	3 1/4	...
Nowsc g	.24e	332	12 1/4	12 3/8	+ 1/8
Nytest		870	1 3/16	1 1/4	− 1/32
-O-O-O-					
OMNI		1	3 3/8	3 5/8	...
ORS Cp		434	1 15/16	2	+ 1/8
Odysey s		34	1 1/2	1 3/4	− 1/8
OfcClub		137	11 1/2	11 3/4	+ 1/4
OlKnt pf	1.82	2	35 3/4	36 1/4	...
OlyBdc h		5	2 1/2	3 1/4	...
Oncor		50	1 11/16	1 13/16	− 1/16
Opticrp		189	3 7/16	3 9/16	− 3/16
ORFA pf		20	25	27	+ 3
Overmy	.20	22	3 3/4	4	...
Ovonic		56	2 1/4	2 1/2	...
Ovonc un		55	2 3/8	2 7/8	...
-P-Q-					
Panigp s		3	3 1/4	3 3/4	...
Parlux		33	7 1/4	7 1/2	− 1/4
Pathe		10	3/4	1	...
vjPergr		150	9/32	11/32	...
Periphl		2158	2 5/8	2 3/4	+ 5/16
PerCpt s		17	4	4 1/2	...
PerDia		30	2 13/16	2 15/16	− 1/16
Petro		124	11/32	3/8	...
PtHel vtg	.04e	1	13	13 3/4	− 1/4
PtHel nv	.04e	12	13 1/4	13 3/4	...
Phrmtc		6	3 1/2	3 5/8	...
PhnxAd		3740	9/32	5/16	...
PicktSu	1.10	6	7	7 1/2	...
Piemnt		20	3	3 1/4	...
PiedMn		10	7/8	15/16	+ 1/16
Piezo		131	1/16	3/32	...
PlasmT		139	11/16	27/32	...
PlexusR		50	2 3/8	2 5/8	+ 1/16
PirMol		1381	3 7/8	3 15/16	+ 1/16
PolrM wt		365	5	5 1/16	+ 3/8
Polydex		220	1 1/16	1 1/8	− 1/8
PopRad		84	12	12 1/4	...
PrabRbt		4	4 7/8	5 1/4	...
PresAr h		70	11/16	3/4	...
PrestoT		618	7/16	5/8	...
Primag		53	2	2 3/16	− 1/8
PrvB pf	.32	10	2 1/8	2 3/8	+ 1/4
PrftTc		250	3 1/4	3 3/8	...
ProB un		5	4	4 3/8	...
PubcoC		120	23/32	3/4	...
Purflw s		229	4 1/16	4 3/16	...
Qdrax		224	2 1/2	2 7/8	+ 1/8
Quartzl		15	4 1/2	5	...
-R-R-R-					
RCM		778	3 15/16	4 1/16	+ 1/16
RCM unB		10	5 1/4	5 3/4	...
RF&P		4	31	31 1/2	...
RHNB	.40	2	13	14 1/2	...
RadaEl		122	1 7/8	2	...
RadtnDs		128	3 1/4	3 3/8	+ 1/16
Radyne		214	1	1 1/8	...
RailSvg	.09e	13	5	5 3/4	...
Rapitec		490	13/16	15/16	...
ReaGld		35	2 5/8	2 11/16	+ 1/8
Realist	.20	1	10 3/4	11 1/2	...
RegFdl	.40	2	14 1/2	15 1/2	...
RenGRX		99	1 3/4	1 13/16	...
RntRte		20	11/16	13/16	− 1/16
RschFt		10	5 3/4	6 1/2	...
Ripley	.20	2	7	8 1/2	...
Ritzys s		1	5/8	3/4	...
Roadmst		820	1 25/32	1 27/32	− [illegible]
RockgH		320	[illegible]	[illegible]	[illegible]
RoosInv		[illegible]	[illegible]	[illegible]	[illegible]
[illegible]		[illegible]	[illegible]	[illegible]	− 1/32
[illegible]		[illegible]	1 3/8	1 9/16	...
[illegible]Alen		45	11/16	13/16	...
WetrPr	.42e	7	7 3/4	8 1/2	...
WilyJ B	.98	3	55	57	...
WolfFn		15	5 1/4	6	...
WidwdCpt		70	1 7/8	2 1/8	...
-X-Y-Z-					
Xeta		10	1 1/2	1 7/8	...
Xsirus		65	14 3/4	15	...
YUBAA		21	11/16	13/16	− 1/16

ADRS

Wednesday, March 29, 1989

Stock & Div		Sales 100s	Bid	Asked	Net Chg.
AngSA	.78e	458	21 1/8	21 3/8	− 1/4
AngAG	.44e	486	6 3/4	6 7/8	− 1/4
Blyvoor	.35e	730	3 1/16	3 3/16	...
Buffels	1.45e	184	13 1/4	13 1/2	− 1/2
Burmah	1.38e	...	38 1/4	38 3/4	− 1/4
DBeer	.65e	2193	14 1/2	14 5/8	− 1/8
DriefC s	.65e	518	9 5/8	9 3/4	− 1/4
FreSCn	1.00e	490	8 5/16	8 7/16	...
FujiPh	.16e	56	52 3/4	53	− 1/8
GoldFd	.46e	20	16 7/8	17 1/8	− 1/4
Highvld	.18e	197	4 1/16	4 1/8	− 1/8
JapnAir	.49e	1	236 1/2	240 1/4	...
KloofG	.45e	502	9	9 1/8	− 1/4
Lydnbg	.51e	16	10	10 1/4	− 1/8
Nissan	.16e	152	23 1/4	23 5/8	+ 5/8
OrangF	2.66e	23	20 3/8	20 5/8	− 1/8
RankO	.50e	52	15 1/4	15 3/8	...
StHIGd	1.02e	237	6 13/16	7 1/8	− 9/16
TelMex		4856	5/16	11/32	...
Toyota	.23r	40	38 1/2	39	− 1/8
VaalRf	.61e	1201	8	8 1/8	− 3/16
WelkG	.66e	461	5 7/16	5 5/8	+ 1/16
WDeep	1.84e	197	31 3/4	32 1/8	− 7/8

CONVERTIBLE DEBENTURES

Wednesday, March 29, 1989

Issue	Sales 100s	Bid	Asked	Net Chg.
AmWst 7 1/2 11	15	78 1/2	81	...
ApolCpt 7 1/4 11	...	65 1/2	67	...
Consul 92	...	82	90	+ 1
Costco 11	14	115	117	− 1/2
Hechng cv12	...	82	83 1/2	...
LypMd 12	1	67	69	...
Masco 11	1	73	75	...
MaxiHlt cv10	13	4	4 1/2	+ 1
Policy cv12	6	80	81 1/2	− 1
RbtHlf 12	2	91	93	...
SCI Sy 12	...	75	77	+ 1 1/2
Seagte 12	10	55 1/2	57 1/2	...
SunMic 12	2	96	97	− 1
Telecm 7s12	50	104	105	+ 1 1/2
WstwdOne 01	...	61	62	...

Source: *The Wall Street Journal*, March 30, 1989.

MUTUAL FUNDS

Wednesday, March 29, 1989

Price ranges for investment companies, as quoted by the National Association of Securities Dealers. NAV stands for net asset value per share; the offering includes net asset value plus maximum sales charge, if any.

LehCa	18.02	18.97+	.09
LehInv	16.06	16.91+	.07
MgdGv	11.75	12.37+	.02
MMun	14.73	15.51+	.01
NJMu	11.65	12.26+	.01
NYMu	15.73	16.56+	.01
PrcMM	15.98	16.82−	.13
PrnRet	9.57	NL+	.04
SmCap	14.07	14.81+	.04
Shearson Ports:			
BasVl t	13.23	13.23+	.07
Convt t	13.10	13.10+	.01
GlbBd t	16.06	16.06+	.01
GlbEq t	11.15	11.15+	.04
GvSec t	8.64	8.64+	.02
GrOpr t	15.86	15.86+	.03
Gwth t	12.04	12.04+	.04
HG Bd t	10.14	10.14+	.03
HiInc t	13.57	13.57	.....
IntGv t	10.97	10.97+	.01
Intl t	17.31	17.31+	.25
LT Gv t	7.92	7.92+	.01
MtgSc t	10.49	10.49+	.01
MOPS t	50.57	50.57+	.31
Optin t	13.17	13.17+	.01
PrcMt t	13.95	13.95−	.13
Sectr t	10.42	10.42+	.03
SplEq t	12.72	12.72+	.04
Stratg t	15.00	15.00+	.06
TxEx t	16.62	16.62+	.01
Util t	11.99	11.99+	.02
ShrmD p	7.04	7.04−	.04
Sigma Funds:			
Capit p	8.38	8.91+	.03
ISIGth	6.57	6.99+	.01
ISI TS	10.66	11.34+	.02
Inco p	8.11	8.49	.....
Invst p	10.33	10.99+	.01
PaTax	11.93	12.49+	.01
Spcl p	8.79	9.35−	.01
TxFB p	8.81	9.23+	.01
Trust p	13.48	14.34	.....
USGv p	11.72	12.27+	.01
ValSh p	9.68	10.30+	.03
Vent p	8.54	9.09−	.01
Wrld p	13.35	14.20+	.07
SitNBG	27.67	NL+	.16
SkylBal p	9.61	9.99+	.01
SkySpE p	11.38	11.84−	.02
Smith Barney:			
Equty	13.33	13.89+	.06
IncGro	11.43	12.13+	.03
IncRet	9.09	9.21	.....
MoGvt	11.56	12.04+	.02
MuCal	11.16	11.63+	.01
MunNt	12.10	12.60+	.01
USGvt	12.33	12.84+	.03
SoGen p	17.30	17.97+	.02
SoundSh	13.76	NL+	.01
SAM VT	12.18	12.18+	.01
SthestG t	13.63	13.63+	.01
Sover In	11.42	12.02+	.03
State Bond Grp:			
Com St	6.63	7.25+	.04
Divers	7.76	8.48+	.02
Progrs	9.81	10.72+	.04
TaxEx	10.15	10.63	.....
USGv p	4.66	4.91+	.01
St FarmFds:			
Balan	19.08	19.08+	.06
Gwth	14.13	14.13+	.02
Muni	7.68	7.68+	.01
StStreet Resh:			
Exc	142.21	142.21+	.76
Grwth	81.18	81.18+	.73
Inv r	76.71	77.08+	.44
Steadman Funds:			
Am Ind	2.20	NL−	.01
Assoc	.63	NL	.....
Invest	1.27	NL+	.01
Ocean	3.09	NL−	.01
Stein Roe Fds:			
Cap Op	22.20	NL+	.09
Discv	10.01	NL+	.04
GvtPlu	9.30	NL+	.01
HYMu	11.62	NL	.....
HYBds	9.39	NL+	.02
IntMu	10.27	NL	.....
MgdBd	8.24	NL+	.02
MgdM	8.64	NL	.....
PrimE	9.51	NL+	.05
Specl	16.17	NL+	.07
Stock	15.36	NL+	.10
TotRet	22.71	NL+	.04
Univ	13.12	NL+	.05
Strategic Funds:			
Gold	4.73	5.17+	.07
Invst	3.13	3.42−	.08
Silvr	3.94	4.31−	.05
StratnDv	24.25	NL	.....
Strat Gth	20.12	NL+	.10
Strong Funds:			
Discov	12.01	12.26−	.04
GovSc	10.04	NL	.....
Inco	11.95	NL	.....
Invst	18.11	18.29+	.04
MunBd	9.36	NL	.....
Oppty	18.30	18.67+	.06
ST Bd	10.09	NL	.....
Total	19.87	20.07+	.02
TecuEq	10.19	10.70+	.03
Tecuml	9.72	10.20+	.03
Templeton Group:			
Frgn	20.46	22.36+	.02
Global	7.73	8.45+	.03
Grwth	14.56	15.91+	.01
Inco	10.00	10.93	.....
World	15.02	16.42+	.02
Thomson McKinn:			
CvSec t	10.35	10.35+	.02
Global t	10.93	10.93+	.10
Gwth t	15.12	15.12+	.10
Inco t	9.42	9.42+	.02
Opor t	12.58	12.58+	.03
PrcMet	9.76	9.76−	.10
TaxEx t	10.78	10.78+	.01
USGv t	9.10	9.10+	.02
Trnstin p	10.14	NL+	.01
TrnstGr p	15.16	NL+	.07
TreasFt	9.21	NL−	.01
20th Century:			
BalInv	10.13	NL+	.02
Gift	7.61	NL+	.07
Grwth	13.62	NL+	.14
HerInv	6.62	NL+	.02
LTBnd	88.78	NL+	.04
Select	28.84	NL+	12
TxEIn	95.22	NL−	.03
TxELT	95.79	NL+	.14
Ultra	8.27	NL	.....
USGv	90.99	NL+	.03
Vista	6.76	NL+	.07
TynNwGI	11.57	12.18+	.03
USAA Group:			
AgsvGth	16.74	NL+	.07
Cornst	17.26	NL+	.03
Gold	8.52	NL−	.07
Grwth	12.20	NL+	.03
Inco	10.83	NL+	.02
IncStk	10.74	NL+	.03
Intl	10.76	NL+	.07
TxEH	12.65	NL+	.01
TxEIt	11.63	NL+	.01
TxESh	10.27	NL	.....
Unified Mgmnt:			
Genrl	8.56	8.56+	.01
Gwth	20.18	20.18+	.05
Inco	10.90	10.90−	.01
Indian	8.82	8.82+	.01
Mutl	15.05	15.05+	.03
United Funds:			
Accm	6.78	7.41+	.03
Bond	5.97	6.52	.....
Con Inc	15.17	16.58+	.02
GldGv	7.69	8.40−	.04
GvtSec	4.70	4.91	.....
IntGth	6.50	7.10+	.04
Hi Inc	11.64	12.72+	.02
HiIncII	4.54	4.96	.....
Incom	17.57	19.20+	.06
Muni	6.84	7.14	.....
MunHi	4.83	5.04	.....
NwCcpt	5.05	5.52−	.02
Retire	5.54	6.05+	.01
ScEng	10.18	11.13+	.02
Vang	6.02	6.58	.....
Utd Services:			
GBT	16.12	NL+	.05
GNMA	9.07	NL+	.02
GldShr	3.79	NL−	.09
Grwth	6.63	NL+	.05
Inco	10.39	NL	.....
LoCap r	6.28	NL+	.02
N Pro r	1.23	NL−	.01
Prspc r	.72	NL	.....
RIEst	9.53	NL+	.01
US TF	11.00	NL+	.01
UST Int	8.53	NL	.....
ValFrg	9.82	9.82+	.02
Value Line Fd:			
AggrIn	7.77	NL	.....
Conv	11.11	NL+	.02
Fund	13.78	NL+	.08
Incom	5.97	NL+	.02
Lev Gt	20.05	NL+	.12
MunBd	10.17	NL+	.02
NY TE	9.68	NL+	.02
Spl Sit	12.36	NL+	.10
US Gvt	11.38	NL+	.02
Van Eck:			
GldRs p	4.71	5.09−	.03
IntInv	12.09	13.21−	.15
Wldin p	9.03	9.76+	.03
WldTr p	12.81	13.85+	.06
VanKampen Mer:			
CATF p	15.03	15.80+	.06
Gwth p	15.90	16.72+	.05
HiYld p	13.28	13.96	.....
InTF p	17.14	18.02+	.03
PA TF	15.10	15.88+	.02
TxFH p	16.02	16.85+	.01
USGv p	14.44	15.18+	.02
Vance Exchange:			
CapE	100.41	NL+	.09
DBst	59.73	NL+	.25
Diver	110.83	NL+	.19
ExFd	153.65	NL+	.38
ExBo	140.96	NL+	.50
FidEx	85.41	NL+	.29
SeFid	85.96	NL	.....
Vanguard Group:			
AssetA	10.60	NL+	.04
BdMkt	8.93	NL+	.02
Convrt	x 8.85	NL−	.13
EqInc	x 11.28	NL−	.09
Explr	28.74	NL+	.06
ExplII	20.18	NL+	.02
Morg	10.74	NL+	.06
NaesT	37.91	NL+	.09
Prmcp	e 46.76	NL+	.01
VHYS	14.63	NL+	.05
V Pref	7.83	NL+	.01
V ARP	19.45	NL−	.01
Quant	11.81	NL+	.03
STAR	11.62	NL+	.03
TC Int	x 27.83	NL−	.95
TCUsa	x 28.25	NL−	.61
GNMA	9.13	NL+	.01
HiYBd	8.28	NL	.....
IGBnd	7.73	NL+	.02
ShrtTr	10.13	NL+	.01
STGovt	9.66	NL+	.01
US Tr	9.04	NL+	.04
IdxExt	e 12.39	NL−	.05
Indx 500	x 28.50	NL−	.27
MuHY	9.93	NL+	.02
MuInt	11.74	NL+	.01
MunLd	9.97	NL	.....
MuLg	10.18	NL+	.02
MInLg	11.32	NL+	.03
MuSht	15.11	NL	.....
Cal Ins	9.77	NL+	.02
NJIns	10.04	NL+	.02
NYIns	9.30	NL+	.02
PennIn	9.73	NL+	.02
VSPE r	12.80	NL+	.04
VSPG r	9.54	NL−	.07
VSPH r	19.62	NL+	.07
VSPS r	16.24	NL+	.10
VSPT r	11.00	NL+	.04
WellsI	x 15.45	NL−	.25
Welltn	16.73	NL+	.06
Wndsr	13.82	NL+	.02
Wnds II	13.79	NL+	.04
WldInt	10.24	NL+	.01
WldUS	8.02	NL+	.02
Venture Advisers:			
IncPl	8.20	8.61−	.01
Muni t	9.48	9.48+	.01
NY Ven	8.22	8.63+	.03
RPFB t	6.81	6.81+	.01
RPFE t	19.67	19.67+	.05
VikEqIn	15.16	NL+	.05
Wealth p	7.33	7.33+	.01
Weiss Peck Greer:			
Tudor	22.62	NL+	.10
WPG	21.20	NL+	.14
Govt	9.61	9.61+	.02
Gwth	100.31	NL+	.16
WallSt	6.84	7.24+	.02
WellsF IRA:			
AstAl f	12.25	NL+	.01
Bond f	11.07	NL+	.01
CpStk f	19.98	NL+	.07
SmlCo f	14.96	NL+	.02
Westcore:			
STBd	9.70	9.90+	.01

Vanguard Group's Index 500 (S & P 500)

Source: *The Wall Street Journal*, March 30, 1989.

fund's assets that is generally less than 1 percent of the investment. Net asset values are calculated after management takes its fee.

You can tell if a fund has no load by the symbol *NL* under the offer price or if the offer price and net asset value are identical. If the fund's offer price exceeds its net asset value, it's loaded.

Front-End Loaded Funds charge a one-time admission or sales fee to purchasers of their shares as well as the management fee levied by all funds. This "sales" or commission fee can be as high as 8 percent, which will effectively reduce your overall return depending on how long you hold the fund. A *p* after the fund's name indicates there is a distribution charge, or front-load, on the fund.

Back-End Loaded Funds levy a fee of up to 8 percent when the shares are sold back to the investment company. An *r* indicates *redemption* charge attached. Some back-ended funds vary their fees according to the length of time the shares are held. If you sell your shares after one year, the fee may be as high as 8 percent. But if you hold the shares for a long time (say, 30 years), no fee may be charged. (Remember that *all* funds have built-in management fees in addition to any loads.)

When both redemption and distribution fees are charged, the fund is identified by a *t* after the fund's name.

If there is no letter following the fund name and the offer price exceeds the net asset value, it is impossible to tell from the listing how the fund is loaded; the mutual fund company can provide that information to you.

Since no-load funds are directly marketed and have no outside sales force, there is no commission fee. In order to invest in a no-load fund, you must select the fund (e.g., in response to a newspaper ad or junk mail solicitation) and contact the investment company directly. A broker customarily will not act for you in the purchase of no-load funds because he or she will not receive a commission fee of any kind.

Loaded funds are sold through brokers, which explains the commission fee. The investment company contracts with the broker to act as the fund's marketer.

Some companies offer many funds, each with its own special objective. Take the *Vanguard Group* (pages 187 and 189), for example. In the first column, *NAV* stands for net asset value (per share). As you recall, this is calculated by totaling the market value of all securities owned by the fund, subtracting the liabilities (if any), and then dividing by the number of fund shares outstanding. In short, NAV equals the dollar value of the pool per mutual fund share. For instance, at the close of business on March 29, 1989, Vanguard Groups Index 500 fund, which invests only in the S & P 500, had a net asset value of $28.50. The last column informs you that this was a 27-cent loss from the previous day.

Notice that the offer price of $28.50 is the only figure given because the Index 500 Fund is a no-load fund. Also note that for $28.50 you could have bought a "share" in the S & P 500. Imagine the cost of buying a share in each of these 500 companies.

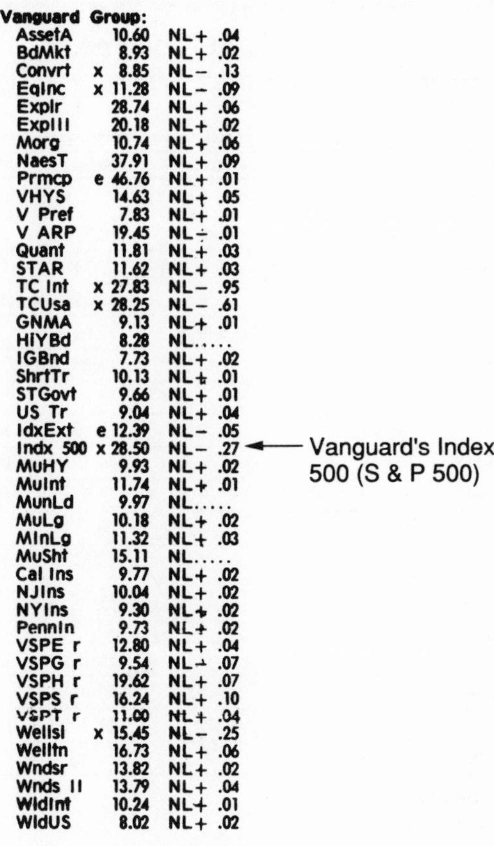

Vanguard Group:				
AssetA		10.60	NL+	.04
BdMkt		8.93	NL+	.02
Convrt	x	8.85	NL−	.13
EqInc	x	11.28	NL−	.09
Explr		28.74	NL+	.06
ExplII		20.18	NL+	.02
Morg		10.74	NL+	.06
NaesT		37.91	NL+	.09
Prmcp	e	46.76	NL+	.01
VHYS		14.63	NL+	.05
V Pref		7.83	NL+	.01
V ARP		19.45	NL+	.01
Quant		11.81	NL+	.03
STAR		11.62	NL+	.03
TC Int	x	27.83	NL−	.95
TCUsa	x	28.25	NL−	.61
GNMA		9.13	NL+	.01
HiYBd		8.28	NL.....	
IGBnd		7.73	NL+	.02
ShrtTr		10.13	NL+	.01
STGovt		9.66	NL+	.01
US Tr		9.04	NL+	.04
IdxExt	e	12.39	NL−	.05
Indx 500	x	28.50	NL−	.27
MuHY		9.93	NL+	.02
MuInt		11.74	NL+	.01
MunLd		9.97	NL.....	
MuLg		10.18	NL+	.02
MInLg		11.32	NL+	.03
MuSht		15.11	NL.....	
Cal Ins		9.77	NL+	.02
NJIns		10.04	NL+	.02
NYIns		9.30	NL+	.02
PennIn		9.73	NL+	.02
VSPE r		12.80	NL+	.04
VSPG r		9.54	NL+	.07
VSPH r		19.62	NL+	.07
VSPS r		16.24	NL+	.10
VSPT r		11.00	NL+	.04
Wellsl	x	15.45	NL−	.25
Welltn		16.73	NL+	.06
Wndsr		13.82	NL+	.02
Wnds II		13.79	NL+	.04
WldInt		10.24	NL+	.01
WldUS		8.02	NL+	.02

Source: *The Wall Street Journal*, March 30, 1989.

The *Journal* publishes a report daily on the second-to-last page of the third (C) section called **Mutual Fund Scorecard**. (See the example from the Friday, March 24, 1989 *Wall Street Journal* on page 190). It lists the top and bottom performers of a wide variety of mutual funds.

Here is a list of some of the different kinds of funds that are covered in the *Journal's* **Mutual Fund Scorecard**:

A-Rated Bond
Balanced
BBB-Rated Bond
Capital Appreciation
Closed End Bond
Closed End Equity

Mutual Fund Scorecard/Equity Income

INVESTMENT OBJECTIVE: Dividend income from a portfolio principally made up of equities; may hold some bonds

(Ranked by 12-month return)	NET ASSET VALUE MAR. 23	TOTAL RETURN[1] IN PERIOD ENDING MAR. 23				ASSETS DEC. 31 (In millions)[2]
		4 WEEKS	SINCE 12/31	12 MONTHS	5 YEARS	
TOP 15 PERFORMERS						
Delaware Gr:Decatur II	$12.04	0.58%	6.58%	19.97%	**%	$203.9
Vanguard Equity Income[3]	11.27	0.45	5.11	17.74	**	63.8
Delaware Gr:Decatur I	17.44	– 0.41	6.57	17.19	128.53	1515.5
Olympic Tr-Eq Income[3]	12.27	0.07	6.03	17.09	**	31.3
T. Rowe Price Eq Inco[3]	13.94	– 0.36	4.11	17.08	**	497.3
Equity Port:Income[3]	11.61	– 0.43	5.87	16.86	116.49	435.8
Vanguard Hi Yld Stk[3]	14.54	0.28	2.84	16.40	146.79	158.0
Fidelity Equity-Income[4]	25.87	– 0.40	5.81	16.35	114.03	4064.9
National Total Income	8.06	0.62	4.40	16.01	125.88	141.5
Helmsman:Inco Eq[4]	9.80	– 0.16	4.57	15.77	**	1.2
Lindner Dividend[3]	23.40	0.73	3.22	15.51	97.69	83.8
Fidelity Puritan[4]	13.16	0.14	4.69	14.99	115.50	4295.5
United Income	17.40	– 0.63	4.58	14.69	151.55	1149.3
Franklin Is Tr:Sp Eq Inc[4]	10.84	0.10	5.01	14.18	**	2.0
Cowen Income & Growth	10.39	0.66	5.42	13.97	**	30.3
AVG. FOR CATEGORY		– 0.04%	3.73%	11.63%	97.75%	
NUMBER OF FUNDS		52	53	46	24	
BOTTOM 10 PERFORMERS						
Div/Gro:Div Series[3]	$22.50	– 1.53%	0.92%	0.43%	51.73%	$3.1
Kidder Peabody Eq Inc[3]	16.65	– 0.12	2.45	4.02	**	57.8
Flex Fund:Inc & Growth[3]	17.99	– 1.12	– 2.76	4.09	**	2.1
Amer Natl Income	18.32	0.16	3.74	5.27	66.86	62.3
Royce Total Return[3]	5.01	1.20	5.84	5.72	**	6.0
Fidelity Qualified Dvd[3]	11.56	0.08	0.59	6.46	96.78	66.6
Tower Srs:Equity Income	5.29	– 1.49	2.32	7.42	**	1.0
Founders:Equity Income[3]	7.13	0.28	3.48	8.34	70.89	12.6
Value Line Income[3]	5.92	0.67	3.08	9.00	80.86	133.1
Capital Income Builder	22.92	0.18	2.71	9.27	**	130.6

[1] Change in net asset value with reinvested dividends and capital gains
[2] Some funds may not qualify for daily quotation of net asset values
[3] No initial load
[4] Low initial load of 4.5% or less

*Fund existed only part of period
**Fund didn't exist in period
N.A.=Not available

Source: ***Lipper Analytical Services Inc.***

Source: *The Wall Street Journal*, March 24, 1989.

Convertible Securities
Equity Income
General Municipal Bond
Ginnie Mae
Global
Growth
Growth and Income
High Current Yield
International
Money Market
Natural Resources and Gold
Short–Term Municipal Bond
Small Company Growth
Specialty and Miscellaneous
U.S. Government Bond
Variable Annuity Bond
Variable Annuity Equity
World Income

At this point you may very well feel that the objective outlined in Chapters 1 and 8 has been lost. Mutual funds seem to have no advantage over individual stocks because the choice among funds, even among different kinds of funds, has become tremendously difficult due to the proliferation of funds. What happened to gold vs. stocks?

Don't despair. You can still invest in the overall stock market by selecting an *index fund* that places your capital in one of the better known stock market barometers. For instance, return to page 189 and the *Journal's* March 30, 1989 quote of the Vanguard Group's Index 500 fund: all of its resources are invested in the S & P 500.

You can see for yourself how well this strategy would have worked. Each quarter the *Journal* publishes a review that summarizes the best and worst performers in each type of mutual fund. The Thursday, April 6, 1989 excerpt from the *Journal* (on page 192) serves as an example. Compare the average fund's performance with the S & P 500's performance at the bottom of the table.

So much for the experts and the management fees they charge for deciding how to invest your money.

Note that the average for all funds did not perform as well as the S & P 500.

Investor's Tip

- Give serious consideration to choosing an index fund. It would have done better than the average mutual fund in the 1980s.

How the Biggest Stock Funds Have Performed

Percentage gains for periods ended March 31; assets as of Dec. 31.

FUND NAME	ASSETS (in billions)	FIRST QUARTER	TWELVE MONTHS	FIVE YEARS	TEN YEARS
Fidelity Magellan Fund	$9.0	9.5%	22.3%	160%	1,170%
Windsor Fund	5.8	6.9	24.9	150	545
Fidelity Puritan	4.3	5.9	17.4	117	392
Investment Company of America	4.1	6.9	17.0	128	391
Fidelity Equity-Income	4.1	7.5	19.3	116	511
Templeton World	3.9	6.8	16.8	116	417
Pioneer II	3.8	7.1	18.7	95	394
Affiliated Fund	3.3	3.8	13.4	110	357
Washington Mutual Investors	2.8	7.2	17.3	133	437
American Mutual	2.6	5.8	13.6	114	405
Mutual Shares	2.5	6.6	21.7	137	531
Dreyfus Fund	2.3	4.4	9.2	85	310
American Capital Pace	2.3	8.4	15.7	69	546
Twentieth Cent: Sel	2.3	8.1	11.2	104	582
Dean Witter Div Growth	1.7	9.0	19.8	128	N.A.
Templeton Growth	1.7	6.0	19.4	116	356
Putnam Growth & Income	1.6	5.4	18.1	121	396
AMCAP Fund	1.6	8.0	13.9	100	406
Pru-Bache Utility	1.6	5.3	22.0	192	N.A.
Fidelity Cap Apprec.	1.6	7.1	25.6	N.A.	N.A.
Delaware Gr: Decatur I	1.5	8.6	21.2	129	437
Windsor II	1.5	9.5	25.1	N.A.	N.A.
Fidelity Destiny I	1.4	8.6	19.6	132	531
Pioneer Fund	1.4	6.1	14.5	91	287
Evergreen Total Return	1.3	5.4	11.6	109	418
T Rowe Price Growth Stock	1.3	4.5	9.6	107	202
Putnam Opt Income II	1.3	4.5	12.1	N.A.	N.A.
Fidelity Freedom Fund	1.2	8.3	13.4	121	N.A.
IDS Stock	1.2	6.8	14.6	100	274
Twentieth Cent:Gro	1.2	11.9	15.7	108	503
United Income	1.1	6.5	18.3	154	410
Fidelity Gro & Income	1.1	8.4	21.7	N.A.	N.A.
Growth Fund of Amer	1.1	9.8	17.6	113	473
Fidelity Overseas	1.1	3.0	6.0	N.A.	N.A.
Nicholas Fund	1.1	8.1	14.8	113	498
Mutual Qualified Fund	1.1	6.8	21.6	141	N.A.
Merrill Basic Value A	1.1	6.0	18.9	129	457
Mass Investors Trust	1.1	7.5	15.9	98	291
Vanguard Index:500 Pt	1.1	7.0	17.8	119	334
Strong Total Return	1.0	7.3	16.5	118	N.A.
GENERAL EQUITY FUNDS AVERAGE		6.6%	13.4%	89.5%	325.1%
S&P 500 (with dividends)		7.1%	18.1%	124%	354%

N.A. =Not available

Source: Lipper Analytical Services Inc.

Average mutual fund performance compared to S&P 500

Source: *The Wall Street Journal*, April 6, 1989.

RISKY BUSINESS

Options

If you are confident a stock will rise, you may purchase it and realize your gain if your prediction proves true. But there are a number of ways you can *leverage* your purchase in order to increase your gain (i.e., you can capture the increase on a larger number of shares of stock than you can currently afford to purchase). Your *leverage* is the ratio between the value of the shares you control and the amount of capital (money) you have invested. The smaller your investment and the larger the value of the shares you control, the greater your leverage.

For instance, under current regulations set by the Fed, you may borrow from your broker up to half the initial value of the shares of stock you purchase, which provides leverage of two to one. It's called *buying on margin*. If you buy $200 worth of stock from your broker, with a margin of $100 (50 percent margin) and a $100 loan from the broker, and the stock doubles in value (from $200 to $400), you have made $200 on a $100 investment (less interest cost) instead of $100 on a $100 investment that was not margined. That's leverage.

Options provide another opportunity to leverage your investment. They give you the right (option) to buy or sell stock at a stated price for future delivery at a small premium (cost to buy the option). People do this for the same reason they buy or sell any stock: they think it's going up or down in value. Only in this case, they believe the stock will be higher or lower than the price at which they agreed to buy or sell it. Options are another way to invest in the stock market.

For instance, suppose you had the option to buy a share of stock for $25 in a few months' time that currently trades at 23 1/2, and you were convinced the stock would be trading at 28 by then. Wouldn't you pay a premium for the right to buy a $28 stock for $25? That's a good deal, as long as the premium is smaller than the spread between $25 and the $28 price at which you think the stock will trade. Conversely, if you were convinced that a stock, currently trading at 23 1/2, would fall to 18, wouldn't you pay a fee (premium) for the right to sell it at $20, knowing you could obtain it at $18?

The excerpt from the Friday, March 31, 1989 *Journal* presents a summary of options trading on Thursday, March 30 (see page 194). This report, called **Listed Options Quotations**, appears daily and you

LISTED OPTIONS QUOTATIONS

Thursday, March 30, 1989

Options closing prices. Sales unit usually is 100 shares.
Stock close is New York or American exchange final price.

	Option & NY Close	Strike Price	Calls–Last			Puts–Last		
			Apr	May	Jun	Apr	May	Jun
	AMag o	11 7/8	5/8	s	r	r	s	5/8
	Blkbst	20	r	s	r	r	s	1/4
	26	22 1/2	r	r	r	r	3/8	5/8
	26	25	1 5/8	2	r	1/2	1	r
	BrisMy	45	1 5/8	2 1/16	2 11/16	1/4	1/2	11/16
	46 5/8	50	1/16	r	7/16	r	r	r
	Bruns	15	5 1/8	5 1/4	5 3/8	r	r	r
	20 1/4	17 1/2	2 1/2	3 1/4	3 3/8	r	3/8	3/4
	20 1/4	20	1 1/4	1 3/4	2	15/16	1 1/4	1 5/8
	20 1/4	22 1/2	s	s	1 1/8	s	s	3 3/8
	Chamln	25	r	r	r	r	1/16	r
	30 1/4	30	1	r	1 5/8	r	3/4	1 1/8
	30 1/4	35	r	1/8	3/8	r	r	r
	30 1/4	40	r	s	1/16	r	s	r
	CompSc	50	r	1 9/16	r	r	r	r
	Dow Ch	80	s	s	r	s	s	1/4
	91 1/2	85	7	s	r	1/4	s	3/4
	91 1/2	90	2 3/4	4	5	7/8	r	2 1/4
	91 1/2	95	11/16	1 1/2	2 3/8	3 1/2	r	4 1/4
	91 1/2	100	r	9/16	1 1/16	r	r	r
	Ford	45	4 1/8	4 1/8	4 1/2	r	5/16	1/2
	48 7/8	50	9/16	1	1 1/2	1 1/2	2 3/8	2 5/16
	48 7/8	55	1/16	1/8	3/8	r	r	6 1/2
	48 7/8	60	r	s	1/8	r	s	11 1/4
	Fuqua	30	r	r	1	r	r	r
	Gap	35	4 1/8	r	r	r	r	r
	38 7/8	40	r	r	2	r	r	r
	Gencp	15	2 3/8	2 7/8	r	r	r	r
	17 1/4	17 1/2	1/2	3/4	1 1/4	r	r	r
	17 1/4	20	1/16	5/16	1/2	r	r	r
	Gen El	40	r	5	5 1/4	r	r	r
	44 1/2	45	1/2	1 1/8	1 9/16	7/8	1	1 1/2
	44 1/2	50	r	1/8	3/16	r	r	r
GM	G M	35	s	s	r	s	s	3/16
GM	41	37 1/2	s	s	4 1/4	s	s	3/8
GM	41	40	1 5/8	2	2 1/8	5/16	15/16	1 1/16
GM	41	42 1/2	3/8	3/4	1	1 5/8	2 1/8	2 3/8
GM	41	45	1/16	1/4	3/8	4	4 1/4	4 3/8
GM	41	47 1/2	r	s	3/16	r	s	6 1/2
GM	41	50	s	s	1/8	s	s	r
	GlfWn	45	2 3/4	3 1/4	3 7/8	3/8	1 3/16	1 11/16
	46 5/8	50	1/2	1 1/16	1 1/2	r	r	r
	46 5/8	55	r	r	11/16	r	r	r
	Hanson	15	1/2	r	r	r	r	r
	Heinz	45	r	r	r	r	r	7/16
	49 3/8	50	7/8	1 1/2	1 15/16	r	1 3/4	2
	49 3/8	55	r	r	3/8	r	r	r
	I T T	50	r	2 3/4	3 1/8	r	r	r
	51 7/8	55	r	3/8	13/16	r	r	r
	K mart	35	r	r	r	1/16	1/16	r
	38 3/4	40	5/16	3/4	1 1/8	r	r	r
	Litton	75	2	r	3 5/8	1	r	r
	MayDS	30	r	s	8 1/4	r	s	r
	38	35	3	3 3/8	3 3/4	r	r	r
	38	40	r	3/8	3/4	2	r	r
	Mc Don	50	1 7/8	2 5/8	3 1/8	5/16	7/8	1 3/8
	51 1/2	55	1/16	3/8	7/8	r	r	r
	Mid SU	17 1/2	r	r	1/4	r	r	r
	N C R	50	5 1/2	r	7 1/8	r	3/8	r
	55 3/4	55	1 7/8	3	4 3/8	r	1 7/8	2 1/2
	55 3/4	60	5/8	1 1/4	2 1/16	5 1/4	r	6
	55 3/4	65	r	5/8	1 1/16	r	r	r
	55 3/4	70	1/4	s	3/4	r	s	r
	NorSo	30	2 5/8	3 1/8	r	r	r	r
	32 3/4	35	1/4	5/8	3/4	r	2 7/8	r
	32 3/4	40	r	r	1/4	r	r	r
	NorTel	15	r	1/2	r	r	r	r
	Oracle	15	s	s	10 1/8	s	s	r
	25 1/4	17 1/2	s	s	7 5/8	s	s	r
	25 1/4	20	4 3/8	r	5 3/8	r	r	1/4
	25 1/4	22 1/2	2 5/8	r	3 1/2	3/8	r	11/16
	25 1/4	25	15/16	1 1/2	2 1/4	r	r	1 1/2
	25 1/4	30	r	r	1/2	r	r	r
	Pall	30	r	r	1	r	2 1/16	r
	RalPur	75	r	r	r	r	r	5/8
	81 1/8	80	2	2 1/2	3 5/8	1	r	1 3/4
	81 1/8	85	1/4	1/2	1 1/4	r	r	r

Option & NY Close	Strike Price	Calls–Last			Puts–Last		
		Apr	May	Jul	Apr	May	Jul
36 3/4	40	1/4	3/4	1 3/4	3 1/2	r	r
36 3/4	45	1/8	s	3/4	8 3/4	s	8 7/8
36 3/4	50	r	s	s	13 3/4	s	s
Merck	55	10 3/8	s	r	r	s	r
65 1/8	60	5 5/8	6	7 1/4	r	r	13/16
65 1/8	65	1 7/16	2 1/4	3 5/8	1	r	2 1/8
65 1/8	70	3/16	7/16	1 3/8	r	r	r
Micron	20	3/8	r	r	r	r	r
MdwAir	12 1/2	1	r	r	1/8	r	r
13 3/8	15	3/16	r	r	r	r	r
M M M	65	2 7/8	r	4 1/4	3/8	r	1 3/8
66 7/8	70	5/16	13/16	1 9/16	3 1/4	r	3 7/8
Monsan	85	r	s	11 3/8	r	s	13/16
93 1/2	90	4 3/4	r	r	r	1 1/4	2 1/4
93 1/2	95	1 1/2	r	5	2 3/8	r	r
93 1/2	100	r	r	2 1/2	r	r	r
N W A	50	19	s	r	r	s	1/8
68 1/4	55	13 3/4	r	r	r	r	5/8
68 1/4	60	8 3/4	9 3/4	12 1/4	1/8	3/4	1 1/2
68 1/4	65	4 3/4	6 3/8	9	1 1/8	2 3/4	3 3/8
68 1/4	70	2 1/4	3 3/4	5 3/4	3 3/4	5	r
68 1/4	75	1 3/16	2 3/8	3 3/4	8	r	r
NatEdu	20	1 1/2	r	r	r	r	r
21	22 1/2	r	7/8	1 1/4	r	r	r
Norton	45	r	r	r	7/16	r	r
PaineW	17 1/2	3/8	r	r	1/2	r	r
Pennz	75	9 1/8	s	r	r	s	r
83 5/8	80	4 1/8	r	r	1/8	r	7/8
83 5/8	85	3/4	1 3/4	2 7/8	1 3/4	r	r
Pepsi	35	9 1/8	s	r	r	s	r
44 1/8	40	4 1/2	r	5 1/2	1/16	r	7/16
44 1/8	45	7/16	1 1/8	2 1/8	1 5/16	1 5/8	2
44 1/8	50	r	r	5/8	r	r	r
Polar	30	7	r	7 5/8	r	r	1/4
36 7/8	35	2 1/8	2 3/4	3 3/4	3/8	3/4	1 1/4
36 7/8	40	3/16	1/2	1 1/4	3 1/8	r	4
36 7/8	45	1/16	r	3/8	8 1/2	r	8 3/4
36 7/8	50	1/16	s	s	r	s	s
Rockwl	20	1 3/4	r	2 1/8	1/8	r	1/2
22	22 1/2	3/8	5/8	1 1/8	1	r	r
22	25	1/16	r	r	r	r	r
S C I	12 1/2	r	r	1 1/8	r	r	r
StJude	22 1/2	4 1/2	r	r	r	r	r
28 1/2	25	3 3/8	4	4 1/4	r	r	7/8
28 1/2	30	r	1	1 1/2	r	r	r
Sears	35	8 7/8	s	9 1/2	r	s	r
43 1/2	40	4	4 1/4	4 7/8	1/16	5/16	5/8
43 1/2	45	5/8	1 3/16	1 15/16	1 3/4	r	2 3/8
43 1/2	50	1/8	7/16	5/8	r	r	r
Squibb	65	2 7/8	r	5	r	r	r
67 1/4	70	9/16	1 1/8	2 1/2	r	r	4
Teldyn	330	r	s	r	r	s	2 5/8
348 1/2	340	r	r	r	1 7/16	r	4 7/8
348 1/2	350	r	r	r	r	7	r
348 1/2	360	1 1/2	3 7/8	r	r	r	13 1/4
Tex In	35	3 1/2	4 1/4	r	1/8	r	r
38 3/8	40	7/16	1	2 1/16	1 7/8	r	r
Upjohn	25	3 1/4	r	3 3/4	1/8	r	r
28	30	1/8	7/16	1 1/16	2	2 1/4	2 3/8
28	35	1/16	r	1/4	r	r	r
WstPP	50	r	s	r	1/8	s	1/8
57 1/2	55	r	r	r	5/16	r	3/8
57 1/2	60	r	r	1/16	r	r	r
Weyerh	25	2	r	r	r	r	r
26 3/4	30	1/16	r	3/8	r	r	3 1/2
Winnbg	10	r	r	3/8	1 1/8	r	r
Xerox	50	r	s	r	r	s	1/2
58 7/8	55	4 1/4	r	r	r	1/2	1 3/8
58 7/8	60	15/16	1 15/16	3 1/4	1 5/8	2 3/8	3 3/8
58 7/8	65	1/4	5/8	1 1/2	6 3/4	r	6 1/4
58 7/8	70	1/16	s	1/2	r	s	r
Zayre	25	3/4	r	1 5/8	r	r	r
		Apr	May	Aug	Apr	May	Aug
Amdahl	15	r	2 1/4	2 3/4	r	7/16	1
16 5/8	17 1/2	1/4	5/8	1 3/8	1	1 3/8	r
16 5/8	20	r	1/4	r	3 1/2	r	r
A E P	25	r	r	1 7/8	r	r	7/16

Source: *The Wall Street Journal*, March 31, 1989.

can find it listed in the front-page indexes of the first (A1) and last (C1) sections. This excerpt takes GM as an example (first column).

The first column informs you that GM closed at $41 (41) on Thursday, March 30, 1989.

The second column lists the *strike prices* ($35, $37.50, $40, $42.50, $45, $47.50, and $50) at which you have the option of buying or selling (striking a deal for) the stock in the future. Note that some prices are higher and some are lower than the current price ($41). Think of the strike price as the price at which you strike a deal.

The third through the fifth columns list the premium you must pay per share to purchase the option to *call* (buy) GM stock at the applicable strike price by the third Friday of the months listed (April, May, June). Take April as an example. On March 30 you had to pay a premium of 38 cents (3/8 of a dollar) for the right (option) to buy a share of GM stock at $42.50 (42½) by the close of trading on April 21, 1989 (third Friday of April). Once the deal was struck, the seller (writer) of the option would be bound to deliver the stock to you at that price at any time before April 21, 1989, *at your option*.

Why would you buy such a contract? Because you were convinced that GM would trade at more than $42.88 (strike price of $42.50 plus premium of $0.38) at any time before the third Friday in April. Then you would have the option to buy it at $42.50 (the strike price) from the option writer and sell it at the higher market price. When a call exceeds the strike price, it is said to be *in the money*.

Trading is done in round lots of 100 shares. Suppose your forecast is correct, and GM trades at $48 by April 21, 1989. You paid a $38 premium (100 × $0.38) to buy the option to call 100 shares at $42.50 a

Option & NY Close	Strike Price	Calls—Last			Puts—Last		
		Apr	May	Jun	Apr	May	Jun
GM	35	s	s	r	s	s	3/16
41	37½	s	s	4¼	s	s	3/8
41	40	1 5/8	2	2 1/8	5/16	15/16	1 1/16
41	42½	3/8	3/4	1	1 5/8	2 1/8	2 3/8
41	45	1/16*	1/4	3/8	4	4¼	4 3/8
41	47½	r	s	3/16	r	s	6½
41	50	s	s	1/8	s	s	r

— GM

Source: *The Wall Street Journal*, March 31, 1989.

share. You now exercise your option and acquire 100 shares for $4,250 (100 × $42.50). Those shares are worth $4,800 (100 × $48) on the market. Thus, you've obtained $4,800 of securities for $4,250, less your premium of $38, for a net gain of $512 on your $4,250 investment. That's leverage.

Thus, if you buy a call, you're speculating that the stock's price will rise sufficiently to earn you a return (spread) over and above the premium you must pay to buy the option. But suppose it doesn't? Suppose the stock rises only a little, or even falls in value, so that you have the an option to buy a stock at a price greater than market value? For instance, you may have purchased the April option to call GM at $42.50, expecting its price to rise. But in reality, on April 21 the price GM acutally only rose to $42.88 at close. Which would mean the market value of 100 shares is $4,288 and it would cost $4,250 minus your premium of $38 to exercise your option for no gain on your $4,250 investment ($4,288 − $4,250 = $38 − $38 = $0). What then? Would you have to buy the stock from the option writer at the strike price ($42.50)? No, because you have only purchased an *option* to buy. There's no requirement to do so. You can let the option expire without exercising it, and you have only lost your premium of $38.

You've probably noticed that the $40 strike price is already in the money (i.e., below the market price). You might think you should buy those options now and make a killing today. Why not exercise the option to buy the stock below market value and sell it immediately at the market price? Because the premium for all months exceeds the spread ($1) between the strike price ($40) and the current market price ($41). For example the April option to buy a call at $40 carries a premium of $1.63 (1⅝), which, when added to the strike price ($40 + $1.63 = $41.63), exceeds the current market price of $41. And you would also have to pay your broker's fee. Clearly, no option writer (the person selling you the option to buy) would want to risk a loss by selling you the option to buy a stock at less than market value unless he or she can make up the difference in the premium you must pay for the option.

A *rising* market motivates investors to buy calls. They hope the price of *their* stock will shoot up and they will be able to exercise their option and recover their premium, and then some. This does not necessarily mean that option writers (people who sell the option) are counting on the market to stay flat or even fall. The call writer may have decided to sell a stock if it reaches a certain target level (i.e., take his or her gain after the stock rises a certain number of points). If it does rise, the call writer will receive the increment and the premium; and even if it doesn't, he or she will still receive the premium. Thus, income is the primary motive for writing the option. Instead of waiting for the stock to move up to the target level, the seller writes a call. If it doesn't move up to that price, he or she will still have earned the premium. If it does, he or she will get premium plus capital gain.

Now let's consider the other kind of option. If you believed that GM stock would fall to a value below the current price of $41, you could purchase a *put* contract, and the option writer would have to buy the put at the strike price, regardless of current market value. Your option to sell at the strike price would give you an opportunity to buy at the lower market value (assuming your forecast was correct) and profit on the difference.

The last three columns in the example on page 195 provide the put contract premiums for April, May and June. A strike price of $42.50 is already in the money, so you could buy GM stock at the current market price of $41 and put (sell) it to the option writer for $42.50 before the option expiration date. You would make $1.50 on each share of stock ($42.50 − $41 = $1.50. However, your premium $1.63 (1 5/8) would be greater than the spread, and when added to transactions cost (brokerage fee) would remove any incentive to buy the put.

But it would be a different story if GM fell to 38 before the April 21 expiration date and you held an April put. With an April put at $42.50, your premium would be $162.50 (100 × $1.625). If GM fell to $38 you could buy 100 shares at $3,800 (100 × $38) in the market and exercise your option to sell for $4,250 (100 × $42.50) for a gain of $450, less the premium of $162.50 for a net gain of $287.50. (Again, you have to subtract the broker's fee from your profit.)

If the market rose, so that the market price exceeded the strike price, you wouldn't want to exercise your option to sell at a price below market. Instead, you would permit your option to expire without exercising it. Your loss would be only the premium you paid.

Why would someone write a put? Because he or she is prepared to buy a stock if it should drop to a particular price. The writer earns the premium whether or not the option is exercised. If he or she believes the stock will rise in price, then the writer has little concern that an option holder will put it to him or her at less than the market price. And the writer has collected the premium. But if the market does fall, and falls sufficiently that the contract comes in the money, the writer will have to buy the stock at the contract price, which will be above market. That's not necessarily bad, since the writer had already planned to buy the stock if it fell to the strike price, and he or she has collected a premium, too.

Incidentally, put and call premiums will rise and fall with the market value of the stock. Therefore, even if your option comes in the money, you need not exercise it, because you will be able to sell it on the market and make a gain without buying or selling the underlying stock.

In addition to simply playing the options market for profit, an investor can buy options to hedge against price fluctuations of his or her investment in the underlying security. This is a sophisticated investment strategy.

Finally, buying *index options* (see page 200) is another way to invest (or speculate) in the entire market. Instead of buying all the stocks in one of the stock market averages (or buying an index mutual fund), you can buy a put or call on an index option (such as the S & P 100), just as you can invest in options on individual stocks. These index options are more widely traded than options on individual securities.

Many of these possibilities sound intriguing, easy, and potentially profitable. Keep in mind, however, that there are substantial commission costs. Furthermore, as in any leveraged situation, the potential for considerable loss exists. Options are not for novices, and even buying on margin exposes you to up to twice the risk of simply buying a stock with your own money. With leverage you can move a big rock with a small stick—but the stick can also break off in your hands, and the rock can roll back over your feet.

In fact, the whole options game is tricky and multi-faceted. Consequently, before you can invest in options, your broker will evaluate your past investment experience and your current financial position. It will not be easy to qualify.

Short Interest

Instead of speculating on a price increase, some investors borrow stock from their broker in the hope of a price *decrease*. They sell the stock and leave the proceeds of the sale with their broker. If the stock falls, the borrower buys it back at the lower price and returns it to the broker, at which time the broker returns the funds from the original sale to the borrower. The advantage to the borrower is obvious: he or she pockets the difference between the high price when he or she borrowed and sold the stock and the low price when he or she bought and returned the stock.

For example, if you borrow a $2 stock from your broker and sell it, you have $2. If it falls to $1, you can buy it on the market and return the stock to the broker and you keep the other dollar. This is called *selling short*. But what advantage does the broker gain? Brokers lend stocks because you have to leave the cash from your sale of the stock with them as collateral for the borrowed stock, and they can then lend (or invest) the cash at interest.

Around the twentieth of each month *The Wall Street Journal* reports **Short Interest Highlights** for each of the Exchanges: NYSE, AMEX, and NASDAQ (OTC) (check the front-page index of the first and third sections). *Short interest* is the number of borrowed shares that have not been returned to the lender. A great deal of short interest in a stock indicates widespread speculation that a stock will fall. Remember, however, that these shares must be repaid, and that those who owe stock must buy it in order to repay it. Their stock purchases could bid the stock up.

The Friday, July 21, 1989 *Journal* article on page 201 serves as an example. It reports that short interest on the NYSE and AMEX fell for the month ending July 14, 1989, indicating reduced sentiment on the part of the short-sellers that the market will fall.

Foreign Markets

Finally, you can buy shares of stock on **Canadian Markets**, **U.S. Regional Markets**, and on Foreign Markets called **Overseas Markets**. The *Journal* provides daily listings, and you can find them in the front-page index. Representative samples are included on pages 202 and 203 from the Thursday, April 20, 1989 edition. Remember that when you invest in foreign markets you must be concerned with the fluctuation of foreign currency values as well as the value of the shares you purchase.

INDEX TRADING

Tuesday, May 23, 1989.

OPTIONS

Chicago Board

S&P 100 INDEX

Strike Price	Calls–Last Jun	Calls–Last Jul	Calls–Last Aug	Puts–Last Jun	Puts–Last Jul	Puts–Last Aug
260	42¼	....	....	⅛	7/16	13/16
265	....	....	....	3/16	⅝	1⅛
270	31	34	....	¼	1	1 11/16
275	26	....	....	7/16	1 5/16	1 15/16
280	20½	25⅝	25¾	¾	1⅞	3
285	15½	20⅛	....	1 3/16	2⅝	3¾
290	11⅜	15	17½	1 15/16	3¾	4⅞
295	7½	12¼	14¾	3⅛	5⅛	7
300	4½	8¼	10⅜	5⅜	7⅜	8½
305	2½	5¾	8¼	8⅝	10	11¼
310	1¼	3⅞	5⅜	12⅜	13¼	13⅝
315	9/16	2½	4⅜	....	....	....

Total call volume 81,471 Total call open int. 220,842
Total put volume 75,577 Total put open int. 282,933
The index: High 301.56; Low 297.40; Close 297.62, −3.93

S&P 500 INDEX

Strike Price	Calls–Last Jun	Calls–Last Jul	Calls–Last Sep	Puts–Last Jun	Puts–Last Jul	Puts–Last Sep
225	....	....	....	....	⅛	....
250	....	....	....	....	....	⅜
275	....	....	....	....	....	1
280	....	....	....	3/16	....	1¼
285	37⅛	....	....	3/16	....	....
290	31⅞	....	....	5/16	....	2
295	26⅝	....	....	⅜	....	2 9/16
300	20½	....	27½	¾	....	3
305	15¾	19⅞	....	1⅛	2 3/16	4
310	11⅝	....	....	1⅝	3¾	5⅛
315	8	12¾	....	3	4⅜	7¼
320	4¾	9⅞	12⅞	4⅞	6	9
325	2⅝	....	....	7¾	....	10
330	1 13/16	....	8	11½	....	....
335	¾	2⅞	6½	....	....	....
350	⅛	....	2 9/16	30⅛	....	26

Total call volume 24,784 Total call open int. 186,342
Total put volume 15,573 Total put open int. 222,848
The index: High 321.98; Low 318.20; Close 318.32, −3.66

American Exchange

MAJOR MARKET INDEX

Strike Price	Calls–Last Jun	Calls–Last Jul	Calls–Last Aug	Puts–Last Jun	Puts–Last Jul	Puts–Last Aug
425	....	....	....	3/16	....	....
430	....	....	....	3/16	....	....
435	....	....	....	¼	....	....
440	....	....	....	⅜	....	....
445	....	....	....	½	....	....
450	39¼	....	....	⅝	1¾	....
455	36¾	....	....	⅞	2 3/16	....
460	....	....	36¾	1 5/16	2⅞	4¼
465	27	....	....	1 13/16	....	....
470	22½	....	....	2 5/16	4¼	....
475	16¾	....	....	3¼	5⅞	....
480	12¾	....	....	4½	7½	....
485	9⅝	15¾	....	6⅛	9	....
490	7¼	13⅛	....	8½	10⅛	13
495	5	....	14⅛	11¼	12⅛	....
500	3⅜	8⅜	....	14⅞	16¼	17⅝
505	2 3/16	6⅛	....	....	....	....
510	1 5/16	4¾	....	1 15/16	....	....
515	⅞	....	....	....	....	....
520	½	....	....	....	....	....

Total call volume 9,989 Total call open int. 17,013
Total put volume 9,590 Total put open int. 19,641
The index: High 491.49; Low 485.58; Close 486.14, −5.35

INTERNATIONAL MARKET INDEX

Strike Price	Calls–Last Jun	Calls–Last Jul	Calls–Last Aug	Puts–Last Jun	Puts–Last Jul	Puts–Last Aug
300	....	....	....	2.50	....	....
305	....	9.50	....	3.88	....	....
310	2.50	6.50	....	6.63	....	....

Total call volume 170 Total call open int. 725
Total put volume 55 Total put open int. 640
The index: High 307.06; Low 304.52; Close 304.56, −2.34

COMPUTER TECHNOLOGY INDEX

Strike Price	Calls–Last Jun	Calls–Last Jul	Calls–Last Aug	Puts–Last Jun	Puts–Last Jul	Puts–Last Aug
100	6½	....	....	....	....	....

Total call volume 1 Total call open int. 30
Total put volume 0 Total put open int. 72
The index: High 107.44; Low 105.03; Close 105.08, −0.85

OIL INDEX

Strike Price	Calls–Last Jun	Calls–Last Jul	Calls–Last Aug	Puts–Last Jun	Puts–Last Jul	Puts–Last Aug
200	....	10⅝	....	....	....	....
205	4¼	....	....	1 15/16	....	....
210	1 13/16	....	....	....	....	....

Total call volume 7 Total call open int. 322
Total put volume 75 Total put open int. 180
The index: High 207.14; Low 205.73; Close 205.89, −1.25

INSTITUTIONAL INDEX

Strike Price	Calls–Last Jun	Calls–Last Jul	Calls–Last Aug	Puts–Last Jun	Puts–Last Jul	Puts–Last Aug
305	....	....	....	1¼	3⅞	....
310	10½	....	....	....	3¼	....
325	3¼	....	....	....	....	....
330	1⅝	....	....	....	....	....
336	⅝	....	....	....	....	....

Total call volume 123 Total call open int. 31,865
Total put volume 186 Total put open int. 26,725
The index: High 321.04; Low 316.48; Close 316.65, −4.39

N.Y. Stock Exchange

NYSE INDEX OPTIONS

Strike Price	Calls–Last Jun	Calls–Last Jul	Calls–Last Aug	Puts–Last Jun	Puts–Last Jul	Puts–Last Aug
170	....	....	....	7/16	....	....
172½	....	....	....	⅝	....	....
175	4 15/16	....	....	1¼	2¼	....
177½	3⅝	....	....	1⅞	....	....
180	1 13/16	4½	....	3 7/16	3¾	....
185	9/16	2¼	....	....	....	....

Total call volume 401. Total call open int. 9,388.
Total put volume 637. Total put open int. 6,774.
The index: High 179.34; Low 177.56; Close 177.61, −1.74

Pacific Exchange

FINANCIAL NEWS COMPOSITE INDEX

Strike Price	Calls–Last Jun	Calls–Last Jul	Calls–Last Sep	Puts–Last Jun	Puts–Last Jul	Puts–Last Sep
210	....	....	....	....	5/16	....
215	....	12	....	....	¾	....
220	....	7	....	....	1 9/16	....
225	....	3⅝	....	....	3⅜	....
230	....	....	....	....	6⅛	....
235	....	....	5	....	....	....

Total call volume 136 Total call open int. 2,955
Total put volume 446 Total put open int. 3,001
The index: High 227.28; Low 224.08; Close 224.25, −3.03

Philadelphia Exchange

GOLD/SILVER INDEX

Strike Price	Calls–Last Jun	Calls–Last Jul	Calls–Last Aug	Puts–Last Jun	Puts–Last Jul	Puts–Last Aug
90	1 5/16	2¾	....	....	....	....

Total call volume 40 Total call open int. 255
Total put volume 0 Total put open int. 160
The index: High 86 83; Low 85.55; Close 85.58, −0.81

VALUE LINE INDEX OPTIONS

Strike Price	Calls–Last Jun	Calls–Last Jul	Calls–Last Aug	Puts–Last Jun	Puts–Last Jul	Puts–Last Aug
275	....	....	....	¾	....	....
290	....	....	....	8⅛	....	....

Total call volume 0 Total call open int. 1,673
Total put volume 32 Total put open int. 699
The index: High 281.93; Low 280.60; Close 280.67, −1.23

NATIONAL O-T-C INDEX

Total call volume 0 Total call open int. 126
Total put volume 0 Total put open int. 28
The index: High 316.80; Low 314.62; Close 314.69, −2.15

UTILITIES INDEX

Strike Price	Calls–Last Jun	Calls–Last Jul	Calls–Last Aug	Puts–Last Jun	Puts–Last Jul	Puts–Last Aug
190	15⅝	....	....	....	....	....
200	5	....	....	....	....	....
205	1¾	....	....	2⅛	....	....

Total call volume 511 Total call open int. 3,138
Total put volume 2 Total put open int. 2,630
The index: High 205.74; Low 204.05; Close 204.30, −1.57

FUTURES

S&P 500 INDEX (CME) 500 times index

	Open	High	Low	Settle	Chg	High	Low	Open Interest
June	322.60	322.85	319.75	320.10	− 3.50	325.00	263.80	123,884
Sept	327.00	327.25	324.15	324.45	− 3.55	329.40	271.50	17,286
Dec	331.40	331.40	328.30	328.65	− 3.60	333.60	298.90	1,295

Est vol 47,059; vol Mon 53,670; open int 142,466, +813.
Indx prelim High 321.98; Low 318.20; Close 318.30−3.66

NYSE COMPOSITE INDEX (NYFE) 500 times index

	Open	High	Low	Settle	Chg	High	Low	Open Interest
June	179.75	179.90	178.35	178.50	− 1.75	181.05	149.60	5,407
Sept	182.15	182.25	180.80	180.85	− 1.80	183.50	153.90	1,342
Dec	184.50	184.50	183.95	183.20	− 1.90	185.70	161.10	415

Est vol 6,890; vol Mon5,900; open int 7,223, +16.
The index: High 179.34; Low 177.56; Close 177.61 −1.73

MAJOR MKT INDEX (CBT) $250 times index

	Open	High	Low	Settle	Chg	High	Low	Open Interest
June	491.90	492.20	488.00	488.60	− 4.85	496.40	442.50	2,285
July	495.00	495.20	491.50	491.80	− 4.90	499.60	469.10	564

Est vol 4,000; vol Mon 2,472; open int 2,849, −12,563.
The index: High 491.49; Low 485.58; Close 486.14 −5.35

KC VALUE LINE INDEX (KC) 500 times index

	Open	High	Low	Settle	Chg	High	Low	Open Interest
June	283.80	283.85	282.20	282.60	− 1.90	285.60	245.65	1,264
Sept	287.65	287.65	286.60	286.80	− 1.90	289.10	267.40	133

Est vol 105; vol Mon 181; open int 1,400, −1.
The index: High 281.93; Low 280.60; Close 280.67 −1.23

CRB INDEX (NYFE) 500 times index

	Open	High	Low	Settle	Chg	High	Low	Open Interest
July	233.15	234.45	232.60	232.65	− .10	250.50	232.60	1,409
Sept	234.90	235.50	234.15	234.20	− .30	249.10	234.15	247
Dec	235.50	235.50	235.15	234.70	− .30	245.25	235.15	278

Est vol 822; vol Mon1,095; open int 1,984, +228.
The index: High 234.08; Low 232.45; Close 232.45 −.87

–OTHER INDEX FUTURE–

Settlement price of selected contract. Volume and open interest of all contract months.

KC Mini Value Line (KC) 100 times index
Jun 282.60 −1.90; Est. vol. 15; Open Int. 104

CBT–Chicago Board of Trade. CME–Chicago Mercantile Exchange. KC–Kansas City Board of Trade. NYFE–New York Futures Exchange, a unit of the New York Stock Exchange.

FUTURES OPTIONS

S&P 500 STOCK INDEX (CME) $500 times premium

Strike Price	Calls–Settle Jun-c	Calls–Settle Jly-c	Calls–Settle Sp-c	Puts–Settle Jun-p	Puts–Settle Jly-p	Puts–Settle Sep-p
310	11.70	17.05	19.40	1.65	2.85	5.35
315	7.85	13.30	16.05	2.80	4.00	6.80
320	4.85	10.00	12.85	4.75	5.60	8.55
325	2.65	7.20	10.10	7.55	....	10.60
330	1.40	4.95	7.80	11.25	....	13.15
335	0.65	3.35	5.85	....	....	....

Est. vol. 4,369; Mon vol. 3,190 calls; 2,578 puts
Open interest Mon; 22,226 calls; 29,134 puts

NYSE COMPOSITE INDEX (NYFE) $500 times premium

Strike Price	Calls–Settle Jun-c	Calls–Settle Jly-c	Calls–Settle Aug-c	Puts–Settle Jun-p	Puts–Settle Jly-p	Puts–Settle Aug-p
174	5.50	8.50	9.15	1.00	1.70	2.45
176	4.00	7.05	7.80	1.55	2.25	3.00
178	2.80	5.70	6.50	2.25	2.85	3.00
180	1.75	4.50	5.35	3.20	3.65	4.45
182	1.15	3.45	4.30	4.50	4.60	5.40
184	0.65	2.60	3.40	6.00	5.70	6.50

Est. vol. 119, Mon vol. 38 calls, 80 puts
Open interest Mon 696 calls, 1,080 puts
CBT–Chicago Board of Trade. CME–Chicago Mercantile Exchange. NYFE–New York Futures Exchange, a unit of the New York Stock Exchange.

Source: *The Wall Street Journal*, May 24, 1989.

Short Interest On Big Board And Amex Falls

Drop in Month Exceeds 8% On New York Exchange, Is Under 1% on American

By Pamela Sebastian

Staff Reporter of The Wall Street Journal

NEW YORK—Short interest fell on both the New York Stock Exchange and American Stock Exchange for the month ended July 14.

The Big Board said short interest dropped 8.35% to 484,818,847 shares from a revised 528,985,908 shares a month earlier. A year ago short interest was 453,067,175 shares.

The American Stock Exchange said short interest slipped 0.89%, or 436,718 shares, to 48,617,319 from the previous month's adjusted record of 49,051,037 shares. A year earlier, Amex short interest was 33,732,498.

A trader who sells short borrows stock and sells it. Simply put, the trader bets that the stock's price will decline, so that he can buy the shares back at a lower price later for return to the lender.

Short interest is the number of shares that haven't yet been purchased for return to lenders. Although a substantial short position reflects heavy speculation that a stock's price will decline, some investors consider an increase in short interest bullish because the borrowed shares eventually must be bought back.

Fluctuation in short interest of certain stocks also may be caused partly by arbitraging. The figures occasionally include incomplete transactions in restricted stock.

The level of negative sentiment as measured by the Big Board's short interest ratio widened a bit. Newton Zinder, market analyst at Shearson Lehman Hutton Inc., New York, calculated the ratio at 2.99, up from the previous month's 2.89. The ratio is the number of trading days, at the average trading volume, that would be required to convert the total of short interest positions.

Mr. Zinder and others believe that the ratio has lost much of its value as an indicator since the advent in recent years of options and other derivative contracts. "Just about all short positions can be hedged with options and other instruments," he noted. Nonetheless, some technical analysts still value the short interest reading on many bellwether stocks.

For instance, short interest on **International Business Machines** Corp. fell 6.56% to 2,657,653 shares from 2,844,114 shares in June. And **Exxon** Corp. again topped the Big Board's list of largest short positions, although the total number of the oil giant's shorted shares slid 7.56% to 8,794,081.

The largest volume increase was logged by **Computer Associates International** Inc., which reported slower than expected revenue growth in July. Short interest in Computer Associates stock soared to 2,776,209 shares from 400,868 shares the previous month. **Integrated Resources** Inc. also showed a big jump in short interest to 2,632,226 shares from 1,365,330. And **Avon Products** Inc., which has been the subject of takeover rumors lately, recorded a big jump in short interest to 1,263,071 shares from 667,459 shares the month before.

Several big utility stocks, which pay hefty dividends, were among the largest volume decliners. Among them were **Panhandle Eastern** Co., **Public Service Co. of Colorado** and **Public Service Co. of New Hampshire**. Topping the list of decliners was **USF&G** Corp., with short interest down to 292,340 shares from 4,738,981 shares the previous month.

The adjacent tables show the Big Board and Amex issues in which a short interest position of at least 100,000 shares existed as of mid-July or in which there was a short position change of at least 50,000 shares since mid-June.

SHORT INTEREST HIGHLIGHTS

Largest Short Positions

Rank	Jul. 14	Jun. 15	Change
NYSE			
1 Exxon	8,794,081	9,512,787	−718,706
2 Tosco	6,621,060	5,285,946	1,335,114
3 Varity	6,503,090	6,746,566	−243,476
4 Texaco	5,445,480	5,413,838	31,642
5 Blockb Entn	5,103,032	5,685,191	−582,159
6 LTV	4,787,954	4,753,942	34,012
7 Cineplex Ode	4,572,769	4,423,958	148,811
8 AT&T	4,512,551	4,599,791	−87,240
9 Consol Ed	4,120,634	2,551,613	1,569,021
10 Genl Elec	3,488,086	4,094,075	−605,989
11 Genentech	3,393,145	3,560,451	−167,306
12 Student Ln Mktg	3,384,224	1,517,475	1,866,749
13 Lilly Eli	3,376,053	3,163,744	212,309
14 Pan Am	3,363,275	2,998,338	364,937
15 Valero Engy	3,082,624	3,268,612	−185,988
16 Genl Motors	2,985,109	3,214,148	−229,039
17 Circle K	2,945,154	3,118,592	−173,438
18 Pac Telesis	2,942,184	2,451,677	490,507
19 Pac G&E	2,917,976	2,611,006	306,970
20 Freeport–McM	2,837,203	2,447,263	389,940
AMEX			
1 Texas Air	3,679,215	3,459,665	219,550
2 OMI Corp	2,240,547	2,403,594	−163,047
3 Home Shop Netw	1,620,090	1,660,030	−39,940
4 Horn Hardart	1,546,612	1,474,112	72,500
5 IGI	1,512,397	1,451,950	60,447

Largest Changes

Rank	Jul. 14	Jun. 15	Change
NYSE			
1 Cptr Assoc	2,776,209	400,868	2,375,341
2 Student Ln Mktg	3,384,224	1,517,475	1,866,749
3 Consol Ed	4,120,634	2,551,613	1,569,021
4 Allstate Mun II	1,370,210	0	1,370,210
5 Tosco	6,621,060	5,285,946	1,335,114
6 Integ Res	2,632,226	1,365,330	1,266,896
7 Columbia Pic	2,695,526	1,575,838	1,119,688
8 Harcourt Brace	2,084,067	1,105,775	978,292
1 USF&G	292,340	4,738,981	−4,446,641
2 Repsol	1,362,411	4,375,342	−3,012,931
3 Panh Eastern	1,692,791	4,170,961	−2,478,170
4 PS Colo	562,064	1,927,500	−1,365,436
5 Western Union	1,802,943	3,051,383	−1,248,440
6 SCEcorp	2,084,617	3,213,704	−1,129,087
7 Houston Ind	1,884,108	2,947,928	−1,063,820
8 PSNH	767,239	1,799,801	−1,032,562
AMEX			
1 Lionel	1,159,875	683,000	476,875
2 Bergen Bruns A	996,085	557,948	438,137
3 Am Tr IBM sc	745,145	384,600	360,545
4 Texas Air	3,679,215	3,459,665	219,550
1 BAT Ind	898,500	1,483,097	−584,597
2 T/SF Comm	4,500	381,657	−377,157
3 Delmed	14,336	314,701	−300,365
4 Amdahl	188,042	430,450	−242,408

NYSE Short Interest
(In millions of shares)

600 550 500 450 400 350

Short Interest Ratio
(NYSE)

4.5 4.0 3.5 3.0 2.5 2.0

J A S O N D J F M A M J J
1988 1989

The short interest ratio is the number of days it would take to cover the short interest if trading continued at the average daily volume for the month.

Largest Short Interest Ratios

	Jul. 14 Short Int	Avg Dly Vol-a	Days to Cover
NYSE			
1 LTV	4,787,954	65,085	74
2 ICN Pharm	1,788,325	33,550	53
3 Southwest PS	2,197,230	47,570	46
4 Reading&Bates	1,289,841	29,290	44
5 USG	2,635,380	61,155	43
6 Hadson	1,546,888	39,565	39
7 Biocraft Labs	1,114,468	31,135	36
8 NBD Bancorp	1,971,492	56,305	35
9 Ideal Basic	1,905,675	54,850	35
10 Cineplex Ode	4,572,769	139,885	33
11 Consol Ed	4,120,634	126,145	33
12 Zenith Labs	1,325,580	41,215	32
13 Coleco Indus	1,276,836	39,835	32
14 Mylan Labs	1,815,801	58,580	31
15 Student Ln Mktg	3,384,224	111,530	30
16 Ranger Oil	1,463,460	50,840	29
17 Home Owners Sav	1,221,291	42,430	29
AMEX			
1 Organogene	1,087,928	23,277	47
2 Horn Hardart	1,546,612	40,222	39
3 Home Shop Netw	1,620,090	49,836	33
4 Bolar Pharm	945,950	38,572	25
5 Telesphere	827,535	34,986	24

a-Includes securities with average daily volume of 20,000 shares or more.

r-Revised. The largest percentage increase and decrease sections are limited to issues with previously established short positions in both months.

Largest % Increases

Rank	Jul. 14	Jun. 15	%
NYSE			
1 TCW Conv	56,446	93	60594.6
2 Huntingdon Int	242,200	3,802	6270.3
3 Freept McM Eng	55,093	4,183	1217.1
4 Motel 6	354,600	37,900	835.6
5 Cabl Syst	134,740	15,100	792.3
6 Beckman Instr	77,281	11,123	594.8
7 Cptr Assoc	2,776,209	400,868	592.5
8 Bowater	224,200	39,256	471.1
9 Arco Chem	220,838	38,700	470.6
10 Anchor Glass	253,421	47,421	434.4
11 Fed Mogul	69,303	13,540	411.8
12 Minn Pwr & Lt	122,763	24,054	410.4
13 Shell T+T(new)	99,488	22,800	336.4
14 Svc Mdse	86,595	19,918	334.8
15 Broad Inc.	127,040	39,340	222.9
16 Cullinet Sftw	414,343	133,153	211.2
17 Bank New Eng	113,825	37,674	202.1
18 Genrad	196,317	66,070	197.1
19 Vista Chem	413,003	146,491	181.9
20 Greyhound	374,876	136,503	174.6
AMEX			
1 Phil Lg Dist Tel	88,305	1,605	5,401.9
2 MC Ship	58,500	3,000	1,850.0
3 Fruit Loom	224,927	56,244	299.9
4 Fur Vault	77,674	19,640	295.5
5 Am Tr AT&T sc	101,506	33,117	206.5

Largest % Decreases

Rank	Jul. 14	Jun. 15	%
NYSE			
1 Georgia Pwr prD	1,600	66,800	−97.6
2 Harcourt Br pf	11,185	337,764	−96.7
3 Chem Bkng C	15,830	340,700	−95.4
4 Chem Bkng adj	15,673	268,036	−94.2
5 USF&G	292,340	4,738,981	−93.8
6 Chem Bkng dep	4,000	57,000	−93.0
7 BCE Inc	10,755	129,643	−91.7
8 Am Health Prop	11,308	124,844	−90.9
9 Western Co	12,416	116,509	−89.3
10 Worldcorp	56,456	488,295	−88.4
11 Allst Mun Inco	27,531	220,767	−87.5
12 News Corp	49,069	384,633	−87.2
13 Thiokol (new)	27,352	196,598	−86.1
14 Brit Tel	27,000	187,767	−85.6
15 Ashland Oil	55,932	381,788	−85.3
16 Analog Dev	15,600	92,020	-83.0
17 Timken	58,743	341,099	−82.8
18 FedHomeLn sr pf	33,050	184,507	−82.1
19 Nortek	35,156	186,724	−81.2
20 Shelby Will	16,565	74,961	−77.9
AMEX			
1 T/SF Comm	4,500	381,657	−98.8
2 AmTrKodak prm	5,497	189,600	−97.1
3 Delmed	14,336	314,701	−95.4
4 Dataprod	22,350	108,350	−79.4
5 Am Tr Philip sc	81,972	219,288	−62.6

Source: *The Wall Street Journal*, July 21, 1989.

CANADIAN MARKETS

Quotations in Canadian Funds
Quotations in cents unless marked $
Wednesday, April 19, 1989

TORONTO

Sales	Stock	High	Low	Close	Chg.
14563	Abti Prce	$19¾	19½	19⅝	+ ⅛
1210	Agnico E	$11⅛	11	11	− ⅛
163822	Air Canada	$11⅜	11⅛	11⅜	+ ¼
23748	Alt Energy	$16⅝	16¼	16½	+ ⅛
1900	Alta Nat	$16½	16¼	16¼	− ¼
16530	A Barick	$25¾	25⅜	25½	
54115	Atco I f	$10⅛	10	10⅛	+ ⅛
316674	BCE Inc	$37¼	37	37⅛	+ ⅛
37433	BCED	320	315	315	
55944	BP Canada	$17½	16¾	17¼	+ ¼
796438	Bank N S	$15⅜	15	15⅜	+ ⅜
1000	Baton	$12⅝	12⅝	12⅝	− ⅛
50300	BCE Mobl	$31⅛	30⅝	30⅞	− ¼
28800	Bralorne	32	30	30	− 2
5400	Bramalea	$31½	30¾	31	
34425	BC Phone	$31¾	31	31½	+ ½
1400	Brunswk	$11¾	11⅝	11¾	+ ⅛
228332	CAE	$12¾	12⅜	12¾	+ ½
1132	CCL A	$10¼	10	10¼	
1200	CCL B f	$10⅛	9⅞	9⅞	− ⅛
3100	Cambior	$13	13	13	
24557	Campeau	$17½	17⅜	17⅜	+ ⅛
6300	C Nor West	$8⅛	8⅛	8⅛	
1650	C Packrs	$14½	14½	14½	− ¼
304335	CI Bk Com	$28⅜	27⅞	28¼	+ ⅜
1510	CP Forest	$43	42⅞	42⅞	− ½
116119	CP Ltd	$23⅜	23¼	23¼	
242165	CTire A f	$20⅜	20¼	20¼	− ⅛
6920	C Util B	$20⅜	20¼	20¼	+ ⅛
1100	Canfor	$25¼	25¼	25¼	− ¼
15800	Cara	$16¾	16½	16⅝	− ⅛
5350	Celanese	$32⅞	32½	32¾	+ ⅝
1100	Celanes 1 p	$30	30	30	
1203	Cntrl Cap	$11⅜	11⅜	11⅜	− ⅜
53400	Cineplex	$17⅜	16⅞	17	− ½
58668	Corona A f	$8	7¾	7¾	− ¼
4200	Crownx	$12	11¾	12	
1563	Denison A p	$5¼	5⅛	5¼	+ ⅛
11565	Denison B f	495	490	490	
13350	Derlan	$12⅞	12⅝	12⅝	− ⅛
89920	Dicknsn A f	$5⅜	5¼	5¼	− ¼
24	Dicknsn B	$7	7	7	− 2
99950	Dofasco	$27⅝	27⅜	27½	+ ⅛
1400	Donohue	$14	13¾	13¾	
14700	Du Pont A	$25	24¾	25	+ ⅛
60858	Dylex A f	$11⅞	11⅝	11⅞	+ ⅜
36800	Equty Svr A	415	400	405	− 5
1400	FCA Intl	$9¼	9¼	9¼	− ¼
7064	FPI Ltd	$8¾	8½	8½	− ¼
405822	Flcnbrdge	$31¼	30⅝	30⅝	− ⅝
46150	Fed Ind A	$15⅞	15⅝	15⅝	− ⅛
12100	Fed Pion	$12⅞	12⅞	12⅞	− ⅛
400	F City Fin	$24⅜	24⅜	24⅜	− ⅛
1386	Flet CCan A	$18⅛	18⅛	18⅛	− ¼
85536	Flet C Inv	$21⅛	20⅞	21⅛	+ ¼
1405	Gendis A	$20⅝	20½	20½	
5000	GE Canada	$20¼	20¼	20¼	
13150	Goldcorp f	485	470	470	−15
58158	Hayes D	$14¼	13¾	14¼	+ ¼
53895	Hees Intl	$31¼	31	31	− ⅜
51674	Hemlo Gld	$14	13⅝	13⅝	− ⅜
95400	Hollingr I	$14	13⅞	14	+ ⅛
13601	H Bay Co	$26⅛	26	26⅛	
49154	Imasco L	$31	30⅞	30⅞	− ⅛
14706	Inland Gas	$13⅞	13¼	13¾	+ ½
34050	Intl Thom	$16¼	16⅛	16⅛	
559	Interhome	$46	45¾	45¾	− ¼
3822	Ipsco	$18¾	18¼	18½	
2700	Ivaco A f	$11¾	11⅝	11⅝	
27407	Jannock	$18	17⅞	18	+ ⅛
1100	Kerr Add	$20¼	19⅞	20¼	+ ⅝
61476	Labatt	$23	22¾	22⅞	
15700	Loblaw Co	$12⅝	12⅛	12¼	+ ⅛
17400	Lumonics	$7½	7½	7½	
48600	Magna A f	$13¼	12¾	13⅛	− ¼
200572	Mclan H X	$12⅝	12⅜	12⅜	− ⅛
3188	Maritime f	$16¼	16⅛	16⅛	
3313	Mark Res	$8⅝	8½	8⅝	+ ⅛
1300	Minnova	$20¼	20¼	20¼	
44995	Molson A f	$33⅛	33	33⅛	+ ¼
3000	Molson B	$33	33	33	+ ⅛
8263	N-W Gr	$5½	5⅛	5⅜	+ ⅛
31050	Noranda F	$13¾	13⅝	13⅝	− ⅛
144274	Noranda I	$22⅜	22⅛	22¼	+ ⅛
40193	Norcen	$24½	23¾	24⅜	+ ¾
214422	Nova Cor f	$12⅛	11⅞	11⅞	
10700	Nowsco W	$16	15⅝	16	+ ½
208108	Onex C f	$14	13½	14	+ ½
14190	Oshawa A f	$24	23¾	24	
48077	PWA Corp	$15¾	15⅝	15¾	+ ⅛
100	Pamour	$7¼	7¼	7¼	− ¼
62300	PanCan P	$26⅞	26½	26¾	+ ½
59042	Placer Dm	$15⅝	15½	15⅝	
85460	Poco Pete	$7⅜	7⅛	7¼	+ ⅛
100	Que Sturg o	200	200	200	
6750	Rayrock f	$8⅛	8	8	
11070	Redpath	$20	20	20	− ⅛
136647	Renisanc	$15⅛	14¾	14⅞	
2500	Roman	$11⅝	11⅜	11⅜	− ⅜
2983	Rothman	$61	61	61	
388578	Royal Bnk	$40¾	40⅜	40½	
58351	RyTrco A	$16⅝	16⅜	16⅝	+ ⅛
11748	Sceptre R	415	405	410	
32726	Scotts f	$16¼	16	16⅛	− ⅛
25651	Sears Can	$12½	12⅜	12⅜	
2067	SHL Systm	$10	10	10	
87600	Shell Can	$45⅞	45¼	45¾	+ ¼
85942	Sherritt	$14⅝	14¼	14½	+ ⅛
31740	Southam	$31¾	31⅜	31⅜	− ⅜
2778	Spar Aero f	$14⅝	14½	14½	− ⅛
47065	Stelco A	$22⅞	22½	22⅞	+ ¼
30550	TCC Bev	$9¼	8⅞	9	− ⅛
500	Teck Cor A	$19⅛	19⅛	19⅛	− ⅜
34764	Teck B f	$18⅝	18⅜	18½	
2830	Tex Can	$40½	40¼	40¼	− ¼
49750	Thom N A	$27⅜	27⅛	27⅛	− ⅛
251635	Tor Dm Bk	$39⅜	39	39⅛	+ ¼
21676	Torstar B f	$32¼	32	32⅛	
3773	Trns Mt	$15	14⅝	14⅝	− ¼
73336	TrnAlta U	$13⅞	13¾	13¾	− ⅛
237389	TrCan PL	$16⅜	16¼	16⅜	
1904	Trimac	375	370	370	− 5
23650	Trilon A	$19½	19¼	19¼	
51458	Trizec A f	$34⅜	34	34⅛	+ ¼
730454	Turbo	84	76	80	+ 3
187	Unicorp A f	$7½	7½	7½	
200	Un Carbid	$25⅛	25⅛	25⅛	− ⅞
5929	U Entprise	$9⅞	9⅞	9⅞	
35000	U Keno	350	320	335	− 5
21650	Wrdair A f	$16⅛	16⅛	16⅛	
16168	Wrdair B	$16⅛	16	16	− ¼
9642	Westmin	$10¼	10⅛	10¼	+ ¼
17325	Weston	$37¾	37½	37½	+ ¼
15511	Woodwd A	$5⅛	5	5	

Total sales 28,102,645 shares

MONTREAL

Sales	Stock	High	Low	Close	Chg.
174910	Bank Mont	$29⅞	29½	29½	
36549	BombrdrA	$11⅝	11½	11½	
85318	BombrdrB	$11⅝	11⅜	11⅝	+ ⅛
1400	CB Pak	$19⅛	19⅛	19⅛	− ⅛
12145	Cascades	$06⅜	06¼	06¼	
48756	DomTxtA	$14¼	13⅞	14	
13260	Memotec	$10⅝	10⅜	10⅝	+ ¼
681283	NatBk Cda	$13⅝	12⅞	12½	+ ⅝
16439	Noverco	$11¾	11½	11⅝	
101265	Power Corp	$15¼	14¾	15⅛	+ ¼
96125	Provigo	$09¼	09	09⅛	+ ⅛
597	SteinbrgA	$38⅜	38¼	38¼	− ¼
11574	Videotron	$16⅝	16½	16½	+ ⅛

Total Sales 8,033,666 shares.

Source: *The Wall Street Journal*, April 20, 1989.

U.S. REGIONAL MARKETS

Dually Listed Issues Excluded
Wednesday, April 19, 1989

PACIFIC

Sales	Stock	High	Low	Close	Chg.
2500	Adacorp	⅜	5-16	5-16	.....
100	AlaskGld	7-16	7-16	7-16	+1-16
100	AFn pfD	10¾	10¾	10¾	.....
100	AFn pfE	10⅝	10⅝	10⅝	− ¼
1000	AFin Ent	19½	19½	19½	.....
1000	AmPac	9½	9½	9½	.....
9000	BetaPhse	15-16	15-16	15-16	+ ⅛
2000	BigSky	9-32	9-32	9-32	.....
7500	BrockCp	2	1¾	2	+ ⅛
12800	CanSoPt g	3 7-16	3⅛	3 7-16	+3-16
200	ClaryCp	¾	¾	¾	.....
2000	CliniTh	7-32	7-32	7-32	−5-32
200	viCwthO	3-32	3-32	3-32	.....
3000	ConsOG	⅜	5-16	5-16	.....
1000	CrysO pf	⅜	⅜	⅜	.....
3000	GldStd	3 1-16	3 1-16	3 1-16	.....
53200	HCA pf	16⅛	15⅞	16	.....
2500	Imreg	3⅝	3⅝	3⅝	− ⅛
4000	MagelPt	1 7-16	1 5-16	1 7-16	+ ⅛
400	MatrxMd	5-16	5-16	5-16	+ ⅛
200	MiniCptr	5-16	5-16	5-16	.....
10100	NVF	5-32	⅛	5-32	+1-16
26900	OKC LP un	3¼	3⅛	3¼	− ⅛
61500	Pengo	1-16	1-16	1-16	.....
1400	PE Cp	1-16	1-16	1-16	.....
300	PopeRs	29½	29	29	− ¼
29700	viPSNH wt	¾	11-16	¾	.....
1500	Purecyc	5-16	5-16	5-16	.....
100	RckwdN	1⅜	1⅜	1⅜	.....
2200	SharnSt	7-16	7-16	7-16	+1-32
4900	SoetPS	9⅞	9½	9½	− ⅜
300	SCGspfA	15½	15½	15½	+ ⅛
2300	TxAir pfG	11⅞	11⅝	11⅞	+ ¼
3000	TxAir pfH	3½	3½	3½	− ⅛
2500	TxAr pfI	5⅞	5¾	5¾	− ⅛
53200	viTexIn	1-16	1-16	1-16	.....
2500	WldAr wt	2 5-16	2 5-16	2 5-16	.....

BONDS

Sales	Stock	High	Low	Close	Chg.
23000	AFinl 10s99	84¾	84¼	84¾	+ ½
20000	AFinl 12s99	97⅜	97⅜	97⅜	−2⅛
2000	AFinl 13½04	101⅜	101⅜	101⅜	− ⅛
2000	viCwO 10s01	7½	7½	7½	− ¼
25000	Paprcft 15s00	10½	10	10	−1½
179000	TWA 12s01	57¾	57½	57½	− ½
30000	TWA 12s08	54	54	54	− ¼

Total sales .... 7,333,000 shares.

BOSTON

Sales	Stock	High	Low	Close	Chg.
100	Bailey	2⅞	2⅞	2⅞	+ ⅛
2500	Canton	¾	¾	¾	.....
10000	CliffEng	1	1	1	+ ⅛
6300	Cstl Carib	⅜	5-16	⅜	+1-16
500	CommGrp	3	2⅞	3	.....
15700	Digicon	1-16	1-16	1-16	−1-64
100	Exolon Co	10½	10½	10½	+ ¼
500	LoJack	4 13-16	4 13-16	4 13-16	−3-16
26600	MemSv	2¾	2⅛	2[illegible]	+1⅛
5000	NewGenFds	1½	1½	1½	− ⅛
1000	Pantepec	11-32	11-32	11-32	−1-32
1400	PremrR	3-16	3-16	3-16	−1-16

Total sales 3,100,000 shares.

PHILADELPHIA

Sales	Stock	High	Low	Close	Chg.
20400	AmFilmTch	2¾	2⅝	2¾	+ ⅛
2000	AppldRs	2¼	2¼	2¼	+ ⅛
11300	Arlen	¼	15-64	15-64	−3-64
2200	PSNCom	1¾	1½	1⅝	− ⅛
27500	PopeEvR	7-32	5-32	5-32	.....
5400	Preway	3-64	3-64	3-64	+1-64
200	RelInsCo pfA	23¾	23¾	23¾	.....
300	Ronson	2¾	2¾	2¾	+ ⅝
500	StWstA	⅞	⅞	⅞	.....
300	Wash Co	7	7	7	.....

Total sales 3,623,000 shares.

MIDWEST

Sales	Stock	High	Low	Close	Chg.
200	FstMich	12½	12½	12½	.....
1600	GreifBr	43⅞	43⅝	43⅝	.....

Total stocks sales 13,352,000

Source: *The Wall Street Journal*, April 20, 1989.

OVERSEAS MARKETS

Wednesday, April 19, 1989

TOKYO
(in yen)

	Close	Prev. Close
ANA	1780	1790
Aiwa	940	944
Ajinomoto	2650	2700
Alps Elec	1540	1530
Amada Co	1520	1550
Ando Elec	2400	2400
Anritsu	1980	1980
Asahi Chem	1270	1270
Asahi Glass	2460	2440
Bank of Tokyo	1660	1650
Bk of Yokohama	1410	1460
Banyu Pharm	1530	1530
Bridgestone	1690	1490
Brother Ind	1040	1060
C. Itoh	1110	1130
CSK	4780	4800
Canon Inc	1660	1660
Canon Sales	2730	2700
Casio Computer	1410	1430
Chubu Pwr	4200	4200
Chugai Pharm	1520	1530
Citizen Watch	998	1010
Dai Nippon Print	2280	2300
Dai-Ichi Kangyo	3310	3350
Daiei	2320	2330
Daiichi Seiyaku	2600	2620
Dainippon Pharm	2260	2260
Daiwa Danchi	995	994
Daiwa House	1980	2000
Daiwa Securities	2250	2270
Eisai	1930	1940
Ezaki Glico	1210	1230
Fanuc	5770	5850
Fuji Bank	3400	3470
Fuji HI	965	972
Fuji Photo Film	3360	3400
Fujisawa Pharm	1660	1660
Fujitsu	1420	1450
Furukawa Elec	1160	1170
Green Cross	1540	1550
Hasegawa Komtn	1330	1320
Hirose Elec	3790	3790
Hitachi Cable	1300	1270
Hitachi Credit	1400	1410
Hitachi Ltd	1510	1520
Hitachi Maxell	2390	2400
Hitachi Metals	1790	1770
Hitachi Sales	905	898
Honda Motor	1890	1900
Hosiden Elec	880	860
Hoya	2210	2200
IHI	1230	1230
Ind Bank Japan	4170	4200
Intec	3490	3490
Isetan	2270	2330
Isuzu	994	975
Ito-yokado	3510	3550
Iwatsu Elec	1230	1260
JAL	16100	16000
JEOL	1900	1670
JUSCO	1700	1700
Japan Aviat El	1600	1610
Japan Radio	1750	1770
Jujo Paper	1370	1320
KDD	18100	18300
Kajima	2350	2380
Kandenko	3320	3290
Kansai Elec	4310	4350
Kao Corp	1640	1630
Kawasaki HI	1070	1070
Kawasaki Steel	966	950
Kinki Elec Con	2870	2870
Kirin	1950	1940
Kobe Steel	922	935
Kokusai Elec	2800	2850
Kokuyo	2890	2890
Komatsu Ltd	1330	1350
Konica	1140	1160
Kubota	1270	1260
Kumagai Gumi	1850	1870
Kuraray	1430	1400
Kureha Chem	1320	1270
Kyocera	4680	4750
Kyowa Hakko	1510	1510
Kyushu Matsushit	2550	2590
Lion	1020	1010
Makino Milling	1010	1020
Makita Elec	1670	1660
Marudai Food	1450	1460
Marui	2670	2680
Matsushita Com	2650	2690
Mats' Elec Ind	2340	2360
Mats' Elec Wrks	1890	1860
Mazda	974	959
Meiji Seika	1030	1060
Minolta	989	1010
Misawa Homes	1880	1880
Mitsubishi Bank	3110	3160
Mitsubishi Corp	1620	1600
Mitsubishi Elec	1120	1130
Mitsubishi Real	2480	2480
Mitsubishi HI	1090	1090
Mitsubishi Kasei	1200	1170
Mitsubishi Metal	1270	1280
Mitsubishi Trust	2600	2610
Mitsubishi Whse	1760	1740
Mitsui Bank	2250	2280
Mitsui Real	2480	2480
Mitsui Trust	1990	2010
Mitsui & Co	1170	1160
Mitsukoshi	2370	2410
Mochida Pharm	3330	3310
NCR Japan	1860	1870
NEC	1790	1830
NGK Spark	1440	1440
NIFCO	1670	1700
NKK	939	935
NTN Toyo Bearing	1050	1070
NTT	1420000	1430000
Nihon Unisvs Ltd	1520	1530
Nikon Corp	1480	1490
Nippon Chemi-con	1290	1200
Nippon Columbia	1260	1270
Nippon El Glass	2350	2370
Nippon Express	1470	1490
Nippon Hodo	2820	2810
Nippon Meat	1990	1970
Nippon Mining	1020	1030
Nippon Oil	1740	1730
Nippon Sanso	1270	1260
Nippon Seiko	1050	1040
Nippon Shinpan	1310	1300
Nippon Steel	942	932
Nissan Motor	1510	1540
Nissin Food	3320	3370
Nitsuko	1340	1340
Nomura Securities	3300	3310
Odakyu Railway	1510	1510
Ohbayashi Corp	1730	1750
Oji Paper	2080	2060
Oki Elec Ind	1080	1060
Okuma Mach	1360	1360
Olympus Optical	1240	1250
Ono Pharm	4070	4150
Onoda Cement	1120	1100
Onward	1630	1650
Orient Finance	1350	1350
Osaka Kiko	959	965
Pioneer Electron	3180	3180
Renown	1020	1000
Ricoh Co	1210	1230
Royal Co	2220	2300
Ryobi	937	940
Secom	5180	5200
SMK	859	853
Sankyo Co	2400	2410
Sanwa Bank	2540	2580
Sanyo Elec	918	923
Sapporo Brewery	1730	1730
Sekisui House	1760	1790
Seven-eleven	6460	6480
Sharp	1290	1300
Shimizu Corp	2110	2140
Shin-etsu Chem	2100	2080
Shionogi	1540	1530
Shiseido	1680	1670
Showa Denko	1410	1380
Skylark	2490	2500
Sony	6740	6770
Sumitomo Bank	3450	3520
Sumitomo Chem	1040	1030
Sumitomo Corp	1400	1430
Sumitomo Elec	1600	1610
Sumitomo Marine	1270	1270
Sumitomo Metal	898	879
Sumitomo Realty	1860	1840
Sumitomo Trust	2580	2620
Suzuki Motor	881	890
TDK	4240	4140
Taisei Corp	1780	1780
Taisho Mar&Fire	1290	1290
Taisho Pharm	2200	2220
Taiyo Yuden	1580	1380
Takeda Chem	2320	2300
Tanabe Seiyaku	1660	1690
Teijin	902	874
Toa Nenryo	1730	1720
Toho Co	24500	23900
Tokio Mar&Fire	2010	2020
Tokyo Denki Kom	1630	1640
Tokyo Elec Power	5830	5900
Tokyo Electron	2980	3050
Tokyo Gas	1100	1120
Tokyo Style	1650	1620
Tokyu Corp	1650	1660
Toppan Print	1920	1920
Toray	1040	990
Toshiba	1220	1230
Toto	2100	2080
Toyo Seikan	2440	2440
Toyobo	945	910
Toyoda Mach	1390	1400
Toyota Motor	2470	2480
Tsugami	968	965
Uny	1880	1870
Ushio	1250	1110
Wacoal	1180	1170
Yamaha	1740	1760
Yamaichi Sec	1790	1800
Yamanouchi Phm	3350	3360
Yamatake-Hnywl	1930	1980
Yamato Transport	1670	1680
Yamazaki Baking	1420	1420
Yasuda Fire	1290	1300
Yokogawa Elec	1830	1870

LONDON
(in pence)

	Close	Prev. Close
Allied-Lyons	443	444
Amstrad	141	141
Argyll Group	187.5	187
Assoc Brit Fds	339	337
Barclays	434	433
Bass	925	912
BAT Indus	555	549.5
Beecham	634	620
Blue Circle	525	525
BOC Group	497	491
Boots	267	268
Borland	80	80
Bowater Indus	490	486
BPB Indus	246	249
Brit & Com	205	205
British Aero	575	575
British Airwys	196	195
British Gas	180.5	177
British Pete	283.5	279
British Telcom	269.5	274.5
BTR	368	364
Burmah Oil	549	557
Burton Group	207	206
Cable&Wireless	495	495
Cadbury Schwp	348	347
Charter Cons	501	503
Coats Viyella	163	164
Commercial Un	373	372
Cnsldtd Gld Fld	1315	1290
Courtaulds	313.5	310
Dixons	150	153
Eng Ch Clay	525	522
Fisons	303	295
Gateway Corp	187	187.5
GEC	236	235
Genrl Accidnt	939	951
GKN	375	367
Glaxo Hldgs	1398	1388
Granada	377	377
Grand Metrop	559	545
Guardian Royal	201.5	198.5
Guinness	463	459
Hanson PLC	186.5	185.25
Hawker Sidley	675	651
Hillsdown	265	265
Imp Chem Ind	1180	1166
Jaguar	302	302
Johnson Mathy	398	403
Kingfisher	288	287
Ladbroke Grp	547	539
Land Securs	570	568
Legal & Genl	319	320
Lloyds Bank	348	354
Lonrho	331	324
Lucas	635	640
Marks&Spencer	166	163.5
MEPC	556	558
Midland Bank	444	445
Nat Wstmntr Bk	594	585
NFC	234	232
P & O	679	673
Pearson	716	717
Pilkgtn Bros	251	248
Plessey	257	258
Prudential	177	177
Racal Elect	398.5	398
Rank Org	932	938
Reckit&Colman	1128	1120
Redland	537	538
Reed Intl	395	395
Reuters	703	706
RMC	656	651
Royal Insur	408	409
RTZ Corp	529	525
Stchi&Stchi	283	285
J Sainsbury	230	228.5
Sears	123.5	124.5
Sedgwick Grp	235	234
Shell Trnspt	402	398
Smith&Nephew	144	144.75
Std Chartrd	518	523
STC	308	307
Storehouse	162	168
Sun Alliance	1099	1088
Tarmac	303	305
Tate & Lyle	241	241
Tesco	167.5	166.5
Thorn EMI	684	691
Trafalgar Hse	384	379
Trusthse Forte	290	285
TSB Group	109	109.5
Ultramar	307	308
Utd Biscuits	323	321.5
Unilever	540	542
Wellcome	492	486
WPP Group	670	669

South African Mines ADRs
(in U.S. dollars)

	Close	Prev. Close
Bracken	0.70	0.70
Deelkraal	3.20	3.20
Doornfontein	1.25	1.25
Durban Deep	3.62	3.62
E. Rand Gold	3.50	3.50
E. Rand Prop	3.75	3.75
Elandsrand	6.00	5.85
Elsburg	0.65	0.65
Grootvlei	1.00	1.00
Harmony	5.50	5.62
Hartebstftn	6.12	6.20
Impala Pltm	x12.06	x12.31
Kinross	9.75	9.75
Leslie	3.88	3.63
Libanon	2.00	1.95
Loraine	1.85	1.85
Randfontein	5.50	5.50
Rustenburg	15.00	15.25
Southvaal	34.00	35.00
Stilfontein	3.12	3.12
Unisel	3.62	3.75
West Areas	1.12	1.12
Winkelhaak	14.50	14.50
(in British pounds)		
Gencor	12.25	12.28

x-Not ADR

FRANKFURT
(in marks)

	Close	Prev. Close
AEG	224	223.1
Allianz	1843	1845
Asko	830.5	829
BASF	303.5	304.2
Bayer	304	305.7
Byr Vereinsbk	399	399
BMW	526	527
Commerzbank	258	257
Continental	267	269.1
Daimler Benz	696	700
Degussa	452	456
Deutsche Bank	555.5	554.3
Dresdner Bank	333	333.8
Hochtief	755	753.5
Hoechst	305	306.9
Karstadt	479.3	474.8
Kaufhof	460	461
Linde	740	745
Lufthansa	171	172.3
Mannesmann	230.3	233
MAN	278.2	280.5
Metallges	427.5	434
Munchen Ruck	2250	2250
Nixdorf	315.8	317.8
Porsche	709.5	724.5
RWE	277	279.7
SEL	315	323
Schering	617.5	628
Siemens	539.5	541
Thyssen	231.3	235
Veba	300	300.5
VEW	171.5	169.5
Volkswagen	357.5	359.6

BRUSSELS
(in Belgian francs)

	Close	Prev. Close
Arbed	5600	5610
Bnque Lambrt	3640	3580
Bekaert	14775	14825
GB Inno	1320	1324
Gevaert	8510	8540
Gen de Bnque	6340	6330
Intercom	3845	3825
Metal Hoboken	18575	18600
Petrofina	13050	12950
Soc Gen Belg	4690	4690
Solvay	13925	13750

MILAN
(in lire)

	Close	Prev. Close
Banca Com	4258	4259
Benetton	11250	11251
Ciga	4750	4750
CIR	5778	5760
FIAT Com	9485	9464
FIAT Pref	6037	6040
Generali	42600	42980
Mediobanca	21590	21580
Montedison	2139	2142
Olivetti Com	9345	9385
Olivetti NC	4905	4985
Pirelli Co	8525	8700
Pirelli SpA	3416	3445
Rinascente	4710	4630
RAS	30610	30990
Saipem	3200	3190
SIP	2960	2940
Snia	2790	2800

PARIS
(in French francs)

	Close	Prev. Close
Air Liquide	584	579
Avions Dassault	670	670
BSN-Gervais	709	706
Carrefour	3958	3923
CGE	427.80	426
Club Med	570	565
Elf Aquitaine	468.80	455
Generale Eaux	1716	1700
Hachette	360	346
Imetal	390	390
Lafarge Coppee	1544	1535
LVMH	3870	3833
Machines Bull	106.80	107
Matra	283.80	279.50
Michelin	196.80	194.30
L'Oreal	4399	4380
Paribas	489	489.70
Pernod Ricard	1345	1364
Peugeot	1787	1785
Saint Gobain	613	614
Sanofi	830	848
Source Perrier	1771	1772
Suez	317.50	315
Thomson CSF	238.80	239.20
Total Francais	422.10	414.10

STOCKHOLM
(in crowns)

	Close	Prev. Close
AGA	255	245
Alfa Laval	555	550
Asea	488	485
Astra	236	238
Atlas Copco	327	326
Electrolux	316	313
Ericsson	449	446
Pharmacia	178	179
Saab Scania	246	245
SE Bank	175	176
Skanska	483	485
SKF	481	480
Volvo	462	451

SWITZERLAND
(in Swiss francs)

	Close	Prev. Close
Brown Boveri	3545	3550
Ciba-Geigy	3440	3450
Credit Suisse	2850	2910
Hoff LaRoche	153750	152750
Roche Baby	15350	15300
Jacobs Suchrd	7510	750
Nestle Bearer	7515	752
Nestle Reg	6730	671
Sandoz	10775	1080
Sulzer	473	46
Swiss Aluminum	990	96
Swiss Bnk Cp	325	32
Swiss Reinsur	10700	1035
Swissair	1050	106
UBS	3250	333
Zurich Ins	5050	507

AMSTERDAM
(in guilders)

	Close	Prev. Close
ABN	44	44.1(
Aegon	100.50	100.50
Ahold	104.70	103.70
Akzo	155	155.50
AMEV	50.10	50.40
AMRO Bank	83.40	83.40
Buhrmn-Tett	72.80	73
DSM	120.90	120.40
Elsevier	68.50	68.40
Fokker	44.50	44.90
Gist-Brocades	37.10	37.10
Heineken	150	149.80
Holec	28.10	29.20
Hoogovens	100.30	101.80
KLM	46.60	46.60
Nat-Ndrlndn	64.10	63.90
Nedlloyd	398	413.50
Oce-van Grntn	324	322
Philips	38.90	38.80
Robeco	105.50	105.30
Rolinco	102.50	102.20
Rorento	61.50	61.50
Royal Dutch	137.30	135.10
Unilever	133.50	133.60
VOC	45	45.60
Wessanen	81.60	81.90

HONG KONG
(in Hong Kong dollars)

	Close	Prev. Close
Bank E Asia	16.40	16.50
Cathay Pacific	9.35	9.25
Cheung Kong	10.80	10.80
China L & P	14.80	14.60
Hang Seng Bk	25.60	25.70
HK Electric	8.30	8.20
HK Land	11.40	11.40
HK Shanghai	6.55	6.50
HK Telecom	5.45	5.30
Hutchsn Whmp	11.30	11.30
Jardine Mathsn	22.40	21.80
Sun Hung Kai	14.90	14.80
Swire Pacific	21.90	21.50
Wharf Holdings	11.60	11.50

SYDNEY
(in Australian dollars)

	Close	Prev. Close
Amcor	4.15	4.05
ANZ Group	4.82	4.75
Ashton	1.14	1.14
Bell Group	1.15	1.20
Bond Corp	1.38	1.43
Boral	3.12	3.02
Bougainville	2.65	2.55
Brambles Inds	11.40	11
Brokn Hill Prp	0.52	0.52
Coles Myer	8.24	8.10
Comalco	3.55	3.48
Centrl Norsemn	0.71	0.71
Centrl P Mnrl	1.02	1
CRA	8.30	7.98
CSR	4.10	3.98
Elders IXL	2.61	2.57
Gld Mns Kalgo	0.95	0.95
Goodman	2	1.92
Leighton	0.60	0.60
MIM Holdings	1.69	1.67
Nat Aust Bnk	6.08	5.94
News Corp	12.15	11.85
Nrthrn Brk Hill	2.32	2.27
Pacific Dunlop	4.10	3.90
Pancontinental	1.70	1.72
Poseidon	2.50	2.50
Renison Gldflds	7	6.90
Santos	3.84	3.67
S Pac Pet	0.43	0.43
TNT Ltd	3.09	3
Western Mining	5.02	4.92
Westpac	5.20	5.02
Woodside	2.18	2.17
Woolworth Ltd	3.70	3.70

Source: *The Wall Street Journal*, April 20, 1989.

EARNINGS AND DIVIDENDS

Many investors focus so heavily upon the potential capital gain (increase in price) of their stock that they ignore the dividends it pays. These dividends can be an important part of a stock's total return, so take a moment to consider corporate earnings and dividends.

Corporations issue stock to raise capital; investors buy shares of it to participate in the growth of the business, to earn dividends, and to enjoy possible capital gains. The ability of a corporation to pay dividends and the potential for increase in the value of a share of stock depend directly on the profits earned by the corporation: the greater the flow of profit (and anticipated profit), the higher the price investors will pay for that share of stock.

The ownership value of assets depends on the income they generate, just as the value of farmland reflects profits that can be reaped by raising crops on it and the value of an apartment building reflects rent that can be collected. Similarly, the value of a share in the ownership of a corporation ultimately depends on the ability of that corporation to create profits. Note that the value of an asset depends not only on the income it is currently earning but also on its potential for greater earnings and on investors' willingness to pay for these actual and potential earnings.

A corporation's profit is one of the most important measures of its success. Profit indicates the effectiveness and efficiency with which its assets are managed and employed. Profits calibrate the ability of a firm to make and sell its product or service for more than the cost of production. Profit means that the firm has efficiently combined the labor, material, and capital necessary to produce and market its product at a price that people will pay and that will provide the owners with the financial incentive to expand the operation. When costs exceeds revenues and the firm takes a loss, the amount that the public is willing to pay for the firm's product no longer justifies the cost of producing it.

If you are a stock owner, then, in addition to following the market indexes, you will need to monitor the earnings of particular stocks. You can do so by using *The Wall Street Journal's* **Digest of Earnings Report**, listed as **Earnings Digest** in the front-page index. **The Digest of Earnings Report** can be found in either the second or third section of the *Journal*.

DIGEST OF EARNINGS REPORTS

L.A. GEAR INC. (N)

Quar Feb. 28:	1989	1988
Sales	$66,070,000	$28,451,000
Net income	5,358,000	1,725,000
Avg shares	8,655,000	a8,104,000
Shr earns:		
Net income .	.62	a.21

a-Adjusted to reflect two-for-one stock split paid in August 1988.

MORRISON INC. (O)

13 wk Feb 25:	1989	a1988
Revenues	$207,081,000	$176,445,000
Inco cnt op	8,804,000	7,062,000
Loss dis op	4,000	c235,000
Net income	8,800,000	7,297,000
Shr earns (com & com equiv):		
Inco cnt op ..	.50	.38
Net income .	.50	.40
39 weeks:		
Revenues	598,604,000	512,900,000
Inco cnt op	23,074,000	20,236,000
Inco dis op	428,000	590,000
Net income	23,502,000	20,826,000
Shr earns (com & com equiv):		
Inco cnt op ..	1.30	1.07
Net income .	1.32	1.11

a-Restated to reflect discontinued operations. c-Income.

NATIONAL MEDICAL ENTERP (N)

Quar Feb 28:	1989	1988
Revenues	$939,067,000	$817,008,000
Net income .	49,433,000	43,416,000
Avg shares .	74,301,000	72,752,000
Shr earns (primary):		
Net income	.67	.60
Shr earns (fully diluted):		
Net income	.60	.54
9 months:		
Revenues	2,686,269,000	2,333,449,000
Net income .	137,871,000	127,424,000
Avg shares .	74,039,000	74,298,000
Shr earns (primary):		
Net income	1.86	1.72
Shr earns (fully diluted):		
Net income	1.69	1.56

OXFORD INDUSTRIES INC (N)

13 wk Mar 3:	1989	1988
Sales	$132,920,000	$138,483,000
Net income	1,113,000	d4,732,000
Shr earns:		
Net income .	.11	....
39 weeks:		
Sales	434,611,000	440,876,000
Net income	7,357,000	d2,381,000
Shr earns:		
Net income .	.74	....

d-Loss; includes a charge of $7,500,-000 related to restructuring.

RAMADA INC (N)

Year Dec 29:	1988	a1987
Revenues	$476,645,000	$407,622,000
Loss cnt op	1,765,000	6,764,000
Loss dis op	3,898,000	c13,041,000
Loss	5,663,000	c6,277,000
Extrd item	b563,000	e1,365,000
Net loss	5,100,000	c4,912,000
Shr earns:		
Loss	....	c.15
Net loss	....	c.12
13 weeks:		
Revenues	123,740,000	91,774,000
Loss cnt op	8,245,000	4,889,000
Loss dis op	1,265,000	c2,851,000
Net loss	9,510,000	2,038,000

a-Restated to reflect discontinued operations. b-Credit. c-Income. e-Debit.

(N) New York Stock Exchange (A) American Exchange (O) Over-the-Counter (Pa) Pacific (M) Midwest (P) Philadelphia (B) Boston (T) Toronto (Mo) Montreal (F) Foreign.

ABBREVIATIONS

A partial list of frequently used abbreviations: Net inv inc (net investment income); Loss dis op (Loss from discontinued operations); inco cnt op (income from continuing operations.)

ROBERT C. BROWN & CO. (O)

Year Dec. 31:	1988	a1987
Revenues	$23,791,848	$20,848,392
Loss	1,019,081	c169,593
bExtrd cred ...	202,170	313,995
Net loss	816,911	483,588
Shr earns:		
Loss	....	c.06
Net loss	....	c.18
Quarter:		
Revenues	5,608,237	5,913,317
Loss	420,555	213,494
Extrd cred	....	b244,822
Net loss	420,555	c31,328
Shr earns:		
Net loss	....	c.01

a-Restated. b-Gain on retirement of debt. c-Income.

SIERRACIN CORP. (A)

Year Dec 31:	1988	1987
Revenues	$82,729,000	$72,832,000
Income	3,116,000	1,630,000
Extrd cred	....	a400,000
Net income	3,116,000	2,030,000
Shr earns:		
Income	.92	.48
Net income .	.92	.60
Quarter:		
Revenues	21,133,000	17,912,000
Net income	1,222,000	530,000
Shr earns:		
Net income .	.36	.16

a-Tax benefit from tax-loss carryforwards.

STANDARD BRANDS PAINT (N)

Year Jan 29:	1989	a1988
Sales	$304,356,000	$305,475,000
Inco cnt op	4,806,000	8,756,000
Loss dis op	1,135,000	2,315,000
Income	3,671,000	6,441,000
Extrd chg	....	b1,041,000
Acctg adj	e1,145,000	....
Net income	4,816,000	5,400,000
Avg shares	5,715,000	10,760,000
Shr earns:		
Inco cnt op ..	.57	.79
Income	.37	.57
Net income .	.57	.47
Quarter:		
Sales	68,211,000	68,932,000
Inco cnt op	f364,000	d4,840,000
Loss dis op	681,000	1,475,000
Loss	317,000	6,315,000
Extrd chg	....	b1,041,000
Net loss	317,000	7,356,000

a-Restated and for 53 and 14 weeks. b-From early extinguishment of debt. d-Loss. e-Credit; cumulative effect on prior periods of an accounting change for income taxes. f-Share earnings not shown; preferred dividend requirement exceeded income from continuing operation.

SYMS CORP. (N)

Year Dec 31:	1988	1987
Sales	$282,555,000	$256,756,000
Net income	18,736,000	17,780,000
Avg shares	17,650,000	17,650,000
Shr earns:		
Net income .	1.06	1.01
Quarter:		
Sales	89,908,000	84,676,000
Net income	8,813,000	8,320,000
Shr earns:		
Net income .	.50	.47

TANDON CORP. (O)

Year Dec 31:	1988	a1987
Sales	$309,346,000	$289,086,000
Loss cnt op	19,868,000	b17,076,000
Inco dis op	....	3,966,000
Loss	19,868,000	b21,042,000
Extrd cred	....	c2,413,000
Net loss	19,868,000	b23,455,000
Shr earns:		
Loss cnt op .	....	b.31
Loss	....	b.38
Net loss	....	b.42
Quarter:		
Sales	90,334,000	95,089,000
Loss cnt op	21,090,000	b6,325,000
Inco dis op	....	3,049,000
Loss	21,090,000	b9,374,000
Extrd cred	....	c2,413,000
Net loss	21,090,000	b11,787,000
Shr earns:		
Loss cnt op .	....	b.11
Loss	....	b.16
Net loss	....	b.20

a-Restated. b-Income. c-Includes gain from tax-loss carryforwards, partially offset by charge from settlement of litigation.

VORNADO INC. (N)

Year Jan. 28:	1989	1988
Revenues	$82,263,000	$73,804,000
Net income	10,121,000	9,880,000
Shr earns (com & com equiv):		
Net income .	4.17	3.74
13 weeks:		
Revenues	23,638,000	20,844,000
Net income	1,688,000	1,296,000
Shr earns (com & com equiv):		
Net income .	.71	.52

WATERHOUSE INVESTOR SVC (O) — Waterhouse

Quar Feb 24:	1989	1988
Revenues	$5,010,000	$3,234,000
Net income	302,000	4,500
Shr earns:		
Net income .	.12	....
6 months:		
Revenues	8,878,000	7,684,700
Net income	326,200	237,500
Shr earns:		
Net income .	.13	.09

WIENER ENTERPRISES (A)

Year Jan 28:	1989	1988
Sales	88,112,000	$84,711,000
Net income	360,000	847,000
Shr earns:		
Net income .	.15	.36
13 weeks:		
Sales	20,473,000	21,586,000
Net loss	654,000	478,000

WORLDCORP INC. (N)

Year Dec. 31:	1988	1987
Revenues	$167,528,000	$143,784,000
Inco cnt op	8,635,000	a20,951,000
Inco dis op	3,200,000	d13,726,000
Net income	11,835,000	7,225,000
Shr earns (primary):		
Inco cnt op ..	.75	1.73
Net income .	1.03	.57
Shr earns (fully diluted):		
Inco cnt op ..	.75	1.46
Net income .	1.03	.50
Quarter:		
Revenues	43,334,000	36,731,000
Inco cnt op	2,054,000	2,338,000
Inco dis op	....	4,357,000
Net income	2,054,000	6,695,000
Shr earns (primary):		
Inco cnt op ..	.19	.19
Net income .	.19	.54
Shr earns (fully diluted):		
Inco cnt op ..	.18	.19
Net income .	.18	.54

a-Includes pre-tax gain of $17,578,-000 on disposition of assets. d-Loss.

Source: *The Wall Street Journal*, March 30, 1989.

WATERHOUSE INVESTOR SVC (O)		
Quar Feb 24:	1989	1988
Revenues	$5,010,000	$3,234,000
Net income	302,000	4,500
Shr earns:		
Net income .	.12	....
6 months:		
Revenues	8,878,000	7,684,700
Net income	326,200	237,500
Shr earns:		
Net income .	.13	.09

Waterhouse

Source: *The Wall Street Journal*, March 30, 1989.

Find the Waterhouse Investor Service Corporation in the Thursday, March 30, 1989 reprint on page 205 (last column, third from the top). The statement reports earnings for the quarter and six-month period ending February 24, 1989 and compares them with figures for the same period one year earlier. Look for revenues, net income, and net income per share (i.e., total earnings divided by total shares of stock outstanding). As you can see, Waterhouse Investors Service's sales, revenue, and profits improved.

Improved earnings are important because (among other things) they permit corporations to pay dividends, an important source of income for many stockholders. The stock pages list current annual dividends, and you can also use the *Journal's* daily **Corporate Dividend News** (see the Friday, March 31, 1989 excerpt), listed in the front-page indexes of the first and last sections, to be informed of future dividend payments.

The March 31, 1989 report provides dividend news for March 30 (see page 207). The companies listed under the heading **Regular** will pay regular cash dividends on the payable date to all those who were stockholders on the record date.

For instance, the March 31 excerpt on page 208 reported that Horizon Bank announced a quarterly dividend of 6 cents per share payable on April 18, 1989 to all stockholders of record on April 7, 1989.

Some companies prefer to pay dividends in extra stock rather than cash. Returning to the report, you can see that Spartech Corporation announced a stock split effective April 28, 1989 for all holders of record on April 15, 1989. This was a 5 percent stock dividend.

CORPORATE DIVIDEND NEWS

METROBANK, Los Angeles, declared an annual of 12 cents a common share, a 20% increase from the 10 cents it paid in each of the past two years. The dividend is payable May 12 to stock of record April 18. The business bank said its policy is to distribute annual dividends equal to either 10% of net income or 10 cents a share, whichever is greater. Metrobank had 1988 net of $4.8 million, or $1.16 a share, up from $3.4 million, or $1 a share, a year earlier.

* * *

AVERY INTERNATIONAL Corp., Pasadena, Calif., increased its quarterly dividend to 14 cents a share from 12 cents, payable June 21 to stock of record at the close of business June 7. Avery makes self-adhesive base materials, labels, tapes, office products and specialty chemicals.

* * *

Stocks Ex-Dividend April 3

Company	Amount
ACM Govt Spectrum	.084½
Allstate M Inco Op	.06½
Allstate Muni Inco	.06½
Allstate Muni Prem	.05
AllstateMuniIncoII	.072
Amer Express Co	.21
AmerTrAmEx primes	.19¾
AmTrAmEx units	.19¾
AmerTrBrstlMyrs pr	.98¾
AmerTrBrstlMyrs un	.98¾
Bristol-Myers Co	.50
Cedar Fair LP	.27¾
Centel Corp	.46½
Centrl Secs prefD	.50
Dean Witter Govt	.077
EastGroup Props	.65
Excel Industries	.10
Fleetwood Enterp	.16
Flexible Bond Tr	.08¼
Friedman Indus	.05
Friedman Indus	5%
HealthCarePropInv	.50¾
High Inco Adv III	.08

Company	Amount
High Inco Advant	.10
High Inco Adv II	.10
Honda Motor ADR	t
t-Five-for-one American Depositary Share split.	
Hydraulic Co	.39½
Louisiana 12.64%pf	.79
LouisianaPL19.20%p	1.20
Mesa L.P.	.50
Mesa LP prefA	.37½
Nortek Inc	.02½
OppenheimerMutlGvt	.076
PHH Group Inc	.28
Pacific TelesisGrp	.47
Pennwalt Corp	.60
Raytheon Co	.55
Scotty's Inc	.13
Sierra CapRlty VII	.035½
SierraCapRl VIIpfd	.0414
SierraCapRltyTrVI	.0189
SierraCapRtyVI7%pf	.022
Signet Banking	.35

Dividends Reported March 30

Company	Period	Amount	Payable date	Record date
REGULAR				
A.L. Laboratories	Q	.03	4–28–89	4–14
Carson Pirie Scott	Q	.02½	6– 2–89	5–19
CrownCentrlPetro pfA	Q	.48	5– 1–89	4–10
CrownCentrlPetro pfB	Q	.56¼	5– 1–89	4–10

Company	Period	Amount	Payable date	Record date
Del-Val Finl	M	.15	6– 1–89	5–18
Excel Bancorp	Q	.17	4–21–89	4– 7
First Fed S&L Coeur	Q	.09	5–15–89	5– 1
Horizon Bank	Q	.06	4–18–89	4– 7
Laidlaw Trans clA	Q	b.06	5–15–89	5– 1
Laidlaw Trans clB	Q	b.06	5–15–89	5– 1
Montana Power	Q	.69	4–26–89	4–10
Norton Co	Q	.50	6– 5–89	5–15
Pilgrim's Pride	Q	.01½	6–30–89	6– 9
Repap Enterp	Q	b.07	4–28–89	4–10
Rogers Corp	Q	.03	5–15–89	4–14
Varity Corp pfA	Q	.32½	5– 1–89	4–21
Wells Fargo adj pfA	Q	.83¾	6–30–89	6–15
WstrnFedSvgsBk PR	Q	.20	4–21–89	3–31
IRREGULAR				
Countrywide Credit	–	.06	4–25–89	4–11
Metrobank	–	.12	5–12–89	4–18
FUNDS - REITS - INVESTMENT COS - LPS				
AmerCapCorpBd	M	.06	4–14–89	3–31
AmerCapGovtSecs	M	.08½	4–14–89	4– 3
AmerCapHiYldInv	M	.09¾	4–14–89	3–31
AmerCapMuniBd	M	.11¼	4–14–89	3–31
Blackstone Income	M	.0917	4–28–89	4–14
Blackstone Target	M	.0833	4–28–89	4–14
CommonSenseGrth&Inco	–	.06¾	4–14–89	3–31
Liberty Fund	Q	h.098	3–30–89	3–30
Phoenix Hi Quality	M	.057	4– 6–89	3–30
Phoenix Hi Yld	M	.086	4– 6–89	3–30
VanKampMerIntermed	–	.096	4–28–89	4–17
STOCK				
Spartech Corp	–	5%	4–28–89	4–15

Horizon Bank

Spartech Corporation

INCREASED

Company	Period	Amounts New	Amounts Old	Payable date	Record date
Great Bay Bkshrs	Q	.12	.10	4–24–89	4–10
Universal Foods	Q	.22	.18	5– 5–89	4–19

A-Annual; Ac-Accumulation; b-Payable in Canadian funds; F-Final; G-Interim; h-From Income; k-From capital gains; M-Monthly; Q-Quarterly; S-Semi-annual.

* * *

Source: *The Wall Street Journal*, March 31, 1989.

Company	Period	Amount	Payable date	Record date	
Del-Val Finl	M	.15	6- 1-89	5-18	
Excel Bancorp	Q	.17	4-21-89	4- 7	
First Fed S&L Coeur	Q	.09	5-15-89	5- 1	
Horizon Bank	Q	.06	4-18-89	4- 7	← Horizon Bank
Laidlaw Trans clA	Q	b.06	5-15-89	5- 1	
Laidlaw Trans clB	Q	b.06	5-15-89	5- 1	
STOCK					
Spartech Corp	–	5%	4-28-89	4-15	← Spartech Corporation

Source: *The Wall Street Journal*, March 31, 1989.

INDUSTRY GROUPS

This chapter began with a look at the **Markets Diary**, which appears on the first page (C1) of the *Journal's* third section (see page 166). That discussion mentioned the Dow Jones Equity Index (June 30, 1982 = 100) and the 700-odd companies that the index comprises.

Each day the *Journal* breaks out the performance of these stocks in the **Dow Jones Industry Groups** (you can find the index on page C1). In addition, the five industries that enjoyed the greatest relative gain in value the previous trading day and the five that suffered the biggest loss are presented together with the three most important contributing firms in each case. You can use this information to compare the performance of your stock with the average for the entire industry or to compare the performance of a variety of industries. For instance, under **Industrial** in the Friday, March 31, 1989 report, note that Pollution control had increased six-fold since June 30, 1982, while under **Energy**, Oil-drilling had fallen.

Every few months Dow Jones revises its list of companies in the **Industry Group Components** and the *Journal* publishes this list on these occasions, as in the Monday, April 24, 1989 report on page 211.

INSIDER TRADING

Finally, if you want to see what the officers and directors of the company in which you own stock are doing, you can follow the **Inside Track**

DOW JONES INDUSTRY GROUPS

March 30, 1989, 4:30 p.m. Eastern Time

GROUPS LEADING (and strongest stocks in group)

GROUP	CLOSE	CHG	% CHG
Banks,money center	**212.91**	**+ 6.91**	**+ 3.35**
Bankers Tr NY	41⅞	+ 2¼	+ 5.68
Chemical Bk	35⅜	+ 1¾	+ 5.20
Mfrs Hanover	35⅜	+ 1½	+ 4.43
Heavy construction	**187.42**	**+ 3.29**	**+ 1.79**
Fluor Corp	23¼	+ ⅞	+ 3.91
Stone & Webstr	78⅛	+ ⅛	+ 0.16
Kasler Corp	10⅝	unch	unch
Cosmetics	**278.20**	**+ 4.79**	**+ 1.75**
Avon Products	22½	+ 1¼	+ 5.88
Neutrogena	27¾	+ 1⅛	+ 4.23
Gillette Co	36	+ ½	+ 1.41
Semiconductor	**174.01**	**+ 3.00**	**+ 1.75**
Intel Corp	25¼	+ ¾	+ 3.06
Appld Materls	23¾	+ ⅜	+ 1.60
Adv Micro Dvc	8¼	unch	unch
Restaurants	**352.54**	**+ 3.52**	**+ 1.01**
Shoney's Inc	8⅜	+ ⅛	+ 1.52
McDonald's	51½	+ ¾	+ 1.48
TW Services	31⅝	+ ¼	+ 0.80

GROUPS LAGGING (and weakest stocks in group)

GROUP	CLOSE	CHG	% CHG
Medical/Bio tech	**235.76**	**– 6.81**	**– 2.81**
Genentech Inc	17¾	– 1⅝	– 8.39
Cetus Corp	13¾	– ⅜	– 2.65
Stryker Corp	25¼	– ¼	– 0.98
Home construction	**373.93**	**– 6.41**	**– 1.69**
U S Home Corp	1⅞	– ⅛	– 6.25
PHM Corp	12	– ⅜	– 3.03
Kaufman Hm	10¼	– ⅛	– 1.20
Casinos	**465.01**	**– 5.78**	**– 1.23**
Circus Circus	36⅞	– ¾	– 1.99
Caesars World	30	– ¼	– 0.83
Golden Nugget	17½	– ⅛	– 0.71
Commu-w/AT&T	**282.81**	**– 3.40**	**– 1.19**
AT&T	30¾	– ½	– 1.60
Gen Instrument	27⅞	– ⅜	– 1.33
Motorola Inc	41⅛	+ ¼	+ 0.61
Containers/pkging	**520.16**	**– 6.07**	**– 1.15**
Sonoco Prod	33½	– ¾	– 2.19
Ball Corp	28½	– ½	– 1.72
Federal Paper	25⅛	– ⅜	– 1.47

INDUSTRY GROUP PERFORMANCE (June 30, 1982=100)

GROUP	CLOSE	CHG	% CHG
Basic Materials	305.50	+ 0.84	+ 0.28
Aluminum	281.65	+ 2.23	+ 0.80
Other non-ferrous	196.22	+ 1.52	+ 0.78
Chemicals	354.13	+ 1.41	+ 0.40
Forest products	226.11	+ 0.02	+ 0.01
Mining,diversified	243.38	+ 1.49	+ 0.62
Paper products	347.73	– 0.01	– 0.00
Precious metals	238.85	+ 1.05	+ 0.44
Steel	135.42	– 0.99	– 0.73
Conglomerate	301.51	– 1.67	– 0.55
Consumer,Cyclical	339.76	+ 0.35	+ 0.10
Advertising	299.51	– 2.11	– 0.70
Airlines	318.25	– 2.03	– 0.63
Auto manufacturers	338.06	– 1.41	– 0.42
Auto parts & equip	275.28	– 0.79	– 0.29
Casinos	465.01	– 5.78	– 1.23
Home construction	373.93	– 6.41	– 1.69
Home furnishings	218.01	+ 0.85	+ 0.39
Lodging	371.08	+ 2.03	+ 0.55
Media	453.46	+ 0.30	+ 0.07
Recreation products	235.69	+ 0.72	+ 0.31
Restaurants	352.54	+ 3.52	+ 1.01
Retailers,apparel	644.22	– 1.41	– 0.22
Retailers,broadline	370.84	+ 1.70	+ 0.46
Retailers,drug-based	256.13	+ 1.57	+ 0.62
Retailers,specialty	318.98	– 0.00	– 0.00
Textiles and apparel	448.21	+ 3.20	+ 0.72
Consumer,Non-Cycl	364.97	+ 0.73	+ 0.20
Beverages	384.06	– 0.39	– 0.10
Consumer services	289.85	– 1.50	– 0.51
Cosmetics	278.20	+ 4.79	+ 1.75
Food	493.22	+ 3.47	+ 0.71
Food retailers	468.31	+ 1.74	+ 0.37
Health care	222.31	– 1.73	– 0.77
Household products	351.84	– 0.15	– 0.04
Medical supplies	263.96	+ 1.09	+ 0.41
Pharmaceuticals	334.17	+ 0.27	+ 0.08
Energy	220.31	– 1.04	– 0.47
Coal	218.69	– 0.99	– 0.45
Oil drilling	81.21	– 0.83	– 1.01
Oil-majors	257.19	– 1.23	– 0.48
Oil-secondary	205.81	– 0.87	– 0.42
Oilfield equip/svcs	104.22	– 0.40	– 0.38
Pipelines	183.75	– 0.95	– 0.51
Financial	274.42	+ 1.95	+ 0.72
Banks,money center	212.91	+ 6.91	+ 3.35
Banks,regional	304.10	+ 1.35	+ 0.45
Banks-Central	351.85	+ 0.74	+ 0.21
Banks-East	317.15	+ 2.32	+ 0.74
Banks-South	247.55	+ 0.41	+ 0.17
Banks-West	329.82	+ 1.99	+ 0.61
Financial services	276.96	+ 1.16	+ 0.42
Insurance,all	280.63	+ 0.34	+ 0.12
Ins-Full line	216.22	+ 0.21	+ 0.10
Ins-Life	335.00	+ 1.57	+ 0.47
Property/Casualty	334.33	+ 0.21	+ 0.06
Real estate	459.23	– 2.01	– 0.44
Savings & loans	422.52	+ 0.66	+ 0.16
Securities brokers	258.97	+ 0.81	+ 0.31
Industrial	286.51	– 0.11	– 0.04
Air freight	183.84	– 1.76	– 0.95
Building materials	410.37	+ 2.92	+ 0.72
Containers/pkging	520.16	– 6.07	– 1.15
Elec comp/equip	272.39	– 0.11	– 0.04
Factory equipment	254.51	+ 0.10	+ 0.04
Heavy construction	187.42	+ 3.29	+ 1.79
Heavy machinery	167.03	+ 0.08	+ 0.05
Industrial services	312.84	– 1.77	– 0.56
Industrial,divers	252.91	+ 0.09	+ 0.04
Marine transport	508.60	– 2.93	– 0.57
Pollution control	605.05	+ 4.15	+ 0.69
Railroads	271.37	– 0.75	– 0.28
Transportation equip	269.31	– 0.15	– 0.06
Trucking	225.22	+ 0.23	+ 0.10
Technology	235.35	– 0.42	– 0.18
Aerospace/Defense	328.15	+ 2.04	+ 0.63
Commu-w/AT&T	282.81	– 3.40	– 1.19
Commu-wo AT&T	168.53	+ 0.98	+ 0.58
Comptrs-w/IBM	207.51	– 1.04	– 0.50
Comptrs-wo/IBM	261.95	– 0.31	– 0.12
Diversified tech	208.17	+ 1.26	+ 0.61
Industrial tech	219.11	+ 0.40	+ 0.18
Medical/Bio tech	235.76	– 6.81	– 2.81
Office equipment	244.23	+ 0.72	+ 0.30
Semiconductor	174.01	+ 3.00	+ 1.75
Software	817.44	+ 5.63	+ 0.69
Utilities	210.85	+ 0.20	+ 0.09
Telephone	280.27	+ 1.11	+ 0.40
Electric	169.50	– 0.29	– 0.17
Gas	164.89	– 0.64	– 0.39
Water	380.65	+ 2.62	+ 0.69
DJ Equity Market	274.60	+ 0.19	+ 0.07

History compiled by Dow Jones and Shearson Lehman Hutton Inc.

Oil drilling

Pollution Control

Source: *The Wall Street Journal*, March 31, 1989.

Energy	**Energy**	**220.31**	**–**	**1.04**	**–**	**0.47**
	Coal	218.69	–	0.99	–	0.45
	Oil drilling	81.21	–	0.83	–	1.01 ← Oil drilling
	Oil-majors	257.19	–	1.23	–	0.48
	Oil-secondary	205.81	–	0.87	–	0.42
	Oilfield equip/svcs	104.22	–	0.40	–	0.38
	Pipelines	183.75	–	0.95	–	0.51

Industrial	**Industrial**	**286.51**	**–**	**0.11**	**–**	**0.04**
	Air freight	183.84	–	1.76	–	0.95
	Building materials	410.37	+	2.92	+	0.72
	Containers/pkging	520.16	–	6.07	–	1.15
	Elec comp/equip	272.39	–	0.11	–	0.04
	Factory equipment	254.51	+	0.10	+	0.04
	Heavy construction	187.42	+	3.29	+	1.79
	Heavy machinery	167.03	+	0.08	+	0.05
	Industrial services	312.84	–	1.77	–	0.56
	Industrial,divers	252.91	+	0.09	+	0.04
	Marine transport	508.60	–	2.93	–	0.57
	Pollution control	605.05	+	4.15	+	0.69 ← Pollution control
	Railroads	271.37	–	0.75	–	0.28
	Transportation equip	269.31	–	0.15	–	0.06
	Trucking	225.22	+	0.23	+	0.10

and **Insider Trading Spotlight** in Wednesday's *Wall Street Journal*. An example from the July 26, 1989 issue is provided.

GREED VS. FEAR

Perhaps this chapter has made clear to you how complex the stock market can be, and how many ways there are to invest in stocks. No wonder that even major investors feel they need an expert's advice before they venture their capital.

There is a saying, "Greed and fear drive the stock market." For example, greedy investors fueled the blaze of speculative gains before the crash of 87, while fear held the market back after the crash.

So far there has been no discussion of investors' psychological dynamics, the herd instinct created by greed and fear. Instead, these chapters treated the fundamentals of investing in terms of the analysis of the out-

DOW JONES INDUSTRY GROUP COMPONENTS

BASIC MATERIALS

• Aluminum:
Alcoa
Maxxam Inc.
Reynolds Metals

• Other Non-ferrous:
Asarco Inc.
Brush Wellman Inc.
Magma Copper Co. "B"
Phelps Dodge Corp.

• Chemicals:
Air Prod & Chem.
Amer Cyanamid
Aristech Chemical
Betz Labs
Cabot Corp.
Dow Chemical
DuPont de Nemours
Ethyl Corp.
Georgia Gulf Corp.
Goodrich (B.F.)
Grace (W.R.) & Co.
Great Lakes Chemical
Hercules Inc.
Int'l Minerals & Chem.
Lubrizol Corp.
Monsanto Co.
Morton Thiokol
Nalco Chemical
Olin Corp.
Pennwalt Corp.
Quantum Chemical
Rohm & Haas Co.
Sigma Aldrich Corp.
Union Carbide
Vista Chemical

• Forest Products:
Boise Cascade
Champion Int'l.
Georgia Pacific
Louisiana Pacific
Potlatch Corp.
Weyerhaeuser Co.
Willamette Indus.

• Diversified Mining:
AMAX Inc.
Cleveland-Cliffs
Freeport McMoRan
Newmont Mining

• Paper Products:
Bowater Inc.
Consol. Papers
Glatfelter (P.H.) Co.
Gt. Northn Nekoosa
Int'l. Paper Co.
James River Corp.
Kimberly-Clark
Mead Corp.
Scott Paper Co.
Union Camp Corp.
Westvaco Corp.

• Precious Metals:
ASA Ltd.
Battle Mountain Gold "A"
Hecla Mining
Homestake Mining

• Steel:
Allegheny Ludlum
Armco Inc.
Bethlehem Steel
Inland Steel Indus.
LTV Corp.
Nucor Corp.
Worthington Industries

ENERGY

• Coal:
Cyprus Minerals
NACCO Indus. "A"
Pittston Co.
Pyro Energy
Westmoreland Coal

• Oil, Drilling:
Energy Service Co.
Helmerich & Payne
Parker Drilling
Reading & Bates
Rowan Cos.

• Oil, Integrated Majors:
Amoco Corp.
Atlantic Richfield
Chevron Corp.
Exxon Corp.
Masco Corp.
Owens-Corning
Sherwin-Williams
USG Corp.
Vulcan Materials

• Containers & Packaging:
Ball Corp.
Crown Cork & Seal
Federal Paper Board
Sonoco Products
Stone Container

• Electrical Components:
AMP Inc.
Emerson Electric
Grainger (W.W.)
Square D Co.
Tecumseh Products
Thomas & Betts
Westinghouse

• Factory Equipment:
Cincinnati Milacron
Interlake Corp.
Keystone Int'l
Nordson Corp.
Parker Hannifin

• Heavy Construction:
Fluor Corp.
Foster Wheeler Corp.
Kasler Corp.
Morrison Knudsen
Stone & Webster

• Heavy Machinery:
Caterpillar Inc.
Clark Equipment
Deere & Co.
Harnischfeger Indus.
Manitowoc Co.

• Industrial & Commercial Services:
Comdisco Inc.
Commerce Clearing Hse.
Deluxe Corp.
Donnelley & Sons
Dun & Bradstreet
Ecolab Inc.
Equifax Inc.
Flightsafety Inc.
Harland (John H.)
Kelly Services "A"
National Education Corp.
National Service Ind.
Ryder System Inc.
Safety-Kleen
ServiceMaster L.P.
XTRA Corp.

• Industrial Diversified:
Allied-Signal
Combustion Engineering
Cooper Industries
Crane Co.
Dexter Corp.
Dover Corp.
Emhart Corp.
Engelhard Corp.
FMC Corp.
Harsco Corp.
Henley Group Inc.
IDI Industries
Illinois Tool Wks.
Ingersoll-Rand Co.
Norton Co.
Penn Central Corp.
PPG Industries
Raychem Corp.
Stanley Works
Tenneco Inc.
Trinova Corp.
Tyco Labs Inc.

• Marine Transportation:
Alexander & Baldwin
American Pres. Cos.
OMI Corp.
Overseas Shipholding
Sea Containers Ltd.

• Pollution Waste Mgt.:
Browning-Ferris Indus.
Ogden Corp.
Rollins Environmental
Waste Management Inc.
Wheelabrator Group

• Railroads:
Burlington Northern
CSX Corp.
Consolidated Rail
Golden Nugget
Showboat
Webb (Del E.)

• Home Construction:
Centex Corp.
Kaufman & Broad
NV Ryan L.P.
PHM Corp.
U.S. Home Corp.

• Home Furnishings/Appliances:
Black & Decker
Leggett & Platt
Maytag Corp.
Ohio Mattress
Whirlpool Corp.

• Lodging:
Hilton Hotels
Holiday Corp.
Marriott Corp.
Prime Motor Inns
Ramada Inc.

• Media:
Belo (A.H.) "A"
Cablevision Sys. "A"
CBS Inc.
Capital Cities/ABC
Dow Jones
Gannett Co.
Harcourt Brace J
Knight-Ridder
LIN Broadcasting
McGraw-Hill
Multimedia Inc.
New York Times "A"
Tele-Communications Inc.
Time Inc.
Times Mirror "A"
Tribune Co.
Washington Post "B"

• Recreation Products:
Brunswick Corp.
Carnival Cruise Lines "A"
Columbia Pictures
Disney (Walt)
Eastman Kodak
Hasbro Inc.
MCA Inc.
Outboard Marine
Polaroid
Warner Commun.

• Restaurants:
McDonald's Corp.
Shoney's Inc.
Sysco Corp.
TW Services
Wendy's Int'l.

• Retailers, Apparel:
Gap Inc.
General Cinema
Limited Inc.
Mercantile Stores Inc.
Nordstrom Inc.
Petrie Stores Inc.
U.S. Shoe Corp.

• Retailers, Broadline:
Carter Hawley Hale
Dillard Dept. Stores "A"
Dayton Hudson
Penney (J.C.)
K mart
May Dept. Stores
Sears, Roebuck & Co.
Wal-Mart Stores
Woolworth (F.W.)
Zayre Corp.

• Retailers, Drug-Based:
Longs Drug Stores
McKesson Corp.
MedcoContainmentSvcs.
Rite Aid
Walgreen

• Retailers, Specialty:
Circuit City Stores
Home Depot Inc.
Jostens Inc.
Lowes Cos.
Melville Corp.
Pep Boys-Manny Moe & Jack
Pic 'N' Save
Price Co.
Tandy Corp.
Toys "R" Us
Kellogg Co.
Lance Inc.
McCormick & Co.
Quaker Oats Co.
Ralston Purina
Sara Lee Corp.
Tyson Foods Inc. "A"
Whitman Corp.
Wrigley (Wm.) Jr. Co.

• Food Retailers:
Albertson's Inc.
American Stores
Bruno's Inc.
Circle K Corp.
Fleming Cos.
Food Lion "B"
Great Atlantic Pacific Tea
Giant Food "A"
Kroger Co.
Super Valu Stores
Vons Cos.
Winn-Dixie Stores

• Health Care Providers:
Amer Medical Int'l.
Community Psych. Ctrs.
Humana Inc.
Manor Care Inc.
National Medical Enterp.

• Household Products:
American Brands
Clorox Co.
Colgate-Palmolive
Johnson & Johnson
Philip Morris Cos.
Procter & Gamble
Rubbermaid Inc.
UST Inc.
Universal Corp.

• Medical Supplies:
Abbott Laboratories
Acuson Corp.
Baxter International Inc.
Bard (C.R.) Inc.
Becton, Dickinson Co.

• Pharmaceuticals:
American Home Products
Bausch & Lomb
Bristol-Myers
Lilly (Eli) & Co.
Marion Labs
Merck & Co.
Pfizer Inc.
Rorer Group
Schering-Plough
SmithKline Beckman
Squibb Corp.
Syntex Corp.
Upjohn Co.
Warner-Lambert

TECHNOLOGY

• Aerospace & Defense:
Boeing Co.
E-Systems Inc.
Gencorp Inc.
General Dynamics
Grumman Corp.
Lockheed Corp.
Loral Corp.
McDonnell Douglas
Martin Marietta
Northrop Corp.
Precision Castparts
Sundstrand Corp.

• Communications:
AT&T Co.
Communications Satellite
General Instruments
Harris Corp.
Motorola Inc.

• Communications (Less AT&T):
Communications Satellite
General Instruments
Harris Corp.
Motorola

• Computers&Information:
Amdahl Corp.
Apple Computer
Compaq Computer
Control Data
Cray Research

• Medical/Bio Technology:
Amgen Inc.
Cetus Corp.
Genentech Inc.
Medtronic Inc.
Stryker Corp.

• Office Equipment:
AM International
Nashua Corp.
Pitney Bowes
Xerox Corp.

• Semiconductor & Related:
Advanced Micro Devices
Applied Materials Inc.
Avnet Inc.
Intel Corp.
Nat'l. Semiconductor

• Software & Processing:
Ashton-Tate
Autodesk Inc.
Automatic Data Process
Computer Associates Int'l
Computer Sciences Corp.
Lotus Development
Microsoft Corp.
Novell Inc.
Oracle Systems Corp.

FINANCIAL SERVICES

• Banks, Money Center:
Bankamerica
Bankers Trust N.Y.
Chase Manhattan
Chemical Banking Corp.
Citicorp
First Chicago Corp.
Manufacturers Hanover
Morgan (J.P.) & Co.

• Banks, Central:
Ameritrust Corp.
Banc One Corp.
Boatmen's Bankshares
Comerica Inc.
First Bank System
First Nat'l Cincinnati
Fifth Third Bancorp
Huntington Bancshares
Manufacturers National
Michigan National Corp.
National City Corp.
NBD Bancorp
Northern Trust
Norwest Corp.
Society Corp.

• Banks, Eastern:
BayBanks Inc.
Bank of Boston
Bank of New England
Bank of New York
CoreStates Financial
First Fidelity Bancorp.
Fleet/Norstar Financial
Keycorp
Mellon Bank Corp.
Meridian Bancorp. Inc.
Midlantic Corp.
MNC Financial Inc.
PNC Financial Corp.
Republic New York
Shawmut National Corp.
State Street Boston
United Jersey Banks

• Banks, Southern:
Amsouth Bancorp
Barnett Banks Inc.
Citizens & Southern Corp.
Crestar Financial
Dominion Bankshares
First Union Corp.
First Wachovia
NCNB Corp.
Signet Banking Corp.
Southeast Banking Corp.
Sovran Financial
Suntrust Banks

• Banks, Western:
Bancorp Hawaii
First Interstate Bancorp.
Security Pacific Corp.
United Banks Colorado
U.S. Bancorp.
Wells Fargo & Co.
St. Paul Cos.
USF&G

• Real Estate Investment:
Federal Nat'l Mortgage Assoc.
Federal Realty Invest Trust
First Union Real Estate Equity
Rockefeller Center Properties
Rouse Co.

• Savings & Loans:
Ahmanson (H.F.) Co.
CalFed Inc.
Golden West Financial
Glenfed Inc.
Great Western Financial
Meritor Financial

• Securities Brokers:
Bear Stearns Cos.
Edwards (A.G.) Inc.
Merrill Lynch & Co.
Morgan Stanley Group
PaineWebber Group
Quick & Reilly Group
Salomon Inc.

UTILITIES

• Telephone Systems:
Alltel Corp.
Ameritech
Bell Atlantic Corp.
BellSouth Corp.
Centel Corp.
Cincinnati Bell
Contel Corp.
GTE Corp.
Metro Mobile CTS "A"
MCI Communications
NYNEX Corp.
Pacific Telesis Group
So. NE Telecom
Southwestern Bell
US West Inc.
Utd Telecommunications

• Electric Utilities:
Allegheny Power System
American Electric Power
Atlantic Energy
Baltimore Gas & Electric
Carolina Power & Light
Centerior Energy
Central Illinois Pub Svc.
Central & So. West Corp.
Cincinnati Gas & Elec.
CMS Energy
Commonwealth Edison
Consolidated Edison
Delmarva Power & Light
Detroit Edison
Dominion Resources
DPL Inc.
Duke Power
Duquesne Light
Florida Progress
FPL Group Inc.
General Public Utils.
Gulf States Utilities
Houston Industries
Idaho Power Co.
Illinois Power Co.
Ipalco Enterprises
Kansas City P&L
Kansas Gas & Electric
Kentucky Utilities
Long Island Lighting
Louisville Gas & Elec.
Middle South Utilities
Montana Power Co.
NIPSCO Industries
New England Elec. Sys.
New York State E&G
Niagara Mohawk Power
Northeast Utilities
Northern States Power
Ohio Edison
Oklahoma Gas & Elec.
PSI Holdings
Pacific Corp.
Pacific Gas & Electric
Pennsylvania Pwr & Lt
Philadelphia Electric
Pinnacle West Capital

Source: *The Wall Street Journal*, April 24, 1989.

Mobil Corp.
Phillips Petroleum
Sun Co.
Texaco Inc.
Unocal Corp.

• **Oil, Secondary:**
Amerada Hess
Anadarko Petroleum
Ashland Oil
Hamilton Oil
Kerr-McGee Corp.
Louisiana Land
MAPCO Inc.
Mesa L.P.
Murphy Oil Corp.
Noble Affiliates
Occidental Petrol
Pennzoil
Quaker State Corp.
Sun Explor & Prod.
Union Texas Pet. Hldgs
USX Corp.

• **Oilfield Equipment:**
Baker Hughes
Dresser Indus.
Halliburton Co.
McDermott Int'l.
Schlumberger Ltd.

• **Pipelines:**
Burlington Resources
Coastal Corp.
Enron Corp.
Enserch Corp.
Panhandle Eastern
Sonat Inc.
Texas Eastern Corp.
Transco Energy
Williams Cos.

INDUSTRIAL

• **Air Freight/Couriers:**
Air Express Intl.
Airborne Freight
Expiditers Int'l. Wash.
Federal Express
Harper Group

• **Building Materials:**
Armstrong World
CalMat Co.
Manville Corp.
Norfolk Southern
Santa Fe Southern
Union Pacific

• **Transportation Equip.:**
Cummins Engine
Eaton Corp.
Navistar Int'l.
Paccar Inc.
Trinity Indus.

• **Trucking:**
Carolina Freight
Consol. Freightways
Hunt (J.B.) Transpt.
Roadway Services
Yellow Freight Sys.

CONSUMER, CYCLICAL

• **Advertising:**
Foote Cone Belding
Grey Advertising
Interpublic Group
Ogilvy Group
Omnicom Group

• **Airlines:**
AMR Corp.
Alaska Air Group
Delta Air Lines
NWA Inc.
Pan Am Corp.
Southwest AirLines
Texas Air Corp.
UAL Corp.
USAir Group

• **Automobile Mfg.:**
Chrysler
Ford Motor
General Motors

• **Automobile Parts:**
Dana Corp.
Echlin Inc.
Genuine Parts
Goodyear Tire
Johnson Controls
Masco Industries
Snap-On Tools
Timken Co.

• **Casinos:**
Caesars World
Circus Circus

• **Textiles & Apparel:**
Brown Group
Hartmarx Corp.
Interco Inc.
Liz Claiborne
Nike Inc. "B"
Reebok Int'l
Russell Corp.
Spring Industries
VF Corp.

CONSUMER, NON-CYCLICAL

• **Beverages:**
A&W Brands Inc.
Anheuser-Busch
Brown-Forman "B"
Coca-Cola Bottling
Coca-Cola Co.
Coca-Cola Entrp.
Coors (Adolph) "B"
PepsiCo Inc.

• **Consumer Services:**
Block (H&R) Inc.
CPI Corp.
Kinder-Care Inc.
Rollins Corp.
Service Corp. Int'l

• **Cosmetics/Personal Care:**
Avon Products
Gillette Co.
Int'l. Flavors & Frag.
Noxell Corp. "B"
Neutrogena
Tambrands

• **Food:**
Archer Daniels Midland
Borden Inc.
CPC International
Campbell Soup
Castle & Cooke Inc.
ConAgra Inc.
Dean Foods Co.
Flowers Industries
General Mills Inc.
Gerber Products
Heinz (H.J.)
Hormel (George A.)
Hershey Foods
Data General
Digital Equipment
Hewlett-Packard
IBM
NCR
Prime Computer
Seagate Technology
Sun Microsystems
Tandem Computers
Unisys Corp.
Wang Labs "B"
Zenith Electronics

• **Computers & Information (Less IBM):**
Amdahl Corp.
Apple Computer
Compaq Computer
Control Data
Cray Research
Data General
Digital Equipment
Hewlett-Packard
NCR
Prime Computer
Seagate Technology
Sun Microsystems
Tandem Computers
Unisys Corp.
Wang Labs "B"
Zenith Electronics

• **Diversified Technology:**
Corning Glass Works
EG&G Inc.
Honeywell Inc.
Litton Industries
Minnesota Mining & Mfg.
Perkin-Elmer Corp.
Raytheon
Rockwell International
TRW Inc.
Tektronix Inc.
Texas Instruments
United Technologies
Varian Associates

• **Industrial Technology:**
Analog Devices
Ametek Inc.
General Signal
Intergraph Corp.
Millipore Corp.
Pall Corp.
Zions Bancorp.

• **Financial Services, Diversified:**
Alexander & Alexander Svcs.
American Express
Beneficial Corp.
Dreyfus Corp.
Household Int'l.
Marsh & McLennan Cos.
Primerica Corp.
Transamerica Corp.

• **Insurance, Full Line:**
Aetna Life & Casualty
American General
Aon Corp.
CIGNA Corp.
Kemper Corp.
Lincoln National
Travelers Corp.

• **Insurance, Life:**
American National
Broad Inc.
Capital Holding
Jefferson-Pilot
Provident Life "B"
Torchmark Corp.
UNUM Corp.
USLIFE Corp.

• **Insurance, Property & Casualty:**
American International
Chubb Corp.
Cincinnati Financial
Continental Corp.
Fireman's Fund
GEICO Corp.
General RE Corp.
Loew's Corp.
Ohio Casualty Corp.
Progressive Corp.
Safeco Corp.
Portland General
Potomac Electric
Public Service Colorado
Public Service Enterprise
Puget Sound P&L
San Diego Gas & Elec.
SCANA Corp.
SCEcorp
Southern Co.
Southwestern Pub. Svc.
TECO Energy
Texas Utilities
Tucson Elec. Power
Union Electric
Washington Water Power
Wisconsin Energy Corp.

• **Gas Companies:**
Arkla Inc.
Columbia Gas System
Consolidated Natural Gas
Equitable Resources
Kansas Power & Light
Nicor Inc.
Oneok Inc.
Pacific Enterprises
Peoples Energy
Questar Corp.

• **Water Companies:**
American Water Works
California Water Service
Consumer Water
Hydraulic Co.
United Water Resources

CONGLOMERATES

General Electric
Greyhound Corp.
Gulf & Western
ITT Corp.
Teledyne Inc.
Textron Inc.

Source: *The Wall Street Journal*, April 24, 1989.

look for stocks vs. gold and then applied that analysis to a variety of stock market indicators. Here is a brief summary of these approaches.

Fundamental analysis tries to determine the intrinsic value of stocks by discovering their future earnings potential within the context of the business environment, and then concludes whether or not their present market value accurately reflects that intrinsic value.

This book's version of fundamental analysis began with a review of business cycle conditions and inflation's outlook, and the impact of monetary and fiscal policy on them. From there, the analysis proceeded to a discussion of profits under a variety of cyclical and inflationary settings, and delved into the importance of these settings for stocks and gold. At the same time it dealt with the importance of the price-earnings ratio and the importance of current stock market valuation as a determinant of potential appreciation.

Three Johnson & Johnson Officials Sold Part of Their Stake in Company in June

INSIDE TRACK

By John R. Dorfman
And Alexandra Peers
Staff Reporters of The Wall Street Journal

Three officers at **Johnson & Johnson** sold portions of their company stock in June.

Clark H. Johnson, chief financial officer of the big New Brunswick, N.J., health-care products concern, sold 6,000 shares, or one-third of his holding, June 7 and 9, according to Securities and Exchange Commission filings.

He received a total of about $316,000, or an average price of $52.80 a share. That's slightly above yesterday's closing price of $49.875. The issue fell 25 cents in New York Stock Exchange composite trading.

Robert Z. Gussin, vice president, science and technology, sold 8,100 shares between June 16 and June 26 for about $408,000, or an average price of $50.42 a share. That was about half his stock, taking into account indirect holdings.

A smaller sale was made by Francis H. Barker, vice president, public affairs. Mr. Barker parted with 2,482 shares June 7 at $52.125 each, or a total of $129,374. He still has 10,332 shares remaining.

A company spokesman said Mr. Johnson sold to fund a divorce settlement, and that Mr. Barker sold to pay taxes and pay off loans connected with an earlier exercise of stock options. The spokesman said, "None of these transactions has any implication for the company's performance or prospects."

Both Mr. Johnson and Mr. Barker declined to be interviewed. Mr. Gussin was traveling and couldn't be reached.

Analysts were generally unfazed by the selling. Mimi Willard, a health care analyst at Shearson Lehman Hutton Inc., called Johnson & Johnson "a classic high-quality, sleep-at-night growth stock." She is excited about EPO, an anti-anemia compound the company has developed in a joint venture with Amgen Inc.

She also thinks Sucralose, a heat-stable artificial sweetener, will be approved by regulators in 1990 or 1991. And she is im-

INSIDER TRADING SPOTLIGHT

Biggest Individual Trades

(Based on reports filed with the SEC last week)

COMPANY NAME	EXCH.	INSIDER'S NAME[1]	TITLE[2]	$ VALUE (000)	NO. OF SHRS. IN TRANS. (000)	% OF HLDNG.	TRANSACTION DATES
BUYERS							
Firemans Fund	N	G. Gabetti x,s	O	**2,131**	61.9	389	6/14-28/89
ICH Corp	A	J. W. Gardiner	P	**671**	173.0	217	6/19-20/89
Storage Equities	N	K. Q. Volk Jr x	CB	**615**	47.9	62	6/9-30/89
United Insurance	O	R. L. Jensen x	CB	**398**	37.1	4	6/30/89
Davox	O	M. D. Kaufman x	D	**380**	96.0	11	6/19-21/89
Neuromedical Tech	O	C. Kovens s	O	**337**	168.5	19	6/7/89
Medco Research	O	W. C. Govier	VP	**310**	37.0	26	6/7-13/89
Landsing Pacific Fund	O	G. K. Bar	P	**279**	32.8	143	6/30/89
Old Kent Financial	O	R. M. Devos	D	**253**	9.3	94	6/2/89
Deposit Guaranty	O	W. H. Holman Jr	D	**238**	7.5	25	6/28/89
SELLERS							
Gantos	O	L. D. Gantos x	O	**9,761**	446.1	22	7/5/89
Uno Restaurant	O	A. D. Spencer x	CB	**6,500**	500.0	12	6/29/89
Telecom-USA	O	C. E. McLeod	Z	**4,372**	140.8	16	7/5-14/89
American Medical Intl	N	M. H. Meyerson	D	**4,051**	154.3	46	7/10/89
Morrison-Knudsen	N	V. V. Morrison x	D	**3,175**	74.8	100	6/2/89
Autodesk	O	G. P. Lutz x	D	**2,114**	57.5	13	6/14/89
Meredith Corp	N	E. T. Meredith III	O	**1,800**	50.0	4	6/15/89
H.J. Heinz	N	J. W. Connolly	VP	**1,657**	30.0	21	7/10/89
Raytheon	N	P. A. Phalon	VP	**1,515**	20.0	74	7/7/89
Intl Technology	N	M. H. Hutchison	CB	**1,408**	250.0	11	6/26/89

Companies With Biggest Net Changes

(Based on actual transaction dates in reports filed through last Friday)

		NET % CHG. IN HOLDINGS OF RECENT TRADERS[3]		LATEST 8 WKS.		LATEST 24 WKS.	
COMPANY NAME	EXCH.	LATEST 8 WEEKS	LATEST 24 WEEKS	NO. OF BUYERS-SELLERS	MULTIPLE OF HIST. NORM[4]	NO. OF BUYERS-SELLERS	MULTIPLE OF HIST. NORM[4]
BUYING							
Cumberland Federal Bancorp	O	**137**	25	3-0	4.5*	5-0	2.5
Data Switch	O	**75**	2	3-0	4.5	4-1	2.0
Data I/O	O	**62**	99	3-0	1.7	5-0	1.0
Sheldahl	O	**38**	49	2-0	1.1	3-0	0.6
Comstock Ptnrs Strategy	N	**25**	42	3-0	1.0*	3-0	0.3
Peoples Bancorp Worcester	O	**18**	14	5-1	3.5*	11-1	2.5
United Insurance	O	**5**	8	3-0	2.0*	4-1	0.9
SELLING							
XL/Datacomp	O	− **80**	− 46				
Wetterau	[illegible]						
Koger Pr[illegible]							

Source: *The Wall Street Journal*, July 26, 1989.

This chapter provided some additional assistance in the fundamental analysis of a particular stock. You learned how to compare that stock's performance to its industry's performance, and then compare the industry to the overall market. A company's earnings and its price-earnings ratio are also ingredients in fundamental analysis. Final steps include an appraisal of a company's management as well as a forecast of future prospects founded upon its marketing and technological outlook and the ability to control costs.

If that makes sense, you must nonetheless keep in mind that *technical analysis*, a school with a number of passionate advocates, takes a different approach. It studies the historical price trend of the stock market, a group of stocks, or a single stock to forecast future trends. Technical analysis makes extensive use of charts to comprehend historical developments and thereby predict price movements. This reduces an understanding of the psychology of the market and the forces of greed and fear to an analysis of charts of past price movements. For instance, if stock prices (or the price of a stock) rise and then fall back, only to rise again above the previous high, one school of technical analysis views this as a sign of market strength. On the other hand, failure of the stock to surpass its earlier peak is viewed as a sign of weakness.

Investor's Tip

- To avoid greed and fear, take the long-run view developed in these chapters.

CONCLUSION

You *can* make money in the stock market if you have the time and expertise required to study it closely. But as you know from Chapters 1 and 8, timing is crucial. You have to know when to get in and when to get out, because it's very difficult to find a stock that will buck the market's trend for long. Just remember that you can invest in that trend, without investing in an individual stock, by investing in an index fund.

CHAPTER 10

COMMODITIES & PRECIOUS METALS

INTRODUCTION

Chapters 1 and 8 observed that stocks and gold move in opposite directions, each reacting differently to the rate of inflation. Chapter 9 reviewed investment opportunities in the stock market. It's now time to turn to gold. But before you do let's take a historical step backward to gain a little perspective on the commodity markets, where gold (among other things) is traded.

Drastic price fluctuations plagued the farmers and producers of commodities throughout our nineteenth-century westward expansion. After a period of rapid western settlement, new farms and ranches flooded the market with their output. Prices plummeted, devastating farmers and ranchers who had hoped for higher prices to cover their debts. Only after the market absorbed the excess capacity did prices firm and rise again, instigating a new round of price increases and cyclical expansion.

Wildly fluctuating prices for cotton, grain, and meat hurt the farmer and rancher as well as the textile manufacturer, flour miller, and meat packer. In order to protect themselves from unpredictable swings in market prices, these "producers" and "consumers" began contracting to buy and sell output *(commodities)* at predetermined prices for future delivery *(futures contracts)*. The *futures price* is the market's best advance estimate of the market price at the time of delivery *(cash* or *spot price)*.

Regardless of the spot price at the time of delivery, parties to these futures contracts were obligated to perform the contract at the agreed upon futures price. In this way producers, such as farmers and ranchers, who contracted to sell their output for future delivery, shielded themselves from potentially low spot (cash) prices, while foregoing the possibility that the actual cash prices might be higher at the time of delivery. Conversely, manufacturers, millers, packers, and other commodity consumers, who contracted to buy goods for future delivery, forewent the potentially low spot prices at time of delivery to avoid the possible risk of high prices later. Futures and forward contracts limit both the potential risk and the potential reward of the cash market for producers and consumers.

Futures contracts are subject to standard size and trading requirements imposed by the exchanges. For instance, in the case of gold, a single contract is 100 troy ounces of gold, priced on a per ounce basis for delivery every other month in February, April, June, August, October, and December. There are nine major futures exchanges in the United States, several in London, and one in Canada; the Chicago Board of Trade (CBT) is the world's largest. The exchanges are nonprofit organizations whose members purchase seats on the open market.

The futures market protects buyers and sellers of commodities, but it also provides a market for speculative trading. Speculators do not produce or consume the commodities they trade; they hope to profit from fluctuations in commodity prices. Speculation is important to the futures market because it provides liquidity by increasing sales and purchases of future contracts. The business of the exchange is conducted by traders who make a market for others and buy and sell on their own account.

LONG POSITION

Miller and manufacturer enter into futures contracts to buy commodities for future delivery at a set price. This is called a *long* position.

Investors also take long positions (i.e., buy futures contracts) when they expect market prices at the time of delivery to be higher than the present futures price. If the investors' predictions about future cash prices are accurate, they will profit by selling at a high spot price the commodity they purchased for a low futures price. For instance, if you expect gold prices to be higher in October than the current October gold futures contract, you will buy that contract. If you are correct, and in October the spot prices *are* higher than the October futures contract price, your gain will be the difference between the low futures price at which you purchased the gold and the high spot price at which you sell it.

In practice, however, fewer than 5 percent of all futures contracts are actually held to delivery; investors rarely trade the actual commodity. An investor who has taken a long position (i.e., bought a contract for future delivery) can sell the contract before the delivery date. Again, as above, if you are correct and gold prices are rising, the October contract will have risen as well because market forces push future prices toward spot prices as the date of delivery approaches. You will be able to sell your contract to buy gold to someone else at a higher price than you paid for it.

Don't worry if this seems a little confusing. There will be a detailed example below.

SHORT POSITION

Farmers, ranchers, and miners enter into futures contracts to sell commodities for future delivery at an agreed upon price. This is known as a *short* position.

Investors take short positions when they anticipate that spot prices will be lower than present futures prices. If, for example, you anticipate falling gold prices and feel that spot prices will be lower than present futures contract prices, you can take a short position in gold and thereby contract to sell gold at favorable futures prices. If you wait until the time of delivery, you can buy gold in the cash market at the low spot price and then complete or perform the contract to sell the gold at the higher contracted futures price.

But as you learned earlier, futures contracts are rarely performed; they are generally cancelled with an opposing trade. As gold prices fall, and therefore futures prices with them, you can buy a contract at the new low price and discharge your obligation to sell a contract at the old high price. Your gain is the difference between the two prices.

Finally, be aware that whether you buy (long position) or sell (short position) a futures contract, your broker will ask you for only a small portion (say, 10 percent) of the contract's value. This margin deposit will protect the broker in the event that prices fall, should you have gone long or rise if you have sold short. The broker can liquidate your position quickly, as soon as prices move the wrong way, and cover the loss from your deposit. Obviously, your margin can disappear in a hurry.

INVESTING IN GOLD FUTURES

The Wall Street Journal reports commodity prices on a daily basis (see the first or last section's index). **Commodity Futures Prices** provides quotes for future delivery of specified amounts of each commodity (see page 220 for a blowup of the excerpt from the Wednesday, March 15, 1989 *Wall Street Journal* report on the next page). The line in boldface across the top tells you the name of the commodity, the exchange where it is traded, the size of a contract, and the unit in which the price is quoted. Take gold as an example. This commodity trades on the Commodity Exchange in New York City (CMX) in contracts of 100 troy ounces at prices quoted in dollars per troy ounce. The quotations are for delivery in March, April, June, August, October, and December of 1989 and February, April, June, August, October, and December of 1990.

Using December 1989 as your example, note how the following information is provided by column:

Open—opening price: $419.50 for December 1989 delivery.

High—highest price for trading day: $421.50.

Low—lowest price for trading day: $419.50.

Settle—settlement price or closing price for the trading day: $420.40.

Change—difference between the latest settlement price and that of previous trading day: increase of $1.90 for December 1989 delivery.

Lifetime High—highest price ever for the December 1989 contract: $514.50.

Lifetime Low—lowest price ever: $403.30.

Open Interest—number of contracts outstanding for delivery (for the previous trading day): 18,143 contracts have not been offset by an opposing trade or fulfilled by delivery.

The bottom line provides the estimated volume (number of contracts) for the day (34,000) as well as the actual volume for the previous trading day (27,402). Finally, the total open interest is given for all gold contracts (169,294), along with the change in the open interest from the previous trading day (–1,077). Since the previous day, 1,077 contracts were cancelled by a reversing trade.

Suppose that after having studied Chapters 1 and 8, you expect gold prices to fall. How can you profit from your forecast? Recall that you

COMMODITY FUTURES PRICES

Tuesday, March 14, 1989.

Open Interest Reflects Previous Trading Day.

–GRAINS AND OILSEEDS–

CORN (CBT) 5,000 bu.; cents per bu.

	Open	High	Low	Settle	Change	Lifetime High	Lifetime Low	Open Interest
Mar	277½	278¾	276	278¼	+ 1¼	370	193½	7,135
May	281¼	282½	280¼	282	+ 1¼	369	207½	88,011
July	284½	285½	283¼	285¼	+ 1¼	360	233	49,605
Sept	277	277½	276½	277½	+ ½	317¾	245	8,885
Dec	274¾	275¼	273½	274¼	– 1	295	234	34,761
Mr90	281¼	281¼	280	281	– ¾	286½	257½	2,820
May	283¼	283¼	282½	283	– ½	289½	275½	781

Est vol 30,000; vol Mon 21,937; open int 191,998, –1,678.

OATS (CBT) 5,000 bu.; cents per bu.

	Open	High	Low	Settle	Change	Lifetime High	Lifetime Low	Open Interest
Mar	210	210	209	209½	– ¼	367¾	161	380
May	215	215½	213	214½	– ¼	340	187	5,306
July	219¼	219¼	217½	218¾	+ ½	277	201½	2,840
Sept	220½	221	219	220½	– ¼	243	200	1,002
Dec	228½	228½	227	228½	+ ½	247	218	893

Est vol 1,000; vol Mon 966; open int 10,421, +144.

SOYBEANS (CBT) 5,000 bu.; cents per bu.

	Open	High	Low	Settle	Change	Lifetime High	Lifetime Low	Open Interest
Mar	770	771	762	769	+ ½	1023	579	1,784
May	782	784¾	775	781½	– ½	1003	647	45,873
July	793	794	784	790½	– ½	986	685	32,281
Aug	787	788	779¾	785½	+ 1½	951	725	5,398
Sept	763½	764	757	761	– 1	835	701	4,540
Nov	748	749¾	743½	748	+ ½	793	663	24,70
Ja90	755½	756	751½	754¾	+ ¼	763	684	1,771
Mar	762	762	760	761	– ½	770	684	462

Est vol 37,000; vol Mon 36,782; open int 116,901, –1,189.

SOYBEAN MEAL (CBT) 100 tons; $ per ton.

	Open	High	Low	Settle	Change	Lifetime High	Lifetime Low	Open Interest
Mar	243.50	243.90	241.50	243.40	+ .90	308.00	193.50	6,133
May	241.80	242.20	239.50	241.10	+ .60	304.00	200.50	31,218
July	240.50	240.50	237.20	239.20	+ .60	300.00	221.00	14,511
Aug	238.50	238.50	236.00	237.20	+ .70	298.00	217.50	[illegible]
Sept	233.50	233.50	232.00	232.50	+ .50	290.00	214.00	[illegible]
Oct	229.00	229.50	226.00	227.20	+ .20	237.00	203 [illegible]	[illegible]
Dec	226.50	226.50	224.50	226.00	....	270.00	[illegible]	[illegible]
Ja90	225.00	225.00	225.00	225.00	– .50	23[illegible]	[illegible]	[illegible],359

Est vol 15,500; vol Mon 11,569; oper[illegible] 3,523

SOYBEAN OIL (CBT) 60,000 lb[illegible] [illegible]04.20 627

	Open	High	Low	Settle	Change	Lifetime High	Lifetime Low	Open Interest
Mar	23.10	23.24	22.98	23.[illegible]	[illegible]	[illegible]	[illegible]	[illegible]
May	23.52	23.69	23.42	[illegible]	[illegible]	[illegible]	[illegible]	[illegible]
July	24.10	24.35	24[illegible]	[illegible]	.10	170.50	103.50	280
Aug	24.30	24.53	[illegible]	[illegible]	– .30	168.50	135.50	3,103
Sept	24.55	[illegible]	[illegible]	[illegible]4.50	– .10	166.50	144.30	1,602
Oct	24.[illegible]	[illegible]	[illegible]00	152.50	+ .30	157.00	144.80	1,483
Dec	[illegible]		....	152.50	– .10	156.00	145.30	385
Ja9[illegible]								

[illegible],348, –126.

[illegible] $ per ton

[illegible] vol Mon 211; open int 6,863, –42.

[illegible]G) 20 metric tons; Can. $ per ton

	Open	High	Low	Settle	Change	Lifetime High	Lifetime Low	Open Interest
[illegible]	....	....	....	156.50	+ 3.00	178.00	149.60	71
[illegible]	152.20	152.50	151.50	151.50	....	171.50	150.00	757
July	....	....	....	151.60	+ .10	164.00	151.00	730
Oct	148.00	148.70	148.00	148.70	+ .70	154.00	146.30	230

Est vol 60; vol Mon 30; open int 1,788, +1.

–LIVESTOCK & MEAT–

CATTLE–FEEDER (CME) 44,000 lbs.; cents per lb.

	Open	High	Low	Settle	Change	Lifetime High	Lifetime Low	Open Interest
Mar	81.40	81.42	80.95	81.15	– .05	84.95	74.00	2,146
Apr	81.20	81.35	80.70	80.75	– .35	84.50	74.40	2,982
May	80.95	81.17	80.35	80.52	– .35	84.15	76.00	5,384
Aug	80.10	80.25	79.55	79.65	– .35	83.27	77.50	2,371
Sept	79.97	80.00	79.40	79.40	– .25	83.10	77.35	644
Oct	79.85	79.95	79.20	79.20	– .42	83.00	77.40	708
Nov	80.50	80.50	80.10	80.30	– .17	83.50	78.05	556
Ja90	80.85	80.85	80.50	80.65	+ .05	83.75	80.30	205

Est vol 2,532; vol Mon 1,669; open int 14,996, –19.

CATTLE–LIVE (CME) 40,000 lbs.; cents per lb.

	Open	High	Low	Settle	Change	Lifetime High	Lifetime Low	Open Interest
Apr	78.15	78.32	77.35	77.42	– .70	78.45	67.20	38,826
June	74.85	74.95	74.05	74.10	– .57	75.90	68.75	28,510
Aug	72.20	72.25	71.65	71.72	– .42	73.80	69.35	13,102
Oct	71.50	71.55	71.02	71.15	– .25	74.00	68.60	12,544
Dec	72.65	72.70	72.10	72.15	– .50	73.95	70.00	1,615
Fb90	72.50	72.50	72.30	72.40	– .27	73.70	71.72	334

Est vol 20,085; vol Mon 14,805; open int 94,984, –1,653.

HOGS (CME) 30,000 lbs.; cents per lb.

	Open	High	Low	Settle	Change	Lifetime High	Lifetime Low	Open Interest
Apr	43.85	43.90	43.62	43.75	+ .12	51.65	40.60	13,554
June	48.80	48.95	48.40	48.60	+ .02	56.25	42.50	6,512
July	48.90	49.15	48.75	48.92	+ .02	56.00	46.10	4,717
Aug	47.75	47.90	47.50	47.55	– .07	51.00	45.05	2,350
Oct	44.40	44.45	44.15	44.35	– .05	47.00	42.30	1,354
Dec	45.85	45.85	45.50	45.52	– .02	47.25	44.20	513

Est vol 4,332; vol Mon 4,734; open int 29,100, –192.

PORK BELLIES (CME) 40,000 lbs.; cents per lb.

	Open	High	Low	Settle	Change	Lifetime High	Lifetime Low	Open Interest
Mar	38.20	38.30	37.90	38.25	+ .20	66.35	37.10	736
May	38.40	38.50	37.95	38.20	+ .20	65.50	37.45	8,025
July	38.40	38.57	38.15	38.37	+ .22	64.50	37.65	8,672
Aug	37.85	38.00	37.35	37.50	– .02	58.25	36.40	4,381
Fb90	51.70	51.70	51.40	51.70	+ .02	61.60	42.00	381

Est vol 4,831; vol Mon 3,335; open int 22,225, –187.

–FOOD & FIBER–

COCOA (CSCE)–10 metric tons; $ per ton.

	Open	High	Low	Settle	Change	Lifetime High	Lifetime Low	Open Interest
Mar	1,540	1,585	1,540	1,575	+ 50	2,088	1,125	452
May	1,405	1,447	1,405	1,440	+ 40	2,088	1,152	12[illegible]
July	1,375	1,403	1,375	1,396	+ 34	1,985	1,17[illegible]	[illegible]
Sept	1,380	1,390	1,375	1,384	+ 25	1,850	[illegible]	[illegible]
Dec	1,375	1,393	1,375	1,385	+ 18	1[illegible]	[illegible]	[illegible]
Mr90	1,378	1,385	1,372	1,381	+ [illegible]	[illegible]	[illegible]	310
May	1,375	1,381	1,372	1,379	[illegible]	[illegible]	[illegible]	[illegible]
July	....	....	....	1[illegible]	[illegible]	[illegible]	[illegible]	[illegible]

Est vol 4,848; vol M[illegible] –102.

COFFEE (CSCE[illegible] [illegible] per lb.

	Open	High	Low	Settle	Change	Lifetime High	Lifetime Low	Open Interest
[illegible]	[illegible]	[illegible]	[illegible]	[illegible]	[illegible]	[illegible]75.50	134.00	634
[illegible]	[illegible]	[illegible]	[illegible]	[illegible]	.20	173.50	132.00	2,669
Mar	134.00	1[illegible]	[illegible]	[illegible]	+ .05	171.80	132.00	1,705
May	13[illegible]	[illegible]	[illegible]	145.20	+ .40	170.10	132.00	1,235
July	[illegible]	[illegible]	[illegible]00	141.70	+ .60	166.50	129.40	350
[illegible]	[illegible]	[illegible]5	140.20	141.15	+ .90	149.25	127.50	102

[illegible]0; vol Mon 1,234; open int 6,791, +129.

–METALS & PETROLEUM–

COPPER-STANDARD (CMX)–25,000 lbs.; cents per lb.

	Open	High	Low	Settle	Change	Lifetime High	Lifetime Low	Open Interest
Mar	142.00	145.00	140.70	144.60	+ 1.90	155.00	66.50	4,195
Apr	....	....	....	140.50	+ 1.60	143.40	125.00	236
May	134.90	138.50	133.50	138.30	+ 2.00	146.00	73.15	19,056
July	127.80	132.00	126.60	131.50	+ 2.30	138.50	76.00	8,499
Sept	121.00	124.25	121.00	125.00	+ 2.70	131.50	76.00	1,732
Dec	117.00	118.30	116.75	119.00	+ .70	126.00	77.45	2,040

Est vol 12,000; vol Mon 9,483; open int 35,758, –228.

GOLD (CMX)–100 troy oz.; $ per troy oz.

	Open	High	Low	Settle	Change	Lifetime High	Lifetime Low	Open Interest
Mar	395.00	395.00	395.00	396.20	+ 1.80	513.00	380.00	12
Apr	397.50	400.00	396.50	398.10	+ 1.70	550.00	382.50	48,533
June	402.50	404.50	401.20	402.80	+ 1.80	570.00	386.50	46,472
Aug	407.00	409.40	406.90	408.40	+ 1.90	575.00	399.50	18,773
Oct	413.70	413.70	413.70	414.40	+ 1.90	575.50	399.50	8,516
Dec	419.50	421.50	419.50	420.40	+ 1.90	514.50	403.30	18,143
Fb90	427.20	427.50	427.20	426.30	+ 1.80	516.00	410.90	5,738
Apr	....	....	....	432.20	+ 1.70	525.80	416.80	4,635
June	....	....	....	438.20	+ 1.60	497.00	422.40	8,312
Aug	....	....	....	444.20	+ 1.60	487.00	428.30	6,153
Oct	....	....	....	450.20	+ 1.50	472.00	434.30	1,725
Dec	....	....	....	456.30	+ 1.50	454.50	437.50	2,282

Est vol 34,000; vol Mon 27,402; open int 169,294, –1,077.

EXCHANGE ABBREVIATIONS
(for commodity futures and futures options)

CBT-Chicago Board of Trade; CME-Chicago Mercantile Exchange; CMX-Commodity Exchange, New York; CRCE-Chicago Rice & Cotton Exchange; CTN-New York Cotton Exchange; CSCE-Coffee, Sugar & Cocoa Exchange, New York; IPE-International Petroleum Exchange; KC-Kansas City Board of Trade; MCE-MidAmerica Commodity Exchange; MPLS-Minneapolis Grain Exchange; NYM-New York Mercantile Exchange; PBOT-Philadelphia Board of Trade; WPG-Winnipeg Commodity Exchange.

PLATINUM (NYM)–50 troy oz.; $ per troy oz.

	Open	High	Low	Settle	Change	Lifetime High	Lifetime Low	Open Interest
Mar	....	....	....	549.30	+ 6.90	546.00	508.00	1
Apr	546.00	552.00	545.00	549.30	+ 6.90	643.50	482.00	9,308
July	546.50	551.00	545.00	549.30	+ 6.90	640.00	501.00	4,873
Oct	544.50	551.00	544.50	548.80	+ 7.10	609.00	505.00	4,241
Ja90	548.00	548.00	548.00	550.30	+ 7.10	646.00	459.00	1,358

Est vol 5,238; vol Mon 4,834; open int 19,802, –598.

PALLADIUM (NYM) 100 troy oz.; $ per troy oz.

	Open	High	Low	Settle	Change	Lifetime High	Lifetime Low	Open Interest
Mar	146.75	146.75	145.00	145.30	+ .20	150.25	115.50	546
June	146.00	146.50	144.50	145.30	+ .20	148.50	114.00	4,037
Sept	142.75	142.75	142.00	142.05	+ .20	144.00	119.00	1,233
Dec	139.00	139.00	139.00	139.05	– .05	142.00	122.25	754

Est vol 331; vol Mon 318; open int 6,644, +65.

SILVER (CMX)–5,000 troy oz.; cents per troy oz.

	Open	High	Low	Settle	Change	Lifetime High	Lifetime Low	Open Interest
Mar	610.0	619.0	610.0	617.6	+ 9.8	1073.0	573.0	395
May	616.0	627.0	614.0	625.5	+ 9.5	965.0	582.5	49,789
July	627.0	639.5	626.0	637.7	+ 10.0	985.0	594.0	15,819
Sept	639.0	650.0	639.0	649.8	+ 10.5	861.0	605.5	7,720
Dec	658.0	670.0	655.5	667.1	+ 11.0	886.0	621.0	9,766
Mr90	684.0	684.0	679.5	684.2	+ 11.5	910.0	640.0	5,276
May	....	....	....	695.6	+ 11.7	910.0	651.0	2,760
July	....	....	....	707.1	+ 11.9	761.5	661.0	1,995
Sept	710.0	710.0	710.0	719.2	+ 12.1	760.0	675.0	64[illegible]
Dec	....	....	....	736.3	+ 12.3	708.5	696.0	

Est vol 26,000; vol Mon 15,107; open int 94,322.

SILVER (CBT)–1,000 troy oz.; cents per tr[illegible]

	Open	High	Low	Settle	Change	Lifetime High	Lifetime Low	Open Interest
Apr	611.0	622.0	609.0	622.0	+ 11.5	8[illegible]	[illegible]	[illegible]28
June	623.0	633.0	620.0	632.5	+ 10.[illegible]	[illegible]	[illegible]	213
Aug	634.0	644.0	632.0	644.0	+ [illegible]	[illegible]	[illegible]125	240
Oct	654.0	654.0	652.0	654[illegible]	[illegible]	[illegible]	[illegible]	[illegible]
Dec	658.0	665.0	655.0	[illegible]	[illegible]	[illegible]	[illegible]	[illegible]

[illegible],993, +1,354.

Est vol 1,500; vol M[illegible] [illegible] ton

CRUDE OIL, Li[illegible]

	Open	High	Low	Settle	Change	Lifetime High	Lifetime Low	Open Interest
[illegible]	[illegible]	[illegible]	[illegible]	[illegible]00	[illegible]	154.50	117.25	15,530
[illegible]	[illegible]	[illegible]	[illegible]	[illegible]	+ 1.25	147.75	115.00	6,655
Apr	19.13	[illegible]	[illegible]	[illegible].00	+ 1.25	146.75	112.75	4,981
May	18[illegible]	[illegible]	[illegible]	144.00	+ 1.75	144.75	110.75	1,697
June	[illegible]	[illegible]	[illegible]8.00	148.50	....	148.50	138.00	189
Ju[illegible]	[illegible]	[illegible]00	149.50	149.50	+ 2.00	150.25	137.00	360

[illegible] vol 6,595; open int 30,492, +735.

–WOOD–

LUMBER (CME)–150,000 bd. ft.; $ per 1,000 bd. ft.

	Open	High	Low	Settle	Change	Lifetime High	Lifetime Low	Open Interest
Mar	176.80	178.10	175.50	175.50	– 1.00	192.20	171.00	215
May	182.20	183.80	182.20	182.90	+ 1.20	194.50	170.10	3,698
July	186.30	187.20	186.10	186.80	+ .90	196.00	175.10	1,924
Sept	186.30	187.10	186.20	186.80	+ 1.10	194.70	175.10	816
Nov	182.90	183.80	182.90	183.20	+ .80	190.60	177.00	222

Est vol 1,030; vol Mon 1,244; open int 6,947, +240.

Source: *The Wall Street Journal*, March 15, 1989.

sell futures contracts when you expect commodities prices to fall. You want to be able to satisfy your commitment to sell at a high price in the future with a purchase at a lower price.

With this in mind, turn to page 221, and note that on Wednesday, February 8, 1989 the price of an October 1989 gold contract was \$415.00. Suppose at that time you sold short 10 October gold futures contracts because you believed gold prices would fall. Your broker would credit your account by \$415,000 (\$415 × 100 troy ounces per contract × 10 contracts) to reflect the sale and ask for a good faith

FUTURES PRICES

Tuesday, March 14, 1989.

Open Interest Reflects Previous Trading Day.

	Open	High	Low	Settle	Change	Lifetime High	Lifetime Low	Open Interest
–GRAINS AND OILSEEDS–								
CORN (CBT) 5,000 bu.; cents per bu.								
Mar	277½	278¾	276	278¼	+ 1¼	370	193½	7,135
May	281¼	282½	280¼	282	+ 1¼	369	207½	88,011
July	284½	285½	283¼	285¼	+ 1¼	360	233	49,605
Sept	277	277½	276½	277½	+ ½	317¾	245	8,885
Dec	274¾	275¼	273½	274¼	– 1	295	234	34,761
Mr90	281¼	281¼	280	281	– ¾	286½	257½	2,820
May	283¼	283¼	282½	283	– ½	289½	275½	781
Est vol 30,000; vol Mon 21,937; open int 191,998, –1,678.								
OATS (CBT) 5,000 bu.; cents per bu.								
Mar	210	210	209	209½	– ¼	367¾	161	380
May	215	215½	213	214½	– ¼	340	187	5,306
July	219¼	219¼	217½	218¾	+ ½	277	201½	2,840
Sept	220½	221	219	220½	– ¼	243	200	1,002
Dec	228½	228½	227	228½	+ ½	247	218	893
Est vol 1,000; vol Mon 966; open int 10,421, +144.								
SOYBEANS (CBT) 5,000 bu.; cents per bu.								
Mar	770	771	762	769	+ ½	1023	579	1,784
May	782	784¾	775	781½	– ½	1003	647	45,873
July	793	794	784	790½	– ½	986	685	32,281
Aug	787	788	779¾	785½	+ 1½	951	725	5,398
Sept	763½	764	757	761	– 1	835	701	4,540
Nov	748	749¾	743½	748	+ ½	793	663	24,70
Ja90	755½	756	751½	754¾	+ ¼	763	684	1,771
Mar	762	762	760	761	– ½	770	684	462
Est vol 37,000; vol Mon 36,782; open int 116,901, –1,189.								

	Open	High	Low	Settle	Change	Lifetime High	Lifetime Low	Open Interest
–WOOD–								
LUMBER (CME)–150,000 bd. ft.; $ per 1,000 bd. ft.								
Mar	176.80	178.10	175.50	175.50	– 1.00	192.20	171.00	215
May	182.20	183.80	182.20	182.90	+ 1.20	194.50	170.10	3,698
July	186.30	187.20	186.10	186.80	+ .90	196.00	175.10	1,924
Sept	186.30	187.10	186.20	186.80	+ 1.10	194.70	175.10	816
Nov	182.90	183.80	182.90	183.20	+ .80	190.60	177.00	222
Est vol 1,030; vol Mon 1,244; open int 6,947, +240.								
–METALS & PETROLEUM–								
COPPER-STANDARD (CMX)–25,000 lbs.; cents per lb.								
Mar	142.00	145.00	140.70	144.60	+ 1.90	155.00	66.50	4,195
Apr	....	....	....	140.50	+ 1.60	143.40	125.00	236
May	134.90	138.50	133.50	138.30	+ 2.00	146.00	73.15	19,056
July	127.80	132.00	126.60	131.50	+ 2.30	138.50	76.00	8,499
Sept	121.00	124.25	121.00	125.00	+ 2.70	131.50	76.00	1,732
Dec	117.00	118.30	116.75	119.00	+ .70	126.00	77.45	2,040
Est vol 12,000; vol Mon 9,483; open int 35,758, –228.								
GOLD (CMX)–100 troy oz.; $ per troy oz.								
Mar	395.00	395.00	395.00	396.20	+ 1.80	513.00	380.00	12
Apr	397.50	400.00	396.50	398.10	+ 1.70	550.00	382.50	48,533
June	402.50	404.50	401.20	402.80	+ 1.80	570.00	386.50	46,472
Aug	407.00	409.40	406.90	408.40	+ 1.90	575.00	399.50	18,773
Oct	413.70	413.70	413.70	414.40	+ 1.90	575.50	399.50	8,516
Dec	419.50	421.50	419.50	420.40	+ 1.90	514.50	403.30	18,143
Fb90	427.20	427.50	427.20	426.30	+ 1.80	516.00	410.90	5,738
Apr	....	....	....	432.20	+ 1.70	525.80	416.80	4,635
June	....	....	....	438.20	+ 1.60	497.00	422.40	8,312
Aug	....	....	....	444.20	+ 1.60	487.00	428.30	6,153
Oct	....	....	....	450.20	+ 1.50	472.00	434.30	1,725
Dec	....	....	....	456.30	+ 1.50	454.50	437.50	2,282
Est vol 34,000; vol Mon 27,402; open int 169,294, –1,077.								

Gold Futures

Source: *The Wall Street Journal*, March 15, 1989.

deposit of, say, 10 percent in the event prices rise. By April 19, 1989 (see the Wednesday, April 20, 1989 *Journal* excerpt on page 221) your forecast has borne fruit with the drop in the October gold contract price to $397 per ounce. Gold futures fell, reflecting declines in the spot market and investors' anticipation of falling inflation. On May 23, 1989 the October gold contract is trading for $370.80 and you decide to cash in by asking your broker to *buy* an October contract for that price in order to meet your obligation to sell, thereby realizing the difference between the original, high futures price at which you sold and the present low price at which you bought. Your net gain on May 23, 1989, after only three months, is $44,200 ($415,000 that you earn for selling your contracts less $370,800—$370.80 per oz. × 100 oz. × 10 contracts—that you owe for the offsetting purchase).

Investor's Tip

- Take a long position in gold futures when you expect rising gold prices and a short position when you think they'll fall.

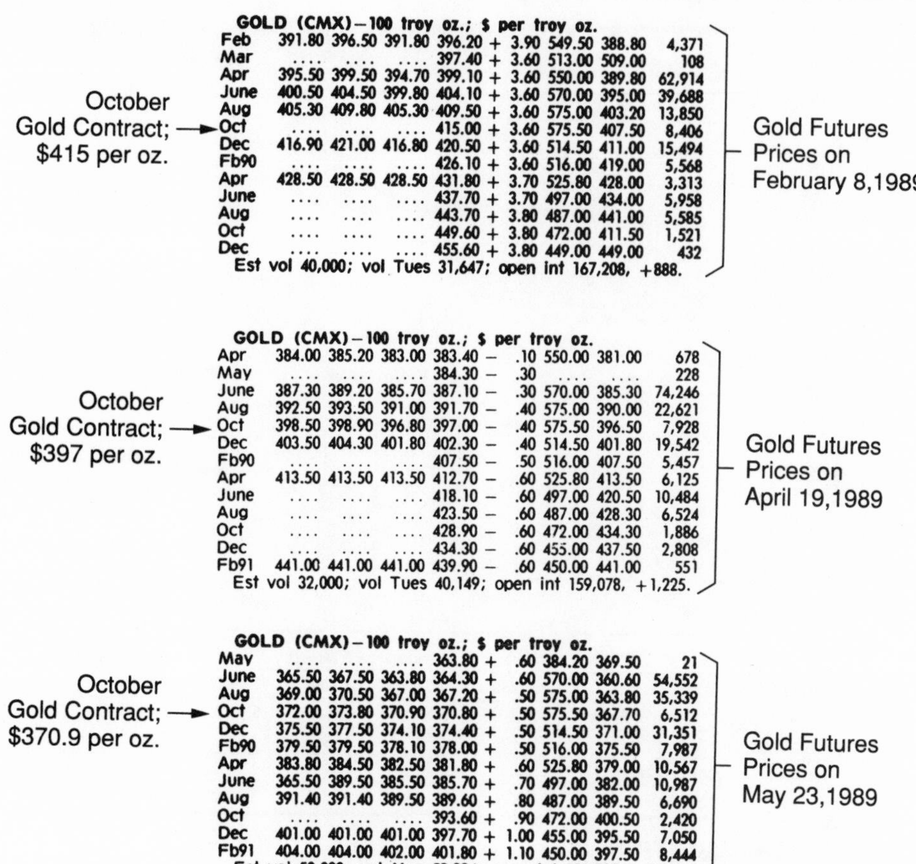

GOLD (CMX)—100 troy oz.; $ per troy oz.								
Feb	391.80	396.50	391.80	396.20	+ 3.90	549.50	388.80	4,371
Mar	....	....	....	397.40	+ 3.60	513.00	509.00	108
Apr	395.50	399.50	394.70	399.10	+ 3.60	550.00	389.80	62,914
June	400.50	404.50	399.80	404.10	+ 3.60	570.00	395.00	39,688
Aug	405.30	409.80	405.30	409.50	+ 3.60	575.00	403.20	13,850
Oct	....	....	....	415.00	+ 3.60	575.50	407.50	8,406
Dec	416.90	421.00	416.80	420.50	+ 3.60	514.50	411.00	15,494
Fb90	....	....	....	426.10	+ 3.60	516.00	419.00	5,568
Apr	428.50	428.50	428.50	431.80	+ 3.70	525.80	428.00	3,313
June	....	....	....	437.70	+ 3.70	497.00	434.00	5,958
Aug	....	....	....	443.70	+ 3.80	487.00	441.00	5,585
Oct	....	....	....	449.60	+ 3.80	472.00	411.50	1,521
Dec	....	....	....	455.60	+ 3.80	449.00	449.00	432

Est vol 40,000; vol Tues 31,647; open int 167,208, +888.

GOLD (CMX)—100 troy oz.; $ per troy oz.								
Apr	384.00	385.20	383.00	383.40	– .10	550.00	381.00	678
May	....	....	....	384.30	– .30	....	....	228
June	387.30	389.20	385.70	387.10	– .30	570.00	385.30	74,246
Aug	392.50	393.50	391.00	391.70	– .40	575.00	390.00	22,621
Oct	398.50	398.90	396.80	397.00	– .40	575.50	396.50	7,928
Dec	403.50	404.30	401.80	402.30	– .40	514.50	401.80	19,542
Fb90	....	....	....	407.50	– .50	516.00	407.50	5,457
Apr	413.50	413.50	413.50	412.70	– .60	525.80	413.50	6,125
June	....	....	....	418.10	– .60	497.00	420.50	10,484
Aug	....	....	....	423.50	– .60	487.00	428.30	6,524
Oct	....	....	....	428.90	– .60	472.00	434.30	1,886
Dec	....	....	....	434.30	– .60	455.00	437.50	2,808
Fb91	441.00	441.00	441.00	439.90	– .60	450.00	441.00	551

Est vol 32,000; vol Tues 40,149; open int 159,078, +1,225.

GOLD (CMX)—100 troy oz.; $ per troy oz.								
May	....	....	....	363.80	+ .60	384.20	369.50	21
June	365.50	367.50	363.80	364.30	+ .60	570.00	360.60	54,552
Aug	369.00	370.50	367.00	367.20	+ .50	575.00	363.80	35,339
Oct	372.00	373.80	370.90	370.80	+ .50	575.50	367.70	6,512
Dec	375.50	377.50	374.10	374.40	+ .50	514.50	371.00	31,351
Fb90	379.50	379.50	378.10	378.00	+ .50	516.00	375.50	7,987
Apr	383.80	384.50	382.50	381.80	+ .60	525.80	379.00	10,567
June	365.50	389.50	385.50	385.70	+ .70	497.00	382.00	10,987
Aug	391.40	391.40	389.50	389.60	+ .80	487.00	389.50	6,690
Oct	....	....	....	393.60	+ .90	472.00	400.50	2,420
Dec	401.00	401.00	401.00	397.70	+ 1.00	455.00	395.50	7,050
Fb91	404.00	404.00	402.00	401.80	+ 1.10	450.00	397.50	8,444

Est vol 50,000; vol Mon 52,224; open int 181,920, –2,696.

Source: *The Wall Street Journal*, February 9, 1989, April 20, 1989, and May 24, 1989, respectively.

TRACKING COMMODITIES

Every day, on the first page (C1) of the third section, *The Wall Street Journal* summarizes recent commodities activity under the **Markets Diary** heading. A sample from the Wednesday, March 15, 1989 edition appears on page 222. The chart presents the Commodities Research Bureau's (CRB) Futures Index and spot prices for gold, oil, wheat, and steers are also given.

The Wall Street Journal carries a commodities article daily in the third section; on Mondays the **Dow Jones Commodity Indexes** chart is

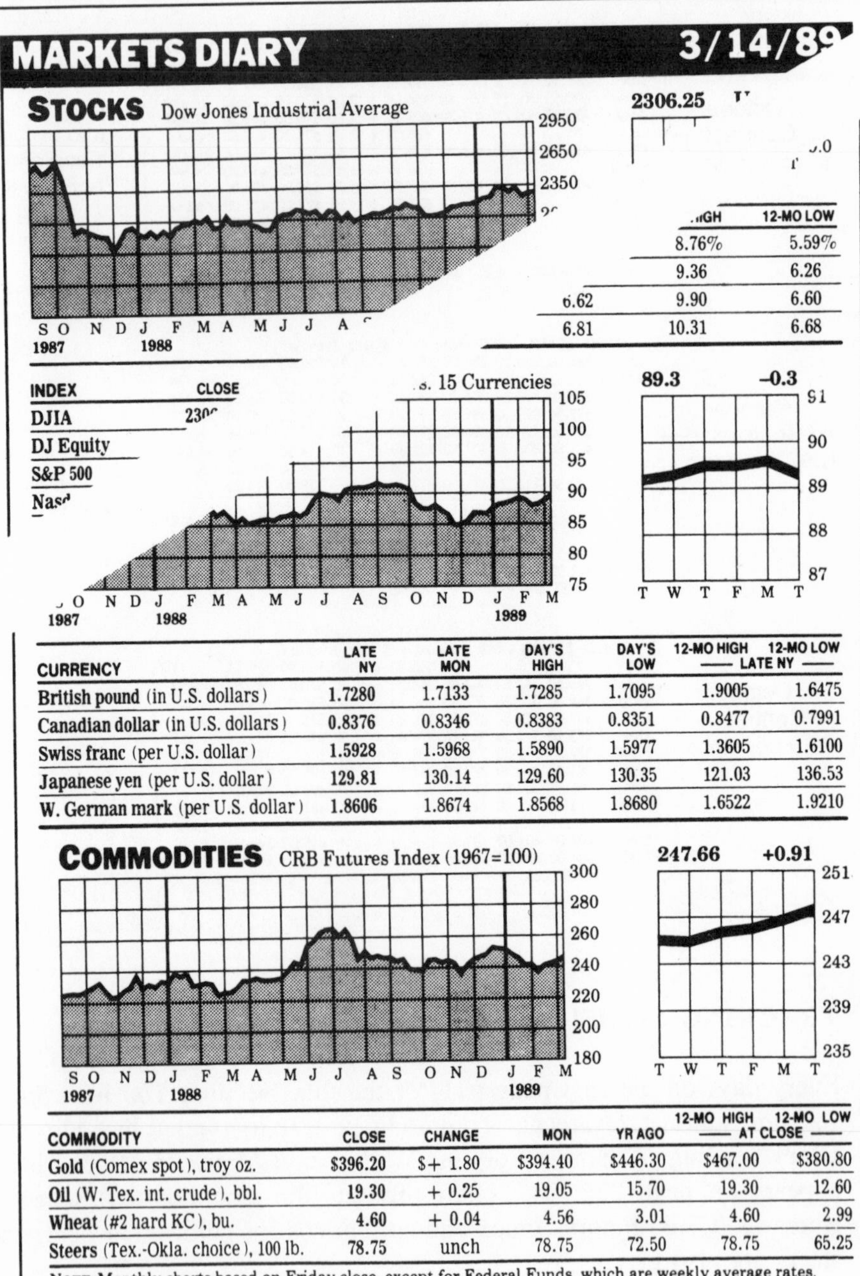

MARKETS DIARY 3/14/89

STOCKS Dow Jones Industrial Average

	..IGH	12-MO LOW
	8.76%	5.59%
	9.36	6.26
6.62	9.90	6.60
6.81	10.31	6.68

INDEX	CLOSE
DJIA	230..
DJ Equity	
S&P 500	
Nas..	

CURRENCY	LATE NY	LATE MON	DAY'S HIGH	DAY'S LOW	12-MO HIGH — LATE NY —	12-MO LOW — LATE NY —
British pound (in U.S. dollars)	**1.7280**	1.7133	1.7285	1.7095	1.9005	1.6475
Canadian dollar (in U.S. dollars)	**0.8376**	0.8346	0.8383	0.8351	0.8477	0.7991
Swiss franc (per U.S. dollar)	**1.5928**	1.5968	1.5890	1.5977	1.3605	1.6100
Japanese yen (per U.S. dollar)	**129.81**	130.14	129.60	130.35	121.03	136.53
W. German mark (per U.S. dollar)	**1.8606**	1.8674	1.8568	1.8680	1.6522	1.9210

COMMODITIES CRB Futures Index (1967=100)

COMMODITY	CLOSE	CHANGE	MON	YR AGO	12-MO HIGH — AT CLOSE —	12-MO LOW — AT CLOSE —
Gold (Comex spot), troy oz.	**$396.20**	$+ 1.80	$394.40	$446.30	$467.00	$380.80
Oil (W. Tex. int. crude), bbl.	**19.30**	+ 0.25	19.05	15.70	19.30	12.60
Wheat (#2 hard KC), bu.	**4.60**	+ 0.04	4.56	3.01	4.60	2.99
Steers (Tex.-Okla. choice), 100 lb.	**78.75**	unch	78.75	72.50	78.75	65.25

NOTE: Monthly charts based on Friday close, except for Federal Funds, which are weekly average rates.

Source: *The Wall Street Journal*, March 15, 1989.

included. See the examples from the Monday, March 13 and Wednesday, March 15, 1989 issues. You can also use the daily CRB **Commodities** in the **Markets Diary** chart (mentioned in the last paragraph) to follow commodity price movements. These indexes will be your most sensitive barometers of inflation.

COMMODITIES

Oil Market's Price Rally Is Stoked by Indication Of Further Cuts in Supplies by Saudis and Qatar

FUTURES MARKETS

By James Tanner
Staff Reporter of The Wall Street Journal

HOUSTON—More bullish news and a strong technical underpinning stoked the oil markets' price rally.

In U.S. futures trading, West Texas Intermediate crude for April delivery rose 26 cents a barrel to settle at $19.29. That was one cent above this year's previous high for any near-month crude—$19.28 Jan. 19—and the highest close for any near-month crude since November 1987.

Prices on European spot markets also surged. North Sea crudes generally traded 40 cents to 65 cents a barrel higher.

Further bullish news—which analysts said could have an impact on trading today—came after the U.S. futures market closed yesterday: The American Petroleum Institute's latest weekly report on U.S. oil statistics showed major declines in inventories of crude oil, heating oil and gasoline.

Among earlier developments were further indications of reductions in world oil supplies. According to Dow Jones International Petroleum Report, Saudi Arabia cut April volume 30% for its Japanese contr[illegible] customers. Qatar, a much sma[illegible] producer, is expected t[illegible] 150,000 barrels [illegible], but it's being weeks fo[illegible] [illegible]ntal things which, indi- [illegible] wouldn't have caused it to take [illegible], said R.B. Hoover, energy futures broker for Prudential-Bache Securities Inc. But he said that even though the market "still looks strong," it may be "overdone on a technical standpoint."

Some others also suggested that they expect some retrenchment in the oil market, where prices have climbed $6 to $7 a barrel since last October. "It will be strong through the first week of April," said Peter Beutel, assistant director-energy group for Elders Futures Inc. After that, based on his study of oil market cycles, he expects a six-week to seven-week correction.

At the moment, however, the outlook for the oil market remains positive, traders said. They cited the latest figures on U.S. oil inventories as a particularly bullish signal. According to the American Petroleum Institute report, gasoline inventories fell 4.7 million barrels last we[illegible] distillate fuels were down by [illegible] barrels and crude-oil in[illegible] million barrels [illegible] rebounded to

There [illegible] early decline that hi[illegible] [illegible]day's losses. The May con- [illegible]ended with a gain of two cents a pound, at $1.3830, after dropping to as low as $1.3350. A factor contributing to the recovery was a report that a strike at a Peruvian iron company has spread to the company's mine, an analyst said. While that labor problem had nothing to do with copper, the analyst emphasized, it inflamed concern that an uneasy Peruvian labor situation could in time spread to the copper industry. As for the periods of weakness that have developed in futures, the analyst said they are taking place while the market's fundamentals are still bullish. "At the moment, it isn't clear whether the market is topping out or just shaking out a little prior to returning to its old highs," he said.

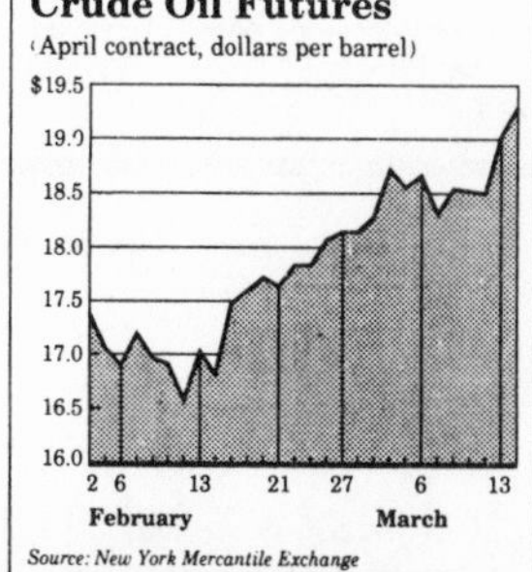

Source: New York Mercantile Exchange

PRECIOUS METALS: Futures prices rose, led by platinum. There was improved demand for the metal from the Far East and concern among traders that the move to oust P.W. Botha as president of South Africa could lead to production disruptions. South Africa is the world's leading producer of platinum. April delivery platinum rose $6.90 an ounce to $549.30. April gold was up $1.70 an ounce to $398.10, while May silver climbed 9.5 cents an ounce to $6.2550. In addition, a U.S. Commerce Department report that showed February retail sales eased 0.4% from January was regarded as non-inflationary, according to an analyst. However, he noted, Britain's chancellor of the exchequer was quoted as saying, "The rate of inflation is unmistakably picking up in industrial nations."

COCOA: Futures prices rose because a stumbling block was set aside in the negotiations of the International Cocoa Organization in London. The May contract rose $40 a metric ton to $1,440. According to one analyst, consumer member dele[illegible] decided not to debate the lev[illegible] the manager of the [illegible] wheat Agreement's [illegible], Texas and mark[illegible] [illegible]ncing above-normal [illegible] and a lack of moisture, con- [illegible] that are threatening the crop. Soybean futures prices settled "narrowly mixed," traders said, amid a dearth of farmer selling and slackening pressure from Brazil, which isn't far enough into the harvest to sell its crop until mid-April. Corn futures rose slightly, reflecting a firmer cash market and reports that South Korea, Jordan and Egypt offered to buy a total of 350,000 metric tons of corn.

	Close		Net Chg.	Yr. Ago
Dow Jones Futures	141.88	+	.31	132.30
Dow Jones Spot	138.80	+	.32	129.63
Reuter United Kingdom	2002.0	+	0.7	1721.3
C R B Futures*	247.66	+	.91	225.76

*Division of Knight-Ridder.

U.S. Electricity Production

Last week's electricity output in the U.S. (excluding Alaska and Hawaii) was reported by the Edison Electric Institute as follows (figures are in millions of kilowatt hours):

Geographic Area	Week Ended 03-11-89	Pct. Chg. From Like 1988 Week	Week Ended 03-04-89
New England	2,449	+ 19.9	2,409
Mid Atlantic	7,979	+ 14.1	7,838
Central Industrial	11,469	+ 10.7	11,590
West Central	3,896	+ 9.3	3,947
Southeast	12,463	+ 15.2	12,352
South Central	7,371	+ 19.2	6,667
Rocky Mountain	2,504	+ 5.4	2,495
Pacific Northwest	3,405	+ 13.7	3,426
Pacific Southwest	4,104	+ 2.2	4,133
Total	55,640	+ 12.8	54,857

Source: *The Wall Street Journal*, March 15, 1989.

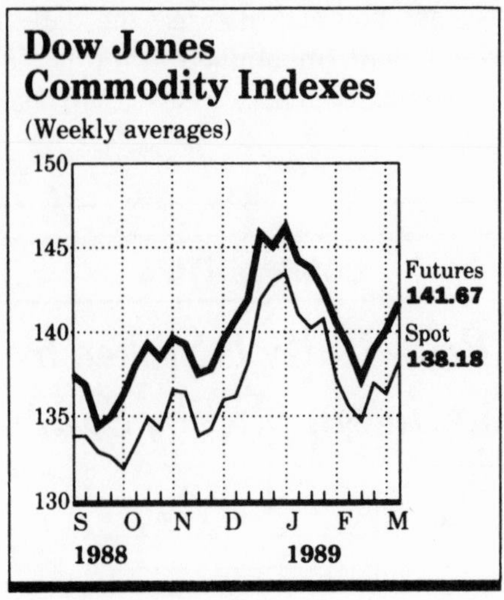

Source: *The Wall Street Journal*, March 13, 1989.

The Wall Street Journal reports **Cash Prices** for immediate delivery on a wide variety of commodities on a daily basis. Thus, on Wednesday, March 15, 1989, the *Journal* published cash prices for Tuesday, March 14, 1989 (see page 225).

All of these series can be located using the indexes on the front pages of the first and last sections.

CONCLUSION

Commodities investing is far riskier than stock market investing because positions are highly leveraged. You can lose your entire investment if prices move the wrong way. Moreover, individual commodities can be drastically affected by world events—droughts, floods, wars, political upheavals. Yet these markets present tremendous opportunities for those who can accurately forecast inflation's trend.

CASH PRICES

Tuesday March 14, 1989.
(Quotations as of 4 p.m. Eastern time)

	Tues	Mon	Yr.Ago
GRAINS AND FEEDS			
Barley, top-quality Mpls., bu	n4.15-.60	4.15-.60	2.10
Bran, wheat middlings, KC ton	101.00	102.00	80.00
Corn, No. 2 yel. Cent-Ill. bu	bp2.67½	2.66	1.89
Corn Gluten Feed, Midwest, ton ..	88.-125.	88.-125.	110.00
Cottnsd Meal, Clksdle,Miss. ton ..	190.-192½	190.-192½	136.25
Hominy Feed, Cent-Ill. ton	85.00	85.00	71.00
Meat-Bonemeal, 50% pro. Ill. ton.	260.00	260.00	237.50
Oats, No. 2 milling, Mpls., bu	n2.39-.60	2.39-.60	1.95
Sorghum, (Milo) No. 2 Gulf cwt ...	5.05	5.03	3.78
Soybean Meal,			
Decatur, Illinois ton.........	239½-240½	238½-239½	186.00
Soybeans, No. 1 yel Cent.-Ill. bu ...	bp7.67½	7.68½	6.02
Sunflwr Sd No. 1 Duluth/Supr cwt	z	z	8.55
Wheat, Spring 14%-pro Mpls. bu	4.62¾-.64¾	4.63	3.11
Wheat, No. 2 sft red, St.Lou. bu	4.43½	4.43½	2.92
Wheat, No. 2 hard KC, bu	4.59¾	4.55½	3.01¼
FOODS			
Beef, 700-900 lbs. Mid-U.S.,lb.fob .	1.11	1.11	1.03
Broilers, Dressed "A" NY lb	x.6653	.6704	.5058
Butter, AA, Chgo., lb.	1.30½	1.30½	1.30½
Cocoa, Ivory Coast, $metric ton ...	g1,832	1,768	1,857
Coffee, Brazilian, NY lb.	n1.28	1.28	1.28
Eggs, Lge white, Chgo doz.	.90-.95	.90-.95	.54
Flour, hard winter KC cwt	10.95	10.90	7.70
Hams, 17-20 lbs, Mid-US lb fob	.59	.59	.78
Hogs, Iowa-S.Minn. avg. cwt	41.00	40.50	43.00
Hogs, Omaha avg cwt	40.50	40.50	43.30
Pork Bellies, 12-14 lbs Mid-US lb ..	.30	.29	.44
Pork Loins, 14-17 lbs. Mid-US lb ...	1.00	.97	.93
Steers, Tex.-Okla. ch avg cwt	78.75	78.75	72.50
Steers, Feeder, Okl Cty, av cwt ...	91.85	92.85	91.90
Sugar, cane, raw, world, lb. fob ...	.1194	.1193	.0808
FATS AND OILS			
Coconut Oil, crd, N. Orleans lb. ...	xxn.26½	.26½	.23½
Corn Oil, crd wet mill, Chgo. lb. ...	n.21¼	.21¼	.21½
Corn Oil, crd dry mill, Chgo. lb. ...	n.20	.20	.23¼
Cottonseed Oil, crd Miss Vly lb. ...	n.a.	n.a.	.19¼
Grease, choice white, Chgo lb.......	n.13	.13	.15½
Lard, Chgo lb.	.14	.14	.17
Linseed Oil, raw Mpls lb.	n.a.	n.a.	n.a.
Palm Oil, ref. bl. deod. N.Orl. lb. .	n.19⅝	.19⅝	.19
Peanut Oil, crd, Southeast lb.	n.30½	.30½	.29
Soybean Oil, crd, Decatur, lb.	.2233	.2217	.1984
Tallow, bleachable, Chgo lb.	.14½	.14½	.17½
Tallow, edible, Chgo lb.	n.16¼	.16¼	.18½
FIBERS AND TEXTILES			
Burlap, 10 oz. 40-in. NY yd	n.2825	.2825	.2775
Cotton 1 1/16 in str lw-md Mphs lb	.5550	.5550	.6086
Print Cloth, poly/cot. 48-in. NY yd	s n.a.	n.a.	.52½
Wool, 64s, Staple, Terr. del. lb.	4.18	4.18	4.25
METALS			
Aluminum ingot lb. del. Midwest	q1.02½-.06½	1.02½-.06½	1.07
Copper cathodes lb	p1.47-.51	1.47¾-.52	1.10½
Copper Scrap, No 2 wire NY lb	k1.00	.98	.77
Lead, lb.	p.35	.35	.34
Mercury 76 lb. flask NY	q320-330	320.-330.	350.00
Steel Scrap 1 hvy mlt Chgo ton	113.-118.	113.-118.	116.50
Tin composite lb.	q5.5354	5.5382	4.2538
Zinc Special High grade lb	p.95-.95½	.95-.95½	.47
MISCELLANEOUS			
Rubber, smoked sheets, NY lb.	n.56½	.56¼	.55
Hides, hvy native steers lb., fob ...	1.00	1.00	.98
PRECIOUS METALS			
Gold, troy oz			
Engelhard indust bullion	396.32	393.82	443.60
Engelhard fabric prods	416.14	413.51	465.78
Handy & Harman base price	395.00	392.50	442.20
London fixing AM 394.30 PM ...	395.00	392.50	442.20
Krugerrand, whol	a397.75	395.75	447.00
Maple Leaf, troy oz.	a409.00	407.00	461.75
American Eagle, troy oz.	a408.25	406.25	461.75
Platinum, (Free Mkt.)	545.00	538.50	501.50
Platinum, indust (Engelhard)	547.50	546.00	489.75
Platinum, fabric prd (Engelhard)	647.50	646.00	589.75
Palladium, indust (Engelhard) ...	146.25	145.50	123.00
Palladium, fabrc prd (Englhard)	161.25	160.50	138.00
Silver, troy ounce			
Engelhard indust bullion	6.180	6.045	6.250
Engelhard fabric prods	6.613	6.468	6.688
Handy & Harman base price	6.140	6.035	6.280
London Fixing (in pounds)			
Spot (U.S. equiv. $6.0595)	3.5365	3.5140	3.3840
3 months	3.6520	3.6290	3.4590
6 months	3.7670	3.7390	3.5395
1 year	3.9815	3.9465	3.6920
Coins, whol $1,000 face val	a4,480	4,430	4,930

a-Asked. b-Bid. bp-Country elevator bids to producers. c-Corrected. d-Dealer market. e-Estimated. f-Dow Jones International Petroleum Report. g-Main crop, ex-dock, warehouses, Eastern Seaboard, north of Hatteras. l.-f.o.b. warehouse. k-Dealer selling prices in lots of 40,000 pounds or more, f.o.b. buyer's works. n-Nominal. p-Producer price. q-Metals Week. r-Rail bids. s-Thread count 78x54. x-Less than truckloads. z-Not quoted. xx-f.o.b. tankcars.

Source: *The Wall Street Journal*, March 15, 1989.

CHAPTER 11

LONG-TERM INTEREST RATES

INTRODUCTION

"Gold vs. stocks" is shorthand for the concept that paper assets do well in times of low inflation while tangible assets do not, and vice versa.

Chapter 9 investigated the stock market; this chapter will examine long-term debt instruments. You will discover why they, like stocks, appreciate when prices are stable but become poor investments when inflation turns severe. Begin your investigation with a general discussion of the origin of these investments.

Governments and businesses turn to the credit markets and issue long-term debt instruments to raise large sums whenever their internally generated funds, such as tax revenues or profits, fall short of their current or capital expenditures. The federal government, for instance, had to borrow over a trillion dollars in the capital markets during the 1980s because recessions and tax cuts in the early years of the decade suppressed revenue growth while expenditures continued to climb.

Corporations, on the other hand, issue debt (i.e., sell bonds that are redeemed after a long period throughout which they pay interest) in order to finance the purchase of new plant and equipment. Take public utilities for example. Profits cannot cover the cost of new generating and switching stations, satellites, and transmission lines, so the difference has to be made up by borrowing. Since the projects of public utility companies are long-term and generate income for these companies over several decades of useful life, it's appropriate that the financing be long-term too. The stretch-out in earnings on these assets will provide for the regular payment of interest and principal.

You already know that corporations can raise funds by selling shares via the stock market (see Chapter 9). In that process, the ownership of a corporation is subdivided by the issue of new stock. The situation is very different when corporations borrow funds in the credit markets. Ownership does not change hands although, of course, the debt burden is increased.

New credit market debt, whether sold by government or business, is subdivided into discrete units called notes or bonds and issued for a specified length of time. At the conclusion of that period, the issuer redeems the note or bond and repays the initial purchase price. Notes are medium-term debt instruments that are redeemed in one to ten years, whereas bonds are issued with maturities of more than ten years. (Chapter 12 discusses debt instruments with maturities of less than a year.)

Notes and bonds have a specific face or **par value** (such as $1,000) and pay a specified annual, semiannual, or quarterly amount, known as **coupon interest.** When you purchase a bond, expect to receive an interest return determined by the relationship between the price of the bond and the periodic payment of coupon interest. If you hold the bond to maturity (i.e., until it is redeemed by the issuer), you will also receive back its par value.

But you need not hold the note or bond to maturity because there is a secondary market for notes and bonds that is separate from the initial-issue market. The existence of this secondary or resale market makes it much easier for government and business to sell bonds in the initial primary market. If note and bond buyers could not sell and resell these instruments over and over again, it would be very difficult for government and business to issue them in the first place. Now you know why these instruments are issued in discrete units (such as $1,000) for convenient trading.

There are three principal issuers of bonds: the United States government and its agencies; corporations; and state and local governments. Examine each of their issues in turn.

TREASURY AND AGENCY ISSUES

Both the U.S. Treasury and a variety of federal agencies issue long-term debt instruments. Treasury debt is classified as bonds, notes, and bills. The Treasury bill will be discussed in Chapter 12. Treasury notes (maturities of 1 to 10 years) and bonds (over 10 years) are issued in $1,000 denominations and pay a stated coupon interest payment semiannually.

Treasury bills, bonds, and notes are referred to collectively as Treasury Securities. These securities are the safest of all debt instruments because they are backed by the full taxing power of the U.S. Government.

The government sells Treasury securities when it needs funds. These primary market sales are made at auction to bond dealers. Dealers then resell them on the secondary market to investors, where they are traded freely until maturity. *The Wall Street Journal* reports activity in the primary and secondary markets for long-term Treasury securities in its daily **Credit Markets** article in the third (C) section (see front page index).

The Treasury announces its auction of 2-year notes four times a year on Wednesdays in the middle of February, May, August, and November. The auction takes place about one week after the announcement and the notes are issued on the last day of the month. Five-year, two-month (62–month) notes are auctioned and issued with the two-year notes.

The Treasury generally auctions 3-year notes, 10-year notes, and 30-year bonds during the second week of February, May, August, and November and issues them shortly afterward, on the 15th of the same month. Page 229 has an excerpt from *The Wall Street Journal's* February 8, 1989 issue describing the previous day's primary market for three-year Treasury notes, as well as *The Wall Street Journal's* description of the March 29 auction of 4-year notes.

Four-year notes are auctioned in the third week of March, June, September, and December and issued the last day of the month. Finally, seven-year notes are usually auctioned in the middle of January, April, July and October and issued on the 15th of the month.

Bonds and notes are almost always issued in denominations of $1,000, which is referred to as the par value of the bond. Each bond has a coupon rate indicating the dollar amount the security will pay annually until maturity. Interestingly, bonds are seldom auctioned at precisely their par value because market conditions will influence buyers' bids at the aution.

Look at the February 15, 1989 *Journal* excerpt (bottom of next page) report on the 8⅞ percent 10-year note issue and you will notice that on the average buyers paid 99.771 percent of par at the auction. So a $1,000 10-year note cost $997.71 (on the average), which is $2.29 less than par. The coupon rate is listed at 8⅞ percent (8.875%) or $88.75 annually per $1,000 bond, but since buyers were willing to pay only $997.71, the true yield is 8.91 percent. Therefore,

Here are details of yesterday's auction:

Rates are determined by the difference between the purchase price and face value. Thus, higher bidding narrows the investor's return while lower bidding widens it.

3–Year Notes	
Applications	$31,264,420,000
Accepted bids	$9,760,690,000
Accepted at low price	26%
Accepted noncompetitively	$1,750,000,000
Average price (Rate)	99.859 (9.18%)
High price (Rate)	99.884 (9.17%)
Low price (Rate)	99.833 (9.19%)
Interest rate	9⅛%

The notes are dated Feb. 15 and mature Feb. 15, 1992.

3-Year Treasury Note Auction

On February 7, 1989, the Treasury auctioned 3-year notes in the primary market which had a yield of 9.18%.

Here are additional details of the Treasury's four-year note sale yesterday:

Rates are determined by the difference between the purchase price and face value. Thus, higher bidding narrows the investor's return while lower bidding widens it.

4-Year Notes	
Applications	$26,085,664,000
Accepted bids	$7,509,765,000
Accepted at low price	48%
Accepted noncompetitively	$1,419,000,000
Average price (Rate)	99.756 (9.70%)
High price (Rate)	99.789 (9.69%)
Low price (Rate)	99.756 (9.70%)
Interest rate	9⅝%

The notes are dated March 31 and mature March 31, 1993.

4-Year Treasury Note Auction

On March 29. 1989, the Treasury auctioned 4-year notes in the primary market which had a yield of 9.70%.

Source: *The Wall Street Journal*, March 30, 1989.

10-Year Treasury Note Auction

On February 14, 1989 the Treasury auctioned 10-year notes in the primary market which had a yield of 8.91%.

Here are auction details:

Rates are determined by the difference between the purchase price and face value. Thus, higher bidding narrows the investor's return while lower bidding widens it.

10–Year Notes	
Applications	$22,739,693,000
Accepted bids	$9,502,032,000
Accepted at low price	76%
Accepted noncompetitively	$522,000,000
Average price (Rate)	99.771 (8.91%)
High price (Rate)	99.837 (8.90%)
Low price (Rate)	99.706 (8.92%)
Interest rate	8⅞%

The notes are dated Feb. 15 and mature Feb. 15, 1999.

Source: *The Wall Street Journal*, February 15, 1989.

the yield on the 10-year notes of 8.91% is slightly higher than the coupon rate of 8.75%.

You can make a rough estimate of the true yield by calculating the current yield as follows:

$$\begin{aligned}\text{Current yield} &= \frac{\text{Coupon payments}}{\text{Auction price}} \\ &= \frac{\$88.75}{\$997.71} \\ &= 0.08895 \\ &= 8.895\%\end{aligned}$$

If the notes had sold at par, the coupon rate and current yield would be the same.

$$\begin{aligned}\text{Current yield} &= \frac{\$88.75}{\$1000} \\ &= 0.08875 \\ &= 8.875\%\end{aligned}$$

Thus, the yield increased as the auction price fell below par.

Your bank or broker can act as your agent if you wish to purchase a Treasury note or bond in the *secondary* (resale) market. This market is very liquid, which means that you should have no trouble buying or selling securities on any business day. The third section of *The Wall Street Journal* reports trading on the secondary market for Treasury notes and bonds on a daily basis under **Treasury Bonds, Notes & Bills**. (See the report for Friday, March 17, 1989 in the Monday, March 20, 1989 *Wall Street Journal*. You can locate it using the front-page index of the first or last section.)

The first three columns describe the bond or note in question. Begin with column one (*Rate*), the coupon rate. If it is 11¼, a $1,000 note or bond will pay $112.50 annually (11¼% of $1,000). The second and third columns, titled *Mat. Date* (maturation date), provide the year and month of maturity. If the security has two maturity dates, such as 2005-10, the bond matures in 2010 but can be called (redeemed) by the Treasury as early as 2005. Thus, if market interest rates drop below the 2005-10 bond's rate, the Treasury may redeem the security in 2005 and reissue the debt at the lower interest rate. For instance, the 12¾ 2005-10 pays

U.S. Treasury Bonds & Notes

TREASURY BONDS, NOTES & BILLS

Friday, March 17, 1989

Representative Over-the-Counter quotations based on transactions of $1 million or more as of 4 p.m. Eastern time.

Hyphens in bid-and-asked and bid changes represent 32nds; 101-01 means 101 1/32. a-Plus 1/64. b-Yield to call date. d-Minus 1/64. k-Nonresident aliens exempt from withholding taxes. n-Treasury notes. p-Treasury note; nonresident aliens exempt from withholding taxes.

Source: Bloomberg Financial Markets

U.S. TREASURY BONDS AND NOTES

Rate	Mat. Date		Bid	Asked	Bid Chg.	Yld.
11¼	1989	Mar p	100-01	100-04	.....	6.75
6⅜	1989	Mar p	99-27	99-30	+01	8.20
7⅛	1989	Apr p	99-21	99-24	.....	9.10
14⅜	1989	Apr n	100-06	100-09	-03	9.81
6⅞	1989	May p	99-16	99-19	-01	9.32
9¼	1989	May n	99-28	100	.....	8.96
8	1989	May p	99-20	99-23	-01	9.22
11¾	1989	May n	100-08	100-11	-01	9.13
7⅜	1989	Jun p	99-11	99-14	.....	9.27
9⅝	1989	Jun p	99-30	100-01	-02	9.32
7⅝	1989	Jul p	99-07	99-10	-02	9.47
14½	1989	Jul n	101-13	101-16	-02	9.47
7¾	1989	Aug p	99-03	99-06	-03	9.61
6⅝	1989	Aug p	98-23	98-27	-02	9.51
13⅞	1989	Aug n	101-20	101-24	-02	9.31
8½	1989	Sep k	99-08	99-12	-03	9.73
9⅜	1989	Sep p	99-22	99-26	-02	9.73
11⅞	1989	Oct n	101-03	101-06	-01	9.66
7⅞	1989	Oct p	98-27	98-31	-01	9.62
6⅜	1989	Nov p	97-24	97-28	-05	9.78
10¾	1989	Nov n	100-17	100-21	-01	9.65
12¾	1989	Nov p	101-23	101-27	-04	9.72
7¾	1989	Nov p	98-17	98-21	-03	9.76
7⅞	1989	Dec p	98-13	98-17	-04	9.84
8⅜	1989	Dec p	98-26	98-30	-04	9.79
7⅜	1990	Jan k	97-27	97-31	-06	9.85
10½	1990	Jan n	100-12	100-16	-04	9.82
3½	1990	Feb	94-25	95-11	+10	8.94
6½	1990	Feb k	97-01	97-05	-05	9.83
7⅛	1990	Feb k	97-15	97-19	-05	9.84
11	1990	Feb p	100-26	100-30	-07	9.87
7¼	1990	Mar p	97-12	97-16	-04	9.86
7⅜	1990	Mar p	97-13	97-17	-06	9.95
10½	1990	Apr n	100-14	100-18	-08	9.92
7⅝	1990	Apr p	97-17	97-21	-07	9.88
7⅞	1990	May k	97-22	97-26	-07	9.91
8¼	1990	May	98-09	98-15	-04	9.66
8⅛	1990	May p	97-28	98	-08	9.92
11⅜	1990	May p	101-12	101-16	-08	9.94
7¼	1990	Jun p	96-25	96-29	-06	9.86
8	1990	Jun p	97-21	97-25	-06	9.86
10¾	1990	Jul n	100-30	101-02	-06	9.85
8⅜	1990	Jul p	98-02	98-06	-05	9.81
7⅞	1990	Aug k	97-09	97-13	-09	9.88
9⅞	1990	Aug p	99-28	100	-09	9.86
10¾	1990	Aug n	101-01	101-05	-08	9.84
8⅝	1990	Aug	98-06	98-10	-11	9.90
6¾	1990	Sep p	95-18	95-22	-07	9.85
8½	1990	Sep p	97-29	98-01	-09	9.91
11½	1990	Oct n	102-07	102-11	-09	9.84
8¼	1990	Oct p	97-14	97-18	-12	9.91
8	1990	Nov p	97-02	97-06	-10	9.87
9⅝	1990	Nov k	99-16	99-20	-12	9.86
13	1990	Nov n	104-15	104-19	-14	9.90
8⅞	1990	Nov p	98-11	98-15	-12	9.86
6⅝	1990	Dec p	94-21	94-25	-13	9.88
9⅛	1990	Dec p	98-26	98-30	-11	9.77
9	1991	Jan p	98-15	98-19	-12	9.83
11¾	1991	Jan n	102-29	103-01	-13	9.87
7⅜	1991	Feb p	95-21	95-25	-13	9.85
9⅛	1991	Feb k	98-22	98-26	-12	9.81
9⅜	1991	Feb p	99-06	99-10	-12	9.77
6¾	1991	Mar p	94-11	94-15	-11	9.82
12⅜	1991	Apr n	104-15	104-19	-15	9.86
8⅛	1991	May p	96-19	96-23	-13	9.84
14½	1991	May n	109-27	109-31	-12	9.27
7⅞	1991	Jun n	95-29	96-01	-15	9.85
13¾	1991	Jul n	107-24	107-28	-17	9.86
7½	1991	Aug p	95	95-04	-14	9.82
8¾	1991	Aug p	97-19	97-23	-13	9.83
14⅞	1991	Aug n	111-06	111-10	-17	9.50
9⅛	1991	Sep k	98-09	98-13	-17	9.85
12¼	1991	Oct p	105-06	105-10	-17	9.85
6½	1991	Nov p	92-08	92-12	-14	9.83
8½	1991	Nov p	96-29	97-01	-13	9.79
14¼	1991	Nov n	110-28	111	-17	9.45
8¼	1991	Dec k	96-02	96-06	-17	9.84
11⅝	1992	Jan p	104-05	104-09	-17	9.84
6⅝	1992	Feb p	92	92-04	-14	9.80
9⅛	1992	Feb p	98-12	98-16	-17	9.72
14⅝	1992	Feb n	112-13	112-17	-17	9.58
7⅞	1992	Mar p	94-29	95-01	-17	9.81
11¾	1992	Apr	104-27	104-31	-16	9.83
6⅝	1992	May k	91-10	91-14	-17	9.84
13¾	1992	May n	110-12	110-16	-17	9.79
8¼	1992	Jun p	95-18	95-22	-18	9.81
10⅜	1992	Jul p	101-13	101-17	-23	9.81
4¼	1987-92	Aug	94-02	94-20	-09	6.02
7¼	1992	Aug	92-28	93	-19	9.71
8¼	1992	Aug p	95-13	95-17	-19	9.82
8¾	1992	Sep p	96-28	97	-20	9.77
9¾	1992	Oct p	99-24	99-28	-21	9.79
8⅜	1992	Nov p	95-20	95-24	-21	9.78
10½	1992	Nov n	102-01	102-05	-19	9.78
9⅛	1992	Dec p	98-05	98-09	-19	9.67
8¾	1993	Jan p	96-24	96-28	-22	9.74
4	1988-93	Feb	94-05	94-19	-09	5.56
6¾	1993	Feb	90-04	90-22	-19	9.66
7⅞	1993	Feb	94-10	94-15	-19	9.60
8¼	1993	Feb p	95-04	95-08	-21	9.74
10⅞	1993	Feb n	103-15	103-19	-21	9.74
7⅜	1993	Apr p	92-03	92-07	-18	9.73
7⅝	1993	May	92-26	92-30	-19	9.73
10⅛	1993	May n	101-04	101-08	-22	9.74
7¼	1993	Jul p	91-03	91-07	-28	9.78
7½	1988-93	Aug	91-26	91-30	-26	9.79
8⅝	1993	Aug	96-10	96-18	-26	9.60
8¾	1993	Aug p	96-17	96-21	-21	9.70
11⅞	1993	Aug n	107-10	107-14	-26	9.75
7⅛	1993	Oct p	90-11	90-15	-26	9.76
8⅝	1993	Nov	96-02	96-08	-26	9.64
11¾	1993	Nov n	107-08	107-12	-26	9.73
9	1993	Nov p	97-16	97-20	-21	9.63
7	1994	Jan p	89-20	89-24	-26	9.71
9	1994	Feb	98-01	98-05	-26	9.47
8⅞	1994	Feb p	96-28	97	-24	9.63
7	1994	Apr p	89-08	89-12	-26	9.70
4⅛	1989-94	May	93-25	94-11	-16	5.40
·13⅛	1994	May p	113-12	113-16	-1-01	9.72
9½	1994	May p	99-12	99-16	-26	9.61
8	1994	Jul n	92-31	93-03	-28	9.69
8¾	1994	Aug	96-22	96-30	-26	9.48
12⅝	1994	Aug p	112-01	112-05	-26	9.68
9½	1994	Oct p	99-10	99-14	-24	9.63
10⅛	1994	Nov	101-26	101-30	-29	9.67
11⅝	1994	Nov	108-04	108-08	-31	9.69
8⅝	1995	Jan p	95-14	95-18	-26	9.63
3	1995	Feb	93-26	94-12	-20	4.08
10½	1995	Feb	103-23	103-27	-29	9.63
11¼	1995	Feb p	106-27	106-31	-29	9.67
8⅜	1995	Apr p	94-07	94-11	-28	9.62
10⅜	1995	May	103-11	103-15	-30	9.61
11¼	1995	May p	107-06	107-10	-29	9.64
12⅝	1995	May	114-09	114-13	-30	9.48
8⅞	1995	Jul p	96-16	96-20	-29	9.59
10½	1995	Aug p	103-28	104	-1-00	9.64
8⅝	1995	Oct p	95-07	95-11	-28	9.59
9½	1995	Nov p	99-12	99-16	-31	9.60
11½	1995	Nov	109-02	109-06	-30	9.59
9¼	1996	Jan	98-13	98-17	-30	9.54
8⅞	1996	Feb p	96-10	96-14	-30	9.59
7⅜	1996	May p	88-15	88-19	-30	9.61
7¼	1996	Nov p	87-11	87-15	-30	9.60
8⅝	1997	Aug k	94-19	94-23	-1-00	9.55
8½	1997	May k	94	94-04	-29	9.55
8⅞	1997	Nov p	96	96-04	-1-01	9.54
8⅛	1998	Feb p	91-18	91-22	-1-00	9.53
9	1998	May p	96-29	97-01	-1-03	9.49
9¼	1998	Aug p	98-11	98-15	-1-04	9.50
7	1993-98	May	84-19	84-23	-1-04	9.54
3½	1998	Nov	93-13	93-31	-21	4.27
8⅞	1998	Nov p	95-30	96-02	-1-04	9.50
8⅞	1999	Feb p	96-03	96-07	-1-03	9.47
8½	1994-99	May	93	93-04	-1-05	9.57
7⅞	1995-00	Feb	88-21	88-25	-1-06	9.55
8⅜	1995-00	Aug	91-30	92-02	-1-04	9.53
11¾	2001	Feb	115-31	116-05	-1-04	9.46
13⅛	2001	May	125-19	125-25	-1-22	9.50
8	1996-01	Aug	89-12	89-18	-1-30	9.44
13⅜	2001	Aug	127-20	127-26	-1-30	9.51
15¾	2001	Nov	147-13	147-19	-1-30	9.28
14¼	2002	Feb	135-15	135-21	-1-26	9.42
11⅝	2002	Nov	115-29	116-03	-1-21	9.49
10¾	2003	Feb	109-10	109-16	-1-21	9.50
10¾	2003	May	109-13	109-19	-1-21	9.50
11⅛	2003	Aug	112-18	112-24	-1-21	9.48
11⅞	2003	Nov	118-17	118-23	-1-21	9.48
12⅜	2004	May	122-26	123	-1-21	9.48
13¾	2004	Aug	134-12	134-18	-1-21	9.44
11⅝	2004	Nov k	117-06	117-12	-1-19	9.47
8¼	2000-05	May	89-17	89-23	-1-23	9.51
12	2005	May k	120-21	120-27	-1-21	9.45
10¾	2005	Aug k	110-13	110-19	-1-22	9.46
9⅜	2006	Feb k	99-17	99-23	-1-21	9.41
7⅝	2002-07	Feb	84-14	84-20	-1-11	9.42
7⅞	2002-07	Nov	86-10	86-16	-1-10	9.42
8⅜	2003-08	Aug	90-15	90-21	-1-12	9.43
8¾	2003-08	Nov	93-24	93-30	-1-12	9.43
9⅛	2004-09	May	96-28	97-02	-1-16	9.45
10⅜	2004-09	Nov	106-15	106-21	-1-20	9.54
11¾	2005-10	Feb	117-21	117-27	-1-19	9.54
10	2005-10	May	103-18	103-24	-1-19	9.54
12¾	2005-10	Nov	126-06	126-12	-1-29	9.55
13⅞	2006-11	May	135-28	136-02	-2-04	9.55
14	2006-11	Nov	137-14	137-20	-2-04	9.55
10⅜	2007-12	Nov	107-03	107-09	-1-22	9.53
12	2008-13	Aug	121-08	121-14	-2-01	9.55
13¼	2009-14	May	132-24	132-30	-2-06	9.54
12½	2009-14	Aug k	126-07	126-13	-2-04	9.54
11¾	2009-14	Nov k	120-04	120-10	-2-04	9.49
11¼	2015	Feb k	117-31	118-05	-2-03	9.37
10⅝	2015	Aug k	112-03	112-09	-2-03	9.36
9⅞	2015	Nov	104-20	104-26	-2-03	9.38
9¼	2016	Feb k	98-18	98-24	-2-04	9.38
7¼	2016	May k	79-10	79-14	-1-19	9.35
7½	2016	Nov k	81-22	81-26	-1-22	9.35
8¾	2017	May k	93-27	93-31	-2-01	9.36
8⅞	2017	Aug k	95-10	95-14	-1-28	9.33
9⅛	2018	May k	97-26	97-30	-2-01	9.33
9	2018	Nov	96-21	96-25	-2-01	9.32
8⅞	2019	Feb k	95-19	95-23	-1-30	9.30

U.S. Treas. Bills

Mat. date	Bid (Discount)	Asked (Discount)	Yield
-1989-			
3-23	8.31	8.19	8.31
3-30	8.61	8.54	8.68
4- 6	8.41	8.34	8.49
4-13	8.33	8.21	8.37
4-20	8.96	8.89	9.08
4-27	8.96	8.92	9.13
5- 4	8.94	8.90	9.13
5-11	9.06	8.99	9.23
5-18	8.88	8.84	9.09
5-25	8.91	8.87	9.14
6- 1	8.88	8.84	9.13
6- 8	8.88	8.84	9.14
6-15	8.86	8.83	9.15
6-22	8.86	8.82	9.15
6-29	8.83	8.79	9.14
7- 6	8.91	8.87	9.24
7-13	8.89	8.85	9.23
7-20	8.94	8.90	9.30
7-27	8.93	8.89	9.31
8- 3	8.96	8.92	9.36
8-10	8.94	8.90	9.35
8-17	8.90	8.86	9.33
8-24	8.90	8.86	9.34
8-31	8.95	8.91	9.42
9- 7	8.95	8.91	9.43
9-14	8.93	8.89	9.43
9-28	8.96	8.92	9.47
10-26	8.98	8.94	9.51
11-24	9.01	8.97	9.57
12-21	8.94	8.90	9.53
-1990-			
1-18	8.94	8.90	9.57
2-15	8.94	8.90	9.62
3-15	8.94	8.90	9.67

Source: *The Wall Street Journal*, March 20, 1989

10⅜	2004-09	Nov.............	106-15	106-21	−1-20	9.54
11¾	2005-10	Feb.............	117-21	117-27	−1-19	9.54
10	2005-10	May............	103-18	103-24	−1-19	9.54
12¾	2005-10	Nov.............	126-06	126-12	−1-29	9.55
13⅞	2006-11	May............	135-28	136-02	−2-04	9.55
14	2006-11	Nov.............	137-14	137-20	−2-04	9.55
10⅜	2007-12	Nov.............	107-03	107-09	−1-22	9.53
12	2008-13	Aug.............	121-08	121-14	−2-01	9.55
13¼	2009-14	May............	132-24	132-30	−2-06	9.54
12½	2009-14	Aug k...........	126-07	126-13	−2-04	9.54

A 12 3/4 bond pays $127.50 per $1,000 bond.

Source: *The Wall Street Journal*, March 20, 1989.

$127.50 per $1,000 bond. If in 2005 the current interest rates fall to 10 percent, the Treasury can redeem the 12¾ 2005-10 bonds and reissue new securities with lower coupon payments, thus reducing the Treasury's annual coupon obligation.

The letter *n* following the month indicates that the security was issued as a note, and the letter *p* describes a note that is not subject to withholding tax if purchased by nonresident aliens. (The letter *k* describes the same status for bond issues.) All other issues are bonds. You will notice that in the Monday, March 20, 1989 example, there are no *n*'s or *p*'s after February 1999 because no notes are issued with maturities greater than 10 years. The bond issues that mature in less than 10 years (those with no letter or with a *k* following the month) are seasoned issues, sold sometime in the past. Remember that the listings with short maturity dates may have been issued long ago.

The fourth (*Bid*) and fifth (*Asked*) columns represent the prices buyers were bidding or offering and sellers were asking. The price quoted is a percentage of par ($1,000) value, with the number after the hyphen representing 32nds. Thus a price of 100–01 for the March 1989, 11¼ note, means that at 4 p.m. March 17, 1989, buyers were willing to pay 100⅟32 percent of the par value, or $1,000.313 (100 + 0.03125 percent of par, or $1,000 × 1.0003125). Whenever the price exceeds par value, the security is trading at a *premium;* securities priced below par are trading at a *discount*. The second to last column is the change in bid price, expressed in 32nds, from the previous trading day. The last column is the yield to maturity. This yield is calculated using a complex yield-to-maturity formula that most would have a difficult time computing. You can obtain a rough estimate of the yield to maturity by using an approximate yield-to-maturity formula:

Take the 7⅞ March 1992 note yielding 9.81 percent as an example.

Approximate yield to maturity

$$= \frac{\text{Annual coupon payment} + \left(\text{Face value} - \text{Market price}\right) \,/\, \text{\# years to maturity}}{(\text{Face value} + \text{Market value})/2}$$

$$= \frac{\$78.75 + (\$1{,}000 - \$949.06)/3}{(\$1{,}000 + \$949.06)/2}$$

$$= \frac{95.73}{974.53}$$

$$= 9.82\%$$

In this particular example the approximate yield to maturity almost exactly equals the actual yield to maturity. That will not always be true; the formula may be slightly off. But it nonetheless offers a good approximation.

Why do securities sell at premiums (prices that rise above the par value of $1,000) and discounts (prices that fall below par)? Once again, market forces provide the answer. The yield on seasoned Treasuries, which is determined both by coupon rate and price, must keep pace with new issues of similar maturity. For example, if the Treasury issues new 10-year notes with a 12 percent coupon rate, buyers of older Treasury securities will pay prices that reflect the yield which can be obtained on the new issue. A seasoned bond that also matures in ten years but has lower coupon payments (say 10 percent), will sell for a lower price to compensate for its lower coupon payment. On the other hand, a buyer will pay a premium (price above par) to purchase older securities with coupon payments greater (say 14 percent) than those currently offered in

8½	1991	Nov p..............	96-29	97-01–	13	9.79
14¼	1991	Nov n..............	110-28	111 –	17	9.45
8¼	1991	Dec k..............	96-02	96-06–	17	9.84
11⅝	1992	Jan p..............	104-05	104-09–	17	9.84
6⅝	1992	Feb p..............	92	92-04–	14	9.80
9⅛	1992	Feb p..............	98-12	98-16–	17	9.72
14⅝	1992	Feb n..............	112-13	112-17–	17	9.58
7⅞	1992	Mar p..............	94-29	95-01–	17	9.81
11¾	1992	Apr................	104-27	104-31–	16	9.83
6⅝	1992	May k..............	91-10	91-14–	17	9.84
13¾	1992	May n..............	110-12	110-16–	17	9.79
8¼	1992	Jun p..............	95-18	95-22–	18	9.81

← The 7 7/8 1992 March note yields 9.81 percent.

Source: *The Wall Street Journal*, March 20, 1989.

the primary market. Thus, the yield a note or bond offers is a reflection of both the coupon rate of the security and the price paid for the security.

To illustrate this, note that two Treasury notes with similar maturity dates can pay markedly different coupon rates, although they have similar yields. For example, the $8\frac{1}{8}$, May 1990 *p* note yields 9.92 percent whereas the $11\frac{3}{8}$, May 1990 *p* note yields 9.94 percent. Why is there so little difference in the yields when there is a large difference in the coupon payments? Because these notes have different prices. The $8\frac{1}{8}$ note's coupon is less than that offered by new issues and therefore sells at a discount price of $97\frac{28}{32}$ or $978.75 for a $1,000 note. The $11\frac{3}{8}$ note, on the other hand, offers a coupon greater than that currently offered on new issues, so the buyer will pay a premium price of $101\frac{12}{32}$ or $1,013.75. Thus, differing prices will ensure that Treasury bonds and notes with similar maturity dates and features will have similar yields whether or not the coupon is markedly different.

Treasury bonds are almost risk-free to maturity, but you do run the risk of loss if you must sell your bonds before they mature. Suppose you purchased the $9\frac{1}{8}$ May 2004-09 bond issue for $100\frac{22}{32}$ of par in the secondary market on Monday, January 30, 1989. (See the excerpt from the January 31, 1989 issue of *the Wall Street Journal.*) A million dollars (face or par value) of these bonds would have cost you $1,006,875.

Now suppose that instead of holding your bonds until maturity, you realize on March 17, that you owe more taxes than anticipated and you must sell the bonds to cover this unexpected expense. On March 17, 1989, the market price was $96\frac{28}{32}$ ($968.75), which means the bonds you bought for $1,006,875 will now sell for $968,750, or a loss of $38,125.

In a different scenario, suppose there were no problem with your tax situation and on April 26, 1989 an attractive investment appeared that prompted you to liquidate your bond holdings. On that day, the price was $100\frac{1}{32}$ of par, or $1,000,312.50, for a loss of only $6,562.50.

On the other hand, if another investor had purchased the same bonds

---

Similar Maturity Dates, May 1990
Different Rates, 8 1/8 and 11 3/8%
have similar yields: 9.92 & 9.94%

$8\frac{1}{8}$	1990	May p............	97-28	98	– 08	9.92
$11\frac{3}{8}$	1990	May p............	101-12	101-16	– 08	9.94

Source: *The Wall Street Journal*, January 31, 1989.

8¾	2003-08	Nov............	97-15	97-21–	13	9.00	
9⅛	2004-09	May...........	100-22	100-28–	15	9.02	← Price of $1,000,000 bonds on January 30, 1989: $1,006,875.00
10⅜	2004-09	Nov............	110-30	111-04–	17	9.04	
11¾	2005-10	Feb............	122-11	122-17–	15	9.06	

8¾	2003-08	Nov............	93-24	93-30–	1-12	9.43	
9⅛	2004-09	May...........	96-28	97-02–	1-16	9.45	← Price of $1,000,000 bonds on March 17, 1989: $968,750.00
10⅜	2004-09	Nov............	106-15	106-21–	1-20	9.54	
11¾	2005-10	Feb............	117-21	117-27–	1-19	9.54	
10	2005-10	May...........	103-18	103-24–	1-19	9.54	

9⅛	2004-09	May...........	100-01	100-07–	02	9.10	← Price of $1,000,000 bonds on April 26, 1989: $1,000,312.00

Source: *The Wall Street Journal*, January 31, 1989, March 20 1989, and April 27, 1989, respectively.

on March 17, 1989 for $968,750 and sold them on April 26, 1989 for $1,000,312.50, he or she would have earned a profit of $31,562.50. You can now see why many investors speculate on falling yields and rising prices.

Bond prices converge on par and fluctuate very little as the maturity date approaches. Thus, bonds with the longest time to maturity offer the greatest opportunities for speculation and the greatest risk of loss.

Investor's Tip

- Bonds are a good investment in low inflation times because falling interest rates send bond prices upward.
- Unload your bonds when inflation threatens because rising interest rates will depress bond prices.

Since fluctuations in market interest rates are crucial in determining the value of your investment, make a habit of tracking **Key Interest Rates** in Tuesday's *Wall Street Journal* (check the last section's index). See Tuesday, March 14, 1989's report for the week ending March 10, 1989.

The Treasury is not the only government agency that has issued long-term debt. A number of others have also been granted the authority. The *Journal* publishes a **Government & Agency Issues** report daily which you can find using the front–page index of the first or last sections (under Treasury). The Tuesday, March 14, 1989 edition covered Monday, March 13, 1989 trading activity for these agencies: FNMA, Federal Farm Credit, Student Loan Marketing, Federal Land Bank, Federal Home Loan Bank, World Bank Bonds, GNMA, and InterAmerican Development Bank. The columns read **Rate, Mat., Bid, Asked,** and **Yld** and provide the same information as Treasury securities.

FNMA (called "Fannie Mae") stands for the Federal National Mortgage Association, a publicly owned corporation sponsored by the federal government and established to provide a liquid market for mortgage investors. Fannie Mae buys mortgages from mortgage bankers and other mortgage writers, earning the interest payments made by homeowners and paying for these mortgages with the sale of bonds (debentures) to investors in $10,000 and $5,000 denominations. Pension funds, insurance companies, mutual funds, and other large institutional investors are the principal purchasers of these bonds, which are called Fannie Maes.

Key Interest Rates

Annualized interest rates on certain investments as reported by the Federal Reserve Board on a weekly-average basis:

	Week Ended:	
	Mar. 10, 1989	Mar. 3, 1989
Treasury bills (90 day)-a	8.64	8.67
Commrcl paper (Dealer, 90 day)-a	9.82	9.88
Certfs of Deposit (Resale, 90 day)	9.94	10.00
Federal funds (Overnight)-b	9.83	9.80
Eurodollars (90 day)-b	10.03	10.03
Treasury bills (one year)-c	9.39	9.40
Treasury notes (three year)-c	9.43	9.43
Treasury notes (five year)-c	9.37	9.42
Treasury notes (ten year)-c	9.27	9.33
Treasury bonds (30 year)-c	9.09	9.15

a-Discounted rates. b-Week ended Wednesday, March 8, 1989 and Wednesday March 1, 1989. c-Yields, adjusted for constant maturity.

Source: *The Wall Street Journal*, March 14, 1989.

GOVERNMENT & AGENCY ISSUES

Monday, March 13, 1989

Mid-afternoon Over-the-Counter quotations usually based on large transactions, sometimes $1 million or more.

Hyphens in bid-and-asked represent 32nds; 101-01 means 101 1/32. a-Plus 1/64. b-Yield to call date. d-Minus 1/64.

Source: Bloomberg Financial Markets

"Fannie Mae"

FNMA Issues

Rate	Mat	Bid	Asked	Yld
7.55	4-89	99-21	99-27	9.42
9.30	6-89	99-24	99-28	9.60
9.50	6-89	99-28	99-31	9.40
8.00	7-89	99-05	99-15	9.56
10.05	8-89	99-29	100-04	9.64
13.13	8-89	101-01	101-09	9.72
12.10	10-89	100-31	101-05	9.94
12.65	3-14	110-19	110-29	9.83
0.00	7-14	10-10	10-20	9.06
10.35	12-15	107-17	107-27	9.53
8.20	3-16	86-20	86-30	9.56
8.95	2-18	93-30	94-08	9.54
0.00	10-19	6-21	6-30	8.92

Federal Farm Credit

Federal Farm Credit

Rate	Mat	Bid	Asked	Yld
8.45	4-89	99-28	99-31	8.72
9.00	4-89	99-29	100-01	8.26
12.50	4-89	100-07	100-12	8.30
8.30	5-89	99-22	99-26	9.46
8.88	5-89	99-27	99-30	9.26
7.35	6-89	99-12	99-15	9.68
7.90	6-89	99-16	99-19	9.62
8.85	6-89	99-23	99-27	9.36
9.25	6-89	99-25	99-29	9.67
9.25	7-89	99-26	99-30	9.29
13.70	7-89	101-14	101-20	8.74
8.38	8-89	99-10	99-13	9.89
9.20	8-89	99-23	99-27	9.52
7.75	9-89	98-25	98-31	10.00
8.75	9-89	99-11	99-15	9.92
9.50	9-89	99-22	99-26	9.89
8.65	10-89	99-06	99-10	9.95
10.60	10-89	100-05	100-11	9.97
15.65	10-89	102-31	103-09	9.90
12.45	10-89	101-07	101-13	9.97
8.45	11-89	98-30	99-02	9.99
8.95	12-89	99-05	99-09	9.98
9.30	1-90	99-12	99-16	9.93
10.95	1-90	100-18	100-28	9.83
11.15	1-90	100-28	101-01	9.83
9.15	2-90	99-06	99-10	9.96
10.85	2-90	100-18	100-23	9.95
9.60	3-90	99-18	99-22	9.94
11.35	4-90	101-12	101-18	9.80
14.10	6-90	104-12	104-21	9.90
8.30	7-90	97-29	98-01	9.93
9.55	7-90	99-15	99-21	9.81
10.40	7-90	100-11	100-17	9.95
12.50	9-90	103-14	103-24	9.70
8.80	10-90	98-14	98-18	9.82
10.60	10-90	100-27	101-01	9.88
7.65	3-91	95-27	96-01	9.92
7.55	4-91	95-17	95-23	9.84
14.10	4-91	108-01	108-07	9.68
9.10	7-91	97-30	98-08	9.94
14.70	7-91	109-22	110	9.82
10.60	10-91	101-02	101-12	9.98
13.65	12-91	108-21	108-31	9.79
11.50	1-92	103-19	103-29	9.88
15.20	1-92	113-26	114	9.47
13.75	7-92	110-20	110-30	9.83
10.65	1-93	103-07	103-17	9.52
11.80	10-93	107-11	107-21	9.69
12.35	3-94	110-25	110-31	9.52
14.25	4-94	118-20	118-26	9.50
13.00	9-94	114-05	114-15	9.54
11.45	12-94	107-22	108	9.59
11.90	10-97	112-25	113-03	9.62
9.63	10-98	98-14	98-18	9.86

"Sallie Mae"

Student Loan Marketing

Rate	Mat	Bid	Asked	Yld
8.00	6-89	99-13	99-17	9.48
7.90	7-89	99-10	99-14	9.62
12.85	9-89	101-11	101-17	9.38
13.15	9-89	101-11	101-17	9.66
10.90	2-90	100-22	100-26	9.98
6.95	8-90	95-22	96	10.01
7.90	9-90	96-29	97-07	9.92
8.45	12-90	97-07	97-17	10.04
7.63	2-91	95-18	95-28	10.05
8.55	5-91	96-27	97-05	10.00
7.75	6-91	95-09	95-19	10.01
7.60	6-91	94-29	95-07	10.03
5.60	8-91	90-16	90-26	10.03
8.00	8-91	95-20	95-30	9.95
9.45	2-92	98-08	98-18	10.03
9.50	2-92	98-12	98-22	10.02
8.25	6-92	95-04	95-22	9.81
9.25	9-92	97-25	98-03	9.91
9.25	9-92	97-25	98-03	9.91
8.80	12-92	97-09	97-19	9.58
9.47	2-93	97-31	98-17	9.93
10.50	4-93	102-25	103-03	9.57
7.35	5-93	91-17	91-27	9.79
8.20	5-93	94-11	94-21	9.78
9.38	2-94	97-15	97-25	9.95
8.50	7-94	94-12	94-16	9.85
0.00	11-94	57-14	58	9.91
7.75	12-96	88-24	88-30	9.81
7.63	1-97	87-29	88-03	9.83
9.50	9-97	99-01	99-19	9.57
9.34	7-98	96-17	96-23	9.88
9.78	1-98	98-30	99-02	9.93
9.80	9-00	98-27	98-31	9.95
0.00	5-14	9-05	9-15	9.59
0.00	10-22	5-21	5-31	8.58

Federal Land Bank

Rate	Mat	Bid	Asked	Yld
8.20	1-90	98-10	98-16	10.05
7.95	4-91	96-05	96-15	9.84
7.95	10-96	90-08	90-18	9.73
7.35	1-97	87-10	87-20	9.63

FHL Bank

Fed. Home Loan Bank

Rate	Mat	Bid	Asked	Yld
6.90	3-89	99-26	99-29	9.21
7.45	3-89	99-25	99-30	8.88
9.05	3-89	99-29	100	8.88
6.90	4-89	99-11	99-21	9.69
7.35	4-89	99-20	99-23	9.57
7.38	4-89	99-20	99-23	9.60
8.95	4-89	99-29	100	8.84
9.40	12-92	98-23	98-29	9.74
9.35	1-93	98-17	98-21	9.77
10.70	1-93	102-25	103-03	9.71
9.50	1-93	98-31	99-09	9.72
8.05	2-93	94-23	95-01	9.59
8.10	3-93	94-25	94-31	9.63
10.80	3-93	103-23	104-01	9.57
7.55	4-93	92-07	92-17	9.79
8.13	5-93	94-11	94-21	9.70
8.90	5-93	97-03	97-09	9.70
10.75	5-93	103-07	103-17	9.70
7.75	7-93	92-25	93-03	9.72
9.00	7-93	97-17	97-21	9.66
11.70	7-93	106-15	106-21	9.78
7.45	8-93	91-13	91-23	9.79
9.38	8-93	98-11	98-21	9.75
11.95	8-93	107-11	107-21	9.78
7.95	9-93	93-19	93-25	9.67
7.88	10-93	93-01	93-11	9.69
8.80	10-93	96-25	96-31	9.62
7.38	11-93	90-27	91-05	9.76
9.13	11-93	97-25	97-31	9.67
7.38	12-93	90-31	91-05	9.72
9.55	12-93	98-17	98-27	9.85
12.15	12-93	109-07	109-13	9.64
9.60	2-94	98-29	99-07	9.80
7.30	1-94	90-05	90-11	9.84
7.45	2-94	90-19	90-25	9.85
12.00	2-94	109-02	109-08	9.60
8.50	4-94	94-18	95-04	9.73
8.88	6-95	95-21	95-25	9.78
10.00	6-95	100-21	100-31	9.78
10.30	7-95	102-09	102-15	9.76
9.50	12-95	98-17	98-21	9.77
8.10	3-96	91-15	91-21	9.77
7.75	4-96	89-14	89-20	9.81
8.25	5-96	92-02	92-08	9.77
8.25	6-96	92-02	92-08	9.76
8.00	7-96	90-23	90-29	9.76
7.70	8-96	89-02	89-08	9.76
8.25	9-96	91-24	91-30	9.79
7.88	2-97	89-23	90-01	9.70
7.65	3-97	88-21	88-27	9.68
9.20	8-97	98-04	98-14	9.47
9.25	11-98	96-24	96-28	9.75
9.30	1-99	97-04	97-08	9.74
9.50	2-04	98-13	98-17	9.69

World Bank Bonds

World Bank Bonds

Rate	Mat	Bid	Asked	Yld
11.00	10-89	100-20	101-04	9.82
4.50	2-90	95-01	95-17	9.03
5.38	7-91	91-29	92-05	8.94
16.63	11-91	115-31	116-15	9.57
15.13	12-91	115-10	115-26	9.23
5.38	4-92	88-31	89-15	9.28
14.75	6-92	113-18	114-02	9.70
13.63	9-92	110-15	110-31	9.96
10.90	3-93	105-02	105-18	9.43
10.38	5-93	101-01	101-17	10.06
5.88	9-93	86-19	87-03	9.43
6.50	3-94	89-08	89-24	9.10
6.38	10-94	87-27	88-11	9.10
11.63	12-94	107-28	108-20	9.79
8.63	8-95	94-15	95-07	9.81
8.13	8-96	91-10	92-02	9.81
9.88	10-97	101	101-05	9.70
9.35	12-00	96-06	96-22	9.90
8.85	7-01	94-23	95-02	9.58
8.38	12-01	90-03	90-13	9.75
8.25	5-02	89	89-11	9.75
8.35	8-02	89-20	90-20	9.75
12.38	10-02	120-24	121-24	9.61
8.25	9-16	86-24	87-03	9.63
8.63	10-16	89-22	90-30	9.70
9.25	7-17	95-30	96-13	9.67
8.88	3-26	92-01	92-16	9.67

"Ginnie Mae"

GNMA Issues

Rate	Mat	Bid	Asked	Yld
8.00		86-19	86-23	10.15
8.50		89-10	89-14	10.24
9.00		91-31	92-03	10.35
9.50		94-17	94-21	10.47
10.00		97-05	97-09	10.57
10.50		99-18	99-22	10.71
11.00		101-28	102	10.87
11.50		103-18	103-22	11.11
12.00		105-05	105-09	11.37
12.50		106-25	106-31	11.60
13.00		108-15	108-21	11.84
13.50		110-16	110-22	12.01
14.00		111-13	111-17	12.37
15.00		112-07	112-11	11.85

Inter-Amer. Devel. Bk.

Rate	Mat	Bid	Asked	Yld
14.63	8-92	113-06	113-22	9.91
12.13	10-93	107-19	107-31	10.00
13.25	8-94	113-17	113-31	9.95
11.63	12-94	108-01	108-25	9.75
11.38	5-95	106-19	107-11	9.91
7.50	12-96	87-27	88-06	9.77
9.50	10-97	100-09	100-16	9.40
9.00	2-01	94-23	95-14	9.76
8.38	6-02	89-20	90-20	9.79
9.63	1-04	97-30	98-14	9.89
12.25	12-08	121-22	122-06	9.75
8.50	3-11	89-11	89-24	9.68

Source: *The Wall Street Journal*, March 14, 1989.

The **Federal Farm Credit Agency** assists farmers by helping financial institutions, such as small commercial banks and savings and loan associations (S&Ls), provide credit to farmers for the purchase and sale of commodities and the financing of buildings and new equipment. It is an independent agency of the U.S. Government primarily funded by short-term debt, although it also issues longer-term notes that trade in the secondary market and are listed in the report.

Federal Land Banks are privately owned organizations, backed by the federal government and organized to finance agricultural activities. They primarily provide first mortgage loans on farm properties with original maturities of around 20 years and fund these mortgages by issuing Consolidated Federal Farm Loan Bonds. The Federal Farm Credit Agency examines the activities of the Federal Land Bank.

The Federal Home Loan Bank (FHLB) is a federally chartered, privately owned company charged with regulating the S & L industry. The FHLB borrows by issuing bonds in $10,000 denominations to provide funds to weaker S & Ls with temporary liquidity problems.

Student Loan Marketing ("Sallie Mae") is a privately owned, government-sponsored corporation that provides a secondary market for government-guaranteed student loans. Sallie Mae sells bonds to investors to raise funds for the purchase of these student loans from financial institututions. The yields on these issues tend to be higher than other government agency issues because of the higher risk of default on student loans.

World Bank Bonds are debt instruments issued by the International Bank for Reconstruction and Development (World Bank) to finance its lending activities to less-developed countries.

GNMA ("Ginnie Mae"), the Government National Mortgage Association, is a government-owned corporation that purchases, packages, and resells mortgages and mortgage purchase commitments in the form of mortgage-backed securities called Ginnie Maes. Each Ginnie Mae bond is backed by a package of residential mortgages, and the holder of a GNMA bond thereby owns a portion of these underlying mortgages. New GNMA bonds cost $25,000, but older, partially repaid GNMAs can cost as little as $5,000.

Mortgage payments of interest and principal are "passed through" to the Ginnie Mae holders. Thus, unlike holders of Treasuries, who receive their principal at maturity, investors in Ginnie Maes are paid interest and principal each month.

Ginnie Maes don't have stated maturity dates because the bond's flow of income depends on the repayment of the underlying mortgages. If all homeowners pay their mortgages regularly for the mortgage's life, with no prepayments, the Ginnie Mae holder receives regular monthly checks for 30 years. However, a homeowner may choose to pay off his or her mortgage prior to maturity, or may pay additional principal in some months. The prepayment or excess principal payments are passed through to the Ginnie Mae holder, who receives a larger monthly check. This prepayment reduces the subsequent monthly payments and the Ginnie Mae's par value.

Ginnie Maes offer higher rates than Treasury bonds because of the unpredictable nature of interest and principal payments. The U.S. Treasury backs these government bonds to remove the risk of homeowner default.

Finally, you can see the mortgage interest rates associated with the various Ginnie Mae pools, as well as the range of prices that determine these bonds' yields.

CORPORATE BONDS

Corporations are the second principal issuer of long-term debt and, like the government and government agencies, issue credit instruments in order to finance long-term needs.

You may wish to purchase or keep track of a particular corporate bond. If this bond is traded on the New York Stock Exchange, you will find it listed in *The Wall Street Journal* under **New York Exchange Bonds**. Consult the front page of the first or last section for the daily listing. An example from the Tuesday, March 14, 1989 issue is on page 241. (American Stock Exchange Bonds appear under **AMEX BONDS** on page 243.)

The top portion of the New York Exchange Bonds quotations provides important information about the previous trading day. **Volume** is the par value of bonds traded on Monday, March 13, 1989, even though bond prices fluctuate from par. On March 13, 1989, $26,320,000 worth of bonds traded, on this exchange—only a fraction of all the bonds traded on that day because most bonds are traded over the counter and directly among market makers (mostly brokerage houses) on behalf of institutional investors and not on any organized exchange. Thus, the NYSE generally deals in small lots of bonds on behalf of individuals.

Issues traded lists the number of different bonds sold on that day. **Advances** is the number of bonds that traded at a price higher than the previous day; **Declines** is the number that traded at a price below the previous trading day's, and **Unchanged** is the number of those whose price did not change. **New highs** lists the number trading at all-time highs.

Dow Jones Bond Averages is a straight arithmetic summary and average of 20 selected utility and industrial bonds.

If you wish to follow the performance of a particular bond, consider the following illustration from the Tuesday, March 14, 1989 edition.

Bonds	*Cur Yld*	*Vol.*	*Close*	*Net Chg.*
AT&T 5 5/8 95	7.0	60	80 1/2	. . .
Fruf 13 1/2 96	18.8	9	72	. . .

(A *cv* in the current yield column indicates a convertible bond that gives the holder the option of converting the bond into some other form of security, generally common stock.)

In the case of the AT&T bond shown above, the coupon rate at issue per $1,000 bond (5⅝ percent) and the year of maturity (1995, the year the bond is due for redemption) follow the company's name. (You'll find an *s* after the interest rate when a fraction is absent.)

Corporate bonds are issued in denominations of $1,000, and this particular AT&T bond originally paid an annual fixed-dollar interest return of $56.25 (5⅝ percent of $1,000 = $56.25). Thus, AT&T promised to pay the bearer $56.25 a year until it redeemed the bond at maturity.

You can see from the next column that the current yield is 7 percent. How can that be true if the bonds were issued at 5⅝ percent? For the answer, remember the earlier Treasury bond discussion of prevailing Treasury rates. Look at the columns following the volume column. (Volume is reported in thousands of dollars—60 bonds with a face value of $1,000 were traded on March 13, 1989.) You can see the closing prices for the day. Since bonds are issued in deniminations of $1,000, the reported prices are a percentage of the face value of $1,000. Thus,

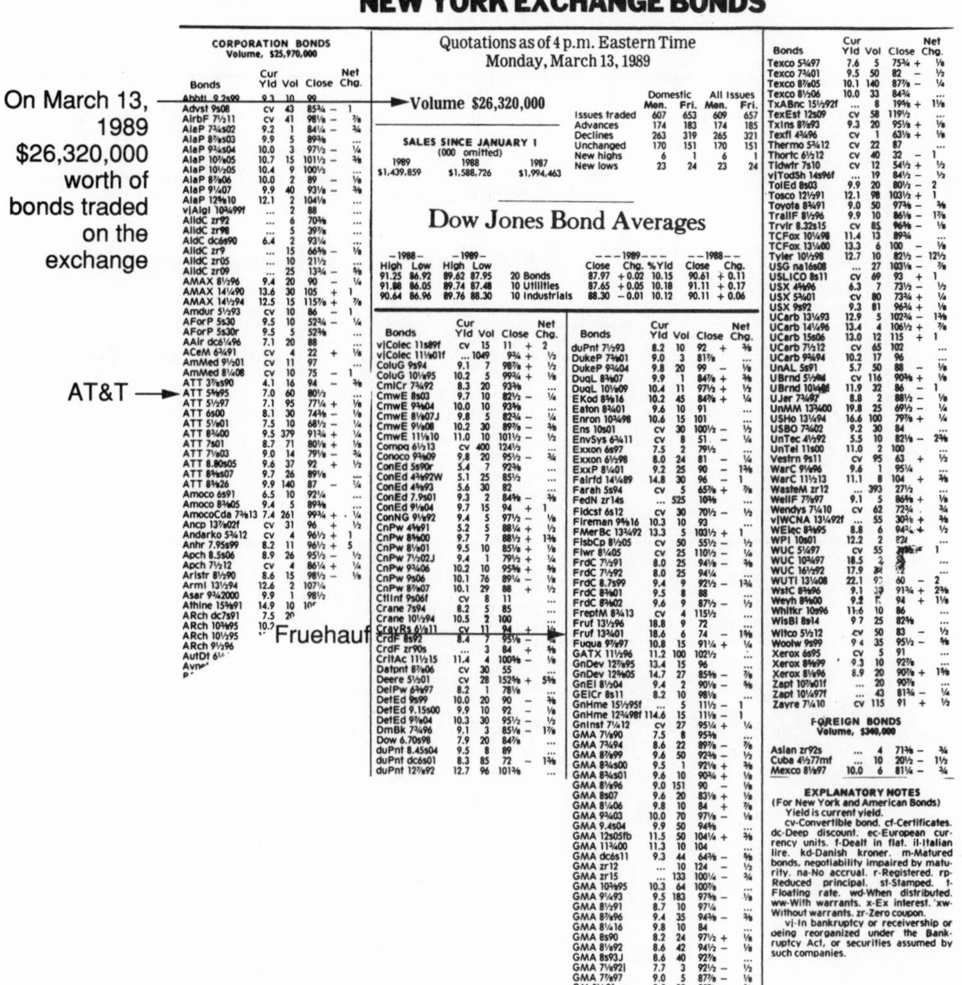
On March 13, 1989 $26,320,000 worth of bonds traded on the exchange
AT&T
Fruehauf

NEW YORK EXCHANGE BONDS

Quotations as of 4 p.m. Eastern Time
Monday, March 13, 1989

CORPORATION BONDS
Volume, $25,970,000

Bonds	Cur Yld	Vol	Close	Net Chg.
Abbtl 9.2s99	9.3	10	99	
Advst 9s08	cv	43	85¾	− 1
AirbF 7½11	cv	41	98⅛	− ⅞
AlaP 7¾s02	9.2	1	84¼	− ¾
AlaP 8⅞s03	9.9	5	89⅜	...
AlaP 9¾s04	10.0	3	97½	− ¼
AlaP 10⅞s05	10.7	15	101½	− ⅜
AlaP 10½05	10.4	9	100½	...
AlaP 8⅞06	10.0	2	89	− ⅛
AlaP 9¼07	9.9	40	93⅛	− ⅜
AlaP 12⅝10	12.1	2	104⅛	...
vjAlgl 10¾99f	...	2	88	...
AlldC zr92	...	6	70⅜	...
AlldC zr98	...	5	39⅞	...
AldC dc6s90	6.4	2	93¼	...
AlldC zr9	...	15	66⅝	− ⅛
AlldC zr05	...	10	21½	...
AlldC zr09	...	25	13¾	− ⅝
AMAX 8½96	9.4	20	90	− ¼
AMAX 14¼90	13.6	30	105	+ 1
AMAX 14½94	12.5	15	115⅞	+ ⅞
Amdur 5½93	cv	10	86	− 1
AForP 5s30	9.5	10	52¾	− ¼
AForP 5s30r	9.5	5	52⅜	...
AAir dc6¼96	7.1	20	88	...
ACeM 6¾91	cv	4	22	+ ⅛
AmMed 9½01	cv	11	97	...
AmMed 8¼08	cv	10	75	− 1
ATT 3⅞s90	4.1	16	94	− ⅜
ATT 5⅝95	7.0	60	80½	...
ATT 5½97	7.1	95	77¼	+ ⅛
ATT 6s00	8.1	30	74⅜	− ⅛
ATT 5⅛01	7.5	10	68½	− ¼
ATT 8¾00	9.5	379	91¾	+ ¼
ATT 7s01	8.7	71	80⅛	+ ⅛
ATT 7⅛03	9.0	14	79⅛	− ¾
ATT 8.80s05	9.6	37	92	+ ½
ATT 8⅝s07	9.7	26	89⅛	...
ATT 8⅝26	9.9	140	87	− ¼
Amoco 6s91	6.5	10	92¼	...
Amoco 8⅜05	9.4	5	89⅜	...
AmocoCda 7⅜13	7.4	261	99¾	+ ¼
Ancp 13⅞02f	cv	31	96	+ ½
Andarko 5¾12	cv	4	96½	+ 1
Anhr 7.95s99	8.2	11	96½	+ 5
Apch 8.5s06	8.9	26	95½	− ½
Apch 7½12	cv	4	86¼	+ ¼
Aristr 8½90	8.6	15	98½	− ⅛
Arml 13½94	12.6	2	107¼	
Asar 9¾2000	9.9	1	98½	
Athlne 15⅝91	14.9	10	10	
ARch dc7s91	7.5	20		
ARch 10⅜95	10.2			
ARch 10½95				
ARch 9½96				
AutDt 6¼				
Avne				

Volume $26,320,000

SALES SINCE JANUARY 1
(000 omitted)

1989	1988	1987
$1,439,859	$1,588,726	$1,994,463

	Domestic Mon.	Domestic Fri.	All Issues Mon.	All Issues Fri.
Issues traded	607	653	609	657
Advances	174	183	174	185
Declines	263	319	265	321
Unchanged	170	151	170	151
New highs	6	1	6	1
New lows	23	24	23	24

Dow Jones Bond Averages

−1988− High	−1988− Low	−1989− High	−1989− Low		−1989− Close	−1989− Chg.	−1989− %Yld	−1988− Close	−1988− Chg.
91.25	86.92	89.62	87.95	20 Bonds	87.97	+0.02	10.15	90.61	+0.11
91.88	86.05	89.74	87.48	10 Utilities	87.65	+0.05	10.18	91.11	+0.17
90.64	86.96	89.76	88.30	10 Industrials	88.30	−0.01	10.12	90.11	+0.06

Bonds	Cur Yld	Vol	Close	Net Chg.
vjColec 11s89f	cv	15	11	+ 2
vjColec 11⅛01f	...	1049	9¾	+ ½
ColuG 9s94	9.1	7	98⅞	+ ½
ColuG 10⅛95	10.2	5	99¾	+ ⅛
CmlCr 7¾92	8.3	20	93⅜	...
CmwE 8s03	9.7	10	82½	− ¼
CmwE 9⅜04	10.0	10	93⅝	...
CmwE 8⅛07J	9.8	5	82¾	− ¼
CmwE 9⅛08	10.2	30	89⅞	− ⅜
CmwE 11⅛10	11.0	10	101½	− ½
Compq 6½13	cv	400	124½	...
Conoco 9⅜09	9.8	20	95½	− ¾
ConEd 5s90r	5.4	7	92⅜	...
ConEd 4⅜92W	5.1	25	85½	...
ConEd 4⅝93	5.6	30	82	...
ConEd 7.9s01	9.3	2	84⅝	− ⅜
ConEd 9⅛04	9.7	15	94	+ 1
ConNG 9⅛92	9.4	5	97½	− ⅛
CnPw 4⅝91	5.2	5	88¼	+ ½
CnPw 8⅝00	9.7	7	88½	+ 1⅜
CnPw 8⅛01	9.5	10	85⅛	+ ⅛
CnPw 7½02J	9.4	1	79½	+ ¼
CnPw 9¾06	10.2	10	95⅝	+ ⅝
CnPw 9s06	10.1	76	89¼	− ⅛
CnPw 8⅞07	10.1	29	88	+ ½
Ctllnf 9s06f	cv	8	11	...
Crane 7s94	8.2	5	85	...
Crane 10½94	10.5	2	100	...
CrayRs 6⅛11	cv	11	94	+ ½
CrdF 8s92	8.4	7	95⅛	− ¼
CrdF zr90s	...	3	84	+ ⅝
CritAc 11½15	11.4	4	100⅝	− ⅛
Datpnt 8⅞06	cv	30	55	...
Deere 5½01	cv	28	152⅝	+ 5⅝
DelPw 6⅜97	8.2	1	78⅛	...
DetEd 9s99	10.0	20	90	− ⅜
DetEd 9.15s00	9.9	10	92	− ⅛
DetEd 9⅞04	10.3	30	95½	− ½
DmBk 7¾96	9.1	3	85⅛	− 1⅞
Dow 6.70s98	7.9	20	84⅞	...
duPnt 8.45s04	9.5	8	89	...
duPnt dc6s01	8.3	85	72	− 1⅜
duPnt 12⅞92	12.7	96	101⅜	...
duPnt 7½93	8.2	10	92	+ ⅜
DukeP 7⅜01	9.0	3	81⅞	...
DukeP 9¾04	9.8	20	99	− ⅛
DuqL 8⅜07	9.9	1	84⅞	+ ⅜
DuqL 10⅛09	10.4	11	97½	+ ½
EKod 8⅝16	10.2	45	84⅞	+ ¼
Eaton 8¾01	9.6	10	91	...
Enron 10¾98	10.6	15	101	...
Ens 10s01	cv	30	100½	− ½
EnvSys 6¾11	cv	8	51	− ¼
Exxon 6s97	7.5	2	79½	...
Exxon 6½98	8.0	24	81	− ¼
ExxP 8¼01	9.2	25	90	− 1⅜
Fairfd 14¼89	14.8	30	96	− 1
Farah 5s94	cv	5	65⅞	+ ⅞
FedN zr14s	...	525	10⅜	...
Fldcst 6s12	cv	30	70½	− ½
Fireman 9⅝16	10.3	10	93	...
FMerBc 13¾92	13.3	5	103½	+ 1
FisbCp 8½05	cv	50	55½	− ½
Flwr 8¼05	cv	25	110½	− ¼
FrdC 7½91	8.0	25	94⅛	− ⅜
FrdC 7½92	8.0	25	94¼	...
FrdC 8.7s99	9.4	9	92½	− 1¾
FrdC 8⅜01	9.5	8	88	...
FrdC 8⅜02	9.6	9	87½	− ½
FreptM 8¾13	cv	4	115½	...
Fruf 13½96	18.8	9	72	...
Fruf 13¾01	18.6	6	74	− 1⅝
Fuqua 9⅞97	10.8	15	91¼	+ ¼
GATX 11½96	11.2	100	102½	...
GnDev 12⅞95	13.4	15	96	...
GnDev 12⅝05	14.7	27	85⅝	− ⅞
GnEl 8½04	9.4	2	90⅛	− ⅝
GElCr 8s11	8.2	10	98⅛	...
GnHme 15½95f	...	5	11½	− 1
GnHme 12¾98f	114.6	15	11⅛	− 1
GnInst 7¼12	cv	27	95¼	+ ¼
GMA 7⅛90	7.5	8	95⅜	...
GMA 7¾94	8.6	22	89⅞	− ⅞
GMA 8⅞99	9.6	50	92⅜	− ½
GMA 8¾s00	9.5	1	92⅛	+ ⅜
GMA 8¾s01	9.6	10	90¾	+ ⅛
GMA 8⅛96	9.0	151	90	− ⅛
GMA 8s07	9.6	20	83⅛	+ ⅛
GMA 8¼06	9.8	10	84	+ ⅞
GMA 9¾03	10.0	70	97⅛	− ⅛
GMA 9.4s04	9.9	50	94⅝	...
GMA 12s05fb	11.5	50	104¼	+ ⅜
GMA 11¾00	11.3	10	104	...
GMA dc6s11	9.3	44	64⅜	− ⅝
GMA zr12	...	10	124	− ½
GMA zr15	...	133	100¼	− ¾
GMA 10⅜95	10.3	64	100⅞	...
GMA 9¼93	9.5	183	97⅝	− ⅛
GMA 8½91	8.7	10	97¼	...
GMA 8⅞96	9.4	35	94⅜	− ⅜
GMA 8¼16	9.8	10	84	...
GMA 8s90	8.2	24	97½	+ ⅛
GMA 8⅛92	8.6	42	94½	− ⅛
GMA 8s93J	8.6	40	92⅞	...
GMA 7⅛92l	7.7	3	92½	− ½
GMA 7⅞97	9.0	5	87⅞	− ⅛
GM 8⅛91	8.5	38	95⅞	− ⅝
GTE 9⅜99	9.6	15	97⅜	− ¼

Bonds	Cur Yld	Vol	Close	Net Chg.
Texco 5¾97	7.6	5	75¾	+ ⅛
Texco 7¾01	9.5	50	82	− ½
Texco 8⅞05	10.1	140	87⅞	− ¼
Texco 8½06	10.0	33	84¾	...
TxABnc 15½92f	...	8	19⅝	+ 1⅛
TexEst 12s09	cv	58	119½	...
TxIns 8⅞93	9.3	20	95⅛	+ ⅛
Texfl 4¾96	cv	1	63⅛	+ ⅛
Thermo 5¾12	cv	22	87	...
Thortc 6½12	cv	40	32	− 1
Tidwtr 7s10	cv	12	54½	+ ½
vjTodSh 14s96f	...	19	84½	− ½
TolEd 8s03	9.9	20	80½	− 2
Tosco 12½91	12.1	98	103½	+ 1
Toyota 8¾91	9.0	50	97⅜	− ⅜
TrailF 8½96	9.9	10	86⅛	− 1⅞
Trvlr 8.32s15	cv	85	96⅝	− ⅛
TCFox 10¼98	11.4	13	89¾	...
TCFox 13¼00	13.3	6	100	− ⅛
Tyler 10½98	12.7	10	82½	− 12½
USG na16s08	...	27	103⅛	− ⅞
USLICO 8s11	cv	69	93	+ 1
USX 4⅝96	6.3	7	73½	− ½
USX 5¾01	cv	80	73¾	+ ¼
USX 9s92	9.3	81	96¾	+ ⅛
UCarb 13¼93	12.9	5	102¾	− 1⅜
UCarb 14¼96	13.4	4	106½	+ ⅞
UCarb 15s06	13.0	12	115	+ 1
UCarb 7½12	cv	65	102	...
UCarb 9¾94	10.2	17	96	...
UnAL 5s91	5.7	50	88	− ⅛
UBrnd 5½[illegible]	cv	116	90⅝	+ ⅛
UBrnd 10[illegible]	11.9	32	86	− 1
UJer 7¾97	8.8	2	88½	− ⅛
UnMM 13¾00	19.8	25	69½	− ¼
USHo 13¼94	16.6	100	79⅞	+ ¼
USBO 7¾02	9.2	30	84	...
UnTec 4½92	5.5	10	82⅛	− 2⅜
UnTel 11s00	11.0	2	100	...
Vestrn 9s11	cv	95	63	+ ½
WarC 9⅛96	9.6	1	95¼	...
WarC 11½13	11.1	8	104	+ ⅜
WasteM zr12	...	393	27½	...
WellF 7⅞97	9.1	5	86⅝	+ ⅛
Wendys 7¼10	cv	62	72¾	¾
vjWCNA 13¼92f	...	55	30⅜	+ ⅜
WElec 8⅜95	8.8	6	94¾	+ ½
WPI 10s01	12.2	2	82	...
WUC 5¼97	cv	55	[illegible]	1
WUC 10¾97	18.5	2	[illegible]	...
WUC 16½92	17.9	[illegible]	[illegible]	...
WUTI 13¼08	22.1	[illegible]	60	− 2
WstC 8⅜96	9.1	[illegible]	91¾	+ 2⅜
Weyh 8⅝00	9.2	[illegible]	94	+ 1⅛
Whitkr 10s96	11.6	10	86	...
WisBl 8s14	9.7	25	82⅝	...
Witco 5½12	cv	50	83	− ½
Woolw 9s99	9.4	35	95½	− ⅝
Xerox 6s95	cv	5	91	...
Xerox 8⅝99	9.3	10	92⅞	...
Xerox 8⅛96	8.9	20	90⅞	+ 1⅝
Zapt 10⅞01f	...	20	90⅞	...
Zapt 10¼97f	...	43	81¾	− ¼
Zayre 7¼10	cv	115	91	+ ½

FOREIGN BONDS
Volume, $340,000

Bonds	Cur Yld	Vol	Close	Net Chg.
Asian zr92s	...	4	71⅜	− ¾
Cuba 4½77mf	...	10	20½	− 1½
Mexco 8⅛97	10.0	6	81¼	− ¾

EXPLANATORY NOTES
(For New York and American Bonds)

Yield is current yield.

cv-Convertible bond. cf-Certificates. dc-Deep discount. ec-European currency units. f-Dealt in flat. il-Italian lire. kd-Danish kroner. m-Matured bonds, negotiability impaired by maturity. na-No accrual. r-Registered. rp-Reduced principal. st-Stamped. t-Floating rate. wd-When distributed. ww-With warrants. x-Ex interest. xw-Without warrants. zr-Zero coupon.

vj-In bankruptcy or receivership or being reorganized under the Bankruptcy Act, or securities assumed by such companies.

Source: *The Wall Street Journal*, March 14, 1989.

80½ means a price of $805 (80½ percent of $1,000 = $805). This bond was bought and sold for $805 at the day's close. The last column informs you that the March 13 closing price was no different from the previous close, as indicated by the three dots. Now, if you bought this bond on March 13, your yield would be 7 percent, not 5⅝ percent,

Quotations as of 4 p.m. Eastern Time
Monday, March 13, 1989

On March 13,1989 $26,320,000 worth of bonds traded on the exchange → **Volume $26,320,000**

SALES SINCE JANUARY 1
(000 omitted)

1989	1988	1987
$1,439,859	$1,588,726	$1,994,463

	Domestic Mon.	Domestic Fri.	All Issues Mon.	All Issues Fri.
Issues traded	607	653	609	657
Advances	174	183	174	185
Declines	263	319	265	321
Unchanged	170	151	170	151
New highs	6	1	6	1
New lows	23	24	23	24

Dow Jones Bond Averages

–1988– High	–1988– Low	–1989– High	–1989– Low		–1989– Close	–1989– Chg.	–1989– %Yld	–1988– Close	–1988– Chg.
91.25	86.92	89.62	87.95	20 Bonds	87.97	+0.02	10.15	90.61	+0.11
91.88	86.05	89.74	87.48	10 Utilities	87.65	+0.05	10.18	91.11	+0.17
90.64	86.96	89.76	88.30	10 Industrials	88.30	–0.01	10.12	90.11	+0.06

Source: *The Wall Street Journal*, March 14, 1989.

Amdur 5½93	cv	10	86	– 1
AForP 5s30	9.5	10	52¾	– ¼
AForP 5s30r	9.5	5	52⅜	...
AAir dc6¼96	7.1	20	88	...
ACeM 6¾91	cv	4	22	+ ⅛
AmMed 9½01	cv	11	97	...
AmMed 8¼08	cv	10	75	– 1
ATT 3⅞s90	4.1	16	94	– ⅜
ATT 5⅝95	7.0	60	80½	...
ATT 5½97	7.1	95	77¼	+ ⅛
ATT 6s00	8.1	30	74⅜	– ⅛
ATT 5⅛01	7.5	10	68½	– ¼
ATT 8¾00	9.5	379	91¾	+ ¼
ATT 7s01	8.7	71	80⅛	+ ⅛
ATT 7⅛03	9.0	14	79⅛	– ¾
ATT 8.80s05	9.6	37	92	+ ½

Excerpt from page 241 → ATT 5⅝95

FisbCp 8½05	cv	50	55½	– ½
Flwr 8¼05	cv	25	110½	– ¼
FrdC 7½91	8.0	25	94⅛	– ⅜
FrdC 7½92	8.0	25	94¼	...
FrdC 8.7s99	9.4	9	92½	– 1¾
FrdC 8⅜01	9.5	8	88	...
FrdC 8⅜02	9.6	9	87½	– ½
FreptM 8¾13	cv	4	115½	...
Fruf 13½96	18.8	9	72	...
Fruf 13¾01	18.6	6	74	– 1⅝
Fuqua 9⅞97	10.8	15	91¼	+ ¼
GATX 11½96	11.2	100	102½	...
GnDev 12⅞95	13.4	15	96	...

Excerpt from page 241 → Fruf 13½96

Source: *The Wall Street Journal*, March 14, 1989.

AMEX BONDS

Volume $2,810,000

SALES SINCE JANUARY 1		
1989	1988	1987
$122,080,000	$128,330,000	$159,290,000

	Mon.	Fri.	Thu.	Wed.
Issues traded	83	86	78	82
Advances	30	34	29	30
Declines	32	32	25	29
Unchanged	21	20	24	23
New highs	4	2	0	4
New lows	1	1	2	4

Bonds	Cur Yld	Vol	Close	Net Chg.
Angles 12½95	15.3	1	81½	– 1½
Arrow 12s98	13.1	12	91½	+ ½
Arrow 9s03	cv	8	66	...
BSN 7¾01	cv	1	69	+ 2½
BergBr 7⅝10	cv	15	110¼	– ¾
ChtMd 15.85s08f	...	23	105	– 1½
ChckFul 8s06	8.4	108	95	+ 3
CircE 13½97	23.1	20	58½	– ½
CmpC 7¾98	cv	7	78½	+ ¾
ContAir 11s96	13.9	20	79	+ 1
ContHlt 14⅛96	14.5	5	97¼	...
DamsO 13.2s00f	...	28	30	...
DamsO 12s03f	...	30	33	+ 1
DiagR 8½98	cv	20	83½	...
vjEAL 5s92f	cv	82	49	+ 2⅛
vjEAL 4¾93f	cv	168	45	+ 1¼
vjEAL 11½99f	cv	629	53½	+ 1¼
vjEAL 11¾05f	cv	107	54⅜	+ 1⅜
vjEAL 17½97f	...	108	101	– ½
vjEAL 17½98f	...	97	100½	– ½
vjEAL 11¾93f	...	42	93	– ¼
Eckerd 11⅛01	12.1	5	92	...
Elsinre 15½99	18.2	52	85	+ ½
Fthill 9½03	cv	21	104	...
FruitL 12⅜03	13.3	17	93	...
GeoRs 13s91f	...	25	54	+ 3
GeoRs 13¾96f	...	30	54¼	– ¾
HarteH 04f	...	1	91½	+ ¼
HlthCr 14⅜95	14.9	11	96¾	+ 1
HlthCh 10⅜99	cv	9	67¼	+ ¼
HomShp 11¾96	12.9	7	90¾	– ¼
HudFd 8s06	cv	28	69	+ 1¾
HudFd 14s08	cv	13	110	...
Intmk 7⅜07	7.3	5	101	+ 2
IntBkn 10s98	11.5	10	86¾	+ 2⅝
IroBr 12s99	16.0	17	75	...
MagCop 98f	...	85	104	– 1
MarkIV 7s11	9.4	11	74½	– ½
Maxam 13½00	14.1	3	95½	+ ½
Moog 9⅞06	cv	1	78½	...
NV Ry 10s02	cv	18	86	...
NV Ry 13¾97	cv	10	99½	...
Nich 14⅞99	17.0	46	87¼	– 1¾
Oakwd 7½01	cv	28	74	...
OBrien 7¾02	cv	15	127	– 1
Olsten 7s13	cv	10	94½	– ½
Openh 12¾02	13.7	2	93⅛	– ⅜
ResrtInt 16⅝04	18.4	81	90¼	– 1¾
ResrtInt 10s98	13.7	35	73	– ½
ResrtInt 11⅜13	17.7	50	64¼	– ¼
RyanM 11¾13I	11.6	1	101½	...
RyanM 11½13J	11.3	4	101½	– 1
RyanM 12⅜13M	12.0	2	103	– 1
RyanM 12⅞14	12.4	11	103½	...
RyanM 12s14	11.6	2	103½	+ 1
Sage 8½05	cv	60	62½	– ½
SvcMer 11¾96	12.9	10	91¼	+ ¼
SCE8⅛94 Y	8.7	7	93¼	+ ⅝
SCE 9⅝03	9.9	20	97⅝	+ ½
SwBell 8¾07	9.6	27	91¼	– ⅛
SwBell 6⅞11	9.4	10	73¼	– ¼
SwBell 7¾09	9.6	10	80⅞	– ⅜
SwBell 8¼14	9.7	10	84¾	+ 1¼
SwBell 9¼15	9.9	27	93	+ ½
SwBell 8¼17	9.9	6	83¾	+ ½
SwBell 8¾18	9.8	5	89	– ½
Storer 10s03	12.2	5	82	– ½
TeamI 13s04	cv	19	115½	+ ½
TxAir 15¾92	16.5	21	95½	– 1
TxAir 15¾92b	16.5	39	95½	– 1½
TxAr 14⅜90	14.8	30	97	...
TmpTaj 14s98	14.1	73	99½	– ½
TurnBd 10¼93	10.8	50	94½	...
Ultrs 7¾06	cv	39	82½	– ½
Wang 7¾08	cv	5	75⅝	+ ⅜
Wang 9s09	cv	15	85¾	...
WarC 7⅝s94	8.6	14	89	...
WstInv 8s08	cv	3	95	...
Wickes 12s94	13.3	25	90½	– ⅝
Wickes 7½-10s05	12.5	11	60	...
Wickes 15s95	14.9	50	101	+ 1½
Wickes 11⅜97	14.4	15	79	– ½
Wickes 11⅞01	14.2	10	83⅜	+ ⅝

Source: *The Wall Street Journal*, March 14, 1989.

because on March 13 the bond had a value of $805, not $1,000. An annual return of $56.25 on an investment of $805 is the equivalent of 7 percent, not 5⅝ percent.

If the current yield on securities of similar risk and maturity as the AT&T bond rises above the coupon rate of 5⅝ percent (as they have here), an investor will pay less than the par value for the bond.

When commentators speak of the bond market rising and falling, they mean the *price* of the bond, not the *interest rate*. Bondholders want interest rates to fall so that the value of their bonds will rise. You can see that the AT&T bond went from $1,000 to $805 as its yield rose from 5⅝ percent to 7 percent.

Investor's Tip

- Rising inflation, or fear of inflation, which drives interest rates up, hurts corporate bonds as well as Treasuries. Bond prices fall as interest rates rise.

Not only interest rates, but also the relative strength of the issuing company will affect the price of its bonds. AT&T is an investment of high quality because of its healthy financial condition and secure earnings potential. On the other hand, the Fruf 13½ 96 bonds, issued by Fruehauf, a truck-trailer manufacturer, have markedly higher coupon payments and yields than AT&T. That issue was speculative because it was a much weaker company. Hence, Fruehauf had to pay a higher return to attract investors' funds.

On March 13, 1989, you could have bought this bond for $720, held it for seven years (during which you would have received an 18.8 percent annual interest return of $135), and then cashed it in for $1,000, at a gain of $280 per bond (*assuming* the company survived). Substantial capital gains can be made in the bond market for an equivalent risk.

Compare the two bonds one last time. They will mature a year apart for $1,000 each. Yet you would have had to pay $805 for the AT&T bond and received a 7 percent return, whereas the Fruehauf bond would have cost you $720 for an 18.8 percent return. A wide range of investment opportunities and risks awaits you in the bond market.

"Junk" bonds (like Fruehauf's) offer higher rates of interest because of their inherently risky nature and are issued by companies that have high debt-to-equity ratios and high debt-to-cash flow ratios. These companies must pay high rates to attract investors' money because any fluctuation in the business of the issuing corporation could affect the timely payment of interest and the repayment of principal on the bonds.

The *Journal* can help you sort bonds according to creditworthiness. Each day it publishes **Credit Ratings,** summarizing the actions of Standard & Poor's and Moody's, the nation's major bond-rating services. (See the example from the March 14, 1989 *Journal.*) These services rate bonds according to the likelihood of payment of principal and

---

CREDIT RATINGS

Fruehauf Corp. Kept On S&P Credit Watch With Positive Rating

By a WALL STREET JOURNAL *Staff Reporter*

NEW YORK—Standard & Poor's Corp. said **Fruehauf** Corp. remains on its CreditWatch list, although the rating agency has revised its rating implications to positive from negative.

S&P placed the Detroit truck-trailer and auto parts maker on its CreditWatch list in late December 1988, citing continued poor performance of its truck trailer unit. It changed the ratings implication following Fruehauf's announcement Tuesday that it will sell its trailer and maritime operations to **Terex** Corp.

About $560 million of single-B-rated senior and triple-C-plus subordinated debt could be affected by any ratings change.

S&P said the sale of the trailer and marine businesses will enable Fruehauf "to cut its large debt burden and will leave it with the profitable Kelsey-Hayes division, a leading maker of wheels and brakes for cars and light trucks."

Source: *The Wall Street Journal*, March 14, 1989.

interest. The rating services arrive at their decision by investigating the profitability and strength of the companies issuing the bonds. You will notice that different companies pay varying rates of interest on their debt according to the ratings they have received.

You can also follow **New Securities Issues** daily in the *Journal* (check the index in the first or last section). It lists all new corporate, municipal, government agency and foreign Bonds. (See the excerpt from the Monday, April 10, 1989 *Journal*.) You can also find out what securities will be offered in the current week by reading Monday's **Securities Offering Calendar** (see the excerpt from the April 10, 1989 edition).

NEW SECURITIES ISSUES

The following were among Friday's offerings and pricings in the U.S. and non-U.S. capital markets, with terms and syndicate manager, as compiled by Dow Jones Capital Markets Report:

CORPORATES

Exxon Capital Ventures Inc.—$250 million of notes due March 15, 1990, priced at par to yield 10.30%. The issue is noncallable and was priced 35 basis points above the Treasury's 7⅜% issue due March 1990. Rated triple-A by Moody's Investors Service Inc. and Standard & Poor's Corp., the issue will be sold through underwriters led by Goldman, Sachs & Co.

Unilever Capital Corp.—$150 million of 10.44% guaranteed notes due Oct. 1, 1990, priced at par. The issue, which is noncallable for one year, was priced at 59 basis points over the Treasury two-year note. Rated triple-A by Moody's and S&P, the issue will be sold through underwriters led by Goldman Sachs.

PHH Corp.—$130 million of 10.6%, noncallable medium-term notes due March 30, 1990, priced at par. The issue was priced 63 basis points above the Treasury's 7⅜% issue due 1990. Rated single-A-2 by Moody's and single-A-plus by S&P, the issue will be sold through underwriters led by Goldman Sachs.

ITT Corp.—$100 million of notes due Oct. 1, 1990, priced at par to yield 10.7%. The notes are noncallable until April 1, 1990, and were priced 85 basis points above the Treasury two-year note. Rated single-A-2 by Moody's and single-A by S&P, the issue will be sold through underwriters led by Salomom Brothers Inc.

Republic National Bank of New York—$100 million of 10.4% notes due March 15, 1994, at various prices. The notes are initially being offered at 99.812 to yield 10.447%, which is a spread of 80 basis points above the Treasury five-year note. The notes are noncallable for three years. Rated double-A-1 by Moody's and double-A by S&P, the issue will be sold through underwriters led by Kidder, Peabody & Co.

Procter & Gamble Co.—$100 million of notes due Sep. 15, 1990, priced at par to yield 10.45%. The issue is noncallable for a year and was priced 60 basis points above the Treasury two-year note. Rated double-A-1 by Moody's and double-A-plus by S&P, the issue will be sold through underwriters led by Goldman Sachs.

Transamerica Corp.—$100 million of notes due March 15, 1990, priced at par to yield 10.55%. The issue is noncallable and was priced 60 basis points above the Treasury 7⅜% issue due March 1990. Rated single-A-2 by Moody's and single-A by S&P, the issue will be sold through underwriters led by Goldman Sachs.

MORTGAGES

Federal National Mortgage Association-$250 million of Remic mortgage securities being offered in six classes by Prudential-Bache Securities Inc. The offering, Series 1989-18, is backed by Fannie Mae 15-year, 9½% securities. Yields range from 10.43%, a spread of 85 basis points over seven-year Treasurys, to 10.81%, a spread of 105 basis points over three-year Treasurys.

Federal National Mortgage Association—$200 million of stripped mortgage securities in principal-only and interest-only classes through Drexel Burnham Lambert Inc. The issue, Fannie Mae's strips Trust 54, brings Fannie Mae 1989 strips volume to $1.3 billion and its total strips issuance to $15.4 billion. The strips program began in January 1987. The collateral consists of Fannie Mae 8% securities.

EUROBONDS

Guaranteed Mortgage-Backed Securities International No. 1 Ltd. (special purpose vehicle, secured on a pool of residential mortgages originated by the United Building Society of New Zealand)—$100 million of 10½% bonds due March 30, 1992, priced at 101¼ to yield 10.55% less fees via Bankers Trust International. Guaranteed by Financial Security Assurance. Fees 1⅜.

CIR International S.A. Luxembourg (Italian parent)—100 billion lire of 13% bonds due April 20, 1994, priced at 101½ to yield 13.11% less full fees, via Banco di Napoli. Guaranteed by Cie. Industriali Riunite(CIR). Fees 1⅞.

Source: *The Wall Street Journal*, April 10, 1989.

SECURITIES OFFERING CALENDAR

The following U.S. Treasury, corporate and municipal offerings are tentatively scheduled for sale this week, according to Dow Jones Capital Markets Report:

U.S TREASURY

Today

$14.4 billion of 13-week and 26-week bills.

Wednesday

$7 billion of seven-year notes.

CORPORATE

One Day This Week

Long Island Lighting Co.–$375 million of debentures, via Shearson Lehman Hutton.

Bytex Corp.–1,350,000 common shares, via Alex Brown & Sons.

Chemdesign Corp.–2,750,000 common shares, via Prudential-Bache.

Chieftan International Inc.–8,250,000 common shares, via Bear, Stearns & Co.

MUNICIPAL

Tuesday

Massachusetts–$200 million of general obligation bonds, consolidated loan of 1989, Series B, with serial bonds and serial and/or term bonds, via competitive bid.

Pima County, Ariz.–$54 million of general obligation bonds, 1989 Series, via competitive bid.

One Day This Week

Indiana Bond Bank–$240 million of composite advance funding program notes, 1989 Series, a Shearson Lehman Hutton Inc. group.

California Housing Finance Agency–$205 million of home mortgage revenue bonds, including $80 million of 1989 Series A non-alternative minimum (amt) tax bonds and $125 million of 1989 Series B AMT bonds, via a Merrill Lynch Capital Markets group.

Salt River Project Agricultural Improvement and Power District, Ariz.–$150 million of Salt River Project electric system revenue bonds, 1989 Series A, via a Shearson Lehman Hutton Inc. group.

Connecticut–$75 million of general obligation capital appreciation bonds, College Savings Plan, 1989 Series A, via a Prudential-Bache Capital Funding group.

South Dakota Health and Education Facilities Authority–$67 million of hospital revenue refunding bonds, McKennan Hospital, via a Dougherty Dawkins Strand & Yost Inc. group.

Source: *The Wall Street Journal*, April 10, 1989.

MUNICIPAL BONDS

Finally, you may wish to purchase municipal (state and local government) or tax-exempt bonds, as they are sometimes called, because earnings from these bonds are not subject to federal income tax and may not be subject to income tax in your state. These bonds were granted tax exemption in order to reduce the borrowing cost of the states, cities, and local districts that issue them. Investors purchase them knowing their return is not taxable and will therefore be satisfied with an interest return below that of comparable federal or corporate bonds. State and local governments save billions in interest costs as a result of this indirect subsidy.

Each Friday the *Journal* publishes a **Municipal Bond Index** prepared by Merrill Lynch (see the last section's index). The excerpt from the February 24, 1989 *Journal* serves as an example. In addition to an overall

---

Municipal Bond Index

Merrill Lynch 500

Week ended Wednesday, Feb. 22, 1989

The following index is based on yields that about 500 major issuers, mainly of investment grade, would pay on new long-term tax-exempt securities. The securities are presumed to be issued at par; general obligation bonds have a 20-year maturity and revenue bonds a 30-year maturity. The index is prepared by Merrill Lynch, Pierce, Fenner & Smith Inc., based on data supplied by Kenny Information Systems, a unit of J.J. Kenny Co. Inc.

–OVERALL INDEX–

7.67 –0.04

–REVENUE BONDS–

Sub-Index 7.73 –0.03

	2-22	Change In Week
AAA-Guaranteed	7.59	– 0.03
Airport	7.75	– 0.03
Electric-Retail	7.65	– 0.08
Electric-Wholesale ...	7.68	– 0.07
Hospital	7.78	– 0.04
Housing	7.79	unch
Miscellaneous	7.61	– 0.05
Pollution Control/ Ind. Dev.	7.83	– 0.04
Transportation	7.67	–0.07
Utility	7.65	– 0.07

–GENERAL OBLIGATIONS–

Sub-Index 7.51 –0.04

Cities	7.58	– 0.01
Counties	7.52	– 0.06
States	7.41	– 0.03
Other Districts	7.57	– 0.06

The transportation category excludes airports; utility excludes electrics. Other districts include school and special districts.

Source: *The Wall Street Journal*, February 24, 1989.

WEEKLY TAX-EXEMPTS

Friday March 17, 1989

Valuations of some widely held but inactively traded municipal issues. Yield is to maturity.

Issue	Coupon	Mat.	Bid	Ask	Yld.
Bat Park City Auth NY	6.375	11-01-14	83½	87½	7.48
Fla Bd of Ed (FBE)	7.250	03-01-10	94½	98½	7.39
Intrmtn Pwr Auth (IPA)	9.000	07-01-19	106	110	8.18
Mass Muni Whlsl El Rev	6.375	07-01-15	76	80	8.25
Mass Muni Whlsl El Rev	13.375	07-01-17	111	115	11.56
Massachusetts GO	6.500	06-01-00	91¾	95¾	7.05
NYC MAC	6.875	07-01-07	89½	93½	7.53
NYC MAC	7.500	07-01-92	99¾	103¾	6.21
NYC MAC	7.500	02-01-95	99¾	103¾	6.71
New Jersey Turnpike Auth	7.200	01-01-18	93¼	94¼	7.70
NY St Pwr (NYS Pwr)	6.750	01-01-12	88¾	92¾	7.41
New York St Pwr ESCR	9.500	01-01-01	108	112	7.91
New York St Pwr	6.675	01-01-10	87	91	7.48
New York St Urban Dev	6.000	11-01-13	79¾	83¾	7.45
NC Catawba Pwr Agy	7.375	01-01-20	92	96	7.71
Oregon GO	7.875	03-01-08	101	105	7.58
Port of NY & NJ	7.000	11-01-11	90⅞	94⅞	7.47
Puerto Rico	7.125	07-01-02	92⅞	96⅞	7.56
Salt River Proj Arizona	7.250	01-01-16	93	97	7.51
Sikeston Elec	7.400	06-01-09	85	89	8.55
So Car Pub Svc Auth	7.300	07-01-21	91½	95½	7.68
So Ca Pub Pwr (SCAPPA)	7.375	07-01-21	94½	98½	7.50
Tex Muni Pwr Au (TMPA)	7.250	09-01-11	90½	94½	7.77
Washington PPSS 1	15.000	07-01-17	139½	143½	10.25
Washington PPSS 1	7.750	07-01-17	94¾	98¾	7.85
Washington PPSS 2	14.750	07-01-12	120¼	124¼	11.69
Washington PPSS 2	6.000	07-01-12	76	80	7.89
Washington PPSS 3	13.875	07-01-18	117¾	121¾	11.31
Washington PPSS 4-5	6.000	07-01-15	7	9	Flat
Washington PPSS 4-5	12.500	07-01-10	7½	9½	Flat

Source: J.J. Kenny Co. Inc.

Source: *The Wall Street Journal*, March 20, 1989.

index, this report presents the latest yield on a variety of municipal bond categories. Also, the *Journal* publishes a weekly listing of inactively traded municipal bonds on Mondays under the heading **Weekly Tax-Exempts**. (See the excerpt from Monday, March 20, 1989 *Journal*.)

Before deciding on the purchase of a tax-exempt municipal bond, an investor must consider three things: the yield available on the municipal bond, the yield on a taxable bond with the same maturity, and the investor's tax bracket.

If, for example, you are in a 28 percent tax bracket, use the "equivalent tax-exempt yield formula" to calculate your after-tax yield on a security whose income is taxable. This is the minimum yield a municipal bond must pay you to be of equivalent value to the taxable bond. Here's an instance using a 10 percent yield on the security whose interest is taxable.

$$\begin{aligned}\text{Equivalent tax-exempt yield} &= (1 - \text{tax bracket}) \times \text{ taxable yield}\\ &= (1 - .28) \times .10\\ &= .072\\ &= 7.2 \text{ percent}\end{aligned}$$

Thus, in your 28 percent tax bracket, a 7.2 percent tax-exempt yield is the equivalent of a 10 percent taxable yield.

Therefore, if you had the opportunity, you would purchase an 8 percent tax-exempt bond rather than a 10 percent taxable bond with similar maturity and creditworthiness.

TRACKING THE BOND MARKET

It's now time to wrap up this discussion by detailing how you can use the *Journal* every day to follow the bond market. You should begin your daily analysis of bond activity with a glance at the **Bonds** reports on the first page of the third section under **Markets Diary** (see the excerpt from the Tuesday, March 14, 1989 edition), which lists five important indexes that track bond market performance. The graph portrays the Shearson Lehman Hutton Treasury Bond Index, a composite index of Treasury securities' yield and price performance. The DJ 20 Bond Index

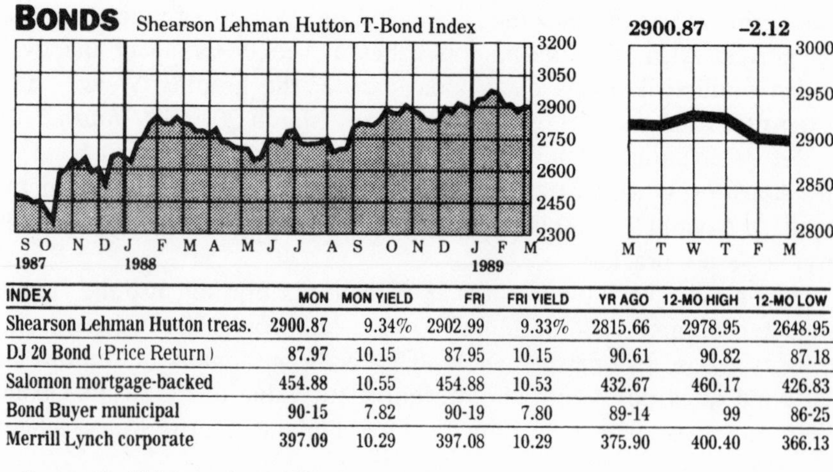

INDEX	MON	MON YIELD	FRI	FRI YIELD	YR AGO	12-MO HIGH	12-MO LOW
Shearson Lehman Hutton treas.	2900.87	9.34%	2902.99	9.33%	2815.66	2978.95	2648.95
DJ 20 Bond (Price Return)	87.97	10.15	87.95	10.15	90.61	90.82	87.18
Salomon mortgage-backed	454.88	10.55	454.88	10.53	432.67	460.17	426.83
Bond Buyer municipal	90-15	7.82	90-19	7.80	89-14	99	86-25
Merrill Lynch corporate	397.09	10.29	397.08	10.29	375.90	400.40	366.13

Source: *The Wall Street Journal*, March 14, 1989.

provides the average price and yield of 10 public utility bonds and 10 industrial bonds. You became acquainted with it in the discussion of NYSE bonds. The Salomon mortgage–backed index covers mortgage-backed securities such as Ginnie Maes, Fannie Maes, and Freddie Macs. The Bond Buyer municipal index is compiled by *The Bond Buyer*, a publication that specializes in fixed-income securities, and covers AA-rated and A-rated municipal bonds. The Merrill Lynch corporate bond index, like the Dow index, is a corporate bond composite.

The Bond Yields chart depicts three series. The top line describes the interest that financially healthy public utilities must pay on debt instruments maturing in 10 years or more, the second line describes the interest rate that the federal government must pay on debts that mature in 15 years or more, and the bottom line lists the rate paid by state and local governments. The chart appears in Monday's *Wall Street Journal* with the **Credit Markets** article as shown in this sample from the September 18, 1989 issue.

The Journal publishes its **Bond Market Data Bank** daily toward the center of Section C (see the Monday, May 22, 1989 example). The Data Bank thoroughly covers the bond market for the preceding trading day and contains more information than you may ever want to know.

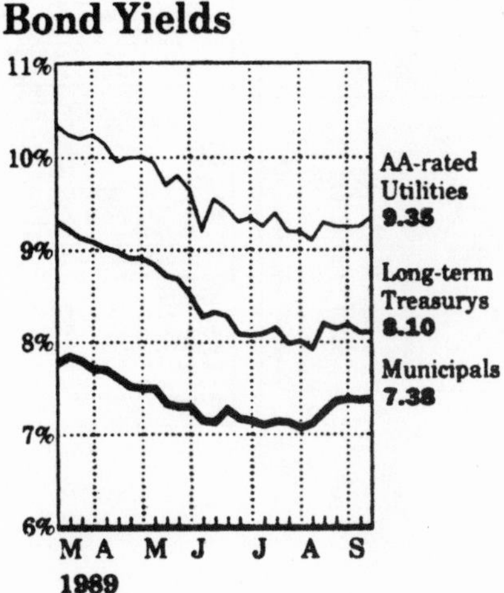

Source: *The Wall Street Journal*, September 18, 1989.

BOND MARKET DATA BANK 5/19/89

MAJOR INDEXES

HIGH	LOW (12 MOS)		CLOSE	NET CHG	% CHG	12-MO CHG	% CHG	FROM 12/31	% CHG
U.S. TREASURY SECURITIES (Shearson Lehman Hutton indexes)									
2636.16	2427.77	Intermediate	2636.16	+ 4.29	+ 0.16	+ 207.38	+ 8.54	+ 111.50	+ 4.42
3081.78	2650.28	Long-term	3081.78	+ 18.86	+ 0.62	+ 432.83	+ 16.34	+ 180.51	+ 6.22
1277.75	1194.42	Long-term (price)	1277.75	+ 7.51	+ 0.59	+ 74.11	+ 6.16	+ 31.68	+ 2.54
2736.42	2477.40	Composite	2736.42	+ 7.79	+ 0.29	+ 260.41	+ 10.52	+ 128.09	+ 4.91
U.S. CORPORATE DEBT ISSUES (Merrill Lynch)									
412.27	366.13	Corporate Master	412.27	+ 2.15	+ 0.52	+ 45.20	+ 12.31	+ 19.75	+ 5.03
312.23	285.45	1-10 Yr Maturities	312.23	+ 1.08	+ 0.35	+ 26.24	+ 9.18	+ 12.42	+ 4.14
303.85	262.17	10+ Yr Maturities	303.85	+ 2.16	+ 0.72	+ 40.62	+ 15.43	+ 16.71	+ 5.82
181.09	163.21	High Yield	181.09	+ 0.54	+ 0.30	+ 17.73	+ 10.85	+ 6.24	+ 3.57
295.98	263.87	Yankee Bonds	279.05	− 16.56	− 5.60	+ 14.49	+ 5.48	− 2.67	− 0.95
TAX-EXEMPT SECURITIES (Bond Buyer; Merrill Lynch: Dec. 31, 1986 = 100)									
93-22	86-25	Bond Buyer Municipal	93-22	+ -9	+ 0.30	+ 6-25	+ 7.84	+ 2-5	+ 2.36
108.71	98.75	New 10-yr G.O. (AA)	108.71	+ 0.02	+ 0.02	+ 10.02	+ 10.15	+ 3.96	+ 3.78
111.00	96.14	New 20-yr G.O. (AA)	111.00	+ 0.02	+ 0.02	+ 14.51	+ 15.04	+ 5.78	+ 5.49
123.67	100.88	New 30-yr revenue (A)	123.67	+ 0.76	+ 0.62	+ 22.86	+ 22.68	+ 8.47	+ 7.35
MORTGAGE-BACKED SECURITIES (current coupon; Merrill Lynch: Dec. 31, 1986 = 100)									
116.75	104.73	Ginnie Mae (GNMA)	116.75	+ 0.47	+ 0.40	+ 11.88	+ 11.33	+ 5.97	+ 5.39
117.95	106.22	Fannie Mae (FNMA)	117.95	+ 0.29	+ 0.25	+ 11.72	+ 11.03	+ 5.43	+ 4.83
116.30	103.78	Freddie Mac (FHLMC)	116.30	+ 0.29	+ 0.25	+ 12.47	+ 12.01	+ 5.86	+ 5.31
CONVERTIBLE BONDS (Merrill Lynch: Dec. 31, 1986 = 100)									
116.27	101.05	Investment Grade	116.27	+ 0.08	+ 0.07	+ 15.21	+ 15.06	+ 10.97	+ 10.42
113.46	98.82	High Yield	113.31	− 0.15	− 0.13	+ 14.24	+ 14.37	+ 10.39	+ 10.10

CORPORATE BONDS

Quotes of representative taxable issues at mid-afternoon New York time, provided by First Boston/CSFB Ltd.

ISSUE (RATING: MOODY'S/S&P)	COUPON	MATURITY	PRICE	CHANGE	YIELD	CHANGE
FINANCIAL						
Citicorp (A2/AA−)	9.000	04/15/99	96.050	0.459	9.625	− 0.075
Ford Credit Co (Aa2/AA)	8.875	05/15/94	97.466	0.291	9.526	− 0.074
GMAC (Aa3/AA−)	8.000	10/15/93	94.525	0.267	9.555	− 0.070
GMAC (Aa3/AA−)	7.875	03/01/97	90.805	0.391	9.578	− 0.072
Household Fin (A1/AA−)	7.750	10/01/99	88.008	0.600	9.599	− 0.101
IBM Credit (Aaa/AAA)	8.000	08/15/90	98.444	0.072	9.369	− 0.031
UTILITY						
Commonwlth Ed (Baa1/BBB+)	11.125	05/01/18	104.158	0.227	10.657	− 0.025
Pacific G&E (A1/A)	8.125	01/01/97	92.529	0.391	9.528	− 0.072
Sou Bell Tel (Aaa/AAA)	8.625	09/01/26	91.942	0.944	9.406	− 0.100
Sou Cal Ed (Aa2/AA)	9.375	02/15/17	95.712	0.228	9.825	− 0.025
Sowest Bell Tel (Aa3/AA−)	11.875	10/18/21	110.433	0.242	10.715	− 0.025
INDUSTRIAL						
Amoco (Aaa/AAA)	8.625	12/15/16	92.172	0.908	9.425	− 0.100
Capital Cities (A1/A+)	8.750	03/15/16	89.655	0.637	9.850	− 0.075
Du Pont & Co (Aa2/AA)	6.000	12/01/01	74.977	0.463	9.453	− 0.072
Exxon Shipping (Aaa/AAA)	Zero	09/01/12	14.513	0.097	8.474	− 0.019
East Kodak (A2/A−)	9.125	03/01/98	96.627	0.428	9.701	− 0.074
Mobil (Aa2/AA)	8.625	07/01/94	96.897	0.301	9.403	− 0.072
FOREIGN						
Australia (Aa1/AA+)	7.625	09/15/97	90.296	0.409	9.327	− 0.073
Hydro-Quebec (Aa3/AA−)	8.250	04/15/26	89.322	0.697	9.275	− 0.075
Int Bk Recon Dev (Aaa/AAA)	9.875	10/01/97	103.559	0.433	9.249	− 0.076
Sweden (Aaa/AAA)	8.125	11/01/96	93.527	0.259	9.352	− 0.048

TAX-EXEMPT BONDS

Representative prices for several active tax-exempt revenue and refunding bonds, based on institutional trades. Changes rounded to the nearest one-eighth. Yield is to maturity. n-New. Source: The Bond Buyer.

ISSUE	COUPON	MAT	PRICE	CHG	BID YLD
Atlanta Rpd Trans Auth	7.250	07-01-10	100	+ ⅛	7.25
Broward Airport	7.625	10-01-13	100	+ ⅜	7.62
Broward North 84	7.950	12-01-08	103¼	+ ¼	7.63
Calif Housing Fin	8.000	08-01-29	101	+ ¼	7.92
D.C. Washn Ser 89A	7.500	06-01-09	101⅞	+ ⅜	7.32
Fairfax Co Va Dev	7.750	02-01-11	102⅛	+ ¼	7.55
Fla 89 Dade Roads	7.375	07-01-19	101½	+ ⅜	7.25
Fla Trans Tpke	7.500	07-01-19	101⅜	+ ¼	7.38
Fla Trans Tpke	7.600	07-01-14	102⅝	+ ¼	7.37
Hudson Co NJ	7.600	12-01-21	101½	+ ¼	7.48
Ill Sports Facil	7.875	06-15-10	102⅞	+ ⅜	7.60
Los Ang Conv Exhbtn	7.000	08-15-20	98⅝	+ 2⅛	7.11
Los Ang Conv Exhbtn	7.375	08-15-18	100¾	+ ⅜	7.31
Los Ang Dept Wtr Ca	7.375	02-01-29	101⅛	+ ½	7.29
Mass G.O. Ser. 88	7.375	12-01-08	100⅝	+ ¼	7.32
Md Hlth & Higher Ed.	7.500	07-01-20	102	+ ⅛	7.33
N Minn Muni Pwr	7.250	01-01-16	99⅞	+ ⅛	7.26
NY MTA	8.000	07-01-18	103⅛	+ ¼	7.73
NY MTA Transit	7.500	07-01-17	101⅝	+ ¼	7.36
NYC Muni Wtr Fin	7.625	06-15-16	100⅞	+ ¼	7.55
NYC Muni Wtr Fin	7.625	06-15-17	102¼	+ ⅛	7.43
NYS Enrgy R & D Auth	7.750	01-01-24	101⅝	+ ¼	7.61
NYS Med Care Fac	7.800	02-15-19	101⅞	+ ⅛	7.64
Oaklnd Ca Pension	7.600	08-01-21	102⅜	+ ¼	7.39
Okla Tpke Auth	7.700	01-01-22	103¾	+ ¼	7.40
Okla Tpke Auth	7.875	01-01-21	103¼	+ ¼	7.60
Orlando Expwy Auth	7.625	07-01-18	102⅝	+ ⅜	7.41
P.R. G.O. Pub Imprv	7.750	07-01-17	102⅝	+ ⅛	7.53
Pa. Tpke Comm	7.500	12-01-19	102⅛	+ ¼	7.32
Pasco Fla Waste	7.800	04-01-11	102⅜	+ ¼	7.57
Pa Tpke Comm Rev	7.625	12-01-17	102¾	+ ¼	7.40
Port Auth NY & NJ 63	7.875	03-01-24	102	+ ¼	7.71
Port Of Oakland Ca	7.250	11-01-16	100¾	+ ¼	7.19
Port Of Oakland Ca	7.600	11-01-16	101⅜	+ ⅜	7.48
Salt River Agri	7.500	01-01-27	101⅝	+ ⅜	7.37
Salt Rvr Project	7.500	01-01-29	101⅜	+ ¼	7.37
San Diego Wtr Auth	7.300	05-01-09	100⅝	+ ⅛	7.24
Texas Wtr Res Fin	7.500	08-15-13	101⅜	+ ¼	7.36
Texas Wtr Res Fin	7.625	08-15-08	101¼	+ ⅛	7.50
Triboro Brdg & Tun	7.700	01-01-19	102⅞	+ ⅜	7.46

MORTGAGE-BACKED SECURITIES

Representative issues, quoted by Salomon Brothers Inc.

	REMAINING TERM (Years)	WTD-AVG LIFE (Years)	PRICE (JUN) (Pts.-32ds)	PRICE CHANGE (32ds)	CASH FLOW YIELD*	YIELD CHANGE (Basis pts.)
30-YEAR						
GNMA 8.0%	28.0	12.7	89-22	+ 18	9.76%	− 10
FHLMC 8.0%	28.0	9.6	90-16	+ 17	9.80	− 11
FNMA 8.0%	28.0	9.5	90-28	+ 18	9.82	− 12
GNMA 10.0%	29.5	11.2	99-28	+ 12	10.16	− 7
FHLMC 10.0%	29.2	9.2	98-26	+ 10	10.20	− 6
FNMA 10.0%	29.0	9.0	99-10	+ 10	10.22	− 7
GNMA 12.0%	25.2	6.7	106-26	+ 6	10.44	− 7
FHLMC 12.0%	20.0	6.0	104-12	+ 4	10.72	− 5
FNMA 12.0%	22.9	5.8	104-22	+ 2	10.77	− 4
15-YEAR						
GNMA 9.5%	14.5	6.7	99-14	+ 11	9.73%	− 8
FHLMC 9.5%	14.4	6.3	98-03	+ 10	9.87	− 8
FNMA 9.5%	14.5	6.3	98-14	+ 10	9.92	− 8

*Based on projections from Salomon's prepayment model, assuming interest rates remain unchanged from current levels

COLLATERALIZED MORTGAGE OBLIGATIONS

Spread of CMO yields above U.S. Treasury securities of comparable maturity, in basis points (100 basis points = 1 percentage point of interest)

MAT	SPREAD	CHG FROM PREV DAY
NEW ISSUES		
2-year	100	− 3
5-year	113	− 2
10-year	135	− 3
20-year	145	− 5
SEASONED ISSUES		
2-year	95	− 3
5-year	108	− 2
10-year	130	− 3
20-year	140	− 5

GUARANTEED INVESTMENT CONTRACTS

Source: T. Rowe Price GIC Index

	1 YEAR		2 YEARS		3 YEARS		4 YEARS		5 YEARS	
	RATE	CHG	RATE	CHG	RATE	CHG	RATE	CHG	RATE	CHG
High	9.31%	−0.02	9.33%	+0.03	9.40%	+0.02	9.43%	+0.03	9.50%	−0.03
Low	7.39	unch	8.44	unch	8.64	unch	8.91	unch	8.91	unch
INDEX	8.83	−0.03	9.04	−0.03	9.14	−0.02	9.21	−0.03	9.25	−0.03
TOP QUARTILE RANGE	9.31% - 9.12%		9.33% - 9.25%		9.40% - 9.30%		9.43% - 9.33%		9.50% - 9.41%	
SPREAD vs. TREASURYS	−0.05		+0.14		+0.29		+0.38		+0.47	

GIC rates quoted prior to 3 pm (Eastern) net of all expenses, no broker commissions. Rates represent best quote for a $2-$5 million immediate lump sum deposit with annual interest payments. Yield spreads based on U.S. Treasury yields, as of 3 pm (Eastern), over the index rate unadjusted for semi vs. annual interest payments. CHG reflects change in basis points from previous day. INDEX is average of all rates quoted. Universe is investment grade.

INTERNATIONAL GOVERNMENT BONDS

Prices in local currencies, provided by Salomon Brothers Inc.

	COUPON	MATURITY (Mo./yr.)	PRICE	CHANGE	YIELD*
JAPAN (3 p.m. Tokyo)					
#89	5.10%	6/96	101.580	+ 0.110	4.83%
#40	3.80	6/90	98.946	unch	4.82
#8	5.30	9/08	101.650	+ 0.100	5.16
#111	4.60	6/98	95.410	+ 0.270	5.24
#71	6.80	1/95	110.040	+ 0.040	4.76
UNITED KINGDOM (5 p.m. London)					
	10.00%	4/93	97.719	− 0.094	10.72%
	9.50	4/05	99.406	− 0.094	9.56
	9.00	10/08	97.500	− 0.031	9.27
	11.00	10/91	99.625	+ 0.375	11.17
	10.50	5/99	101.469	− 0.063	10.25
WEST GERMANY (5 p.m. London)					
	7.75%	11/90	100.550	+ 0.150	7.28%
	7.50	1/93	100.850	unch	7.20
	7.00	1/95	99.600	+ 0.150	7.08
	6.13	7/97	93.950	+ 0.300	7.12
	6.75	1/99	97.950	+ 0.400	7.04
CANADA (3 p.m. EDT)					
	10.25%	12/98	102.750	+ 0.750	9.80%
	10.00	6/08	102.500	+ 0.800	9.71
	10.25	2/94	101.450	+ 0.400	9.85
	10.25	6/92	100.000	unch	10.25
	10.25	3/14	104.375	+ 0.825	9.78

*Equivalent to semi-annual compounded yields to maturity

Total Rates of Return on International Bonds

In percent, based on Salomon Brothers' world government benchmark bond indexes

	LOCAL CURRENCY TERMS					U.S. DOLLAR TERMS				
	1 DAY	1 MO	3 MOS	12 MOS	SINCE 12/31	1 DAY	1 MO	3 MOS	12 MOS	SINCE 12/31
Japan	+0.14	+ 0.10	− 0.38	+ 3.21	− 0.62	− 0.05	− 4.55	− 8.77	− 6.99	− 10.65
Britain	+0.10	+ 1.11	+ 1.00	+ 5.76	+ 3.94	− 0.15	− 4.65	− 6.66	− 8.25	− 7.16
West Germany	+0.26	− 0.44	+ 1.00	+ 2.30	− 0.62	− 0.04	− 6.09	− 5.71	− 11.90	− 9.96
France	+0.36	+ 0.39	+ 4.19	+ 10.51	+ 2.13	+ 0.25	− 5.39	− 2.04	− 4.87	− 6.84
Canada	+0.60	+ 2.93	+ 5.70	+ 8.45	+ 6.56	+ 0.74	+ 2.53	+ 5.89	+ 12.14	+ 6.70
Netherlands	unch	− 0.93	+ 0.32	+ 1.32	− 1.30	− 0.07	− 6.52	− 6.16	− 13.18	− 10.56
Non-U.S.	NA	NA	NA	NA	NA	+ 0.11	− 4.11	− 3.91	− 5.51	− 6.41
World*	+0.27	+ 0.60	+ 1.84	+ 4.66	+ 1.59	+ 0.16	− 3.38	− 3.20	− 4.57	− 5.35

*Includes U.S. Treasury benchmark index NA=not applicable

EURODOLLAR BONDS

Provided by First Boston/CSFB Ltd.

ISSUE (RATING: MOODY'S/S&P)	COUPON	MATURITY	PRICE	CHANGE	YIELD	CHANGE
Canada (Aaa/AAA)	9.000	02/27/96	99.686	− 0.085	8.853	0.015
Alberta (Aa1/AA+)	7.375	12/09/91	95.151	− 0.050	9.367	0.045
Belgium (Aa1/NR)	9.625	07/10/98	99.816	− 0.265	9.427	0.045
Italy (Aaa/NR)	9.000	07/28/93	98.229	− 0.153	9.302	0.050
Int Bk Recon Dev (Aaa/AAA)	9.000	07/07/93	98.682	− 0.156	9.179	0.051
Int Bk Recon Dev (Aaa/AAA)	9.000	08/12/97	97.215	− 0.127	9.277	0.025
Lincoln Natl (A1/AA)	9.750	10/20/95	99.366	− 0.145	9.632	0.031

Source: *The Wall Street Journal*, May 22, 1989.

YIELD COMPARISONS

Based on Merrill Lynch Bond Indexes, priced as of midafternoon Eastern time.

	3/22	3/21	−52 Week− High	Low
Corp.-Govt. Master	9.92%	9.99%	9.99%	8.38%
Treasury 1-10 yr	9.80	9.90	9.89	7.68
10+ yr	9.44	9.50	9.63	8.85
Agencies 1-10 yr	10.14	10.19	10.19	8.01
10+ yr	9.78	9.82	10.19	9.44
Corporate				
1-10 yr High Qlty	10.24	10.28	10.28	8.99
Med Qlty	10.57	10.61	10.61	9.54
10+yr High Qlty	10.24	10.27	10.38	9.73
Med Qlty	10.65	10.67	10.82	10.16
Yankee bonds(1)	10.23	10.28	10.28	9.43
Current-coupon mortgages				
GNMA 10.50%	10.91	11.00	11.00	9.32
FNMA 10.50%	11.03	11.07	11.07	8.60
FHLMC 11.00%	10.99	11.13	11.13	9.52
High-yield corporates	13.43	13.42	13.43	12.80
New tax-exempts				
10-yr G.O. (AA)	7.30	7.30	7.30	6.70
20-yr G.O. (AA)	7.60	7.60	8.15	7.15
30-yr revenue (A)	8.05	8.05	8.45	7.61

Note: High quality rated AAA-AA; medium quality, A-BBB/Baa; high yield, BB/Ba-C.

(1) Dollar-denominated, SEC-registered bonds of foreign issuers sold in the U.S.

Source: *The Wall Street Journal*, March 23, 1989.

Finally, you can compare the yield of a variety of long-term instruments by using the **Yield Comparisons** table that appears daily with the **Credit Markets** article (see the excerpt from the Thursday, March 23, 1989 issue.)

MUTUAL FUNDS

If you recall our discussion of mutual funds in Chapter 9, you will remember that mutual funds often specialize in particular types of investments. Bond funds are mutual funds that invest primarily in debt instruments, which allows you to diversify in bond investments without venturing large sums of capital. For example, new Ginnie Mae issues require a $25,000 minimum investment, which would be out of reach of the small investor. Mutual funds pool large sums of money in order to invest in instruments like Ginnie Maes from which small individual investors can then benefit.

CLOSED-END BOND FUNDS

Tuesday, March 21, 1989

Unaudited net asset values of closed-end bond fund shares, reported by the companies as of Friday, March 17, 1989. Also shown is the closing listed market price or a dealer-to-dealer asked price of each fund's shares, with percentage of difference.

Fund Name	Stock Exch.	N.A. Value	Stock Price		% Diff.
Bond Funds					
ACM Govt Inco Fund	NYSE	10.20	10¾	+	5.39
ACM Govt Oppor Fd	NYSE	8.96	8⅝	–	3.74
ACM Govt Securities	NYSE	10.26	10⅝	+	3.56
ACM Govt Spectrum	NYSE	8.66	8¾	+	1.04
ACM Managed Inco	NYSE	8.94	8⅞	–	0.73
AMEV Securities	NYSE	a10.05	10¼	+	1.99
American Capital Bond	NYSE	b20.15	19	–	1.99
American Capital Inco	NYSE	a8.84	8⅞	+	0.40
American Govt Income	NYSE	6.69	7½	+	12.11
American Govt Portf	NYSE	8.59	9¼	+	7.68
American Govt Term	NYSE	9.18	10	+	8.93
Blackstone Inco Tr	NYSE	8.24	9	+	9.22
Blackstone Target Tr	NYSE	9.00	9½	+	5.56
Bunker Hill Income	NYSE	17.57	16½	–	6.09
CIGNA High Income	NYSE	9.07	10	+	10.25
CNA Income Shares	NYSE	11.06	11½	+	3.98
Circle Income Shares	OTC	11.97	12⅜	+	3.38
Colonial Int High Inco	NYSE	9.26	9⅜	+	1.24
Comstock Ptr Strategy	NYSE	a9.40	9	–	4.26
Current Income Shares	NYSE	11.66	11⅜	–	2.44
Dean Witter Govt Inco	NYSE	8.97	9	+	0.33
Dreyfus Strt Gov Inco	NYSE	10.74	10½	–	2.23
1838 Bond-Deb Trad	NYSE	19.50	19¼	–	1.28
Excelsior Inco Shares	NYSE	a16.29	14¾	–	9.45
First Boston Inco Fd	NYSE	8.47	8¼	–	2.60
First Boston Strategic	NYSE	10.70	11¼	+	5.14
Flexible Bd Tr	AMEX	9.17	9	–	1.85
Ft Dearborn Income	NYSE	14.36	13¾	–	4.25
John Hancock Income	NYSE	a14.92	14¼	–	4.49
John Hancock Invest	NYSE	a20.08	20⅛	+	0.22
Hatteras Income Secs	NYSE	ae15.79	15	–	5.00
High Income Adv Tr	NYSE	8.88	9⅛	+	2.76
High Income Adv II	NYSE	9.19	9⅛	–	0.71
High Income Adv III	NYSE	9.27	9⅞	+	6.53
High Yield Income Fd	NYSE	8.93	8⅞	–	0.62
High Yield Plus Fund	NYSE	9.09	8⅝	–	5.12
INA Investments	NYSE	17.21	16⅞	–	1.95
Independence Sq	OTC	16.40	15	–	8.54
Intercapital Income	NYSE	19.00	20	+	5.26
Kemper High Inco Tr	NYSE	10.58	11½	+	8.70
Kemper Inter Govt Tr	NYSE	9.02	9⅛	+	1.16
Kemper Multi Inco Tr	NYSE	11.04	11½	+	4.17
Lincoln Natl Dir Place	NYSE	27.77	25	–	9.97
Lomas Mtge Sec Fd	NYSE	a10.84	11⅝	+	7.24
MFS Gov Mkts Inco	NYSE	8.92	10	+	12.11
MFS Inco & Oppor Tr	NYSE	9.49	9⅞	+	4.06
MFS Intermed Inco Tr	NYSE	8.88	9	+	1.35
MFS Multimkt Inco Tr	NYSE	8.75	9⅞	+	12.86
MFS Multimkt Ttl Ret	NYSE	9.20	8½	–	7.61
Montgomery Street	NYSE	18.42	17⅞	–	2.96
Mutual Omaha Int Shs	NYSE	a13.17	14	+	6.30
New America Hi Inco	NYSE	a8.31	9¾	+	17.33
Oppenhmr Multi-Govt	NYSE	9.05	8¾	–	3.31
Oppenhmr Multi-Sectr	NYSE	10.89	10	–	8.17
Pacific Amer Inco Shs	NYSE	b14.85	14⅝	–	1.52
Prospect St Hi Inco Fd	NYSE	a9.13	9⅜	+	2.68
Prudential Interm Inco	NYSE	a8.85	8⅝	–	2.54
Prudential Strat Inco	NYSE	a8.68	8⅝	–	0.63
Putnam Int Govt Inco	NYSE	9.09	9	–	0.99
Putnam Mstr Inco Tr	NYSE	9.21	9¼	+	0.43
Putnam Mstr Int Inco	NYSE	9.10	8⅞	–	2.47
Putnam Prem Inco Tr	NYSE	8.78	9¼	+	5.35
RAC Income Fund	NYSE	11.05	10⅝	–	3.85
State Mutual Securities	NYSE	10.48	10⅝	+	1.38
Transamerica Income	NYSE	22.12	22⅝	+	2.28
USF&G Pacholder Fd	AMEX	18.71	18⅝	–	0.45
USLIFE Income Fund	NYSE	9.53	8⅝	–	9.50
Van Kmpn Merr Inter	NYSE	9.24	9⅝	+	4.17
Vestaur Securities	NYSE	13.22	12⅜	–	6.39
Convertible Bond Funds					
Lincoln Natl Convert	NYSE	14.37	12⅛	–	15.62
Putnam Hi Inco Conv	NYSE	8.44	7⅞	–	6.69
International Bond Funds					
First Australia Prime	AMEX	9.84	8¾	–	11.08
Global Government	NYSE	8.65	9¼	+	6.94
Global Income Plus	NYSE	9.36	9¼	–	1.18
Global Yield Fund	NYSE	a9.02	9½	+	5.32
Kleinwort Benson Aust	NYSE	10.48	9⅜	–	10.54
Templtn Glbl Gov Inco	NYSE	9.04	9½	+	5.09
Templeton Global Inco	NYSE	a8.88	8⅞	–	0.06
World Income Fund	AMEX	a9.45	9¼	–	2.12
Municipal Bond Funds					
Allstate Muni Inco Op	NYSE	9.45	10	+	5.82
Allstate Muni Inco Tr	NYSE	10.13	10¼	+	1.18
Allstate Muni Inco II	NYSE	9.75	9⅝	–	1.28
Allstate Muni Pr Inco	NYSE	9.36	9¼	–	1.18
Colonial Hi Inco Muni	NYSE	9.26	10	+	7.99
Colonial Muni Inco Tr	NYSE	8.91	9⅞	+	10.83
Dreyfus Cal Muni Inco	AMEX	9.17	9⅜	+	2.24
Dreyfus Muni Inco	AMEX	9.32	9⅛	–	2.09
Dreyfus NY Muni Inco	AMEX	9.18	9¼	+	0.76
Dreyfus Strategic Muni	NYSE	9.78	10¼	+	4.81
Kemper Muni Inco Tr	NYSE	11.13	11⅜	+	2.20
MFS Muni Income Tr	NYSE	9.23	9⅞	+	6.99
MuniEnhanced Fund	NYSE	11.11	11⅝	+	4.64
MuniInsured Fd Inc	AMEX	9.82	10¾	+	9.47
MuniVest Fund Inc	AMEX	a9.24	9⅜	+	1.46
New York Tax-Exmpt	AMEX	9.81	9¼	–	5.71
Nuveen CA Muni Inco	NYSE	11.44	11½	+	0.52
Nuveen CA Muni Val	NYSE	9.74	9⅞	+	1.39
Nuveen Muni Inco	NYSE	11.33	11½	+	1.50
Nuveen Muni Value	NYSE	9.78	9¾	–	0.31
Nuveen NY Muni Inco	AMEX	11.37	11⅜	+	0.04
Nuveen NY Muni Val	NYSE	9.89	10	+	1.11
Nuveen Prem Inco	NYSE	14.10	14⅜	+	1.95
Putnam Mgd Mun Inco	NYSE	9.25	9⅞	+	6.76
VanKmpn M CA Muni	AMEX	9.13	9⅝	+	5.42
VanKmpn Mer Muni	NYSE	9.34	9¼	–	0.96

a-Ex-dividend. b-Fully diluted. e-Thursday's market close.

Source: Lipper Analytical Services, Denver Colorado.

Source: *The Wall Street Journal*, March 22, 1989.

Mutual funds come in two forms, open-ended and closed-ended. Open-ended funds issue shares as needed, and you will no doubt recall the earlier discussion when you review the example. A closed-end fund's shares are limited and fixed. Once all the shares are sold, no more shares will be issued. On Wednesdays, the *Journal* reports the **Closed-End Bond Fund** and you can see an example from the March 22, 1989 edition.

CONCLUSION

If all this detail has set your head swimming, regain your perspective by recalling that stocks' and bonds' values should move together in the long haul and that both are paper investments that thrive in low inflation.

CHAPTER 12

MONEY MARKET INVESTMENTS

INTRODUCTION

Maybe the risk and bother of investing in stocks, bonds, and commodities inhibit you. If that's so, you may be satisfied with an investment whose return just covers the rate of inflation, provided that you can readily convert it to cash. In other words, you want your money's purchasing power to be unchanged a year or two from now and you want the assurance that you can get your hands on your money at will.

Many circumstances might justify this point of view. Everyone's future involves some degree of uncertainty. If you are retired, your nest egg may have to meet unexpected medical bills. You don't want to be penalized for cashing out in a hurry. And investors of every age may wish to park their funds for brief periods in anticipation of other planned uses of their funds. Whatever the situation, you might have a number of good reasons not to tie up your funds in riskier investments even if they offer higher returns.

If you wish to make a short-term investment that is relatively risk-free and can be quickly converted to cash, the money market offers a variety of selections that range from one day to one year and may be obtained for large or small amounts. Most of these are probably familiar to you: bank savings accounts, interest–bearing checking accounts (money market checking accounts), certificates of deposit, money market mutual funds, and Treasury bills (T-bills). Their rate of interest is determined by market forces, and the markets for all are interrelated.

As a general rule, the greater the liquidity (ease with which it is converted into cash) and safety of an investment, the lower the yield. A smaller investment commitment and a shorter maturity also reduce the yield.

This chapter describes the money market investments available to individual investors and shows you how to track those investments in *The Wall Street Journal*.

CONSUMER SAVINGS AND INTEREST-EARNING CHECKING ACCOUNTS

Your interest-earning checking account, NOW (negotiable order of withdrawal), or savings account at the bank or savings and loan company (S&L) is a short-term liquid investment because you can withdraw your funds quickly and easily with relatively few restrictions. Moreover, these accounts are insured up to $100,000 by either the Federal Deposit Insurance Corporation (FDIC) or the Federal Savings and Loan Insurance Corporation (FSLIC). In the hierarchy of short-term interest rate yields, consumer checking and savings rates tend to be on the bottom because of their liquidity and safety, and because of the inertia preventing many savers from shopping for the higher yields available on alternative investments.

BANK MONEY MARKET ACCOUNTS

You can open a money market account with a minimum daily balance ranging from $500 to $5,000, depending on the bank. This is a highly liquid investment because you can withdraw from the account at any time simply by writing a check, although most banks have restrictions regarding the number and frequency of checks written. These accounts offer relatively low yields because of their check-writing privilege, although the return tends to be a little higher than on savings accounts due to higher required minimum balances. They are also insured up to $100,000 by the FDIC and FSLIC.

Every Thursday *The Wall Street Journal* publishes **Consumer Savings Rates** (check the third section's index), a listing prepared by the Bank Rate Monitor that reports on the average rate paid by 100 banks on the previous day for a variety of money market and certificate of deposit (CD) accounts. See the excerpt from the March 23, 1989 *Journal*.

Consumer Savings Rates

Money Market Deposits-a	6.33%
Super-NOW Accounts-a	5.09%
Six-month Certificates-a	8.82%
One-year Certificates-a	8.98%
Thirty-month Accounts-a	8.91%
Five-Year Certificates-a	8.85%
U.S. Savings Bonds-b	7.35%

a-Average rate paid yesterday by 100 large banks and thrifts in the 10 largest metropolitan areas as compiled by Bank Rate Monitor.
b-Current annual yield. Guaranteed minimum 6%.

Source: *The Wall Street Journal*, March 23, 1989.

According to this report, money market deposits paid 6.33 percent on March 22, 1989, Super–NOWs paid less, and a variety of certificates of deposit as well as U.S. Savings Bonds earned more.

On Friday of each week, the *Journal* publishes the **Banxquote Money Markets** together with **High Yield Savings** and **High Yield Jumbos**, and the excerpt from the March 24, 1989 *Journal* provides an example. The Banxquote Money Market report lets you compare your yield on a variety of money market accounts and certificate of deposit accounts at different maturities with the average earned nationally (Bank Average) and in six key states: New York, California, Pennsylvania, Illinois, Texas, and Florida. You can also find the weekly change in the national average. On March 23, 1989, for instance, the average short-term account earned 6.94 percent and had increased 0.03 percent over the previous week. The High Yield Savings figures represent the rates available at individual institutions for accounts requiring a small minimum balance (some as low as $500), and the High Yield Jumbos are rates offered with minimum balances of $95,000 to $100,000.

Banks and S&Ls created the money market accounts to stem withdrawals of funds lost to competing money market mutual funds offering

Savings Avg: 6.94 percent →

BANK AVERAGE								
Savings	6.94%	z	z	8.45%	8.87%	9.17%	9.15%	9.13%
Jumbos	7.38%	9.16%	9.25%	9.42%	9.71%	9.85%	9.61%	9.51%

Source: *The Wall Street Journal*, March 23, 1989

BANXQUOTE® MONEY MARKETS

Survey ended Thursday, March 23, 1989

AVERAGE YIELDS OF MAJOR BANKS

	MMI*	One Month	Two Months	Three Months	Six Months	One Year	Two Years	Five Years
NEW YORK								
Savings	8.31%	z	z	9.01%	9.46%	9.80%	9.66%	9.53%
Jumbos	8.31%	9.57%	9.71%	9.87%	10.28%	10.51%	10.00%	9.75%
CALIFORNIA								
Savings	6.36%	z	z	7.38%	8.50%	8.53%	8.62%	8.67%
Jumbos	6.79%	8.35%	8.45%	8.85%	9.15%	9.20%	9.20%	9.23%
PENNSYLVANIA								
Savings	6.11%	z	z	8.62%	8.92%	9.66%	9.31%	9.25%
Jumbos	7.41%	9.34%	9.40%	9.48%	9.56%	9.71%	9.67%	9.47%
ILLINOIS								
Savings	7.15%	z	z	8.36%	8.80%	9.02%	9.41%	9.14%
Jumbos	8.03%	9.45%	9.52%	9.67%	9.97%	10.17%	9.57%	9.43%
TEXAS								
Savings	7.10%	z	z	8.58%	8.81%	9.25%	9.39%	9.35%
Jumbos	7.10%	9.24%	9.30%	9.39%	9.81%	9.89%	9.91%	9.82%
FLORIDA								
Savings	6.61%	z	z	8.42%	8.75%	8.77%	8.77%	8.83%
Jumbos	6.61%	9.03%	9.14%	9.28%	9.51%	9.59%	9.55%	9.45%
BANK AVERAGE								
Savings	6.94%	z	z	8.45%	8.87%	9.17%	9.15%	9.13%
Jumbos	7.38%	9.16%	9.25%	9.42%	9.71%	9.85%	9.61%	9.51%
WEEKLY CHANGE (in percentage point)								
Savings	+0.03	z	z	+0.13	+0.10	+0.14	+0.12	+0.05
Jumbos	+0.03	+0.16	+0.16	+0.17	+0.25	+0.25	+0.14	+0.08

Savings Average: 6.94 percent

SAVINGS CD YIELDS OFFERED THROUGH LEADING BROKERS

	Three Months	Six Months	One Year	Two Years	Five Years
BROKER AVERAGE	9.80%	9.98%	10.09%	9.97%	9.72%
WEEKLY CHANGE	+0.28	+0.19	+0.26	+0.23	+0.09

*Money Market Investments include MMDA, NOW, savings deposits, passbook and other liquid accounts.

Each depositor is insured by the Federal Deposit Insurance Corp. (FDIC) or Federal Savings and Loan Insurance Corp. (FSLIC) up to $100,000 per issuing institution.

COMPOUND METHODS: c-Continuously. d-Daily. w-Weekly. m-Monthly. q-Quarterly. s-Semi-annually. a-Annually. si-Simple interest.

YIELD BASIS: A-365/365. B-360/360. C-365/360.

The information included in this table has been obtained directly from broker-dealers, banks and savings institutions, but the accuracy and validity cannot be guaranteed. Rates are subject to change. Yields, terms and creditworthiness should be verified before investing.

z-Unavailable.

HIGH YIELD SAVINGS

Small minimum balance, generally $500 to $10,000

Money Market Investments	Rate		Yield
Chevy Chase, Laurel Md	9.40%	mA	9.82%
Eastern Savings, Baltimore Md	9.30%	dA	9.74%
Chase Bank, Baltimore Md	9.25%	dA	9.69%
Haymarket Bank, Boston Ma	9.27%	mA	9.67%
Barclays Bank, New York Ny	9.20%	dA	9.64%

One Month CDs	Rate		Yield
New South FSB, Birmingham Al	9.30%	siA	9.30%
Columbia Svgs, Newport Beach Ca	8.80%	dA	9.20%
Hallmark Savings, Plano Tx	9.00%	siA	9.00%
Bank Of New England, Boston Ma	9.00%	siA	9.00%
North American, San Antonio Tx	8.88%	siA	8.88%

Two Months CDs	Rate		Yield
New Haven Svgs, New Haven Ct	9.00%	mA	9.38%
New South FSB, Birmingham Al	9.30%	siA	9.30%
Columbia Svgs, Newport Beach Ca	8.80%	dA	9.20%
North American, San Antonio Tx	9.00%	siA	9.00%
Rancho Bernardo, Escondido Ca	8.50%	dC	9.00%

Three Months CDs	Rate		Yield
Merchants Bank, Boston Ma	10.00%	mA	10.47%
Compass Bank, New Bedford Ma	9.80%	mA	10.25%
Home Loan, Providence RI	10.00%	siC	10.14%
Columbia Svgs, Newport Beach Ca	9.60%	dA	10.07%
Bank Of Boston, Boston Ma	10.00%	siA	10.00%

Six Months CDs	Rate		Yield
CBT, Hartford Ct	10.00%	mA	10.47%
Merchants Bank, Boston Ma	10.00%	mA	10.47%
Citytrust, Bridgeport Ct	10.00%	mA	10.47%
Columbia Svgs, Newport Beach Ca	9.80%	dA	10.29%
Home Loan, Providence RI	10.00%	siC	10.14%

One Year CDs	Rate		Yield
CBT, Hartford Ct	10.00%	MA	10.47%
Citytrust, Bridgeport Ct	10.00%	MA	10.47%
Firstbanc Svgs, Missouri City Tx	10.00%	qA	10.38%
Bank Of New England, Boston	10.00%	qA	10.38%
Columbia Svgs, Newport Beach Ca	10.10%	sA	10.36%

Two Years CDs	Rate		Yield
CBT, Hartford Ct	10.00%	mA	10.47%
Mercantile Bank, Boston	10.00%	mA	10.47%
Commonwealth Svgs, Houston Tx	9.95%	dA	10.46%
Firstbanc Svgs, Missouri City Tx	10.00%	qA	10.38%
Bank Of New England, Boston	10.00%	qA	10.38%

Five Years CDs	Rate		Yield
Commerce Savings, Dallas	9.85%	dA	10.35%
Benjamin Franklin, Houston Tx	9.75%	qA	10.11%
Independence Fed, Wash DC	9.75%	qA	10.11%
First Republic, Los Angeles	9.62%	dA	10.10%
Columbia Svgs, Newport Beach Ca	9.85%	sA	10.09%

HIGH YIELD JUMBOS

Large minimum balance, generally $95,000 to $100,000

Money Market Investments	Rate		Yield
Bexar Savings, San Antonio Tx	10.00%	dA	10.52%
Banco De Bogota, New York	9.75%	siC	[illegible]
Chevy Chase, Laurel Md	[illegible]		

Six Months Jumbo CDs	Rate
New Braunfels, [illegible]	

Source: *The Wall Street Journal*, March 24, 1989

higher rates than savings accounts. Although interest paid by the money market accounts fluctuates with short-term market rates, these accounts do not enjoy yields as high as those paid by money market mutual funds.

MONEY MARKET MUTUAL FUNDS

Investment companies establish mutual funds to pool the capital of many investors and thus create a large shared portfolio of investments. (Recall the earlier discussions of mutual funds in Chapter 9.) Individuals invest in mutual funds by purchasing shares in the fund, and the return on the portfolio is passed through to the investor according to the number of shares held. An enormous variety of mutual funds is available, designed for different types of investors and bearing a wide variety of yields.

Money market mutual funds invest principally in short-term investment instruments such as Treasury bills, commercial paper, bank certificates of deposit, bankers acceptances, and other liquid assets denominated in large amounts and therefore unavailable to the small investor. A money market mutual fund permits you to participate in the return on a variety of short-term investments and enjoy the benefits of diversification without employing large sums of your own capital. You also take advantage of the professional management skills of the investment company.

Most money market mutual funds are *no-load funds*. They do not charge a sales commission fee because they are directly marketed by the investment company. However, "management" fees are subtracted from the yield you receive. Money market mutual funds are issued and trade at a par value of one dollar. The dividends you receive are expressed as percentage yield.

Although money market funds sell their shares for a dollar each, most have minimum investment requirements ranging from $1,000 to $20,000. As an incentive, many money market funds also have check-writing privileges. Although these funds are not insured by the federal government, they are safe and liquid investments whose yields tend to be higher than the yields on bank money market accounts.

In the early 1980s, when the Federal Reserve applied a chokehold on the economy and interest rates climbed to the sky, money market mutual funds became popular among investors and savers. Since banks and S&Ls at the time were prohibited from offering above-passbook rates to small depositers, huge sums poured into the money market funds as their yields climbed above the legal passbook minimums. When the interest rate ceilings were removed from small denomination accounts at banks and S&Ls, and these accounts began to offer rates that moved with market conditions (and thus competed with the money market mutual funds), some investors deserted the money market funds. However, money market fund rates generally outdo those at the banks and consequently remain very popular.

You can use a variety of reports in *The Wall Street Journal* to compare the performance of your money fund with others.

Examine the **Short-Term Rate Surge** . . . article (on page 262) from the Monday, January 30, 1989 *Journal*. The **Climbing Short-Term Yields** chart depicts the hierarchy of rates that prevailed in 1988 among bank money market accounts, money market mutual funds, six-month CD rates, and six-month T-bills. Note that the gap between money market mutual funds and bank money market accounts widened as interest rates rose.

Each Friday the *Journal* publishes a report on the size of money market funds' assets, which, as you can see from the March 24, 1989 excerpt on page 263, had climbed to $300 billion by the late 80s. Note in particular the surge in late 1988 and early 1989 as investors took advantage of these funds' relatively higher rates.

The *Journal* reports money market fund yields on Thursdays. For instance, the March 23, 1989 edition of the *Journal* (pages 264 and 265) states that the seven-day compounded yield for the preceding week averaged 9.35 percent while the top performing funds had yields exceeding 10 percent. Notice that the average maturity of the investments in these funds (T-bills, CDs, commercial paper, etc.) was 31 days. Many fund managers lock in longer yields on longer maturities if they think interest rates will fall, and shorter maturities when they believe rates will rise.

Money Market Mutual Funds, published every Thursday in the *Journal,* lists the most popular money market mutual funds (see the index on page C1). Several statistics are given for each: the average maturity of the investments in the fund, the 7-day yield for the week (average yield), the effective 7-day yield (after reinvesting and compounding interest earned), and the total assets in millions of dollars as of the previous day. (See the example from the March 23, 1989 *Journal* on pages 266 and 267.) You can track the performance of your money market mutual fund and most others with this report. For instance, Merrill Lynch's Cash Management fund had an average maturity of 35 days, yields of 8.82 percent and 9.22 percent, and assets of $23.09 billion.

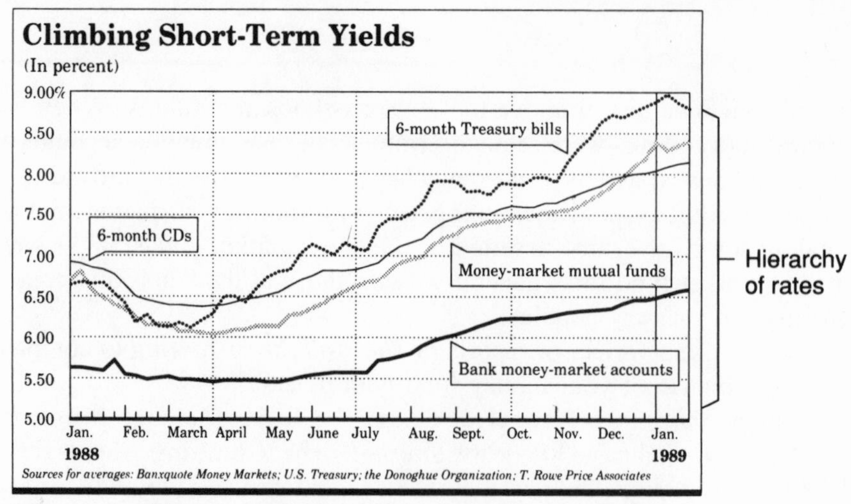

Short-Term Rate Surge Sets Off Feeding Frenzy Among Investors

YOUR MONEY MATTERS

By GEORGETTE JASEN
Staff Reporter of THE WALL STREET JOURNAL

NEW YORK—If print advertisements could scream, these would.

In large type they call out: "Look What $50,000 Can Earn When It's Hungry" and "Why Gamble With Interest Rates?" Bank accounts brandish names such as Power Savings or the Hungry Savers Fund.

Many investors are eager to take advantage of the surge in short-term interest rates, now hovering at the highest point in nearly five years. But there are lots of places they can put their cash.

Banks and money funds are out to nab the money. The U.S. Treasury doesn't advertise, but T-bills offer even better yields. What to do with your dollars? The choice depends on a number of factors.

The prevailing wisdom is to stay short. Most short-term rates have jumped almost 2½ percentage points in the past year, while long-term rates have barely budged.

For example, the annualized yield on a six-month T-bill bought at auction was 8.79% last week, up sharply from 6.50% a year ago. Yet the yield on 30-year Treasury bonds was also around 8.8%, not much above the 8.625% of a year before.

Federal Reserve Chairman Alan Greenspan recently called inflation too high, suggesting that short-term rates are likely to continue climbing. "Short-term rates could go a lot higher," says Paul W. Boltz, vice president and financial economist at T. Rowe Price Associates, a mutual-fund concern.

"If the investor thinks that the fight against inflation has just begun, he should stay in the shortest instruments possible and roll them over every three months," says Maury Harris, chief economist at PaineWebber Group Inc. But Mr. Harris cautions: "Sometimes if you wait for what you think is the peak, you can miss the train."

The shortest-term investments are the money-market mutual funds and bank money-market accounts. Interest rates for both generally are adjusted weekly and funds can be added or withdrawn easily.

MONEY-MARKET MUTUAL FUNDS: Money funds, which like other mutual funds are pools of investors' money managed by professionals, currently offer considerably higher yields than competing bank accounts. According to Donoghue's Money Fund Report, a newsletter based in Holliston, Mass., the latest seven-day average yield on taxable funds was 8.38% a year. On a compounded basis, which assumes that the current yield continues for a year and dividends are reinvested, it was 8.73%. The best-performing funds are yielding slightly more than 9% on an an-

Please Turn to Page C23, Column 1

Source: *The Wall Street Journal*, January 30, 1989.

Money-Fund Assets Increased $2.8 Billion In the Latest Week

By a WALL STREET JOURNAL *Staff Reporter*

NEW YORK—Assets of the nation's 461 money-market funds rose $2.8 billion, to $299.4 billion, in the week ended Wednesday.

Money Market Fund Assets

The Investment Company Institute said that assets of 228 general-purpose funds rose $1.3 billion, to $97.42 billion; 94 broker-

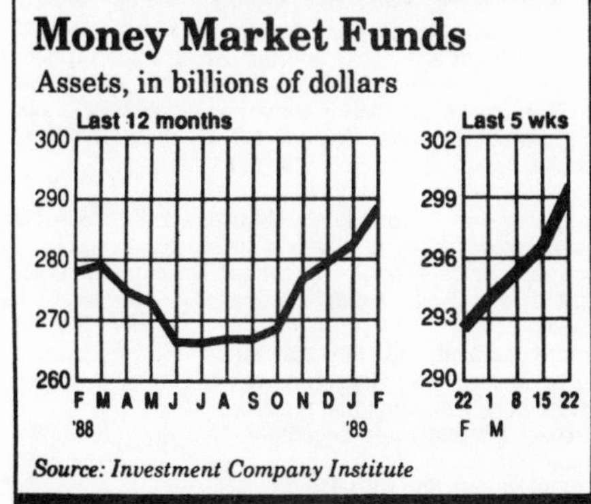

dealer funds rose $1.08 billion, to $129.05 billion; and 139 institutional funds rose $449.1 million, to $72.97 billion.

"As the yields paid by money-market funds kept increasing their advantage over the yields of other financial instruments available to individual investors, assets of money-market funds continued to climb," said Jacob Dreyer, vice president and chief economist for the Washington trade association.

"The surge in assets was concentrated in the general-purpose and broker-dealer categories of funds, a pattern prevailing since the beginning of the year and indicative of the dominant effect of short-term interest-rate movements on liquid asset flows," he said. "Last week, this pattern was most likely reinforced by the sell-off in the stock and bond markets and the ensuing placement of proceeds from sales of stock and bonds in money-market accounts."

Source: *The Wall Street Journal*, March 24, 1989.

Money Fund Yields Reach Double Digits

By Georgette Jasen
Staff Reporter of The Wall Street Journal

Yields on money market mutual funds are moving into double digits.

The three top-performing money funds in the latest week had seven-day compounded yields of more than 10%, according to Donoghue's Money Fund Report.

And more funds will cross into double digits in coming weeks, predicts Susan Cook, editor of the newsletter, based in Holliston, Mass. She notes that the No. 4 fund in the latest week offered a 9.97% yield.

Among the top 10 funds, the lowest seven-day compounded yield was 9.80%. (Compounded yields assume that the rate continues for a year and that dividends are reinvested.)

Average Maturity

Average maturity of the 361 funds tracked by Money Fund Report remained short, at 31 days, indicating that fund managers expect interest rates to continue to rise.

That will be just fine with individual investors, who have poured billions of dollars into money funds since rates began rising last spring. But it could be more bad news for the stock market. Investors able to get 10% with little risk on money funds are apt to feel that the potential rewards of stocks simply aren't great enough to justify the added risk.

Money Market fund yield

The average seven-day compounded yield of 9.35% on money funds, up from 9.24% last week, is still higher than most yields on bank certificates of deposit. But six-month Treasury bills sold at Monday's auction had an effective yield of 9.60%, and two-year Treasury notes to be auctioned Tuesday are expected to yield between 9.5% and 10%.

Money funds remain more than two percentage points ahead of bank money market investments, which also offer check-writing and easy withdrawal. Banxquote Money Markets, a New York-based information service, reported earlier this week that the average yield on those bank accounts was just 6.94%.

Six-month CDs offered by banks were

Yields for Consumers

Average compounded yields in percent; money market funds yield is 7-day average; CD yields are for deposits of $50,000 or less at major banks

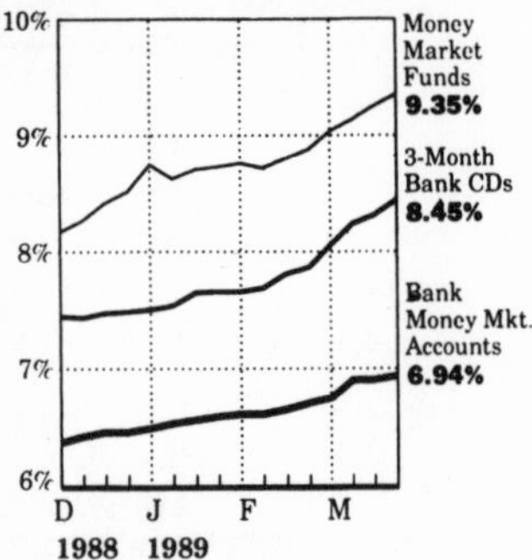

Sources: Banxquote Money Markets; Donoghue's Money Fund Report

Source: *The Wall Street Journal*, March 23, 1989.

Average Maturity–Fifth Paragraph

Average maturity of the 361 funds tracked by Money Fund Report remained short, at 31 days, indicating that fund managers expect interest rates to continue to rise.

Excerpt from page 264

Money Fund Yields–Seventh Paragraph

The average seven-day compounded yield of 9.35% on money funds, up from 9.24% last week, is still higher than most yields on bank certificates of deposit. But six-month Treasury bills sold at Monday's auction had an effective yield of 9.60%, and two-year Treasury notes to be auctioned Tuesday are expected to yield between 9.5% and 10%.

Excerpt from page 264

Source: *The Wall Street Journal*, March 23, 1989.

MONEY MARKET MUTUAL FUNDS

The following quotations, collected by the National Association of Securities Dealers Inc., represent the average of annualized yields and dollar-weighted portfolio maturities ending Wednesday, March 22, 1989. Yields are based on actual dividends to shareholders.

Fund	Avg. Mat.	7Day Yld.	e7Day Yld.	Assets
Money Market:				
AALMnv	32	8.68	9.06	127
AARP	27	8.58	8.95	288
AMA TrP	7	8.65	9.03	16
AMA PrP	52	8.97	9.38	121
AMEV	23	8.83	9.22	75
ASO Pr	26	9.17	9.59	275
ASO US	22	8.76	9.15	100
ActAsGv	40	8.68	9.06	244
ActAsMnv	46	9.00	9.41	2955
AlexBwn	34	9.13	9.55	1095
AlxBGvt	36	9.02	9.43	238
AlgerMM	31	9.71	10.20	46
AlliaCpRs	45	8.62	9.00	1519
AlliaGvRs	31	8.49	8.86	458
AlturaPr	20	9.23	9.66	211
AlturUS		....	....	......
AmCRs a	23	8.96	9.38	517
AmNatl	28	8.48	8.84	15
ArchFd	22	9.28	9.72	337
AsocCap	19	9.82	10.31	46
AutCsh	35	9.12	9.54	950
AutGvt	22	8.94	9.35	2566
AxeHgh	15	8.98	9.39	120
Babson	25	8.68	9.06	82
BaysCsh	31	9.24	9.68	413
BaysUS	54	8.88	9.29	73
BedfdGvt	25	8.67	9.05	44
BedfdMM	34	8.94	9.34	153
BinchGv	1	9.07	9.49	8
WmBRdy	32	9.01	9.42	246
BostCo	18	8.92	9.32	405
BostGvt	61	8.67	9.05	45
BullBDlr	29	8.83	9.22	103
CAM		....	....	......
Bradfd	20	9.01	9.42	305
CIMCO		....	....	......
CalSoc af	16	9.03	9.45	106
CapCash	12	8.86	9.26	3
CapPrsv	34	8.29	8.64	2523
CapPre II	1	8.87	9.27	620
CardinGvt	33	9.21	9.46	467
Carillon	33	9.18	9.61	93
Carnegie	18	8.84	....	......
CshAset	30	9.19	9.62	253
CashEqM	28	8.90	9.30	6238
CshEqGv	10	9.14	9.56	2401
CshMgtA a	20	9.15	9.58	1274
CentnGv	5	8.76	9.15	143
Centen	16	9.01	9.42	303
ChchCsh	22	9.14	9.56	210
CignCsh	34	9.16	9.22	119
CigMM h	37	8.89	9.30	175
ColonIGv	50	8.58	8.95	96
ColDIn af	29	8.89	9.30	613
ComSens	25	8.86	9.27	33
CompCs	30	8.98	9.39	365
CompUS	32	8.69	9.07	148
CmpCs a	41	8.72	9.11	221
CoreFd	32	9.24	9.67	145
CortldGn	27	8.81	9.20	716
CortldUS	28	8.40	8.76	83
CnslCR	42	9.29	9.73	213
CtryCa	25	8.44	8.80	15
CritPrm	22	9.29	9.72	158
Curentln	19	8.42	8.78	100
CurntlUS	24	9.21	9.63	84
DBL Port	33	8.76	9.15	1607
DBL Gvt	32	8.25	8.60	283
DailCsh 1	14	9.18	9.61	3590
DailDlr	31	8.75	9.14	93
DailyInco	34	8.95	9.36	472
DlyPasp f	33	8.77	9.15	1364
DWitrLq	47	9.10	9.52	9530
DWitrUS	39	8.61	8.99	693
DelaCR f	40	8.82	9.22	1094
DelaTr	45	8.28	8.63	34
DryInst	29	9.01	9.42	618
DryfLA	34	8.85	9.25	7737
DryGvt	8	8.89	9.29	692
DryInG	5	9.07	9.49	242
DryMM	25	8.90	9.30	395
DryUSGr	57	8.17	8.51	139
DryWld	71	10.19	10.72	136
EatVCsh	37	8.97	9.37	206
EmblPr	34	9.12	9.54	208
EmblUS	27	8.55	8.92	119
EvrgMM	35	9.41	9.86	270
FBL	23	8.92	9.33	46
FFB Csh	49	9.19	9.62	508
FFB US	21	9.23	9.66	237
FFB US	34	8.79	9.18	118
FedMstr	33	9.16	....	2154
FdShtUS	26	9.35	9.79	819
FidCshR	48	9.08	9.50	11486
FidDIn b	31	8.92	9.33	3172
FidDMM	32	9.21	9.65	631
FidDUS	5	9.13	9.56	513
FidGvPr	12	9.30	9.74	513
FidDom	26	9.38	9.83	1083
FidUS Tr	3	9.38	9.83	359
FidelUS	13	8.80	9.20	1601
FinDlInc	24	9.12	9.54	363
FnclRsv	32	9.30	9.74	449
FstAmer	30	9.25	9.69	136
FtBost	22	9.33	9.77	209
FtInvCs f	20	9.11	9.50	254
FtLkMM	19	8.84	9.23	223
FtLkGv	15	8.55	8.92	149
FtVarG f	17	8.64	9.02	366
FlexFd	31	9.37	9.81	205
FtWash	34	8.83	9.22	59
Founders	18	8.74	9.13	55
FountSq	43	8.85	9.25	124
FrkMny a	33	8.83	9.23	1609
FrkFdl b	1	8.59	8.96	169
FrnkGvt	14	9.75	...	59
FrnkIFT	31	9.52	....	133
FremntMM	17	9.12	9.54	......
FdGvtInv	18	8.74	9.13	645
FdSrce	29	8.83	9.22	113
FdSMony	55	9.17	9.59	126
FSWash	30	9.02	9.43	120
Gab OC DP	27	9.53	9.99	239
GalaxyGv	17	9.09	9.51	210
GalxyMM	24	9.22	9.65	251
GnGvSec	22	8.62	8.99	274
GnMMkt	25	8.58	8.95	723
GovtInvTr a	21	8.88	9.28	169
GvtSec f	26	9.06	9.33	15
GradCshR	35	8.94	9.34	520
GradUS	34	8.03	8.35	28
GranitMM	25	8.85	9.25	33
GrdCsFd	25	9.31	9.75	248
GrdCsMg	25	9.24	9.67	23
HTInsgtCs	48	9.06	9.47	76
HTInsgtGv	43	8.88	9.26	53
Harbor a	54	9.52	9.98	51
HelmsPr	30	9.21	9.64	324
HelmsUS	29	8.97	9.38	40
HrtgCsh	38	9.02	9.43	331
HiMrkDv	46	9.04	9.45	448
HiMrkUS	19	8.90	9.30	86
HiMrkUST	52	8.72	9.10	223
HYCT	33	9.24	....	105
HilrdLyon	25	8.49	8.85	84
HomeCsh	32	8.79	9.18	443
HomeGvt	48	8.50	8.86	107
HorznPr	29	9.35	9.80	433
HorznTr	36	9.06	9.47	231
Hummer	23	8.88	9.28	140
IDS CshM	22	9.04	9.45	1400
IMGLiq	18	8.50	8.87	82
IMG TE	10	5.98	6.16	12
IndCsh f		...	...	....
ILAGOVY af	22	9.20	9.63	2188
ILAPOP af	33	9.45	9.90	3829
ILATRSY af	16	8.98	9.39	1627
ILAMMP af	36	9.47	9.92	781
IntegCsh	10	8.81	9.18	73
IntegMM	30	8.78	9.17	459
InvCshRsv	28	8.21	7.95	20
IvyMny	23	8.96	9.37	......
JHanCshM	16	8.90	9.30	262
KemperGvt	11	9.36	9.80	387
KemperM	28	9.33	9.77	6156
KeyLqd	25	8.65	9.03	640
KidPeGv	32	8.69	9.07	358
KidPePr	39	8.90	9.30	964
LdmkCs	43	8.80	9.18	323
LaurlGv	34	9.19	9.62	78
LaurlPr	30	9.44	9.89	62
LaurPrII	33	9.48	9.93	30
LazCsh	25	9.04	9.42	270
LazGvt	23	8.93	9.33	93
LazdInCsh	16	9.37	9.81	68
LazdInGv	28	9.46	9.91	173
LazdInPr	22	9.51	9.97	124
LazdInTr	4	9.31	9.75	38
LegMCR f	26	8.83	9.22	552
LexGvSc a	28	8.29	8.60	16
Lexingt a	33	8.91	9.31	95
LibtyUS	25	8.66	9.03	1378
LiqCapital	43	9.09	...	...
LiqCshTr f	1	9.77	...	542
LadGrTr	31	8.71	9.09	408
LrdAbCR	30	8.81	9.21	220
LuthrnBr	36	8.68	9.06	334
MFS Life	25	7.84	8.15	159
MIMLIC	21	8.78	9.17	153
Map Gvt	46	8.54	8.91	32
MacKySh	32	8.97	9.38	106
MarinCsh	33	9.18	9.61	690
MarineGv	21	9.12	9.54	263
MarinerUS	36	8.88	9.28	122
MassCash a	26	8.98	9.38	699
MassCsGv	19	8.88	9.27	55
MassMtl	24	8.74	9.13	50
McDonald	36	8.37	8.72	236
ML CBAMon	38	9.18	9.61	493
ML CMAGv a	12	9.14	9.57	2446
ML CMAMn a	35	8.82	9.22	23090
MerLyGv a	22	8.92	9.33	1417
MerLyIn af	37	9.24	9.68	1417
MerLyRdy	37	8.80	9.20	9680
MerLyRet a	33	8.86	9.26	3748
MerLyUSA	12	8.90	9.31	276
MetLfStMM	30	9.06	9.47	62
MdIncTrGvt	18	8.47	8.83	109
Mon&ManPr	18	8.94	9.35	101
MonManGvt	23	8.50	8.87	14
MonMMgt f	32	8.74	9.12	200
MonMkTrst	33	9.19	....	1567
MonitorGov	30	8.90	9.30	77
MonitorMM	29	9.12	9.54	297
MutlOmah	39	8.72	9.10	184
MtlOmahC	40	8.54	8.91	47
NLR Cash	32	8.91	9.31	1526
NLR Gvt	29	8.43	8.79	98
NatlCash	32	9.11	9.54	53
NatwMM	32	8.94	9.35	460
NeubCsh	32	9.20	9.63	198
NeubGvt	44	7.70	8.00	166
NEMMkt	33	9.02	9.43	904
NEUSGvt	30	8.59	8.96	58
Newton	36	9.18	9.61	98
Nicholas	45	8.93	9.33	48
OppMoney	15	9.11	9.53	855
PSB Gov	10	9.02	9.43	30
PcHrzGvt	41	8.69	9.07	919
PcHzMMP	36	9.15	9.57	898
PW Cash	34	9.18	9.61	4406
PW MstrM b	20	8.56	8.93	52
ParkPr	23	9.10	9.52	450
ParkUS	33	8.74	9.13	176
ParkCsh	42	8.52	8.89	115
Phonix	46	8.97	9.38	143
PilgrmGov		....	....	.....
Pinacle	14	8.92	9.32	92
PionrCs	25	8.84	9.23	66
PiprMM	28	8.70	9.13	804
PiprUS	25	8.60	8.97	33
PrimeCsh	15	9.30	9.74	295
PrVlCsh	35	9.19	9.62	362
PrVlRdy	40	8.96	9.37	102
PrincorCash	19	8.47	8.83	117
PruBGv	48	8.95	9.35	189
PruBMy	34	9.18	9.60	2060
PrVlUS	31	8.93	9.33	293
PrudBGvt	39	8.86	9.25	457
PrudBMart	29	9.13	9.55	6236
PruInMM	51	9.40	9.84	236
PruInDom	8	7.93	8.25	21
PruInGov	11	9.43	9.87	85
PutDDiv	28	8.96	9.37	777
PW RMA	28	9.30	9.74	2432
PW Retr	29	8.88	9.29	1212
PW RM US	34	8.50	8.87	328
QuestValue	15	9.13	9.55	493
RNC Liq	25	9.08	9.50	103
RenaisGvt	6	8.91	9.32	56
RenaisMM	3	9.20	9.64	308
RsveCsh		....	....	......
ReserveFd	25	8.87	9.27	1672
ResrveFd Gvt	5	8.90	9.31	641
RetirPl	15	8.78	9.17	36
RodSMM	25	9.19	9.62	634
RdSqUS	18	9.03	9.44	266
Rushmore	20	8.91	9.31	67
TRwPr f	32	8.99	9.40	4184
TRwPU f	30	8.30	8.64	296
SBSF MM	49	8.98	9.38	26
SEI LqTr	16	9.04	9.45	2475
SEI LqGv	20	9.06	9.48	338
SEI LqPr	23	9.29	9.73	1915
SEI LqCl	21	9.28	9.71	165
SEI CsFd	6	8.96	9.36	33
SEI CsGv	36	9.09	9.51	167
SEI CsMM	23	9.14	9.57	361
SEI CsPr	26	9.50	9.95	215
SEI LqTII	6	9.07	9.49	121
SPIFqFed	27	9.38	9.82	1583
SPIFqTFd	26	9.22	9.65	1482
SPIFqTCs	38	9.62	10.09	689
SPIFqTmp	46	9.60	10.07	5027
Safeco f	30	9.06	9.48	178
StClair	31	9.03	9.44	84
ScudCshIn	30	8.72	9.33	1501
ScudGovt	19	8.45	8.82	161
ScudTr	19	5.95	9.36	65
SeagtePr	39	8.67	9.05	121
SeagtTrs	44	8.12	8.45	118
SlectGv	26	8.75	...	...
Slectin	38	9.11	...	.....
SecurityCsh	14	8.76	9.15	47
SeligCsh Gvt	1	8.73	9.12	26
SeligCsh pr	29	8.76	9.15	337
SentinelCsh	29	8.65	9.03	[illegible]
ShearDDv	44	8.94	9.34	13035
ShearsonGv	46	8.47	8.83	5073
ShrtTrmMM	33	8.82	9.22	[illegible]
ShTrinUS	37	8.03	8.35	200
ShrtTrA	11	9.02	9.43	48
Sigma	15	8.70	9.09	18
SouFarm	55	8.35	8.70	17
Standby	32	8.91	9.31	375
SteinroeCRs	37	8.88	9.26	996
SteinroeGvt	25	8.78	9.06	51
Strong	58	9.42	9.86	544
SumtCsh	33	8.94	9.35	593
TecuPrm	42	9.01	9.42	328
TecuUS	24	8.52	8.89	119
TempltnM	15	9.05	9.45	123
ThmMcNtl	24	9.21	9.64	2441
ThmMcGv	25	8.73	9.11	58
ThoroPO	23	8.97	9.38	344
ThoroUS	82	8.84	9.23	109
TowerCsh	27	8.84	9.24	77
Money Market:				
TransamCs	22	9.28	9.72	465
Trinity	26	9.18	9.62	493
TCU MMP	15	9.65	10.12	142
TrstShtGv	28	9.12	....	3786
TrstUSTrOb	22	9.06	....	4864
TuckAnthny	28	8.90	9.30	893
TuckrGvt	23	8.48	8.84	168
TwCntCs	21	8.95	9.35	567
UMB Fed	25	8.72	9.10	141
UMB Prim	27	9.33	9.77	116
USAA Mutl	32	8.98	9.39	804
US Treas	33	8.33	8.68	147
UST Gvt	10	9.03	9.45	235
UST Mny	14	9.30	9.74	367
UtdCshM a	58	8.98	9.39	355
ValLin	25	9.10	9.52	631
VnEckUS	46	7.56	7.85	42
VanKmpMM	53	8.40	8.76	48
VangFdl f	30	9.11	9.53	1404
VangPr f	34	9.35	9.79	8553
VangUST	31	8.85	9.24	169
VantgCsh	28	8.85	9.25	655
VantgGvt	31	8.46	8.82	82
VentGen	17	8.18	8.52	13
VentGov	34	8.02	8.34	19
Viking	26	8.95	9.35	34
VisnMM	31	8.97	9.38	76
VisnTr	12	7.86	8.17	35
VistaUS	17	8.81	9.21	266
WPG Sht	42	8.79	9.18	72
WebsCshR	39	8.89	9.29	1857
WoodGv	18	9.20	9.64	157
WoodMM	33	9.41	9.87	292
WorkAsets	22	8.60	8.97	152
Tax Exempt:				
AT OhioTx	55	6.25	6.44	258
ActAstTx	28	6.42	6.62	1119
AlliaTax	39	6.11	6.30	706
AllTxCal	37	6.09	6.28	136
AllTxNY	17	5.80	5.97	40
AlturTF	23	6.77	7.00	34
ArchFd	29	6.51	6.72	79
BdfdTxFr	29	6.27	6.47	95
BenhCal	30	6.21	6.40	439
BenhNtl	31	6.51	6.72	90
BostonCo	52	6.15	6.34	145
CIGNATx	31	5.99	6.17	53
CMA Cal TE	32	6.14	6.33	713
CMA NY TE	56	5.67	5.83	303
CalDaly	24	6.06	6.24	71
CalTRw	18	6.07	6.25	81
CalTF	29	6.38	6.58	84
CalvTxFr	51	6.58	6.80	870
CardTx	25	6.75	6.72	75
CarnegTx	68	6.19	.....	......
CashEq	13	6.48	6.69	2006
CentenTx	32	6.14	6.32	484
ColTEx	41	6.45	6.66	58
CompTx	36	6.59	6.81	126
ConnDlv	64	5.95	6.13	237
CortldTx	31	6.35	6.55	150
CounslNY	23	5.99	6.17	56
DBL Tax	31	6.21	6.40	406
DailTx c	15	6.27	6.47	751
DWSears	33	6.45	6.66	975
DWSrCal	26	6.34	6.55	281
DelaTax	56	5.93	6.11	66
DreyCalTx	33	5.94	6.12	272
DrNJTE	53	6.77	7.00	372
DrNYTE	50	5.75	5.92	452
DreyTxEx c	47	6.14	6.33	2401
EatnVn	36	6.22	6.42	64
Emblem	29	6.49	6.70	74
EmpirTxF	51	5.66	5.81	177
EvgrnTE	35	6.86	7.10	60
EvrgCA	16	6.75	6.98	27
FFB TF	41	6.32	6.52	132
FN Netwk	45	6.20	6.39	102
FedTxF c	51	6.17		2435
FidlCal	28	6.22	6.42	725
FidlNJ	33	6.83	7.07	230
FidlNY	49	5.69	5.85	715
FidPa	38	6.72	6.95	139
FidTxE c	38	6.32	6.52	3041
FidMassTx	44	6.24	6.44	639
FidDlvTE	43	6.14	6.33	207
FinclTxFr	36	6.12	6.31	30
FtInvTax	57	5.89	6.05	39
FtLkTE	35	6.22	6.41	129
FrkCal	33	6.04	6.22	847
FrkNYTE	38	5.91	6.09	60
FrkTx c	48	5.97	6.15	221
Gab OC TE	70	6.60	6.82	60
GalxyTE	48	6.24	6.43	120
GnCalTE	39	5.88	6.05	76
GnNYTE	45	5.47	5.62	52
FdTxFr	45	6.12	6.31	46
GnTxEx	42	5.98	6.16	360
HTInsgh	54	6.16	6.35	116
Helmsmn	41	6.56	6.77	50
HiMrkCal	40	6.00	6.18	163
HiMrk	40	6.18	6.37	41
HmeFdTF	22	6.22	6.41	81
HmeNY	50	5.57	5.72	26
HorznTE	36	6.83	7.07	
IDS Tx c	61	6.04	6.22	
ITADIV acf	38	6.37	6.57	
IntegTFr	8	6.31	6.51	
KmprMM	16	6.79	7.03	
KiddrPeaTx	49	6.11	6.29	
KidP CalT	39	6.02	6.20	
LndmkNY	44	5.54	5.69	
LdmkTxFr	34	6.29	6.48	
LaurlTE	30	6.48	6.69	
LazdInTF	30	6.73	6.96	
LazTex	27	6.08	6.26	
LegMTE	27	6.32	6.23	
LexingTx c	61	5.84	6.01	
LqdGrTx	69	6.09	6.28	
MarinTx	44	6.34	6.54	
MarinNY	78	5.51	5.66	
MassMM	78	6.02	6.20	
McDld	70	5.66	5.82	
MerLyCMA	45	6.28	6.48	
MerLyIns	16	6.63	6.85	
MetNYTF	31	5.61	5.77	
MdwstGrp	71	5.82	5.96	
MdwOHTF	29	6.14	6.33	
MnyMgt	26	5.97	6.15	
MonitorTF	38	6.30	6.50	
NeubBMu	59	6.39	6.59	
NETxEx	53	6.01	6.19	
TRPNY	24	5.45	5.60	
NYMuniCT	42	5.87	....	
NuvCal	38	6.30	6.50	
NuvnMas	45	6.25	6.45	
NuvNY	50	5.88	6.06	
NuvTxEx	51	6.49	6.70	
NuvnTFRs	56	6.17	6.36	
PacHorz	22	6.37	6.57	
PWRMA CA	31	6.20	6.40	
PWRMA NY	63	6.01	6.19	
PW RM Tx	49	6.14	6.33	
ParkTF	51	6.25	6.45	
PiperTE MM	51	6.12	6.31	
PrBCdTx	44	6.19	6.38	
PruBNY	70	5.48	5.63	
PrudBchTx	52	5.85	6.02	
PruInTE	15	6.41	6.62	
PutCA	29	6.18	6.37	
PutNY	74	5.36	5.50	
PutTE	38	6.25	6.4[illegible]	
RsrvConn	56	5.86	6.0[illegible]	
ResrvInt	47	5.98	6.1[illegible]	
ResrvNY	65	5.59	5.7[illegible]	
RdSqTE	14	6.55	6.7[illegible]	
TRPTx cf	15	6.49	6.7[illegible]	
SEI TFPt	40	6.32	6.5[illegible]	
SEI InTF	10	6.53	6.7[illegible]	
SPIFqMCa	34	6.42	6.6[illegible]	
SPIFMNY	35	6.07	6.2[illegible]	
SPIFGMCs	40	6.55	6.7[illegible]	
SPIFqMFd	42	6.38	6.5[illegible]	
SAFC TF	37	6.42	6.6[illegible]	
StClair	35	6.14	6.3[illegible]	
ScudCal	25	6.07	6.2[illegible]	
ScudNY	29	5.74	5.9[illegible]	
ScudTxF cf	26	6.23	6.4[illegible]	
Seagate	23	6.45	6.66	60
SlectTE	34	6.29	...	.....
SeligCATx	5	5.69	5.85	8
ShearCal	26	6.29	6.49	476
ShearDTx	46	6.22	6.41	3206
ShearNY	55	6.07	6.25	332
Standby c	54	6.26	6.46	70
SteinR	39	6.34	6.55	279
StrngMu	32	6.55	6.76	78
TxExCA	14	6.22	6.42	189
TaxFrCsh	30	6.41	6.61	240
TxFreeFd	3	5.95	6.13	13
TaxFrInst	42	6.27	6.46	1322
TxFreeM c	42	6.39	6.60	1017
TecuTx	47	6.16	6.35	115
ThMcTax	47	6.05	6.24	259
TuckAntTxE	35	6.07	6.25	206
UMBTxF	45	6.29	6.48	65
USAATxEx	70	6.24	6.43	804
UST Master	49	6.48	6.69	534
ValLinTxE	35	6.10	6.29	47
VanKmpTF	87	5.86	6.03	51
VangCA	55	6.41	6.61	376
VangNJ	60	6.70	6.92	[illegible]
VangPA	19	6.54	6.75	[illegible]
VangMB	58	6.52	6.74	2101
VentTF	58	5.11	5.24	[illegible]
VistaTF	32	6.16	6.35	106
VistaNY	28	5.57	5.72	220
WPG TX	33	6.58	6.80	33
WoodTE	47	6.35	6.55	200

Source: *The Wall Street Journal*, March 23, 1989.

Merrill Lynch Cash Management Account →

Fund	Avg. Mat.	7Day Yld.	e7Day Yld.	Assets
ML CMAMn a	35	8.82	9.22	23090

The Wall Street Journal, March 23, 1989.

CERTIFICATES OF DEPOSIT

Certificates of deposit (CDs) are like savings accounts for which you receive a "certificate of deposit" from the bank or savings and loan company. Banks and S&Ls issue certificates of deposit to compete with Treasury bills and commercial paper for the investor's dollar. CDs that have maturities of one year or less are part of the money market.

CDs offer higher rates than bank money market accounts and money market mutual funds with the same maturities. But you pay a price in penalties for early withdrawal of funds. Jumbo ($90,000–$100,000) certificates purchased through a broker are the only exception and then only if the broker can sell the CD to another investor. When you tie up your funds until maturity, the CD becomes a nonliquid asset. This disadvantage is offset to some extent by FDIC or FSLIC deposit insurance.

You can often get a higher CD rate from your broker than your local bank or S&L because your broker can shop nationally for the highest CD rate. You won't pay a fee for this service because the bank pays the broker.

Every Wednesday *The Wall Street Journal* publishes an article on current certificates of deposit yields which accompanies the **Banxquote Index.** An example from the March 22, 1989 issue is provided on page 268. The Banxquote Index presents the average yields paid by 18 leading banks for one, two, three, and six months and for one, two, and five years on savings CDs (minimum balance of $500 to $10,000) and jumbos (minimum balance of $90,000 to $100,000) along with the weekly interest rate change.

Two days later, on Fridays, the *Journal* publishes the more comprehensive **Banxquote Money Markets, High Yield Savings,** and **High Yield Jumbos.** Return to the March 24, 1989 example on page 259 (and blown-up on page 269). It reports CD interest rates by locale, maturity, and size. Note that CDs are

CD Yields Surge, But Rate-Watchers See More Rises

By GEORGETTE JASEN
Staff Reporter of THE WALL STREET JOURNAL

NEW YORK—Yields on certificates of deposit are surging to new highs—and there's more to come.

Yields on jumbo CDs (deposits of more than $95,000) and on CDs sold through brokers were up most in the past week. They gained more than a quarter of a percentage point in some maturities, according to Banxquote Money Markets, a New York-based information service.

On most smaller-denomination savings CDs, (generally less than $50,000), banks are paying at least a tenth of a percentage point more than they were a week ago, Banxquote said yesterday.

The increases, which bring CD yields to their highest level since late 1984, follow the jump in interest rates on Treasury bills sold at Monday's auction. Large-denomination CDs and CDs sold by brokers tend to react more quickly to interest rate trends.

But yields can be expected to rise even higher, said Norberto Mehl, chairman of Banxquote. As a result, he said, investors should buy CDs maturing in 12 months or less "to be able to ride the yield curve in a rising interest rate environment."

The highest yields are currently on one-year CDs, with banks paying an average of 9.17% on deposits of less than $50,000 and brokers offering an average of 10.09%. For jumbos, the average yield paid by banks is 9.86%.

The average yield on a six-month bank CD of less than $50,000 rose to 8.87% in the latest week. Three-month CD yields rose to an average of 8.45%.

Average Six-Month CD & Three-Month CD Yields

Some banks are paying well above the national averages, however. In part, this reflects competition among banks, which is particularly stiff in the Northeast.

The highest yield offered by a bank on deposits of less than $50,000, according to Banxquote, is 10.67% on a three-month CD at **Home Loan Bank** in Providence, R.I.

New York banks also continue to pay among the highest yields, with **Citicorp**'s Citibank, for example, offering 9.58% on a six-month CD and **Manufacturers Hanover Trust** Co. paying 9.25% on a three-month CD.

For CDs sold by brokers, yields rose to an average of 9.98% for six-month and 9.80% for three-month money.

Average yields offered by banks on jumbo CDs were 9.72% for six months and 9.43% for three months.

The effective annual yield on T-bills sold at Monday's auction was 9.60% for six months and 9.34% for three months. T-bills require a minimum investment of $10,000.

On longer-term CDs of less than $50,000, average yields were 9.15% for two years and 9.13% for five years. On jumbo CDs, the averages were 9.61% and 9.51%, respeotively.

Broker-sold CDs were yielding an average of 9.97% for two years and 9.72% for five years.

Bank money market accounts continue to lag behind other investments by a significant margin. Like CDs, these accounts offer yields that are adjusted periodically in response to interest-rate trends, but they also offer check-writing and are considered more liquid. Banxquote reported that the average yield on money-market investments of less than $50,000 was 6.94% in the latest week; on jumbo deposits, it was 7.38%.

BANXQUOTE® INDEX

Tuesday, March 21, 1989

AVERAGE YIELDS OF 18 LEADING BANKS

	Savings Yield	Wkly Chg.	Jumbo Yield	Wkly Chg.
Money Market	6.94	+0.03	7.38	+0.03
1 Month CD	....	....	9.17	+0.17
2 Month CD	....	....	9.26	+0.17
3 Month CD	8.45	+0.13	9.43	+0.18
6 Month CD	8.87	+0.10	9.72	+0.26
1 Year CD	9.17	+0.14	9.86	+0.26
2 Year CD	9.15	+0.12	9.61	+0.14
5 Year CD	9.13	+0.05	9.51	+0.08

CD Yields

AVERAGE YIELDS OF LEADING BROKERS

	3 Mo.	6 Mo.	1 Yr.	2 Yr.	5 Yr.
Savings CD	9.80	9.98	10.09	9.97	9.72
Weekly Change	+0.28	+0.19	+0.26	+0.23	+0.09

Source: BANXQUOTE MONEY MARKETS, N.Y.

Source: *The Wall Street Journal*, March 22, 1989.

quoted by rate and yield. The more frequently interest is compounded, the higher the yield for each rate. Look under **High Yield Savings**, One-year CDs and you'll notice that both CBT in Hartford, Connecticut and Firstbanc Savings in Missouri City, Texas quote rates of 10 percent. However, because CBT compounds monthly (denoted by *MA*) and Firstbanc compounds quarterly (*qA*), the yield is higher at CBT (10.47 percent) than at Firstbanc (10.38 percent).

It pays to shop. You can see that while the average 3-month CD paid 8.45 percent, the broker average was 9.8 percent, and Merchant's Bank in Boston paid 10.47 percent.

Bank Average: 8.45% for 3-month CD

BANK AVERAGE

Savings	6.94%	z	z	8.45%	8.87%	9.17%	9.15%	9.13%
Jumbos	7.38%	9.16%	9.25%	9.42%	9.71%	9.85%	9.61%	9.51%
WEEKLY CHANGE (in percentage point)								
Savings	+0.03	z	z	+0.13	+0.10	+0.14	+0.12	+0.05
Jumbos	+0.03	+0.16	+0.16	+0.17	+0.25	+0.25	+0.14	+0.08

SAVINGS CD YIELDS OFFERED THROUGH LEADING BROKERS

Broker Average: 9.83% 3-month yield

	Three Months	Six Months	One Year	Two Years	Five Years
BROKER AVERAGE	9.80%	9.98%	10.09%	9.97%	9.72%
WEEKLY CHANGE	+0.28	+0.19	+0.26	+0.23	+0.09

*Money Market Investments include MMDA, NOW, savings deposits, passbook and other liquid accounts.

Each depositor is insured by the Federal Deposit Insurance Corp. (FDIC) or Federal Savings and Loan Insurance Corp. (FSLIC) up to $100,000 per issuing institution.

COMPOUND METHODS: c-Continuously. d-Daily. w-Weekly. m-Monthly. q-Quarterly. s-Semi-annually. a-Annually. si-Simple interest.

YIELD BASIS: A-365/365. B-360/360. C-365/360.

The information included in this table has been obtained directly from broker-dealers, banks and savings institutions, but the accuracy and validity cannot be guaranteed. Rates are subject to change. Yields, terms and creditworthiness should be verified before investing.

z-Unavailable.

HIGH YIELD SAVINGS

Small minimum balance, generally $500 to $10,000

Money Market Investments	Rate		Yield
Chevy Chase, Laurel Md	9.40%	mA	9.82%
Eastern Savings, Baltimore Md	9.30%	dA	9.74%
Chase Bank, Baltimore Md	9.25%	dA	9.69%
Haymarket Bank, Boston Ma	9.27%	mA	9.67%
Barclays Bank, New York Ny	9.20%	dA	9.64%

One Month CDs	Rate		Yield
New South FSB, Birmingham Al	9.30%	siA	9.30%
Columbia Svgs, Newport Beach Ca	8.80%	dA	9.20%
Hallmark Savings, Plano Tx	9.00%	siA	9.00%
Bank Of New England, Boston Ma	9.00%	siA	9.00%
North American, San Antonio Tx	8.88%	siA	8.88%

Two Months CDs	Rate		Yield
New Haven Svgs, New Haven Ct	9.00%	mA	9.38%
New South FSB, Birmingham Al	9.30%	siA	9.30%
Columbia Svgs, Newport Beach Ca	8.80%	dA	9.20%
North American, San Antonio Tx	9.00%	siA	9.00%
Rancho Bernardo, Escondido Ca	8.50%	dC	9.00%

Merchant's Bank

Three Months CDs	Rate		Yield
Merchants Bank, Boston Ma	10.00%	mA	10.47%
Compass Bank, New Bedford Ma	9.80%	mA	10.25%
Home Loan, Providence RI	10.00%	siC	10.14%
Columbia Svgs, Newport Beach Ca	9.60%	dA	10.07%
Bank Of Boston, Boston Ma	10.00%	siA	10.00%

Six Months CDs	Rate		Yield
CBT, Hartford Ct	10.00%	mA	10.47%
Merchants Bank, Boston Ma	10.00%	mA	10.47%
Citytrust, Bridgeport Ct	10.00%	mA	10.47%
Columbia Svgs, Newport Beach Ca	9.80%	dA	10.29%
Home Loan, Providence RI	10.00%	siC	10.14%

CBT

Firstbanc Savings

One Year CDs	Rate		Yield
CBT, Hartford Ct	10.00%	MA	10.47%
Citytrust, Bridgeport Ct	10.00%	MA	10.47%
Firstbanc Svgs, Missouri City Tx	10.00%	qA	10.38%
Bank Of New England, Boston	10.00%	qA	10.38%
Columbia Svgs, Newport Beach Ca	10.10%	sA	10.36%

Two Years CDs	Rate		Yield
CBT, Hartford Ct	10.00%	mA	10.47%
Mercantile Bank, Boston	10.00%	mA	10.47%
Commonwealth Svgs, Houston Tx	9.95%	dA	10.46%
Firstbanc Svgs, Missouri City Tx	10.00%	qA	10.38%
Bank Of New England, Boston	10.00%	qA	10.38%

Five Years CDs	Rate		Yield
Commerce Savings, Dallas	9.85%	dA	10.35%
Benjamin Franklin, Houston Tx	9.75%	qA	10.11%
Independence Fed, Wash DC	9.75%	qA	10.11%
First Republic, Los Angeles	9.62%	dA	10.10%
Columbia Svgs, Newport Beach Ca	9.85%	sA	10.09%

Source: *The Wall Street Journal*, March 24, 1989.

TREASURY BILLS

Our national debt made the news when it passed $2 trillion, and it continues to grow. Treasury bills (T-bills) constitute about a quarter of the total national debt, and this huge dollar volume makes Treasury bills one of the most important short-term investment instruments.

The U.S. Treasury borrows by selling bills at *auction* (primary market) every Monday in New York, and in the following day's *Journal* you will find a summary of the U.S. Treasury's Monday auction of 13- and 26-week bills at the end of the **Credit Markets** article. (You can find it using the indexes at the front of the first and last sections.) See the example drawn from the Tuesday, March 14, 1989 edition of the *Journal* on page 272.

One-year Treasury bills are auctioned every four weeks. The auction is announced on the fourth Friday and conducted the following Thursday. See the example from the Wednesday, February 15, 1989 edition of the *Journal* on page 272.

Treasury bills are sold on a discount basis. Buyers pay less than the $10,000 face value (par value), the amount they will receive when the bill matures and is redeemed by the U.S. Treasury. If bidding is strong and the price is high, the effective rate of interest will be low and vice versa.

To understand how this works, place yourself in the role of a buyer. If you pay $9,750 for a bill maturing in 91 days (about a quarter of a year), your effective annual yield is approximately 10 percent. Remember, $250 in a quarter-year is the equivalent of $1,000 in a year, or 10 percent of a $10,000 base. (Use $10,000 as the base for calculating the discount rate, rather than $9,750, because Treasury bills' yields are usually quoted on a discount basis; that is, the discount—$250—is measured against face value—$10,000.) If strong bidding drives the price to $9,875, your yield falls to 5 percent. If weak bidding or selling pressure permits the price to fall to $9,500, the effective yield rises to 20 percent; the more you pay for the Treasury bill, the lower your yield and vice versa. The examples are summarized here. You can easily approximate the following discount rates using this simple chart.

Face (redemption) Value	$10,000	$10,000	$10,000
Selling Price (note: prices falling)	$9,875	$9,750	$9,500
Discount (difference)	$125	$250	$500
Approximate Yield (Discount Rate) (note: yield rising)	5%	10%	20%

Most short-term rates also rose. For example, rates were higher on new three-month and six-month Treasury bills.

Elsewhere in the markets, the Federal Home Loan Banks plan a record $6.94 billion debt offering today. Some analysts think the issue will sell briskly because of wide spreads between the issue and comparable Treasury issues.

But several agency traders say the sheer size of the offering, particularly the weighty one-year to three-year parts of the six-pronged financing, will make investors cautious. The three biggest issues each total $1.4 billion to $1.8 billion. Several traders say they expect yields of more than 10% on these issues.

FHLB's February offering of $6.38 billion was the previous record package, a sale that far exceeded the $4.73 billion sold in January.

At the February sale, one-year and two-year FHLB bonds were priced to yield 18 and 19 basis points above their equivalent Treasury notes; a basis point is 1/100 a percentage point. Some traders say these new issues will carry spreads that are around double those in February.

Here are details of the Treasury's auction yesterday of new short-term bills:

Rates are determined by the difference between the purchase price and face value. Thus, higher bidding narrows the investor's return while lower bidding widens it. The percentage rates are calculated on a 360-day year, while the coupon equivalent yield is based on a 365-day year.

	13-Week	26-Week
Applications	$22,864,050,000	$27,209,475,000
Accepted bids	$7,216,160,000	$7,203,225,000
Accepted at low price	36%	77%
Accepted noncompet'ly	$1,436,560,000	$1,201,275,000
Average price (Rate)	97.803 (8.69%)	95.571 (8.76%)
High price (Rate)	97.813 (8.65%)	95.576 (8.75%)
Low price (Rate)	97.801 (8.70%)	95.571 (8.76%)
Coupon equivalent	9.01%	9.29%

Both issues are dated March 16. The 13-week bills mature June 15, and the 26-week bills mature Sept. 14.

13-Week & 26-Week Treasury Note Auction

Source: *The Wall Street Journal*, March 14, 1989

Treasury Securities

Bond dealers are bracing for another large wave of Treasury borrowing soon.

The government today is expected to announce plans to sell new two-year and five-year notes next week. Traders generally expect the Treasury to sell about $9.25 billion of two-year notes next Wednesday, followed by around $7.75 billion of five-year notes the following day.

The government's new 30-year bonds fell yesterday to 97 17/32, down 17/32 point from Monday. The yield rose to 9.12% from 9.06%. The bonds were auctioned last Thursday by the Treasury at an average annual yield of 8.91%.

The Treasury's new 10-year notes fell to 97 28/32 from 98 2/32, while the yield climbed to 9.21% from 9.18%.

The average annual yield of 9.32% on the new 52-week bills sold yesterday was the highest since March 1985, a Treasury spokesman said.

The yield on 13-week bills rose to 8.84% bid from an average of 8.80% set at Monday's auction. The yield on 26-week bills climbed to 9.12% from 9.05%.

Here are details of yesterday's 52-week bill sale:

Rates are determined by the difference between the purchase price and face value. Thus, higher bidding narrows the investor's return while lower bidding widens it. The percentage rates are calculated on a 360-day year, while the coupon equivalent yield is based on a 365-day year.

52-Week Treasury Bill Auction

	52-Week
Applications	$27,737,330,000
Accepted bids	$9,031,770,000
Accepted at low price	78%
Accepted noncompetitively	$1,46,660,000
Average price (Rate)	91.315 (8.59%)
High price (Rate)	91.365 (8.54%)
Low price (Rate)	91.315 (8.59%)
Coupon equivalent	9.32%

The bills are dated Feb. 16 and mature Feb. 15, 1990.

Source: *The Wall Street Journal*, February 15, 1989.

Take a moment to review the method used to compute the discount rate in the bottom row of the table on page 270. The following calculations show how the 10 percent rate was obtained. Discount rate (Yield) = Discount expressed as a percentage of par (yield) × Time factor multiplier (which is needed to generate the annual rate).

$$\text{Approximate discount rate (yield)} = \frac{\text{Discount}}{\text{Face or par value}} \times 4 \quad \text{(because 91 days are about a quarter of a 365-day year)}$$

$$= \frac{\$250}{\$10{,}000} \times 4$$

$$= 2.5\% \times 4$$

$$= 10\%$$

The true discount rate formula is very close to this approximation. The "time factor multiplier" is somewhat different because the "year" is 360 days. Again returning to the example, the discount rate would be calculated as follows:

$$\text{Discount rate} = \frac{\text{Discount}}{\text{Par value}} \times \text{Time multiplier}$$

$$= \frac{\$250}{\$10{,}000} \times \frac{360}{91}$$

$$= 0.0989$$

$$= 9.89\%$$

You can see that the true discount rate of 9.89 is less than the 10 percent approximation calculated above because the time multiplier (360/91) is less than 4.

The discount rate is only an approximation of the true yield to maturity or coupon equivalent. In the first place, the purchase price of the T-bill was not $10,000. It was only $9,750. So in the fraction, $10,000 should be replaced by $9,750. And secondly, a year is 365 days, not 360. Thus, the correct time multiplier is 365/91.

Now calculate the actual yield, called the investment yield to maturity, for the same example.

$$\text{Yield to maturity} = \frac{\text{Discount}}{\text{Purchase price}} \times \text{Time factor}$$
$$= \frac{\$250}{\$9{,}750} \times \frac{365}{91}$$
$$= 0.1029$$
$$= 10.29\%$$

You can see that the discount rate of 9.89% is less than the true yield of 10.29 percent because the discount is expressed as a percentage of the purchase price rather than par, and the year is calculated at 365 rather than 360 days.

Now that you understand the relationship between the discount rate and the yield to maturity (coupon equivalent), look at the illustration from the Tuesday, March 14, 1989 *Journal*. On the average, the U.S. Treasury received $9,780.30 (97.803 percent of face value) for each $10,000 bill auctioned on Monday, March 13, 1989 for a discount rate of 8.69 percent and a coupon equivalent yield of 9.01 percent.

Here is how you calculate the discount rate using the Treasury auction figures on page 271 and blown-up below.

$$\text{Discount rate} = \frac{\text{Discount}}{\text{Par value}} \times \text{Time multiplier}$$
$$= \frac{\$219.70 \text{ (i.e., } \$10,000 - \$9,780.30)}{\$10,000} \times \frac{360}{91}$$
$$= 0.0869$$
$$= 8.69\%$$

Here are details of the Treasury's auction yesterday of new short-term bills:

Rates are determined by the difference between the purchase price and face value. Thus, higher bidding narrows the investor's return while lower bidding widens it. The percentage rates are calculated on a 360-day year, while the coupon equivalent yield is based on a 365-day year.

	13-Week	26-Week
Applications	$22,864,050,000	$27,209,475,000
Accepted bids	$7,216,160,000	$7,203,225,000
Accepted at low price	36%	77%
Accepted noncompet'ly	$1,436,560,000	$1,201,275,000
Average price (Rate)	97.803 (8.69%)	95.571 (8.76%)
High price (Rate)	97.813 (8.65%)	95.576 (8.75%)
Low price (Rate)	97.801 (8.70%)	95.571 (8.76%)
Coupon equivalent	9.01%	9.29%

Both issues are dated March 16. The 13-week bills mature June 15, and the 26-week bills mature Sept. 14.

Treasury Bill Auction

On Monday, March 13, 1989 the Treasury auctioned 13-week bills in the primary market which had a discount rate of 8.69 percent; and a coupon equivalent yield of 9.01%

Source: *The Wall Street Journal*, March 14, 1989.

You can also compute the true (coupon equivalent) yield as follows.

$$\begin{aligned}\text{Yield to maturity} &= \frac{\text{Discount}}{\text{Purchase price}} \times \text{Time multiplier}\\ &= \frac{\$219.70}{\$9{,}780.30} \times \frac{365}{91}\\ &= 0.0901\%\\ &= 9.01\%\end{aligned}$$

Your motivation for buying Treasury bills is probably quite simple: you have idle cash on which you wish to earn an interest return. If you and all other bidders for Treasury bills have ample funds and are eager to buy, you will drive the price close to $10,000 and earn a low rate of return. If you and all other bidders do not have ample funds, you can be enticed only by a very low price for the right to receive $10,000 in 91 days, and you will earn a high rate of return.

Now, this discussion has been presented as if you could participate in the bidding for Treasury bills. Well, you can't. The auction is conducted in New York by the Fed, acting as the Treasury's agent, and is reserved for a closed list of large firms that deal in, and make a market for, Treasury bills. They bid for the bills at the weekly Monday auction (primary market) so they can resell them at a markup on any business day (secondary market). You *can* go to your local regional Federal Reserve Bank and buy Treasury bills, but you'll have to do so noncompetitively at the average rate (discount) established at the New York auction. (For instance, the 8.69 percent discount rate and 9.01 percent yield in the example on page 274.)

There are two ways to buy T-bills from the Fed: immediately or by opening an account that permits purchases at a later date. If you want to purchase Treasuries right away, obtain what is called a "Tender" form from the Fed or your bank, fill out the "Direct Deposit" section and include a money order or certified check for $10,000. The Fed will mail you your change (the discount) and return the $10,000 at maturity (91 days). If you wish to open an account to purchase Treasuries in the near future, complete and return the "New Account Application." Once the application is received and you are given an account number, you can then contact the Fed by phone and purchase Treasuries with a tender offer and certified check.

If you purchase a Treasury bill from the Fed, you must hold it to maturity, which is not the case if you have purchased it from your bank or broker. Your bank or broker can sell it on the open or secondary market for you at any time, but be prepared to pay a flat fee of $25 to $50 per transaction. In order to gain clients with large assets, some brokerage houses do not charge a fee if an investor purchases more than $100,000 of Treasury bills.

The Wall Street Journal reports on activity in the secondary market each day, under the heading **Treasury Bonds, Notes & Bills**. Find this table by using the index on the front page or the index on the first page of Section C.

Look at the excerpt from the Tuesday, September 19, 1989 *Journal* on page 277 and 278. The data represent quotations for Monday, September 18, 1989 at 4 P.M. Eastern time. Keep in mind that these bills are auctioned on Mondays, issued on Thursdays, and mature 13 weeks later (also on a Thursday). Thus, using the report for Monday, September 18, 1989, you know that the latest 91-day bill included in the report was auctioned on Monday, September 11, 1989, and issued on Thursday, September 14, 1989. It will mature 13 weeks later, on Thursday, December 14, 1989. On September 14, that bill carried an interest rate (bid) of 7.61 percent. This figure is located in the row opposite the date under the column headed "Bid." Buyers (bidders) paid a price (less than $10,000) that would yield 7.61 percent if the Treasury bill were held to maturity and cashed in for $10,000. Sellers on September 18 were asking a higher price (lower interest rate) equivalent to 7.57 percent. The last column gives the true yield of 7.82 percent. (The other maturity dates are for older bills and for bills with maturities of more than 91 days.)

It is now time to complete this discussion of short-term interest rates with a description of how you can track the yield on your own interest-earning investments and compare them with market rates.

TRACKING SHORT-TERM INTEREST RATES

Every day you can use the **Markets Diary** report on the left side of the first page (C1) of the *Journal's* last section to follow some of the most important short-term interest rates. Consult the excerpt from the Monday, March 20, 1989 edition on page 278, starting with the chart labeled **Interest**, which displays the federal funds rate for the preceding 18 months. This is the rate banks charge one another for overnight loans of reserves in

TREASURY BONDS, NOTES & BILLS

Monday, September 18, 1989

Representative Over-the-Counter quotations based on transactions of $1 million or more as of 4 p.m. Eastern time.

Decimals in bid-and-asked and bid changes represent 32nds; 101.01 means 101 1/32. Treasury bill quotes in hundredths. a-Plus 1/64. b-Yield to call date. d-Minus 1/64. k-Nonresident aliens exempt from withholding taxes. n-Treasury notes. p-Treasury note; nonresident aliens exempt from withholding taxes.

Stripped Treasuries -- a-Stripped interest. b-Treasury bond; stripped principal. c-Treasury note; stripped principal.

Source: Bloomberg Financial Markets

GOVT. BONDS & NOTES

Rate	Maturity	Bid	Asked	Bid Chg.	Yld.
8.50	Sep 89p	99.28	99.31	−.01	9.18
9.37	Sep 89p	99.29	100.00	−.01	8.98
11.87	Oct 89n	100.05	100.08	...	7.93
7.87	Oct 89p	99.29	100.00	+.01	7.64
6.37	Nov 89p	99.20	99.24	...	7.84
10.75	Nov 89n	100.08	100.12	...	8.00
12.75	Nov 89p	100.18	100.22	...	7.91
7.75	Nov 89p	99.26	99.29	−.01	8.05
7.87	Dec 89p	[illegible]	[illegible]	[illegible]	[illegible]
[illegible]	[illegible]	[illegible]	[illegible]	...	7.68
[illegible]	May 91p	100.27	100.31	−.03	8.11
7.87	Jun 91n	99.15	99.19	−.02	8.11
8.25	Jun 91p	100.03	100.07	−.02	8.10
7.75	Jul 91p	99.09	99.13	−.03	8.09
13.75	Jul 91n	109.07	109.11	−.03	8.11
7.50	Aug 91p	98.27	99.00	−.02	8.07
8.75	Aug 91p	100.31	101.03	−.05	8.11
14.87	Aug 91n	112.23	112.27	−.04	7.50
8.25	Aug 91p	100.06	100.09	−.03	8.09
9.12	Sep 91p	101.25	101.29	−.04	8.09
12.25	Oct 91p	107.18	107.22	−.06	8.13
6.50	Nov 91p	96.25	96.29	−.03	8.09
8.50	Nov 91p	100.20	100.24	−.05	8.10
14.25	Nov 91n	112.19	112.23	−.04	7.72
8.25	Dec 91p	100.04	100.09	−.05	8.10
11.62	Jan 92p	107.04	107.09	−.03	8.11
6.62	Feb 92p	96.21	96.25	−.04	8.12
9.12	Feb 92p	102.02	102.06	−.03	8.10
14.62	Feb 92n	115.04	115.08	−.03	7.56
7.87	Mar 92p	99.12	99.16	−.03	8.10
11.75	Apr 92k	108.02	108.07	−.05	8.14
6.62	May 92p	96.12	96.16	−.03	8.11
9.00	May 92p	101.31	102.03	−.04	8.10
13.75	May 92n	113.04	113.08	−.03	8.09
8.25	Jun 92p	100.09	100.13	−.02	8.08
10.37	Jul 92p	105.14	105.18	−.05	8.12
4.25	Aug 87-92	92.00	92.29	−.03	6.99
7.25	Aug 92	97.25	97.31	−.03	8.04
8.25	Aug 92p	100.07	100.11	−.08	8.11
7.87	Aug 92p	99.14	99.17	−.03	8.05
8.75	Sep 92p	101.20	101.24	−.02	8.09
9.75	Oct 92p	104.08	104.12	−.04	8.11
8.37	Nov 92p	100.18	100.23	−.02	8.11
10.50	Nov 92n	106.15	106.19	−.03	8.08
9.12	Dec 92p	102.23	102.27	−.02	8.11
8.75	Jan 93p	101.23	101.27	−.02	8.10
4.00	Feb 88-93	91.28	92.23	−.03	6.41
6.75	Feb 93	95.29	96.15	−.03	7.95
7.87	Feb 93	98.20	98.27	−.03	8.27
8.25	Feb 93p	100.10	100.14	−.01	8.10
10.87	Feb 93n	107.30	108.02	−.03	8.11
9.62	Mar 93p	104.15	104.19	−.04	8.10
7.37	Apr 93p	97.20	97.24	−.04	8.11
7.62	May 93p	98.11	98.15	−.03	8.11
10.12	May 93n	106.05	106.09	...	8.10
8.12	Jun 93p	100.02	100.05	−.03	8.07
7.25	Jul 93p	97.03	97.07	−.05	8.11
7.50	Aug 88-93	97.18	97.27	−.03	8.15
8.62	Aug 93	101.22	101.26	−.03	8.07
8.75	Aug 93p	101.31	102.04	−.03	8.10
11.87	Aug 93n	112.07	112.11	−.04	8.12
7.12	Oct 93p	96.19	96.23	−.04	8.08
8.62	Nov 93	101.22	101.28	−.03	8.08
11.75	Nov 93n	112.13	112.18	−.01	8.12
9.00	Nov 93p	102.31	103.04	−.03	8.09
7.00	Jan 94p	96.02	96.06	−.04	8.06
9.00	Feb 94	103.06	103.10	−.03	8.09
8.87	Feb 94p	102.25	102.29	−.02	8.07
7.00	Apr 94p	95.29	96.02	...	8.04
4.12	May 89-94	91.29	92.14	−.03	6.01
13.12	May 94p	119.03	119.07	...	8.08
9.50	May 94p	105.09	105.13	−.02	8.07
8.00	Jul 94p	99.21	99.26	−.03	8.04
8.62	Aug 94p	102.03	102.07	−.02	8.05
8.75	Aug 94	102.18	102.30	−.03	8.01
12.62	Aug 94p	117.29	118.01	−.03	8.09
9.50	Oct 94p	105.18	105.22	−.04	8.11
10.12	Nov 94	108.09	108.13	−.03	8.09
11.62	Nov 94p	114.14	114.18	−.03	8.11
8.25	Nov 94p	100.26	100.29	−.03	8.02
8.62	Jan 95p	102.01	102.05	−.03	8.11
3.00	Feb 95	92.01	93.04	−.03	4.44

Rate	Maturity	Bid	Asked	Bid Chg.	Yld.
10.50	Feb 95	110.08	110.12	...	8.09
11.25	Feb 95p	113.08	113.12	−.03	8.14
8.37	Apr 95p	101.00	101.04	−.04	8.12
10.37	May 95	109.28	110.00	−.07	8.13
11.25	May 95p	113.21	113.27	−.07	8.14
12.62	May 95	120.05	120.10	−.03	8.07
8.87	Jul 95p	103.07	103.12	−.01	8.13
10.50	Aug 95p	[illegible]	[illegible]	[illegible]	[illegible]
[illegible]	[illegible]	[illegible]	[illegible]	−.03	8.21
[illegible]	Aug 03-08	101.01	101.07	−.03	8.22
8.75	Nov 03-08	104.03	104.09	−.03	8.23
9.12	May 04-09	107.07	107.13	−.03	8.24
10.37	Nov 04-09	117.15	117.21	−.07	8.30
11.75	Feb 05-10	129.11	129.17	−.06	8.31
10.00	May 05-10	114.23	114.29	−.08	8.28
12.75	Nov 05-10	138.25	138.31	−.05	8.32
13.87	May 06-11	149.14	149.20	−.05	8.31
14.00	Nov 06-11	151.08	151.14	−.05	8.32
10.37	Nov 07-12	119.07	119.13	−.06	8.29
12.00	Aug 08-13	134.27	135.01	−.06	8.30
13.25	May 09-14	147.15	147.21	−.06	8.29
12.50	Aug 09-14k	140.15	140.21	−.06	8.29
11.75	Nov 09-14k	133.15	133.21	−.06	8.28
11.25	Feb 15k	131.31	132.05	−.02	8.21
10.62	Aug 15k	125.17	125.23	−.04	8.21
9.87	Nov 15k	117.22	117.28	−.05	8.20
9.25	Feb 16k	111.06	111.12	−.06	8.19
7.25	May 16k	90.01	90.05	−.05	8.16
7.50	Nov 16k	92.21	92.25	−.05	8.16
8.75	May 17k	106.04	106.08	−.05	8.17
8.87	Aug 17k	107.18	107.22	−.04	8.17
9.12	May 18k	110.19	110.23	−.04	8.15
9.00	Nov 18k	109.13	109.17	−.01	8.14
8.87	Feb 19k	108.04	108.08	...	8.13
8.12	Aug 19k	100.10	100.14	−.02	8.08

STRIPPED TREASURIES

Rate	Maturity	Bid	Asked	Bid Chg.	Yld.
.00	Aug 89a	99.21	99.22	...	7.94
.00	Nov 89a	98.24	98.25	...	7.89
.00	Feb 90a	96.26	96.27	...	8.02
.00	May 90a	94.29	94.31	...	8.04
.00	Aug 90a	93.00	93.03	−.01	8.05
.00	Nov 90a	91.05	91.09	−.01	8.05
.00	Feb 91	89.12	89.16	...	8.05
.00	May 91a	87.18	87.24	−.02	8.06
.00	Aug 91	85.31	86.05	−.02	7.97
.00	Nov 91a	84.04	84.11	−.02	8.06
.00	Feb 92a	82.15	82.22	−.02	8.06
.00	May 92a	80.26	81.02	−.03	8.06
.00	Aug 92a	79.08	79.16	−.01	8.05
.00	Nov 92a	77.22	77.31	−.01	8.04
.00	Feb 93a	76.07	76.16	−.01	8.02
.00	May 93a	74.23	75.02	−.02	8.01
.00	Aug 93a	73.13	73.23	−.01	7.96
.00	Nov 93a	71.30	72.09	−.01	7.97
.00	Feb 94a	70.10	70.21	...	8.04
.00	May 94a	68.30	69.10	−.01	8.03
.00	Aug 94a	67.24	68.04	...	7.98
.00	Nov 94a	66.06	66.18	...	8.05
.00	Feb 95a	64.26	65.07	...	8.07
.00	May 95a	63.15	63.29	−.01	8.08
.00	Aug 95a	62.06	62.19	−.01	8.09
.00	Nov 95a	60.29	61.11	−.01	8.10
.00	Feb 96a	59.21	60.03	−.01	8.11
.00	May 96a	58.15	58.29	−.01	8.11
.00	Aug 96a	57.08	57.23	−.01	8.12
.00	Nov 96a	56.02	56.17	−.01	8.13
.00	Feb 97a	54.29	55.12	−.01	8.14
.00	May 97a	53.26	54.09	−.01	8.14
.00	Aug 97a	52.22	53.06	−.01	8.15
.00	Nov 97a	51.21	52.04	...	8.15
.00	Feb 98a	50.18	51.02	−.01	8.16
.00	May 98a	49.18	50.01	−.01	8.16
.00	Aug 98a	48.16	49.00	−.01	8.17
.00	Nov 98a	47.17	48.01	−.01	8.17
.00	Feb 99a	46.19	47.03	−.01	8.17
.00	May 99a	45.21	46.05	−.01	8.17
.00	Aug 99a	44.23	45.08	−.01	8.17
.00	Nov 99a	43.24	44.08	−.01	8.19
.00	Feb 00a	42.28	43.12	−.01	8.19
.00	May 00a	42.00	42.17	−.01	8.19
.00	Aug 00a	41.05	41.22	−.01	8.19
.00	Nov 00a	40.12	40.28	−.01	8.18
.00	Feb 01a	39.14	39.30	−.02	8.21

Rate	Maturity	Bid	Asked	Bid Chg.	Yld.
.00	May 01a	38.20	39.05	−.03	8.21
.00	Aug 01a	37.26	38.10	−.02	8.22
.00	Nov 01a	37.01	37.18	−.03	8.22
.00	Feb 02a	36.09	36.26	−.03	8.22
.00	May 02a	35.18	36.03	−.02	8.22
.00	Aug 02a	34.27	35.12	−.02	8.22
.00	Nov 02a	34.04	34.21	−.03	8.22
.00	Feb 03a	33.14	33.31	−.01	8.22
.00	May 03a	32.25	33.09	−.01	8.22
.00	Aug 03a	32.03	32.20	−.02	8.22
.00	Nov 03a	31.16	32.01	...	8.21
.00	Feb 04a	30.25	31.09	−.01	8.23
.00	May 04a	30.05	30.21	−.01	8.23
.00	Aug 04a	29.17	30.02	−.02	8.23
.00	Nov 04a	28.30	29.15	−.01	8.23
.00	Feb 05a	28.12	[illegible]	[illegible]	[illegible]
[illegible]	[illegible]	[illegible]	[illegible]	[illegible]	7.97
[illegible]	May 16a	12.03	12.16	−.04	7.96
.00	Aug 16a	11.29	12.09	−.04	7.95
.00	Nov 16a	11.22	12.02	−.03	7.94
.00	Feb 17a	11.16	11.28	−.03	7.93
.00	May 17a	11.11	11.22	−.03	7.91
.00	Aug 17a	11.06	11.17	−.02	7.89
.00	Nov 17a	11.00	11.11	−.02	7.88
.00	Feb 18a	10.28	11.07	−.02	7.85
.00	May 18a	10.22	11.01	−.03	7.84
.00	Aug 18a	10.16	10.28	−.03	7.83
.00	Nov 18a	10.14	10.26	−.03	7.78
.00	Feb 19a	10.11	10.22	−.02	7.75
.00	Aug 19a	10.18	10.30	−.03	7.54
.00	Nov 04b	29.04	29.13	−.01	8.24
.00	May 05b	28.00	28.09	−.01	8.23
.00	Aug 05b	27.15	27.25	−.01	8.22
.00	Feb 06b	26.12	28.20	−.01	7.77
.00	Feb 15b	13.11	13.18	−.01	8.02
.00	Aug 15b	12.26	13.01	−.01	8.02
.00	Nov 15b	12.20	12.27	−.01	8.00
.00	Feb 16b	12.15	12.22	−.01	7.97
.00	May 16b	12.11	12.19	−.01	7.93
.00	Nov 16b	11.28	12.03	−.01	7.93
.00	May 17b	11.16	11.22	...	7.91
.00	Aug 17b	11.11	11.18	−.01	7.88
.00	May 18b	10.27	11.02	−.01	7.83
.00	Nov 18b	10.17	10.24	−.01	7.80
.00	Feb 19b	10.14	10.21	−.01	7.76
.00	Nov 94c	66.07	66.14	+.01	8.09
.00	Feb 95c	64.30	65.06	...	8.08
.00	May 95c	63.21	63.29	+.01	8.08
.00	Aug 95c	62.13	62.21	+.01	8.08
.00	Nov 95c	61.05	61.13	...	8.08
.00	Feb 96c	59.30	60.07	...	8.08
.00	May 96c	58.24	59.01	...	8.08
.00	Nov 96c	56.15	56.24	+.01	8.08
.00	May 97c	54.07	54.16	+.01	8.09
.00	Aug 97c	53.05	54.01	+.01	7.94
.00	Nov 97c	52.03	53.00	+.01	7.94
.00	Feb 98c	51.02	51.31	+.01	7.94
.00	May 98c	50.01	50.31	...	7.94
.00	Aug 98c	49.02	50.00	+.01	7.94
.00	Nov 98c	48.03	49.01	+.01	7.94

TREASURY BILLS

Rate	Maturity	Bid	Asked	Bid Chg.	Yld.
.00	Sep 21 '89	7.56	7.44	...	7.55
.00	Sep 28 '89	7.51	7.29	...	7.40
.00	Oct 05 '89	7.51	7.39	...	7.52
.00	Oct 12 '89	7.66	7.54	−.05	7.68
.00	Oct 19 '89	7.66	7.54	...	7.69
.00	Oct 26 '89	7.74	7.67	+.05	7.84
.00	Nov 02 '89	7.68	7.62	+.06	7.80
.00	Nov 09 '89	7.65	7.58	+.05	7.77
.00	Nov 16 '89	7.70	7.66	+.06	7.86
.00	Nov 24 '89	7.74	7.70	+.05	7.92
.00	Nov 30 '89	7.70	7.67	+.36	7.90
.00	Dec 07 '89	7.63	7.60	+.05	7.84
.00	Dec 14 '89	7.61	7.57	+.06	7.82
.00	Dec 21 '89	7.65	7.59	+.08	7.85
.00	Dec 28 '89	7.57	7.50	+.06	7.77
.00	Jan 04 '90	7.58	7.50	+.02	7.78
.00	Jan 11 '90	7.60	7.53	+.07	7.82
.00	Jan 18 '90	7.66	7.59	+.08	7.90
.00	Jan 25 '90	7.74	7.70	+.14	8.03
.00	Feb 01 '90	7.72	7.68	+.12	8.02
.00	Feb 08 '90	7.74	7.70	+.14	8.05
.00	Feb 15 '90	7.71	7.67	+.11	8.03
.00	Feb 22 '90	7.70	7.66	+.14	8.03
.00	Mar 01 '90	7.64	7.58	+.10	7.96
.00	Mar 08 '90	7.65	7.61	+.09	8.00
.00	Mar 15 '90	7.69	7.65	+.14	8.06
.00	Apr 12 '90	7.74	7.70	+.16	8.13
.00	Apr 19 '90	7.73	7.69	+.11	8.12
.00	May 10 '90	7.70	7.66	+.12	8.10
.00	Jun 07 '90	7.58	7.54	+.10	7.99
.00	Jul 05 '90	7.58	7.54	+.09	8.02
.00	Aug 02 '90	7.57	7.54	+.09	8.05
.00	Aug 30 '90	7.55	7.52	+.09	8.06

Source: *The Wall Street Journal*, September 19, 1989.

On Monday, September 18, 1989, the 91-day T-bill rate on the open (secondary) market was 7.61 percent for bills auctioned on September 11 (Monday), issued on September 14 (Thursday), and maturing 13 weeks later on December 14 (Thursday). →

TREASURY BILLS

.00	Sep 21 '89	7.56	7.44	...	7.55
.00	Sep 28 '89	7.51	7.29	...	7.40
.00	Oct 05 '89	7.51	7.39	...	7.52
.00	Oct 12 '89	7.66	7.54	-.05	7.68
.00	Oct 19 '89	7.66	7.54	...	7.69
.00	Oct 26 '89	7.74	7.67	+.05	7.84
.00	Nov 02 '89	7.68	7.62	+.06	7.80
.00	Nov 09 '89	7.65	7.58	+.05	7.77
.00	Nov 16 '89	7.70	7.66	+.06	7.86
.00	Nov 24 '89	7.74	7.70	+.05	7.92
.00	Nov 30 '89	7.70	7.67	+.06	7.90
.00	Dec 07 '89	7.63	7.60	+.05	7.84
.00	Dec 14 '89	7.61	7.57	+.06	7.82
.00	Dec 21 '89	7.65	7.59	+.08	7.85
.00	Dec 28 '89	7.57	7.50	+.06	7.77
.00	Jan 04 '90	7.58	7.50	+.02	7.78
.00	Jan 11 '90	7.60	7.53	+.07	7.82
.00	Jan 18 '90	7.66	7.59	+.08	7.90
.00	Jan 25 '90	7.74	7.70	+.14	8.03
.00	Feb 01 '90	7.72	7.68	+.12	8.02
.00	Feb 08 '90	7.74	7.70	+.14	8.05
.00	Feb 15 '90	7.71	7.67	+.11	8.03
.00	Feb 22 '90	7.70	7.66	+.14	8.03
.00	Mar 01 '90	7.64	7.58	+.10	7.96
.00	Mar 08 '90	7.65	7.61	+.09	8.00
.00	Mar 15 '90	7.69	7.65	+.14	8.06
.00	Apr 12 '90	7.74	7.70	+.16	8.13
.00	Apr 19 '90	7.73	7.69	+.11	8.12
.00	May 10 '90	7.70	7.66	+.12	8.10
.00	Jun 07 '90	7.58	7.54	+.10	7.99
.00	Jul 05 '90	7.58	7.54	+.09	8.02
.00	Aug 02 '90	7.57	7.54	+.09	8.05
.00	Aug 30 '90	7.55	7.52	+.09	8.06

Source: *The Wall Street Journal*, September 19, 1989.

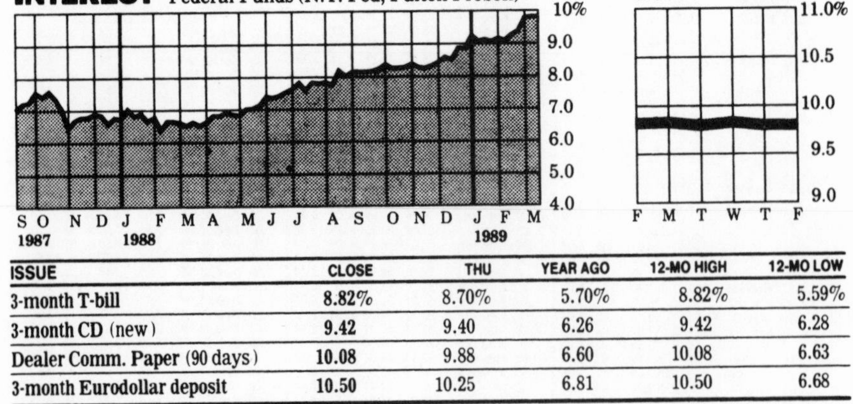

ISSUE	CLOSE	THU	YEAR AGO	12-MO HIGH	12-MO LOW
3-month T-bill	8.82%	8.70%	5.70%	8.82%	5.59%
3-month CD (new)	9.42	9.40	6.26	9.42	6.28
Dealer Comm. Paper (90 days)	10.08	9.88	6.60	10.08	6.63
3-month Eurodollar deposit	10.50	10.25	6.81	10.50	6.68

Source: *The Wall Street Journal*, March 20, 1989.

amounts of $1 million or more. The federal funds rate was 9.80 percent on March 17,1989. Four more interest rates follow. Except for Treasury bills, which were discussed above, these quotes are for instruments purchased by financial institutions in very large amounts. Nonetheless, they provide a good daily snapshot of current short-term rates. Note that the yields increase with increased risk and reduced liquidity. The March 17, 1989 rates were 3-month T-bills, 8.82 percent, new 3-month certificates of deposit, 9.42 percent, 90-day commercial paper (short-term corporate debt), 10.08 percent; and 3-month Eurodollar deposits ("dollar" denominated deposits held at European banks), 10.5 percent.

You can follow an even larger array of interest rates each day in **Money Rates**, a report that lists the current yields on most of the major money market interest-rate instruments. Look for it in the front-page index of the first and last sections. The example from the Monday, March 20, 1989 *Journal* on page 280 reports the rates for Friday, March 17, 1989. **Money Rates** tracks the following domestic rates: *Prime Rate* (rate banks charge their corporate customers), *Federal Funds*, *Discount Rate* (rate the Federal Reserve charges its member banks), *Call Money* (rate banks charge brokers), *Commercial Paper, Certificates of Deposit, Bankers Acceptances* (rates on corporate or business credit used in international trade, backed by a bank), *Treasury Bills, Federal Home Loan Mortgage Corp.* (rates on a variety of mortgages), *Federal National Mortgage Association* (also rates on a variety of mortgages), and *Merrill Lynch Ready Assets Trust* (a money market mutual fund), *Money Rates* also tracks foreign money market rates including: *London Late Eurodollars, London Interbank Offered Rates* (similar to federal funds), and *Foreign Prime Rates* of different countries. These interest rates are discussed more thoroughly below.

Federal Funds Rate

Banks lend reserves to one another overnight at the federal funds rate. This practice is profitable for lender banks because they earn interest on funds ($1 million or more) that would otherwise be idle, and it is profitable for the borrower banks because they acquire reserves that enable them to make additional loans and still meet their reserve requirement. Arrangements for the transfer of funds are managed by telex.

Notice that under *Federal Funds* in the *Money Rates* column on page 280, four different percentages are listed: 9⅞ percent high, 9½ percent

MONEY RATES

Friday, March 17, 1989

The key U.S. and foreign annual interest rates below are a guide to general levels but don't always represent actual transactions.

Prime Rate, 11 1/2%	**PRIME RATE:** 11½%. The base rate on corporate loans at large U.S. money center commercial banks.
Federal Funds Rate, 9 7/8%	**FEDERAL FUNDS:** 9⅞% high, 9½% low, 9⅞% near closing bid, 10% offered. Reserves traded among commercial banks for overnight use in amounts of $1 million or more. Source: Fulton Prebon (U.S.A.) Inc.
Discount Rate, 7%	**DISCOUNT RATE:** 7%. The charge on loans to depository institutions by the New York Federal Reserve Bank.
Call Rates, 10 1/2%	**CALL MONEY:** 10½% to 10⅞%. The charge on loans to brokers on stock exchange collateral.
	COMMERCIAL PAPER placed directly by General Motors Acceptance Corp.: 9.80% 18 to 32 days; 9.90% 33 to 59 days; 9.80% 60 to 89 days; 9.70% 90 to 119 days; 9.60% 120 to 149 days; 9.50% 150 to 179 days; 9.30% 180 to 270 days.
Commercial Paper, 10.075%	**COMMERCIAL PAPER:** High-grade unsecured notes sold through dealers by major corporations in multiples of $1,000: 9.975% 30 days; 10.025% 60 days; 10.075% 90 days.
Certificates of Deposit, 9.42%	**CERTIFICATES OF DEPOSIT:** 9.24% one month; 9.33% two months; 9.42% three months; 9.66% six months; 9.86% one year. Average of top rates paid by major New York banks on primary new issues of negotiable C.D.s, usually on amounts of $1 million and more. The minimum unit is $100,000. Typical rates in the secondary market: 10.10% one month; 10.30% three months; 10.60% six months.
Bankers Acceptances, 9.93%	**BANKERS ACCEPTANCES:** 9.85% 30 days; 9.90% 60 days; 9.93% 90 days; 10% 120 days; 10% 150 days; 10% 180 days. Negotiable, bank-backed business credit instruments typically financing an import order.
London Late Eurodollars	**LONDON LATE EURODOLLARS:** 10¼% to 10⅛% one month; 10⅜% to 10¼% two months; 10½% to 10⅜% three months; 10⅝% to 10½% four months; 10 13/16% to 10 11/16% five months; 10 15/16% to 10 13/16% six months.
London Interbank Offered Rates	**LONDON INTERBANK OFFERED RATES (LIBOR):** 10 1/16% one month; 10 3/16% three months; 10½% six-months; 10 13/16% one year. The average of interbank offered rates for dollar deposits in the London market based on quotations at five major banks.
Foreign Prime Rates	**FOREIGN PRIME RATES:** Canada 12.75%; Germany 7%; Japan 3.375%; Switzerland 6.50%; Britain 13%. These rate indications aren't directly comparable; lending practices vary widely by location.
Treasury Bills, 8.69%	**TREASURY BILLS:** Results of the Monday, March 13, 1989, auction of short-term U.S. government bills, sold at a discount from face value in units of $10,000 to $1 million: 8.69% 13 weeks; 8.76% 26 weeks.
Federal Home Loan Mortgage Corp.	**FEDERAL HOME LOAN MORTGAGE CORP.** (Freddie Mac): Posted yields on 30-year mortgage commitments for delivery within 30 days. 11.28%, standard conventional fixed-rate mortgages; 8.75%, 2% rate capped one-year adjustable rate mortgages. Source: Telerate Systems Inc.
Federal National Mortgage Association	**FEDERAL NATIONAL MORTGAGE ASSOCIATION** (Fannie Mae): Posted yields on 30 year mortgage commitments for delivery within 30 days (priced at par) 11.35%, standard conventional fixed rate-mortgages; 10.70%, 6/2 rate capped one-year adjustable rate mortgages. Source: Telerate Systems Inc.
Merrill Lynch Ready Assets Trust	**MERRILL LYNCH READY ASSETS TRUST:** 8.80%. Annualized average rate of return after expenses for the past 30 days; not a forecast of future returns.

Source: *The Wall Street Journal*, March 20, 1989.

low, 9⅞ percent near closing bid, and 10 percent offered. These numbers show that during trading on Friday, March 17, 1989, 9⅞ percent was the highest interest rate proposed by a potential lender bank, and 9½ percent was the lowest interest rate proposed by a prospective borrower. The last two percentages describe the state of trading near the end of the day: Lender banks were offering 10 percent, and borrower banks were still bidding 9⅞ percent. Use the closing bid (9⅞ percent) when following this interest rate.

This rate is closely watched as an indicator of Federal Reserve monetary policy. A rising federal funds rate is a sign that the Fed is draining reserves from the banks via its open market operations, forcing some banks to borrow excess reserves from other banks and thereby driving up the federal funds rate. A falling rate would indicate an easy money policy. But beware: sharp fluctuations occur from day to day. This is such a short-term market that the rate changes on an "as needed" basis.

Investor's Tip

- Follow the federal funds chart under **Interest** in the **Markets Diary** on page C1, because it presents a weekly average that smooths out sharp daily movements.

Commercial Paper

You can see from the excerpt on page 280 that 10.075 percent was the going rate on 90-day commercial paper on March 17, 1989. Commercial paper is short-term, unsecured debt issued by the very largest corporations. It is the equivalent of the Treasury bill, so in order to attract investors, its rate of interest has to be higher.

Corporations issue commercial paper to avoid the higher interest rate (prime rate) levied by banks on business borrowers and it is issued for maturities up to 270 days. There are very large minimums set on commercial paper purchases (often in excess of $1 million), and this instrument is very popular with money market funds.

Prime Rate

This is the rate that large commercial banks charge their best corporate customers. Although it does not change as frequently as other market rates, it is an important indicator of supply and demand in the capital markets. Banks raise the prime rate whenever they have difficulty meeting the current demand for funds, or when the Federal Reserve drains away their reserves through its open market operations.

Bankers Acceptances

Bankers Acceptances are used to finance international trade. Large institutions, investment companies, and money market mutual funds purchase bankers acceptances because they offer high yields for relatively short periods of time. Individual investors benefit from the higher yields when they invest in funds that include these instruments.

Call Rates

The call rate is the rate that banks charge brokers, who generally add 1 percent on loans to their clients.

Key Interest Rates

Every Tuesday, under the heading **Key Interest Rates**, the *Journal* reports the weekly average of most important interest rates, including long-term rates. See the example from the March 21, 1989 edition of the *Journal*. In the week ended March 17, Treasury bills averaged 8.74 percent; commercial paper, 9.92 percent; CDs, 10.09 percent; and federal funds, 9.83 percent. Once again, notice the interest rate hierarchy.

Short-Term Interest Rates Chart

Also, the *Journal* provides a **Short-Term Interest Rates** chart each Thursday in the daily **Credit Markets** report (consult the front-page index of the first and last sections for location of the *Credit Markets* article), as in the example from the Thursday, March 23, 1989 edition of

Treasury Bills, 8.74%
Commercial Paper, 9.92%
CDs, 10.09%
Federal Funds, 9.83%

Key Interest Rates

Annualized interest rates on certain investments as reported by the Federal Reserve Board on a weekly-average basis:

	Week Ended: Mar. 17, 1989	Mar. 10, 1989
Treasury bills (90 day)-a	8.74	8.64
Commrcl paper (Dealer, 90 day)-a	9.92	9.82
Certfs of Deposit (Resale, 90 day)	10.09	9.94
Federal funds (Overnight)-b	9.83	9.83
Eurodollars (90 day)-b	10.10	10.03
Treasury bills (one year)-c	9.56	9.39
Treasury notes (three year)-c	9.61	9.43
Treasury notes (five year)-c	9.49	9.37
Treasury notes (ten year)-c	9.35	9.27
Treasury bonds (30 year)-c	9.17	9.09

a-Discounted rates. b-Week ended Wednesday, March 15, 1989 and Wednesday March 8, 1989. c-Yields, adjusted for constant maturity.

Source: *The Wall Street Journal*, March 21, 1989.

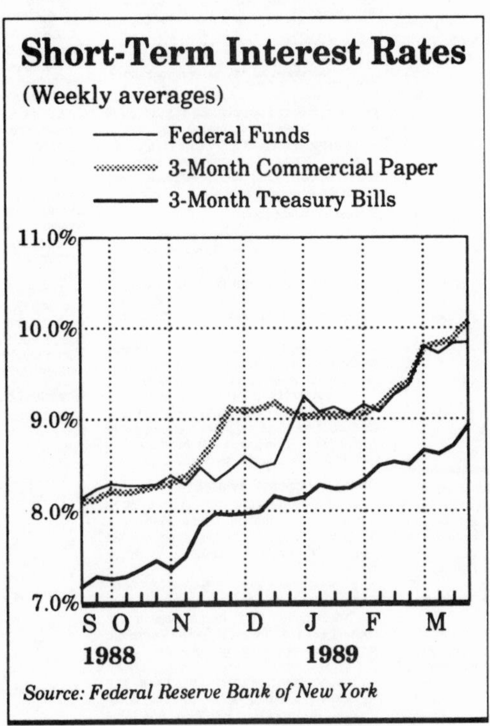

Source: *The Wall Street Journal*, March 23, 1989.

Bond Prices Rally as Report on Durable Goods Suggests to Some the Economy May Be Slowing

By Constance Mitchell
And Laurence Bauman
Staff Reporters of The Wall Street Journal

NEW YORK—News pointing to slower economic growth calmed inflation fears and helped to spark a bond market rally.

Treasury bond prices rose about half a point, or $5 for each $1,000 face amount, while most short-term interest rates eased. Prices of some mortgage-backed securities rose even more than Treasury bonds.

"We saw real money in the market," said Michael Moore, manager of government trading at Continental Illinois Bank in Chicago. He was referring to institutional and foreign investors that had been absent from the market. "There was not an avalanche of activity, but we saw more interest than we've seen in some time."

Bond prices were flat in early morning trading, then rose immediately after the Commerce Department reported that orders for durable goods fell 3.6% in February. The decline, which followed a 2.9% drop in January, was interpreted by some investors as a sign that the economy has begun to slow down. That's considered positive news for credit markets because it suggests that inflation might not rise as rapidly as some economists have predicted. The fear of inflation has been responsible for driving up interest rates in recent months.

Another factor helping to buoy bonds was comments by Federal Reserve Board Vice Chairman Manuel Johnson. At a conference here sponsored by the Securities Industry Association, Mr. Johnson said that the latest inflation data, notably the back-to-back 1% increases in the producer price index, overstate current inflationary trends. "The underlying rate of inflation is more behaved" than the data would indicate, he said. "Two months do not make a trend."

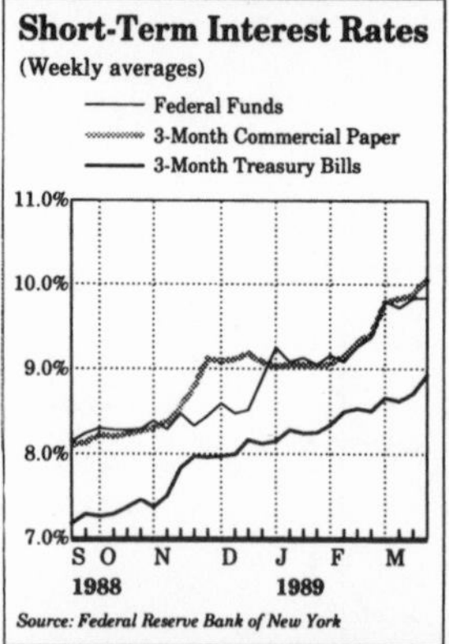

Such remarks were taken as a sign that the Federal Open Market Committee, which has a regularly scheduled meeting Tuesday, probably will vote to leave policy steady until more economic data come out, especially the March employment report, due April 7.

"Even the hawks on the FOMC are inclined to wait and see wh...

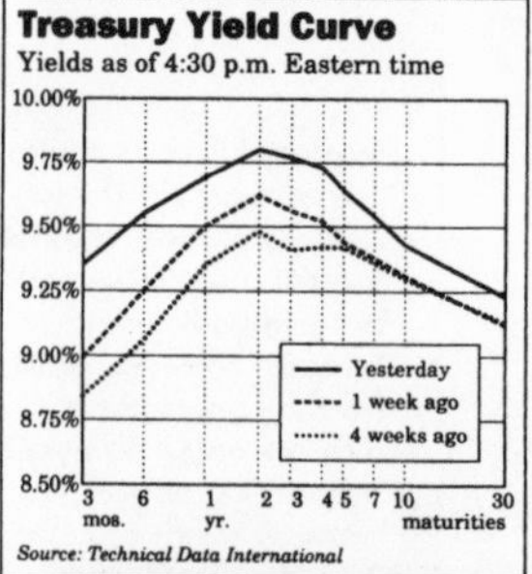

YIELD COMPARISONS

Based on Merrill Lynch Bond Indexes, priced as of midafternoon Eastern time.

	3/22	3/21	–52 Week– High	Low
Corp.-Govt. Master	9.92%	9.99%	9.99%	8.38%
Treasury 1-10 yr	9.80	9.90	9.89	7.68
10+ yr	9.44	9.50	9.63	8.85
Agencies 1-10 yr	10.14	10.19	10.19	8.01
10+ yr	9.78	9.82	10.19	9.44
Corporate				
1-10 yr High Qlty	10.24	10.28	10.28	8.99
Med Qlty	10.57	10.61	10.61	9.54
10+yr High Qlty	10.24	10.27	10.38	9.73
Med Qlty	10.65	10.67	10.82	10.16
Yankee bonds(1)	10.23	10.28	10.28	9.43
Current-coupon mortgages				
GNMA 10.50%	10.91	11.00	11.00	9.32
FNMA 10.50%	11.03	11.07	11.07	8.60
FHLMC 11.00%	10.99	11.13	11.13	9.52
High-yield corporates	13.43	13.42	13.43	12.80
New tax-exempts				
10-yr G.O. (AA)	7.30	7.30	7.30	6.70
20-yr G.O. (AA)	7.60	7.60	8.15	7.15
30-yr revenue (A)	8.05	8.05	8.45	7.61

Note: High quality rated AAA-AA; medium quality, A-BBB/Baa; high yield, BB/Ba-C.

(1) Dollar-denominated, SEC-registered bonds of foreign issuers sold in the U.S.

year notes next Tuesday and $7.5 billion of four-year notes the following day.

Individual investors are expected to buy a large amount of the two-year notes. In when-issued trading late yesterday, those notes were quoted at 9.81%.

Treasury Securities

Treasury bond prices headed higher, and short-term interest rates eased.

The Treasury's bellwether 30-year bond rose to 96 11/32 from 95 26/32 Tuesday. The issue's yield, which moves in the opposite direction of its price, fell to 9.24% from 9.29%.

Shorter-term issues posted smaller gains. The government's 10-year notes rose 14/32 point to 96 13/32 to yield 9.44%.

Among short-term rates, the latest six-month bills were quoted late yesterday at a discount rate of 8.99%, down from an average of 9.07% Tuesday. Their bond equivalent yield was quoted at 9.56%.

Mortgage-Backed Securities

Helped by the rumored purchase of as much as $750 million of Ginnie Maes by a big bank, the mortgage securities market ended with moderate gains of ½ to ⅝ point.

First Union Corp., a North Carolina-based bank, is said to have bought the Ginnie Maes in the morning. A First Union spokesman said the bank doesn't comment on any rumored mortgage securities activity.

Traders describe First Union Corp. as a significant participant in the mortgage market in recent years with a sizable mortgage-backed portfolio...

Meanwhile, battered adjustable-rate mortgage securities posted modest gains in response to price increases for one-year Treasury bills and two-year Treasury notes.

Corporate Issues

In corporate trading, industrial bonds also posted gains in moderate activity.

Moody's Investment Grade Corporate Bond Index, which measures price movements on 80 corporate bonds with maturities of five years or longer, edged up 0.12 to 295.32.

Activity focused on several recent new issues. **Merrill Lynch & Co.** came to market for the third time in a week, selling $200 million of 10⅝% notes due in two years. The issue was priced at par.

Foreign Bonds

The U.S. bond market's rise sparked small rallies in several European bond markets.

In Great Britain, West Germany and France, prices of government bonds rose ⅛ to ¼ of a point on news that U.S. durable goods orders fell in February. But trading activity was light, in part because the four-day Easter holiday weekend is approaching. "It doesn't require much buying to get this market moving," said senior trader Malcolm Holliday of Daiwa Europe Ltd. in London.

Britain's benchmark 11¾% Treasury issue due 2003/2007 rose ⅛ point to 116 19/32 to yield 9.56%. The 11¾% issue due 1991 was up 3/32 to 100 21/32 to yield 11.31%.

The West German government's 6½% issue due 1999 rose 0.15 point to 96.85 to yield 6.945%. The 6% notes due 1993 firmed 0.10 point to 96.80 to yield 6.855%. Among French Treasurys, the 9.8% issue due 1996 finished at 103.86, up 0.26 from late Tuesday in Paris, to yield 9.00%.

Japanese government bond prices ended little changed after an afternoon sell-off erased early morning gains. Traders said the selling was prompted by renewed rumors that members of the Takeshita cabinet would be forced to resign.

Japan's benchmark No. 111, 4.6% issue due 1998 closed at 96.08, down 0.06 yen for each 100 yen face value from Monday. The issue's yield was 5.23%, up one basis point. Tokyo markets were closed Tuesday for a national holiday.

Municipal Issues

Municipal bonds preserved ⅛ to ½ point gains on the day, propelled largely by early session short-covering after the latest economic statistics.

The modest price advances reversed three consecutive sessions of rather sharp losses.

The New Jersey Turnpike Authority's 7.20% bonds due 2018 were quoted at 93⅜, up ½ from Tuesday. They yielded about 7.78%, down two basis points.

The market's tone improved out of the gate, with the report of the drop in February durable goods orders.

"I think it was mostly short-covering after the data fueling the gains and then some of the regional guys picking up cheaper paper for retail," said one N... York trader...

Source: *The Wall Street Journal*, March 23, 1989.

the *Journal*. The Short-Term Interest Rate chart portrays Federal Funds, 3-Month Commercial Paper, and 3-Month T-Bill rates over the past six months. You will notice that Treasury securities rates are well below the others because they are safer and more liquid.

Treasury Yield Curve

The yield curve charts the relationship between interest rates and length of maturity for all debt instruments at a particular time. A normal yield curve slopes upward, with higher yields for longer-term investments. Thus, short-term Treasury bills will usually have relatively low rates and long-term Treasury bonds will have higher rates. Abnormal yield curves can be flat, inverted, or peaked in the middle (higher short-term rates than long-term rates).

The Wall Street Journal publishes a yield curve chart daily with the Credit Markets article. The yield curve assumed an abnormal bell shape for the first part of 1989, as you can see in the excerpt from the Thursday, January 19, Thursday, March 23, and the Friday, April 21, 1989 editions of the *Journal* on pages 284 and 286. The conventional wisdom at the time said that the Fed had driven up short-term rates to cool the economy, which also boosted medium-term but not long-term rates.

Buying and Borrowing

Each Monday, the *Journal* reports a variety of figures that investors follow, under the heading *Buying & Borrowing*, including bank money market deposit account rates and effective mortgage rates along with a Dow Industrial figure and corporate bond yields. See the Monday, March 20, 1989 example on page 287.

Bank Credit Card Rates

At the beginning of each month, the *Journal* publishes a representative listing of the rates banks charge for the use of their credit cards. See the **Bank Credit Card Interest Rate** article on page 288 from the Monday, February 6, 1989 edition of the *Journal*.

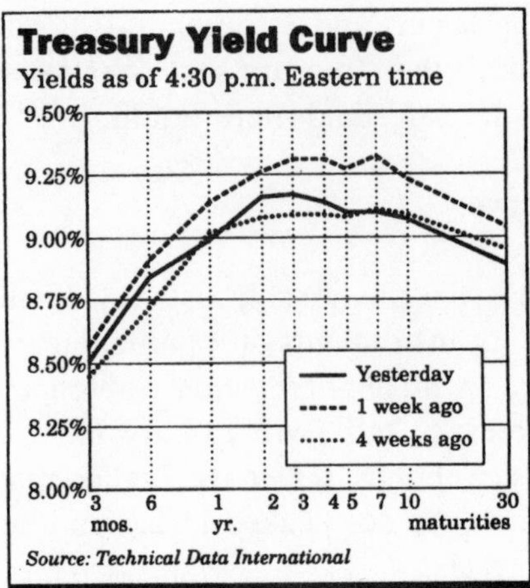

Source: *The Wall Street Journal*, January 19, 1989.

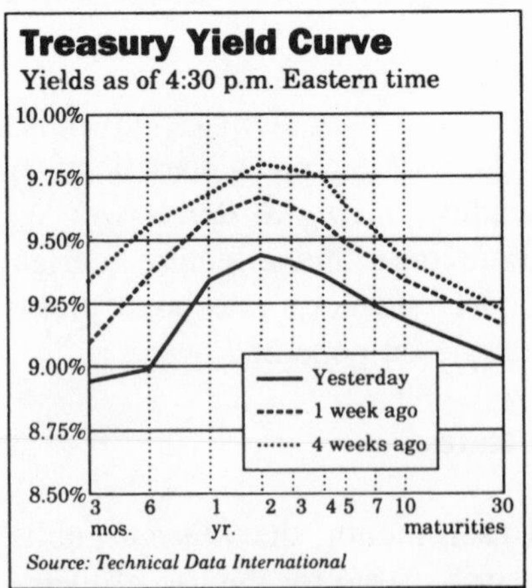

Source: *The Wall Street Journal*, April 21, 1989.

Buying & Borrowing

Here are some recent figures on financial trends affecting consumers and individual investors.

—DOW JONES INDUSTRIALS—
Close: 2292.14. Year earlier: 2087.37.

—MOODY'S CORPORATE YIELDS—
Average for double-A-rated bonds:
9.93%. Year earlier: 9.57%.

—FEDERAL HOME LOAN BANK—
Average effective rate for conventional fixed-rate mortgage on new homes:
11.17%. Year earlier: 10.97%.
Average price on new homes:
$156,200. Year earlier: $150,100.

—BANK MONEY MARKET DEPOSITS—
Rates for accounts with minimum balance of $2,500:
At one major commercial bank: 7.7%.
At one major savings & loan association: 5.25%.

Source: *The Wall Street Journal*, March 20, 1989.

CONCLUSION

If the risk and bother of investing in stocks, bonds, and commodities seems excessive to you, a wide variety of relatively risk-free and highly liquid money market instruments is available to you. Use *The Wall Street Journal's* data services to check the hierarchy of rates and then choose the instrument that's right for you.

Bank Credit Card Interest Rates

February 1989

Banks or savings institutions with low interest rates offering bank credit cards nationally. Rates shown are for regular, not premium cards. Though not listed, some cards may be through affiliate or agent banks. Temporary or promotional interest rates are excluded. Grace period (interest free period for cardholders paying purchase balance in full each month) is calculated from the date of billing unless footnoted.

Bank / Location	Int. Rate	Annual Fee	Grace Days
Arkansas Fed Svg, Little Rock	11.40%	$35.00	z0
Home Plan S&L, Des Moines	12.90	25.00	25
People's Bank, Bridgeport, Conn.	c13.50	25.00	25
Empire of America, Buffalo	13.75	18.00	z0
Republic S&L, Milwaukee	13.92	10.00	x0
Republic S&L, Milwaukee	v14.25	20.00	x0
Amalgamated Trust, Chicago	14.50	0.00	25
First Atlanta, Wilmington	14.88	24.00	28
Security Pacific, Seattle	v15.00	18.00	25
Connecticut B&T, Fairfield	c15.00	25.00	25
USAA Fed Svg, Tulsa	v15.21	0.00	25
Manufacturers, Wilmington	v15.90	0.00	x0
Hibernia Natl, New Orleans	15.90	12.00	25
Chevy Chase Svg, Chevy Chase, Md.	15.90	20.00	25
Mercantile, St. Louis	15.90	20.00	25
Fidelity Natl, Atlanta	v16.20	22.00	25
Bank of Hawaii, Honolulu	16.50	15.00	25
Star Bank, Cincinnati	v16.50	20.00	25
SF Fed Svg, San Francisco	v16.50	21.00	25
Chittenden, Rutland, Vt.	16.75	18.00	25
Shawmut, Boston	v16.86	24.00	25
Bank of NY, Newark, Del.	16.98	18.00	25
Gem Savings, Dayton	v17.00	20.00	25
Bank of Boston, Boston	17.04	21.00	25
Union Natl, Temple, Okla.	v17.10	20.00	z0

Banks without any annual fee offering credit cards nationally.

Bank / Location	Interest Rate Structure	Grace Days
Amalgamated Trust, Chicago	(14.5% fixed)	25
USAA Fed Svg, Tulsa	2x26wkTB14%min	25
Manufacturers, Wilmington	(26wk TB + 8%)	x0
Dauphin Dep, Harrisburg, Pa.	17.9-16.4%tiered	25
Security B&T, Southgate, Mich.	(18.0% fixed)	25
Household Bk, Salinas, Calif.	(19.8% fixed)	25
Harris Tr, BuffaloGrove, Ill.	(19.8% fixed)	25
Imperial Savings, San Diego	(19.8% fixed)	25
Peoples First, Salt Lake City	(21.9% fixed)	28
First Natl Omaha, Omaha, Neb.	u(1mo.CP +13%)	z0

The most common interest rates offered by the ten largest U.S. issuers.

Bank	Int. Rate	Annual Fee Regular	Annual Fee Premium	Grace Days
Citibank	s19.80%	$20.00	$50.00	30
Chase Manhattan	17.50	20.00	45.00	30
Bank of America	19.80	18.00	36.00	25
First Chicago	s19.80	w20.00	35.00	25
Wells Fargo	s20.00	18.00	45.00	25
Mfrs Hanover	17.80	20.00	40.00	25
First Interstate	s21.00	20.00	40.00	25
Maryland Natl	17.90	e18.00	e30.00	25
Bank of New York	s16.98	18.00	40.00	30
Security Pacific	s20.40	15.00	45.00	25

v-Variable rate. t-Tiered (or lower) rates based on account balance. c-Higher rate charged for cash advances. w-Fee waived under special conditions. x-Interest charged from date of purchase. z-Interest charged from date of posting. s-Special lower rate available on some cards. e-estimated amount, actual fees not disclosed. TB-Treasury Bill Rate. Prime-Prime Rate.

Source: RAM Research Bankcard Update/Barometer, Frederick, Md.

Source: *The Wall Street Journal*, February 6, 1989.

APPENDIX TO PART II

FURTHER REFERENCES*

BASICS

American Association of Individual Investors
625 North Michigan Avenue, Suite 1900
Chicago, IL 60611
(312) 280-0170

Member benefits include a subscription to the excellent monthly, *AAII Journal*. The Association also publishes home study courses, audio tapes, and presents seminars. There is a local chapter network. (Annual membership, $49.00.)

Classics: An Investor's Anthology, edited by Charles D. Ellis.

This is one of the most concentrated sources of Wall Street wisdom. The book presents the practical ideas and philosophies of 97 gifted thinkers and writers on financial analysis, investment, and portfolio management from the past 60 years (759 pages, hardbound, $37.50).

BUSINESS ONE IRWIN One-Hour Guide Series

a. *How to Be a Successful Investor* by Bailard, Biehl & Kaiser (230 pages, $10.95)
b. *How To Set and Achieve Your Financial Goals* by Bailard, Biehl, and Kaiser (229 pages, $10.95)

---

*The author gratefully acknowledges the assistance of Bob Meier and Jane O'Neil in compiling these references.

Available in bookstores, or order from BUSINESS ONE IRWIN, 1818 Ridge Road, Homewood, IL 60430. Customer Service 1-800-634-3961; in Illinois, 708-957-5800.

CONSUMER PROTECTION

The Guide to Investor Protection by Mary E. Calhoun
Overture Publishing
P. O. Box 99
Newton, MA 02162
(617) 924-4484

The author is a highly regarded investor protection advocate. Her book provides common sense advice on a wide range of topics including investor rights and arbitration of broker disputes (160 pages, $11.95).

What Every Investor Should Know
Consumer Information Center-K
P. O. Box 100
Pueblo, CO 81002

Basic information on choosing and safeguarding investments, trading securities, and protections guaranteed by law. Written by the Securities & Exchange Commission. When ordering, make check payable to the "Superintendent of Documents" and include the publication number, #146V. (35 pages, $1.25.)

HISTORY

The Lore and Legends of Wall Street by Robert M. Sharp

This book contains over 50 vignettes of market history from colonial times to the present. Entertaining and informative (246 pages, $18.95.)

Available in bookstores, or order from BUSINESS ONE IRWIN, 1818 Ridge Road, Homewood, IL 60430. Customer Service 1-800-634-3961; in Illinois 708-957-5800.

PSYCHOLOGY

Investment Psychology Consulting, Inc.
1410 East Glenoaks Blvd.
Glendale, CA 91206

Books and audio cassettes by Dr. Van K. Tharp to help investors and traders overcome the psychological barriers to objective interpretation of economic news and successful investment decisions. (Write for catalog.)

GENERAL REFERENCE

Amling, Frederick, and Droms, William G. *Dow Jones-Irwin Guide to Personal Financial Planning*. Homewood: Dow Jones-Irwin, 1987.

Chambliss, H. Darden, Jr. *The Bank of America Guide to Making the Most of Your Money,* Homewood: Dow Jones-Irwin, 1989.

Fabozzi, Frank, and Zarb, Frank, eds. *Handbook of Financial Markets*. Homewood: Dow Jones-Irwin, 1986.

Frank, Al. *The Prudent Speculator*. Homewood: Dow Jones-Irwin, 1989.

Graham, Benjamin. *The Intelligent Investor*. New York: Harper & Row, 1965.

Harper, Victor L. *New York Institute of Finance, Investor's Desk Reference*. New York: New York Institute of Finance; Prentice Hall, 1988.

Hirsch, Michael D. *Multifund Investing: How to Build a High Performance Portfolio of Mutual Funds*. Homewood: Dow Jones-Irwin, 1987.

Hirt, Geoffrey, and Block, Stanley B. *The Complete Investor: Instruments, Markets and Methods* Homewood: Dow Jones-Irwin, 1987.

Kinsman, Robert. *Always a Bull Market: Conservative Investing in Stocks, Bonds and Gold*. Homewood: Dow Jones-Irwin, 1989.

Lori, James H., and Hamilton, Mary T. *The Stock Market: Theories and Evidence*. Chicago: Irwin, 1975.

Malkiel, Burton G. *A Random Walk Down Wall Street, 4th Ed*. New York: W.W. Norton & Company, 1985.

Murphy, Joseph E., Jr. *With Interest: How to Profit from Interest Rate Fluctuations*. Homewood: Dow Jones-Irwin, 1987.

Nichols, Donald R. *Starting Small, Investing Smart: What to Do with $5 to $5,000*. Homewood: Dow Jones-Irwin, 1986.

Pressin, Allan H., and Ross, Joseph A. *Words of Wall Street* and *More Words of Wall Street*, Homewood: Dow Jones-Irwin, 1986.

Scott, David L. *Wall Street Words: Financial Literacy for a Changing Market*. Boston: Houghton Mifflin, 1988.

Veale, Stuart R., ed. *Stocks, Bonds, Options, Futures: Investments and Their Markets*. New York: New York Institute of Finance; Prentice Hall, 1987.

STOCKS

Droms, William G., and Heerwagon, Peter D. *No Load Mutual Funds, 1986 Edition*. Homewood: Dow Jones-Irwin, 1986.

Nix, William E., and Nix, Susan W. *The Dow Jones-Irwin Guide to Stock Index Futures and Options*. Homewood: Dow Jones-Irwin, 1987.

Pierce, Phyllis, ed. *The Dow Jones Averages, 1885 to 1985*. Homewood: Dow Jones-Irwin, 1986.

Pierce, Phyllis, ed. *The Dow Jones Investor's Handbook*. Homewood: Dow Jones-Irwin, 1989.

Pring, Martin J. *Technical Analysis Explained, 2nd Ed.* New York: McGraw-Hill, 1985.

Sharp, Robert M. *Calculated Risk: A Master Plan for Common Stocks*. Homewood: Dow Jones-Irwin, 1986.

Stillman, Richard J. *The Dow Jones Industrial Average*. Homewood: Dow Jones-Irwin, 1986.

Rugg, Donald D. *The Dow Jones-Irwin Guide to Mutual Funds, 3rd Ed.* Homewood: Dow Jones-Irwin, 1987.

Weinstein, Stan. *Stan Weinstein's Secrets for Profiting in Bull & Bear Markets*. Homewood: Dow Jones-Irwin, 1988.

Zweig, Martin E. *Understanding Technical Forecasting: How to Use Barron's Market Laboratory Pages*. Homewood: Dow Jones-Irwin, 1978.

TECHNICAL ANALYSIS

Technical Analysis Explained by Martin J. Pring
Pring Market Review
P.O.Box 329
Washington, CT 06794

Considered by many to be the definitive reference on the topic. The book, now in its second edition, includes over 150 charts and illustrations. Japanese, German, Spanish, and Danish editions are also available. (432 pages, $47.50.)

Stan Weinstein's Secrets for Profiting in Bull and Bear Markets by Stan Weinstein.

Professional Tape Reader
P.O. Box 2407
Hollywood, FL 33022

A popular book with the primary emphasis on technical analysis of stocks. (348 pages, $24.95.)

COMMODITIES AND PRECIOUS METALS

Babcock, Bruce. *The Dow Jones-Irwin Guide to Commodity Futures Trading Systems*. Homewood: Dow Jones-Irwin, 1989.

Belveal, L. Dee. *Speculation in Commodity Contracts and Options*. Homewood: Dow Jones-Irwin, 1986.

Belveal, L. Dee. *Charting Commodity Price Market Behavior*. 2nd Ed. Homewood: Dow Jones-Irwin, 1987.

Classing, Henry K. *The Dow Jones-Irwin Guide to Put and Call Options*. Homewood: Dow Jones-Irwin, 1987.

Kroll, Stanley. *Kroll on Futures Trading Strategy*. Homewood: Dow Jones-Irwin, 1987.

Labuszewski, John W., and Sinquefield, Jeanne Cairns. *Inside the Commodity Option Markets*. New York: John Wiley & Sons, 1985.

Markham, Jerry W. *The History of Commodity Futures Trading and Its Regulation*. New York: Praeger, 1987.

Nix, William E., ed. *Futures Markets: Their Economic Role*. Washington D.C.: American Enterprise Institute for Public Policy Research, 1985.

Schwartz, Edward W., Hill, Joanne M., and Schneeweis, Thomas. *Financial Futures: Fundamentals, Strategies and Applications*. Homewood: Dow Jones-Irwin, 1987.

Seidel, Andrew D., and Ginsberg, Philip M. *Commodities Trading: Foundations, Analysis and Operations*. Englewood Cliffs: Prentice-Hall, 1983.

FUTURES & OPTIONS

Futures & Options Trading Kit
Stotler FMO
Attn: Tony Raia, Consumer Affairs
Suite 1600A
141 W. Jackson Blvd.
Chicago, IL 60604

Collection of basic "how-to" brochures, article reprints, and other information on the potential risks and rewards of futures and options trading, including managed accounts and funds. Indicate any special areas of interest. (Free.)

LONG-TERM INTEREST RATES AND MONEY MARKET INVESTMENTS

Berlin, Howard M. *The Dow Jones-Irwin Guide to Buying and Selling Treasury Securities*. Homewood: Dow Jones-Irwin, 1986.

Nichols, Donald R. *The Dow Jones-Irwin Guide to Zero Coupon Investments*. Homewood: Dow Jones-Irwin, 1987.

Rosen, Lawrence R. *The Dow Jones-Irwin Guide to Calculating Yields*. Homewood: Dow Jones-Irwin, 1987.

Stigum, Lawrence R. *The Dow Jones-Irwin Guide to Interest: What You Should Know About the Time Value of Money*. Homewood: Dow Jones-Irwin, 1987.

Stigum, Marcia, with Mann, John. *Money Market Calculations: Yields, Break Evens and Arbitrage*. Homewood: Dow Jones-Irwin, 1987.

Stigum, Marcia, and Fabrozzi, Frank. *The Dow Jones-Irwin Guide to Bond and Money Market Investments*. Homewood: Dow Jones-Irwin, 1987.

COMPUTERS

Wall Street Computer Review
5615 West Cermak Road
Cicero, IL 60650

This monthly magazine offers news of the latest in hardware, investment and economic databases, and software. It features many special product and service directory supplements. (Annual subscription, $49.00.)

FINANCIAL AND ECONOMIC ON-LINE DATA RETRIEVAL

A number of computer information subscription services provide up-to-the-minute financial and economic information.

Dow Jones News Retrieval (DJN/R): 1-609-452-1511
Compuserve: 1-800-848-8990.
GEnie: 1-800-638-9636
The Source: 1-800-336-3366

These services will give you access to many of the following:

- S & P Online
- Value Line Data Base
- Futures Focus
- Money Market Services
- OTC News
- Bond Prices and Volumes
- Stock Quotes
- Commodities/Futures Prices
- Company Information
- *and much more*

CHART SERVICES

Commodity Research Bureau
30 S. Wacker Drive, Suite 1820
Chicago, IL 60601

Weekly and monthly chart services, plus yearbooks, covering all commodity futures and options on futures contracts. (Write for catalog.)

Chartcraft, Inc.
Investors Intelligence
30 Church Street, Box 2046
New Rochelle, NY 10802

Fifteen different chart service combinations, featuring the point and figure charting method. (Write for catalog.)

Securities Research Company
208 Newbury Street
Boston, MA 02116

Monthly and quarterly chart services covering 1,000 stocks each, plus wall charts and books. (Write for catalog.)

Standard & Poor's Corporation
25 Broadway
New York, NY 10004

Comprehensive subscriber package, including the Trendline Chart Service, tracking over 1,400 active stocks, and the Security Owner's Stock Guide, presenting statistics on over 5,300 stocks. (Write for Catalog.)

PART III

FINE TUNING: REFINING YOUR SENSE OF THE ECONOMY AND THE RIGHT INVESTMENT DECISIONS

CHAPTER 13

LEADING ECONOMIC INDICATORS

Now that you have examined the business cycle in detail and learned to use *The Wall Street Journal's* statistical series, you may be looking for a device to make analysis somewhat easier. Perhaps, while wading through the stream of data, you felt the need for a single indicator that could predict changes in the business cycle. You wanted something akin to the meteorologist's barometer, to inform you of rain or shine without a detailed examination of cloud formations.

Unfortunately, economists have never agreed on a *single* economic indicator to predict the future. Some indicators are better than others, but none is consistently accurate; all give a false signal on occasion. To deal with this, economists have devised a *composite* or combination of statistical series drawn from a broad spectrum of economic activity, each of which tends to move up or down ahead of the general trend of the business cycle. These series are referred to as *leading* indicators because of their predictive quality, and 11 have been combined into the *composite index of leading economic indicators.*

The components of the index are as follows:

1. Average weekly hours of production or non-supervisory workers, manufacturing.
2. Average weekly initial claims for unemployment insurance, state programs.
3. Manufacturers' new orders in 1982 dollars, consumer goods and materials industries.
4. Vendor performance—slower deliveries diffusion index.
5. Contracts and orders for plant and equipment in 1982 dollars.
6. New private housing units authorized by local building permits.

7. Change in manufacturers' unfilled orders in 1982 dollars, durable goods industries.
8. Change in sensitive materials prices.
9. Stock prices, 500 common stocks.
10. Money supply—M2—in 1982 dollars.
11. Index of consumer expectations.

There are three general criteria for inclusion in the index. First, each series must accurately lead the business cycle. Second, the various series should provide comprehensive coverage of the economy by representing a wide and diverse range of economic activity. And, third, each series must be available monthly, with only a brief lag until publication, and must be free from large subsequent revisions.

The leading indicators meet these criteria, and weaving these series into a composite provides a statistic that is more reliable and less erratic than any individual component by itself.

Finally, some of the indicators measure activity in physical units, others in current dollars, still others in constant dollars, and some with an index form. This variety of measurements is reduced to an index with 1982 assigned a base value of 100. All other months and years are expressed as a percentage of the base year.

The January 1989 index, published in the Monday, March 6, 1989 issue of *The Wall Street Journal*, is representative. The series usually appears around the first of the month. The chart accompanying the article and the second paragraph inform you that the index rose 0.6 percent to 145.7 (1982 = 100) in January. (See page 302.)

Chart 13–1 on page 304 confirms that this was an all-time high, and you will notice the index has historically turned prior to the cycle. In January 1989 there was no recession in sight.

You can see that the index did a good job of forecasting all recessions, leading the downturn by at least five months in every instance except 1981–1982. And in that case you should observe that the two-month lead is a difficult call because the index double-clutched just prior to the recession's start. The first pump on the clutch is at least a half-year before the downturn begins.

But you can also see the false alarms of 1962, 1966, 1984, and 1987. In each case the index fell for at least three consecutive months although no recession followed. The 1962 decline followed on the heels of President Kennedy's forced rollback of Big Steel's price increase.

Data Show Economy Isn't Weakening

Leading Index Climbed 0.6% In January, but Orders To Manufacturers Fell

By Hilary Stout
Staff Reporter of The Wall Street Journal

WASHINGTON—Despite a hint of softness in manufacturing, the economy still shows few signs of significantly slowing, the latest government figures indicate.

Index of Leading Indicators

The government's principal economic forecasting gauge, the index of leading indicators, climbed 0.6% in January after rising 0.7% in December, the Commerce Department reported. During the same month, the department said, new orders received by manufacturers fell 1.3% after rising 4.7% in December. But much of the decline, and much of the December rise, came in categories such as transportation equipment, where the size of individual transactions makes monthly figures erratic. Excluding transportation, orders rose 0.2% in January.

The rise in the index of leading indicators, which is designed to predict economic activity about six to nine months ahead, was the first time since April that it has recorded consecutive monthly increases. Many economists had viewed the sawtoothed pattern of the index as a signal that the economy, now in its seventh year of expansion, was headed for a slowdown.

But after the latest report, in which eight of the 11 indicators in the index advanced, the outlook for the economy appeared heartier than ever.

"At a minimum you'd have to say there certainly is no sign that the economy is imminently in a weakening state," said Thomas Juster, an economist at the University of Michigan's Institute for Social Research.

That view is likely to be welcomed by the Bush administration, which is counting on vigorous economic activity to bring in enough tax revenue to reduce the federal budget deficit.

But it is unlikely to be well received at the Federal Reserve, which believes the current economic momentum carries risks of accelerating inflation. With that in mind, policy makers at the nation's central bank have been nudging up interest rates to increase the cost of borrowing and reduce demand, which they hope will stem price increases.

Some economists remain wary of the precision of the leading indicators index—which comprises an array of statistics on areas as diverse as building permits and factory shipments—in forecasting future economic activity. (See chart on page one.)

"I think people place too much emphasis on it," said Evelina Tainer, senior domestic economist at First National Bank of Chicago.

Of the latest index, she said, "It says the economy is going to continue to grow, but I think it has limited power" to predict.

In the January report, the Commerce Department added two indicators to the index and dropped two others in an effort to more accurately gauge the economy.

The new components are an "index of consumer expectation," compiled by researchers at the University of Michigan, and monthly factory orders for durable goods—items such as cars, machinery and household appliances, expected to last at least three years.

The department dropped measures of outstanding credit and business inventories, largely because they aren't available when analysts initially compile the index. "That meant we often made major revisions," said Larry Moran, an economist in the department's Bureau of Economic Analysis. "The major advantage (in changing the index) is that we remove those big revisions."

Standing alone, January factory orders, which fell to $235.83 billion, suggested faltering in the manufacturing sector. But the figures were tugged down by steep drops in orders for both transportation and defense equipment, which fell 8.5% and 33.9% respectively. In December, transportation orders jumped 22.1% and defense orders soared 24%.

In a sign of continued investment in plant and equipment, orders for capital goods outside the defense area continued to increase in January, growing 1.6% on top of a particularly strong 10.1% rise in December. Orders for nondurable goods rose 0.5% after climbing 1.5% in January.

Durable goods are more closely tied to interest rates than nondurables. In January orders of durable goods declined 2.7% after rising 7.4% in December, leading some analysts to suggest that rising interest rates may be starting to show an effect. But others maintained that December's increase was so large that orders in January were bound to fall.

Statistical Summary

LEADING INDICATORS

Here are the net contributions of the components of the Commerce Department's index of leading indicators. After various adjustments, they produced a 0.6% rise in the index for January and a 0.7% rise for December.

	Jan. 1989	Dec. 1988
Workweek	0.07	−0.22
Unemployment claims	0.05	−0.04
Orders for consumer goods	−0.12	0.16
Slower deliveries	0.06	0.04
Plant and equipment orders	0.04	0.18
Building permits	−0.11	0.09
Durables order backlog	0.05	0.17
Materials prices	0.12	0.07
Stock prices	0.17	0.11
Money supply	−0.22	0.03
Consumer expectations	0.33	−0.06

The seasonally adjusted index numbers (1967=100) for January, and the change from December, are:

Index of leading indicators	145.7	0.6
Index of coincident indicators	132.9	1.0
Index of lagging indicators	118.1	0.1

The ratio of coincident to lagging indicators was 1.13% in January, up from 1.10 in December.

Source: *The Wall Street Journal*, March 6, 1989.

Leading Indicators

In percent (1982=100).

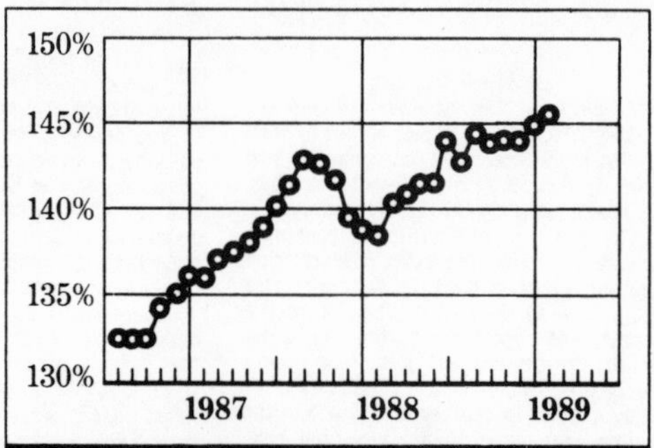

COMPOSITE of key indicators of future economic activity rose in January to 145.7% of the 1982 average from a revised 144.9% in December, the Commerce Department reports.

Source: *The Wall Street Journal*, March 6, 1989.

Leading Index – Second Paragraph

The government's principal economic forecasting gauge, the index of leading indicators, climbed 0.6% in January after rising 0.7% in December, the Commerce Department reported. During the same month, the department said, new orders received by manufacturers fell 1.3% after rising 4.7% in December. But much of the decline, and much of the December rise, came in categories such as transportation equipment, where the size of individual transactions makes monthly figures erratic. Excluding transportation, orders rose 0.2% in January.

Source: *The Wall Street Journal*, March 6, 1989.

Statistical Summary – End of Article

LEADING INDICATORS

Here are the net contributions of the components of the Commerce Department's index of leading indicators. After various adjustments, they produced a 0.6% rise in the index for January and a 0.7% rise for December.

	Jan. 1989	Dec. 1988
Workweek	0.07	−0.22
Unemployment claims	0.05	−0.04
Orders for consumer goods	−0.12	0.16
Slower deliveries	0.06	0.04
Plant and equipment orders	0.04	0.18
Building permits	−0.11	0.09
Durables order backlog	0.05	0.17
Materials prices	0.12	0.07
Stock prices	0.17	0.11
Money supply	−0.22	0.03
Consumer expectations	0.33	−0.06

The seasonally adjusted index numbers (1967=100) for January, and the change from December, are:

Index of leading indicators	145.7	0.6
Index of coincident indicators	132.9	1.0
Index of lagging indicators	118.1	0.1

The ratio of coincident to lagging indicators was 1.13% in January, up from 1.10 in December.

Source: *The Wall Street Journal*, March 6, 1989.

The stock market went into shock and business activity slowed, but you can see that the setback was brief. This decline was clearly a random event and of no cyclical significance.

The indicators' 1966 setback was more like developments in the 1980s. The Vietnam War had begun and inflation was climbing. The Fed tightened in response, in order to raise interest rates and curb consumer and business demand. Housing starts crashed and it was "nip-and-tuck" for a while, but the Fed quickly eased when alarm spread so that recession never took hold.

The Fed faced similar conditions and tightened in 1984 as the cycle came roaring back from the 1981–1982 recession. The economy went into the doldrums temporarily and the leading indicators fell, but once again the Fed eased as soon as inflation subsided and the economy emerged with only a scratch.

The October 1987 stock market crash was as severe as 1962's decline, but this time the market's own dynamic created the problem, rather than the actions of the president. Nonetheless, fears of recession swirled about for several months and the composite index headed south. Soon, how-

CHART 13–1
Composite Index of 11 Leading Indicators

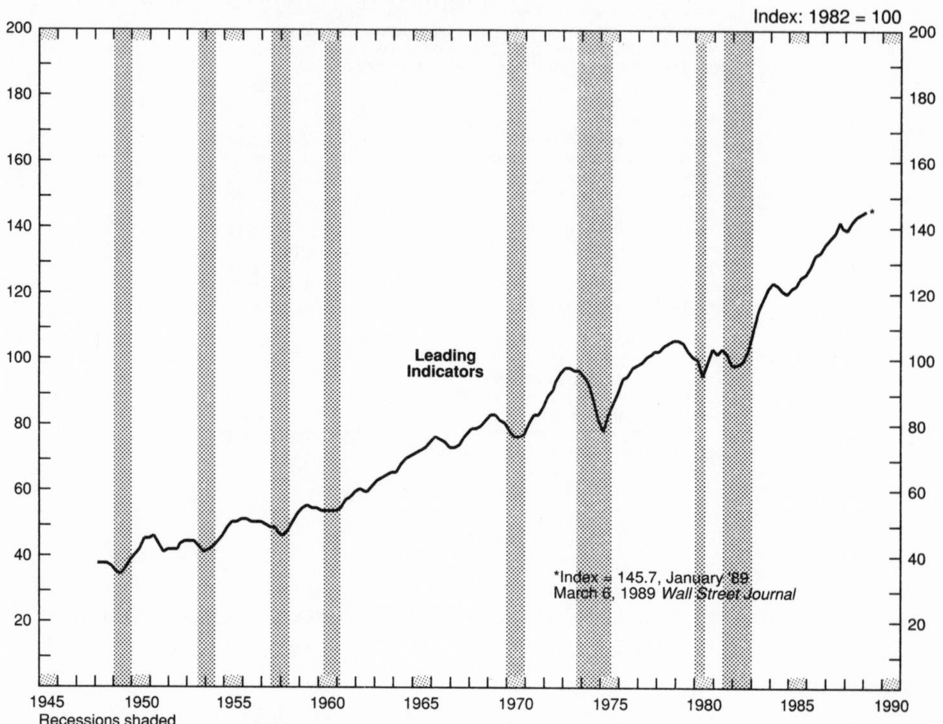

Source: U.S. Department of Commerce, *Business Conditions Digest* and *Handbook of Cyclical Indicators*, series 910.

ever, everyone realized the crash had nothing to do with the economy's fundamentals, and concern evaporated as the index snapped back.

Moreover, keep in mind that this statistic is not an analytical tool that permits you to probe beneath the cycle's surface in order to analyze its dynamic. The composite does not provide a step-by-step diagnosis that reveals the cycle's rhythm. It does not disclose the forces that lead from one set of conditions to another. It only averages a number of convenient series that are themselves leading indicators, but are otherwise unrelated.

This series is of interest *solely* because it provides an omen of future events. You need all the statistical reports appearing in the *Journal* in order to build an understanding of the timing, direction, and strength of the business cycle. After all, a meteorologist needs more than a barometer, and most Americans who make decisions in the business community, or wish to be fully informed of current economic events, need far more than a crude, general directional signal to guide their long-range planning.

Investor's Tip

- The composite index of leading economic indicators is not the square root of the universe. There is no single index or formula that provides all the answers to the problem of business forecasting.

CHAPTER 14

INVENTORIES

A DESTABILIZING FORCE

Inventories are stocks of goods on hand: raw materials, goods in process, or finished products. Individual businesses use them to bring stability to their operations, and yet you'll see that they actually have a destabilizing effect on the business cycle.

Businesses view inventories as a necessary evil. A manufacturer, wholesaler, or retailer can't live from hand to mouth, continually filling sales orders from current production. Stocks of goods "on the shelf" are a cushion against unexpected orders and slowdowns in production. On the other hand, inventories are an investment in working capital and incur an interest cost. If the firm borrows capital to maintain inventories, the direct interest cost is obvious. Even if the firm has not borrowed, however, working capital tied up in inventories represents an interest cost. Any funds invested in inventories could have earned the going interest rate in the money market, and this loss can substantially crimp profits.

Therefore, business attempts to keep inventories at an absolute minimum consistent with smooth operations. For a very large business, literally millions of dollars are at stake. This is why you see modern automated cash registers (i.e., the ones that automatically "read" the black and white bar code on packages) in large chain supermarkets and retail establishments. These cash registers came into use not chiefly because they record your purchases more quickly (which of course they do), but because they also tie into a computer network that keeps track of inventories of thousands of items on a daily basis.

But why do inventories, so necessary to the smooth functioning of an individual business, exacerbate the business cycle?

Consider the upswing of the cycle first. As demand increases rapidly, businesses must boost production to meet the growing volume of orders. If they are not quick enough, and sales grow more rapidly than output, an unplanned drawdown of inventories will occur as orders are filled. This is known as *involuntary inventory depletion*. If inventories are severely depleted, shortages can result and sales may be jeopardized. To protect itself against such developments once it is confident of the unfolding expansion, business will expand output and defensively accumulate inventories more rapidly than its sales are growing. Since all firms are stockpiling to prevent shortages, industrial production increases more vigorously than it otherwise would, accentuating the cyclical expansion and the swift rise in capacity utilization. For the entire economy, production grows more rapidly than sales. This, of course, hastens the inevitable decrease in labor productivity and increase in unit labor costs associated with this phase of the cycle. Hence, inventory accumulation adds to inflationary pressures.

Now consider the downswing of the cycle. No firm willingly maintains production in a sales slump because unsold goods would pile up on the shelf. As sales weaken and fall, business curtails production in order to prevent *involuntary inventory accumulation*. Indeed, once business recognizes the severity of the slump, it will begin to liquidate the large volume of (now unnecessary) inventories built up during the previous expansion. These stockpiles of goods are no longer needed and can be disposed of. But as goods are sold from inventories, output and employment are reduced more than sales, since orders can be filled from inventories rather than from current production. This aggravates the cycle's downturn.

Thus, inventories play an important destabilizing role in the cycle through their influence on industrial production, boosting output during expansion and depressing it during slump. This destabilizing influence is compounded by inventory's impact on inflation. When rapid expansion is heightened by inventory accumulation, contributing to inflationary pressures, business firms increase their inventory buildup. They want to stockpile goods at current prices and sell them later at inflated prices. And when inventory liquidation in a recession contributes to deflationary pressures, falling prices can trigger a panic sell-off, which drives prices down even more steeply.

Here's how it works. Business stockpiles goods during the expansionary phase of the cycle to prevent involuntary inventory depletion and shortages, and prices start to rise. Firms quickly discover that goods held in inventory increase in value along with the general rise in prices. They have an incentive to buy now while prices are low, hold the goods in inventory, and sell them later at higher prices and profits. If prices are rising rapidly enough, widespread speculation can set in, which adds to the general increase in production and reinforces the inflation.

Recall, for example, the rapid increase in sugar prices in 1973–1974. Sugar manufacturers and industrial users of sugar (canners, soft drink bottlers, confectioners, and bakers) produced sugar and sweetened products and held them in inventory while their prices were low, hoping to make large profits from sales when their prices increased. This speculative stockpiling contributed to the price increase by bidding up production (and costs) out of proportion to sales.

Of course, when the inevitable contraction comes, liquidation of the inventory overhang helps halt the inflationary spiral. Businesses panic when faced with the prospect of sellng at a price that will not recoup interest costs. If sufficiently severe, the sell-off can force prices down. More important, output plummets and layoffs mount as orders are filled from the shelf. Liquidation continues until inventories are in proper relation to sales.

Thus, speculative inventory accumulation and liquidation become a self-fulfilling prophecy. Firms pile up inventories in anticipation of a price increase, and the large volume of orders bids prices upward. When the recession begins, firms sell inventories in haste, afraid of a drop in prices, and the sell-off forces prices downward.

Now you understand why inventories and their relationship to sales are such important economic indicators. They not only confirm the stage of the cycle, they also provide advance warning of turning points and of the strength or severity of impending boom and bust.

RECENT EXPERIENCE

Inventory accumulation and liquidation reinforce the business cycle. The consumer sets the cycle's pace; inventories exacerbate it. The cyclical experience of the early 1970s will serve as an illustration, followed by an examination of more recent developments.

To begin with, *The Wall Street Journal* publishes the Commerce Department's *inventory* and *sales* data around the middle of each month.

Business Inventories Seem Under Control, U.S. Data Indicate

By Hilary Stout

Staff Reporter of The Wall Street Journal

WASHINGTON—Businesses appear to be continuing to keep their inventories under control, the latest government figures indicate.

Inventory/
Sales Ratio

In January, manufacturers, retailers and merchant wholesalers held their stocks to 1.49 months of sales for the second consecutive month, the Commerce Department said. While inventories climbed 0.7% in the month, sales grew 1.0%.

Balancing inventories with sales is tricky but it is as critical to the national economy as it is to individual businesses. If businesses find they can't sell what is on their shelves, they will cut back orders and production, and the chain reaction can lead to a recession. But if reserve stocks are too slim, shortages can spur price increases.

Alan Greenspan, chairman of the Federal Reserve Board, has frequently cited excessive inventory buildup as a warning signal of economic downturn.

But January's figures mean it would take businesses just under a month and a half to sell off their stockpiles at January's sales pace, lower than the 1.53 months of a year earlier.

Inventories
and Sales

January's activity brought total business inventories to $766.21 billion and sales to $513.9 billion, the department said. All the numbers in the report are adjusted for seasonal variations but not for inflation.

The figures did show some areas of softness. Automobile inventories grew 1.9%, while sales fell 1.7%, bringing the inventory level to 2.04 months of sales. In December it equaled 1.97 months of sales.

Retailers increased their inventories 0.9%, while their sales grew only 0.7%. Manufacturers' inventories expanded 0.9% while sales rose only 0.3%.

But manufacturers' inventories still equaled only 1.54 months' sales, just a slight increase from December's level of 1.53. Retailers' inventories equaled 1.64 months' sales, also up slightly from December, when the level was 1.63.

BUSINESS INVENTORIES

Statistical
Summary

Here is a summary of the Commerce Department's report on business inventories and sales in January. The figures are in billions of dollars, seasonally adjusted:

	(billions of dollars)		
	Jan. 1989	Dec. 1988	Jan. 1988
Total business inventories	766.21	760.59	711.03
Manufacturers	357.35	354.16	333.37
Retailers	227.07	225.01	209.43
Wholesalers	181.79	181.42	168.23
Total business sales	513.90	508.89	464.73
Inventory/sales ratio	1.49	1.49	1.53

Source: *The Wall Street Journal*, March 16, 1989.

Inventory/Sales Ratio – Second Paragraph

In January, manufacturers, retailers and merchant wholesalers held their stocks to 1.49 months of sales for the second consecutive month, the Commerce Department said. While inventories climbed 0.7% in the month, sales grew 1.0%.

Inventories and Sales – Sixth Paragraph

January's activity brought total business inventories to $766.21 billion and sales to $513.9 billion, the department said. All the numbers in the report are adjusted for seasonal variations but not for inflation.

Statistical Summary – End of Article

BUSINESS INVENTORIES

Here is a summary of the Commerce Department's report on business inventories and sales in January. The figures are in billions of dollars, seasonally adjusted:

	(billions of dollars)		
	Jan. 1989	Dec. 1988	Jan. 1988
Total business inventories	766.21	760.59	711.03
Manufacturers	357.35	354.16	333.37
Retailers	227.07	225.01	209.43
Wholesalers	181.79	181.42	168.23
Total business sales	513.90	508.89	464.73
Inventory/sales ratio	1.49	1.49	1.53

Source: *The Wall Street Journal*, March 16, 1989.

In the Thursday, March 16, 1989 article, the second paragraph and the statistical summary at the end of the article inform you that inventories were 1.49 times sales. The sixth paragraph states that inventories were $766.21 billion and sales were $513.9 billion.

Inventories and sales are straightforward concepts. The *inventory-sales ratio* tells you how many months it would take to sell off inventories at the prevailing sales pace. You can calculate the ratio by dividing monthly inventory by monthly sales. Typically, inventories have been roughly 1.5 times sales over the cycle. A rise in the ratio indicates that inventories are growing out of proportion to sales and that inventory liquidation and recession are imminent. A fall in the ratio informs you that sales are outpacing inventory growth and that economic expansion is under way. This is a key indicator; you should follow it closely.

Return to the *Journal* article after examining the inventory cycle of the early 1970s (see Chart 14–1 on page 312). This cycle concluded with a good example of inventory accumulation and speculation followed by inventory liquidation. To trace these events, follow the steep rise in inventories from 1972 through 1974 and the 1975 liquidation; note the decline in the inventory-sales ratio in 1971–72 and the increase in 1973 and 1974; and note that the inventory and sales curves are nearly congruent, with inventories lagging behind sales by a year or so.

You can observe the decline of the inventory-sales ratio as the business cycle moved from recovery to expansion in 1971–1972. Sales were expanding, but it was still too early for business to rebuild inventories.

As increasing demand boosted sales, 1973 displayed all the symptoms of the expansion-to-peak phase of the cycle: strong and rapidly growing sales, strained capacity utilization and slower deliveries, and a rising rate of inflation. Under these circumstances, business sought to defend itself against possible shortages by adding to inventories more rapidly than sales grew. The long decline in the inventory-sales ratio was reversed, and speculation began. business boosted inventories in the expectation of rising prices, hoping to make a profit as goods increased in value. This intensified inflationary pressure (recall sugar) as a share of production went on the shelf instead of toward satisfying consumer demand. You can see that the inventory run-up dwarfed all other postwar increases up to that date.

As the cycle's peak approached, in 1974, sales stopped growing. Unplanned inventory accumulation became a problem; the inventory-sales ratio rose even more rapidly; and business firms had to deal with ever-larger stockpiles of goods. Sensing that a sell-off was around the corner, they tried to bring inventories under control. Unfortunately, this was more easily said than done. Orders had to be cancelled and production curtailed more than once because business underestimated the situation's severity.

But beginning in late 1974 and continuing into 1975, inventory liquidation finally began. Under panic conditions, business desperately dumped goods on the market. Despite the sell-off, you'll notice that the

CHART 14–1
Manufacturing and Trade Sales and Inventories, Inventory-Sales Ratio (monthly basis), **and Change in Book Value of Manufacturing and Trade Inventories**

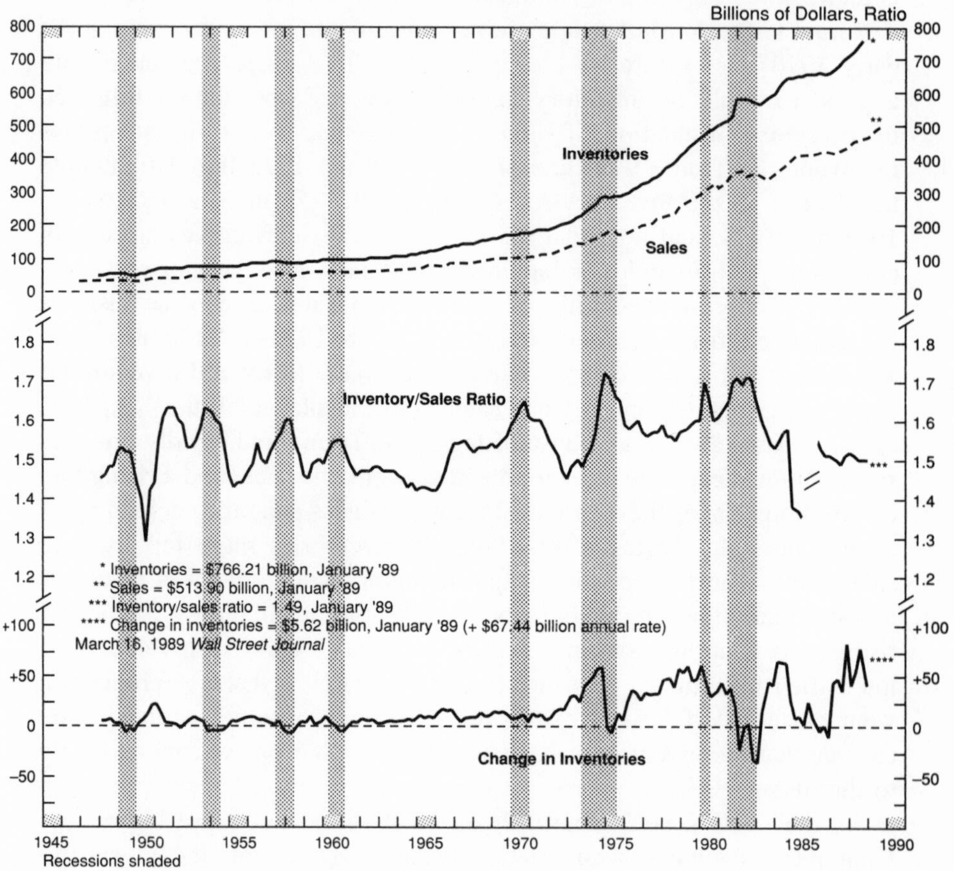

Source: U.S. Department of Commerce *Business Conditions Digest* and *Handbook of Cyclical Indicators*, series 31, 56, and 71, and *Survey of Current Business*.

inventory-sales ratio remained high until early 1975. This is evidence of the collapse in sales and the recession's severity—the reason business went to such lengths to unload its stocks of goods.

Other postwar recessions had been mild by comparison. Industrial production plunged as business firms cut output sharply and filled the meager volume of orders from overstocked inventories. Two million workers were laid off between the fall of 1974 and the spring of 1975, and the unemployment rate brushed 10 percent. There is no doubt that inventory accumulation and liquidation played a key role in the recession's harshness.

Unlike the cycle of the early 70s, the 1981–82 recession can't be used as a typical example of inventory accumulation and liquidation because of the Fed's role in aborting the 1981 recovery. Sales were doing well and the inventory-sales ratio was low when the Fed's tight money policy clamped a vise on the economy in 1981. Sales shrank and involuntary inventory accumulation drove up both inventories and the inventory-sales ratio. As soon as possible, business began a massive inventory liquidation program that continued through early 1983. As you can tell from Chart 14–1 on page 312, the worst recession since World War II was accompanied by the most desperate bout of inventory liquidation.

Recovery began as soon as the Fed provided easier credit conditions. And you can see that business did not wait long before it began restocking its depleted inventories. By early 1984 inventory accumulation set a new record. Massive inventory accumulation was an important contributor to the economy's explosive growth immediately after the 1981–82 recession. Yet sales were so strong that the inventory-sales ratio declined throughout 1983 and remained low in 1984. There was no indication that inventory growth had outstripped sales or that the economy was near a cyclical peak.

Nevertheless, the Fed was concerned that the recovery and expansion were proceeding too rapidly. It fine-tuned the slowdown of mid-84, and inventory accumulations began to subside. By 1985 and early 1986 inventory accumulation was down to a moderate level.

To a large extent, the inventory run-up of 1984 and the subsequent drop to a moderate pace in 1985–86 were a one-time reaction to the extreme inventory depletion during the 1981–82 recession. These developments were not part of the ordinary cyclical scene; they were a reaction to the credit conditions imposed on the economy by the Fed. In a way, the decks were cleared for a resumption of normal cyclical patterns by the second half of the 80s.

As the economy's pace improved in the late 80s, inventory accumulation picked up once again. Although inflation was minimal and therefore speculation was probably not the motive behind this build-up, business was probably exercising precaution to ensure that it had ample stocks to meet the expected rise in orders.

THE OUTLOOK

Return to the March 16, 1989 *Journal* article on pages 309 and 310. It informs you that the inventory-sales ratio was 1.49, and you will observe from Chart 14–1 on page 312 that the ratio had fallen to a very low figure by the mid-80s. This is partly a consequence of the improved technology that enables business to keep a closer watch over its inventories. But it's also a sign of a lean economy, showing that the big inventory expansion of the late 80s was not a symptom of the excesses of inventory speculation, but rather an attempt by management to build stocks in proportion to the rapid increase in sales. In the late 1980s, the expansion still had a way to go.

How long will the inventory-sales ratio remain low, and how long will it be before inventory accumulation exacerbates the expansion and contributes to the next recession? That depends on the strength of the expansion as determined by the growth in consumer demand. If demand grows too quickly and inflation speeds up, business will begin stockpiling for self-protection and speculation, and the inventory-sales ratio will start to climb. This will be a dead giveaway that inventory accumulation is contributing to boom conditions and that the peak of the cycle cannot be far off. On the other hand, if the expansion is restrained, the inventory-sales ratio should remain flat for a long time. In that case, inventory accumulation will not aggravate the expansion and the business cycle will not be brought to a peak prematurely.

Investor's Tip

- Watch these figures carefully. If boom conditions drive inventories out of moderate proportion to sales and the inventory-sales ratio rises rapidly and exceeds 1.6, you know recession can't be far behind.

CHAPTER 15

BUSINESS CAPITAL EXPENDITURES

WHY BUSINESS INVESTS

John Maynard Keynes could not have known America's modern consumer economy when he wrote his *General Theory* in 1936 (see Chapters 3 and 5). Keynes assumed the absence of any dynamic in British consumer expenditures and believed consumption behaved passively, expanding and contracting with consumer income. As far as Keynes was concerned, business investment determined the cycle's dynamic. So Keynes built his theory of aggregate economic activity around the forces that determine business investment in plant and equipment.

But business's expenditures on factories, warehouses, offices, machinery, and equipment, like its accumulation of inventories, reinforce the business cycle; they do not lead it. Business waits for its signal from the economy before committing its capital. Similarly, only after the expansion is over does business begin to cut back on capital expenditures in anticipation of reduced sales.

There are six principal factors influencing business decisions to spend on new plant and equipment.

First, old facilities may wear out and need to be replaced.

Second, the rate of capacity utilization may be high. Putting it simply, if sales are strong, business will invest in new machinery and equipment in order to have the capacity necessary to fill the orders. During a recession, however, the rate of capacity utilization is low and business has more than enough plant and equipment on hand to satisfy the low volume of orders. Why add to plant and equipment when the existing level is already more than adequate?

Third, old facilities, whether fully utilized or not, will be scrapped and replaced by new if operating costs can be sufficiently reduced through innovation in the process of production. Competition leaves business no choice: if equipment is no longer cost-effective, it must be replaced even though it could still be used.

Fourth, new plant and equipment may be required to produce a new or redesigned product even if existing facilities are operating at full capacity and have a continued useful life. Model and style changes have forced the automobile industry to spend billions replacing still-functional equipment, for instance.

Fifth, spending on plant and equipment is sensitive to current and anticipated profits. Business will invest in additional facilities if it expects long-range profit growth beyond any short-run cyclical fluctuation. In addition, profits plowed back into the business provide the cash flow necessary to finance capital expenditures. A recession will limit business's ability to finance capital expenditures; an expansion will generate the necessary cash flow.

The final factor is interest rates. Business must borrow to finance plant and equipment expenditures if internally generated funds are not adequate. When interest rates are very high the cost of borrowing may be prohibitive, and so business firms postpone or cancel their capital expenditure plans. Or they may feel that for the time being they can get a better return by investing their own funds at high rates of interest than by making expenditures on new productive facilities.

Keep these factors in mind when evaluating business's capital expansion plans and their role in the current cycle. You can keep abreast of capital expenditures by following three series published monthly in *The Wall Street Journal*: the Commerce Department report on new orders for nondefense capital goods, the National Machine Tool Builders' Association report on machine tool orders, and the F.W. Dodge report on building awards.

NONDEFENSE CAPITAL GOODS

The Wall Street Journal publishes preliminary data for *nondefense capital goods*, such as the Thursday, March 23, 1989 release, on the Thursday or Friday of the next-to-the-last week of the month, and then publishes the final report about a week later. You will have to keep your

Durables Orders Decreased 3.6% For February

Drop Is for Second Month In a Row; Data Suggest The Economy Is Cooling

By David Wessel
Staff Reporter of The Wall Street Journal

WASHINGTON—Factory orders for durable goods declined in February for the second month in a row, their first back-to-back drop in three years. The report is another sign that the economy is cooling off.

The Commerce Department said orders for durable goods, those manufactured products intended to last three years or more, fell 3.6% in February following a 2.9% decline in January.

"It's significant that the decline was quite widespread across most industries," said Jerry Jasinowski, chief economist of the National Association of Manufacturers. He termed the report "solid evidence" that the economy is slowing.

And Federal Reserve Board Chairman Alan Greenspan yesterday suggested that the economy is likely to continue to slow. Testifying on Capitol Hill, he said the U.S. still hasn't felt the full impact of the tighter monetary policy that the Fed began carrying out a year ago. "There are significant lags," he said.

Other government measures also are sending signals of a slowing economy. The Commerce Department said factory shipments declined in February for the second consecutive month. Factory payrolls, which had been growing strongly, declined. And the Fed's industrial production index failed to climb in February for the first time in a year.

Hints that the pace of economic activity is retarding may relieve some of the pressure on the Fed to tighten credit when policy makers convene next week for a regularly scheduled meeting. Pressure on the Fed mounted last week with a government report that producer prices shot up 1% for the second month in a row—and the inflation threat still looms large.

Moderation Trend

Speaking in New York, Fed Vice Chairman Manuel Johnson said he sees signs that the economy is moderating. "One month, as I want to stress, should never be the basis of a policy decision," Mr. Johnson said, "but the longer trends suggest some moderation."

Mr. Johnson cautioned, though, that good weather probably made government economic data for January look unusually strong. That accounts for some of the decline in economic indicators in February, he suggested.

The Commerce Department figures for new orders, though volatile and often revised substantially, suggest that after a two-year boom, the best times may be past for manufacturers. "We're not going to see investment growing quite as fast as last year. Blame some of that on interest rates," said Priscilla Trumbull of Wefa Group Inc., a Bala Cynwyd, Pa., consulting company. "And we're not going to see exports growing as fast as we did . . . because the big declines in the dollar are over." A cheaper dollar makes U.S. goods more attractive to foreigners.

But she and other economists cautioned that while the pace of growth seems to be slowing, it's too soon to conclude that a downturn is at hand. "At least temporarily, manufacturing is running out of gas," said Robert Dederick, an economist at Northern Trust Co. "Is this a little stutter step or is it tripping? Unfortunately, we can't tell yet."

Softer Orders

The Commerce Department said nearly all major industries reported softer orders. In all, orders for durable goods totaled $123.7 billion in February, down from $128.3 billion in January.

Transportation equipment, where orders swing widely from one month to the next, accounted for most of the decline, falling 8.5%. Orders for primary metals were off 3.3%; the Commerce Department said softer orders for steel were largely responsible. Orders for nonelectrical machinery, a category that includes computers, farm equipment and metal-working machines, were off 2.3%. But orders for electrical machinery—which ranges from toasters to electrical transmission gear—were up 0.6%.

Orders for non-defense capital goods, a closely watched gauge of business capital spending plans, fell 8.9% in February after rising 2.2% in January. — Non-defense Capital Goods

Factory shipments of durable goods were off 2.5% to $120.6 billion in February after slipping 0.4% in January. It was the first back-to-back drop in that measure since the spring of 1987. All major industries except nonelectrical machinery reported downturns; higher shipments of farm machinery and special-industry machines boosted shipments in that category.

Manufacturers reported their backlog of unfilled orders grew 0.7% to $455.5 billion. The aircraft industry accounted for much of the increase. Backlogs in the computer industry declined, the government said.

Source: *The Wall Street Journal*, March 23, 1989.

Non-defense Capital Goods – Third Paragraph from End of Article

Orders for non-defense capital goods, a closely watched gauge of business capital spending plans, fell 8.9% in February after rising 2.2% in January.

eyes open for these figures because they are part of an overall report on *durable goods*. The revised data, appearing a week later, is included with a general release on *factory orders*. The Friday, March 31, 1989 article is a good example.

You will notice that the third from the last paragraph of the March 23 durable goods article states that orders for nondefense capital goods fell 8.9 percent in February, but that the statistical summary at the end of the March 31 factory orders article revises that to a decline of 8.2 percent and provides a figure of $37.06 billion.

This series presents new orders received by manufacturers of durable goods other than than military equipment. (*Durable goods* are defined as those having a useful life of more than three years.) Nondefense capital goods represent approximately one fifth to one third of all durable goods production. The series includes engines; construction, mining, and materials handling equipment; office and store machinery; electrical transmission and distribution equipment and other electrical machinery (excluding household appliances and electronic equipment); and railroad, ship and aircraft transportation equipment. Military equipment is excluded because new orders for such items do not respond directly to the business cycle.

Chart 15–1 on page 320 provides a good illustration of the relationship between capacity utilization (see Chart 7–3 on page 120) and equipment expenditures. Orders for nondefense capital goods expanded swiftly as capacity utilization rose rapidly through early 1984. Then, capacity utilization leveled off at 80 percent during the mid-80s, and nondefense orders stopped growing.

Orders for nondefense capital goods began growing again in 1987, this time leading capacity utilization upward. Businesses invested in new equipment despite moderate levels of capacity utilization in order to replace worn out and obsolete equipment, produce new products, and

Factory Orders Declined 2.3% For February

Figures Again Are Hinting At Economic Slowdown, Though Backlog Grew

By David Wessel
Staff Reporter of The Wall Street Journal

WASHINGTON — Factory orders fell 2.3% in February after dropping 1.2% in January, another hint that the U.S. economy may be slowing down.

Shipments from factories also declined, and inventories increased. But the backlog of unfilled orders continued to grow, the Commerce Department said.

Several government economic indicators suggest that the economy slowed in February and January after a strong December, but economists warn that it's too soon to conclude that several years of prosperity are over.

Commerce Undersecretary Robert Ortner, who has said he wouldn't be surprised if the U.S. enters a recession in the next year, warned, "It's premature to call a downturn. It would take several more months of decline before you would say that."

Indeed, factories booked $230.68 billion in new orders in February, more than any single month in 1988 except December. The figures are adjusted for seasonal fluctuations, but not for inflation.

Nonetheless, factory orders haven't fallen two months in a row since early 1986, and the declines were widespread. Industries that have exhibited substantial strength lately—including chemicals, paper and rubber—reported drops in orders in February.

The department added that orders booked by the computer industry, in which fears of a slowdown have spooked investors, were down 11.6% in February after rising 0.5% in January and 3.6% in December. Shipments dropped 4.1% in February, and the backlog of unfilled orders fell 2.7%.

New orders for nondurable goods, those intended to last less than three years, fell 1% to $106.48 billion in February after rising 0.8% in January. Orders for durable goods fell a revised 3.3% to $124.2 billion after falling 2.8% in January. In an earlier report, the department estimated the February decline at 3.6%.

Factory shipments dropped 1.7% to $227.61 billion in February after increasing 0.3% in January. Shipments of both durable and nondurable goods declined.

Factory inventories rose 0.5% to $359.09 billion on top of a 0.9% increase in January. Inventories equaled 1.58 months of shipments, up from 1.54 months in January. Economists consider an increase in that ratio a harbinger of a recession, but the ratio is still within the narrow band in which it has stayed for several months.

The backlog of unfilled orders rose 0.6% in February to $476.52 billion after rising 1.0% the month before. Most unfilled orders are for durable goods.

FACTORY ORDERS

Here are the Commerce Department's latest figures for manufacturers in billions of dollars, seasonally adjusted.

	Feb. 1989	Jan. 1989	%Chg.
All industries	230.68	236.08	− 2.3
Durable goods	124.20	128.48	− 3.3
Nondurable goods	106.48	107.60	− 1.0
Capital goods industries	45.40	47.17	− 3.7
Nondefense	37.06	40.35	− 8.2
Defense	8.34	6.82	+ 22.4
Total shipments	227.61	231.49	− 1.7
Inventories	359.09	357.46	+ 0.5
Backlog of orders	476.52	473.45	+ 0.6

Nondefense Capital Goods

Source: *The Wall Street Journal*, March 31, 1989.

March 31, 1989 – Statistical Summary – End of Article

FACTORY ORDERS

Here are the Commerce Department's latest figures for manufacturers in billions of dollars, seasonally adjusted.

	Feb. 1989	Jan. 1989	%Chg.
All industries	230.68	236.08	− 2.3
Durable goods	124.20	128.48	− 3.3
Nondurable goods	106.48	107.60	− 1.0
Capital goods industries	45.40	47.17	− 3.7
Nondefense	37.06	40.35	− 8.2
Defense	8.34	6.82	+ 22.4
Total shipments	227.61	231.49	− 1.7
Inventories	359.09	357.46	+ 0.5
Backlog of orders	476.52	473.45	+ 0.6

Source: *The Wall Street Journal*, March 31, 1989.

CHART 15–1
Nondefense Orders of Capital Goods

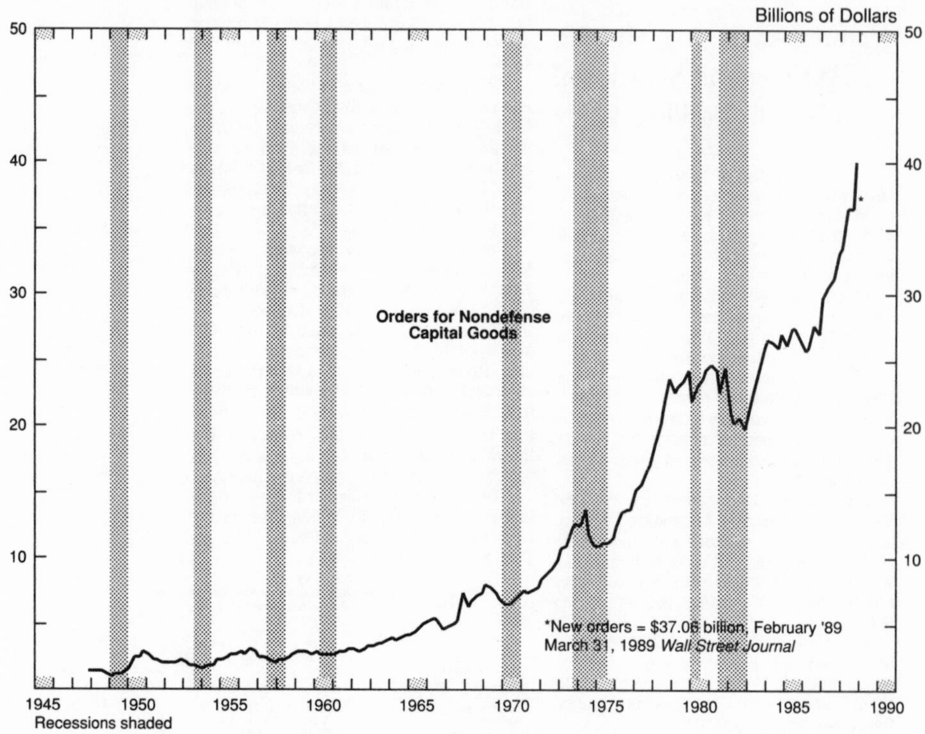

Source: U.S. Department of Commerce, *Business Conditions Digest* and *Handbook of Cyclical Indicators*, series 24.

introduce new methods of production. Export markets also began to perk up in 1987.

By the late 80s, nondefense orders were hovering around $40 billion and had advanced rapidly over the past half-decade. This was a good sign of a strong and robust economy, but also indicated an economy on the verge of resurgent inflation.

MACHINE TOOL ORDERS

Machine tools are used to shape parts for all durable goods; therefore, orders for new machine tools reliably herald industry's plans to add to plant and equipment. The National Machine Tool Builders' Association reports data for new machine tool orders; *The Wall Street Journal* publishes this data around the last Monday of each month, just after the Commerce Department's preliminary release on new orders for nondefense capital goods. Take a look at the Monday, March 27, 1989 *Journal* article.

You can see from the second paragraph that new machine tool orders were $282.3 million in February 1989, up 22 percent from January, but 5.3 percent less than new machine tool orders a year earlier. Note that the $282.3 million figure is the sum of the new orders totals for metal-cutting and metal-forming machines contained in the statistical summary at the end of the article. Compare these figures with the data in Chart 15–2 on page 323. While machine tool orders in the late 80s had recovered from their recession lows at the start of the decade, they remained at little more than half the peak levels reached in the late 70s. And as the text of the March 27, 1989 article makes clear, imports were as much to blame as the threat of rising interest rates.

New Orders for Machine Tools – Second Paragraph

Machine-tool orders in February bounced back from a January drop and were only slightly below the average monthly rate for 1988, according to the Association for Manufacturing Technology. Bookings at domestic machine-tool plants last month totaled $282.3 million, down 5.3% from the year earlier but up 22% from January.

Statistical Summary – End of Article

Comparative new orders for metal-cutting machines:

	Feb. 1989	Jan. 1989	Feb. 1988
Domestic	$191,600,000	$145,400,000	$217,950,000
Foreign	23,650,000	21,600,000	32,450,000
Total	$215,250,000	$167,000,000	$250,400,000

Two-month total for 1989: $382,250,000; for 1988: $474,350,-000.

Metal-forming machine orders:

	Feb. 1989	Jan. 1989	Feb. 1988
Domestic	$57,050,000	$56,600,000	$40,900,000
Foreign	9,950,000	7,250,000	6,750,000
Total	$67,000,000	$63,850,000	$47,650,000

Two-month total for 1989: $130,850,000; for 1988: $121,200,-000.

Source: *The Wall Street Journal*, March 27, 1989.

Orders for Machine Tools Rebounded In February From Month-Earlier Drop

By Ralph E. Winter
Staff Reporter of The Wall Street Journal

The inflation scare and rising interest rates haven't curtailed spending on factory equipment, machine-tool executives say. But some worry that orders will slow later this year if interest rates climb further.

Machine Tool Orders

Machine-tool orders in February bounced back from a January drop and were only slightly below the average monthly rate for 1988, according to the Association for Manufacturing Technology. Bookings at domestic machine-tool plants last month totaled $282.3 million, down 5.3% from the year earlier but up 22% from January.

Machine tools are complex, often computer-controlled, machines that shape most metal parts, and thus are a barometer of factory spending. Orders have been on a plateau at about $300 million a month since the first of last year.

"I've had only one customer really upset over interest rates, and I think he's going ahead with his project," says James R. Roberts, vice president, world-wide sales and marketing, for Giddings & Lewis Inc., a unit of **AMCA International** Corp. "The payback is so fast on most of these programs" that it overwhelms the rise in the cost of money.

"There are more compelling reasons to buy capital goods than the level of prices or interest rates," says Edson I. Gaylord, chairman and chief executive of **Ingersoll Milling Machine** Co., Rockford, Ill. Companies order Ingersoll's production systems because they need better productivity to be competitive, he says, and that need doesn't evaporate if interest rates rise.

"We've never seen interest rates impact our orders," says William T. Bournias, vice president of **Litton Industries** Inc. and president of its machining and assemblies group. If auto and truck sales drop sharply, automotive companies and their suppliers "would rethink some of their programs," he says, "but we don't sense anything happening now."

Also, while short-term interest rates have climbed sharply in recent months, "the cost of long-term borrowing hasn't gone up appreciably from a year ago," says Adrian T. Dillon, chief economist for **Eaton** Corp., a maker of truck parts, electrical products and other capital goods. Major companies arrange long-term financing for large capital investments.

However, the Federal Reserve Board's public concern about inflation and its explicit intent to slow the economy's growth "raises the uncertainty level" for manufacturers, Mr. Dillon says. But it probably won't affect capital spending until the second half, he says, and even then is more likely to slow the rate of increase than to cause a spending cutback.

Christopher C. Cole, group vice president for machine tools at **Cincinnati Milacron** Inc., agrees. "Based on a very bullish West Coast trade show this month and the proposals we're working on, I think orders will continue strong for at least several more quarters," he says. A boom in commercial-aircraft orders leads subcontractors to buy machine tools, Mr. Cole says. And producers of bearings have aggressive investment plans.

"However, longer-term, we have to get the cost of capital down if we're going to be internationally competitive," says Milacron's Mr. Cole. "The current rise in interest rates probably isn't going to torpedo too many projects." But capital costs for U.S. companies are higher than for Japanese and European concerns, which over time will discourage vital product and plant investment.

Short of a severe recession, a rise in the value of the dollar is the greatest threat to durable-goods manufacturers—and the machine-tool companies that equip them. Should foreign investors rush in to scoop up U.S. bonds and other investments carrying high interest rates, the dollar could soar, as it did from 1980 to 1985. So far, however, the dollar has remained relatively stable.

"The key to continued strong sales is the currency ratio," says Mr. Roberts of Giddings & Lewis, which had a 40% order increase in the first two months over a year earlier. "So long as the dollar remains at about 130 yen or below, everybody can export and keep their plants busy," he says.

Orders in February for lathes, milling machines, machining centers, boring mills, grinders and other machines to shape metal by cutting totaled $215.3 million, down 14% from a year earlier but up 29% from January, the NMTBA said. February 1988 was one of last year's strongest months for cutting-type machine tools.

February orders for metal-forming presses and other machines to shape metal with pressure totaled $67 million, the association said, up 41% from a year earlier and 4.9% higher than January.

Machine Tool Orders

Comparative new orders for metal-cutting machines:

	Feb. 1989	Jan. 1989	Feb. 1988
Domestic	$191,600,000	$145,400,000	$217,950,000
Foreign	23,650,000	21,600,000	32,450,000
Total	$215,250,000	$167,000,000	$250,400,000

Two-month total for 1989: $382,250,000; for 1988: $474,350,000.

Metal-forming machine orders:

	Feb. 1989	Jan. 1989	Feb. 1988
Domestic	$57,050,000	$56,600,000	$40,900,000
Foreign	9,950,000	7,250,000	6,750,000
Total	$67,000,000	$63,850,000	$47,650,000

Two-month total for 1989: $130,850,000; for 1988: $121,200,000.

Comparative shipment of metal-cutting machines:

	Feb. 1989	Jan. 1989	Feb. 1988
Domestic	$133,550,000	$89,500,000	$97,000,000
Foreign	17,350,000	13,350,000	11,900,000
Total	$150,900,000	$102,850,000	$108,900,000

Two-month total for 1989: $253,750,000; for 1988: $180,100,000.

Metal-forming machine shipments:

	Feb. 1989	Jan. 1989	Feb. 1988
Domestic	$66,400,000	$42,200,000	$48,100,000
Foreign	11,150,000	7,150,000	9,450,000
Total	$77,550,000	$49,350,000	$57,550,000

Two-month total for 1989: $126,900,000; for 1988: $129,700,000.

Source: *The Wall Street Journal*, March 27, 1989.

CHART 15–2
Machine Tool Orders

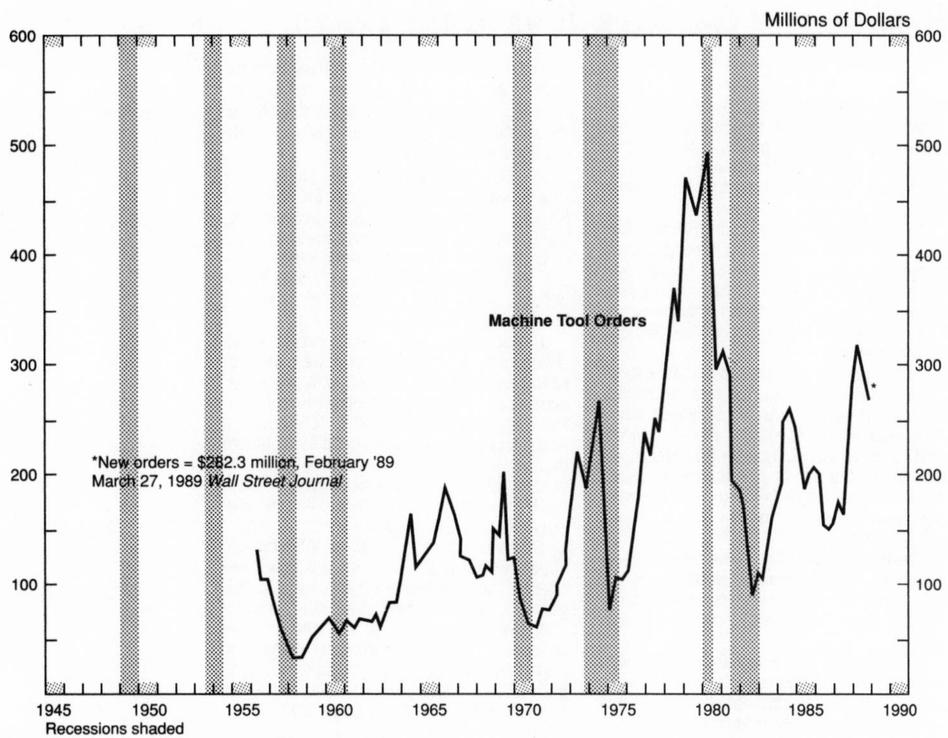

Source: U.S. Department of Commerce, *Business Statistics* and *Survey of Current Business.*

NONRESIDENTIAL BUILDING

You have examined two sources of data on *equipment* expenditures. Turn now to a series on *plant* expenditures. *The Wall Street Journal* publishes F.W. Dodge's report on building awards at the turn of the month. See the Tuesday, March 7, 1989 article on page 324.

Focus on the sixth paragraph and the statistical summary at the end of the article: these report that nonresidential building, including factories, offices, and retail and wholesale establishments, was $87.5 billion in January 1989. You can ignore the data on residential building because this refers to home construction, which has already been covered in Chapter 6, and on nonbuilding construction because this refers primarily

January Construction Contracts Fell 5%; Residential Cutback Was Main Factor

By James T. Areddy
Staff Reporter of The Wall Street Journal

NEW YORK—New residential building dropped in January, pulling the value of new construction contracts down 5% to an annualized $243.6 billion for the month from $256.2 billion in December.

In January, however, commercial and industrial construction was stronger than in recent months. This sector has largely been swayed by moves in the public works category of construction, according to F.W. Dodge Group, the forecasting division of McGraw-Hill Inc.

Although January got 1989 off to a weak start, "one month hardly sets a trend," said George A. Christie, vice president and chief economist of Dodge. "But if the Federal Reserve stands firm in its determination to tighten credit further as inflationary pressures continue to mount, the coming months could make January look good," he added.

Residential building was down 8% in January, after seasonal adjustment, to $120.1 billion. Contracting for both single-family and multifamily dwellings was off.

"One-family home building, which was the only major category of construction to show a gain last year, holds the key to this year's outcome as well," Mr. Christie said. "Stable mortgage rates would again let housing demand offset the continuing weakness in commercial building. But if rates rise, as is more likely, the lone support of the housing market will be lost," the economist added.

In January, nonresidential contracting rose to its highest level since last August, as starts on commercial, industrial and institutional buildings increased 8% to an annualized $87.5 billion. — Nonresidential Building

An office building at the Dallas-Fort Worth Airport and an industrial research project in Kalamazoo, Mich., led the rise. Even with manufacturers operating at near capacity, the "overbuilt office market" will probably lead to a decline in industrial construction in 1989 as a whole, Mr. Christie said.

Public-works and utilities construction returned to a normal level in January, an annualized $36.1 billion, off 20% from December's "unusually strong rate of contracting," Mr. Christie said. "December's surge was probably influenced by a change in federal funding due to take place at year end," he said. Highway construction, the biggest factor in the public works category, was up 5% in January.

On an unadjusted basis, at $15.8 billion, January construction contract value exceeded the year-earlier level by 4%. Regionally, the Southern and the Western U.S. registered gains of 3% and 2%, respectively. The North Central region, or upper Midwestern U.S., posted an 18% gain from a weak January 1988, while the Northeast slipped 1%, Dodge said.

Statistical Summary

	a-Jan. '89 Construction Contract Val. (000,000)	Seasonally Adjusted % Change From Prev. Month
Nonresidential bldg.	$87,457	+ 8
Residential building	120,076	− 8
Non-building constr.	36,096	−20
Total construction	243,629	− 5

a-Monthly construction contract values are reported on an annualized, seasonally adjusted basis.

	1 month 1989 (000,000)	1 month 1988 (000,000)	Cumulative % Chg
Nonresidential bldg.	$6,081	5,840	+ 4
Residential building	7,515	6,739	+ 12
Non-building constr.	2,180	2,534	− 14
Total construction	15,776	15,113	+ 4

Source: *The Wall Street Journal*, March 7, 1989.

to government projects, such as roads and bridges, rather than business plant.

You can use the *Journal* article in tandem with Chart 15–3 on page 326. Both reinforce earlier observations that business expansion was well under way again in the late 80s after stalling in mid-decade due to the Fed's tight money policy.

Nonresidential Building – Sixth Paragraph

In January, nonresidential contracting rose to its highest level since last August, as starts on commercial, industrial and institutional buildings increased 8% to an annualized $87.5 billion.

Statistical Summary – End of Article

	a-Jan. '89 Construction Contract Val. (000,000)	Seasonally Adjusted % Change From Prev. Month
Nonresidential bldg.	$87,457	+ 8
Residential building	120,076	– 8
Non-building constr.	36,096	–20
Total construction	243,629	– 5

a-Monthly construction contract values are reported on an annualized, seasonally adjusted basis.

	1 month 1989 (000,000)	1 month 1988 (000,000)	Cumulative % Chg	
Nonresidential bldg.	$6,081	5,840	+	4
Residential building	7,515	6,739	+	12
Non-building constr.	2,180	2,534	–	14
Total construction	15,776	15,113	+	4

Source: *The Wall Street Journal*, March 7, 1989.

CHART 15–3
Nonresidential Building

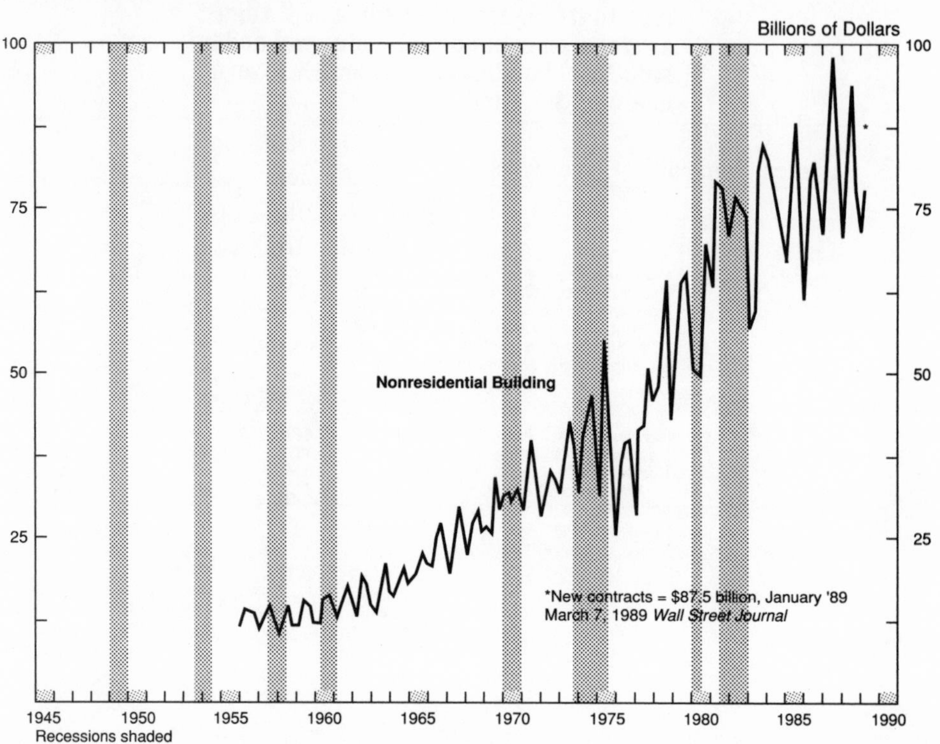

Source: *Dodge Construction Potentials*, McGraw-Hill Information Systems Company; U.S. Department of Commerce, *Business Statistics* and *Survey of Current Business*.

SUMMARY

In conclusion, the data in the *Journal* articles, along with Charts 15–1 through 15–3, illustrates the point that capital expenditures, like inventory accumulation, reinforce the cycle rather than initiate it. Business responds to consumer orders by adding plant and equipment. As the expansion develops into the peak of the cycle and productive capacity is strained, business adds facilities and equipment. Their completion swells the level of demand and contributes to generally inflationary conditions.

After recession begins, some of the investment projects are canceled, but most are completed, and these expenditures ease the downturn. Time elapses before a new cycle's expansionary phase encourages another round of capital expenditures. Until this occurs, the depressed level of plant and equipment expenditures holds demand down and prevents the economy from heating up too quickly. When capital expenditures do recover, the economy is once again approaching the cycle's peak.

Returning one last time to the articles and charts for an overview of the process, despite less than robust levels of capacity utilization in the late 1980s, nondefense orders for capital equipment and nonresidential construction reached new high ground. Although the cycle of the 1980s, because it was so long and stretched out, differed from that of the 1970s, eventually strong business conditions prompted record levels of plant and equipment expenditures.

Investor's Tip

- Treat these statistics like inventory accumulation: too much of a good thing is dangerous.

CHAPTER 16

U.S. INTERNATIONAL TRANSACTIONS

POSTWAR PERSPECTIVE

The phrases of international commerce dominated the financial news of the late 1980s. Foreign exchange rates, IMF, balance of trade, balance of payments, and the other terms used to discuss America's international economic relations can certainly be defined and described in the context of current events. But to understand them thoroughly, you must think back to World War II. Most of our modern international economic institutions were formed at the end of the war and immediately afterward, when the American dollar assumed the central role in the world's economy that it still plays today. Take the time to review postwar international economic developments before plunging into the current data and terminology.

In the summer of 1944, in the resort town of Bretton Woods, New Hampshire, well before World War II came to a close, the United States hosted a conference to plan international monetary affairs for the postwar years, since the Allies were already certain of victory. The United States knew that the war was taking a drastic toll on the rest of the world's economies, while the U.S. economy was growing stronger. Both victor and vanquished would need food, fuel, raw materials, and equipment, but only the United States could furnish these requirements. How were other nations to pay for these imports? They had very little that Americans wanted. If they sold their money for dollars in order to buy goods from us, the strong selling pressure on their currencies and their strong demand for dollars would drive their currencies down in value and the dollar up. Soon the dollar would be so expensive, in terms of foreign currency, that the rest of the world could not afford to buy the American goods necessary to rebuild.

It would have been very easy to say that this was everyone else's problem, not ours, but America's statesmen knew that it was our problem as well. This lesson had been learned the hard way during the aftermath of World War I. Following that war, the United States had washed its hands of international responsibilities; consequently, the world economy had suffered a severe dollar shortage. Many nations were forced to devalue their currencies. Other nations used gold in desperation to settle their accounts with the United States, so America ended up with most of the world's gold supply. Moreover, each nation sought shelter in shortsighted protectionist devices, shattering the world economy. Economic nationalism spilled into the diplomatic arena where its malevolent force accelerated the world into the second global war.

Determined to avoid these mistakes the second time around, the United States convened the Bretton Woods Conference to anticipate such problems and establish institutions to handle them. The conference's principal task was to prevent runaway depreciation of other currencies after the war. It therefore created the *International Monetary Fund* (IMF), a pool of currencies to which all nations (but mostly the United States) contributed and from which any nation could borrow in order to shore up the value of its own currency. If a nation's currency was under selling pressure, and weak and falling in value compared to other currencies, buying pressure designed to drive its price upward could be implemented with strong currencies borrowed from the IMF. For instance, Britain could borrow dollars from the IMF to buy pounds, thus supporting the price of the pound.

The dollar was pegged to gold at $35 an ounce, and all other currencies were pegged to the dollar (e.g., a dollar was worth a fixed number of francs or pounds). At the time, the United States had most of the world's gold and other nations had hardly any, so the entire system was tied to gold through the U.S. dollar. This system of fixed exchange rates was constructed to provide stability in international economic relationships. Traders and investors knew exactly what a contract for future delivery of goods or future return on investment was worth in terms of the foreign exchange in which a contract was written. There was no incentive to speculate on shifting exchange rates, which could wipe out profit margins or generate large losses.

To draw an analogy, consider a shipment of oranges from California to

New York and investments made by Californians on the New York Stock Exchange. Californians must be concerned about the price of oranges in New York and the price of a share of stock on the exchange, but they need not be concerned about fluctuations in the value of New York currency versus California currency, since both states use dollars.

Now think how much more difficult selling and investing in New York would be for Californians if the exchange rate between their currencies fluctuated. The diplomats wished to avoid precisely that problem after World War II, and that's why the Bretton Woods Conference established the IMF and a system of fixed exchange rates.

Unfortunately, after the war the U.S. *balance-of-trade surplus* (the amount by which the revenue of all exports exceeds the cost of all imports) created a greater dollar shortage than the conference had anticipated. Other nations were continually selling their currencies in order to buy American dollars with which to purchase American goods. Selling pressure forced down the price of other currencies despite the IMF, which was not large enough to bail them out, and many of these currencies faced runaway depreciation against the dollar.

The United States responded to this crisis with the Marshall Plan. George C. Marshall, a career soldier, had been chairman of the Joint Chiefs of Staff during the war. At the war's end, President Truman appointed him Secretary of State. Marshall understood that Europe's recovery was hobbled by a shortage of essential items. Food, fuel, raw materials, and machinery and equipment were scarce when available at all. The United States was the only nation that could supply Europe's needs in sufficient quantities. He further understood that the dollar shortage prevented Europe from importing what it needed from the United States. He proposed, and President Truman and Congress approved, a plan whereby the European nations drew up a list of their needs and the United States gave (not loaned) them the dollars they required to satisfy those needs. In that way, the European nations' balances of payments were not strained and their currencies were freed from the pressure of devaluation. American exports, of course, benefited as our dollars bounced right back to us for purchases of American goods.

By the time of the Korean War, everyone was talking about the "economic miracle of Europe." The Marshall Plan had been extended to victor and vanquished alike, probably history's greatest example of benevolence as enlightened self-interest. The United States had learned from its mistakes following World War I. Isolationism was myopic; the United States had to play an active role in world affairs. And our generosity would be repaid many times over as foreign markets for our goods recovered rapidly.

The Marshall Plan became a cornerstone of American foreign policy. The United States provided the rest of the world with desperately needed dollars in this and also a number of other ways, not all of them purposeful. For example, the United States began to maintain a substantial military presence overseas, and our foreign bases salted their host countries with dollars when native civilians were employed at the bases and American personnel spent their paychecks. In addition, American business firms resumed overseas investing, especially in Europe, spending dollars to purchase subsidiaries and to build facilities. Finally, Americans started to travel abroad in great numbers, seeding Europe with funds. All of these activities meant that dollars were sold for foreign exchange (foreign currency) and so they helped offset the constant sale by other nations of their currency in order to buy American goods.

Furthermore, whenever foreign banks, businesses, or individuals received more dollars than were immediately required, they were delighted to deposit those dollars in either American or foreign banks in order to hold them for a rainy day. Since dollars were in vigorous demand because of the continuing need to buy American exports, those dollars could always be sold in the future, and meanwhile they were a handy private reserve.

To summarize, there were four principal outflows of dollars from the United States: foreign aid (such as the Marshall Plan), foreign investment, military presence overseas, and tourism. Two principal influxes of foreign exchange offset these outflows: foreign purchase of American exports, which greatly exceeded our purchases of imports, and foreigners' willingness to hold dollars as a liquid investment. The four outflows of dollars (roughly) equaled the two influxes of foreign exchange.

By the late 50s and early 60s, however, some foreign banks, businesses, and individuals found that they had more dollars than they could use. They did not wish to buy American goods, and they had found making other investments more attractive than holding dollars, so they decided to sell them.

The United States did not have to rely on the IMF to support the dollar and maintain a fixed exchange rate between the dollar and other currencies. Rather, the U.S. Treasury stood ready to redeem dollars with gold whenever selling pressure on the dollar became heavy: the United States propped up the price of the dollar relative to other currencies by buying the dollar for gold. Since a foreign holder of dollars could buy gold at $35 per ounce and sell that gold for foreign exchange anywhere in the world, there was no need to sell dollars below the fixed rate of exchange. Whenever the dollar fell a little, foreigners would buy gold with their dollars and cash that gold in for other currencies at full value, which kept the dollar up. And the U.S. price of $35 per ounce of gold set the world price for gold, simply because the United States had most of the world's supply. As a result, a stream of gold started to leave the United States as dollars were redeemed for it. American holdings of gold were cut almost in half by the time increasing alarm was voiced in the early 60s.

An alternative solution had to be found, or else the U.S. supply of gold would disappear. The foreign central banks stepped in and agreed to support the price of the dollar as part of the their obligation to maintain fixed exchange rates under the Bretton Woods agreement. They had potentially limitless supplies of their own currencies. If a bank, business, or individual in another nation wanted to sell dollars, and this selling pressure tended to force the price of the dollar down in terms of that nation's currency, the foreign central bank would buy the dollars for its currency and thus support the price of the dollar. This could not be accomplished by the U.S. Treasury or the Federal Reserve System because neither had limitless supplies of foreign currency. As long as the foreign central banks were willing to buy and accumulate dollars, private citizens, banks, and businesses in other countries were satisfied. In this way, the system of fixed exchange rates survived.

However, by the late 60s and early 70s the situation had once again become ominous. The United States no longer had a favorable balance of trade. Other nations were selling more to, and buying less from, the United States. America's favorable balance of trade had been the single big plus in its balance of payments, offsetting the outflows of dollars mentioned earlier: foreign aid (the Marshall Plan), American tourism, foreign investment, and the American military presence overseas. Now the dollar holdings of foreign central banks began to swell ever more rapidly as their citizens liquidated dollar holdings. These central banks realized that they were acquiring an asset that ultimately would be of little value to them. Having been put in a position of continually buying dollars they would never be able to sell, they insisted that the United States do something to remedy the situation.

The French suggested that the dollar be officially devalued as a first step, because it had had a very high value in terms of other currencies ever since World War II. They reasoned that if the dollar were worth less in terms of other currencies, American exports would be cheaper for the rest of the world, imports would be more expensive in the United States, and thus the U.S. balance of trade would shift from negative to positive as the United States exported more and imported less. In addition, if foreign currencies were more expensive, Americans would be less likely to travel and invest overseas. This would partially stem the dollar hemorrhage. Others suggested that the foreign central banks stop supporting (buying) the dollar and that the dollar be allowed to float downward to a more reasonable level as foreigners sold off their holdings.

For many years, the United States resisted both devaluation and flotation, until, in a series of developments between 1971 and 1973, the U.S. ceased redeeming the dollar for gold and permitted it to float. It promptly fell, relative to other currencies, because foreign central banks no longer felt obliged to purchase it in order to support its price.

At the same time, the price of gold increased because the United States would no longer redeem dollars with gold. The willingness of the United States to sell gold virtually without limit at $35 per ounce had kept its value from rising, but now the price of gold could increase according to the forces of private supply and demand. Consequently, it fluctuated with all other commodity prices, rising rapidly during the general inflation at the end of the 1970s and then falling with commodity prices after 1980.

The dollar fell until the summer of 1973, and then it fluctuated in value until the end of the 1970s. Although foreign central banks no longer felt an obligation to buy dollars, they occasionally did so to keep it from plummeting too far or too fast. They took this action in their own interest at the suggestion of exporters, who knew that a low value for the dollar and a high value for their own currencies made it difficult to export to the United States. Nevertheless, by the end of the 70s the dollar's value was at a postwar low.

The history of the dollar in the 1980s is a roller coaster ride. At first the dollar's value headed steeply up and rose to a new postwar high by mid-decade. After that it fell once again, so that by the end of the 80s it was not much higher in value than it had been 10 years earlier. What caused these ups and downs, and what does the future hold? You can find an answer in *The Wall Street Journal's* coverage of the balance of payments, the balance of trade, and foreign exchange rates.

These few statistical series portraying America's international transactions have generated more confusion in public perception than perhaps any others, but you will see that they are really not difficult to grasp and follow on a regular basis.

BALANCE OF PAYMENTS AND BALANCE OF TRADE

In order to comprehend the *balance-of-payments* accounts, think of yourself as representing the United States in all dealings with the rest of the world. If you wish to do business with the rest of the world, you must buy its currencies (called *foreign exchange*). Likewise, in order to do business in the United States, the rest of the world must buy dollars.

Now set up an accounting statement. The left side will include all the uses you had for all the foreign exchange you purchased. The right side of the account will include all the uses for the dollars that the rest of the world purchased. The two sides must balance: *for every dollar's worth of foreign exchange that you buy with a dollar, the rest of the world must use a dollar's worth of foreign exchange to buy that dollar.* There are no leaks. It is impossible for you to buy any amount of foreign currency without the seller of that currency buying an equivalent value of dollars. It doesn't matter what you do with the foreign exchange you bought nor what they do with the dollars they bought (even if both of you do *nothing* with your newly purchased money). The balance of payments statement merely records what both parties do with their funds.

Congratulations. You have just constructed a balance-of-payments statement.

U.S. Balance of Payments

Money going out (−)	Money coming in (+)
Uses by United States for all foreign exchange purchased with U.S. dollars	Uses by rest of world for all U.S. dollars purchased with foreign exchange

Once the accounting statement has been set up, you may add other details. Each side of the statement will have a *current account* and a *capital account*. The current account will be subdivided into merchandise trade, services, and foreign aid; the capital account will be subdivided into private investment and central bank transactions.

U.S. Balance of Payments

U.S. purchase of foreign money (debit) (−)	**Foreign purchase of U.S. money (credit) (+)**
Current account payments by United States to rest of world	Current account payments to United States by rest of world
Goods and services imports by United States	Goods and services exports by United States
Merchandise trade imports	Merchandise trade exports
Services for which United States pays rest of world	Services United States sells rest of world
Foreign aid payments by United States to rest of world	Foreign aid payments by rest of world to United States
Capital account outflows of funds from United States	Capital account inflows of funds to United States
Private investment by United States in rest of world	Private investment by rest of world in United States
Central bank transactions such as Fed buys foreign currencies	Central bank transactions such as foreign central banks buy dollars

To summarize: the left side of this account (*debit*) shows what you, representing the United States, are doing with the foreign exchange you purchased with American dollars. The right side of the account (*credit*) shows what the rest of the world is doing with the dollars it purchased with its money. Remember, *the two sides must be equal*; a transaction can take place only if things of equal worth are exchanged. Although the *total* for each side must be equal, however, the *individual categories* need *not* be. Thus, you can balance one category against another in order to arrive at a merchandise trade balance, goods and services balances, and so on. Each category in the balance of payments will be examined in turn.

The Current Accounts

Balance on Goods and Services

Merchandise Trade. You can use the foreign exchange you have purchased to buy foreign goods, and the rest of the world can use dollars to buy American goods. Thus, if you import goods into the United States, you have incurred a debit (–) because you have sold dollars to buy foreign currency in order to make the transaction; in other words, money has left the United States. On the other hand, if the rest of the world buys American goods, you have earned a credit (+). It is customary to talk about the *balance on merchandise trade* by netting imports against exports to determine whether we have an export (+) surplus or an import (–) deficit.

Services. If you use your dollars to buy foreign currency in order to travel in a foreign country, or to use a foreign air carrier, or to pay interest on a foreign debt, all this would be classified as an outflow of funds or a debit (–). On the other hand, if the rest of the world uses the dollars it buys to travel in the United States, or to fly with an American air carrier, or to pay interest on a debt to the United States, that flow of money into the United States would be a credit (+).

If the net credit (+) or debit (–) balance on this account is added to the credit (+) or debit (–) balance of the merchandise trade account, this subtotal is referred to as the *balance on goods and services*.

Foreign Aid

If you use the foreign money you have purchased to make a gift to the rest of the world, that's a debit (–); if the rest of the world uses the dollars it has purchased to make a gift to the United States, that's a credit (+) (and a miracle).

When the foreign aid transaction is combined with the balance on goods and services, it completes the *balance on current account*, which will be a debit (–) balance or a credit (+) balance, depending on whether more funds flowed out of or into the United States.

The Capital Accounts

Private Investments

As a private investor, you may wish to sell U.S. dollars and buy foreign exchange in order to make an investment somewhere else in the world. This could be a direct investment in the form of plant and equipment expenditures or the purchase of a foreign company, or it could be a financial asset, either long-term or short-term. (Stocks and bonds, for instance, are long-term investments, while a foreign bank account or a holding in foreign currency is a short-term investment.) Any of these transactions will be a debit (–) in the American account because dollars have left the United States. Conversely, when a private investor in another country sells foreign exchange in order to have U.S. dollars to make a direct or financial investment in the United States, whether long-term or short-term, this is classified as a credit (+).

Central Bank Transactions

If, as a representative of the Federal Reserve System, you sell dollars in order to buy foreign currency, this too is a debit (–), and when foreign central banks buy dollars, it is a credit (+). These central bank transactions conclude the discussion of balance-of-payments components.

A further point must be made before you plow into the data. References are constantly being made to deficits or surpluses in the balances on trade, goods and services, and current account. Now and then you may encounter a comment about a deficit or a surplus in the balance of payments despite this chapter's assertion that it always balances. How can you explain this apparent paradox?

Trade, goods and services, and current account are easy. You already know that there can be a surplus (+) or a deficit (–) in these separate accounts. But how could anyone speak of a *deficit* in the total balance of payments when it must *always balance*? Because that is the shorthand way of saying that the nation's currency is under selling pressure and that the value of the currency will fall unless some remedial action is taken.

For instance, at the time the foreign central banks were supporting the value of the dollar, their purchases of dollars constituted a "plus" (+) in the American balance of payments because they sopped up the excess dollars that their own economies didn't need. (Had they not done so, the dollar would have fallen in value.) Obviously, if you remove a plus from an accounting system that is in balance, what remains has a negative bottom line. Since the plus that made the account balance was a remedial action and since without it the account would have been negative, reference was made to a deficit in the balance of payments.

When the United States still made sales of gold internationally, in order to redeem the dollar, these sales were plus (+) entries in our balance of payments. If you wonder why the loss of gold is a plus, remember that anything sold by the United States is a plus because the rest of the world must pay us for it. When you remove gold sales from the balance of payments, the remaining items must net out to a negative balance. Therefore, people often referred to the size of the U.S. gold loss as the deficit in the U.S. balance of payments.

And now for one final tip before you look at the data: keep your eyes on the money. That's the best way to determine whether something is a plus (+) or minus (–) in the balance of payments. If *we* pay for it, it's a minus because money is going out. If *they* pay for it, it's a plus.

The Wall Street Journal regularly publishes two Commerce Department reports dealing with the balance of payments and the balance of trade that will be useful to you.

1. *Balance-of-payments* figures for the previous *quarter* appear in the third week of the last month of each quarter.
2. *Monthly balance-of-trade* figures for the previous month are also released in the third week of each month.

Look for the following in the Wednesday, March 15, 1989 balance of payments article: *current account balance, merchandise trade balance, services,* and *foreign aid*. Very few of the items in the capital account are reported, so the article will not present a complete record of the balance of payments.

According to the second paragraph, the current account deficit was $31.91 billion in the fourth quarter of 1988. This was generated by the merchandise trade deficit of $32.02 billion (third paragraph) and foreign aid payments of $4.44 billion (last paragraph), and occurred despite net service income of $4.5 billion (third paragraph).

Put these figures in the accounting framework below:

U.S. Balance of Payments
Fourth Quarter 1988

U.S. purchase of foreign exchange (−)		**Foreign purchase of dollars (+)**	
Merchandise trade deficit	$32.02 billion		
Foreign aid	$ 4.44 billion	Service income	$4.54 billion
Current account deficit	$31.91 billion	(detail may not add to total because of rounding)	
(trade deficit and foreign aid less service income)			

Payments Gap Was Narrower In 4th Quarter

By Hilary Stout
Staff Reporter of The Wall Street Journal

WASHINGTON—The broadest measure of the U.S. trade deficit narrowed in the fourth quarter and finished the year at its smallest level since 1985, the Commerce Department reported.

The deficit in the country's balance of payments on current account—a measure of transactions in services, such as investment, as well as trade in goods—shrank to $31.91 billion in the fourth quarter from $32.61 billion in the third. For the year, it narrowed to $135.33 billion from $153.96 billion in 1987.

A shift in the balance for services to a $4.5 billion surplus from a $200 million deficit accounted for much of the narrowing in the fourth period. The gap between exports and imports of goods during the quarter worsened to $32.02 billion from $29.17 billion.

The current account deficit provides a measure of the amount of money the nation must raise abroad, principally from borrowing, to finance the economy.

The decline in the exchange value of the dollar during the fourth quarter fattened the receipts of American investment abroad in foreign currencies, Commerce Department analysts said.

But a number of economists suspect the days of service surpluses may end this year because foreign holdings in the U.S. are growing rapidly, and the U.S. is relying on foreign investment to finance its federal budget deficit.

At the start of this decade, the U.S. was running surpluses in its current account, because earnings from American investment abroad were so fat that they offset deficits in merchandise trade.

By the end of the year, foreign holdings in the U.S. totaled $71.08 billion, up from $48.10 billion three months earlier. Total U.S. assets overseas grew to $40.18 billion from $39.22 billion during the period.

Overall, exports of goods and services expanded to $136.30 billion in the fourth quarter from $127.85 billion in the third. Imports of goods and services grew to $163.77 billion from $157.24 billion.

Earnings on American direct investment overseas increased to $15.51 billion in the fourth quarter from $10.39 billion in the third while payments for foreign investment in the U.S. dropped, to $3.32 billion from $4.23 billion. Foreign purchases of U.S. Treasury securities rose to $4.13 billion from $3.41 billion.

U.S. government payments abroad, including pension payments and foreign aid grants but not military aid, grew to $4.44 billion in the fourth quarter from $3.21 billion in the third, with nearly all the grants going to Israel.

Margin labels: Current Account Balance; Services and Merchandise Trade Balance; Foreign Aid

Source: *The Wall Street Journal*, March 15, 1989.

Merchandise trade (deficit)	−$32.02 billion
Service income (surplus)	+ 4.50 billion
Foreign aid (deficit)	− 4.44 billion
Balance on current account (deficit)	−$31.91 billion

(detail may not add to total because of rounding)

The outflow due to the trade deficit and foreign aid swamped service income—hence, the current account deficit.

Use Chart 16–1 to analyze these developments. You can make two observations. First, the merchandise trade balance dropped like a stone

Current Account Balance – Second Paragraph

The deficit in the country's balance of payments on current account—a measure of transactions in services, such as investment, as well as trade in goods—shrank to $31.91 billion in the fourth quarter from $32.61 billion in the third. For the year, it narrowed to $135.33 billion from $153.96 billion in 1987.

Services and Merchandise Trade Balance – Third Paragraph

A shift in the balance for services to a $4.5 billion surplus from a $200 million deficit accounted for much of the narrowing in the fourth period. The gap between exports and imports of goods during the quarter worsened to $32.02 billion from $29.17 billion.

Foreign Aid – Last Paragraph

U.S. government payments abroad, including pension payments and foreign aid grants but not military aid, grew to $4.44 billion in the fourth quarter from $3.21 billion in the third, with nearly all the grants going to Israel.

Source: The Wall Street Journal, March 15, 1989.

in the early 80s and was responsible for the current account deficit. Second, the merchandise trade deficit stopped falling in the late 80s, halting the decline in the current account balance.

The gap between the current account and merchandise trade balances is composed of service income, such as the net earnings that the United States receives from foreign investments, the sale of banking, transport, and insurance services, and foreign tourism in the United States. Notice that until the late 70s and early 80s, U.S. service earnings grew so rapidly that the balance on current account remained positive (+) despite an acutely negative (–) merchandise trade balance.

Why did the merchandise trade balance fluctuate in the late 70s, deteriorate so sharply in the early 80s, and then stabilize at the end of the

CHART 16–1
Balance of Payments (quarterly data): **Current Account Balance, Goods and Services Balance, and Merchandise Trade Balance**

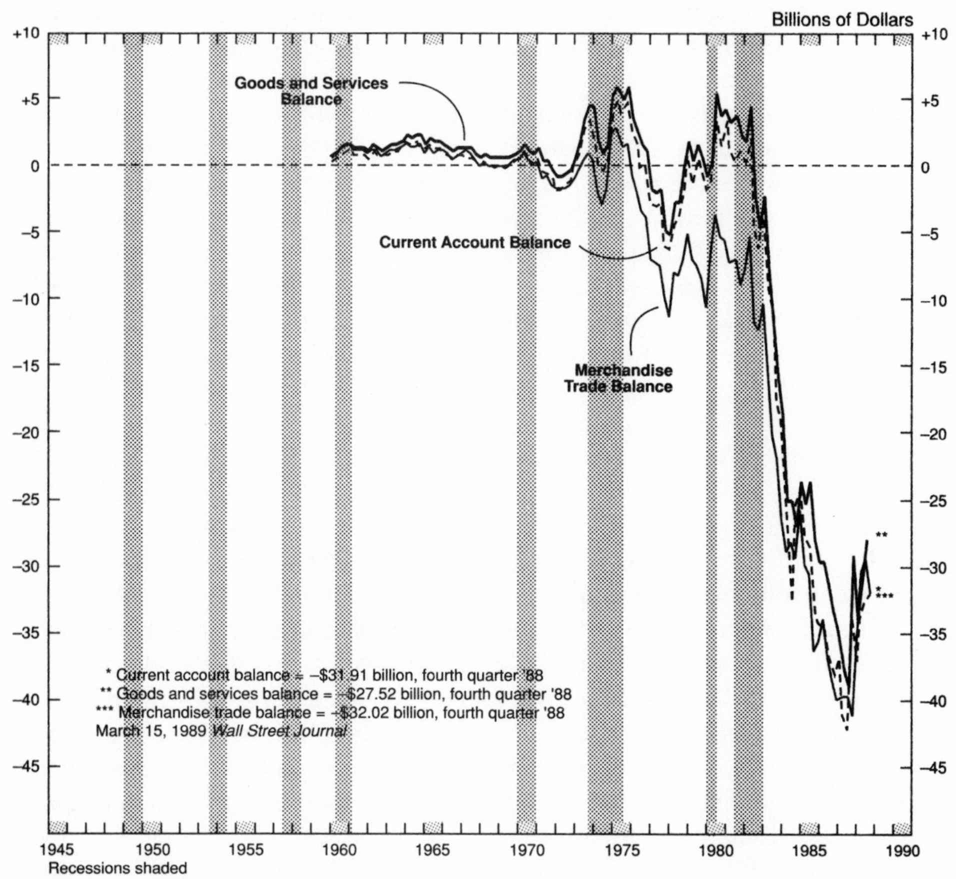

Source: U.S. Department of Commerce, *Business Conditions Digest* and *Handbook of Cyclical Indicators,* series 622 and 667; U.S. Department of Commerce, *Business Statistics;* and *Federal Reserve Bulletin.*

decade? The business cycle and the foreign exchange value of the dollar provide an answer to this question. Imports fell sharply in 1975 because the recession reduced demand, including demand for imports. Exports continued to grow, however, because recession had not yet gripped U.S. trading partners, and thus 1975 was a year of trade surplus. Then, in 1976–77, recession spread internationally and exports began to lag just as U.S. imports increased sharply with economic recovery at home. Hence, our trade balance swung into and remained in deficit as imports and exports grew at similar rates, with a steady gap between them.

Imports fell again during the 1980 recession, while exports continued to grow. As a result, the trade gap narrowed substantially. And imports hardly had a chance to recover before they fell once more during the 1981–82 recession. Consequently, the merchandise trade deficit was smaller than during the economic expansion of 1978. But as recession gripped the rest of the world after 1982 and the American economy recovered and grew, U.S. exports stagnated while imports rose, pushing the merchandise trade deficit to record levels. And it continued to grow in the mid-80s because Europe was recovering only slowly from its slump while our economy expanded. Swiftly improving incomes in the United States boosted demand for imports, whereas exports to Europe languished in sync with the European economy. America's balances on trade and current account hit record lows.

Europe's economies began to break out of their malaise by the end of the 80s. As their incomes grew more rapidly, so did their imports of American goods. This helped stabilize our balance of trade.

In addition, high interest rates in the United States during the 1981–82 recession, and a more favorable investment climate here than abroad, attracted foreign funds to the United States and discouraged American funds from leaving. (The dollar's foreign exchange value is discussed fully below.) The net drop in demand for foreign currencies (increased demand for dollars) pushed up the value of the dollar, making American goods more expensive, cheapening foreign goods, and thus discouraging exports while encouraging imports. The U.S. trade and current account balances suffered accordingly.

By early 1985, however, the balance of trade deficit began to slow the dollar's rise and then initiated a long slide in the dollar's value that lasted until the end of the decade. Americans were buying so much from abroad and hence had such a strong demand for foreign currencies, while the rest of the world's demand for our goods and money was so relatively weak, that the dollar plunged. Also, America's attractiveness as a haven for foreign investment subsided with the continuing decline in our interest rates, further weakening foreign demand for dollars. Finally, the U.S. convinced the foreign central banks to sell off some of their dollar holdings, also contributing to the dollar's decline. We had threatened our trading partners with higher tariffs unless they helped depress the dollar, and our threats were heeded. As the dollar became cheaper and our goods more attractive and theirs less so, the balance of trade stopped deteriorating.

You can use the *Journal* to follow the Commerce Department's monthly *merchandise trade* report. The Thursday, March 16, 1989 article provides data for January 1989. Focus your attention on *imports*, *exports*, and the *balance* between the two. (See page 344.)

According to the first, second and twelfth paragraphs, the United States ran a $9.49 billion trade deficit in January 1989 due to exports of $27.80 billion land imports of $37.29 billion. As time goes by, our exports should rise more rapidly than imports, narrowing the deficit even further.

Investor's Tip

- There is no long-run correlation between our balance of trade and the stock market's or gold's performance. As the trade figures improve, less and less attention will be paid to them. And when the balance of trade is no longer a headline-grabber, the stock and gold markets will pay less attention to it.

FOREIGN EXCHANGE RATES

Each day *The Wall Street Journal* publishes several reports on foreign exchange trading activity. Start with the report on the last section's first page (C1), under the **Markets Diary** heading, labeled **U.S. Dollar**. The excerpt on page 346 from the Friday, May 26, 1989 issue is an example. The Chart provides a record of the dollar's value compared with a trade-weighted average of 15 currencies. You can observe the dollar's advance in early 1989. Below that is a record of the dollar's value against five major currencies.

The excerpt from the Friday, May 26, 1989 edition on page 347 is an example of the daily **Foreign Exchange** article (check the front-page index of the first and last sections). The *Journal* also publishes daily a table of **Exchange Rates** quotations. The May 26, 1989 table is reproduced on pages 348 and 349.

Trade Gap Shrinks to $9.49 Billion, But Surging Oil Prices Pose Threat

Both Imports and Exports Declined in January; Markets Revel in Data

By Hilary Stout
Staff Reporter of The Wall Street Journal

Merchandise Trade Deficit

WASHINGTON—The U.S. merchandise trade deficit shrank to $9.49 billion in January, the Commerce Department reported, a $1.5 billion improvement driven by declining imports.

Exports

The advance came in spite of a $1.25 billion drop in exports, to $27.8 billion in January from a record $29.06 billion in December.

The gap between imports and exports was at its slimmest since October, but it remained fatter than a number of monthly deficits earlier last year. Moreover, revised figures showed December's trade figure worsened during the month instead of improving, as the department initially reported—to $10.99 billion from $10.23 billion. The November deficit was $10.66 billion.

Imports

"I'd say we're on a plateau," said Fred Bergsten, director of the Institute for International Economics here. "Since about the middle of last year, I've read the numbers as essentially indicating the deficit is on a plateau running between a $110 billion and $120 billion annual rate."

A number of other economists echoed his assessment.

'A Mixed Bag'

"I would say it's a mixed bag," said Lawrence Chimerine, chairman of the WEFA group, an economic forecasting concern in Bala Cynwyd, Pa. "On one hand, the improvement is welcome. But I wouldn't read too much into it. The trend of the last six months showed it leveled off."

But some financial markets reveled in the monthly improvement. Stock prices rose, and the dollar climbed against major currencies.

With yesterday's report, the government resumed reporting the trade balance without including the cost of shipping and insurance in the import totals. This "customs value" method is thought to give a more precise accounting of the difference between the amount of goods the U.S. buys from abroad and the amount it sells overseas.

It reduces the reported deficits by about $1.5 billion a month, however, and Congress in 1979 outlawed its use in the d... ment's initial month... year's t...

U.S. Merchandise Trade Deficits
(In billions of U.S. dollars, not seasonally adjusted and including insurance and freight costs)

	JAN. '89	DEC. '88	JAN. '88
Japan	$3.53	$5.07	$3.69
Canada	1.75	0.99	0.84
Western Europe	0.05 (surplus)	1.21	0.99
NICs*	2.40	2.51	2.65

*Newly industrialized countries: Singapore, Hong Kong, Taiwan, South Korea

Source: Commerce Department

Hills, the U.S. trade representative, called the figures "encouraging for continued correction in the trade deficit."

Commerce Secretary Robert Mosbacher said, "The year is starting on a plus note."

While the drop in exports was discouraging, economists were encouraged by the bigger decline in imports, to $37.29 billion from December's record $40.05 billion. Some of the largest declines came in automobiles and consumer goods.

"On its face, that's a very nice development, because generally speaking, the Federal Reserve and the financial markets are reassured to see things indicating the consumer is cooling off a bit," said Frederick Sturm, senior economist at Kleinwort Benson Government Securities in Chicago.

But Mr. Sturm and other analysts were concerned that exports of capital goods fell, reducing the country's surplus in that area. "We want to watch that carefully, because that is the one sector besides agriculture where we have the ability to export. A lot of our export improvement came there" in the past year.

A Rare Surplus

The narrowing of the trade deficit in January reflected a rare trade surplus with Western Europe, the first since 1983. Exports to Western European countries topped imports by $47 million in January, although the U.S. continued to run a deficit with West Germany.

In December, the U.S. registered a $1.2 billion deficit with Western Europe. A Commerce Department analyst said a drop in automobile imports was behind much of the improvement.

Likewise, red... car...

Source: *The Wall Street Journal*, March 16, 1989.

Merchandise Trade Deficit – First Paragraph

WASHINGTON—The U.S. merchandise trade deficit shrank to $9.49 billion in January, the Commerce Department reported, a $1.5 billion improvement driven by declining imports.

Exports – Second Paragraph

The advance came in spite of a $1.25 billion drop in exports, to $27.8 billion in January from a record $29.06 billion in December.

Imports – Twelfth Paragraph

While the drop in exports was discouraging, economists were encouraged by the bigger decline in imports, to $37.29 billion from December's record $40.05 billion. Some of the largest declines came in automobiles and consumer goods.

Source: *The Wall Street Journal,* March 16, 1989.

You can use the *Journal's* daily **Exchange Rates** report to keep abreast of the dollar's value. For instance, on Thursday, May 25, 1989 the British pound was worth approximately $1.59, the Canadian dollar about $0.83, the French franc approximately $0.15, the Japanese yen about $0.007, the Swiss franc approximately $0.57, and the German mark approximately $0.50. You can see that these quotations portray the value of a single unit of foreign exchange in terms of the American dollar. However, foreign currencies are often quoted in units per American dollar. Thus on May 25 the dollar was worth 141.50 Japanese yen and 2.986 German marks.

Most foreign exchange trading is conducted by banks on behalf of their customers. Banks will also provide future delivery of foreign exchange for customers who want a guaranteed price in order to plan their operations and limit risk due to exchange rate fluctuation. The price for future delivery is known as the *forward rate*, and you can see forward quotes for the major currencies immediately beneath the current rate.

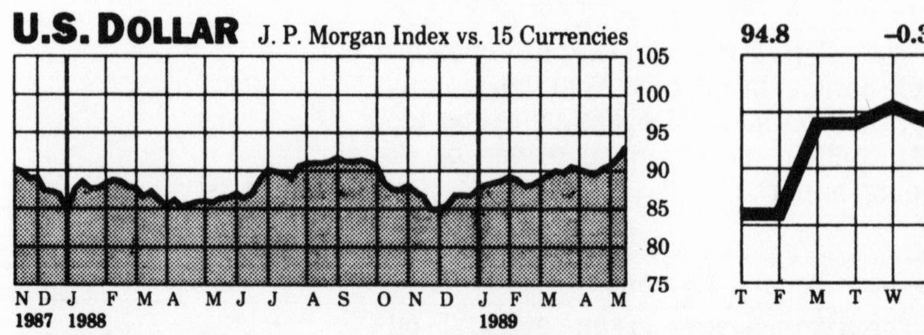

CURRENCY	LATE NY	LATE WED	DAY'S HIGH	DAY'S LOW	12-MO HIGH — LATE NY —	12-MO LOW
British pound (in U.S. dollars)	**1.5910**	1.5695	1.5900	1.5710	1.8680	1.5695
Canadian dollar (in U.S. dollars)	**0.8286**	0.8276	0.8295	0.8203	0.8477	0.8063
Swiss franc (per U.S. dollar)	**1.7425**	1.7855	1.7390	1.7820	1.4260	1.7945
Japanese yen (per U.S. dollar)	**141.20**	142.80	141.20	142.55	121.03	142.80
W. German mark (per U.S. dollar)	**1.9805**	2.0138	1.9780	2.0095	1.7113	2.0138

Source: *The Wall Street Journal*, May 26, 1989.

Future contracts for foreign currencies are also available on a number of exchanges.

Finally the *Journal* also provides exchange rates for major currencies in terms of each other's value. See **Key Currency Cross Rates** from the May 26, 1989 issue.

Recall the brief outline of the dollar's postwar history presented earlier.

You can see from Chart 16–2 on page 350 that the value of foreign currencies in terms of dollars has risen dramatically (i.e., the dollar has fallen in value) since the mid-80s. The French franc has jumped

Key Currency Cross Rates Late New York Trading May 25, 1989

	Dollar	Pound	SFranc	Guilder	Yen	Lira	D-Mark	FFranc	CdnDlr
Canada.........	1.2068	1.9200	.69257	.54092	.00855	.00084	.60934	.18003	......
France.........	6.7035	10.665	3.8471	3.0047	.04748	.00467	3.3848	....	5.5548
Germany.......	1.9805	3.1510	1.1366	.88772	.01403	.00138	....	.29544	1.6411
Italy...........	1434.3	2281.9	823.10	642.87	10.158	....	724.19	213.96	1188.5
Japan..........	141.20	224.65	81.033	63.290	....	.09845	71.295	21.064	117.00
Netherlands....	2.2310	3.5495	1.2803	.....	.01580	.00156	1.1265	.33281	1.8487
Switzerland....	1.7425	2.7723	....	.78104	.01234	.00121	.87983	.25994	1.4439
U.K............	.62854	....	.36071	.28173	.00445	.00044	.31736	.09376	.52083
U.S............	....	1.5910	.57389	.44823	.00708	.00070	.50492	.14918	.82864

Source: Telerate

Source: *The Wall Street Journal*, May 26, 1989.

FOREIGN EXCHANGE

U.S. Currency Declines on Profit-Taking, Intervention and Overseas Rate Jitters

By Michael R. Sesit
Staff Reporter of The Wall Street Journal

The dollar fell on a combination of profit-taking, concerted central-bank intervention and jitters over interest-rate increases abroad.

Late in the New York trading day, the dollar was quoted at 1.9805 marks, down sharply from 2.0138 marks late Wednesday in New York. The U.S. unit was also at 141.20 yen, down from 142.80 yen. Sterling traded at $1.5910, up from $1.5695.

Dealers said the Federal Reserve Bank of New York plus the central banks of Britain, Canada, Switzerland, Holland, France, Italy and Belgium all sold dollars in an attempt to drive the U.S. currency lower. While the Fed bought both marks and yen, the continental banks purchased marks and the Bank of Canada bought yen. The Bank of England purchased pounds.

In Tokyo Friday, the U.S. currency opened for trading at 140.85 yen, down sharply from Thursday's Tokyo close of 142.35 yen.

Once again, the Bundesbank didn't participate in the intervention effort. Moreover, most banks in Germany were closed yesterday for a holiday. Banks in the U.S. and Britain will be closed for a holiday Monday.

Nevertheless, some analysts cautioned about reading too much into yesterday's dollar retreat. "There are a lot of investors and traders with profits in long-dollar positions that have probably wanted to take profits prior to the long holiday weekend, especially in light of market rumors regarding possible central-bank action," said John Lipsky, an international economist at Salomon Brothers Inc.

Indeed, such rumors played a key role in sending the dollar lower yesterday, traders said.

Leading the speculation was an announcement by the Swiss National Bank that it would set its Lombard rate each day at one percentage point above the call-money rate. The policy change means that the Lombard rate will be raised by about two percentage points today.

"Instead of having to move rates up in discrete jumps, they will be able to move them through a series of daily steps that would be less dramatic than larger discrete changes in official interest rates" that prevail under the existing system, said Mr. Lipsky. That, in turn, will enhance the flexibility of Switzerland's monetary policy. The Lombard rate is that at which banks borrow using securities as collateral.

By itself and in calm markets, the Swiss move might not have meant much to currency traders. But the announcement set off speculation that the Swiss move was a prelude to a general rise in European interest rates. Some analysts also speculated that West Germany might adopt a similar policy. On Wednesday, the British government forced British banks to raise their base lending rates a full percentage point to 14%.

For more than a week, many traders and economists have argued that central-bank intervention isn't enough to stem the dollar's rise. What is needed, they contended, are higher interest rates in West Germany and Japan and lower rates in the U.S.

There is speculation in the market that the three major governments are trying arrange a deal whereby Japan would raise its discount rate by three-quarters of a percentage point and Germany by half a point, while the U.S. lowers its discount rate by a quarter point. Narrowing the gap between U.S. and Japanese and German interest rates, should theoretically reduce the dollar's allure to international investors.

Adding to speculation about such a scenario were statements by French Economics Minister Pierre Beregovoy. In a radio interview, he said Japanese interest rates "are no doubt a bit too low, and rates in the U.S. are probably a bit too high."

Mr. Beregovoy emphasized that cooperation in international markets depends on central-bank intervention and on coordinating the level of interest rates. The French minister said he was "concerned by the idea that international cooperation might not be maintained."

Nevertheless, Mr. Beregovoy told journalists that he felt the major industrial countries still cooperated on economic policy. He added that an emergency meeting of the Group of Seven industrial countries—the U.S., Japan, West Germany, France, Britain, Italy and Canada—isn't needed before an economic summit scheduled for mid-July in Paris.

Despite the interest-rate jitters, many traders and analysts remain bullish on the dollar.

"We look for a dollar rally over the summer with the currency climbing towards 2.25 marks and 160 yen," said Anne Parker Mills, a vice president at Shearson Lehman Hutton Inc. Yet she doesn't preclude significant drops interrupting the currency's climb. "If we see coordinated interest-rate action by the G-7 countries over the next several days, this week's profit-taking pullback in the dollar could turn into something bigger."

On the Commodity Exchange in New York, gold for current delivery rose $2.50 to $367 an ounce in moderate trading. Estimated volume was 4.3 million ounces.

In early trading in Hong Kong Friday, gold was quoted at $365.55 an ounce.

Source: *The Wall Street Journal*, May 25, 1989.

EXCHANGE RATES

Thursday, May 25, 1989

The New York foreign exchange selling rates below apply to trading among banks in amounts of $1 million and more, as quoted at 3 p.m. Eastern time by Bankers Trust Co. Retail transactions provide fewer units of foreign currency per dollar.

		U.S. $ equiv.		Currency per U.S. $	
	Country	Thurs.	Wed.	Thurs.	Wed.
	Argentina (Austral) ...	z	z	z	z
	Australia (Dollar)	.7580	.7465	1.3192	1.3395
	Austria (Schilling)	.07102	.07044	14.08	14.19
	Bahrain (Dinar)	2.6528	2.6528	.37695	.37695
	Belgium (Franc)				
	Commercial rate	.02402	.02370	41.62	42.19
	Financial rate	.02396	.02363	41.72	42.31
	Brazil (Cruzado)	.892857	.892857	1.1200	1.1200
British Pound →	**Britain** (Pound)	1.5850	1.5680	.6309	.6377
	30-Day Forward	1.5797	1.5627	.6330	.6399
	90-Day Forward	1.5694	1.5514	.6371	.6445
	180-Day Forward	1.5538	1.5360	.6435	.6510
Canadian Dollar →	**Canada** (Dollar)	.8261	.8275	1.2105	1.2084
	30-Day Forward	.8238	.8250	1.2138	1.2120
	90-Day Forward	.8203	.8216	1.2190	1.2170
	180-Day Forward	.8163	.8175	1.2249	1.2232
	Chile (Official rate) ...	.0039753	.0039753	251.55	251.55
	China (Yuan)	.268672	.268672	3.7220	3.7220
	Colombia (Peso)	.002750	.002750	363.60	363.60
	Denmark (Krone)	.1292	.1272	7.7390	7.8555
	Ecuador (Sucre)				
	Floating rate	.001908	.001908	524.00	524.00
	Finland (Markka)	.2257	.2225	4.4290	4.4925
French Franc →	**France** (Franc)	.1486	.1465	6.7280	6.8240
	30-Day Forward	.1487	.1467	6.7224	6.8187
	90-Day Forward	.1488	.1468	6.7160	6.8130
	180-Day Forward	.1490	.1469	6.7100	6.8080
	Greece (Drachma)	.005917	.005841	169.00	171.20
	Hong Kong (Dollar) ...	.128592	.128592	7.7765	7.7765
	India (Rupee)	.0617665	.0617665	16.19	16.19
	Indonesia (Rupiah)	.0005694	.0005694	1756.00	1756.00
	Ireland (Punt)	1.3290	1.3290	.75244	.75244
	Israel (Shekel)	.5503	.5503	1.8170	1.8170
	Italy (Lira)	.0006954	.0006844	1438.00	1461.00
Japanese Yen →	**Japan** (Yen)	.007067	.006995	141.50	142.95
	30-Day Forward	.007091	.007022	141.01	142.39
	90-Day Forward	.007146	.007072	139.93	141.39
	180-Day Forward	.007215	007138	138.59	140.09
	Jordan (Dinar)	1.8968	1.8968	.5272	.5272
	Kuwait (Dinar)	3.3917	3.3917	.2948	.2948
	Lebanon (Pound)	.001941	.001941	515.00	515.00
	Malaysia (Ringgit)	.37140	.37140	2.6925	2.6925
	Malta (Lira)	2.7816	2.7816	.3595	.3595
	Mexico (Peso)				
	Floating rate	.0004076	.0004076	2453.00	2453.00
	Netherland(Guilder) .	.4466	.4399	2.2390	2.2730
	New Zealand (Dollar)	.5955	.5945	1.6792	1.6820
	Norway (Krone)	.1395	.1379	7.1650	7.2490
	Pakistan (Rupee)	.04830	.04830	20.70	20.70
	Peru (Inti)	.0003691	.0003691	2709.00	2709.00
	Philippines (Peso)	.048543	.048543	20.60	20.60
	Portugal (Escudo)	.006046	.006046	165.39	165.39
	Saudi Arabia (Riyal) ..	.2665	.2665	3.7510	3.7510
	Singapore (Dollar)	.5116	.5116	1.9545	1.9545
	South Africa (Rand)				
	Commercial rate	.3603	.3583	2.7753	2.7908
	Financial rate	.2370	.2356	4.2200	4.2450
	South Korea (Won)	.0014925	.0014925	670.00	670.00
	Spain (Peseta)	.008067	.007936	123.95	126.00
	Sweden (Krona)	.1496	.1479	6.6830	6.7630
Swiss Franc →	**Switzerland** (Franc) ..	.5720	.5595	1.7480	1.7870
	30-Day Forward	.5726	.5605	1.7462	1.7840
	90-Day Forward	.5740	.5619	1.7420	1.7795
	180-Day Forward	.5763	.5642	1.7350	1.7723
	Taiwan (Dollar)	.038911	.038911	25.70	25.70
	Thailand (Baht)	.038910	.038910	25.70	25.70
	Turkey (Lira)	.0004856	.0004856	2059.00	2059.00
	United Arab(Dirham)	.2722	.2722	3.6725	3.6725
	Uruguay (New Peso)				
	Financial	.001811	.001811	552.00	552.00
	Venezuela (Bolivar)				
	Floating rate	.02649	.02649	37.75	37.75
German Mark →	**W. Germany** (Mark) ..	.5035	.4965	2.9860	2.0140
	30-Day Forward	.5047	.4977	2.9812	2.0090
	90-Day Forward	.5065	.4994	2.9741	2.0022
	180-Day Forward	.5087	.5044	1.9657	1.9942
	SDR	1.24085	1.23855	0.805898	0.807396
	ECU	1.03890	1.03555	....	....

Special Drawing Rights (SDR) are based on exchange rates for the U.S., West German, British, French and Japanese currencies. Source: International Monetary Fund.

European Currency Unit (ECU) is based on a basket of community currencies. Source: European Community Commission.

z-Not quoted.

Source: *The Wall Street Journal*, March 26, 1989.

Britain (Pound)	1.5850	1.5680	.6309	.6377
30-Day Forward	1.5797	1.5627	.6330	.6399
90-Day Forward	1.5694	1.5514	.6371	.6445
180-Day Forward	1.5538	1.5360	.6435	.6510
Canada (Dollar)	.8261	.8275	1.2105	1.2084
30-Day Forward	.8238	.8250	1.2138	1.2120
90-Day Forward	.8203	.8216	1.2190	1.2170
180-Day Forward	.8163	.8175	1.2249	1.2232
France (Franc)	.1486	.1465	6.7280	6.8240
30-Day Forward	.1487	.1467	6.7224	6.8187
90-Day Forward	.1488	.1468	6.7160	6.8130
180-Day Forward	.1490	.1469	6.7100	6.8080
Japan (Yen)	.007067	.006995	141.50	142.95
30-Day Forward	.007091	.007022	141.01	142.39
90-Day Forward	.007146	.007072	139.93	141.39
180-Day Forward	.007215	007138	138.59	140.09
Switzerland (Franc) ..	.5720	.5595	1.7480	1.7870
30-Day Forward	.5726	.5605	1.7462	1.7840
90-Day Forward	.5740	.5619	1.7420	1.7795
180-Day Forward	.5763	.5642	1.7350	1.7723
W. Germany (Mark) ..	.5035	.4965	2.9860	2.0140
30-Day Forward	.5047	.4977	2.9812	2.0090
90-Day Forward	.5065	.4994	2.9741	2.0022
180-Day Forward	.5087	.5044	1.9657	1.9942

Excerpts from page 348

Source: *The Wall Street Journal*, March 26, 1989.

from $0.10 to $0.15; the British pound from a little over $1.00 to $1.59; the Swiss franc from $0.35 to $0.57; the Japanese yen from $0.004 to $0.007; and the German mark from $0.30 to $0.50. The balance-of-payments discussion will aid your understanding of the dollar's fall.

CHART 16–2
Foreign Exchange Rates

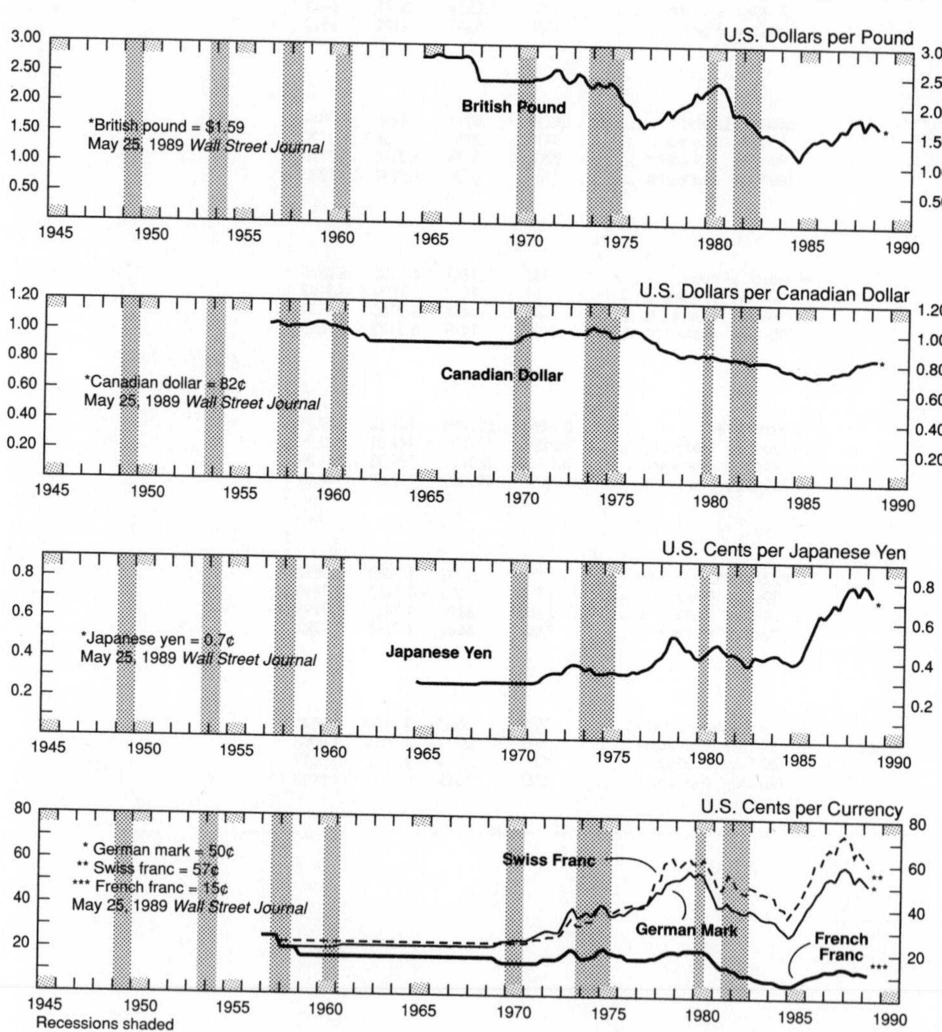

Source: Standard & Poor's, *Statistical Service.*

The dollar fell to its post–World War II low against most currencies in the late 70s because of severe inflation here at home and its impact on our trade balance. (You can observe the increase in value of the key currencies in Chart 16–2.) The merchandise trade balance sank dramatically, as rising prices impeded our ability to sell and whetted our appetite for imports (Chart 16–1 on page 341). Since people in the rest of the world needed fewer dollars (because they weren't buying as many of our goods) and we needed more foreign exchange (because we were buying more of their goods), the dollar's value plunged.

The dollar's rally in the early 80s was a two-phase process. The first phase in 1981–82 had two major causes.

First, high interest rates strengthened the dollar. When interest rates in the United States are higher than interest rates elsewhere, foreign exchange is sold for dollars and the capital accounts will show a net flow of private investment into the United States. The Fed's tight money policy pushed interest rates in the United States higher than those in Europe and Japan, prompting heavy dollar purchases by foreign investors who wished to enjoy the high interest rates available here.

Second, the U.S. balance on current account improved dramatically until late 1982 because of rapidly growing service income and despite a sharply negative balance of trade. This positive element in the American balance of payments not only generated a flow of dollars into the United States but also encouraged private businesses and individuals in the rest of the world to invest in dollars because they believed that the dollar would remain strong in the future.

The second phase in 1983–84 is somewhat more complex. Since mid-82 the interest rate differential between the United States and the rest of the world narrowed (see the first cause listed above), while the balance on current account deteriorated rapidly (see the second cause listed above) due to the plunge in our merchandise trade balance (see Chart 16–1 on page 341). Under these circumstances, the dollar's value should have fallen.

Nevertheless, it improved, because of the continuing flow of investment dollars into the United States and the continuing reduced flow of our investment dollars to the rest of the world. The rest of the world believed America to be the safest, most profitable home for its funds. To foreigners (indeed, to many Americans) President Reagan symbolized America's protection of, and concern for, business interests. Certainly, the United States is a secure haven: investments will not be expropriated nor will their return be subject to confiscatory taxation. And the return was good; even if the interest rate differential between here and abroad had narrowed, U.S. rates were still higher than those in most other countries. Moreover, profits had been strong, and the stock market reflected this. Foreign investors who had a stake in American business were rewarded handsomely.

Thus the dollar remained strong because the huge net capital flow into the United States bid the dollar's price up and forced other currencies down. The rise in the dollar's value, together with the quicker economic expansion here than abroad, depressed our exports and stimulated our imports. Consequently, the deterioration in our merchandise trade balance in 1983 and 1984 was a *result* of the dollar's appreciation, not a *cause* of it.

But by 1985 the merchandise trade balance had deteriorated to such an extent, while American interest rates continued to slide, that the dollar began to weaken. Foreign demand for our currency was not strong enough to offset our demand for the rest of the world's currencies. In addition, we began to pressure our major trading partners, requesting their assistance in reducing our trade deficit by driving the dollar's value down. They (i.e., their central banks) complied by selling dollars, contributing to the dollar's slide. As a result, by the late 80s, the dollar had lost most of the increase of the early 80s.

The dollar stabilized at the end of the decade because our balance-of-trade deficit stopped growing due to rapid export growth. American interest rates rose, and foreign central banks actively supported the dollar once again. These developments stimulated dollar purchase and helped halt the dollar's decline. The foreign central banks had begun to respond to their own industrial interests and were no longer willing to let the dollar fall in order to protect our markets.

This brief history should warn you how hard it is to predict the dollar's value and the course of international economic events. That's why foreign exchange speculation is not for amateurs. Even some pros go broke doing it.

Investor's Tip

- To sum up, the dollar fell in the 70s, rose in the first half of the 80s, and fell in recent years. You will not be able to establish a good correlation between the dollar's value and the stock market's or gold's performance.
- So, once again, don't count on international economic developments to have a lasting impact on the stock market or gold. As time goes by, attention will increasingly focus on the domestic scene.

CHAPTER 17

SUMMARY AND PROSPECT

So what will you have for the 1990s? Stocks and other paper securities, or gold and similar tangible assets? The best investment all depends on the course of inflation and the business cycle.

But, you may ask, didn't we tame both inflation and the business cycle in the 1980s? The decade came to an end after seven good years of steady expansion, with both low unemployment and low inflation. Wasn't this evidence that the Fed had done a great job?

Yes, the Fed did perform admirably and effectively in the 1980s, so that by the end of the decade, escalating debt and inflation and the business cycle's roller coaster ride appeared to be mere relics of the past, confined to the years 1965 through 1980. Could it be that those years, with all their problems, were an exception, a kind of rough patch that is now behind us? Once again, we must turn to the historical record for some perspective.

The early 1960s followed the Eisenhower years, which President Kennedy and his advisers criticized severely for sluggish economic performance and too many recessions. They excoriated the fiscal policy of President Eisenhower's administration and the monetary policy of the Federal Reserve for excessive concern with inflation and complacency about slow economic growth and unemployment. These critics charged that because of the attempt to restrain demand in order to combat "creeping inflation," the economy's growth rate had fallen and recovery from frequent recessions in the 1950s had been weak.

Yet the Eisenhower years had been the best of times for stock market investors. The Dow climbed from 200 in 1950 to almost 1,000 in 1965, a fivefold increase in 15 years. Some said that stocks had been a good hedge against the negligible inflation of those years. In truth, they had done well because of inflation's absence.

But as the middle 60s approached, the economy rapidly gained steam. The low level of inflation (inherited from the Eisenhower years) and the Fed's easy money policy (in response to Kennedy administration requests) were the most important ingredients in the rapid economic expansion that began in the 1960s.

Modest increases in the CPI permitted strong growth in real consumer income. As a result, consumer sentiment steadily improved. This, together with the ready availability of loans at low interest rates, prompted consumers to resort to record levels of mortgage borrowing and consumer credit. Home construction and automobile production set new highs. Business responded by investing heavily in new plant and equipment, so that general boom conditions prevailed by the middle of the decade.

The tax cut proposed by President Kennedy has received most of the credit for this prosperity. Inconveniently, however, it was not enacted until 1964, after his death, and it is difficult to understand how an expansion that began in 1962 can be attributed to a tax cut two years later.

The expansion's relaxed and easy progress was its most important early feature. There was no overheating. Housing starts, auto sales, consumer credit, and retail sales gradually broke through to new highs. By 1965 there had been three solid years of expansion, reflected in a strong improvement in labor productivity and a solid advance in real compensation.

The problems began in the late 60s when the Fed did not exercise enough restraint on the boom. Its half-hearted measures were too little and too late. Most observers blamed the Vietnam War for the inflation, but the federal deficit never exceeded $15 billion in the late 60s. Meanwhile, private borrowing hit $100 billion annually, thereby dwarfing federal fiscal stimuli. *Private* borrowing and spending on residential construction, autos, and other consumer durables and business capital expenditures—not *federal* borrowing and spending on the Vietnam War—generated the inflation of the late 60s.

As the inflation progressed, it created a nightmare for stock and bond holders in the 1970s. During the entire decade, their investments did not gain in value; some even fell. Meanwhile, gold and other precious metals went through the roof.

And as you know from the earlier discussion, the Fed's attempts to deal with inflation remained inadequate throughout the 70s, so that its stop-go policies only exacerbated inflation over the course of the cycle.

It was not until Paul Volcker persuaded the Fed to take a stand in the early 80s with a policy of continued restraint that inflation was brought under control and stability ensured for the rest of the decade. By the end of the 80s, Americans enjoyed better economic conditions than at any time since the early 60s.

Will the 1990s be like the late 80s and the early 60s? Will the economy expand slowly and gradually, bringing prosperity without severe fluctuation and inflation?

Certain features of the late 80s remind us of the early 60s and give hope. The rate of inflation is low, with substantial slack in the economy. Productivity is growing and unit labor costs are under control. All of this augurs well for continued expansion.

But there was an important difference between the late 80s and the early 60s: the Fed had learned its lesson. Twenty-five years earlier, its expansionary policy had held interest rates at bargain basement levels, fueling inflation. In the 80s the Fed's deliberate policy of restraint kept interest rates far higher. What difference will that make?

The Fed's change in direction means that the years from 1965 to 1980 were an anomaly, a bad patch that is now behind us. Spiraling debt and inflation should be a thing of the past as we look forward to continued monetary restraint.

Paradoxically, those tight conditions may help sustain the expansion because overheating is the chief threat now. An easy money policy spawned the boom of the early 60s and the disastrous period of inflation that followed. Monetary restraint in the 1990s will permit the expansion of the late 80s to continue, preventing the inflation that choked off previous periods of prosperity.

And that provides the key to the future. Stocks, bonds, and other paper assets will continue to perform well in the 1990s as long as the Fed maintains plenty of slack by keeping interest rates up. Ironically, interest must remain historically high for continued prosperity. If the Fed lets interest rates stay too low too long, as it did in the 1960s, move your investments into gold and other tangibles, because the economy will surely overheat and return to the bad old days of high inflation and cyclical volatility.

Does that mean that in the middle 60s the Fed created the business cycle by adopting overly expansionary, stop-go policies, and that it has now repealed the business cycle by seeing the error in its ways? No, because the business cycle is part and parcel of all modern capitalist economies. The point is that the Fed's 1965–80 policies exacerbated the cycle, while its policies since then have worked to reduce the cycle's amplitude and severity.

Capitalism is a moving target, always changing and always evolving—constrained by indigenous institutions and shaped by contemporary events. The description of its dynamic, contained in these chapters, is appropriate for the present time and place. This dynamic would not have explained conditions 50 years earlier, nor will it describe them 50 years hence. The system will evolve in ways that no one can predict. Yet for the time being, the Fed has managed to wrestle the business cycle and inflation to the mat, so that they will be restrained, although not absent, in the 1990s.

APPENDIX A

MISCELLANEOUS STATISTICAL INDICATORS

A number of statistical indicators have not yet been discussed although they appear regularly in *The Wall Street Journal*. These indicators are not directly applicable to the earlier chapters' analyses. They are important, however, and the following commentary should help you put them in perspective.

EMPLOYMENT DATA

The Wall Street Journal usually publishes the Labor Department's *monthly employment report* on Monday of the second week. February 1989 data appeared on Monday, March 13, 1989 (see page 358). The third paragraph informs you that *non-farm payrolls* grew by 289,000, which was a good indication at the time of continued robust conditions. You should also track the *average workweek* and *factory overtime* because they, too, portray the economy's strength and are important determinants of consumer sentiment. They appear in the statistical summary at the end of the article, as in the example drawn from the March 13 story.

Appendix Charts 1–1 and 1–2 on pages 359 and 360 clearly show that by the end of the 80s both the workweek and overtime were at very high levels. You should also observe that these indicators improve during expansion, flatten with boom conditions, and plummet in recession. Their relationship to the consumer is probably obvious. True, manufacturing production workers typically do not control the length of their workweek or whether they will work overtime. Yet the extra income afforded by overtime is welcome and bolsters the consumer sentiment of

Fall in Joblessness Raises Inflation Fears; More Fed Tightening Isn't Expected Soon

Unemployment in February Equaled '74 Low of 5.1%; Payrolls Grew by 289,000

By HILARY STOUT
Staff Reporter of THE WALL STREET JOURNAL

WASHINGTON—February's drop in the unemployment rate to 5.1% brings the economy to what many economists consider "full employment," a level they view as a portent of escalating wages, faltering productivity and higher prices.

The civilian jobless rate, which was 5.4% in January, hasn't been lower since December 1973, when it reached 4.9% of the work force. Unemployment also stood at 5.1% in May 1974.

Non-farm payrolls

The Labor Department report confirmed the persistent strength of the economy, which last month generated an increase of 289,000 in non-farm payrolls. The strong job growth followed January's startling increase of 415,000, a revision from the 408,000 reported about a month ago.

The White House hailed the figures, with spokesman Marlin Fitzwater declaring, "Jobs are the best barometer of the economy."

Still, the low jobless rate and continued job growth will put pressure on businesses to raise wages to attract and keep workers. In addition, the shallower pool of available workers means companies in the job market may end up with employees who are less skilled.

Stocks Confound Pessimists

The stock-market bulls really can't complain, but the bears and short-sellers are frustrated. They say they keep seeing the signals for a good downward 'correction,' such as Friday's report of high employment, but the market won't oblige. **(Story on Page C1)**

February's labor report, said Allen Sinai, chief economist for Boston Co. in New York, "is terrific news for certain age groups and ethnic groups that had trouble finding jobs, but it does mean increased cost pressures . . . and inflation."

"In the short run, this is good," said Daniel Van Dyke, senior economist for Bank of America in San Francisco. "But in a longer-term sense, I think it portends additional risk to the economy. . . . Labor costs are about two-thirds of the whole economy, so when they go up you get additional price pressure."

Audrey Freedman, an economist at the Conference Board in New York, said, "They're reaching into every corner for additional workers."

Most of the decline in unemployment occurred in parts of the work force where jobless rates tend to be both higher and more changeable from month to month. Hispanics, who make up only 7.5% of the U.S. work force, accounted for nearly 40% of the February drop in unemployment. In addition, the jobless rate for teen-agers

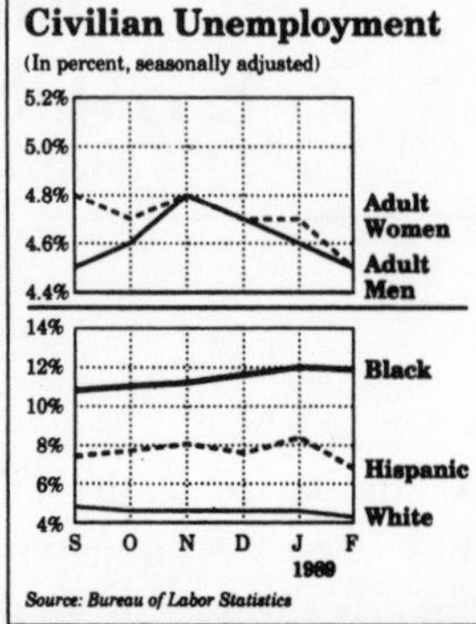

dropped 1.6 percentage points to 14.8%, and the rate among young adults—age 20 through 24 years—declined 1.2 points to 8.1%. Among people over 25, however, the rate barely changed.

Consequently, Janet Norwood, commissioner of the Labor Department's Bureau of Labor Statistics, cautioned in testimony on Capitol Hill, "sudden movements in these more volatile series are frequently followed by similar movements in the opposite direction."

She added: "Additional data are needed to determine whether the February decline will be sustained."

The job growth in February came entirely in the services sector, which added 321,000 positions. Jobs declined by 32,000 in the goods-producing sector, largely because of a drop in construction employment amid harsh winter weather. The figures are adjusted for seasonal factors.

Jerry Jasinowski, chief economist for the National Association of Manufacturers, maintained that the drop doesn't signal weakness in manufacturing. "Apart from autos, manufacturers continue to see orders and production at a strong rate," he said.

Despite the concern over pressure on wages, pay was little changed in February after increasing substantially in January. Average hourly earnings of production or non-supervisory workers edged up to $9.51 in February from $9.50 in January.

Statistical Summary

EMPLOYMENT

Here are excerpts from the Labor Department's employment report. The figures are seasonally adjusted.

	Feb. 1989	Jan. 1989
	(millions of persons)	
Total labor force	124.9	125.1
Total employment	118.5	118.4
Civilian labor force	123.2	123.4
Civilian employment	116.9	116.7
Unemployment	6.3	6.7
Payroll employment	108.3	108.1
Unemployment:	(percent of labor force)	
All workers	5.1	5.4
All civilian workers	5.1	5.4
Adult men	4.5	4.6
Adult women	4.5	4.7
Teen-agers	14.8	16.4
White	4.3	4.6
Black	11.9	12.0
Black teen-agers	32.4	34.5
Hispanic	6.8	8.4
Average weekly hours:	(hours of work)	
Total private nonfarm	34.7	34.8
Manufacturing	41.0	41.0
Factory overtime	3.9	3.9

Source: *The Wall Street Journal*, March 13, 1989.

Statistical Summary – End of Article

EMPLOYMENT

Here are excerpts from the Labor Department's employment report. The figures are seasonally adjusted

	Feb. 1989	Jan. 1989
	(millions of persons)	
Total labor force	**124.9**	**125.1**
Total employment	118.5	118.4
Civilian labor force	**123.2**	**123.4**
Civilian employment	116.9	116.7
Unemployment	6.3	6.7
Payroll employment	**108.3**	**108.1**
Unemployment:	(percent of labor force)	
All workers	5.1	5.4
All civilian workers	5.1	5.4
Adult men	4.5	4.6
Adult women	4.5	4.7
Teen-agers	14.8	16.4
White	4.3	4.6
Black	11.9	12.0
Black teen-agers	32.4	34.5
Hispanic	6.8	8.4
Average weekly hours:	(hours of work)	
Total private nonfarm	34.7	34.8
Manufacturing	41.0	41.0
Factory overtime	3.9	3.9

Source: *The Wall Street Journal*, March 13, 1989.

APPENDIX CHART 1–1
Average Workweek of Production Workers, Manufacturing

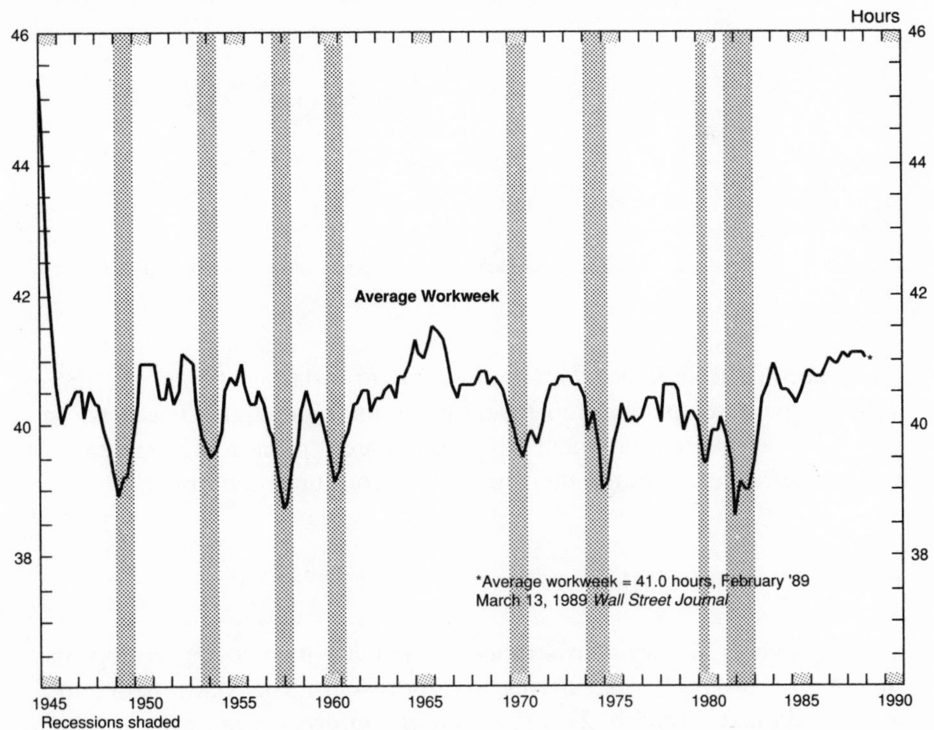

Source: U.S. Department of Commerce, *Business Conditions Digest* and *Handbook of Cyclical Indicators*, series 1.

APPENDIX CHART 1–2
Average Weekly Overtime of Production Workers, Manufacturing

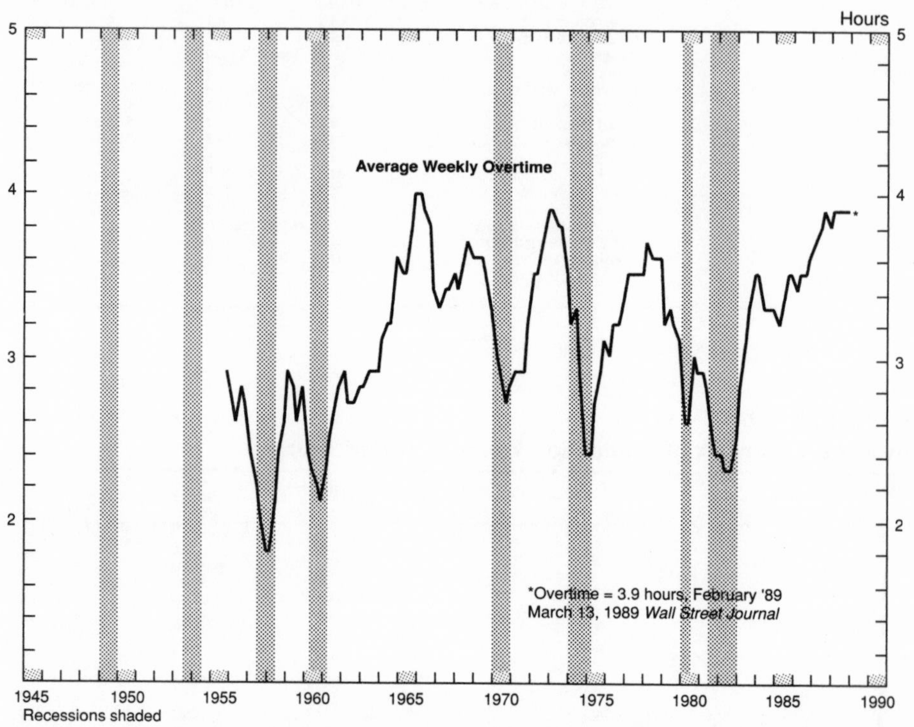

Source: U.S. Department of Commerce, *Business Conditions Digest* and *Handbook of Cyclical Indicators*, series 21.

those earning it. Together with the low rate of inflation, strong overtime helps explain robust consumer sentiment throughout the late 80s. In general, marginal employment adjustments are a reinforcing element of the business cycle through their impact on consumer sentiment.

PERSONAL INCOME

The Commerce Department's monthly personal income report appears in *The Wall Street Journal* during the third week. The fourth paragraph of the Monday, March 27, 1989 article informs you that personal

Consumer Spending Rose 0.5% in February

Most of the Gain Occurred In the Services Category; Income Grew Strong 1%

By David Wessel
Staff Reporter of The Wall Street Journal

WASHINGTON—Total consumer spending showed little sign of slowing in February, but nearly all the growth came in services, Commerce Department figures show.

The department said consumer spending rose 0.5% in February to an annual rate of $3.38 trillion following increases of 0.4% in January and 0.6% in December.

Spending on big-ticket items, durable goods that are intended to last three years or more, dropped for the second month in a row. Analysts said this largely reflects softness in auto sales. Spending on non-durables rose less than 0.1%. Spending on services, which accounts for more than half of all consumer spending, climbed slightly more than 1%.

Personal Income

Total personal income rose a strong 1% in February to an annual rate of $4.315 trillion (see chart on page one). That was far slower than January's 1.7% rise. The February increase partly reflected a big jump in government farm subsidy payments.

"For consumers, the nation's retailers and consumer-product companies, it's all very good news," said Sandra Shaber, an economist with the Futures Group, a consulting firm. "They're earning more. They're continuing to spend more.

"Our friends on Wall Street aren't so happy," she added. "They see more overheating, more sucking in of imports and maybe higher interest rates."

By raising interest rates, the Federal Reserve is attempting to discourage spending in order to brake the economy. February's 0.3% drop in spending on durable goods, which follows a decline of nearly 4% the month before, suggests that higher interest rates are affecting some consumer spending, she said.

Personal savings amounted to 5.9% of after-tax income in February, up from 5.4% the month before.

Analysts cautioned that the increase may not be significant because of the way the government accounts for purchases of autos and other expensive items. Even though consumers generally buy autos with savings or with borrowed money, the Commerce Department counts the entire price of auto purchases against personal income in the month in which the purchases occur. So when auto sales dip, the savings rate rises.

Increasing interest rates showed up both in spending and income. Consumer interest payments to businesses rose 0.6% to an annual rate of $103.2 billion in February. But personal interest income climbed 1.4% to an annual rate of $628.5 billion.

After adjusting for inflation, the Commerce Department said total personal income was up 0.9% in February compared with a 1% rise in January. Consumer spending rose 0.4% after falling 0.3% in January, when consumer prices rose at a much faster clip.

After-tax, or disposable, personal income rose 1.1% to an annual rate of $3.7 trillion in February. It climbed 1.7% in January. After adjusting for inflation, disposable income was up 0.9% in February after climbing 1.0% in January.

Personal disposable income per capita, a measure some economists consider a gauge of living standards, continued to rise in February. After adjusting for inflation, it stood 3.4% above the year-earlier level.

All the figures are adjusted for seasonal changes.

Statistical Summary

Here is the Commerce Department's latest report on personal income. The figures are at seasonally adjusted annual rates in trillions of dollars.

	Feb. 1989	Jan. 1988
Personal income	4.315	4.273
Wages and salaries	2.573	2.558
Factory payrolls	.542	.540
Transfer payments	.614	.612
Disposable personal income	3.700	3.660
Personal outlays	3.480	3.462
Consumption expenditures	3.376	3.358
Other outlays	.104	.104
Personal saving	.220	.198

Source: *The Wall Street Journal*, March 27, 1989.

income grew by 1.0 percent in February 1989, and this paragraph and the statistical summary accompanying the article puts the current figure at $4.315 trillion. (See page 362.) The statistical summary at the end of the article also breaks out the major components of personal income and its disposition.

Personal income is all the income we earn (wages, salaries, fringe benefits, profit, rent, interest, and so on) plus the transfer payments

Personal Income – Fourth Paragraph

Total personal income rose a strong 1% in February to an annual rate of $4.315 trillion (see chart on page one). That was far slower than January's 1.7% rise. The February increase partly reflected a big jump in government farm subsidy payments.

Statistical Summary – End of Article

Here is the Commerce Department's latest report on personal income. The figures are at seasonally adjusted annual rates in trillions of dollars.

	Feb. 1989	Jan. 1988
Personal income	4.315	4.273
Wages and salaries	2.573	2.558
Factory payrolls	.542	.540
Transfer payments	.614	.612
Disposable personal income	3.700	3.660
Personal outlays	3.480	3.462
Consumption expenditures	3.376	3.358
Other outlays	.104	.104
Personal saving	.220	.198

Source: *The Wall Street Journal*, March 27, 1989.

we receive (such as veterans' benefits, social security, unemployment compensation, and welfare), minus the social security taxes we pay to the government. Therefore, the federal government's ability to borrow from banks, and use these borrowed funds to pay out to us in transfer payments more than it receives from us in taxes, provides a cushion that keeps personal income growing even in recession, when earned income is down. The huge federal deficits generated by the 1981–82 recession and the 1981–82–83 tax cuts helped maintain personal income's growth trend despite heavy unemployment in those years. This kept a floor under personal consumption expenditures.

For this reason, as you can see from the historical data (Appendix Chart 1–3 on page 363), personal income has grown so steadily that it is difficult to use as a cyclical indicator. As a first step in improving its usefulness, you would have to adjust it for inflation in order to ascertain trends in real income. This is hardly worth the effort, however, since data on the CPI and consumer expenditures, as presented in Chapter 6, serve the same purpose.

Nonetheless, you can see from the headline accompanying the article on page 361 that this monthly report can be used as an indicator of

APPENDIX CHART 1–3
Personal Income

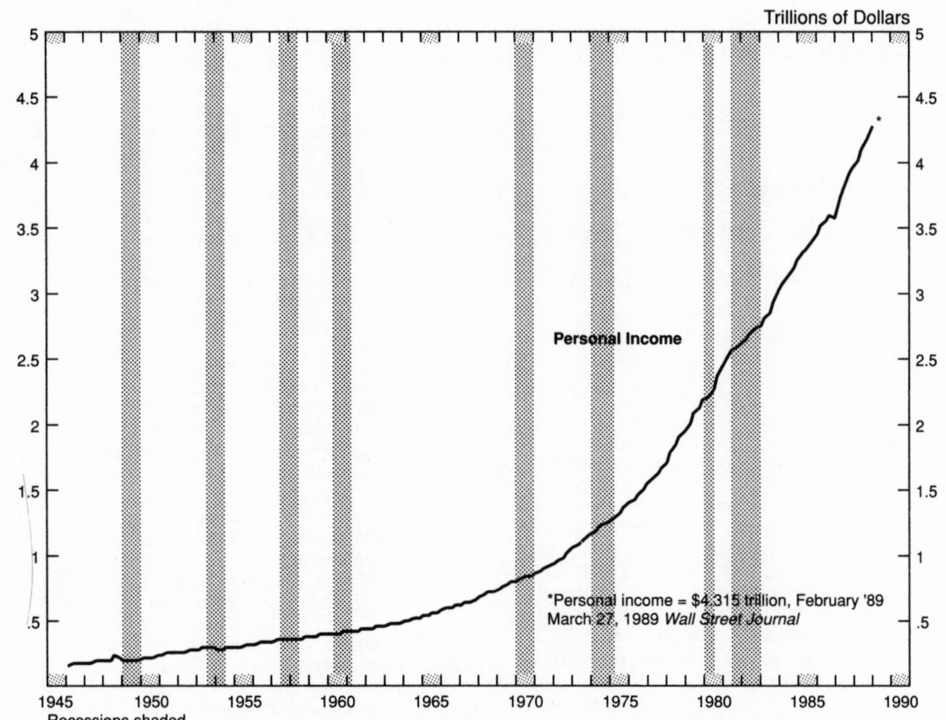

Source: U.S. Department of Commerce, *Business Conditions Digest* and *Handbook of Cyclical Indicators*, series 223.

consumer demand. In February 1989, consumer spending rose by only half as much as consumer income, generating an increase in consumer saving.

RETAIL SALES

The U.S. Department of Commerce's monthly release on *retail sales* appears in *The Wall Street Journal* around the second week. You can see from the headline and fourth paragraph from the end of the Wednesday, March 15, 1989 article on page 364 that retail sales slipped in early

Retailers' Sales Declined 0.4% For February

Slide Indicates That Activity In Key Economic Sector Could Be Slowing Down

By Hilary Stout
Staff Reporter of The Wall Street Journal

WASHINGTON—Retailers from department stores to car dealers saw sales slip in February, a hint that activity in a critical sector of the economy could be slowing.

Sales for retailers of all types fell 0.4% in February, after rising 0.7% in January and dropping 0.3% in December, the Commerce Department said. February's decline matched the largest since retail sales slid 0.9% in October 1987, the month the stock market crashed. In April 1988 retail sales also fell 0.4%. The figures are adjusted for seasonal changes.

Many economists, concerned over inflationary pressures, welcomed the sales report as a clue—but not conclusive evidence—that the pace of the economy's growth may be easing. Analysts have been hoping that the economy, particularly consumer buying, would slow, which they feel would reduce pressure on prices and reduce demand for imports. To achieve this end, the Federal Reserve Board has been gradually pushing up interest rates for the past year to increase the cost of credit.

Auto Sales Take a Dive

Sales of domestic cars and light trucks dropped a greater-than expected 14.8% in early March against the same period in 1988. The decline is fresh evidence of weakness in the auto market, and comes as auto makers wrap up second-quarter production plans. **Story on page A6.**

The Bush administration has been concerned that the Fed's action might stifle the economy, and it took pains yesterday to call attention to the retail sales figures. They "are certainly an indication to me that inflation is not getting away," said Treasury Secretary Nicholas Brady.

Roger Brinner, chief economist at DRI/McGraw Hill, an economic forecasting firm in Lexington, Mass., said the latest numbers suggest the Fed's policy may be having some effect. "I think what you've got is evidence that the consumer notices the Federal Reserve is working very hard to slow down the economy, and that can't be good news for future income growth. So the consumer is going to pick his or her spot to spend—when given an opportunity like an excellent auto rebate plan. . . . They think they now need that extra excuse to commit to big-ticket expenses, and that's going to bring the economy into balance."

While cautioning that recent economic signals "are mixed," John Langum, president of Business Economics Inc. in Chicago, said the retail sales report "is an indication of the slow weakening of the economy which appears to be under way."

He added, "It's very important to slow domestic demand for the purposes of increasing personal savings and to make room for greater exports."

Overall, retail sales fell to $138.23 billion in February from $138.85 billion in January. — Retail Sales

Sales declined in a variety of areas, but auto dealerships showed particular weakness, with sales having fallen 1.7% for two months in a row. General merchandise sales, largely department store items, dropped 0.8% after rising 2.0% in January. Sales of furniture and building materials also declined. Clothing sales edged up 0.5%. Sales at food stores and gasoline and service stations also rose, but some analysts said the higher total might be due to price increases. The figures aren't adjusted for inflation.

Florence Skelly, president of Telematics, a firm specializing in consumer research, said the figures underscore the firm's recent findings that, while the comprehensive economic statistics look good, "I think as you get to the consumer level and the way people live their daily lives, the economy is not so wonderful."

But Mr. Brinner noted that recent studies have shown consumer confidence still running high. "The consumer is not through yet," he said. Of the retail sales report, he declared: "This is encouraging but not definitive."

Source: *The Wall Street Journal*, March 15, 1989.

APPENDIX CHART 1–4
Retail Sales

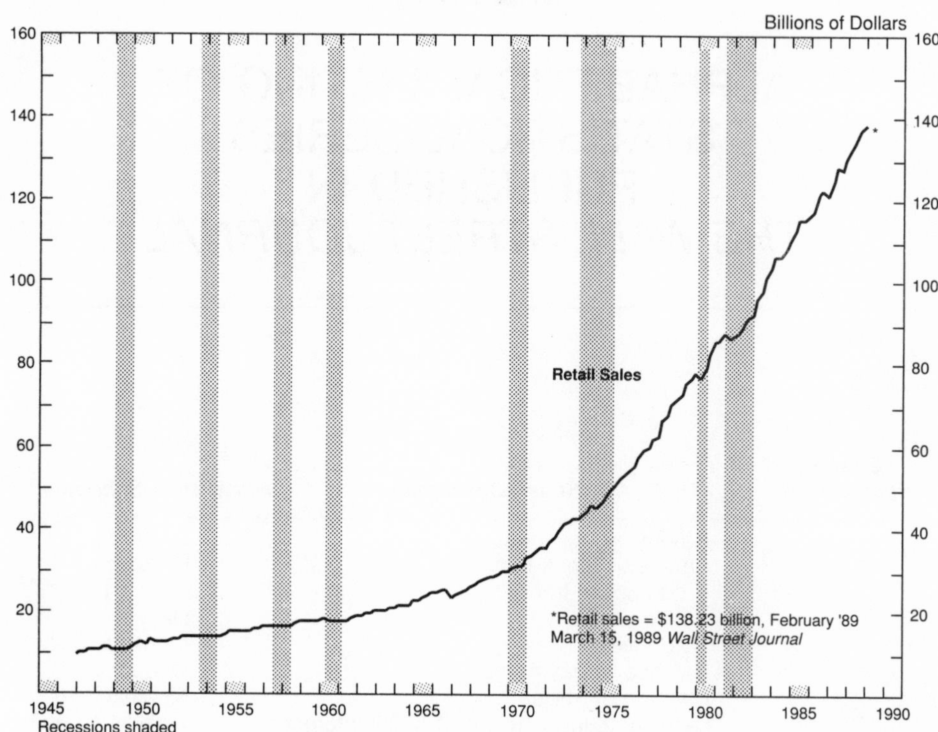

Source: U.S. Department of Commerce, *Business Conditions Digest* and *Handbook of Cyclical Indicators*, series 54.

1989. This reinforces the impression created by the article on personal income, discussed above, that consumer expenditures weakened in those months.

As you can see from Appendix Chart 1–4, however, retail sales has not been a volatile series, so using retail sales to trace the course of the business cycle is not so easy nor satisfactory as using auto sales, housing starts, or consumer credit.

APPENDIX B

ALPHABETICAL LISTING OF STATISTICAL SERIES PUBLISHED IN *THE WALL STREET JOURNAL*

Chapter Introduced	*Series Description*	*Publication Schedule*
9	Advance/decline (stocks)	Daily
9	American Stock Exchange composite transactions	Daily
11	Amex bonds	Daily
6	Auto sales	Monthly
16	Balance of payments	Quarterly
16	Balance of trade	Monthly
12	Banxquote index (deposit & CD interest rates)	Weekly
12	Banxquote money markets (deposit & CD interest rates)	Weekly
11	Bond market data bank	Daily
11	Bond yields (chart)	Weekly
15	Building awards	Monthly
12	Buying and borrowing (interest rates)	Weekly
9	Canadian markets (stocks)	Daily
7	Capacity utilization	Monthly
10	Cash prices (commodities)	Daily
11	Closed end bond funds	Weekly
10	Commodities (article)	Daily
10	Commodity futures prices	Daily
10	Commodity indexes	Daily
6	Consumer confidence	Monthly
6	Consumer credit	Monthly
6	Consumer price index	Monthly
12	Consumer savings rates	Weekly
9	Corporate dividend news	Daily

Chapter Introduced	Series Description	Publication Schedule
8	Corporate profits (Commerce Department)	Quarterly
8	Corporate profits (***The Wall Street Journal*** survey)	Quarterly
11 and 12	Credit markets (article)	Daily
11	Credit ratings	Daily
9	Digest of earnings report	Daily
9	Dow Jones Averages (six-month charts)	Daily
10	Dow Jones commodity indexes (chart)	Weekly
9	Dow Jones industry groups	Daily
15	Durable goods orders	Monthly
Appendix A	Employment	Monthly
4	Federal Reserve data	Weekly
16	Foreign exchange rates	Daily
7	GNP	Quarterly
11	Government agency issues	Daily
6	Housing starts	Monthly
9	Index trading (options)	Daily
7	Industrial production	Monthly
9	Insider trading spotlight	Weekly
11	Interest rate instruments (options)	Daily
14	Inventories	Monthly
9–12	Investment insights	Daily
6	Key currency cross rates	Daily
11 and 12	Key interest rates	Weekly
13	Leading indicators	Monthly
9	Listed options quotations	Daily
15	Machine tool orders	Monthly
15	Manufacturers' orders	Monthly
9–12	Markets diary	Daily
12	Money fund yields	Weekly
12	Money market funds assets	Weekly
12	Money market mutual funds	Weekly
12	Money rates	Daily
4	Money supply (chart)	Weekly
11	Municipal bond index	Weekly
9	Mutual fund quotations	Daily
9	Mutual fund scorecard	Daily
9	NASDAQ bid & asked quotations	Daily
9	NASDAQ national market issues	Daily
11	New securities issues	Daily
11	New York exchange bonds	Daily
9	NYSE composite transactions	Daily
9	NYSE highs/lows	Daily
9	Odd-Lot trading	Daily

Chapter Introduced	*Series Description*	*Publication Schedule*
9	Overseas markets	Daily
8	P/E ratios	Weekly
Appendix A	Personal income	Monthly
7	Producer price index	Monthly
7	Productivity	Quarterly
Appendix A	Retail sales	Monthly
11	Securities offering calendar	Weekly
9	Short interest (stocks)	Monthly
12	Short-term interest rates (chart)	Weekly
9	Stock market data bank	Daily
11 and 12	Treasury auction	Weekly
11 and 12	Treasury bonds, notes and bills	Daily
12	Treasury yield curve	Daily
9	U.S. regional markets	Daily
11	Weekly tax-exempts (bonds)	Weekly

APPENDIX C

STATISTICAL SERIES PUBLISHED IN *THE WALL STREET JOURNAL* IN CHAPTER ORDER

Chapter Introduced	*Series Description*	*Publication Schedule*
4	Federal Reserve data	Weekly
4	Money supply (chart)	Weekly
6	Auto sales	Monthly
6	Consumer confidence	Monthly
6	Consumer credit	Monthly
6	Consumer price index	Monthly
6	Housing starts	Monthly
7	Capacity utilization	Monthly
7	GNP	Quarterly
7	Industrial production	Monthly
7	Producer price index	Monthly
7	Productivity	Quarterly
8	Corporate profits (Commerce Department)	Quarterly
8	Corporate profits (*The Wall Street Journal* survey)	Quarterly
8	P/E ratios	Weekly
9–12	Investment insights	Daily
9–12	Markets Diary	Daily
9	Advance/decline (stocks)	Daily

Chapter Introduced	*Series Description*	*Publication Schedule*
9	American Stock Exchange composite transactions	Daily
9	Canadian markets (stocks)	Daily
9	Corporate dividend news	Daily
9	Digest of earnings report	Daily
9	Dow Jones Averages (six-month charts)	Daily
9	Dow Jones industry groups	Daily
9	Index trading (options)	Daily
9	Insider trading spotlight	Weekly
9	Listed options quotations	Daily
9	Mutual fund quotations	Daily
9	Mutual fund scorecard	Daily
9	NASDAQ bid & asked quotations	Daily
9	NASDAQ national market issues	Daily
9	NYSE composite transactions	Daily
9	NYSE highs/lows	Daily
9	Odd-Lot trading	Daily
9	Overseas markets	Daily
9	Short interest (stocks)	Monthly
9	Stock market data bank	Daily
9	U.S. regional markets	Daily
10	Cash prices (commodities)	Daily
10	Commodities (article)	Daily
10	Commodity futures prices	Daily
10	Commodity indexes	Daily
10	Dow Jones commodity indexes (chart)	Weekly
11	Amex bonds	Daily
11	Bond market data bank	Daily
11	Closed end bond funds	Weekly
11 and 12	Credit markets (article)	Daily
11	Credit ratings	Daily
11	Government agency issues	Daily
11	Interest rate instruments (opinions)	Daily
11 and 12	Key interest rates	Weekly
11	Municipal bond index	Weekly
11	New securities issues	Daily
11	New York exchange bonds	Daily
11	Securities offering calendar	Weekly
11 and 12	Treasury auction	Weekly
11 and 12	Treasury bonds, notes and bills	Daily
11	Weekly tax-exempts (bonds)	Weekly
12	Banxquote index (deposit & CD interest rates)	Weekly

Chapter Introduced	*Series Description*	*Publication Schedule*
12	Banxquote money markets (deposit & CD interest rates)	Weekly
12	Buying and borrowing (interest rates)	Weekly
12	Consumer savings rates	Weekly
12	Money fund yields	Weekly
12	Money market funds assets	Weekly
12	Money market mutual funds	Weekly
12	Money rates	Daily
12	Short-term interest rates (chart)	Weekly
12	Treasury yield curve	Daily
13	Leading indicators	Monthly
14	Inventories	Monthly
15	Building awards	Monthly
15	Durable goods orders	Monthly
15	Machine tool orders	Monthly
15	Manufacturers' orders	Monthly
16	Balance of payments	Quarterly
16	Balance of trade	Monthly
16	Foreign exchange rates	Daily
16	Key currency cross rates	daily
Appendix A	Employment	Monthly
Appendix A	Personal income	Monthly
Appendix A	Retail sales	Monthly

APPENDIX D

LISTING OF STATISTICAL SERIES ACCORDING TO *THE WALL STREET JOURNAL* PUBLICATION SCHEDULE

Day of Month Usually Published in The Wall Street Journal	*Series Description*	*Chapter Introduced*
	Quarterly	
Two months after end of quarter	Corporate profits (*The Wall Street Journal* survey)	8
Middle of last month of quarter	Balance of payments	16
20th of month	GNP	7
20th of last month of quarter	Corporate profits (Commerce Department)	8
First week of last month of quarter	Productivity	7
	Monthly	
1st	Building awards	15
1st	Leading indicators	13
1st week	Manufacturers' orders	15
1st week	Customer confidence	6
5th, 15th, 25th	Auto sales	6
2nd week	Consumer credit	6
Monday of 2nd week	Employment	Appendix A
Middle of 2nd week	Retail sales	Appendix A
3rd Monday	Producer price index	7
Midmonth	Industrial production	7

Day of Month Usually Published in The Wall Street Journal	*Series Description*	*Chapter Introduced*
	Monthly	
Midmonth	Inventories	14
Midmonth	Capacity utilization	7
15th to 20th	Short interest (stocks)	9
3rd week	Balance of trade	16
17th to 20th	Housing starts	6
Thurs or Fri of 3rd week	Durable goods orders	15
4th week	Personal income	Appendix A
4th week	Consumer price index	6
Last Monday	Machine tool orders	15

Day of Week Usually Published in The Wall Street Journal	*Series Description*	*Chapter Introduced*
	Weekly	
Monday	Bond yields (chart)	11
Monday	Buying and borrowing (interest rates)	12
Monday	Dow Jones commodity indexes (chart)	10
Monday	P/E ratios	8
Monday	Securities offering calendar	11
Monday	Weekly tax-exempts (bonds)	11
Tuesday	Key interest rates	11 and 12
Tuesday	Treasury auction	11 and 12
Wednesday	Banxquote index (deposit & CD interest rates)	12
Wednesday	Closed end bond funds	11
Wednesday	Indsider trading spotlight	9
Thursday	Consumer savings rates	12
Thursday	Money market mutual funds	12
Thursday	Money fund yields	12
Thursday	Short-term interest rates (chart)	12
Friday	Banxquote money markets (deposit & CD interest rates)	12
Friday	Federal Reserve data	4
Friday	Money market funds assets	12
Friday	Money supply (chart)	4
Friday	Municipal bond index	11

Series Description	*Chapter Introduced*
Daily	
Advance/decline (stocks)	9
American Stock Exchange composite transactions	9
Amex bonds	11
Bond market data bank	11
Canadian markets (stocks)	9
Cash prices (commodities)	10
Commodities (article)	10
Commodity futures prices	10
Commodity indexes	10
Corporate dividend news	9
Credit markets (article)	11 and 12
Credit ratings	11
Digest of earnings report	9
Dow Jones Averages (six-month charts)	9
Dow Jones industry groups	9
Foreign exchange rates	16
Government agency issues	11
Index trading (options)	9
Interest rate instruments (options)	11
Investment insights	9–12
Key currency cross rates	6
Listed options quotations	9
Markets diary	9–12
Money rates	12
Mutual fund quotations	9
Mutual fund scorecard	9
NASDAQ bid & asked quotations	9
NASDAQ national market issues	9
New securities issues	11
New York exchange bonds	11
NYSE composite transactions	9
NYSE highs/lows	9
Odd-Lot trading	9
Overseas markets	9
Stock market data bank	9
Treasury bonds, notes and bills	11 and 12
Treasury yield curve	12
U.S. regional markets	9

INDEX